D0120214

DEVIL DOGS

Also by Saul David

NON-FICTION

Churchill's Sacrifice of the Highland Division: France 1940

Mutiny at Salerno 1943: An Injustice Exposed

The Homicidal Earl: The Life of Lord Cardigan

Military Blunders

Prince of Pleasure: The Prince of Wales and the Making of the Regency

The Indian Mutiny: 1857

Zulu: The Heroism and Tragedy of the Zulu War of 1879

Victoria's Wars: The Rise of Empire

All the King's Men: The British Soldier in the Era of Sword and Musket

100 Days to Victory: How the Great War Was Fought and Won 1914–1918

Operation Thunderbolt

The Force: The Legendary Special Ops Unit and WWII's Mission Impossible

Crucible of Hell

SBS: Silent Warriors

FICTION

Zulu Hart

Hart of Empire

The Prince and the Whitechapel Murders

DEVIL DOGS

FIRST IN, LAST OUT –
KING COMPANY
FROM GUADALCANAL
TO THE SHORES OF JAPAN

Saul David

WILLIAM
COLLINS

William Collins
An imprint of HarperCollins*Publishers*
1 London Bridge Street
London SE1 9GF

WilliamCollinsBooks.com

HarperCollins*Publishers*
1st Floor, Watermarque Building, Ringsend Road
Dublin 4, Ireland

First published in Great Britain in 2022 by William Collins

1

A catalogue record for this book is available from the British Library

HB ISBN 978-0-00-839576-6
TPB ISBN 978-0-00-839577-3

Maps by Martin Brown

Typeset in Adobe Garamond Pro
by Palimpsest Book Production Ltd, Falkirk, Stirlingshire

Printed and Bound in the UK using
100% Renewable Electricity at CPI Group (UK) Ltd

This book is produced from independently certified FSC™ paper
to ensure responsible forest management.

For more information visit: www.harpercollins.co.uk/green

For Piran

Contents

Illustrations

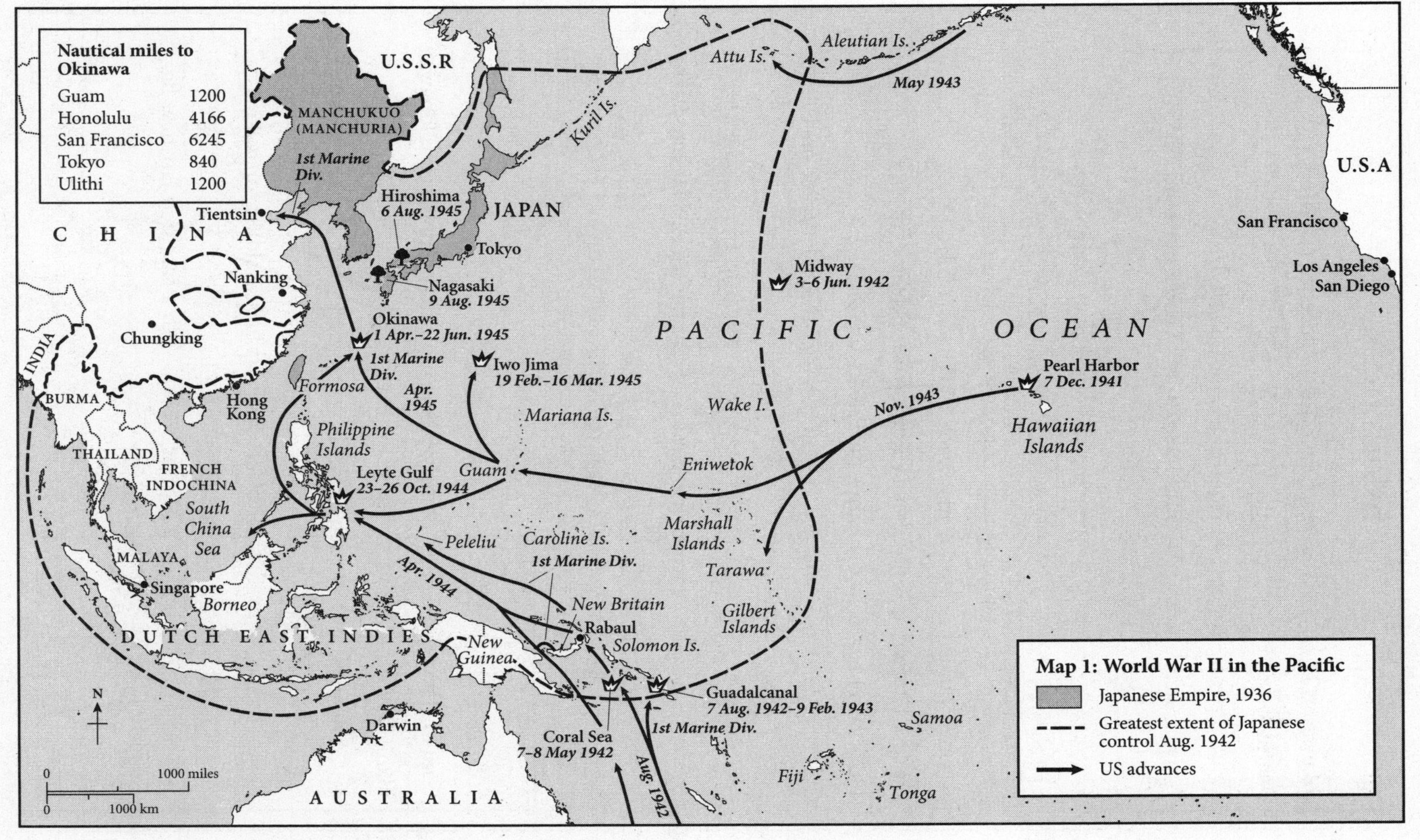
Map 1: World War II in the Pacific
Japanese Empire, 1936
Greatest extent of Japanese control Aug. 1942
US advances
Nautical miles to Okinawa
Guam 1200
Honolulu 4166
San Francisco 6245
Tokyo 840
Ulithi 1200
U.S.S.R
MANCHUKUO (MANCHURIA)
1st Marine Div.
Tientsin
C H I N A
Nanking
Chungking
INDIA
BURMA
THAILAND
FRENCH INDOCHINA
Hong Kong
Formosa
South China Sea
MALAYA
Singapore
Borneo
DUTCH EAST INDIES
Philippine Islands
Leyte Gulf
23–26 Oct. 1944
JAPAN
Hiroshima
6 Aug. 1945
Tokyo
Nagasaki
9 Aug. 1945
Okinawa
1 Apr.–22 Jun. 1945
1st Marine Div.
Apr. 1945
Iwo Jima
19 Feb.–16 Mar. 1945
Mariana Is.
Guam
Peleliu
Caroline Is.
1st Marine Div.
Apr. 1944
New Britain
Rabaul
Solomon Is.
New Guinea
Guadalcanal
7 Aug. 1942–9 Feb. 1943
1st Marine Div.
Coral Sea
7–8 May 1942
Aug. 1942
Darwin
AUSTRALIA
Kuril Is.
Attu Is.
Aleutian Is.
May 1943
Midway
3–6 Jun. 1942
PACIFIC OCEAN
Wake I.
Eniwetok
Marshall Islands
Tarawa
Gilbert Islands
Nov. 1943
Pearl Harbor
7 Dec. 1941
Hawaiian Islands
Samoa
Fiji
Tonga
U.S.A
San Francisco
Los Angeles
San Diego
N
0
1000 miles
0
1000 km

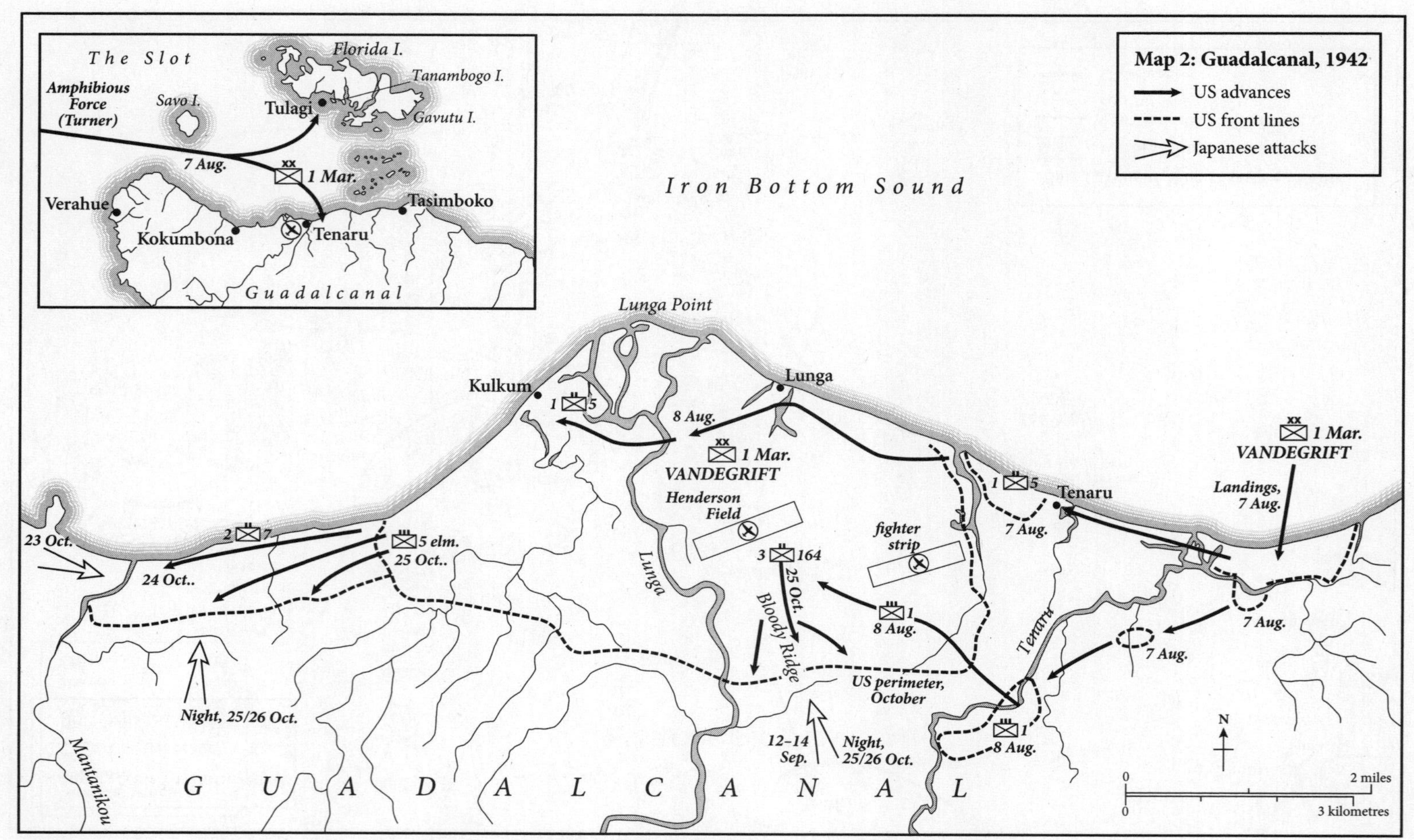
Map 2: Guadalcanal, 1942
US advances
US front lines
Japanese attacks
The Slot
Amphibious Force (Turner)
Savo I.
Florida I.
Tanambogo I.
Tulagi
Gavutu I.
7 Aug.
1 Mar.
Verahue
Tasimboko
Kokumbona
Tenaru
Guadalcanal
Iron Bottom Sound
Lunga Point
Kulkum
Lunga
8 Aug.
1 Mar.
VANDEGRIFT
Henderson Field
fighter strip
Landings, 7 Aug.
7 Aug.
8 Aug.
25 Oct.
Bloody Ridge
US perimeter, October
12–14 Sep.
Night, 25/26 Oct.
23 Oct.
24 Oct..
5 elm.
25 Oct..
Tenaru
Lunga
Mantanikou
G U A D A L C A N A L
N
0
2 miles
3 kilometres

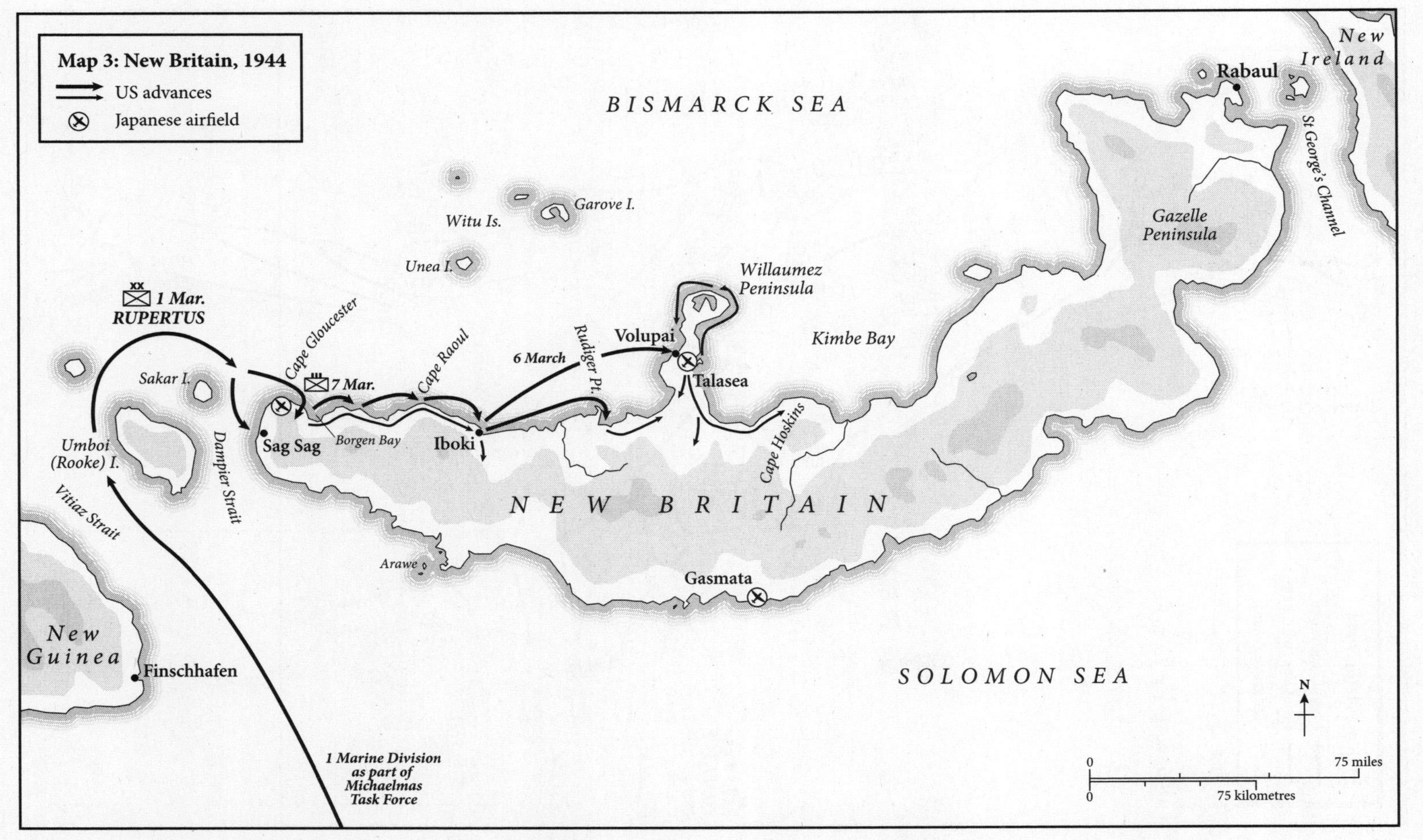
Map 3: New Britain, 1944
US advances
Japanese airfield
BISMARCK SEA
New Ireland
Rabaul
St George's Channel
Gazelle Peninsula
Garove I.
Witu Is.
Unea I.
Willaumez Peninsula
Kimbe Bay
XX
1 Mar.
RUPERTUS
Cape Gloucester
Cape Raoul
7 Mar.
6 March
Rudiger Pt.
Volupai
Talasea
Sakar I.
Sag Sag
Borgen Bay
Iboki
Cape Hoskins
Umboi (Rooke) I.
Dampier Strait
Vitiaz Strait
NEW BRITAIN
Arawe
Gasmata
New Guinea
Finschhafen
SOLOMON SEA
N
1 Marine Division as part of Michaelmas Task Force
0
75 miles
0
75 kilometres

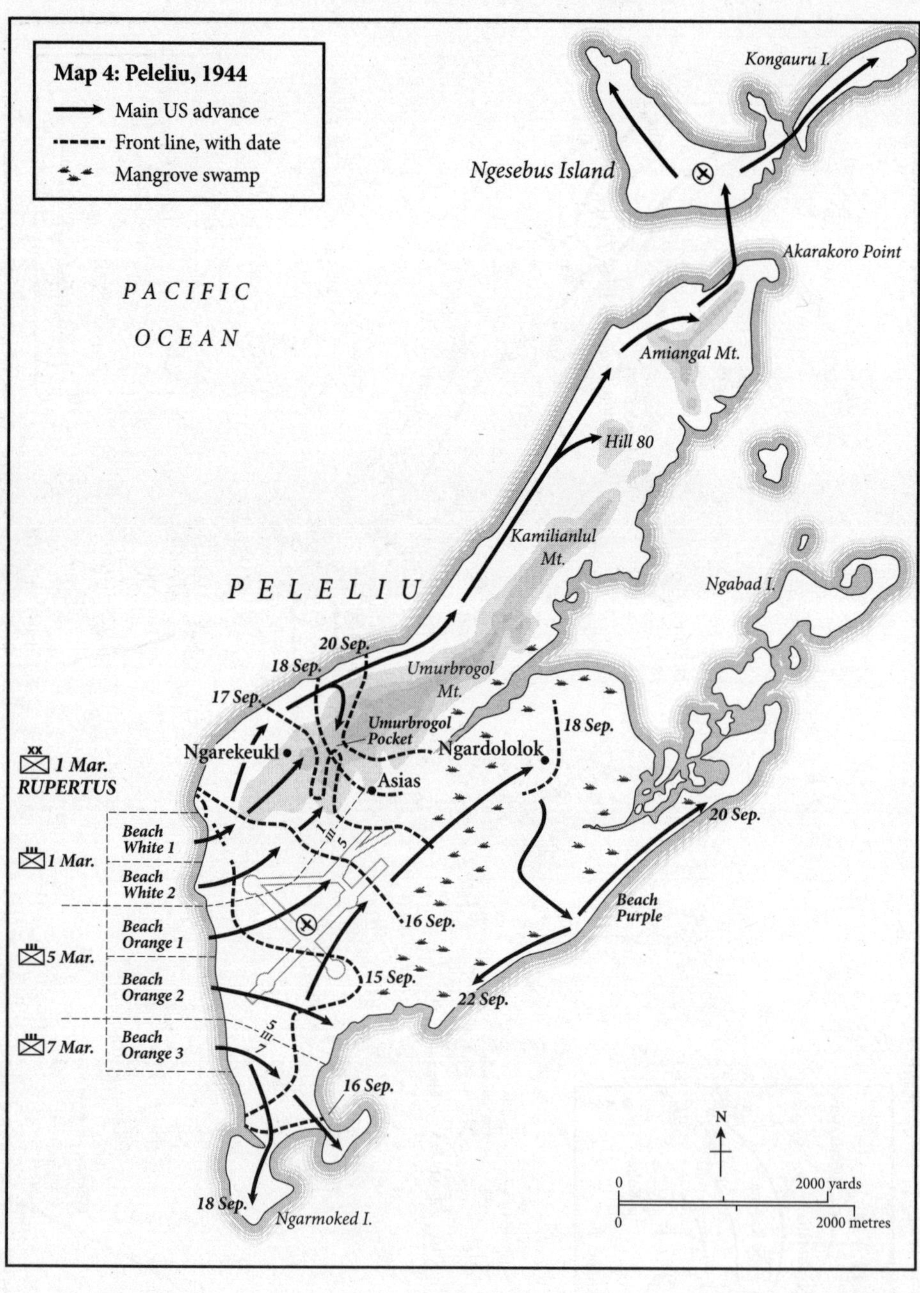

Map 4: Peleliu, 1944
Main US advance
Front line, with date
Mangrove swamp
Kongauru I.
Ngesebus Island
Akarakoro Point
PACIFIC
OCEAN
Amiangal Mt.
Hill 80
Kamilianlul
Mt.
Ngabad I.
PELELIU
20 Sep.
18 Sep.
Umurbrogol
Mt.
17 Sep.
Umurbrogol
Pocket
18 Sep.
1 Mar.
RUPERTUS
Ngarekeukl
Ngardololok
Asias
Beach
White 1
1 Mar.
Beach
White 2
20 Sep.
Beach
Purple
16 Sep.
Beach
Orange 1
5 Mar.
Beach
Orange 2
15 Sep.
22 Sep.
7 Mar.
Beach
Orange 3
16 Sep.
N
0
2000 yards
0
2000 metres
18 Sep.
Ngarmoked I.

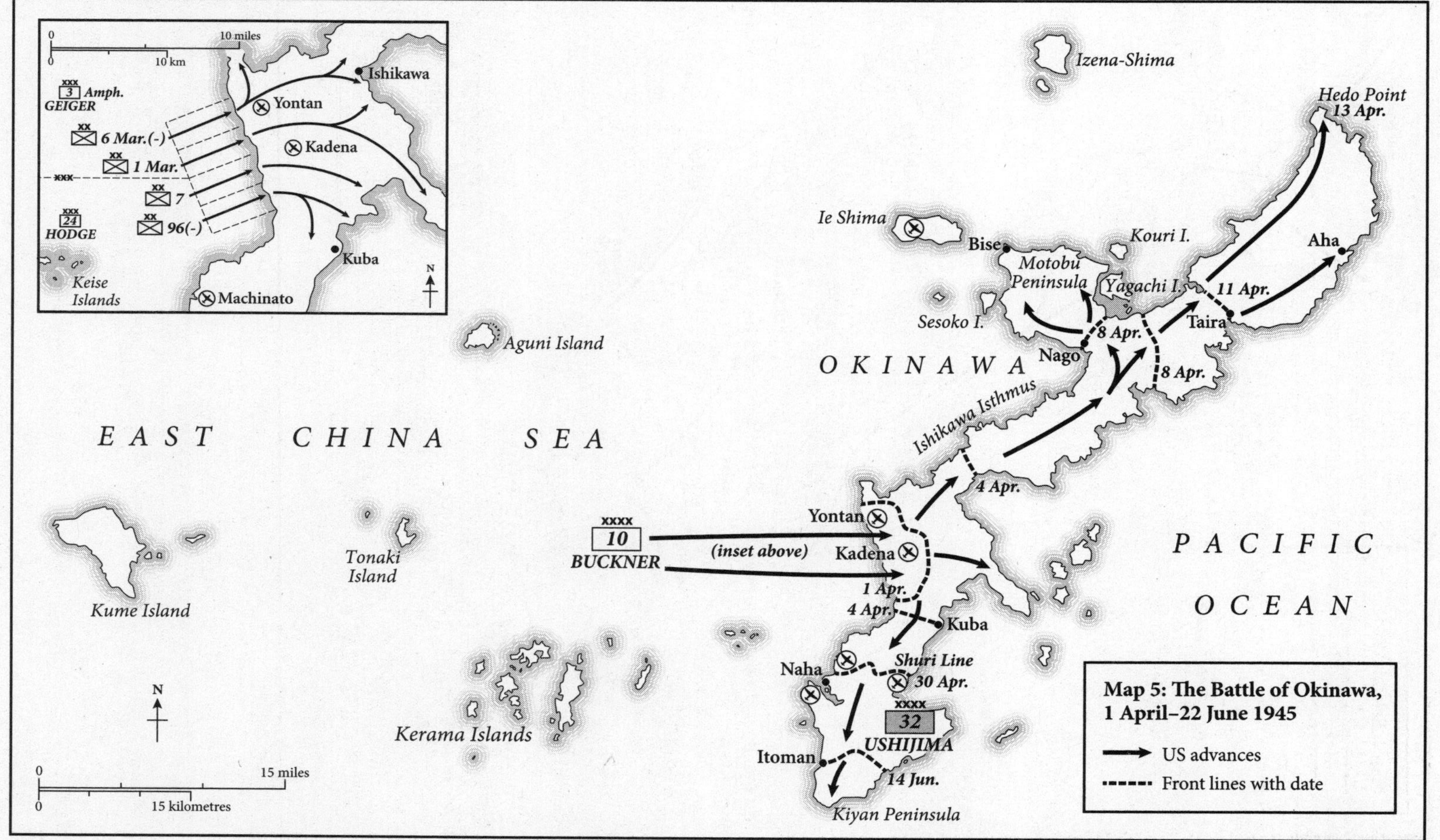

Map 5: The Battle of Okinawa, 1 April–22 June 1945
US advances
Front lines with date
EAST CHINA SEA
PACIFIC OCEAN
OKINAWA
Izena-Shima
Hedo Point
13 Apr.
Aha
11 Apr.
Taira
Kouri I.
Yagachi I.
Ie Shima
Bise
Motobu Peninsula
Sesoko I.
8 Apr.
Nago
8 Apr.
Ishikawa Isthmus
4 Apr.
Aguni Island
Yontan
Kadena
10
BUCKNER
(inset above)
1 Apr.
4 Apr.
Kuba
Naha
Shuri Line
30 Apr.
32
USHIJIMA
Itoman
14 Jun.
Kiyan Peninsula
Kume Island
Tonaki Island
Kerama Islands
15 miles
15 kilometres
10 miles
10 km
3 Amph.
GEIGER
6 Mar.(-)
1 Mar.
7
24
HODGE
96(-)
Ishikawa
Yontan
Kadena
Kuba
Keise Islands
Machinato

Foreword

By W. Henry Sledge

Richard Frank, Pacific War historian, recently asked if I had heard of the forthcoming book by Saul David, called *Devil Dogs.* It is about my father's unit – K Company, 3rd Battalion, 5th Marines, 1st Marine Division – and its journey across the Pacific in World War II. I had not, but I am always happy to hear of any upcoming scholarship concerning the Pacific War. The fact that it follows K/3/5 all the way through the war makes it even better. Rich said, 'I think you would really like it. Sledgehammer is a central character throughout the second half of the book. Would you like to read the manuscript? I'm sure Saul would love for you to.'

Saul sent me the manuscript and I lost no time in diving in. One of the very compelling things about this book was not just that my father had a key role in a significant portion. It was the fact that it covers K/3/5's entire World War II experience, and therefore contextualizes things in a new way. My interest in Pacific War history goes far beyond my father's well-known story. One of the first war books I read as an adolescent was *Helmet for My Pillow* by Robert Leckie. It was the copy that my father had read as he was deeply enmeshed in writing what was to become his own story, the classic *With the Old Breed.* That was only the beginning of what has become a lifelong fascination with the subject of the US Marines in World War II. I was familiar with, for example, Guadalcanal, but it was from the perspective of Robert Leckie and the

1st Marines. I was also very familiar with the fighting at Alligator Creek and Colonel Ichiki's regiment crossing the sandspit, but, again, it was from the perspective of the 1st Marines. As I bonded over the years with my father's story and came to know K/3/5, I wondered, 'Where were they during the fighting for Alligator Creek?'

Devil Dogs addresses the question of what K Company was up to during so many iconic Pacific War battles, where extant written work focuses on other units. Saul David has dug deep and done his research here. Not only does he make good use of published classic material like George McMillan's *The Old Breed*, and Garand and Strobridge's *History of U.S. Marine Corps Operations in World War II*, he skilfully interweaves this with more personal material such as carefully selected quotes from the archival letters of Eugene Sledge. Therefore, one gets the feeling that, rather than merely reading a reinterpretation of already published material with nothing new to add, one is reading a fresh interpretation of established scholarship on the subject, with the added benefit of an intimate view of the central characters. The result is excellent; a book that puts you in the foxholes, in the gun pits, and in the thick of the action with the Marines of K/3/5. *Devil Dogs* will go the distance and serve as a solid companion piece to books like *With the Old Breed*, a vital resource for the reader who wants to learn the panoply of K Company's World War II experience.

Bluff Park, AL 2021

Introduction

The 'Devil Dogs' of K Company, 3rd Battalion, 5th Marines ('K/3/5') – part of the legendary 1st Marine Division, the 'Old Breed' – were among the first American troops to take the fight to the enemy in World War II, and also among the last. They landed on the beaches of Guadalcanal in the British Solomon Islands in August 1942 – the first US ground offensive of the war – and were present when Okinawa, Japan's most southerly prefecture, finally fell to American troops after a bitter struggle in June 1945. In between they fought in the 'Green Hell' of Cape Gloucester on the island of New Britain, and across the coral wasteland of Peleliu in the Palau Islands, a campaign described by one K/3/5 veteran as 'thirty days of the meanest, around-the-clock slaughter that desperate men can inflict on each other'.[1]

Their story encapsulates the American experience in the Pacific: from the shock of the surprise Japanese aerial attack on Pearl Harbor, in December 1941, that brought the United States into the war and encouraged many of the men who would fight in K Company to enlist in the first place; through the brutal recruit training regime in the Marine boot camps at Parris Island, South Carolina, and San Diego, California; to the hurried deployment to the Pacific and the shock of their first taste of combat against a formidable foe; and, for the lucky ones, a blissful period of rest and recuperation in Australia before they were pitched back into the maelstrom in Cape Gloucester in late 1943, Peleliu in late 1944 and Okinawa in the spring of 1945, with only brief periods of recovery in between on the barren island of Pavuvu. Poised that summer to take part in the invasion of Japan proper – an operation that US military chiefs expected to cost at least a million casualties – they were saved by the news that Truman had dropped two atomic bombs and Japan had surrendered.

No US Marine fought in all the Old Breed's battles, because they were typically rotated home after two years of overseas service and/or two campaigns (though some stayed on for three). The wartime adventures of K Company are told, therefore, through the eyes of some of its most interesting characters – officers and enlisted men – whose service overlapped. Ordinary people from very different backgrounds, and drawn from cities, towns and settlements across the United States, the Devil Dogs were asked to do something extraordinary: take on the victorious Imperial Japanese Army, composed of some of the most effective, 'utterly ruthless and treacherous' soldiers in world history, and beat it. This is the story of how they did that while, in the process, creating a brotherhood that remained for the rest of their lives. One veteran wrote:

> Up there, on the line, with nothing between us and the enemy but space (and precious little of that), we'd forged a bond that time would never erase. We were brothers. I left with a sense of loss and sadness, but K/3/5 will always be a part of me.
>
> It's ironic that the record of our company was so outstanding but that so few individuals were decorated for bravery. Uncommon valor was displayed so often it went largely unnoticed. It was expected. But nearly every man in the company was awarded the Purple Heart* . . .
>
> War is brutish, inglorious, and a terrible waste. Combat leaves

* Since 1932, the Purple Heart has been awarded to US servicemen who were wounded or killed in combat (including a retrospective award to casualties of World War I). Its forerunner, the Badge of Military merit, was established by George Washington in 1782 and took the form of a heart made of purple cloth.

> an indelible mark on those who are forced to endure it. The only redeeming factors were my comrades' incredible bravery and their devotion to each other. Marine Corps training taught us to kill efficiently and to try to survive. But it also taught us loyalty to each other – and love. That esprit de corps sustained us.[2]

The proven template for focusing on a single company of World War II combat soldiers is Stephen E. Ambrose's *Band of Brothers*, first published in 1992, which follows the fortunes of Easy Company of the 506th Parachute Infantry Regiment, 101st Airborne Division, through a series of battles in northwest Europe. No author has attempted something similar for the Pacific War. Ambrose's son Hugh went close by publishing *The Pacific* in 2010. But that was a book inspired by the HBO TV mini-series of the same name, rather than the other way around. Instead of following a single unit, it tells the story through the eyes of five main characters who fought in different outfits, who were only loosely connected and in some cases not at all. The result is a tale that ranges across units and campaigns, and lacks *Band of Brothers'* narrative coherence.

I chose K/3/5 as my vehicle for two reasons: it was there from start to finish, having landed on Guadalcanal with the first wave in the morning of 7 August 1942, and being still in action when Okinawa fell in June 1945; but, more importantly, the company contained an unusually high number of talented writers – particularly among its enlisted men – whose letters, first-hand accounts and memoirs provide the colour, emotion and context for this extraordinary story. The best known is Eugene B. Sledge, whose fabled book *With the Old Breed: At Peleliu and Okinawa* is regarded as 'one of the greatest American combat memoirs of the war, if not the greatest'.[3] Sledge was also a prodigious letter writer – both during the war and after – and it is this largely untapped archive of correspondence, held by Auburn University in Alabama, that provides much of the bedrock for the latter half of the book.

Sledge was present for the company's last two campaigns. Fortunately, there are other excellent memoirs that help to complete K/3/5's story.

They include *Earned in Blood* by Thurman Miller, who joined the US Marines in 1940 and served at Guadalcanal and Cape Gloucester; *Hell in the Pacific* by Jim McEnery, who fought from the Canal to Peleliu (making three campaigns in total); and *Islands of the Damned* by R. V. Burgin, who served from Cape Gloucester to Okinawa.

By utilizing these and many other sources – official and private, published and unpublished – it has been possible to portray the 1st Marine Division's four campaigns through the eyes of veterans in a single rifle company. Yet, at the same time, the book attempts to put K/3/5's experience in the broadest possible context by explaining the decisions that were taken by generals, admirals, presidents and emperors at the higher operational, strategic and grand strategic levels. The end result is a unique narrative of the Pacific War that aims to be both authoritative and far-reaching, but also personal and deeply moving.

No K/3/5 veterans emerged from the conflict unscathed. Even those without physical injury would struggle, instead, with survivors' guilt and more or less severe forms of post-traumatic stress disorder (PTSD). What helped them get through this mental turmoil was the comradeship of their fellow Marines and the unshakeable belief that the war, however terrible, was worth fighting.[4]

1

'I would've followed him anywhere'

Southwest Pacific, 6 August 1942

As night fell on 6 August 1942, the officers assembled in the wardroom of the amphibious assault ship USS *Fuller* for a final briefing by the commander of the 3/5 Marines, Lieutenant Colonel Frederick C. Biebush. 'We know from intelligence,' he told them, 'that when we hit the beaches tomorrow we'll run into heavy artillery, machine gun and rifle fire, barbed wire and land mines. Very frankly, the estimate is that nobody who lands in the first wave will come out of it alive. Now it's up to you whether you want to tell your platoons this or you want to keep it to yourselves.'[1]

Among the listeners was Arthur L. 'Scoop' Adams, a 24-year-old second lieutenant from Beacon, New York, who had joined the US Marines after graduating from Colgate University in the summer of 1940. An aspiring journalist, he had acquired his nickname while working on his college newspaper. 'He wasn't a big guy,' noted one of his men. 'Only about five-ten and 165 pounds. But there was something athletic about the way he moved, and he was always on the alert . . . I'd admired him ever since I first met him back at New River in North Carolina. Even after he chewed me out good – and rightfully so – for coming back early from a patrol, I still admired him. And I'm not exaggerating when I say I would've followed him anywhere.'[2]

Adams was the type of officer who had implicit faith in the forty-one men of K Company's 1st Platoon and they, in turn, 'wanted to live up to that confidence'.[3] True to form, he went straight from the wardroom to the platoon quarters below deck, where he found the men sharpening their bayonets on a borrowed grindstone. After repeating word for word what Biebush had told him, he added: 'If there's anybody here who doesn't think he can make it tomorrow, come see me tonight. I'll figure out something so that you don't have to go in.'

The only response was from Private First Class (PFC) Norman R. 'Dutch' Schantzenbach, a 21-year-old former steelworker from East Macungie, Pennsylvania. 'Let's go get them Japs!'[4]

In just a few hours, Adams and his men were scheduled to land on the north shore of Guadalcanal, a mountainous and jungle-covered island in the British Solomon Islands that had been occupied by the Japanese since May 1942. Codenamed Operation Watchtower, the hastily planned recapture of Guadalcanal by the 19,000-strong US 1st Marine Division was the first major American ground offensive of the war and a lot was riding on it. Following the humiliation of the surprise Japanese carrier-borne aerial attack on the US naval base at Pearl Harbor in Hawaii on 7 December 1941 – a pre-emptive strike that sank four American battleships, seriously damaged one and inflicted minor damage on another three* – things went from bad to worse as successive Japanese amphibious operations captured Guam, Wake Island and, in May 1942 (after a five-month campaign that led to the death or imprisonment of around 70,000 US and Filipino troops), the Philippines.

Elsewhere Japanese forces had swept through British and Dutch possessions in southeast Asia: Hong Kong fell on Christmas Day, 1941; the fortress island of Singapore, at the southern tip of the Malay Peninsula, on 15 February 1942, with the loss of its 85,000-strong garrison (causing Churchill to lament that the numerically superior defenders 'should have done better'); Rangoon, the capital of Burma,

* Two cruisers were also seriously damaged, and three destroyers and a minelayer sunk. Total American casualties were 2,403 killed and 1,178 wounded, the heaviest single-day toll of the war (Frank, *Tower of Skulls*, p. 288.)

on 7 March; and Dutch forces surrendered on Java, the main island in the Dutch East Indies, a day later.[5] In its campaigns since 7 December, Japan had killed approximately 65,000 Allied servicemen while losing 15,000 of its own men. Over 300,000 Allied personnel were prisoners of war. The Imperial Japanese Empire now stretched across seven time zones and contained 516 million people, many more than the 360 million under Hitler's control at the height of Nazi Germany's military successes.[6]

The first gleam of light for the Allies was provided by two naval clashes in the Pacific. At the Battle of the Coral Sea near New Guinea in early May, the Imperial Japanese Navy won a tactical victory when its planes sank one of the US Navy's four fleet aircraft carriers (USS *Lexington*) and damaged another, while its own losses were a light aircraft carrier and some smaller warships. But the IJN also sustained serious damage to one of its fleet carriers, *Shokaku*, and the heavy loss of aircraft and aircrew from two of its fleet carriers. They were turned back from the planned invasion of Port Moresby on the south coast of New Guinea, just a few hundred miles from the northern tip of Australia. Coral Sea was, therefore, the first strategic setback for the Japanese.

Having achieved almost all its original war aims by late March 1942, the Imperial General Headquarters (IGHQ) in Tokyo had been faced with a momentous decision: pause and consolidate its conquests, or continue to expand. It chose the more ambitious course, and Port Moresby was on a list of targets that included the occupation of New Guinea and the Solomons (from where they could threaten Australia), while further north they hoped to take American possessions in the western Aleutian Islands off Alaska, and Midway Island in the central Pacific. If successful, they would be able to isolate Pearl Harbor, sever sea routes between the United States and Australia, and provide Japan with bases from which further attacks could be launched. Their fatal miscalculation, however – according to Winston Churchill – was to underestimate the 'latent might of the United States'.

The attack on Midway in early June involved a huge Japanese naval force of four fleet carriers, eleven battleships (including three of the strongest and fastest in the world), and multiple smaller warships and transports. The Americans had only three fleet carriers – including one hastily repaired after Coral Sea – and no battleships. Yet they knew from intercepted signals the timing and direction of the Japanese assault, and were lying in wait. The Japanese struck first, sending planes to knock out the US airfield on Midway Island. But having returned to their aircraft carriers, the surviving planes were being refuelled and rearmed for a second strike when they were caught on their flight decks by an American torpedo- and dive-bomber attack. Three Japanese fleet carriers were set on fire and eventually sank. The fourth, *Hiryu*, dispatched planes that damaged one American fleet carrier (USS *Yorktown*) so severely it was finished off by a Japanese submarine two days later. But the *Hiryu*, in turn, was crippled beyond repair and foundered.

In losing four aircraft carriers to its opponent's one, Japan had suffered its first major defeat. The battle was, in the opinion of eminent naval historian Samuel Eliot Morison, the 'most decisive' of the war. He added:

> Had the Japanese won it, they would have turned Midway Island into an air base, from which they could have rendered Pearl Harbor untenable. They would have set up a defensive perimeter, manned by mutually supporting aircraft and ships, from the western Aleutians through Wake and Midway Islands, to Samoa, the Fijis, New Guinea and Australia, cutting us off completely from 'down under'. After our miraculous victory . . . the Japanese Fleet was thrown on the defensive, an unwelcome role for which they were ill-prepared.[7]

More recent scholarship suggests that the strategy of Admiral Isoroku Yamamoto, the brilliant Commander-in-Chief of the IJN's Combined Fleet, was even more ambitious: that he hoped victory at Midway would lead to the seizure and occupation of the main Hawaiian Islands. This, in turn, would give him around 425,000 civilian hostages that he could use as a bargaining chip to negotiate an early end to the war.[8]

What is not in doubt is that Midway was a hugely significant victory. 'At one stroke,' wrote Winston Churchill, with the benefit of hindsight, 'the dominant position of Japan in the Pacific was reversed. The glaring ascendancy of the enemy, which had frustrated our combined endeavours throughout the Far East for six months, was gone for ever. From this moment all our thoughts turned with sober confidence to the offensive.'[9]

This is going too far. Midway may have shifted the balance of power: but only from Japanese naval domination to something approaching parity. Despite losing four aircraft carriers and 3,000 veteran sailors and airmen, Japan still retained 'a numerical advantage in most categories of deployed naval and air strength' in the Pacific, including five aircraft carriers to the Americans' four and 'several more under construction'. Midway, moreover, had claimed none of Japan's formidable array of battleships, submarines, destroyers, troopships, flying boats or land-based medium bombers, nor had it blunted the 'violence or energy of the Japanese offensive in the South Pacific, where naval, ground, and air forces based at Rabaul on New Britain island were pushing south and east'.[10]

There remained, too, a sneaking suspicion among the American public that the Japanese soldier, man for man, could not be beaten. 'People had come to believe,' recalled one Marine officer, 'that the Japs were supermen, that maybe our American boys really weren't as rugged as the Japs. What people wanted, back in the summer of '42, was a hand-to-hand, battle royal between some Japs and some Americans to see who would really win.'[11]

That the tussle would take place on Guadalcanal – an island most Americans had never heard of – was thanks in no small part to Admiral Ernest J. King, the Commander-in-Chief of the US Fleet and a member of the US Joint Chiefs of Staff. Tall, with thinning dark hair, a Roman nose and a cleft chin, King looked every inch the patrician graduate of Annapolis naval academy. Yet, unlike many of his colleagues, he came from a modest home in Lorain, Ohio, where his father was a foreman in a railroad machine shop. His rapid advance up the naval chain of command was helped by his tireless work ethic and fearsome intellect. He expected similar standards from others and would, according to an aide, 'tolerate almost anything in an officer except incompetence, laziness, or verbosity'. He was rude, obnoxious and, in the opinion of General

George C. Marshall of the US Army, one of his fellow Joint Chiefs, 'a mental bully'.[12]

Yet he got things done and was never as blinkered about the Pacific theatre as his British allies suggested. After meeting King in London in July 1942, General Sir Alan Brooke, chief of the British Imperial General Staff, noted: 'We went on arguing for 2 hours, during which time King remained with a face like a Sphinx, and only one idea, i.e. to transfer operations to the Pacific.' Brooke made a similar accusation at the Casablanca conference in early 1943. King, he wrote, 'is a shrewd and somewhat swollen headed individual. His vision is mainly limited to the Pacific, and any operation calculated to distract from the force available in the Pacific does not meet with his support or approval.'[13]

This was an exaggeration. Along with President Franklin D. Roosevelt and his fellow Joint Chiefs, King never seriously deviated from the 'Germany First' strategy agreed with the British in early 1941 and reaffirmed after Pearl Harbor.* This meant, in effect, devoting the bulk of America's military resources to North Africa and Europe on the grounds that Hitler's defeat would inevitably be followed by the demise of the other Axis powers, Italy and Japan. Conquering Japan, on the other hand, would have little bearing on Germany's military prospects, particularly its titanic struggle with Russia. Yet King was also well aware that Japan could not be left to run amok. To prevent this, at least some of the Allies' resources – particularly naval – were needed in the Pacific. How big a share? King suggested 30 per cent at Casablanca. But even this modest amount was too much for Brooke, who envisaged 'minimum holding operations' in the Pacific while the war was won in Europe.[14]

* Though both King and Marshall, it should be said, were prepared to consider a shift to a 'Pacific First' strategy when Britain persisted in its refusal to consider a cross-Channel invasion in 1942, and argued instead for an invasion of French North Africa. They were stymied by Roosevelt, who backed British plans on the grounds that a North African invasion was better than no action at all in the European theatre. (Mark A. Stoler, 'The "Pacific-First" Alternative in American World War II Strategy', *The International History Review*, 2/3 (July 1980), pp. 432–52.)

King held his ground. His 'strategic genius', noted historian Clark G. Reynolds, 'lay in his general appreciation of the global dimensions of World War II, namely the need to speed up the war in Europe in order to enhance operations in the Pacific, and in particular the nature of Pacific geography and how a strategy of concentration would defeat Japan'. King's strategy was a facsimile of the 'indirect approach' preached by British military theorist Basil Liddell Hart in the 1920s. First, the navy would isolate the Japanese home islands by commerce warfare and blockade to wreck its economy, fight naval battles to destroy the enemy fleet, and seize or neutralize the enemy's overseas possessions and strongholds. Second, the United States would support, supply and encourage a major continental ally – in this case China – so that Japan could be defeated on land.[15]

But even after Midway, King knew that 'Japan posed a threat to Allied territories throughout the South Pacific, and until the theater could be stabilized, there was no prospect of the hypothetical holding action pictured in Allied planning documents'. With danger 'imminent', he urged Marshall to create strategic 'strong points' by transferring men and planes – particularly bombers – to islands such as Samoa, Fiji, New Caledonia and Tonga. But he also wanted to launch a counter-offensive into the Solomons and the Bismarck Archipelago, thus beginning the step-by-step rollback of recent Japanese advances. On 24 June 1942, he gave Admiral Chester W. Nimitz, Commander-in-Chief of the Pacific Fleet, just five weeks' notice to plan for 'the seizure and initial occupation of Tulagi and adjacent islands' in the Solomons. The biggest of those islands was Guadalcanal.[16]

A week later, General Marshall confirmed King's instructions to Nimitz by ordering Allied forces in the Pacific to mount a limited offensive to stop the Japanese drive towards the line of communications from the United States to Australia and New Zealand. There were, at that time, two separate commands in the Pacific: General Douglas MacArthur's Southwest Pacific Area (SWPA), which included the Philippine Islands, the South China Sea, the Gulf of Siam (modern Thailand), the Netherlands East Indies (most of modern Indonesia, with the exception of Sumatra), the Solomon Islands, Australia and the waters to the south;

and Admiral Nimitz's Pacific Ocean Area, a vast tract that encompassed three subordinate areas, the North, Central and South Pacific.

As John Miller, Jr wrote, in the official US Army history of the Guadalcanal campaign,

> The missions assigned to MacArthur and Nimitz were virtually the same. They were to hold those island positions between the United States and Australia which were essential to the security of the line of communications and to the support of air, surface, and amphibious operations against the Japanese; to contain the Japanese within the Pacific; to support the defense of North America; to protect essential sea and air communications; and to prepare major amphibious offensives, the first of which were to be delivered from the South and Southwest Pacific Areas. Each area was to support its neighbor's operations.[17]

As early as May, MacArthur had been preparing plans for an offensive that would forestall Japan's drive south. At the same time, Admiral Nimitz was contemplating an attack on Tulagi in the Solomons, a project which was backed by Admiral King. Nimitz initially thought a single Marine Raider battalion could do the job. By 1 June, however, Admiral King and Generals Marshall and MacArthur were agreed that more troops would be needed. The latter envisaged a broader operation that would encompass the Solomons and New Britain, to the northwest, and that he would command. But as the only available combat troops in the SWPA were the 32nd and 41st Infantry Divisions, and the 7th Australian Division – and none was equipped or trained for amphibious operations – he required both a Marine division and the close support of US aircraft carriers.

He was backed by General Marshall, who told Admiral King on 12 June 'that an attack designed to retake eastern New Guinea and New Britain could be mounted in early July'. But it would require the transfer to MacArthur of the 1st Marine Division, soon to arrive in New Zealand, to make the initial amphibious assault. King's counter-proposal, on

25 June, was for an offensive no later than 1 August by a task force controlled by Admiral Nimitz. The immediate objectives would be positions in the Solomons and also in the Santa Cruz Islands, 370 nautical miles east-southeast of Guadalcanal. The ultimate objectives would be in the New Guinea–New Britain area.

The compromise was for Nimitz to have responsibility for the initial operation in the Solomons and Santa Cruz Islands – under his subordinate commander Vice Admiral Robert L. Ghormley – while MacArthur took charge of the follow-up operations. It was enshrined in the 'Joint Directive for Offensive Operations in the Southwest Pacific Area Agreed on by the United States Chiefs of Staff' on 2 July. Task One – codenamed Operation Watchtower – was the 'seizure and occupation of the Santa Cruz Islands, Tulagi, and "adjacent positions"' by an officer 'designated by Admiral Nimitz' (Ghormley). Tasks Two and Three, including the capture of Japanese airfields on the northeast coast of New Guinea, followed by the seizure of Rabaul on New Britain, were MacArthur's responsibility. To keep Task One entirely within Ghormley's area of responsibility, the boundary between the SWPA and SPA was moved one degree west, to latitude 159° east, just beyond the western end of Guadalcanal. The other Solomon Islands remained in MacArthur's fiefdom.[18]

The unit assigned to Operation Watchtower – the 1st Marine Division under Major General Alexander A. Vandegrift – had only left its training base at New River, North Carolina, a month before Nimitz received his instructions from King. The original plan was to move the division to a semi-permanent camp near Wellington in New Zealand where it would begin six months of intensive training before it was sent into battle. The advance echelon – including the 3/5 Marines – had been in Wellington for only six *days* when Vandegrift was told that the Guadalcanal operation was scheduled for 1 August. 'I could not believe it,' he remembered. 'I read the typewritten words again. There was no mistaking their content.'[19]

The task facing Vandegrift's staff was formidable. They had just a few weeks 'to reconnoiter the objective, get information, study the terrain, make a decision, issue orders, load 31 transport and cargo carriers, embark 20,000 men and 60 days' supply, effect a rendezvous with supporting naval forces and, in addition, conduct a thorough set of joint rehearsal exercises'. Just getting to the target would eat up the bulk of the time available. Moreover the only information to hand was a single navy hydrographic chart of the Tulagi–Guvatu harbour area, corrected to 1910. So Vandegrift sent his chief of intelligence, Lieutenant Colonel Frank B. Goettge, to Australia to glean any information he could from former residents of the Solomons and masters of trading vessels who had plied those waters. At the US Army headquarters in Melbourne, Goettge was given an estimate of the Japanese Order of Battle for the Solomons and reports from coastwatchers who had chosen to stay on after the Japanese occupation. But neither gave accurate information regarding enemy troop dispositions.[20]

Goettge returned to New Zealand in mid-July and 'put together a brief and error-filled report and a rough map of Guadalcanal's northern coast', where the Japanese were building an airfield on an old plantation.[21] According to George McMillan's *The Old Breed*, the classic wartime account of the 1st Marine Division, the map was 'a rough, uncontrolled sketch of the rivers, plains, coconut plantations and wooded areas', and 'the only guide regiments, battalions, and companies were to have'.[22] The reason it was so 'crude and inadequate', wrote Second Lieutenant Thayer Soule, the officer in charge of Goettge's map section, was because there was no reliable topographic information. Instead they were forced to make sketch maps from aerial photos, with large blank areas where cloud had obscured the land.[23]

Goettge estimated the combined Japanese garrison on Guadalcanal and nearby Tulagi to be 8,400 men and planned accordingly. There were in fact only 3,500 troops, of whom 2,300 were on Guadalcanal. Most of the latter were members of two construction units whose task was to build an airfield close to Lunga Point on the island's northern coast.[24]

The problem of supply was just as acute as the lack of reliable intelligence. The 1st Marine Division had arrived in New Zealand as part of an administrative move from one base to another; its ships, as a result, were loaded commercially rather than for 'combat' to save space. With an operation in the offing, everything had to be hurriedly repacked in reverse order of when it would be needed. 'The essence of combat loading,' explained the commander of the 5th Marines to a journalist, 'is not to put the toilet paper on top of the ammunition.'

Hampered by bad weather – which spoiled many of the supplies – and strident local dock unions who insisted on regular tea breaks and perfect working conditions for their members, the reloading took much longer than expected and prompted Admiral King to extend the original landing date to 7 August. But, despite this extra time, supplies were pared to a minimum. Each man would take only what he needed to 'actually live and fight', with all excess clothing, bedding rolls and company property left in storage. Food would last for sixty days, rather than the prescribed ninety, and ammunition reserves were just ten units of fire – each made up of one day's theoretical expenditure – per man.[25]

The dubious honour of being the first men ashore on Guadalcanal had been given to the 1st and 3rd Battalions of the 5th Marines, an outfit that fought so hard during the vicious 1918 defensive battle of Belleau Wood near the Marne River in eastern France that, according to the media, they were nicknamed *Teufel Hunden* ('Devil Dogs') by their German opponents.[26] The name had stuck.

Though the 5th Marines had only been activated in 1917, the pedigree of the United States Marine Corps (USMC) went all the way back to November 1775, at the start of the American War of Independence, when the Continental Congress authorized the raising of two battalions of Marines to serve as a landing force with the fledgling American fleet. Legend has it that the first Marine was recruited in a Philadelphia tavern and sent to a ship in the harbour where the officer-of-the-deck asked: 'What the hell is a Marine? You go aft there and sit down till I find out.'

A few minutes later, a second Marine appeared and was sent to join the first. 'Listen, boy,' said the original Marine, 'you shoulda been in the *old* Corps!'[27]

Since then, Marines had fought in every conflict in US history, including the wars against the Barbary Pirates (1801–5) and Mexico (1846–8) that are commemorated by the opening verse of the Marines' Hymn:

From the Halls of Montezuma
To the shores of Tripoli;
We fight our country's battles
In the air, on land, and Sea;
First to fight for right and freedom
And to keep our honor clean;
We are proud to claim the title
Of United States Marine.

In 1868, around the time the hymn was composed, the Marines first used their famous 'Eagle, Globe, and Anchor' (EGA) emblem. Fifteen years later, they adopted the motto 'Semper Fidelis' (shortened to 'Semper Fi', the Latin for 'Always Faithful'). Playing a relatively minor role in the US Civil War, Marines were far more prominent in the Spanish–American War of 1898 and helped to put down the Boxer Rebellion in China in 1900. But it was during World War I that the US Marines earned their reputation as elite shock troops and expert shots, with numbers rapidly expanding from 13,000 to more than 70,000, including the first female recruits.

Having won more laurels at the battles of Château-Thierry and Saint-Mihiel, and during the hard-fought Meuse–Argonne Offensive in late 1918 – earning it the right to wear the *fourragère*, a braided cord awarded by the French to distinguished military units – 'The Fighting Fifth' was briefly deactivated in 1919 and again in 1930. Raised once more in 1934, it became part of the 1st Marine Brigade – the so-called 'Raggedy-Ass Marines' – which pioneered the practice of amphibious warfare, notably assault landings on hostile shores.

The 'father' of American doctrine on amphibious warfare was Lieutenant Colonel Earl H. 'Pete' Ellis, a Marine Corps intelligence officer who in the early 1920s – following Japan's post-World War I acquisition of former German territories in the Pacific, including the Marshall, Mariana and Caroline Islands – had written the influential paper 'Advance Base Operations in Micronesia'.* Ellis understood, wrote historian Richard Overy,

> that attacking from the sea was fundamentally different from both war on land and conventional naval warfare. His description of future operations against defended shores anticipated in detail the conflict across the central Pacific twenty years later: the need for a large trained force of Marines; channels cleared of mines and obstacles for the approaching of landing craft to the shore; flanking support from naval gunfire to suppress enemy fire; ground support from the naval air arm; artillery and signal battalions brought ashore to assist the Marines in building a beachhead; . . . and rapid ship-to-shore movement to maximize the initial impact of the assault.

Amphibious operations, Ellis believed, would 'entirely succeed or fail practically on the beach'.[28]

Ellis's doctrine was finally adopted by the US Marine Corps in 1934 when it issued the first *Tentative Landing Operations Manual.* A year earlier, the US Navy had authorized the Marine Corps to activate a 3,000-strong Fleet Marine Force dedicated to amphibious operations. It initially consisted of just the 1st Marine Brigade, stationed in Quantico, Virginia; but was soon joined by the 2nd Marine Brigade, based on the west coast in San Diego, California (where its members were known, inevitably, as 'Hollywood Marines'). Beginning in 1934, units of the Fleet Marine Force took part in the annual manoeuvres of the US Fleet in the Caribbean and the Pacific. These exercises, wrote Richard Overy, 'mimicked amphibious operations and provided a solid opportunity to

* Even before World War I, the American military had drafted 'War Plan Orange' for a possible war with Japan. The Pacific remained the American military's chief strategic focus until the outbreak of World War II in Europe.

learn from many mistakes. By the seventh exercise, in 1941, the complexities of a landing against opposition were fully understood.' By then the 1st Marine Brigade was commanded by Brigadier General Holland M. 'Howlin' Mad' Smith, a 49-year-old Alabaman who had served with the Devil Dogs in France in 1917.[29]

When the 1st Marine Division was formed around the nucleus of the 1st Marine Brigade on 1 February 1941, Smith became its first commander and the 5th Marines provided cadres for two new regiments, the 1st and 7th. Yet the 5th's reputation as the finest combat unit in the US Marines seemed to be confirmed by its selection to spearhead the Guadalcanal operation.* The 1st Marine Division was a self-contained fighting unit and the 'first integrated amphibious striking force' in US history. It was organized around its three infantry regiments – the 1st, 5th and 7th Marines – with supporting units of raiders, parachutists, artillery, engineers, special weapons, armour, navy corpsmen and pioneers. But the infantry regiments, each around 3,100 men strong, were the division's unglamorous workhorses and would do most of the fighting. They were made up, in turn, of three infantry battalions, and each battalion of an HQ company, three rifle companies and a weapons company (of three machine-gun platoons, an 81mm mortar platoon and an anti-tank platoon). The 5th Marines, therefore, had nine rifle companies: A, B and C in its 1st Battalion; E, F and G in its 2nd; and I, K and L (there was no J) in its 3rd. The weapons companies, one to a battalion, were designated D, H and M.[†30]

'Scoop' Adams and his men were in K Company (K/3/5). In August 1942 the company was 6 officers and 177 enlisted men strong. It included an HQ, staffed by the company commander or 'Skipper', executive officer

* Barely 20,000 men strong when World War II broke out in Europe in September 1939, the US Marine Corps quickly grew to 54,000 in 1941, 142,000 in 1942 and 385,000 by the end of the war (Garand and Strobridge, pp. 19–20.)

† In combat, the companies were known by their phonetic radio call signs: Able, Baker, Charlie, Dog, Easy, Fox, George, How, Item, King, Love and Mike. There was no J Company because the letter was too similar to I.

or XO, first sergeant and various communications and supply personnel (a total of two officers and twenty-seven men); a weapons platoon of two light machine guns and two 60mm mortars (one officer and twenty-seven men); and three rifle platoons (each composed of a platoon leader and forty-one men). Each rifle platoon was further subdivided into an HQ (one officer and six men), three rifle squads (nine men each) and an automatic rifle squad (eight men).*[31] A Marine might be proud of his battalion, his regiment and even his division. But his first loyalty was to his company. It was his home. Among its men he lived, trained, fought and sometimes died.

K Company was due to land on the left (or eastern) half of a 1,600-yard stretch of Guadalcanal's north coast, dubbed Red Beach, at H-hour, 9.10 a.m. on 7 August. The 1st Battalion would land simultaneously on its right. The main objective of the operation was to capture the half-finished Japanese airfield that lay three miles to the west. But first the two battalions of 5th Marines had to secure a beachhead 2,000 yards long and 600 yards deep. With that accomplished, all three battalions of the 1st Marines would pass through their position and advance a couple of miles towards a feature known as the 'Grassy Knoll' where they would set up a number of all-round defensive perimeters. That, at least, was the plan. 'If we were lucky,' noted a squad leader in Adams's platoon, 'this was all supposed to happen on the first day. If we weren't lucky, nobody knew what would happen. Even at best our defenses would be widely scattered and thinly stretched.'[32]

* Composed of four gunners, armed with the M1918 Browning Automatic Rifle (BAR), and four assistant gunners to help carry ammunition.

2

'Where I'm going will either make or break me'

Southwest Pacific, 6 August 1942

Steaming north towards Guadalcanal at 12 knots, the USS *Fuller* was part of a fleet of eighty-two transports and warships, the largest yet assembled in the Pacific. It included three fleet aircraft carriers – *Enterprise*, *Saratoga* and *Wasp* – the battleship *North Carolina*, cruisers, destroyers, transports, cargo ships, minesweepers and fleet oilers. 'All over the sea and as far out as eye could reach,' noted an *Enterprise* pilot, 'the armada mottled the water. Everybody aboard became excited at the prospect of being part of what looked like the first big American offensive of the war.'[1]

Having left Wellington on 22 July, *Fuller* and the rest of the task force had sailed for Koro Island in Fiji where, six days later, they practised an amphibious landing. It was a fiasco. 'Boat control by boat officers and flotilla commander was unsatisfactory,' noted the 5th Marines' War Diary. 'C.T. [Combat Team] 3 landed on wrong beach. Because of surf and beach conditions, landing was stopped when 75% complete.'[2]

'Scoop' Adams and his men did get ashore, and 'spent the day wandering about the island, looking around', and trying to figure out how to open coconuts. 'When dusk fell,' noted a sergeant, 'we pitched our tents and settled in to watch the sailors, who worked through the night struggling to free their boats from the coral.' He added:

> The coral reef was a bad place to land, the landing craft were in poor condition, ship-to-shore communications were slow, navy

coxswains were inexperienced, Marines were slow to embark, and there was confusion among the destroyers' artillery groups. The reality is that we were damned lucky no one was killed or injured.

This was only a trial run. How would we perform when facing live fire, an entrenched, heavily armed enemy, and an unknown hostile island? We were soon to find out.[3]

Back on board the *Fuller*, the men of the 3/5 Marines spent the next few days preparing for battle. Adams and the other officers attended a series of lectures and briefings at which all eventualities were discussed. They were told, for example, that the terrain on Guadalcanal could not have been tougher. 'From our landing point,' noted one memorandum, 'our forces will have to cross a stream about 20 feet wide and 400 yards south of the beach. The name of the stream is the Ilu and it runs westward and parallel to the shore into the Tenaru River. Actually it is a backwater from the Tenaru and except in the rainy season is still and stagnant. Its banks are steep, boggy and from five to six feet high. The bottom is silty.'

Once over the Ilu, Marines would encounter 'high grass averaging four feet in height which affords possible positions for machine guns, riflemen, etc., with a field of fire extending across the stream toward the beach'. Further to the west, towards the airfield, was the larger Tenaru River, with banks 'eight to ten feet in height' and covered by grass and thick brush, giving the enemy more ambush opportunities. Its current was 4 knots – even faster in the rainy season – and the depth in places was over a man's head.

Beyond the Tenaru was a plantation of coconut trees, arranged in groups of four in a diamond formation that offered lanes of observation in all directions. Then came a stretch of more high grass that led through swampy undergrowth and jungle to the headwaters of Alligator Creek. The woods were dense, noted the memo, with visibility barely five yards. 'There are no roads or paths. Between the trees are thorny vines and thick low underbrush through which it is necessary to cut passage.'[4]

A couple of days before the landing, Colonel LeRoy P. Hunt, commanding the 5th Marines, wrote to the men of his command. Hunt was a legend in the Corps. Born in Newark, New Jersey, but brought up in Berkeley, California, where he later attended university, he had fought with the Devil Dogs as a 26-year-old first lieutenant at Belleau Wood, Soissons, Saint-Mihiel, Blanc Mont Ridge and the Argonne Forest, and was awarded three Silver Stars, the Distinguished Service Cross and the Navy Cross.* When he spoke, his men – the vast majority of whom had not seen action – paid attention. Hunt wrote:

> The coming offensive in Guadalcanal marks the first offensive of the war against the enemy, involving ground forces of the United States. The Marines have been selected to initiate this action which will prove to be the forerunner of successive offensive actions that will end in ultimate victory for our cause. Our country expects nothing but victory from us and it shall have just that . . .
>
> We have worked hard and trained faithfully for this action and I have every confidence in our ability and desire to force our will upon the enemy. We are meeting a tough and wily opponent but he is not sufficiently tough or wily to overcome us because WE ARE MARINES.

Hunt signed off: 'Good luck and God bless you and to hell with the Japs.'[5]

The intention of the regimental commander was to steel his troops to the task in hand. 'He knew what hard fighting was all about,' noted a corporal in Adams's platoon, 'and he was telling us this fight was going to be as hard as they came.' Yet, aside from Hunt and a few other holdovers from World War I, the men of the 1st Marine Division were

* The Silver Star is the US Armed Forces' third highest personal decoration for valour in combat. The second highest personal decorations, after the Congressional Medal of Honor, are the Army's Distinguished Service Cross and the Navy Cross. Because the Marine Brigade in France during World War I was part of the Army's 2nd Infantry Division, Marines were awarded army decorations like the Distinguished Service Cross and navy decorations like the Navy Cross.

as 'green as gourds'. Almost none of them had heard a shot fired in anger and the grim warnings they kept hearing were making people jumpy. Men kept repeating, only half in jest: 'Somebody's gonna get hurt! Somebody's gonna get hurt!'[6]

On 6 August, approaching Guadalcanal, the men of Adams's 1st Platoon spent their last evening on board the 8,000-ton *Fuller* – a former mail ship that had been acquired by the US Navy in 1940 and converted to a fast attack transport – cleaning and checking their weapons and equipment, and packing their gear. After a 'sumptuous dinner', Sergeant Thurman Irving Miller – known to his friends as 'T.I.' – told a man who owed him ten dollars to forget the debt. It was cancelled. He then lit a cigarette with a dollar bill. Why? Because he doubted, after Adams's speech, that he would ever have the opportunity to spend it.[7]

Though just 22 years old, with a pleasant oval face, dark hair and stocky frame, Sergeant Miller was one of the more experienced men in the platoon. Born and brought up in grinding poverty on a subsistence farm near Otsego in rural West Virginia, his earliest memory was of his grandfather hoeing corn. His 'gnarled hands would wrap around the handle of the hoe,' recalled Miller, 'as he worked along the row, the six-feet plus of man blending perfectly with his tool, defining economy of motion as his hoe cut its way smoothly through the dirt and replaced it without leaving weeds or piles . . . He knew how to carve a living from the land and preserve it for coming generations.'

From a huge family of sixteen siblings, Miller was put to work from the age of eight when he was given his own hoe. It was tough labour, making his hands 'hard and rough' and his back stiff. They would store up corn for the winter to feed the livestock and poultry. 'We didn't go hungry,' remembered Miller, 'but we didn't get fat either, and we knew of many who had much less than we did. It was a life that echoed throughout West Virginia, throughout all Appalachia.'

The family's jerry-built home was made of plain timber boards, lined on the inside with scraps of fabric and old magazines for insulation and decoration. There was no electricity, heating system, plumbing or running water. In autumn and winter, it was Miller's job to build the morning fires. He and his siblings would bathe in water heated on the kitchen stove, and brush their teeth with baking soda or just plain soap and a rag.

Despite the hardship, Miller enjoyed his childhood: fighting, playing and hiding in hills 'impenetrably wooded with oak and hickory, with maple and pine and locust'. A low point was in 1931 when a great drought swept across the United States, drying up streams and killing crops. 'There was no corn,' recalled Miller, 'no wheat, no rye, no feed for the livestock. Our cattle began to die, so there was no fresh beef or milk. The horses began to die.' Yet the experience of drought, and of the Great Depression more generally, paid dividends for Miller's generation when war came. He noted: 'We learned the lessons of making do with whatever was at hand, or doing without.'

A determined if not particularly inspired student, Miller graduated from high school and worked in a series of low-paid jobs before he was laid off. He decided to stow away on a freight train to California, but was arrested at the first stop and jailed for thirty days. It was a Damascene moment. He had for some time been mixing in dubious company. 'I didn't have the ambition to be a true criminal,' he admitted, 'but was curious and mischievous.' This short spell in prison made him determined to mend his ways.

In late 1940, with war clouds gathering, Miller decided to join the US Marine Corps. It had, he wrote, a 'well-deserved reputation for being the elite branch, after its success at Belleau Wood and other battles', and 'even though all the branches were seeking recruits, with the war just over the horizon, the Marines had a special place in the armed services, the first to fight, capable of being sent anywhere'. The forces would also offer him, as it had generations of men from West Virginia, 'a path out of the poverty that has marked both the perception and the reality of our most rural areas'.

His father was not convinced. 'Son,' he said, 'I'm afraid you'll spend all your time in a guardhouse.'

'Dad, if I don't go,' replied Miller, 'these people will make a criminal out of me anyway, so where I'm going will either make or break me. If I make good, I'll be back; if not, I'll stay away.'[8]

Boot camp at Parris Island, South Carolina, was for Miller a brutally tough yet necessary training for war. Aside from endless drill and marches, Platoon 99 was put through the obstacle course, practice on cargo nets and munitions training. They were told to scrub their barracks with soap and water, even cleaning the cracks in the floor with a toothbrush. 'They erased all memories of our past lives,' recalled Miller, 'or tried to. It was drilled into us that nothing but strict and immediate obedience to orders given was acceptable.'

As every Marine in the Corps is a rifleman, Miller and his fellow boots 'learned that our rifle was our best friend, to be kept clean and at the ready at all times'. He practised for hours on the range and was eventually rated a Marksman, the lowest of the three levels of proficiency.* He also qualified as a combat swimmer and learnt how to fight with a bayonet, throw a grenade, shoot a .45 automatic pistol and take part in hand-to-hand combat. But hard as he found the training, it was worse for many of the other raw recruits who, unlike him, were not used to meagre rations, 'roaming the hills for days on end, and going without sleep and working hard'.[9]

The suitability of people from Appalachia for military service was confirmed by a historian researching Vietnam-era soldiers. 'Veterans,' she wrote, 'who had grown up in rural areas indicated a better preparedness for the physical requirements of military service. Many Appalachian veterans credit their hunting and weapons skills, developed during childhood, in helping them to survive in combat.'[10] Another study by a veterans' psychologist noted that servicemen from Appalachia were much more likely to die in action than men from other regions, 'either because they were assigned more combat duty or volunteered for hazardous

* The three levels of qualification, in ascending level of ability, were: Marksman; Sharpshooter; Expert.

assignments'. He put this down to a mystique about Appalachian 'heroism and skill and attitudes about God and country', a mindset he dubbed the 'Sergeant York Syndrome' after the Tennessee conscientious objector turned warrior who won the Medal of Honor for capturing ninety German soldiers in World War I.[11]

At boot camp, they learned a new language. The Marine NCOs in charge were called DIs (drill instructors). The recruits themselves were either 'boots' or 'shitbirds', depending on the DI's mood. Food was 'chow', field shoes were 'boondockers' (never boots), gossip was 'scuttlebutt', and their weapon was a 'rifle' (or an '03'), but never a 'gun'. One recruit who got the names mixed up was forced to parade in front of the platoon huts, holding his rifle in one hand and his penis in the other, chanting, as he held them up in turn, 'This is my rifle . . . this is my gun . . . this is for Japs . . . and this is for fun.' He never made the same mistake again.[12]

Once through boot camp, Private Miller was sent with his provisional company to Guantánamo Bay in Cuba where the United States had enjoyed a perpetual lease on the land and waters since 1903. Arriving in December 1940, the company joined the 1st Marine Brigade and later became K Company, 3rd Battalion, 5th Marines (K/3/5). Miller and his fellow Marines 'carved their tent camp from the burning landscape of the desert', breaking rock and mixing and pouring cement for the mess hall base, the head, and other sanitation facilities. They practised 'landing on the beaches of the surrounding islands, assaulting hills, cutting through the jungles of the shoreline'. They were taught to live off the land, a skill Miller acquired quicker than most. Given a potato and two strips of bacon, he built a firepit with pebbles, lit a fire and fried the bacon and slices of potato in his mess kit. The city boys were amazed and, before long, 'small fires popped up all over the beach'.

Assigned to 1st Platoon, Miller's officer was Second Lieutenant 'Scoop' Adams from New York. As Miller noted,

> He was only average sized but had a strong Marine bearing. We found in him the type of officer who recognizes that he can depend on those under his command, and we wanted to live up to that

> confidence. He was always ready to listen, always ready to dispense advice when just that was needed. He never flaunted his rank even as he moved his way up. I recognized his leadership immediately and was proud to serve under his command.[13]

In the summer of 1941, K/3/5 joined the rest of the still understrength 1st Marine Division at its new training base at New River, North Carolina, a sprawling 111,000 acres of 'water, coastal swamp and plain, theretofore inhabited largely by sandflies, ticks, chiggers and snakes'. More landings were practised on Onslow Beach, while a 'Tent City' sprang up to house the ever-growing number of new recruits. That autumn each tent was furnished with a kerosene stove, 'a smelly, ornery, and often dangerous contraption'. If a tent was not set on fire – and many were – it was covered in sooty smoke, causing its occupants to cough 'for a week'.[14]

Among the new recruits was 21-year-old Jim McEnery from an Irish 'blue-collar neighbourhood' in South Brooklyn, New York. A 'scrappy kind of kid' who never 'dodged a challenge or ducked a fight', he was just twelve when his hard-drinking father died of pneumonia. A year later, with his mom struggling to pay the bills, he enrolled in a trade school that promised students good paying jobs in the aviation industry after graduation. But unable to afford the tuition fees for the final two terms, he dropped out and found work as a shipping clerk in a pen company. His salary of $15 a week was more than some men twice his age were paid. He and his family were financially secure for the first time in his life.

Yet McEnery had often thought of joining the military – an ambition first sparked when he attended an Armistice Day parade at the age of seven – and, with international tensions rising, he and a friend took the plunge by visiting an army recruitment office. It was closed, so the pair went to the nearby Navy Building where a 'middle-aged Marine sergeant in dress blues' talked them into joining the Corps. A private's pay was only $21 a month, a third of what McEnery had been earning. But as all his food, clothing and housing would be taken care of, he figured he could send half his monthly pay home to his mom.

He enlisted in September 1940 and, following boot camp at Parris Island – where he qualified as a marksman and became a close buddy of a fellow recruit called Remi Balduck, who would later 'have a Navy ship named after him' – did guard duty at Norfolk naval base in Virginia before he was assigned to K/3/5 at New River.[15]

By now a private first class,* tall and skinny with a pencil-thin moustache and dark curly hair, McEnery joined Adams's 1st Platoon where he became a good buddy of Thurman Miller. 'Jim stood about six feet,' wrote Miller, who was a good five inches shorter, 'and had a distinct Brooklyn accent. I had never been to New York City (or much of anywhere) then, and I always enjoyed listening to him no matter what he was saying, just for the accent. He had a colorful way of expressing himself, too, with a degree of drama.' They had, by coincidence, enlisted on the same day. But because McEnery took a boat from New York to Parris Island, while Miller went by train, the West Virginian got there first and joined an earlier training platoon.[16]

Another key member of Adams's platoon who joined at New River was Sergeant Maurice O. 'Mo' Darsey from Dexter, Georgia. After graduating from high school, Darsey enlisted in the US Marines in 1935, aged twenty, because his family 'was too poor to send him to college'. After boot camp, he was sent to guard the US Embassy in Peking, China, where he witnessed Japanese atrocities at the start of the Sino-Japanese War in 1937. As a result, he would have, noted Miller, 'a better idea of what we'd be facing than did any of the rest of us'. Darsey's next posting was Pearl Harbor, from where he had the good fortune to be 'pulled out' the day before the Japanese attack. It was far from his last encounter with Lady Luck. Miller recalled: 'Mo was a stout, strong man and may have looked overweight compared to

* The enlisted ranks for the US Marine Corps, at this stage of the war, were: private (no insignia); private first class (a single chevron); corporal (two chevrons); 'buck' sergeant (three chevrons); platoon sergeant (three chevrons with a single 'rocker' beneath), first sergeant and gunnery sergeant (three chevrons with a double 'rocker' beneath); sergeant major or master gunnery sergeant (three chevrons with a triple 'rocker' beneath).

the rest of us scrawny Marines, but he was just large and sturdy, and the ravages of battle did not seem to affect him as much as they did others . . . He was a very dedicated sergeant, and all the men of the platoon had great respect for him.'[17]

By the time the 1st Marine Division left New River in May 1942, Darsey had become Adams's platoon sergeant, or number two, with Miller, recently promoted to buck sergeant, as the platoon guide, or third in the chain of command. 'Scoop, Mo and I,' noted Miller, 'made up platoon "headquarters unit," or platoon command post (CP). The CP would be located several yards in the rear of the four squads . . . The command-post strategy started at the top, with the division command post, and on down to regimental, battalion, and company command-post level, as a matter of observing what was happening in front of us, and we could move another squad (or higher up, a regiment or company), to plug any gap.' Jim McEnery, now a corporal, was leader of the platoon's 1st Squad.

Shortly before shipping out, Miller returned to Otsego on leave. It was a tiring trip by train, bus and finally a hitchhike ride. Miller did not care. He had left home eighteen months earlier with few prospects and a reputation as a tearaway. His father had predicted he would end up in jail. Yet the Marine Corps had been the making of him. Given structure, discipline and a sense of belonging, he had found something he could excel at, and was rewarded by three promotions in quick succession, the last, to sergeant, after an examination. He arrived home wearing his smart uniform, the 'best clothes' he had ever owned, and three stripes on his arm. 'I was,' he wrote, 'making good on my promise to Dad.'

During this final leave, Miller popped the question to his sweetheart Recie, a beautiful dark-haired girl he had been dating since she was thirteen, four years his junior. She said yes. But as he was determined not to make her a widow, the marriage would have to wait until he returned – *if* he returned – from service overseas.[18]

3

'Will I run? Will I be afraid?'

British Solomon Islands, 7 August 1942

The men of K/3/5 were woken on USS *Fuller* at 4:00 a.m. after a fitful sleep. With their first experience of combat looming, many asked themselves the questions all soldiers pose sooner or later: *Will I run? Will I be afraid?*

Only time would tell.

It was 7 August 1942, D-Day, and exactly eight months since the 'Day of Infamy' at Pearl Harbor. Now was their opportunity to strike back.[1]

Having rounded Cape Esperance on the northwest corner of Guadalcanal, the task force split into two: some transports headed north for the tiny island of Tulagi; while the majority, *Fuller* included, steamed due east for the landing zone on Red Beach. Sailing just ahead of *Fuller* was the fast attack ship USS *American Legion*, carrying the command group of the 5th Marines and Dick Tregaskis, a 25-year-old Harvard-educated combat correspondent from Elizabeth, New Jersey, who was on his first assignment for the International News Service. The 6ft 7in Tregaskis recalled:

> On the deck, Marines lined the starboard rail, and strained their eyes and pointed their field glasses toward the high, irregular dark mass that lay beyond the sheen of water, beyond the silently moving shapes that were our accompanying ships. The land mass was Guadalcanal Island. The sky was still dark; there was yet no

> pre-dawn glow, but the rugged black mountains were quite distinct against the lighter sky.
>
> . . . The only sounds were the swish of water around our ship, the slight noises of men moving about on the forward deck. Fifteen troop transports and freighters, loaded with 16,000 men of the reinforced First Marine Division, were slipping under the noses of the Japs, without a single sign of protest. And there was only silence across the bay where eight other transports were carrying 3,000 more men to the smaller islands to the north.

As the sun began to rise, the rugged mass of Guadalcanal grew more distinct, revealing the 'sharp shoulders' of high mountains. There was, as yet, no sign of any opposition.

At 6:14 a.m., the escorting heavy cruisers began their bombardment of the coast: brilliant yellow-green flashes, followed by the 'red pencil-lines of the shells arching through the sky', and finally 'flashes on the dark shore' and the 'b-rroom-boom' of the explosion. As the lead transports neared the landing zone, they passed a burning Japanese schooner, set on fire by US Navy dive-bombers. More planes strafed Red Beach and the coast behind with bombs and machine-gun bullets.

The lead ships reached the transport area, four and a half miles off the shore, at 6:51 a.m. No sooner had they stopped than the 'davits began to clank as the boats were lowered away'.[2] The boats in question were LCP(L)s – Landing Craft Personnel (Large) – better known as Higgins boats, after their designer Andrew Higgins. Based on vessels used in swamps, the Higgins was a shallow-draught, barge-like boat just over 36 feet long and under 11 feet wide. Powered by a 225-horsepower diesel engine, it could ferry a platoon-sized complement of thirty-six men to shore at 8 knots. Later in the war they would be supplied with steel ramps at the front, which could be quickly lowered to disembark men and supplies. But these early versions had no front ramps and, to exit, the Marines had to leap over the side. Moreover, the boat's pine plank and plywood construction offered little protection from enemy fire; and, as had been discovered during the disastrous practice landings on Koro Island a week earlier, the Higgins could not easily pass through shallow water or over reefs.

While the boats were being lowered into the water, cargo nets were dropped down the high sides of the transports. Then, at a signal from a sailor, the first Marines, silent and nervous, 'clambered over the rail and swung down the rope nets into the boats'. Once full, the boats pulled away and more took their place, and 'the seeping waterfall of Marines continued to slide over the side'.[3] Unlike the dress rehearsal on Koro, this debarkation went without a hitch. 'There was no noise or confusion,' noted the divisional action report. 'It proceeded with the smoothness and precision of a well-rehearsed peace-time drill.'[4]

Five boats were needed to accommodate K/3/5, with 'Scoop' Adams and most of his 1st Platoon in one of them. 'If so many of us hadn't been so nervous and on edge,' recalled Jim McEnery, 'it would've been a pretty nice day for a boat ride. The sky was pale blue with some big, puffy clouds that looked like gobs of whipped cream. And as our Higgins boat headed for the shore . . . there was hardly a ripple in the sea around us.'

From a distance the island looked quiet and unthreatening: 'white sand beaches framed by clusters of dark green palm trees, with dense jungle undergrowth just behind and blue-green hills rising up in the distance'. Yet, told what to expect, they imagined the place 'to be crawling with Japs, all of them itching to blow us to hell'. Oddly, McEnery did not feel scared; but he was 'tense and excited', and his pulse had quickened. 'I probably *should've* been scared,' he admitted, 'but I just didn't have enough sense to be, and I sure as hell didn't blame anybody that was.'

Though still early in the day, the air was 'already uncomfortably warm and steamy', and the Marines' dungaree uniforms were sticking to their wearers 'like glue'.[5] The uniforms were made of a distinctive olive drab herringbone twill (aka 'dungaree')* that was actually a greyish sage-green

* In the 1930s Marines had worn one or two-piece blue denim fatigues (called 'utilities' or 'dungarees') for work detail. In the summer of 1941, new work

shade. The jacket had three flapless pockets, the one on the left breast being marked with 'USMC' and the famous Eagle, Globe and Anchor insignia of the Corps beneath. The trousers were worn bloused into canvas leggings, and the footwear were the rubber-soled, rough-side-out leather service shoes known as 'boondockers'. Each man wore the standard-issue M-1 helmet, a one-size-fits-all steel construction with chin strap and a hard inner plastic liner with an adjustable sweatband and cotton webbing for comfort (but without the camouflage cover that Marines would wear in later Pacific campaigns). He also had a light-tan webbing belt for spare ammunition, two fragmentation grenades, a bayonet and a metal water bottle. He carried his weapon – a rifle, Browning Automatic Rifle (BAR), submachine gun and/or automatic pistol – and, depending on his speciality, might also be toting ammunition and parts for mortars or machine guns. But he had left his pack on board, and so went ashore without any rations or personal items. He did not even have a specialized entrenching tool.[6]

On the starboard side of the boat, aiming to be first out, was 'Scoop' Adams. Across from him, on the port side, was T. I. Miller, next to the navy coxswain. Halfway to the beach, Adams noticed the coxswain was not the one they had trained with, and who had promised to get them 'all the way up into the coconut trees' if need be. So he crawled over and tapped the new man on the shoulder. 'When we scrape the beach,' said Adams, 'make sure you keep the throttle open until we're all off.'

The coxswain shook his head. 'I'm in charge of the boat, lieutenant, and I'll take you in only far enough that I can safely get the boat back out.'

Adams was about to protest when he saw Miller signal for him not to worry. Confident that the sergeant had matters in hand, he returned to his original position.[7]

With just a couple of hundred yards to go, McEnery noticed members of the platoon 'staring towards the approaching beach with grim expressions and glassy eyes'. Others bowed their heads and muttered silent

---

uniforms were issued made of cotton herringbone twill (HBT). Despite replacing the blue denim uniforms, they were still called 'dungarees'.

prayers. For a moment, McEnery had a mental picture of his mother and sister, and the last letters he had read from them. He assumed others were doing the same, and was grateful that he 'didn't have a wife or kids back home, or even a steady girlfriend, to grieve' for him if anything happened.

He noticed that the man crouching next to him – PFC William Murray, 'a pint-sized kid of eighteen' who served as a platoon scout – was fidgeting with one of the two grenades that each rifleman had hooked to his belt. Suddenly a look of horror came over Murray's face. 'My God!' he said. 'I think I dislodged the pin.'

McEnery leaned forward, grabbed the grenade and forced the pin back into place. 'What the hell are you trying to do?' he shouted. 'You want to blow up the whole damn boat?'

White-faced and shaking, Murray was about to throw the grenade over the side when McEnery stopped him. 'Hand it to me. I'll give you one of mine to replace it.'

'But . . .'

'Just calm down and give it here,' McEnery insisted. 'It'll be okay. That one grenade might save your life this morning.'

To ease the tension, PFC 'Dutch' Schantzenbach, one of the company's keenest beer drinkers, began singing the popular ditty 'Roll out the Barrel'.* He was soon joined by a couple of dozen 'off-key male voices'. McEnery almost laughed: it sounded bad enough to scare the enemy.[8]

Moments later, the boat hit the bottom, but, as Adams had feared, it was still in water too deep for comfort. Then the engine roared and the boat pushed farther up the beach. As Adams went over the side, into just a few inches of water, he looked across at the coxswain. He was out cold and someone else was at the controls. 'T.I. had done what he signalled he would do,' noted Adams. 'The Marines thus made a safe landing.'

* Originally composed in Czechoslovakia in 1927, it was known as the 'Beer Barrel Polka' and later became famous around the world, particularly among World War II soldiers.

It was 9:27 a.m. K Company was on the extreme left (or eastern edge) of Red Beach. The lead companies of the 1/5 Marines had landed away to their right fifteen minutes earlier.

Once on firm ground, Adams and his men hurried up the beach towards the jungle's edge. 'There we waited,' recalled Miller, 'for incoming fire that never came. There were no bullets, no sound except the men behind us as we ran toward the jungle. We had caught the enemy off guard.'[9]

This was partly true. But Major General Vandegrift had premised his plan on the idea that there were 5,000 Japanese soldiers on the island, including an infantry regiment of 2,100 men. He thought the bulk were at Lunga Point, with a detachment near Koli Point, eight miles further east, where they were building another airfield. Which is why he had chosen to land at Red Beach, a 1,600-yard stretch of sand that lay halfway between the two points. The intention was to avoid landing too close to enemy troop concentrations and prepared defences. In fact, there were only 2,300 Japanese soldiers on Guadalcanal, and most of them were rear area construction troops.[10]

But none of Adams's men knew this and, urged on by their officer, they struggled through tangled undergrowth to a low ridge about a hundred yards inland, where they set up a skirmish line. 'We started digging foxholes as fast as we could,' recalled McEnery, 'while some of the guys took cover in the trees and brush and kept their eyes on the jungle and their rifles at the ready. Other guys hacked at the undergrowth with bayonets and machetes, but it took a lot of hacking to make even a small dent in the stuff.'

Every now and again, they would pause, look at each other and ask a question no one could answer: 'Where the hell are the Japs?'[11]

Dick Tregaskis came ashore with Colonel Hunt and the rest of the 5th Marines' Command Group at 9:50 a.m. Jumping carefully from the boat's bow, the lanky journalist 'got only one foot wet, and that slightly; hardly the hell-for-leather leap and dash through the surf, with accompaniment of rattling machine guns' that he had expected.

Within half an hour, anti-aircraft guns were being set up on the beach and the first tank came ashore. The only casualty thus far, Tregaskis discovered, was a Marine who had cut his hand while trying to open a coconut with a machete. Hunt, meanwhile, had moved inland with his staff. Tregaskis followed them by sticking close to the Command Post telephone lines that had 'sprung through the conquered terrain almost instantaneously'. Passing coconut palms, he moved along a path cut through 'shoulder-high parched grass' and into the 'thick, shadowy jungle'. Once over a muddy, stagnant little creek – much smaller than the 20ft-wide stream mentioned by the intelligence reports – he moved easily down a track four feet in width to where Hunt had sited his CP in 'an undistinguished part of the jungle, where communications men were busy installing field telephones'. As it was time for lunch, they 'squatted in matting of soft, wet leaves and opened ration cans'.[12]

Once the 5th Marines had secured the initial beachhead, the three battalions of the 1st Marines came ashore and headed obliquely inland towards the 'Grassy Knoll'. It soon became obvious that this was a mountain, not a knoll, and that it was much farther away than anticipated. Having crossed a tributary of the Tenaru River, the 1st Marines entered Guadalcanal's jungle canopy formed by huge hardwood trees, some more than 150 feet in height, 'draped with brilliant green foliage, spread haughtily over dingy snarls of vines, thorns, and tough roots'. Catcalls from exotic birds 'mocked Marines as they exhausted themselves and dulled machete blades trying to chop a path through the tangle'. Watching from the undergrowth were wild dogs, pigs, lizards and bush rats. Mosquitoes descended in clouds. All around was the stench of rotting vegetation.[13]

Struggling through this difficult and unfamiliar terrain, the 1st Marines slowed to a crawl. 'There was,' noted one report, 'a uniform and lamentable failure to use patrols – control and communication were difficult to maintain.'[14]

At 2:00 p.m., to support the advance of the 1st Regiment, the 1/5 Marines was ordered to extend the western perimeter of the beachhead as far as the east bank of the Tenaru River, a distance of around two miles. At the same time, K Company and the rest of the 3/5 Marines were told to secure the left (east) flank.[15] As they were moving into position, thirty-two Japanese twin-engine 'Betty' bombers and their escort of twenty-four long-range Zero (or 'Zeke') fighters flew overhead. 'They were less than a hundred feet off the ground,' recalled Jim McEnery,

> But they didn't even slow down or take a second look at us. They were after our ships out in the Sealark Channel. We stopped digging in long enough to watch the fireworks. We'd been trained to hit the deck when the enemy planes showed up, but I could see hundreds of Marines up and down the beach just standing there gawking at the planes like they were watching a damn ball game. You'd have thought they were in the bleachers at Yankee Stadium for Pete's sake. If any of those Jap Zeros had decided to make a few strafing runs along the shoreline, it could've been one helluva slaughter.[16]

Fortunately for the American ships, low cloud cover disrupted the Japanese aim and no bomb found its target. A subsequent attack by nine Japanese 'Val' dive-bombers scored only a single hit on the destroyer USS *Mugford*. Total Japanese losses were five Bettys, nine Vals and two Zekes, most of them shot down by Grumman F4F 'Wildcats' from the carrier *Enterprise*. The Wildcats, in turn, lost 50 per cent of their number: the victims of more experienced Japanese pilots and a plane, the Zeke, that was superior in a dogfight.[17]

One of the unintended consequences of these raids was that they held up the unloading of supplies. 'There were tons of the stuff already piled up along the beach,' remembered Jim McEnery, 'but we didn't know where it was or which part was ours. Even if we had, we didn't have enough manpower to go out and haul it in – not when we needed to work on our defenses at the same time.'

As darkness fell, McEnery asked 'Scoop' Adams what the plan was for the following day. 'Where do we go from here? Are we just gonna sit tight and wait for the Nips to come at us or what?'

Adams shrugged. 'Just set up your line and make sure it's solid for tonight. Then we'll talk again in the morning. Captain Patterson's probably waiting to hear from battalion, and battalion's waiting to hear from Colonel Hunt at regiment. Nobody expected the Japs to pull a disappearing act like this. We'll probably send out some patrols tomorrow, but my guess is we won't do much till after the First Marines take the airfield.'

'So should I plan on taking a patrol out tomorrow?' queried McEnery.

'Just sit tight, Mac, and tell your guys to stay on their toes. If I hear anything, I'll let you know.'

McEnery nodded. He regarded Adams as a 'terrific officer and an all-round good guy', the type who would 'stay right up there on the front line with the rest of us' and even do 'some of the digging'. He was not so impressed by the company commander or 'skipper', Captain Lawrence V. Patterson. A pre-war regular, Patterson had joined the Marines as an enlisted man and was promoted from corporal to second lieutenant as a 'meritorious NCO' in the summer of 1938. He should, in theory, have been a solid skipper who saw things from the ordinary Marine's perspective. Yet, as events would prove in Guadalcanal, that was not necessarily the case and, unlike Adams, Patterson tended 'to hide out in a command post' well to the rear.

Despite his confidence in Adams's judgement, McEnery still felt uneasy. He and the rest of K Company had come ashore with just two grenades and a single 'unit of fire' for their bolt-action 1903 vintage Springfield rifles. Some units in the US armed forces had been using the more effective gas-operated .30 M1 Garand, the first semi-automatic military rifle, since 1936; but none of the Marines in the Pacific had them because their superiors still favoured the more accurate and reliable bolt-action Springfield over the quicker firing Garand. A 'unit of fire', moreover, was supposed to equal an average day's expenditure of ammunition. McEnery doubted that, in a firefight, it would last 'half an *hour*'.

Then there was the issue of sustenance. They had landed without rations and only a quart of water each. By nightfall the water was long gone and no one in K Company had eaten since breakfast. McEnery was sharing a foxhole with 31-year-old PFC Bill Landrum, his assistant squad leader from Tallahassee, Florida. A 'good Marine' who had been in the Corps a little longer than McEnery, Landrum was a 'quiet guy who never seemed to have much to say'. That first night on Guadalcanal, he was even quieter than usual. They were both 'thinking about people and things that were far, far away'. McEnery offered to take the first watch, while Landrum got some sleep. 'Pretty soon,' recalled McEnery, 'he was snoring, and I was alone, staring into the darkness in front of me.'

The longer he stared, the more he convinced himself that indeterminate dark shapes could only be the enemy. Men up and down the line had the same problem and, every now and again, a nervous Marine would loose off a few rounds, prompting others to join in. It was a waste of their limited ammo supply, but 'the jitters that caused it were understandable'. McEnery tried to think positive thoughts. It was hard because he 'didn't have the foggiest idea what was going to happen next'. By the same time tomorrow, they might all be dead; or they might be in the same spot, 'wishing for more water and ammo and something to eat'.

He gripped his rifle tighter and asked himself: 'Okay, so how the *hell* did I end up in this godforsaken place, anyway?'[18]

4

'You think we'll ever get off this damned island?'

Guadalcanal, 8–11 August 1942

At first light on 8 August, 'Scoop' Adams passed on orders from Captain Patterson to his platoon. 'The whole company's going on a recon patrol as a unit,' he told his men. 'We'll check out the area to our immediate front. If everything looks okay, we may form a new line further west.'

The first thought that popped into Jim McEnery's head was: *Oh crap, sounds like we're in for more digging!*[1]

He was right. The patrol was part of a general movement west towards the Lunga River which would put Vandegrift's 1st Marine Division in possession of the Japanese airfield. The 1/5 Marines had the easiest job, advancing 'through flat coconut plantations bordering the sea', while the 1st Marines continued their march across 'seemingly impenetrable jungle'.[2]

Moving out at 9:00 a.m., Adams's platoon headed southwest on high alert. 'We advanced maybe 1,500 yards,' noted McEnery, 'using the undergrowth and coconut palms for cover and staying within sight of the beach. After that, we stopped for a break, then started retracing our path back toward our original defense line.'

They had almost made it when a swarm of Betty torpedo-bombers and Zeke long-range fighters flew low overhead, heading for the ships in Sealark Channel. McEnery got a good look at one pilot: he was wearing goggles and the grin on his face 'was a foot wide'.[3]

Minutes later, the 'quick paced whoomp-whoomp of anti-aircraft firing began' and black bursts covered the sky. 'Suddenly,' recalled Dick Tregaskis, watching from the shore, 'I saw the first Jap, a long, flat-shaped two-engined plane moving in among the transports like some preying shark, skimming over the water below the levels of the masts.' Then more planes appeared and began to launch their torpedoes. One, chased by a Grumman Wildcat, trailed smoke and fire before it 'arched into the water' and exploded, sending a 'sheet of flame backfiring a hundred feet into the sky'.[4]

Other planes were shot down by the blizzard of anti-aircraft fire, though one torpedo found its mark when it struck the starboard bow of the destroyer *Jarvis*, killing fifteen men. Another stricken plane flew into the bridge of the transport *George F. Elliott*, causing 'a huge flash of fire, as red as blood', to burst along her upper deck. The burning transport was later scuttled in shallow water, taking with it the supplies for the 2/1 Marines. Only five of the twenty-nine attacking Bettys made it back to their base at Rabaul on the island of New Britain.[5]

The 1/5 Marines, meanwhile, advancing up the coast, had captured two Japanese soldiers in the village of Lunga, a mile short of the point. Interrogated by Japanese speakers, the prisoners gave the first reliable intelligence about the number of defenders on the island. Their forces, said the prisoners, were 'two Navy construction battalions about 1,800 men and under 500 troops'. This was far fewer than the pre-invasion estimate of 5,000 men, including 2,100 'who were supposed to make up a reinforced infantry regiment'. What Japanese defenders there were, moreover, had withdrawn to the west.

Armed with this new information, Vandegrift ordered Colonel Hunt to contract the 5th Marines' front, and to move westward quickly, seizing the village of Kukum a mile beyond Lunga Point before nightfall. This was done. En route, between the Lunga and Kukum rivers, the 1/5 Marines captured intact the main Japanese camp with large supplies of food, ammunition, equipment, motor transport, and electric and radio installations. 'The enemy,' noted the 5th Marines' War Diary, 'had apparently fled in great haste. Only material damage noted was that caused by our naval gunfire prior to the landing.'[6]

In one big tent, Dick Tregaskis found breakfast still on the table, as if the Japanese 'had left by the back door as we came in the front'. There were serving dishes 'filled with meat stew, rice, and cooked prunes', and bowls and saucers still half full of food. Chopsticks had been left propped on dishes, or dropped hastily on the floor. In other tents he saw shoes, mosquito nets, toilet articles and soap, and some had had their canvas ripped by high-explosive shrapnel. A little further on, clusters of coconut palms had been shattered by naval gunfire, and in one little grove were found two fly-covered corpses. 'One body sat at the foot of a tree,' wrote Tregaskis, 'eyes staring straight ahead. The left leg had been nipped off at the knee, and the lower part of the leg, with the shoe still on the foot, lay a few feet to one side.'

The nearby airfield was overrun by the 1st Marines in the early afternoon. When Tregaskis got there he saw 'rows of brand-new wooden barracks – so new that the Japs had not yet moved in'. Hitching a lift to Lunga Point on a tank, he passed a large grey frame-house that contained an electricity plant, and a huge motor pool with at least a hundred trucks, 'Nipponese versions of the Chevrolet'.

Next appeared a cluster of buildings that had housed the Japanese headquarters, complete with iron beds, 'handsome French telephone receivers, radios, riding boots standing in corners'. The main house was well stocked with luxuries that included bottles of sake and wine, a large radio set, and a bathtub, a 'crowning luxury on this hot tropical island'. Outside were stacks of crates 'filled with canned goods, cases of a soda pop labelled "Mitsubichampagne Cider", and two varieties of Japanese beer'.

Tregaskis rejoined Colonel Hunt at his new CP beyond the Lunga River. He had not been there long when he heard rifle shots from a nearby wood. *This is it!* he thought. *This is the trap! They've got us.* The apprehensive look on the faces of the Marines told him they felt the same. Only Hunt – who earlier had been the first man across the Lunga River – seemed unconcerned as he strode into the wood to investigate.

Tregaskis followed to find two dead Japanese soldiers, and a third lying on the ground, breathing hard, 'with a small bloodstain on the back of his shirt, the color of wine'. He was treated by a corpsman* but died soon after.[7]

Back in its original position by 1:00 p.m. on 8 August, K Company was ordered to remain there until the following morning when it and the remainder of the 3/5 Marines would march west to link up with the 1/5 Marines and the regimental CP in the new beachhead perimeter between the Kukum and Tenaru rivers. The news filtered through that the airfield had been captured and the Japanese troop strength on the island was much weaker than anticipated. 'Suddenly,' remembered Jim McEnery, 'everything started looking a lot simpler – and easier – than it had that morning. We felt like we'd gotten a big break. All we had to do now to finish our job on Guadalcanal was find and take care of those few hundred Jap combat troops and get the airfield into operation.'[8]

An hour or so after midnight, as some of the K Company men kept watch from their foxholes, they heard the sound of heavy naval gunfire to the north, from the direction of Savo Island. McEnery and others in the 1st Platoon 'cheered like crazy' when they saw the 'big guns flashing and heard the explosions far out in the channel'. They assumed the US Navy was 'giving the Japs an ass-kicking they'd never forget'. Instead they were watching 'the worst American naval defeat since Pearl Harbor'.[9]

The grim sequence of events had begun earlier the previous evening with a conference of Operation Watchtower's senior officers on board the flagship of the amphibious task force commander, Admiral Richmond Kelly Turner. A short, balding man with beetle eyebrows and steel-rimmed glasses, Turner had a quick temper and a hectoring manner.

* Each Marine battalion was assigned two naval doctors and forty corpsmen (always known individually as 'Doc'). The corpsmen were, in fact, naval ratings – ranking from hospital apprentice 2nd class to chief pharmacist's mate – who had passed courses at Hospital Corps School and Field Medical Service School before being assigned to their individual units. They were Marines in all but name.

With bad news to impart, he made no attempt to sugarcoat it. He told them that Vice Admiral Jack Fletcher, the commander of the aircraft carrier task force, was concerned about the safety of his flat-tops and, as a result, had been given permission to withdraw them from the channel off Guadalcanal eight hours earlier than originally agreed. This meant they would leave that night, thus depriving Turner's transports and cargo ships of air cover. Turner, as a result, would move the rest of the fleet out at sunrise the following day, 9 August. When Vandegrift complained that he needed more supplies, Turner said that the cargo ships could stay and unload for another day. But the warships and troop transports had to leave at dawn.*

Despite receiving patchy and contradictory reports that a Japanese fleet was approaching, Turner made no mention of this at the conference. He was confident, in any event, that reconnaissance flights had searched the approach routes without spotting anything. Those flights, it would later transpire, were cancelled because of poor weather, but Turner was not informed. Other reconnaissance planes that did sight the Japanese misidentified the composition of the Japanese force, which misled Turner on their potential threat. The upshot was that a Japanese naval force of five heavy cruisers, two light cruisers and a destroyer was able to approach Savo Sound – where Turner's warships, cargo vessels and transports were located – under the cover of darkness. The Japanese had long anticipated such an action and were superbly equipped with night optical rangefinders and spotting sights, illumination aids (such as star shells, searchlights and flares), and the excellent Type 93 'Long Lance' 24-inch oxygen torpedo, 24 feet long and weighing more than a ton, tipped with a 1,090-lb high explosive warhead, and capable of a maximum speed of 49 knots.

* What Turner did not mention is that he had failed to inform Fletcher that the unloading plan was falling well behind schedule. Assuming that the bulk of the amphibious shipping would leave after dark on the 8th, Fletcher got Ghormley's approval to withdraw. He was probably right to do so, saving his limited airpower for the inevitable showdown with the Japanese carrier force.

Advancing with his eight ships in a single column, the Japanese commander Vice Admiral Gunichi Mikawa was able to enter Savo Sound undetected. At 1:31 a.m. he signalled, 'Every ship attack.'

The US screening group south of Savo Island was the first to be illuminated by flares dropped by Japanese float planes. Moments later two heavy cruisers, the USS *Chicago* and HMAS *Canberra* (crewed by Australians), were struck by a hail of 8in armour-piercing rounds and Long Lance torpedoes. These were the first explosions and flashes detected by the men of K Company on Guadalcanal, and they were not a cause for rejoicing. Hit by at least twenty rounds, *Canberra* was soon ablaze, deprived of engine power and listing to starboard. A torpedo tore into *Chicago*'s starboard bow soon after. It, too, was out of the fight.

Steaming north at 30 knots, the Japanese force broke into two columns and enveloped the three American cruisers and two destroyers of the northern screening group. Once again, the attack was sudden, swift and deadly. One US cruiser, USS *Quincy*, did fire back and cause serious damage to Mikawa's flagship *Chokai*. But it was an isolated moment of defiance and, within minutes, Japanese shells had destroyed *Quincy*'s bridge and killed all its senior officers, while two torpedo strikes put paid to her propulsion. She quickly sank by the bow, 'her stern with propellers and rudder clearly outlined against the fire-lit sky'.

USS *Vincennes* was the next victim. Hit by more than seventy projectiles from five different Japanese cruisers, she caught fire and sank. The third cruiser, USS *Astoria*, was also pummelled by Japanese shells and left drifting without power and burning fiercely. She sank just after noon. *Canberra* was too badly damaged to join the withdrawal ordered by Turner and, after the crew was removed, was finished off by shells fired by American destroyers. Its floor now littered with sunken ships, the Sealark Channel was henceforth known as Ironbottom Sound. In all, the one-sided Battle of Savo Island cost the US fleet four heavy cruisers (one Australian), while another heavy cruiser and a destroyer were damaged; casualties were 1,077 Allied servicemen killed and 700 wounded. Japanese casualties, by contrast, were 129 killed and 85 wounded (including the men lost when the heavy cruiser *Kako* was torpedoed and sunk by the US submarine *S-44* on 10 August). It was a catastrophic defeat for the US Navy that would have dire consequences for the men on Guadalcanal. But it could have been worse.

Unaware that the US Navy had already withdrawn its aircraft carriers, and with dawn fast approaching, Vice Admiral Migawa chose not to engage the now defenceless transports and cargo ships. Instead he retired at full speed to the northwest. His chief of staff, Commander Ohmae, later explained that the 'Decisive Battle' doctrine – which held that the destruction of the enemy's surface fleet automatically reduced his command of the sea – lay behind Migawa's decision. It was, in any event, a fatal error. 'If the admiral had taken the more aggressive course,' wrote historian Ian W. Toll, 'as some of his officers had urged, Turner's fleet might have been wiped out.' This, in turn, would have left the troops on Guadalcanal without supplies or hope of reinforcement, and the campaign must have ended in ignominious failure. As it was, the outcome was still very much in the balance because Turner had no option but to withdraw his remaining ships on the 9th, leaving the Marines on shore with barely half their supplies and none of their heavy equipment. Observing the burning hulks of *Canberra* and *Astoria*, and watching ship after ship sail away, General Vandegrift asked an aide: 'What's happened to the navy?'

'I don't believe,' the staff officer replied, 'the first team has taken the field.'[10]

Word of the scale of the US Navy's defeat, and its decision to withdraw its remaining warships and transports that day, reached General Vandegrift's CP near Alligator Creek, west of the Tenaru River, an hour or so later. Despite driving rain, Vandegrift called his senior commanders to a council of war. He recalled:

> Singly or in pairs, they straggled to my CP, the colonels, lieutenant colonels, and majors on whom so much depended. They already were a sorry-looking lot with bloodshot eyes and embryonic beards and filthy dungarees. They were tired. They did not talk much as

> they slumped to the wet ground under the coconut palms and huddled over their knees against rain hissing on a pathetic fire. Some smoked, others sipped black coffee from aluminium canteen cups and swore when the hot metal touched chapped lips.

Many watched the pathetic scene on the nearby beach, where small boats were landing survivors from the naval battle 'whose semi-naked bodies black from burns and oil of the sunken ships claimed the ministrations of our doctors and corpsmen'. Offshore they could see the cruiser *Chicago*, 'her bow shot away', limp past transports 'busily hoisting landing craft to their decks'.

Once everyone was present, Vandegrift passed on the bad news: the navy had lost most of its cruisers in a surprise attack and was pulling out. The carriers had already left, depriving the Marines of air cover. 'Please inform the men,' said Vandegrift, 'but tell them from me that this will be no Bataan or Wake Island. There'll be no surrender. We'll get through this.'

The general then called on his operations chief, Lieutenant Colonel Gerald Thomas, to outline the division's three priorities: form a new defensive perimeter around the airfield; move all the supplies within that perimeter; and finish the airfield as quickly as possible, so that planes could be flown in for aerial defence. Vandegrift's division at this stage was split: he had 6,075 Marines on the nearby islands of Tulagi, Gavutu and Tanambogo, including six infantry battalions; while on Guadalcanal there were 10,819 Marines, but only five infantry battalions. A further 1,800 men, mostly from the 2nd Marines, had left in Turner's transports.

Given his limited rifle strength, Vandegrift decided to hold a reduced perimeter with part of his defences facing the sea to stop a potential Japanese landing. He therefore anchored the right or eastern flank of the beach defences at Alligator Creek, with a short 600-yard extension inland along the creek's west bank. The line then moved along the coast to a point 1,000 yards west of Kukum where it extended inland through a chain of low hills. The 5th Marines (less its 2nd Battalion, still on Tulagi) would hold the western half of the 10,000-yard beach defence line, from the Lunga River to the chain of hills; the eastern half, from the Lunga to Alligator Creek, was the responsibility of the 1st Marines (less its 1st Battalion, which was in divisional reserve). The southern perimeter ran mostly through dense jungle and did not need, it was decided, a continuous line of defence. Instead it was covered by artillery and support units grouped along the Lunga and some nearby coral ridges.[11]

When the news filtered through to K Company, still in position near Red Beach (and therefore well outside the new perimeter), it shocked the young Marines. 'Our confidence,' recalled Corporal Jim McEnery, 'sank down to about the same depth as those sunken hulks in Iron Bottom Sound. Less than a day before, we'd thought we were almost home free. Now we knew we were in trouble up to our eyeballs.'

With the navy gone, and the Japanese in control of the sea and air, there was nothing to stop the enemy from 'sending in as many supplies and reinforcements as they needed to pin us down and bleed us to death'. The Japanese on the island, moreover, had freedom of movement, while the Marines had neither the men nor the fortifications to prevent an amphibious landing. 'For the time being, though,' noted McEnery, 'there was nothing for K/3/5 to do but follow orders and move west in a hurry.'

They had with them just a single unit of fire per man: which in McEnery's case was ten five-round clips, and one in his rifle, or fifty-five rounds in total. The men who had shot at shadows for the first two nights ashore had 'considerably less'.

As 1st Platoon began its march along the beach road, Second Lieutenant Adams advised his men: 'Conserve your ammo. When we make contact with the enemy don't waste a single round. Make every shot count. Use your bayonets whenever you can.'

Morale, by this point, was at rock bottom, with some men openly comparing their predicament to the US troops captured in Bataan and Corregidor in the Philippines. Walking beside McEnery was a private in the mortar section. 'Oh Jesus, Mac,' he asked, a pained expression on his face, 'you think we'll ever get off this damned island?'

The honest answer was no, but McEnery tried to be positive. 'Yeah, yeah. We'll be fine.'

An hour later, as they reached a point just south of the airfield, a submarine surfaced in the channel just offshore. 'That's a Jap sub!' shouted one man. 'Hit the deck!'

They did as instructed. But when the submarine's deck gun opened fire, its shells passed well overhead towards the airfield. The explosions stopped after two or three minutes. When someone got up to check, the submarine had vanished. 'Okay,' said Adams. 'Show's over. Let's move out.'[12]

Continuing on for another couple of miles, they reached their new position on a ridge that ran parallel to the coast, overlooking some coconut groves. There, at the extreme southern end of the 5th Marines' line, they were ordered to set up a new defensive perimeter. With a scarcity of picks, axes and shovels, no mines and only a few strands of barbed wire, this was not a simple task. The front line eventually consisted of foxholes and machine gun positions, backed up by 60mm mortars. Much further back, dug in south of the airfield, were two battalions of 75mm pack howitzers and one battalion of 105mm howitzers which could send high-explosive rounds to any threatened point on the perimeter.

The bulk of the supplies, meanwhile, were still piled on Red Beach, exposed to Japanese attack. Fortunately, it never came and, for the next four days, service troops used American and captured Japanese trucks to move the food and ammunition to four dispersed dumps within the perimeter. When added to the Japanese booty, this meant four units of fire and seventeen days of food per person (at two meals a day).

At the same time, the Marine pioneers worked tirelessly to finish the airfield – particularly a 180ft gap in its centre – and, assisted by Japanese construction equipment that included road rollers, handcarts, explosives and gasoline-powered locomotives, they managed this by 12 August. Rechristened Henderson Field – in honour of Marine aviator Major

Lofton Henderson, killed at Midway – the airstrip received its first plane that day. More would follow. A few days later, the runway had been extended to its maximum 3,778 feet, and ran roughly east to west, from Alligator Creek to the east bank of the Lunga River.[13]

Meanwhile, on 10 August, a patrol from the 1/5 Marines had met a small Japanese force five miles southwest of Kukum, beyond the Matanikau River, and suffered three wounded in the ensuing firefight. At least two Japanese were killed and several injured. That same day, a separate patrol brought in an American naval pilot whose plane had been shot down on the 7th. Having bailed out and landed near the beach, he was 'picked up and well cared for by natives' who eventually handed him over to the patrol. The locals – dark-skinned Melanesians who spoke pidgin English and had, until recent times, a reputation for cannibalism – were friendly, said the pilot, 'and did not like the Japs'.[14]

The following day, Japanese planes began a daily ritual of strafing and bombing the airfield and nearby Marine positions. Other planes would fly over at night. While causing limited damage and inflicting few casualties, the attacks jangled the Marines' nerves and kept them on edge. Recalling the night sorties, McEnery wrote:

> The pilot would come in slow and leisurely, like he didn't have a care in the world. He must have known we didn't have a damn thing bigger than .30-caliber or a BAR to fire at him. He'd circle around for a while, then drop one bomb and fly away. A couple of minutes later, another plane would show up and go through the same routine.
>
> The thing that hurt worst was they kept us awake most of the night. Plus they were such arrogant, infuriating sons of bitches. They knew there was nothing we could do against them . . . We called all Jap pilots by the same name – 'washing-machine Charlie'.

Early one morning, McEnery could hear another Marine 'cussing the third or fourth low-flying "Charlie" of the night from a couple of foxholes away'.

The Marine yelled: 'Damn you, you asshole! I'd give a hundred-dollar bill for thirty seconds with a .50-caliber machine gun right now!'

McEnery knew how he felt.

5

The Goettge Patrol

Guadalcanal, 12 August 1942

At 6:00 p.m. on 12 August, a large reconnaissance patrol of four officers and twenty-one enlisted men left the 5th Marines' CP, south of Kukum, and made their way to the coast where they were transported in lighters to a Higgins boat offshore. The patrol's main mission was to land on a beach close to Point Cruz, a mile west of the Matanikau River, and assess the strength of Japanese positions in the nearby village of Horahi that previous reports had described as a 'hornet's nest'. Then it would move south up the left bank of the Matanikau, bivouac for the night and return to American lines 'eastward through the hills to the upper reaches of the Lunga River'.

The initial plan had been for First Sergeant Steven Custer, enlisted chief of the divisional intelligence section (and a distant relative of the legendary general), to lead a patrol of combat troops. But this all changed after a captured Japanese naval rating told his interrogators that some of his former comrades were camped in the bush near Point Cruz and would surrender 'if given the chance'. The claim was supported by a report from a Marine patrol that it had seen 'a white flag flying above the Japanese bivouac'.[1]

This new information prompted Lieutenant Colonel Goettge, Vandegrift's intelligence chief, to include the capture of POWs as one of the mission's objectives. He also persuaded a reluctant Vandegrift that he should lead the patrol in person. This was, in Thayer Soule's opinion, a 'fatal mistake'. He added:

> As division intelligence officer and a full colonel, Goettge's place was in headquarters, but ever since arriving on the island, he had been at the front or ahead of it. He was that kind of man. In Haiti, he had once been on continuous patrol for eighteen months, and he had made similar forays in Nicaragua and Santo Domingo. Only the general or chief of staff could order him to change his ways, and neither of them had the heart to do that. 'Well, Frank,' I heard the general say, 'I'm not going to order you to stay here, but . . .'

As if his decision to lead the patrol was not bad enough, Goettge took with him a group of scouts, intelligence specialists and corpsmen, but no combat troops. They included, wrote Soule, 'some of the most valuable men in the division, most of whom had no good reason to go': Commander Malcolm Pratt, regimental surgeon of the 5th Marines; Captain Wilfrid Ringer, the 5th's regimental intelligence officer; and First Lieutenant Ralph Corry, one of only two Japanese interpreters with the division who could both read and write the enemy's language.[2]

'He just about cleaned out the Divisional intelligence section,' wrote George McMillan in *The Old Breed*, 'not to say a big hunk of the 5th Marines-2 section. Colonel Goettge felt that his men would, among other things, be acting in a humanitarian role: the Japs were said to be starving. He therefore took along [a] surgeon and a language officer, one of the few in the division, to help out.'[3]

Goettge 'wanted to prove to himself and to the Japanese', wrote Thayer Soule, that Marines 'weren't afraid of anybody, least of all a bunch of little brown men who hid in the woods'.[4] This gung-ho attitude was typical of the man. A 46-year-old veteran of World War I – where he had served as a junior officer with the Devil Dogs during the Meuse–Argonne offensive – Goettge was a tough, bearlike figure who had been a football star for the Quantico Marines Devil Dogs, playing against colleges and other military teams in the 1920s, and once turned down an offer to play for the New York Giants. Convinced that his mission beyond the Matanikau would not encounter resistance

– and that, as one member of his party put it, 'no fighting would take place unless absolutely necessary' – his men were not equipped with machine guns, BARs, radios or grenades. Instead they took only their personal weapons (pistols, rifles and submachine guns), 'ponchos, a belt, canteen with no cup, one can of C-rations, and one can of fish'.

They landed on a sandbar, four and a half miles west of Kukum – somewhere between the mouth of the Matanikau River and Point Cruz – at around 10:00 p.m. 'Some of us tried to push the boat off the sandbar,' recalled Sergeant Charles C. 'Monk' Arndt of the 5th Marines intelligence section, 'and I guess we made a lot of noise.'

Arndt then waded to the shore, after the others, and found them having a conference at the back of the 20-yard strip of beach where the jungle began. It was a dark, cloudy night, with no moon or stars visible, and Arndt could just see the outline of a 'few grass huts'. While Goettge discussed the next move with his officers, the men dug shallow foxholes in the sand. Eventually Goettge and one or two others decided to look for somewhere to spend the night. They had only covered a short distance when the waiting Japanese opened fire.[5] Goettge was hit first, struck by a bullet in the chest. The first man to reach him was Platoon Sergeant Frank Few, a swarthy 22-year-old part-Native American from Buckeye, Arizona, who had 'fierce dark eyes, a wiry muscular body' and moved 'with the swift ease of a cat'. Few tried to rouse Goettge, but it was obvious he was dead.

Looking up he saw a figure approach and challenged it. The response was a 'warwoop' as the Japanese soldier charged. Few raised his Reising submachine gun* and pulled the trigger. Nothing. It had jammed –

* First issued to Marine officers and NCOs in 1941, the .45-calibre M50 Reising possessed similar firepower to the more famous Thompson submachine gun (the 'Tommy gun'), yet was more accurate, lighter, better balanced and cheaper and easier to manufacture. On fully automatic fire, it could empty its twenty-round magazine in under two seconds. But it had its drawbacks – it was hard to maintain under combat conditions, and tended to jam. The lack of reliability soon prompted most Marines to replace it with other weapons, usually the M1903 Springfield rifle.

possibly because of sand in the mechanism – and before Few could fix the problem he was bayoneted in the arm and chest. Luckily, he was able to knock the rifle away and choke his assailant, before stabbing him with his own bayonet.

Retiring towards the main group of Marines, Few spotted another Japanese in the fork of a tree. With his own weapon still jammed, he borrowed a pistol from another Marine and shot the Japanese 'seven times'. He then got his Reising to work by loading cartridges in the chamber each time he wanted to fire. This enabled him to blast another attacker in the face, before hitting him with the butt of the gun.

Back with the others, he hastily dug a hole in the sand with his hands and helmet, while the chaotic firefight continued.[6] More Marines were hit, including Sergeant Custer who was shot through the arm. He was patched up by Lieutenant Commander Pratt, the 5th Marines' surgeon, who in Arndt's opinion was 'one of the best doctors the Marine Corps ever had'.

During a lull in the fighting, Captain Wilfrid Ringer, Sergeant Arndt and another Marine crept forward to check on Goettge. They whispered his name, but there was no response. Eventually Ringer reached the colonel's body and found, where his face should have been, a 'big hole'. As they withdrew, the third Marine was jumped and bayoneted.

Moments later, the Japanese opened up with machine guns. 'They stayed back,' recalled Arndt, 'and fired at close range, so close you could feel the air from the muzzles. About that time a corporal went out to the water's edge and started firing tracers, trying to get an SOS back. We didn't have a radio. The fighting went on until about 1 o'clock.'

Outgunned, the Marine casualties steadily mounted. Lieutenant Commander Pratt was hit first in the butt, then the chest. He died soon after. Lieutenant Corry, the 5th Marines' Japanese interpreter (who had worked in the US consulate in Tokyo before the war), was shot in the stomach. Eventually Ringer asked for a volunteer to go back for reinforcements and Arndt put up his hand. 'There was no chance to leave by land,' he recalled, and I was a pretty good swimmer. I went in the water just like a snake, on stomach, hands and knees, and I went like this just as far as I could without swimming at all. Out for about thirty yards.'

To make it easier to swim, he took off his clothes. His shoes he kept on, because the laces were knotted, and also his helmet with his pistol hooked under the chin strap. Japanese bullets narrowly missed him as he crossed the sandbar naked. Once in deeper water, he swam east along the coast, using breaststroke to make as little noise as possible. Every now and again he had to crawl over sharp coral rocks that cut his hands and feet to ribbons. At one point he saw a Japanese soldier and shot him. He remembered:

> I was afraid to go too far out. I was getting pretty tired. But I swam on a while, along the beach sort of, and then I saw a native boat beached. I crawled into it and felt around and saw one end of it was full of bullet holes and I pushed out and got in the other end. There was an old plank in it. I paddled away until I got back down to the boat base and there everybody was challenging me. I didn't know the password so I kept yelling, 'Million, million.' That had a lot of 'l's' in it.* And when I hit the shore and guys started looking at me funny I realized I was bleeding all over. I was cut all the way to the hips from the coral.[7]

Arndt reached the safety of American lines at 5:30 a.m. and, wrapped in a blanket, spoke to Colonel Hunt on a field telephone a few minutes later. He explained that Goettge had been killed and the rest of the patrol was fighting for its life four and a half miles down the beach. Hunt immediately ordered A Company (A/1/5) to set off in boats to rescue the patrol. They left at 6:50 a.m. Half an hour later, a second survivor reached Kukum: Corporal Joseph Spaulding, a New Yorker who worked in the division intelligence section. He confirmed that Pratt, Corry and many others were casualties by the time he entered

* American soldiers believed the Japanese could not pronounce the letter 'l'.

the water. During the swim back, he claimed to have passed a Japanese camp that held an estimated 300 men.[8]

The last survivor to reach Kukum at 8:00 a.m. was Platoon Sergeant Frank Few. It was just beginning to get light, and the Japanese were 'closing in for the kill', when he stripped down to his underclothes and 'made a dash for the water'. As he swam away, Few looked back to see the Japanese overwhelm the Marines' position and cut up the survivors, their Samurai swords 'flashing in the sun'.

In spite of his wounds, Few was able to swim the four and a half miles back to Kukum through shark-infested waters. When he spoke to the journalist Dick Tregaskis a couple of hours later, he was 'still a little shaky from the experience' but 'did not seem physically tired at all'.[9]

As for the others, Few was convinced they had all been killed. It certainly looked that way when A Company and a second rescue party sent by boat – composed chiefly of L Company men – reported by radio in the afternoon that they could find no sign of Goettge's men on the beach. To make certain, both companies disembarked from the boats and marched back towards Kukum, via the Japanese camp on the Matanikau: A Company along the beach, and L Company cutting a trail through the jungle. 'Both patrols started back to camp at 1700 [hrs],' noted the 5th Marines' War Diary. 'It was found that the enemy had fortified both sides of the river. As it was then about dark the order to withdraw had been given and the [A Company] patrol had returned to camp. About 15 Japs were killed and others were wounded.'[10]

The loss of Goettge and so many key intelligence personnel was a devastating blow for Vandegrift. Appointed as Goettge's replacement, Lieutenant Colonel Edmund J. Buckley worked tirelessly to rebuild morale and improve the work of the divisional intelligence section. But it was, as Thayer Soule acknowledged, an uphill battle:

> The patrol had been conceived in arrogance and ignorance. The result could have been expected. Even so, it was a rude shock to the staff and especially to the Intelligence Section. We had lost 30 percent of our personnel, including our colonel and our first

> sergeant. Until then, the war had been impersonal: shellings, bombings, a few skirmishes, and some straggling prisoners. Now it had come into our tent, to a shortwave radio that no longer had an owner, to an empty desk with a family photograph, to empty cots. We would never be the same. Neither would the division. From then on, every move was carefully evaluated, with no more rank-heavy beach parties.[11]

A couple of days later, the 3/5 Marines sent out a number of patrols to search the area where the Goettge ambush had taken place. One of them was composed of K Company's 1st Platoon. Thurman Miller recalled:

> Scoop, Jim, Mo, Slim Somerville, myself, and several others set out along the east side of the [Matanikau] sandspit. Our perimeter of defense did not include the river at this time, and so our approach up the coast through the jungle was made with the utmost caution. We were directed to engage the enemy only if necessary; we had permission to fire only if we ran into trouble. Up through the long stands of coconut trees and dense brush, across a dry wash, we crept single file. We spoke very little.[12]

Moving a little to the north of the rest of the platoon was Jim McEnery's 1st Squad. Before departing, they had been briefed by 'Scoop' Adams. 'Be damn careful out there, Mac,' he said. 'Don't take any unnecessary chances. Don't take any prisoners, either.'

'No chance of that,' replied McEnery. 'We don't need no extra mouths to feed.'

There was also the question of revenge. 'Mad as hell' about what had happened to the Goettge patrol, he and his men were 'itching for some kind of payback'. Looking back, McEnery concluded that the patrol had been 'one big, terrible series of mistakes', not least the belief that Japanese servicemen might surrender. 'To them,' he wrote later, 'surrender was the worst thing they could imagine, and they'd a whole lot rather die than disgrace the family by doing it . . . But we didn't know anything about that in those first days of combat.'

Advancing in single file, they 'waded across a knee-deep stream and climbed the three-foot-high mud bank on the other side'. From there the going was tougher through 'dense undergrowth and a thick grove of coconut palms'. Eventually they circled back towards the beach and made a grim discovery near the water's edge. 'The first thing I saw,' remembered McEnery, 'was the severed head of a Marine. I almost let out a yell because the head was moving back and forth in the water and looked like it was alive. Then I realized it was just bobbing in the small waves lapping at the shore. They would wash it up onto the sand a few inches, then it would float back out again when the waves receded.'

Near the head was a leg, still wearing its boondocker shoe, that had been hacked off at the knee. A few feet away was part of a bloody sleeve from a Marine sergeant's shirt 'with the chevrons still attached'. Other rotting body parts were scattered around. The smell of decomposing flesh was 'overpowering'.

'Holy shit!' said a Marine. 'I think I'm gonna puke!'

He staggered away and gagged. McEnery might have followed suit if he had had something besides black coffee in his stomach. Instead he just stood there, frozen in his tracks, trying to process what he was seeing. His men did the same. They were all thinking the same thing. *I won't ever forget this – not ever! I'll never see a Jap in my life without thinking about it.*

McEnery would, over the next couple of years, see a lot of gruesome sights. But nothing to compare with what he witnessed that morning. There were, he estimated, body parts from four separate corpses. There might have been more in the bushes nearby but he did not want to look. It was obvious what had happened to Goettge and his men: they had been killed to a man, and then butchered like animals.

Standing closest to McEnery was PFC Kenneth Blakesley, a 'skinny blond kid not quite eighteen years old'. Staring wide-eyed at the bodies, shaking his head, he asked: 'For God's sake, Mac, why would anybody do this? Wasn't killing 'em enough? Did they have to make mincemeat out of 'em, too?'

McEnery put his hand on the young PFC's shoulder. 'They just want to scare us, Kenny. They want to show us how tough and mean they are so we'll think they're a bunch of damn supermen. But we're gonna show them a few things, too, before this shit's all said and done.'[13]

A minute or two later, Second Lieutenant Adams appeared with the rest of the platoon. They had found more human remains: a shoe, legging, helmet and shirt, all containing the severed parts of mutilated and dismembered bodies. A particular mystery was why the bodies were here, and what had happened to the rest of them. 'We hadn't made it as far west as the patrol had landed,' noted Thurman Miller, '[and] the remains seemed to be placed for obvious discovery. As we looked over the scattered body parts we could feel the eyes of the Japanese watching us from the jungle.'[14]

McEnery asked Adams: 'What should we do with these bodies, Scoop? You want us to try and bury them?'

The platoon leader shook his head. 'Just leave 'em where they are, Mac,' he replied, fighting back the tears. 'There's no time for it right now. Maybe we can send back a burial detail later, but frankly I'd hate to risk it.'[15]

As they marched away, the men of 1st Platoon were changed for ever. As Thurman Miller wrote:

> That day on the Matanikau we beheld all the horrors of war, all the degrees of degradation to which the human race could descend. We were hardened by much training, and our reflexes were sudden, our minds alert, but now our killing potential was amplified. A second ingredient, hatred, had been added. What kind of warfare was this? . . . The Articles of War seemed to ring hollow. We threw away the book that day on the sandspit on Guadalcanal. From now on, we would do it their way. There were no words of agreement, no fanfare, no loud cursing or crying, only grimness and resolve.

There would be many reasons for American Marines to hate the Japanese: the sneak attack on Pearl Harbor, the booby-trapped corpses, and the enemy's habit of deliberately killing navy corpsmen. But 'no single event fed that hatred more', recalled Miller, 'than the story of the Goettge patrol'. The Japanese, as a result, became 'less than human' to the men of K Company, and many Marines 'descended to their level, not just taking revenge but also taking body parts, even skulls, as souvenirs'. This barbaric practice, noted Miller, although officially condemned, was 'widespread and accepted in American society' in a way that would be difficult to understand today. Miller added: 'Every soldier knew, or should have known, that taking teeth, bones, or any body part of an enemy soldier is a violation of the most basic rules of war, but the spiraling cycle of revenge reduced both sides to base animal instincts. We were killing machines fueled by hatred.'[16]

Heading back to camp, McEnery kept repeating the same words like a mantra: *I won't forget! I won't forget! I won't forget!*

That afternoon, to take his mind off what he had seen, he wrote a letter to his mom. 'Well, here we are on this beautiful tropical island,' it began, 'and everything's just fine . . .'[17]

6

'Boy, they were a sight for sore eyes!'

Guadalcanal, 18 August–14 September 1942

By mid-August, the 1st Marine Division's defensive perimeter on Guadalcanal was 'semicircular in shape, bounded by Ironbottom Sound on the north and the jungle foothills to the south'. It was 5 miles wide (east to west) and 2 miles deep (north to south), and 'covered most of what had been, before the war, the three largest and most prosperous' coconut plantations on the island. The terrain was, for that reason, relatively developed with a 'network of reasonably passable dirt roads running between the beach, Lunga Point, and Henderson Field'.[1]

K Company was defending the left portion of the division's western perimeter, dug in along a low ridge that faced the Matanikau River from the east. Since locating the remains of the Goettge patrol, Adams and his men had been itching for an opportunity to strike back.[2] But when Colonel Hunt planned a three-company assault on the Japanese concentration west of the Matanikau, he ignored K and nominated B (of the 1st Battalion), I and L (of the 3rd Battalion) instead. The plan was for L Company to 'work its way through jungle to back of enemy positions, B Company to attack along the beach starting at the river mouth, and I Company to land near Kokumbona to cut off the enemy if they attempt to retreat along the beach'.

The two-day operation – supported by artillery fire and aerial bombing raids – began on 18 August when L Company crossed the Matanikau and advanced a further 1,000 yards, killing ten Japanese en route. A few hours later B Company set off for the northwest bank of the river 'to be in position to attack by morning'. The following day, L Company 'fought its way through the jungle and took the Jap village by close rifle and bayonet fighting'. B Company, meanwhile, was prevented by machine-gun fire from crossing the mouth of the Matanikau, but did engage the Japanese across the river, 'thereby forcing the enemy to defend his rear as well as his front'. L Company found sixty-five Japanese dead in and around the village, while many more – including wounded – escaped into the hills. Also on the 19th, I Company landed by boat near the village of Kokumbona, further to the west, and drove out its defenders. Overall casualties were light: L Company had four killed – including one platoon commander – and eleven wounded; I Company just one fatality.[3]

The news that L Company, in particular, had got some payback for the Goettge patrol was greeted with whoops of delight by the K Company men in their foxholes on the ridge. They soon had another reason to celebrate. At 4:00 p.m. the next day, 20 August, they watched two Marine air squadrons – nineteen Grumman Wildcat fighters and twelve Douglas Dauntless dive-bombers – arrive at Henderson Field, circle and then land, one by one. The planes had flown the last 190 miles from the escort carrier *Long Island*, which had ferried them from Pearl Harbor. Jim McEnery remembered,

> Boy, they were a sight for sore eyes! In K/3/5's sector of our defensive perimeter about a mile southwest of the airfield, everybody started cheering and waving their arms and throwing their helmets up in the air. Some of the guys actually got all teary-eyed at the sight of those planes. As for me, I didn't shed any tears, but the planes gave me a better feeling in my gut than I'd had since we landed.
>
> The first thing I did when I saw them was get down on my knees and say, 'Thank you, Lord.'

Major General Vandegrift was just as delighted, wringing the hand of the bomber commander and saying, 'Thank God you have come.'

The arrival of the 'Cactus Air Force', as it became known – named after the codename for the island – was thought to be a gamechanger. The planes would give Vandegrift's men protection against attack by air, sea and land, and the chance to interdict enemy ships approaching from the northwest. But all these advantages would be lost if the Japanese landed reinforcements on Guadalcanal and retook the airfield – something they were determined to do. The Marines were just as determined to stop them. But could they?[4]

The first indication of an impending Japanese attack had come two nights before the arrival of the planes when ships were heard passing through Ironbottom Sound from west to east. A few hours later, they were detected moving in the opposite direction. The obvious conclusion was that the ships had dropped off troops to the east of the Marine perimeter. This surmise, as events would prove, was correct.

The initial response of the Japanese to the news of the American landings at Guadalcanal was low key. Imagining at first that the move was just a 'reconnaissance in force', the IGHQ in Tokyo was nevertheless determined to eject the invaders and recover the airfield. But despite evidence that a full Marine division had landed, naval sources insisted that the main body of troops had already withdrawn. This prompted the local army headquarters in Rabaul – the 17th – to assume that a reinforced brigade of Japanese veterans would be sufficient to retake both Guadalcanal and Tulagi. The spearhead – 917 men of Colonel Kiyoano Ichiki's 28th Infantry Regiment (known as the Ichiki Detachment) – was dropped by six destroyers at Taivu Point, 22 miles east of Lunga, on the night of 18/19 August (these were the ships heard by the Marines). Ichiki's task was to retake the airfield if possible and, if not, to secure a lodgement nearby and wait for reinforcements.[5]

The clash came in the early hours of 21 August, when the Ichiki Detachment attempted to storm positions held by the 2/1 Marines on the division's eastern perimeter along Alligator Creek. The first attempt to cross the sandspit at the mouth of the creek was made by a company of 200 Japanese soldiers. Running into a single strand of barbed wire, they were 'hit by small-arms fire and by canister' from a 37mm cannon.

Yet they kept coming, waving their arms 'wildly' and shrieking and jabbering 'like monkeys', as one Marine officer put it.

A Japanese grenade disabled the crew of the 37mm cannon, before other Marines took their place. One Marine corporal had to use a machete to fight off three assailants after his BAR jammed. Another was blinded by grenade fragments, and kept fighting. It was now a brutal, hand-to-hand struggle, but gradually the Marines got the upper hand. Once the first attack had been repulsed, the Japanese tried again along the beach, a little to the north of the sandspit. That charge was also stopped. The commander of the 2/1 Marines noted:

> From about 4 a.m. to daylight, the battle continued more or less as a state of siege, with all weapons firing and no one knowing the exact situation. When daylight came, the gruesome sight on the sandspit became visible. Dead Japs were piled in rows and on top of each other from our gun positions outward. Some were only wounded and continued to fire after playing dead. Others had taken refuge under a two-foot sand embankment and around the trunks of coconut trees, not fifty yards from our lines. But our mortars cleaned them out.[6]

It was now that the 1st Marines' reserve battalion, 1/1, was sent across the headwaters of the creek with a platoon of light tanks to cut off and destroy the remaining 500 men of Ichiki's command. Captain Nikolai 'Steve' Stevenson, the 23-year-old commander of C Company, recalled:

> Suddenly the Japanese rear guard in the coconut grove realized that they were encircled and turned to face us. Leapfrogging our two light machine guns along the beach, we raked them with crossfire, while the riflemen moved up in short, broken-field rushes. Both sides built up a firing line. Casualties mounted as snipers hidden in the tops of the palm trees picked off our men. Seventy yards from the Japanese line, the intense exchange of fire was costing us too much. Some kind of action had to be taken. I gave

> the signal to fix bayonets and the lieutenants did the same. Together we rushed the Japanese position. Seeing this, the enemy, too, fixed bayonets, leapt up and charged straight at us.

In the vicious struggle that followed, 'no quarter was asked or given' as Marines and Japanese 'fought face to face in the swirling gunsmoke, lunging, stabbing and smashing with bayonets and rifle butts'. Shrieks rose above the general tumult 'as cold steel tore through flesh and entrails and men died in agony'.

At last, it was over. The Japanese lay dead or wounded, or pretended to be. Suddenly one of the shammers threw a grenade that landed between Stevenson and a corporal. Both hit the deck and, miraculously, were unhurt by the blast. Rushing up to their assailant, Stevenson placed the muzzle of his .45 automatic pistol next to the man's head and pulled the trigger. 'The top of his head came off,' noted Stevenson. 'I rolled the man onto his back and took a wallet and papers from a blood-soaked tunic pocket. Inside the wallet was a snapshot of his wife and two children smiling primly before a lacquered screen. The papers (delivered to Regimental Intelligence) showed that he was my opposite number, commanding the rearguard. His samurai sword lay beside his lifeless hand.'

To prevent a repeat, the wounded Japanese were finished off by Stevenson's men and the platoon of light tanks. Watching the battle from 1/1 Marines CP, Dick Tregaskis noted:

> It was fascinating to see [the tanks] bustling amongst the trees, pivoting, turning, spitting sheets of yellow flame. It was like a comedy of toys, something unbelievable, to see them knocking over palm trees which fell slowly, flushing the running figures of men from underneath their treads, following and firing at the fugitives. It was unbelievable to see men falling and being killed so close, to see the explosions of Jap grenades and mortars, black fountains and showers of dirt near the tanks, and see the flashes of explosions under their very treads.

> We had not realized there were so many Japs in the grove. Group after group was flushed out and shot down by the tanks' canister shells.[7]

As the dust finally settled, Stevenson was told his XO had been killed and a platoon leader hit in the shoulder. Listening to the dying gasp of 'Mother' from a young Marine shot through the lungs, he thought about the 'extreme youth of all in my company. Most were in their middle or late teens.'[8]

Wrongly remembered as the Battle of Tenaru River – it was actually fought near Alligator Creek – this brief action cost the Marines forty-four killed and seventy-one wounded. Apart from the 15 prisoners and 120 men he had left near Taivu Point to act as a rearguard, Ichiki lost his entire attacking force of more than 770 men. In true Samurai tradition, the defeated commander shot himself, leaving behind a diary that read: '20 Aug. The march by night and the battle. 21 Aug. Enjoyment of the fruits of victory.'[9]

Ichiki's arrogant belief that the experience and fighting spirit of his men would overcome any American opposition had contributed to his downfall. More importantly for the Marines on Guadalcanal, the destruction of the Ichiki Detachment had dispelled for ever the myth of Japanese invincibility. It had also – thanks to the treacherous behaviour of some of the wounded Japanese – left even the men of K Company, who had played no part in the fighting, unwilling to take prisoners in the future. 'We learned,' wrote Jim McEnery, 'that "the only good Jap is a dead Jap," as the saying goes, and we made sure that all the wounded ones left on the field after a firefight got to be "good Japs" just as quick as we could shoot them.'[10]

To a modern audience, McEnery's words sound callous. But they become more understandable when the lessons of the Goettge patrol and the Battle of Tenaru River are factored in. The patrol taught Marines that the Japanese did not take prisoners; the battle that they would not surrender themselves, even after a crushing defeat, preferring death to dishonour. Thereafter, wary of dropping their guard, most

American servicemen exercised extreme caution when taking prisoners and erred on the side of shooting first if the enemy looked even remotely threatening.

On hearing that the Japanese had landed reinforcements on Guadalcanal, Vice Admiral Fletcher moved his aircraft carriers closer to the island to provide more effective air cover. This probe, in turn, delayed the arrival of the Japanese transports carrying Ichiki's 'Second Echelon', the men of his command who had missed the initial landing. But it also brought Fletcher's flat-tops in striking distance of the Japanese carrier fleet and, on 24 August – in a 'confused and scattershot encounter' – he won a modest tactical victory when his force sank a small Japanese carrier, *Ryujo*, and shot down seventy-five enemy aircraft. His losses were one fleet carrier damaged – the *Enterprise* was hit by three bombs, and suffered seventy-five killed and ninety-five wounded – and twenty-five planes. Thus ended the Battle of the Eastern Solomons: an American success, but one that had 'little long-term result, apart from a further reduction in the corps of trained Japanese carrier aviators'. It had, moreover, put a brake on the Japanese reinforcement of Guadalcanal by slow-moving troop transport; but other ways to reach the island would soon be found.[11]

Some of the guys of K Company, meanwhile, 'were starting to feel kind of left out and neglected' because, when it came to combat, they 'never seemed to be where the main action was'.[12] This was again the case on 27 August when the 1/5 Marines was chosen to lead another sweep back down the coast from Kokumbona. But the mission was not a success, chiefly because many of the officers and men were inexperienced and under-trained, and, as a consequence, the battalion commander Lieutenant Colonel William Maxwell did not encourage his subordinates to show initiative.[13]

The result was a slow advance through difficult terrain that was easily stopped by enemy sniper, machine-gun and light mortar fire. The final straw for Colonel Hunt was when he heard by radio that

Maxwell had ordered his men to return to Kukum by boat instead of along the coast. Egged on by Vandegrift, he sacked Maxwell and took personal command that evening. But by the time the 1/5 resumed its sweep next morning, the remaining Japanese had withdrawn into the hills, leaving twenty dead. American losses were modest – five killed and eighteen wounded – but the greater injury was to Marine pride. The whole affair was, noted George McMillan, 'a sad tale of bad leadership and inconclusive results'. The only good to come from the 'faltering foray' was the proof 'that there were relatively few Japs in the area, for if they had been there in strength they would obviously have taken advantage of our fumbling'.[14]

Glad, in retrospect, that it was not part of this discreditable affair, K Company would soon get its first proper taste of combat against the men of Major General Kiyotake Kawaguchi's 35th Infantry Brigade who were landed from barges and destroyers, 6,200-strong, at various locations along the coast – the majority at Taivu Point – in early September. The first and heaviest Japanese blow, however, would fall on the 1st Marine Raider Battalion (with Marine parachutists attached) of Lieutenant Colonel Merritt 'Red Mike' Edson. Having suffered heavy losses in the hard-fought capture of Tulagi, Edson's men were next landed at Taivu Point on 8 September to take the recently arrived Japanese reinforcements from the rear. Fortunately for the Raiders, the bulk of Kawaguchi's men had already moved west to Koli Point, and they were able to capture four 75mm field guns and a large quantity of ammunition and supplies in the village of Tasimboko, not far from Taivu Point, at a cost of just two Marines killed and six wounded.

Re-embarked and transported back to the main perimeter at Guadalcanal, the Raiders were ordered to dig a defensive position on a low ridge dubbed 'the Centipede' (thanks to its two knolls and many spurs that looked, from the air, like legs), a mile south of Henderson Airfield. It was where, coincidentally, Edson expected a future attack by the 4,000 or so Japanese troops who had, until recently, been at Tasimboko. He was right about the direction of assault, but slightly underestimated the numbers.

With barely enough time to string a single strand of barbed wire in front of a chain of mutually supporting strongpoints – rather than a continuous line – Edson's 'mongrel command' of 840 men was attacked on its right flank by the spearhead elements of Kawaguchi's brigade after dark on 12 September. But advancing through difficult and marshy terrain, on the east bank of the Lunga, the Japanese assault was poorly coordinated and easily beaten back by small arms and artillery fire.

The following day, anticipating another attack, Edson told his exhausted command: 'There is nothing but us between the Japs and Henderson Field. If we don't hold, the whole Guadalcanal landing will be a flop.'

Inspired by Edson's words, his men swore they would fight to the finish. But the ferocity of the Japanese attack at 10:00 p.m. took the paratroopers, manning the left of Edson's line, by surprise and they withdrew 150 yards, leaving the flank of the neighbouring Raiders' B Company vulnerable. It, too, was forced back until the last Raider stronghold between the Japanese and Henderson Field was a horseshoe position on a low knoll, manned by Edson and 300 Marines. It was now that Edson replaced the ineffective paratroop commander with his XO, Captain Harry Torgerson, who led a counter-attack that extended Edson's new line to the east (or left).

But still the Japanese attacked, causing the beanpole war correspondent Dick Tregaskis, watching events from division HQ behind Edson's ridge, to fear for his safety. 'We wondered,' he noted in his diary, 'if we could hold our place. If the Japs drove down the ridge in force, and broke through Col. Edson's lines, they would be able to take the CP. If they had already cut in behind our position, as we suspected they had, they would box us in, and perhaps capture the general and his staff.'

While fear gnawed at Tregaskis's insides, Vandegrift seemed calm and unconcerned as he sat on the ground beside the operations tent. 'Well,' he said with a smile, 'it's only a few more hours till dawn. Then we'll see where we stand.'[15]

As wave after wave of Japanese attacks were launched, the fighting became hand to hand. One Japanese officer and sixty men broke through and got as far as the edge of the new grass airstrip, a mile east of Henderson Field, called Fighter One. They overran some engineers and captured two machine guns, but were eventually overwhelmed. By daylight on the 14th it was all over. Edson's men, heavily outnumbered, had held their ground. Their casualties were 31 killed (including Edson's operations officer), 104 wounded and 9 missing. Japanese fatalities were at least 600, with more killed during the mopping-up operations.

The battle, in George McMillan's opinion, was 'the most critical and desperate' of the entire Guadalcanal campaign. The red-headed and softly spoken Edson had led by example, moving his CP onto the forward nose of the ridge and directing troops to where they were needed. 'Listen, you guys,' he told one disorientated group of Marines, 'the only thing those people have got that you haven't is guts.'[16] His calm and steady demeanour under fire was rewarded with the Medal of Honor. Part of the citation read:

> Col. Edson, although continuously exposed to hostile fire throughout the night, personally directed the defense of the reserve position against a fanatical foe of greatly superior numbers. By his astute leadership and gallant devotion to duty, he enabled his men, despite severe losses, to cling tenaciously to their position on that vital ridge.*[17]

Even as Edson's men were fighting to repulse Kawaguchi's main thrust, a subsidiary attack was made against the 3/1 Marines on the eastern perimeter. It was easily beaten off for the loss of seven Marines; the Japanese fatalities were a battalion commander and twenty-seven men. But when a daylight patrol of six light tanks was sent to sweep the area in front of the 3/1 line, three were destroyed by Japanese anti-tank fire.[18]

The final attempt by Kawaguchi's men to capture Henderson Field was made during the early hours of the 14th when a battalion of 1,000

* Known thereafter as 'Bloody' or 'Edson's Ridge'.

Japanese crossed the Matanikau and attacked the low ridge on the western perimeter held by the 3/5 Marines. 'Here,' noted George McMillan, 'the Japs fought fiercely and determinedly, and it looked for a while as if they might carry the ridge.'[19]

The main blow fell against L Company and the neighbouring 2nd Platoon of K Company. As the attack intensified during the morning of 14 September, Jim McEnery was called to the company CP and told by Patterson to collect two men from each of the four squads in 1st Platoon and 'hustle them up to the line' as fast as he could. Recently promoted to buck sergeant and assigned as company reconnaissance NCO, McEnery was no longer a member of 1st Platoon. So having picked two guys from his old squad – one of them the dependable Kenny Blakesley, who had been so upset when they 'stumbled onto the cut-up bodies from the Goettge patrol' – he let the other squad leaders choose the men they wanted to go. 'Come on,' he said, when they were all assembled, 'let's move out.'

Creeping forward, it took them about five minutes to cover the 75 yards to where 2nd Platoon was pinned down by Japanese fire. As they reached the top of a low rise, Blakesley was a couple of yards to McEnery's left, and slightly ahead. A BAR man he did not recognize was further to the left, blazing away. He was, recalled McEnery, 'big and burly', and handled the 19lb weapon 'like it was a water pistol'. Its slugs were 'chewing so hard into a bunch of Japs running towards him that their blood was spraying into the air'.

McEnery emptied a five-round clip from his Springfield, but was not convinced he had hit anything. Blakesley, meanwhile, was 'hugging the ground and easing forward' when a crack sounded from a Japanese rifle. The young Marine grabbed at his chest and rolled over, to reveal 'dark red blood staining the left side of his dungaree shirt'.

'Hit the deck!' yelled McEnery as more Marines came forward. It was the first time he had been under enemy fire, and the shock was severe. He crawled up next to the wounded Marine, and found him pale-faced and groaning. 'No use bothering about me, Mac,' mumbled Blakesley. 'I think he got me in the lung. I'm probably done for.'

McEnery lifted the kid's arm and tore his shirt open for a better look. 'Nah,' he said, hoping to comfort him, 'I think it's between your arm and shoulder, Kenny. Just take it easy. You'll be okay.'

'Don't let the bastards chop me up if I die out here,' whispered Blakesley, his mind on the Goettge patrol. 'Promise me you won't, Mac.'

'Don't worry,' said McEnery, wadding the torn shirtsleeve and pressing it against the wound, 'we're gonna get you out of here. Nobody's gonna chop you up.'

A voice behind them shouted: 'Corpsman! We got a man down here!'

Seconds later, a corpsman appeared and squatted down next to Blakesley. But before he could start treating him, a bullet hit the corpsman square in the chest. He fell across Blakesley's body. 'Stretcher-bearer!' yelled a Marine. 'Now we got two guys hit.'

A second corpsman ran up. He was shot in the head as he tried to lift Blakesley.

McEnery watched in horror. He wanted to fire back, but his head was spinning and he hardly dared raise his rifle in case he was next. *We need to get the hell out of here*, he told himself, *before they pick us all off one at a time*.

Eventually the fire slackened off and McEnery was able to get Blakesley on a stretcher. Others carried him to the rear.* The firefight lasted for two or three hours and, before it was over, the whole of K Company was involved. But accurate artillery fire made the difference, prompting the Japanese to break off the attack and withdraw over the Matanikau. They left behind scores of dead.[20]

K Company's casualties were thirteen killed (including the two corpsmen) and six wounded, an unusually high proportion of dead that is testament to the ferocity of the fighting.[21] It had been a sobering experience for McEnery. Seeing two corpsmen – 'some of the bravest guys in the world' – shot and killed within a few feet of him was particularly hard to take. 'All our corpsmen wanted to do was help people that were hurt,' he wrote. 'I figured out later that was why the

* Blakesley survived his wounds and returned to the United States.

Japs liked to target them so much . . . They thought the more corpsmen they killed, the more of our wounded would die from lack of treatment. And the saddest part about it was they were right.'[22]

7

'A pesthole that reeked of death, struggle and disease'

Guadalcanal, September 1942

By beating off determined Japanese attacks on the eastern, southern and western perimeters of their fragile Guadalcanal beachhead – between 21 August and 14 September 1942 – the men of the Old Breed had shown they were a match for anything their opponents could throw at them. As Jim McEnery wrote,

> Before those battles our mental state hadn't been too good. We didn't know if we could trust ourselves or not. But what happened at Tenaru [sic] and the Ridge gave us a hefty shot of self-confidence . . . After those battles, the Japs knew they couldn't make us break and run with their banzai charge in the middle of the night. At first, the arrogant bastards didn't think we'd stand and fight. They thought we were a bunch of pushovers.
>
> Now they knew better – and so did we.[1]

Vandegrift was delighted. The officers and men, he wrote in a commendation, 'proved themselves to be among the best fighting troops that any service could hope to have'.[2]

Yet the 1st Marine Division's foothold on Guadalcanal was still a precarious one – particularly given the difficulty of reinforcement and resupply – and the multiple challenges of inadequate food, disease and the harsh tropical climate were taking their toll. By early September, the men of K Company were reduced to eating two portions of unpolished 'wormy rice' a day. 'The first day,' recalled Thurman Miller, 'we saw worms in the rice and refused to eat it. The second day we picked out the worms and ate the rest. We ate, we lived. We fought off green flies while trying to eat a spoonful of rice and Eagle brand canned milk we'd captured from the Japanese. If it didn't move, we ate it. Sometimes we ate it if it did move.'

To get extra food, some K Company men joined the work parties sent to unload ships. One guy came back with coffee grounds which were boiled again and again. They were even picked up off the ground after they had been spilt during a Japanese naval bombardment and stuffed back, 'leaves and all', into the can. Having 'cussed everybody in the Marine Corps' for their carelessness, Miller brewed the grounds for an eighth time.[3]

When new supplies arrived for the officers, 'Scoop' Adams was encouraged by his men to get some. At first he refused, but when they kept pushing he gave in. He felt bad, cussing the men and saying he wouldn't be going back until the whole platoon had better food. 'I already respected him,' said Platoon Sergeant Mo Darsey, 'but I really learned to respect a man who'd say, "If my men don't eat, I don't eat." And that's exactly the kind of platoon leader I had on Guadalcanal.'[4]

As if hunger was not bad enough, the men also had to cope with the tropical heat and humidity, swarms of insects and sleepless nights caused by guard duty and Japanese shelling and bombing. Moreover, most of the Old Breed were struck down, at one time or another, with malaria and dysentery, often both together.* A Marine suffering from malarial fever – caused by a bite from a female mosquito that transits malaria parasites, via the bloodstream, into the victim's liver – was often taken

* The number of Marines admitted to hospital on Guadalcanal with malaria was: August – 900; September – 1,724; October – 2,630; November – 2,414; to 10 December – 913. Atabrine anti-malaria tablets were available but not always taken because Marines believed the rumours they would turn your skin yellow and lower your sperm count. Both were untrue. (Frank, *Guadalcanal*, p. 260.)

off the lines to the division field hospital near Lunga Point 'where he and a hundred or so fellow sufferers lay bathed in sweat from head to toe, oscillating between blazing fevers and teeth-rattling chills'. When the fever broke – usually within forty-eight hours – the man 'put his boots on and went back to his foxhole'.[5]

Thurman Miller remembered being constantly bitten by mosquitoes, 'regardless of how much bug repellant we used or how faithfully we later covered ourselves at night with mosquito netting'. He was one of the lucky ones: the parasite would stay dormant in his liver until the campaign was almost over.[6] But many other K Company men were laid low, including 'Scoop' Adams whose first spell in the field hospital was from 30 August to 2 September.[7] Malaria was almost as widespread on Guadalcanal, wrote Jim McEnery, as trench foot and jungle rot: 'They fed us bunches of quinine tablets to try to keep us from getting it – I remember swallowing up to five tablets a day at one point – but most of us were hit with it sooner or later, anyway . . . For most people, symptoms of the disease come and go. You'll be burning up with fever or shaking with chills one day and up playing Ping-Pong the next.'[8]

Chronic dysentery was widespread and rarely required hospitalization. 'It was so bad and so prevalent,' recalled one Marine, 'that a solid bowel movement was a cause for rejoicing.'[9] Fatigue also took its toll, as the men tried to remain vigilant. 'You would wake somebody up careful,' recalled Mo Darsey, 'or you were liable to end up with a rifle or a pistol in your face . . . Night and day you're living under the threat of death, day after day after day, nothing to eat, no sleep, nothing, sometimes no hope.'[10]

For the city kids, in particular, the jungle was a weird and disorientating experience. It was 'like going back to school', said one. 'All we had were barely legible aerial photographs taken from a vertical angle. The fields showed up as white, and the jungle showed up as black. But you had no feeling of topography . . . Being from an industrial town, I had no background in dense, jungle terrain, but suddenly I had to move in the forest quietly, read the stars and other signs to find my location.'

It was easier for country boys like Thurman Miller. The jungle was 'nothing like' his own hills, and the 'stars were out of place', but growing up he learned to 'listen to the land and the animals that inhabit it'. The jungle would, he insisted, 'tell you many things if you let it'. He was also used to privations, having regularly gone without food and water as a young boy; he would often leave home and not know where was going to sleep that night or what he would eat. 'Guadalcanal,' he wrote, 'was just an extreme case of my wanderlust.'[11]

For all the horrors of the campaign – and there were many – the men gradually adjusted to the conditions and made the best of it. Just below a temporary bridge over the Lunga River, built early on, was an enormous tree lying flat in the water. During most daylight hours could be seen a line of naked Marines washing and beating their clothes on the tree trunk. Nearby, over a deep pool, someone had rigged up a diving board. The river water was also used for drinking once it had been purified. 'So the Lunga,' wrote George McMillan, 'served as bath, swimming pool, laundry, spring and, I suspect (though it was strictly forbidden), sometimes as latrine. More than that, it was one of the chief bright spots in the perimeter, a relief from choking dust and sweat.'[12]

Even in the tightest spots, servicemen resort to humour. So it was on Guadalcanal, where one unit put up a sign that read: 'DRIVE CAREFULLY WE LOVE OUR CHILDREN.' Platoon Sergeant Darsey was known for his dry sense of humour. Whenever 'Scoop' Adams complained about the bad food and the harsh living conditions, Darsey would ask him what he was moaning about. 'You're getting a place to sleep and a good meal twice a day, aren't you?'

One of the great characters in 1st Platoon was Corporal Weldon DeLong, a 'husky Marine just under six feet tall' who had been born in Nova Scotia, Canada, but moved to Dover, Massachusetts, as a young boy and joined the US Marines in late 1940. He passed through boot camp with Jim McEnery, who described him as 'a crack shot with either a rifle or a pistol and one of the gutsiest Marines I ever knew – exactly the type of guy you wanted with you when the chips were down'. When

McEnery was made company reconnaissance sergeant, DeLong took over his squad in 1st Platoon.[13]

On the day of his twenty-seventh birthday – 18 September 1942 – DeLong and the rest of the platoon were on a work detail at division headquarters. Noticing that a cake was being baked for a senior officer, DeLong thought he would help himself to a slice. But first, to clear the area, he shouted, 'Air raid!'

Sure enough, everyone headed for the shelters apart from the 1st Platoon work detail. Having pocketed two steaks for himself and 'Scoop' Adams, DeLong started to hand out pieces of cake. 'Unfortunately,' recalled Thurman Miller, 'the colonel came out of his bunker and saw through our plot. He approached our platoon leader, and I wondered how Scoop was going to handle a piece of cake in one hand, a cigarette in the other, and a salute at the same time. I have always admired his quick thinking: he hastily put both hands behind his back, dropped the cigarette, transferred the cake from his right to his left hand, and saluted smartly with his right hand.'[14]

A born leader, Adams had won his platoon's respect by his willingness to share its hardships and danger. The job of a platoon leader was, acknowledged McEnery, the 'toughest one any commissioned officer can have, and the casualty rate's also the highest'. While most officers spent their days and nights in a company, battalion or regimental CP, located well behind the front lines and 'better constructed than an ordinary foxhole', platoon commanders were rarely more than a 'grenade toss' from the enemy in a combat situation.[15]

On patrol, Adams led from the front. On one occasion, using a felled tree to bridge a ravine, he inched his way across until he 'ran out of vines and limbs to hold on to and had to depend on balance alone'. This was fine until he slipped on a piece of rotten bark, 'lost his footing and fell headfirst down through the vegetation, lodging himself in a tangle'. It was left to Mo Darsey to reach down and extract 'the muddy lieutenant from the darkness below'.

On that same patrol, a captured Japanese soldier tried to grab Adams's Reising submachine gun. As they struggled for possession, the lieutenant's chief concern was not for himself, but that one of his men might be killed or wounded in the crossfire. *Can't have that happen*, he told himself. Fortunately, Weldon DeLong intervened, his fist narrowly missing Adams's head 'before it slammed into the Jap's jaw'. Two men escorted the prisoner back to rear headquarters.[16]

On 14 September, in an attempt to reinforce the hard-pressed American troops on Guadalcanal, 4,200 men of the 7th Marines – the last of the 1st Marine Division's three infantry regiments – and supporting artillery left Espiritu Santo in five transport ships. The 7th Marines missed the original landing because it had been sent, in April 1942, to defend the islands of Western Samoa. But with the situation so serious on Guadalcanal, Admiral Kelly Turner thought it worth risking a sortie into seas still dominated by the Imperial Japanese Navy. The decision was doubly brave in that the US Navy had recently suffered two heavy blows to its carrier fleet with the torpedoing of the *Saratoga* and *Wasp* by Japanese submarines on 31 August and 15 September respectively. The *Saratoga* survived, but had to return to Pearl Harbor for repairs; the *Wasp* could not be saved, and was finished off by American destroyers. That left just one fleet carrier in the Pacific, USS *Hornet*, to face up to six opponents.

Despite the loss of *Wasp*, and the withdrawal of the other covering ships (among them the fast battleship USS *North Dakota*, which had also been damaged by a torpedo strike), Turner pressed on with his plan to reinforce the Guadalcanal garrison. He had received intelligence that the bulk of the Japanese fleet was withdrawing to the north, but it was still a big gamble to send unescorted transports into enemy-controlled waters. Fortunately, it paid off and the transports – carrying the 7th Marines and the supporting artillery of the 1/11 Marines – arrived safely off the north coast of Guadalcanal in the morning of 18 September. By nightfall, more than 4,200 Marines, 4,000 drums of fuel, 1,000 tons of rations and 147 vehicles had come ashore, swelling the garrison to ten infantry battalions, one Raider battalion, four battalions of artillery, a small tank battalion and a growing air force. Taken off were 160 casualties and the remains of the 1st Parachute Battalion.

The arrival of these extra troops – talking 'tough and loud' as they came ashore – was a 'terrific morale boost' for Jim McEnery and the rest of K Company. They enabled Vandegrift to establish, for the first time, a complete perimeter defence. It was made up of ten sectors: three fronted the beach (and were manned by support units like the Pioneers and Engineers); the other seven faced inland and were given, two each, to the three infantry regiments, while the last one was under division control. Broadly speaking, the 5th Marines had responsibility for the western perimeter, the 7th the southern perimeter, and the 1st the eastern perimeter. Assuming that any future Japanese attacks would be launched on land from the east, west and south – and particularly from the first two compass points – Vandegrift made plans to meet any Japanese advance not on the perimeter, but at crossing points on the Tenaru and Matanikau, where there was enough room for flanking attacks or amphibious hooks. By ensuring that each infantry regiment always had a battalion in reserve, Vandegrift created a mobile reservoir of three infantry battalions that could be deployed 'to meet a major attack [from] wherever it came'.

Lastly, Vandegrift freshened his senior command group by sacking officers who, in his opinion, had under-performed. They included his chief of staff and personal friend, Colonel William C. James, and the commander of the 5th Marines, Colonel Leroy Hunt. James and Hunt were replaced, respectively, by Colonel Gerald Thomas, Vandegrift's excellent former operations officer, and the aggressive Merritt Edson of the Raiders, who had done so well at Bloody Ridge. Succeeding the commander of the 3/5 Marines, Lieutenant Colonel Frederick Biebush, was his XO, Major Robert Bowen. To soften the blow for the sacked officers, the official line was that they were being sent home to make space for freshly promoted officers and to help train new units.[17]

Also leaving the island was Dick Tregaskis, the combat correspondent, who had worn through his last serviceable pair of shoes and was unable to get a replacement size 14. Instead he was wearing rubber-soled tennis shoes which, he noted, were 'hardly the thing for hiking through the jungle'. When he asked Vandegrift for permission to leave, the major general replied with a chuckle: 'They're putting in a shower for me in few days. And when such luxuries come, the correspondent should go.'

Tregaskis felt less guilty about leaving when Vandegrift assured him that the situation on Guadalcanal was 'brightening a bit'. The major general added: 'The reinforcements have been a great help and I've been assured that the naval protection of our shores will improve.'

The correspondent flew out in a B-17 Flying Fortress bomber on 26 September, acting as nose-gunner on a reconnaissance mission to the Japanese-held island of Bougainville – where he helped to fight off various marauding enemy fighter planes – before landing at Espiritu Santo later that day. His feelings of relief on the one hand, and nostalgia on the other, would be shared by many of the Marines who survived the campaign. 'Men cursed and hated Guadalcanal,' wrote Tregaskis, 'a pesthole that reeked of death, struggle and disease, but the Canal [as the veterans preferred to call it] was like a good-for-nothing cousin or brother. When you make tremendous sacrifices for someone or something, and give your blood or your last drop of muscular effort or sweat, you feel something like affection for that object or person.'[18]

When Tregaskis departed Guadalcanal, he assumed the worst of the fighting was over. He could not have been more wrong. Far from discouraging the Japanese high command, the repeated failures by Colonel Ichiki and Major General Kawaguchi to retake the airfield had, in fact, galvanized the IGHQ, Combined Fleet and 17th Army to redouble their efforts to recapture the whole island. They planned to do this by sending more reinforcements from the 2nd and 38th Infantry Divisions, and by halting the competing campaign to take Port Moresby on New Guinea by overland attack. At the same time the IJN would prevent the arrival of more American troops on Guadalcanal by committing more air units and improving its existing airfields in the Solomons and on New Guinea. Guadalcanal's recapture would be the first step in a new phase of expansion in the southern Pacific that would eventually consume Rabi Island in Fiji, San Cristobal in the Solomons, Port Moresby, the Russell Islands and the Louisiades.

The plan finally agreed was to move Japanese troops, guns and supplies to Guadalcanal in early October by both destroyers (a system known as the 'Rat' convoy) and fast transports. Accompanying the high-speed convoy would be a support fleet of battleships and cruisers whose additional task was to bombard Henderson Field and put it out of action. The tentative date for the completion of the build-up of Japanese troops – known as X-Day – was fixed for 14 October. The start of the new land offensive, Y-Day, was set for six days later.[19]

Major General Vandegrift, meanwhile, was keen to establish an 'advanced battle position' on the muddy Matanikau River, five miles west of the Lunga, from where he anticipated a future assault by the remnants of Kawaguchi's brigade. But his first attempt to dominate the area – a four-day land-and-sea operation from 23 to 27 September, carried out by a mixed force of Raiders, 7th Marines and 2/5 Marines – was a fiasco. 'It had been initiated,' wrote Richard B. Frank in his magisterial *Guadalcanal*, 'without meaningful intelligence on the enemy situation or the terrain, and the attack was characterized by the commitment of battalions along unreconnoitred axes, beyond mutual support range, and without coordination of movements or of air or artillery support.'[20]

More than sixty Marines were killed and one hundred wounded; Japanese losses were much lighter. It was the Marines' first significant defeat on Guadalcanal and an indication, if any was needed, that the combat effectiveness of Japanese troops was far from subdued. This battle, wrote Vandegrift's critical report, was 'unpremeditated' and 'fought without definite purpose other than the natural one of closing with the enemy at once and upon every occasion'. The challenge, in the future, would be to avoid a repeat.[21]

8

'Thirty hours of pure hell'

Guadalcanal, October 1942

K Company got its first opportunity to take the fight to the enemy when it spearheaded the next strike across the Matanikau River on 7 October. The intention was to destroy Japanese forces between the river and Point Cruz, and drive any survivors beyond the range at which artillery could hit Henderson Field. If successful, the Marines would be able to establish a permanent patrol base as far west as Kokumbona.

With the memory of the earlier repulse still fresh in his mind, however, Major General Vandegrift assigned no fewer than six battalions from the 2nd, 5th and 7th Marines to take part in the new operation. The plan was for the 5th Marines (less one battalion) to engage the enemy at the river mouth, while the 7th Marines (also less one battalion) and the 3/2nd Marines,* reinforced by the division scout-sniper detachment – recently raised by Lieutenant Colonel Whaling – crossed the river inland and attacked north towards Point Cruz and Matanikau village. Whaling's group would move down the first ridgeline west of the river, while the two battalions of the 7th did the same along successive

* Attached to the reinforced 1st Marine Division for the Guadalcanal campaign, the 2nd Marines (less one battalion) was in divisional reserve for the initial landing when part of the 3rd Battalion was used to help the paratroopers take the smaller islands of Gavutu and Tanambogo.

ridgelines to the west. Meanwhile the planes of the Cactus Air Force would provide close air support and artillery spotting. If all went well, the 5th Marines would cross the river and pursue the enemy towards Point Cruz where the 7th Marines would close the trap.[1]

The operation was led by K and I Companies of the 3/5 Marines, who had orders to advance down the coastal track and gain a foothold on the east bank of the Matanikau. 'We were told,' recalled Jim McEnery, 'to set up our machine-guns, mortars and rifle squads when we got there, while some of our guys would pretend to be building a bridge. This was supposed to be a trick to draw the enemy to the river, but we never got a chance to do the part about the phony bridge because the Japs came along too soon.'[2]

Having set off at 7:00 a.m. – K on the left and I on the right – they had been on the march for about three hours, and were still 500 yards east of the river, when they ran into a company of Japanese from the 4th Infantry Regiment who were attempting to establish artillery positions for their own counter-attack. Very quickly the two Marine companies sent forward their rifle platoons to set up a skirmish line, supported by mortars and machine guns. While they were doing this, the 2/5 skirted round the enemy strongpoint and reached the river, where it secured a 500-yard stretch of the east bank.[3]

But with the 3/5 Marines facing fierce resistance from the Japanese to their front, Colonel Edson requested support and was sent a company of Raiders from his former outfit. Anticipating their arrival, Edson sent a message to the platoons engaged. It was carried by Jim McEnery, who as reconnaissance sergeant had the job of ferrying messages between Captain Patterson's company CP and 'Scoop' Adams and the other two rifle platoon leaders, Second Lieutenants Sam Carnwath and Thomas O'Neill, in the front line. 'I was pounding along,' remembered McEnery, 'when I caught the attention of a group of four or five Japs, and one of them threw a grenade right at me.'

Fortunately, it hit a tree and bounced off course, giving McEnery enough time to head in the opposite direction. 'I could hear bullets,' he wrote, 'slapping the leaves on the bushes around me – probably from the same bunch of Japs – but I wasn't about to slow down long enough to fire back at them with my '03 Springfield.'[4]

By late afternoon, the 3/5 Marines were holding the Matanikau from the coast to the right flank of the 2/5 Marines, apart from a bulge 400 yards inland that contained the remnants of the Japanese company. As the light was fading, Platoon Sergeant Mo Darsey and Corporal Weldon DeLong went forward to see if they could recover any of K Company's wounded. Darsey recalled:

> It was almost dark, and me and DeLong went out in the direction where we'd been ambushed that afternoon, where we knew [Private Emil] Student was. We got pretty close and DeLong called Stu, and Student told him, 'Don't come out here. Don't come out here. Don't come any closer.' About the time he said that they just sprayed machine gun fire over DeLong and myself, and we just lay flat on the ground. A few minutes later we called for L Company [on the flank] . . . They laid another barrage right down on our heads, so DeLong and myself fell back to our lines at just about dark. Of course DeLong always thought that if we could have gotten to Stu we might have saved his life. He was shot through the stomach.

Even as he was dying, noted Thurman Miller, 'this tough Marine was protecting his buddies. He couldn't move, we couldn't reach him, and he died that night.'[5]

After dark, to distract attention from the crossing downstream by the Whaling group and the 7th Marines, the men of the 5th Marines simulated an assault over the river using LVT-1 amphibian tractors or 'amtracs', welded steel supply vehicles with paddle-type treads that could move over land and water. Heavy rains began that night and continued into the 8th, making 'trails and hills slick, muddy, and treacherous', and grounding the Cactus Air Force. This slowed the offensive, and the K Company men spent much of the day huddling under their ponchos. But they also made efforts to reduce the Japanese positions to their front and at 6:30 p.m., under pressure from three sides, the enemy 'made a final effort to break out of their nearly surrounded bridgehead and retreat across the river mouth'.[6]

Leaving their foxholes, they charged the thinly held Marine right flank where a platoon of Raiders faced them. There was a vicious hand-to-hand fight as the outnumbered Raiders were attacked with bayonet and hand grenades. 'Most of the Raiders were killed,' noted the division report, 'but only after inflicting heavy losses on the enemy. The surviving Japanese broke through but only to find themselves trapped on the inside of the wire barricade we had erected across the sandspit. Sixty-seven dead were found in the wire the next morning.'[7]

Only a handful of Japanese got away. Raider casualties were twelve killed and twenty-two wounded, but the Japanese bridgehead was no more. As Jim McEnery ran messages to the platoon on the right flank, he was shocked to see 'dead Marines from I and K Companies and the Raiders scattered all over the place'. One corpse leaning against a tree, looking like it was asleep, was Private Emil 'Stu' Student. Scattered nearby were thirty Japanese bodies and another dozen Marines.

By now, McEnery had got used to seeing dead Japanese. 'Usually,' he recalled, 'I could step over them and go on about my business. But it still upset me when the bodies belonged to Marines.' That day, as a consequence, he 'couldn't choke down a single mouthful of food'.[8]

Meanwhile Vandegrift had received intelligence that Japanese reinforcements were on their way and a counter-attack was imminent. He therefore scaled back the operation by ordering Whaling and the 7th Marines to return to the perimeter after carrying out their flank manoeuvres on the 9th. The job of K Company and the rest of the 5th Marines was to hold the line of the Matanikau. Part of the revised plan worked beautifully. Taking up a position on a commanding ridge that overlooked the coast, the 1/7 Marines – commanded by Lieutenant Colonel Lewis B. 'Chesty' Puller, an aggressive barrel-chested Virginian with a 'chin like a bulldozer blade' – could see below them a battalion of Japanese in a wooded ravine. Calling in an artillery bombardment, and adding his own mortars to the storm of high explosive, Puller caused havoc.

Unable to close with Puller's men up the steep slope, the surviving Japanese tried to climb the opposite ridge but were cut to pieces by machine-gun fire.

Once he had used all his mortar ammunition, Puller withdrew his men back to the Matanikau, linking up with the Whaling group and the 2/7 Marines en route. By 2:00 p.m. the combined raiding force had 'retired east of the Matanikau through the covering positions of the 5th Marines and the raiders'. Marine casualties for the entire three-day operation were 65 killed and 125 wounded. Japanese fatalities were estimated 'at above nine hundred', with 640 killed in the fight with Puller's 1/7 Marines, according to the captured diary of a Japanese officer.[9]

'Even more important than the enemy casualty figures,' noted Jim McEnery, 'was the fact that the Marines now held a well-fortified position along the Matanikau.'[10]

On 13 October, word reached K Company's CP that the first army troops – 2,850 men of the Americal* Division's 164th Regiment, a National Guard unit that recruited heavily in the rural farming and ranching communities of North and South Dakota – had landed on Guadalcanal. Their arrival was seen as evidence that the American troops were there to stay. 'Hell,' commented a colleague of Jim McEnery, 'they don't send in the Army guys until the tough fighting's over, and the Marines have the situation well in hand.'[11]

Prior to the landings, the escorting task force of US cruisers and destroyers had ambushed a slightly smaller Japanese flotilla in Ironbottom Sound, sinking two ships and badly damaging another at the Battle of Cape Esperance. It was thought to be a decisive American victory. But the margin – given the loss of a US Navy destroyer and damage to two cruisers – was much narrower than the inflated claims in the press.[12]

* So-called because it was activated on the island of New Caledonia in May 1942, having been hurriedly sent there from the US in the wake of Pearl Harbor. The name was a contraction of 'American-New Caledonian Division'. The Americal was the only US infantry division formed outside America during World War II.

This double dose of good news was quickly forgotten, however, as Japanese planes, ships and land-based guns delivered the heaviest bombardment of the campaign, and the 'worst shelling Marines took in World War II'. It began at noon on the 13th as bombs from a fleet of Bettys and Zekes rained down on Henderson Field, destroying twelve Marine aircraft and igniting 5,000 gallons of gasoline, as well as cratering the runway. It was the start, remembered Jim McEnery, of 'thirty hours of pure hell'.

A second Japanese air raid was followed, a few hours later, by the first artillery barrage of the campaign from 150mm howitzers sited beyond the Matanikau: well beyond the retaliation of American guns. But it was the 14in shells* fired by the IJN's battleships *Kongo* and *Haruna* in the early hours of 14 October that did most of the damage, physically and psychologically. Preceded by a series of star shells that 'lit up the whole sky', the massive bombardment – fired at a distance of 29,500 yards – sounded like 'one constant, rumbling roar'. It lasted, recalled McEnery, 'for eighty minutes that seemed like forever. I lay there face-down in the deepest part of my foxhole, hugging my arms around my head. At times, I prayed. At other times, I tried to think about home and visualize my mother's face. Eventually I just went so numb all over that I couldn't think about anything.'[13]

For Thurman Miller, nothing was more terrifying 'than to be crouched in a foxhole in dark of night, wondering if the next shell has your name on it'. He and every other man in K Company would remember the shelling as 'one of the worst experiences' on Guadalcanal. As Mo Darsey put it: 'When we were fighting with small arms, we didn't have time to be scared. But when the shelling started it seemed we were at the mercy of fate.'

Many factors contributed to the mental breakdown of Marines: lack of sleep and food, and seeing their buddies killed. But being bombarded by naval shells as 'heavy as a small car' was, in Miller's opinion, the

* The 14in rounds included armour-piercing, high-explosive and an anti-aircraft incendiary (known as the Type 3) that scattered 470 mini-bombs over a wide area.

greatest single factor.[14] McEnery saw Marines 'crying like babies and beating their fists against the ground', but it was more out of frustration than fear. 'Just shoot me, goddamn it!' yelled one Marine as the shells burst all around. 'I can't stand this shit any longer!'[15]

No one was safe. One near miss forced Major General Vandegrift to dive to the floor of his flimsy shelter. 'Until someone has experienced naval or artillery shelling or aerial bombardment,' he reflected later, 'he cannot easily grasp a sensation compounded of frustration, helplessness, fear and, in the case of close hits, shock.'

Finally, at 3:00 a.m., the battleships ceased fire and withdrew, though Japanese aircraft continued to drop random bombs and, at daylight, the long-range 150mm artillery pieces opened up on Henderson Field again. The worst may have been over, but the price was high: the airfield unusable until the craters could be repaired; nearly all aviation gasoline burned; and more than fifty fighters and bombers damaged and destroyed, leaving fewer than forty to defend the island. Incredibly, amid so much destruction, only forty-one men were killed (including the CO and XO of a newly arrived Marine dive-bombing squadron).[16]

As McEnery and his comrades emerged from their foxholes, they looked like 'drunks after an all-night binge'. The ringing in their ears was so bad they could hardly hear. They shook their heads 'to try to clear them and stared at each other like a bunch of strangers'. Then the private who was always asking stupid questions appeared. 'Oh God, Mac,' he said. 'You think we're ever gonna get off this damn island?'

Fighting off the urge to punch him, McEnery replied. 'Damn right. I'll get off this son of a bitch, and you can make a book on it – but I ain't so sure about you.'[17]

In the wake of the terrible bombardment, American search missions spotted Japanese reinforcements nearing Guadalcanal on six transports and eight destroyers. Vandegrift radioed for 'maximum support of air and surface units', adding that 'aviation gas' was essential. Twenty Wildcats and seventeen torpedo bombers were duly flown in from

Espiritu Santo, as was some fuel. But the navy was in no position to, as Nimitz's staff noted, 'prevent a major enemy landing'.

By 16 October – despite the loss of three transports – more than 5,500 Japanese reinforcements and two-thirds of their supplies and equipment had reached Guadalcanal, bringing the total number on the island to around 14,000. While there were more Americans (23,000 of all services, and another 4,600 on nearby Tulagi), Vandegrift felt that half of them were in no condition to undertake protracted operations. It was, wrote Ian Toll, 'the bleakest moment of the campaign'. Unconvinced that the front-line troops could withstand a sustained assault, the division intelligence staff began burning classified documents. 'We all feared defeat and capture, I think,' remembered a Wildcat crew chief. 'We were afraid they were going to leave us there.'

According to Lieutenant Colonel Merrill B. Twining, Thomas's replacement as division operations chief, Vandegrift had been told by the theatre commander, Admiral Robert L. Ghormley, to surrender his forces if the position became hopeless. The major general was loth to do that, preferring to order contingency plans for a fighting retreat up the Lunga River. Twining favoured a withdrawal to the east, using the rivers as interim defensive lines and retaining the possibility of evacuation by sea.[18] The gloomy outlook was even worse in Washington DC. 'Do you think we can hold Guadalcanal?' a reporter asked Navy Secretary Frank Knox on the 16th.

'I certainly hope so and expect so,' replied Knox, before adding a caveat: 'I will not make any predictions, but every man will give a good account of himself. What I am trying to say is that there is a good stiff fight going on. Everybody hopes we can hold on.'[19]

It was hardly a ringing endorsement. But Vandegrift's cause was helped when Ghormley, believed to be overly pessimistic and lacking in drive, was sacked by Nimitz and King on 18 October, and replaced as commander of the South Pacific Area* with the more aggressive Vice

* The South Pacific Area was, with the North and Central Pacific Areas, part of Admiral Nimitz's huge Pacific Ocean Area. But unlike the NPA and CPA, which were under Nimitz's direct control, the SPA was controlled by a subordinate commander.

Admiral William F. 'Bull' Halsey, fifty-nine, from Elizabeth, New Jersey. A firm believer that the aircraft carrier was the dominant weapon in naval warfare, Halsey had led his carrier task force in a series of hit-and-run raids against the Japanese in early 1942, including the first strike against Tokyo and other targets on mainland Japan by medium-range B-25 bombers that April (the so-called 'Doolittle Raid'), thus providing the American public with the first proper boost to morale after Pearl Harbor. Halsey's slogan, 'Hit hard, hit fast, hit often', became a byword for US Navy operations.

Halsey missed the Battle of Midway because of illness, relinquishing command of the carrier task force to Raymond A. Spruance. It was, he told a class of midshipmen at the US Naval Academy at Annapolis, the 'greatest disappointment' of his career. He added: 'But I am going back to the Pacific where I intend personally to have a crack at those yellow-bellied sons of bitches and their carriers.'

No one was more relieved when he did than Doug MacArthur, commanding the neighbouring Southwest Pacific Area, who regarded Halsey as one of America's 'great sailors'. MacArthur wrote later:

> His one thought was to close with the enemy and fight him to the death. The bugaboo of many sailors, the fear of losing ships, was completely alien to his conception of sea action. I liked him from the moment we met, and my respect and admiration increased with time. His loyalty was undeviating, and I placed the greatest confidence in his judgment. No name rates higher in the annals of our country's naval history.

Soon after taking up his new post, Halsey invited Vandegrift to a command summit on the island of New Caledonia on 23 October, and asked bluntly: 'Are we going to evacuate or hold?'

'I can hold,' said Vandegrift. 'But I have to have more support than I have been getting.'

'All right. Go on back. I'll promise you everything I've got.'[20]

Ten days later, despite the distraction of other global flashpoints –

including the seminal battles of Stalingrad in Russia and El Alamein in Egypt, and the preparations for Operation Torch, the Allied landings in North Africa that were scheduled for early November – President Roosevelt wrote a strongly worded memo to his Joint Chiefs, urging the dispatch of 'every possible weapon' to the Southwest Pacific to help the troops on Guadalcanal. In the event, twenty more ships were sent to the theatre.

At the IGHQ in Tokyo, meanwhile, there was rare agreement among the Army and Navy Sections that Guadalcanal was shaping to become *the* decisive battle between Japan and the United States. Even the bloody repulse of its latest attempts to breach the American perimeter – at the Matanikau on 21 October, and on a ridge south of the airfield on 25/26 October (in a desperate fight that earned machine-gunner Sergeant John Basilone of the 1/7 Marines the Medal of Honor) – did not shake the Japanese high command's conviction that, eventually, it would prevail. To make victory certain, two more infantry divisions – a total of 30,000 men, 300 guns and 3,000 tons of supplies – were to be sent as reinforcements.[21]

Their passage was assisted by a marginal Japanese victory in the naval Battle of the Santa Cruz Islands, east of Guadalcanal – the fourth carrier clash of the Pacific War – that raged from 25 to 27 October and resulted in the destruction of one American fleet carrier, *Hornet*, and one destroyer, and damage to the other fleet carrier (*Enterprise*), a battleship, a cruiser and several destroyers. The Japanese suffered damage to two carriers, but neither was sunk. A more serious setback was the loss of 148 Japanese aviators to twenty-six Americans, and ninety-seven planes (half their total) to the Americans' eighty-one. 'Considering the great superiority of our enemy's industrial capacity,' noted the Japanese naval commander, Admiral Nagumo, 'we must win every battle overwhelmingly. This one, unfortunately, was not an overwhelming victory.'[22]

In late October, K Company's 1st Platoon lost its leader when 'Scoop' Adams suffered another bout of malaria and was hospitalized. He recovered after a week, but did not return to his platoon. Instead he swapped places with the company XO, Lieutenant Rex G. McIlvaine. 'The word,' recalled Jim McEnery, 'was that Adams was stressed out from nearly three months of constant combat conditions and just needed to get off the line for a while. But I think he was physically sick at the time, too.'

The change was a blow for the men of 1st Platoon. McIlvaine, twenty-four, from Wadsworth, Ohio, was a 'good officer', noted McEnery, 'and a regular guy, but he was also on the quiet side, and the guys in the platoon didn't feel the same kind of closeness with him as they had with Adams.'

Even when Adams became the company XO, most of his men hoped it was a temporary posting and that, eventually, he would return to 1st Platoon. It was not to be. In early November, soon after his transfer to the 3/5's I Company, which had taken heavy casualties in a recent battle, he came down with a 'really bad strain of malaria' which 'affected his brain somehow', and he was evacuated back to the United States. 'We all knew,' wrote Thurman Miller, 'we couldn't hold our units together, that the man next to you could be gone in an instant, but I would miss Scoop's leadership for the rest of my time in the Corps.'[23]

9

'It was just a crazy thing to do'

The Battle of Point Cruz, 1–4 November 1942

On 1 November, K Company and the other Devil Dogs were sent on an operation across the Matanikau that, in Jim McEnery's view, changed 'the whole course of the campaign'.[1]

Buoyed by the success of recent defensive battles and Halsey's promise of reinforcements, Major General Vandegrift's intention was to push the Japanese beyond the reach of Henderson Field with their artillery, once and for all. His objective, therefore, was to capture the village of Kokumbona – where Major General Shu'ichi Miyazaki, the chief of staff of the Japanese 17th Army, had established his headquarters – and drive the enemy back across the Poha River. He had selected the 5th Marines to spearhead the attack because it was, compared to other regiments, 'available and rested'. Yet it was also reduced in numbers, thanks to battle casualties and illness, and so Vandegrift supplemented the attack with the reconstituted Whaling Group (scout-snipers and the 3/7 Marines), and placed two battalions of the 2nd Marines from Tulagi in reserve. Fire support was provided by three battalions of artillery, the Cactus Air Force and naval gunfire.

The assault began at first light on 1 November as the 1/5 and 2/5 Marines (on the right and left respectively) crossed footbridges over the Matanikau and moved west. The 3/5 Marines advanced in support, following the tracks of the 2nd Battalion. Facing minimal opposition, the 2/5 had reached its first objective, a ridge south of Point Cruz, by 10:00 a.m. Further inland, the Whaling Group also made good progress.[2]

The 1/5 Marines, on the other hand, had been stopped cold in a coconut grove, 500 yards west of the Matanikau, by a Japanese defensive line 'anchored by at least two 75-millimeter field pieces and about a dozen machine guns'. There were also hundreds of riflemen 'firing from a natural ditch that ran inland from the coast for 100 yards or more'.

C Company, advancing on the left, suffered heavy casualties, including three officers, and was driven back by a Japanese counter-attack. To fill the gap that had opened up between C and A Company (on the right), the reserve B Company was rushed forward. As the shocked survivors tried to take cover in the coconut grove, the Japanese field pieces opened up 'and blasted most of the trees into stumps', pinning the 1/5 down not far from a river at the base of Point Cruz. Sent up in support, I and K Companies of the 3/5 formed a skirmish line behind the 1/5 so the latter could evacuate their wounded and withdraw to a more secure position.

Jim McEnery's job was to meet the casualties and guide them to the aid station on the coast where Higgins boats would take them back to the field hospital. He had already walked 'eight or ten guys back along the same route through the trees' when he spotted another path that he thought might be quicker. He headed down it and 'hadn't gone five steps' when he heard a shot and felt the shockwave of a bullet narrowly miss his head.

'Get down! For Chrissake, get down!' shouted a Marine hiding behind a clump of brush. 'You're in a Nip fire lane!'

McEnery hit the ground, just in time. Seconds later, a Marine officer and his runner came trotting down the same path. Another shot rang out and the bullet caught the runner 'squarely in the throat, and he went down hard, gushing blood'. To McEnery, the wound looked 'really bad', though he 'never knew if the guy lived or died'. Needed at the company CP, he crawled away until it was safe to get back to his feet.[3]

That evening, after consultation with Vandegrift's senior staff officers, Colonel Edson ordered the 2/5 to advance beyond the Japanese strongpoint at Point Cruz and encircle it. This manoeuvre was carried out early on the 2nd, and succeeded in trapping the remnants of two companies of the Japanese 4th Infantry, a dozen guns of the 2nd Anti-tank Gun Battalion, and the 39th Field Road Construction Unit, in a pocket between the coastal trail and the beach west of Point Cruz.[4]

As pressure was exerted on the pocket during 2 November, American casualties mounted, particularly in the shattered coconut grove where men of the 1/5 Marines were still pinned down by machine gun and artillery fire. At around 4:30 p.m., a platoon leader from the 3/5's I Company, 24-year-old Second Lieutenant Charles J. Kimmel from Rushsylvania, Ohio (and a graduate of Ohio State University), decided to do something about it. Addressing the Marines crouched near him – a mixture of I and K Companies – he yelled: 'Those guys are getting murdered by that 75[mm gun] out there. We got to give 'em some relief. Who wants to help me knock out that damn gun?'

One of the first to volunteer was Corporal Weldon DeLong. 'Sure,' said the Canadian-born prankster. 'Let's hit 'em.'

He was quickly joined by two members of K Company's 1st Platoon, PFC Charles 'Slim' Somerville and Private John Teskevich. Somerville was a 'short, skinny West Virginian who talked with a slow drawl but was the fastest man with a BAR' in the company. 'Yeah,' said Somerville, 'I'll go along too.'

Teskevich, a hot-tempered coal miner from Pennsylvania, was known as the 'Mad Russian' because he kept getting into fights. In combat, however, he was as cool as a cucumber. 'Count me in,' he said to Kimmel. 'It'll give my old man another shot at collecting my GI insurance.'

After that, dozens of other Marines from both companies – Platoon Sergeant Mo Darsey among them – shouted, 'Me too! Me too!' This drew the attention of Captain Erskine Wells, commanding I Company, who gave his approval by punching the air with his fist.

'OK,' said Kimmel, 'fix bayonets! And when I say "Charge", just run at the bastards like your pants are on fire.'

Seconds later, almost a hundred Marines formed up in a ragged line, left their cover and, yelling like 'a bunch of lunatics', charged the Japanese-held ditch 50 yards away. 'We all just started runnin',' remembered Darsey, 'hollerin', and shootin'. It was just a crazy thing to do.'[5]

Taken completely by surprise, the Japanese defenders got off only a few shots before the Marines were on them. Some fought; others ran. By leading the bayonet charge, Kimmel had 'encouraged and inspired his men to heights of tremendous endeavour'. But in the hand-to-hand melee at the climax, he was shot in the chest and killed.[6]

K Company casualties were one killed by shrapnel – Corporal Charles Beltrami – and many wounded. The latter included Second Lieutenant John Kelley (recently promoted from platoon sergeant), Sergeant Ralph Rose, and Privates First Class Lou Bors and John Teskevich. Shot in the left leg, the Mad Russian felt lucky to be alive. 'God knows,' he said, 'every one of us damn nearly bought it right here. I almost made my old man $20,000 richer today, but I guess he'll have to wait a while.'

Word of the attack soon filtered back to Captain Patterson at K Company's CP. 'Hey Mac,' said the captain to Jim McEnery, 'get back out there and see what's happening. Then report back to me.'

McEnery was not impressed. 'I thought at the time,' he wrote later, 'if Patterson was the same kind of officer as Lieutenant Kimmel and Captain Wells of I Company, he'd be out on the line himself in a case like this. But I didn't say anything. I just did what I was told.'[7]

Kimmel's attack had sliced through the northern portion of the Japanese pocket as far as the 2/5 Marines. But the southern portion – including a number of anti-tank guns – was still holding out. Next morning, as the temperature nudged a blistering 100 degrees, Captain Wells decided to snuff out the last embers of resistance by leading another I/K bayonet charge. A 24-year-old native of Jackson, Mississippi, Wells had been a popular and active law student at Ole Miss, serving as president of both the YMCA and the Omicron Delta Kappa leadership fraternity. He now put this keen sense of public duty into practice by leading his troops in action.[8]

This time Weldon and Somerville, who had both survived the earlier action, were joined by, among others, Jim McEnery. 'There were,' he recalled, 'at least another hundred guys in this second wave, and I was squarely in the middle. I noticed that PFC Bill Landrum, the assistant leader of my old squad, who'd shared a foxhole with me on our first night in Guadalcanal, was just three or four guys to my right.'

Shortly before jumping off, McEnery heard Landrum tell his neighbour: 'Just give your soul to the Lord, and let's go!'

As they raced forward, Wells at their head, many of their Japanese opponents melted away. 'We went right through the ditch where the main Jap line had been,' remembered McEnery, 'but it had already fallen to pieces. The first wave of the charge had completely ruptured the enemy line. I saw Japs blowing themselves up with grenades and others running like so many scared rabbits . . . They didn't look much like supermen now.'

The lack of serious opposition was probably because the bulk of the defenders were second-line construction troops. Unaware of that, and with their blood up, the Marines showed little mercy. McEnery emptied a clip of his '03, dropping two of the enemy. He then bayoneted their prone bodies to make certain. It was partial revenge for the Marines hit during the charge. They included Bill Landrum, shot in the stomach, and Private Paul Gunter, bayoneted in the heart. Landrum was evacuated to the division field hospital, but died that afternoon.[9]

The greatest heroics that day were performed by two men – Erskine Wells and Weldon DeLong – who were both awarded the Navy Cross. 'Cheering and encouraging his worn men,' read Wells's citation, 'in the midst of heat and severe enemy mortar and machine-gun fire during the latter phases of the assault, he personally led them in hand-to-hand combat, driving the Japanese from their position and completely annihilating them. His extreme valor and outstanding leadership were a constant inspiration to his officers and men.'[10]

DeLong, meanwhile, had demonstrated similar heroism. 'After leading his squad forward in numerous assaults upon enemy positions,' noted his citation, 'Corporal DeLong and two other Marines, when the advance of his company was threatened by a Japanese 37-mm gun firing at almost point-blank range, unhesitatingly rushed forward, seized the gun after disposing of its crew and put it out of action. Finally, in a violent bayonet assault, he advanced to the front of his unit and engaged the enemy in hand-to-hand combat.'[11]

With the main Japanese position captured, it was now a question of mopping up the survivors who, recalled McEnery, were 'scattered over a wide area singly and in small groups. Some were wounded, but they all had weapons of some kind, and they were more than willing to use them.' DeLong took the lead in finishing off the Japanese casualties, 'running back and forth with nothing but a pistol and firing whenever he saw a downed Jap make a move'. He had already put several 'out of their misery' when 'Slim' Somerville noticed the reflections of a group of Japanese hiding in some water behind a log. Realizing that DeLong was out in the open and vulnerable, Somerville shouted a warning. 'Get down! Get down!'

Typically, DeLong was the most alert Marine on patrol, always checking out anything that seemed suspicious. But on this occasion he was so fixated on his task of rooting out fugitives that he did not hear Somerville's warning. Moments later, a shot rang out – fired by one of the soldiers in the water – and the bullet caught DeLong square in the chest. He went down as if poleaxed, and did not move.

While some Marines dealt with the Japanese behind the log, McEnery ran to DeLong's aid. 'He was lying in a puddle of blood,' wrote the sergeant, 'with his eyes wide open and his pistol still in his hand. The bullet had gone straight through his heart. He was as dead as a man could get.'

McEnery was sick to the stomach. DeLong was not only a friend, but the best Marine in his former squad, and maybe the best in 1st Platoon. He had been able to trust the Canadian with any job, no matter how tough. But now, a single moment of carelessness 'had cost him his life'.

Seeing the sergeant so crestfallen, another Marine told him: 'Don't beat yourself up about it, Mac. If you hadn't warned me to keep my head down, I wouldn't be alive now, either.'

McEnery nodded, but he was hardly listening. It was, looking back, one of the worst days of his life; but also one he remembered with no small feeling of pride. 'I was sick at heart about the friends I'd lost,' he wrote, 'and I spent a long time that night with their faces floating through my mind, thinking about them and praying for them. But buried somewhere underneath my grief for DeLong and Landrum and the others was the feeling we'd really accomplished something that day.'[12]

They had. By noon on 3 November, the Japanese pocket near Point Cruz had been reduced to a 'desolate landscape of blocked or blasted caves and clumps of corpses'. The Marines captured a dozen 37mm guns, one field piece and thirty-four machine guns. Japanese fatalities were around three hundred.

Like DeLong, Second Lieutenant Kimmel was awarded a posthumous Navy Cross.* 'Valiantly leading the bayonet charge initiated by his command,' noted his medal citation, 'he was mortally wounded during the fierce hand-to-hand struggle that ensued. As a result of his daring spirit and inspiring leadership, the enemy was completely routed and the company's objective obtained.' By taking part in the only 'authenticated' American bayonet charges of the campaign, the men of I and K Companies had shown they could fight equally well offensively as defensively, and, in the process, beat the Japanese at their own game.[13]

On 4 November – the day after the battle at Point Cruz ended – the 5th Marines and the Whaling Group were relieved by the 2nd Marines and the 1/164th Infantry, and the drive towards Kokumbona continued. But it was soon called off when Vandegrift received word that large numbers of Japanese troops had landed to the east of the division perimeter – at Koli Point and Tetere – and mauled the 2/7 Marines who were moving in that direction. Reinforcements were sent to the 2/7's aid and, on 10 November, they trapped and killed 350 Japanese, and captured fifteen tons of rice, fifty collapsible landing boats and some artillery pieces. American losses were 40 dead and 120 wounded.[14]

Two days earlier, Vice Admiral 'Bull' Halsey had flown in to Guadalcanal to tour the 1st Marine Division's front-line positions and

* In keeping with US Navy tradition, all three winners of the Navy Cross – Kimmel, Wells and DeLong – had warships named after them. The USS *DeLong*, commissioned in 1943, was a Rudderow-class destroyer escort.

get, he hoped, a better understanding of the challenges of holding the island. Wearing Marine dungarees and boondockers, so as not to stand out from the crowd, he drove with Vandegrift in a jeep along the perimeter, refusing his staff's request to stand up and wave. 'It smells of exhibitionism,' he growled. 'To hell with it!'

But he did stop and get out to speak to Marines of all ranks, and was shocked by their 'gaunt, malaria-ridden bodies [and] their faces lined from what seemed like a nightmare of years'. Informed by a Roman Catholic chaplain that many Marines feared Guadalcanal becoming another Bataan, he replied: 'This won't be another Bataan, dammit. We're going to win, and you and I will both see Yamamoto in hell!'

It was clear to him, however, that the 1st Marine Division was at the end of its tether and needed a rest. Having told Vandegrift that his men would be relieved by army troops as soon as possible, Halsey revealed to a press reporter his secret plan to defeat the enemy: 'Kill Japs, kill Japs, and keep killing Japs.' When asked if ultimate victory required an invasion of the Japanese home islands, he replied: 'I hope so.' He looked forward, he added, to the carnage that such an operation would inevitably entail.[15]

10

'We've got the bastards licked!'

Guadalcanal, 7 November–9 December 1942

Following the fight at Point Cruz, K Company was pulled off the line and sent to a rest area close to the airfield. It was during this spell of downtime, on 7 November, that Captain Lawrence Patterson was transferred to the 1/5 Marines and replaced as K/3/5's skipper by Captain Clay M. Murray, newly arrived from the United States.[1]

Though never officially sacked, the timing of Patterson's departure in the wake of the Point Cruz battle suggests that the brass were not happy with his hands-off approach to soldiering. This was what Jim McEnery suspected. 'Patterson,' he wrote later, 'almost never left his command post during a fight, and nobody in the company was more aware of that than I was. After all, I was the guy who ran back and forth with messages from his CP to the platoon leaders out on the line. A lot of them were messages Patterson could've – and I think should've – been close enough to his men to deliver himself.'

For McEnery, there was 'something wrong' with a skipper who needed to send out a runner to locate his company. By contrast, he noted, 'nothing revs up a Marine's fighting spirit more than seeing his CO alongside him when the going gets rough'.[2] The New Yorker had witnessed that at first hand when Captain Wells of I Company won a Navy Cross for leading a bayonet charge. Of Captain Patterson, of course, there had been no sign. But it was not just the company commander who was conspicuous by his absence from reports of the battle. No platoon leader from K Company was mentioned either, and it may not be a coincidence that, bar Rex McIlvaine, they were all replaced at the same time as Patterson.*[3]

Clay Murray, the new company skipper, struck McEnery as 'as being a really good, competent guy'. A devout Roman Catholic from Tulsa, Oklahoma, he had joined the Marine Corps Reserve Officer Training Program while still a student at Notre Dame University in 1936. Since then he had completed an MBA and begun a PhD at Columbia University in New York, but his academic studies were interrupted by the outbreak of war. In 1941 he was sent with the 6th Marines to Iceland to prevent the Nazis from establishing a submarine base there. After Pearl Harbor, the 6th Marines returned to the United States and Murray was eventually transferred to the 5th Marines as a replacement.[4]

Yet to see action, the new skipper was desperate to prove himself. 'He at once tried to turn us back into the spit-and-polish image of the Corps,' recalled the West Virginian Thurman Miller. 'He ordered our platoon leader [Rex McIlvaine] to take us on another combat patrol. Our gunny was wise and led us around within the confines of our own lines, the CO never suspecting.'

On a separate occasion, Miller was ordered by Murray to give a lecture on night patrols. Assuming the company commander was out of earshot, Miller said: 'Personally, if I were given the order to go on night patrol, I would tell whoever gave that order to go to hell.'

Noticing uncomfortable looks on the men's faces, Miller turned to see the skipper, who had heard his comment. Later, in Murray's tent, Miller was asked: 'Were you serious?'

'Yes, sir.'

'Dismissed. Give your lecture tomorrow on barbed wire entanglement instead.'[5]

* * *

* Second Lieutenants Sam Carnwath and Thomas O'Neill were transferred to I and L Companies respectively, and replaced by Second Lieutenants Andrew Chiswick (from the 1/5 Marines) and Albert Fisher (from the 3/5's Weapons Company).

While Murray struggled to win over K Company's veterans, Vice Admiral 'Bull' Halsey was living up to his promise to send army reinforcements to Guadalcanal. Between 8 and 10 November, a fleet of fast transports and cargo ships – and its escort of six cruisers and fourteen destroyers – left New Caledonia and Espiritu Santo with the Americal Division's 182nd Infantry and supplies. The advance elements entered Ironbottom Sound in the early hours of 11 November and, for the next two days, there was a race against time to unload the troops and their equipment before the arrival of a Japanese fleet escorting its own troop transports that US reconnaissance planes had seen approaching from the north. They narrowly won the race, though the heavy cruiser *San Francisco* was damaged and fifteen men killed when an attacking Japanese plane flew into its superstructure.

During the evening of 12 November, the American transport and supply ships withdrew, leaving five cruisers and eight destroyers to take on a much more powerful Japanese fleet, including two battleships, in what many believed was a suicide mission. The one-sided battle began in the early hours of Friday the 13th. 'The action,' noted Admiral Ernest King, 'which lasted 24 minutes, was one of the most furious sea battles ever fought.'

In that short time, two American destroyers were sunk outright while one cruiser and two destroyers sustained fatal damage, sinking later. Every other ship save the destroyer *Fletcher* at the rear of the column was damaged, some like the flagship *San Francisco* severely. Moreover, the American commander, Rear Admiral Daniel J. Callaghan, was killed with most of his staff, as were his deputy Rear Admiral Norm Scott, and a further 1,437 officers and men.*

Almost half the dead were from the light cruiser *Juneau*. Damaged in the night action, it blew up the following morning when it was

* The only American admirals killed in action during a surface battle in World War II, Callaghan and Scott were both awarded posthumous Medals of Honor. Also among the fatalities were five brothers from the same Sullivan family, all serving on *Juneau*.

torpedoed by a Japanese submarine. Around 120 men survived the sinking, but an erroneous location report sent rescuers to the wrong place. After as many as ten days adrift suffering severe thirst, merciless sun exposure and shark attacks (a horrific ordeal that would be repeated on an even greater scale when the heavy cruiser *Indianapolis* was sunk by an enemy submarine in 1945), only ten men survived the sinking. They were joined by four others transferred off the ship that morning before she was torpedoed, making just fourteen ultimate survivors. Japanese losses, by contrast, were one battleship – the *Hiei*, crippled by eighty-five gunfire hits in the night action and ultimately succumbing to US air attacks from Guadalcanal and the carrier *Enterprise* – and two destroyers sunk, and four damaged.[6]

Yet the loss of Callaghan and most of his ships was not in vain. By valiantly standing their ground, they forced the Japanese fleet to turn back temporarily, and gave the supporting US Navy task force of two fast battleships (*Washington* and *South Dakota*) and the fleet carrier *Enterprise* time to reach the area. They also saved the American aircraft on Guadalcanal, and enabled them to play a vital role in the fighting to come. In a later dispatch to 'Bull' Halsey, Vandegrift acknowledged the debt that he and his men owed to the US Navy: 'To Scott, Callaghan, and their men goes our greatest homage. With magnificent courage against hopeless odds, they drove back the first hostile stroke and made success possible. To them the men of Guadalcanal lift their battered helmets in deepest admiration.'[7]

On 14 November, search planes from *Enterprise* located two clusters of Japanese ships approaching Guadalcanal: one was composed of a battleship, three heavy cruisers, a light cruiser and a destroyer; the other of thirteen destroyers and eleven transport ships (carrying the 13,500 men of the 38th Division).

The troop transports were the priority. Halsey recalled,

> We threw in every plane that could take the air – planes from the *Enterprise*, Marine planes from Henderson, Army B-17s from Espiritu, fighters, bombers, dive bombers and torpedo planes. Their

> attacks began at 1000[hrs] and continued until twilight. They would strike, return to base, rearm and refuel, and strike again. When 'the Buzzard Patrol,' as they dubbed themselves, had finished its work, one heavy cruiser and six transports had been sunk, and three other cruisers had been damaged, as had four more transports and two destroyers.

Damage to one other transport turned it back.

As the reports of the naval action reached New Caledonia, Halsey felt they had 'rattled Hirohito's protruding teeth'. The attack on the transports was the climax. Showing the dispatch to his staff, he said: 'We've got the bastards licked!'

The fighting, however, was not over. Late on the 14th, the main US task force of two battleships and four destroyers – under Rear Admiral Willis A. 'Ching' Lee – clashed south of Savo Island with Vice Admiral Nobutake Kondō's bombardment force of one battleship, four cruisers and nine destroyers. Sacrificing themselves to screen the battleships, three American destroyers were sunk and one damaged, as was the battleship *South Dakota*. But this allowed the other battleship, *Washington*, unnoticed at first by the enemy, to engage and eventually sink the Japanese leviathan *Kirishima*. A destroyer was also abandoned by the Japanese. 'Though I am a destroyer man,' noted 'Bull' Halsey, 'I will gladly exchange two [sic] of my destroyers for an enemy battleship whenever the chance is offered.'

Next morning, the four damaged and unprotected transports managed to beach themselves near Tassafaronga Point, northwest of Kokumbona, where they were shelled, bombed and strafed by American artillery, planes and a destroyer. Only about 2,000 Japanese soldiers got ashore with a four-day supply of rice and 260 boxes of shells. 'They must have succeeded,' wrote Halsey, 'only in adding to the misery of the destitute troops already there.'

The air–sea clash of 12–15 November – known collectively as the Battle of Guadalcanal – had cost the Japanese a total of two battleships, one heavy cruiser, three destroyers and ten transports, and damage to another nine warships. American losses were two light cruisers and seven destroyers sunk, and another seven ships damaged. Even at a tactical level, therefore, the US Navy had got one over its IJN counterpart. But strategically the victory was decisive in that it ended Japanese hopes of retaking Guadalcanal once and for all. 'By the morning of November 15,' wrote historian Richard B. Frank, 'Halsey had committed virtually every ship and plane in his command to battle and had suffered grievous losses. But by then the convoy was destroyed and the American grip on Guadalcanal assured.'

The Japanese high command had known what was at stake. 'It must be said,' noted a strategic appreciation of late October, 'that the success or failure in recapturing Guadalcanal Island, and the vital naval battle related to it, is the fork in the road which leads to victory for them or for us.'

That fork had now been reached and the path of American success was all but assured. Acknowledging this fact, Halsey described the battle as the 'third great turning point in the war in the Pacific'. He explained:

> Midway stopped the Japanese advance in the Central Pacific; Coral Sea stopped it in the Southwest Pacific; Guadalcanal stopped it in the South Pacific. . . . If our ships had been routed in this battle, if we had lost it, our troops on Guadalcanal would have been trapped as were our troops on Bataan. We could not have reinforced them or relieved them. Archie Vandegrift would have been our 'Skinny' Wainright,* and the infamous Death March would have been repeated.

That, however, had not happened. 'We didn't lose the battle,' wrote Halsey. 'We won it. Moreover, we seized the offensive . . . Until then he [the enemy] had been advancing at his will. From then on he retreated at ours.'[8]

* * *

* Lieutenant General Jonathan M. 'Skinny' Wainright, commanding Allied troops in the Philippines, who surrendered to the Japanese on 6 May 1942.

While the air-naval Battle of Guadalcanal was being fought, Jim McEnery finally succumbed to a 'nasty' bout of malaria. He thought at first that he was 'just tired and weak from hunger'. But as he was walking in the K Company bivouac area one morning, returning to the CP, he passed out cold on the ground. 'The next thing I knew,' he recalled, 'I was in the sick bay burning up with fever, and the medics were cramming quinine down me. I had a lot of company in that field hospital, too. The place was running over with malaria patients.'

Since so many Marines were now hospitalized with malaria – McEnery was one of 3,213 admitted with the disease in November – the average stay had been reduced from ten days to three or four. The New Yorker was out in two: given a handful of quinine tablets and sent back to the company.[9]

He was not the only one barely fit for service. 'The cumulative effect of long periods of fatigue and strain,' noted the 1st Marine Division's final action report, 'endless labor by day and vigilance by night were aggravated to an alarming degree by the growing malarial rate.' Compounding the effects of malaria was 'a form of secondary anemia which caused the endurance and resistance of the troops to decline rapidly'. By mid-November, as a result, the division was 'no longer capable of offensive operations'.[10]

McEnery was not alone in feeling that the division was 'pretty well whipped by this time'. Not by the Japanese, but by a combination of 'exhaustion, stress, malnutrition, hard labor, and those damned mosquitoes'. They had lived with 'almost constant rain and mud' for nearly three and a half months. Their socks had long since rotted in their shoes. It was time to hand the baton to the Americal Division and the 2nd Marine Division, and let them finish the job.[11]

The Devil Dogs were the first to leave on 9 December, four months and two days since their arrival on the island. Woken at 3:00 a.m., they ate breakfast before helping to load their gear onto landing craft at beaches near Lunga Point. At noon it was their turn to embark.[12] In contrast to their arrival, they were a rag-tag bunch, 'dressed in green dungarees or dirty khaki, often with limbs protruding from shirts chopped back to the shoulders, trousers clipped at the knees, or sleeves and pant legs that ended in fringes of tatters'. Most were dirty, gaunt, and still wracked with malarial parasites.[13] Everyone had lost weight. Thurman Miller, for example, was down from his usual 160 pounds to just 115, and he was one of the few not to get malaria because he had been very diligent about taking the preventive atabrine.[14] But it was the mental condition of the returning veterans that concerned one naval doctor. In his view, 'never before in history' had such a group of 'healthy, toughened, well-trained men' been exposed to such brutal conditions for so long. He added:

> Rain, heat, insects, dysentery, malaria, all contributed – but the end result was not blood stream [*sic*] infection nor gastro-intestinal disease but a disturbance of the whole organism – a disorder of thinking and living, or even wanting to live.
>
> And this incredible strain lasted not one or two days or nights but persisted and increased for months . . . They were alone on this island and their expected relief did not come. They had no way of knowing why it did not arrive. Soon they were sure none of them would get off the island – they were expendable, doomed.[15]

Before they left, many of the K Company men visited the makeshift cemetery near the airport that contained most of the division's 650 dead. The graves were covered with palm fronds and marked with a wooden tombstone or cross, some tacked with the dead man's mess gear and identification tag, and a handwritten farewell. One read:

> And when he goes to Heaven
> To St Peter he'll tell:
> Another Marine reporting, sir,
> I've served my time in hell.[16]

As Thurman Miller looked down at the graves of friends and colleagues, he was convinced a 'higher power' had kept him safe. 'Their faces flashed before my eyes,' he wrote. 'Beltrami. Student. DeLong, and so many others. I had come with many of these men through the pain of boot camp and advanced training. I would leave them there to go again against the enemy on another island and take my chances of joining them.' Yet, at the same time, he felt like he was leaving 'a part of himself on Guadalcanal', and that every man who served there had a right to feel 'a sense of possession about the island, and an interest in the ground that holds his friends'.

Hearing the sand crunch under his feet as he walked to the landing craft, Miller was reminded of his arrival in August. His pack felt much lighter now, and he was able to climb the cargo net of the attack transport USS *President Jackson* unaided; others were weaker and had to be helped up by navy men. They included Jim McEnery, who was 'so tired' he was not even embarrassed. 'I just thanked the swabbies for giving me a hand,' he remembered, 'and looked for the nearest place to sit down.'[17]

That same day, Major General Vandegrift turned over the command of the island to Major General Alexander M. Patch of the Americal Division. In a final message to his troops, he tried to convey his feeling of pride in their 'magnificent accomplishments' and his thanks for their 'unbounded loyalty, limitless self-sacrifice and high courage'. He continued:

> To the soldiers and Marines who have faced the enemy in the fierceness of night combat; to the pilots, Army, Navy and Marines, whose unbelievable achievements have made the name 'Guadalcanal' a synonym for death and disaster in the language of our enemy; to those who have labored and sweated within the lines at all manner of prodigious and vital tasks; . . . to the surface forces of the Navy associated with us in signal triumphs of their own, I say that at all times you have faced without flinching the worst that the enemy could do to us and have thrown back the best that he could send against us.[18]

Though the fighting on Guadalcanal would continue for another two months, the Devil Dogs and the rest of the 1st Marine Division had done their job, repulsing multiple attempts by often superior Japanese forces to drive them from the island.* By December, having broken the back of the enemy's counter-attack, it was no longer a question of whether the Americans could hold on; but rather how long it would take the Japanese high command to admit defeat. The answer came in early February 1943 when the Japanese embarked their remaining garrison of 9,860 men, leaving the corpses of another 25,600 ground troops, 3,543 sailors and 1,200 airmen on or near the island. Total American fatalities, by comparison, were 1,769 Marines and soldiers killed (out of about 60,000 committed), 4,911 sailors† and 420 airmen, a combined total of 7,100.[19]

Guadalcanal, concluded Major General Kawaguchi, was the 'graveyard of the Japanese army'.[20] For US Army Chief of Staff General Marshall, it marked the 'turning point in the Pacific' thanks to 'the resolute defence of these Marines and the desperate gallantry of our naval task forces'.[21] Historian Richard B. Frank agrees:

> The Japanese remained on the offensive in the Southeast Asia area in the summer of 1942, and persisted in an offensive in New Guinea until checked there and forced to focus their attention on the southern Solomons. Moreover, up until the Naval Battle of Guadalcanal the Japanese threatened to crush the attempt of the Allies to move to the offensive. Thus, Guadalcanal, not Midway, represented the actual shift in strategic postures.[22]

* For its 'outstanding gallantry' on Guadalcanal, the 1st Marine Division was given the first of three Presidential Unit Citations for service during the war. Its men had 'not only held their important strategic positions despite determined and repeated naval, air and land attacks, but by a series of offensive operations against strong enemy resistance drove the Japanese from the proximity of the airfield and inflicted great losses on them by land and air attacks'. (McMillan, *The Old Breed*, pp. 465–7.)

† A similar number of American sailors were later killed at Okinawa, often cited as the US Navy's costliest campaign. 'Proportionate to the forces engaged, however,' wrote Richard B. Frank, 'Guadalcanal was much more bloody.' (Frank, *Guadalcanal*, p. 614.)

George McMillan summed up the importance of the battle in *The Old Breed*: 'The Guadalcanal campaign drove a deep wedge into the Japanese Pacific perimeter and at the same time robbed them of a critically large number of their best carrier pilots and finest warships . . . We gained a vital airbase and an important troop-staging area for our drive through the South Pacific, and we rubbed out the myth that the Japs were supermen.'[23]

The moral effect of the victory was also significant. Before the war, Japanese military leaders had questioned America's stomach for a fight. Guadalcanal left them in no doubt that, as Frank puts it, 'American marines and soldiers could meet the enemy in adversity and prevail.' Their eventual triumph on Guadalcanal, after months of uncertainty, 'not merely represented a step forward, but vindicated a generation and the nation's faith inself'.[24]

Such insight came later. According to Thurman Miller, it would take the 'perspective of a few years' to establish the battle 'as a decisive moment in the war, for both sides'. At the time, he and the surviving men of K Company were just relieved to get off Guadalcanal. Yet every one of them felt pride in what they had achieved, and knew that to be identified as a Canal veteran was a badge of honour. 'Less than a year after our fight on the island,' noted Miller, 'the Corps would purchase fifty thousand additional acres at the Marine base in Quantico, Virginia, and immediately name it Guadalcanal Area. The 1st Marine Division adopted the symbol of the Southern Cross as our emblem. For years afterward, everywhere we went people would ask, "You served on the Canal, didn't you?"'[25]

11

'Saviours of Australia'

Brisbane and Melbourne, December 1942–January 1943

On 10 December, a day in to their voyage south, the exhausted men of K Company were resting and enjoying the plentiful food aboard the USS *President Jackson*, confident they were on their way home, when a message came over the ship's loudspeaker. 'Now hear this. This ship is bound for Brisbane, Australia.'[1]

Amid the disappointment, there was also consolation that they would soon be enjoying the creature comforts of a modern city. Four days later, having reached their destination on Australia's northeast coast, a Marine officer described the city as 'low and ugly', but with 'no shooting, plenty of women and few men'.[2] Jim McEnery saw even less to admire. It was 'just as hot and miserable as it was on Guadalcanal', he noted, and everywhere you looked there were banana plantations and 'clouds of mosquitoes'.

It did not help that Brisbane was the headquarters of General Doug MacArthur, the vain and bombastic (but also brilliantly able) Supreme Commander of the Southwest Pacific Area. While commander of Allied troops in the Philippines, MacArthur had left the island fortress of Corregidor in Manila Bay before it and Bataan fell to the Japanese in spring 1942, with the loss of 75,000 US and Filipino troops. Many Marines felt that MacArthur, a US Army general, had 'bugged out' and abandoned his troops – when he had, in fact, been ordered to leave by President Roosevelt – and believed the untrue rumour that he had omitted the 4th Marines from the list of Corregidor and Bataan defenders who were awarded the Presidential Unit Citation.[3]

The Old Breed had been sent to Australia because MacArthur, with only two American infantry divisions under his command, was relying chiefly on Australian troops to drive the Japanese out of New Guinea. The Marines' first task would be to help defend the northern coast of Australia. But MacArthur also hoped to capture the Solomon Islands to the northwest of Guadalcanal – including New Georgia and Bougainville – as well as New Britain in the Bismarck Archipelago, and this type of operation required divisions with amphibious training. Before the 1st Marine Division could be redeployed, however, it needed to rest, refit and replenish its numbers. That this might take longer than expected was abundantly clear to the two staff officers from MacArthur's HQ who came down to the dock to welcome the Marines. 'The men,' recalled a Marine officer who was with the army colonels, 'were ragged, still dirty, thin, anemic, sallow, listless. Just about one out of every ten of them fell down, tumbling limply down the steep ladder on their backs, landing pitifully on the dock.'

Turning to one of the colonels, the Marine officer said bitterly: 'Well, there are your defenders of Australia.'[4]

It was not all doom and despondency. Thurman Miller was grateful for the warm welcome given to the Marines by the citizens of Brisbane who had gathered at the harbour in their thousands. 'They must have wondered,' noted Miller, 'about this motley bunch of men. We were not the well-groomed yanks they expected.' Yet they cheered, nonetheless, convinced the Marines had 'halted, for the time being, the march of the Japanese army toward their continent'.[5]

Units formed on the quay and began to board trucks for the trip to the tented camp inland. As one rifle company completed Inspection Arms, a shot rang out. Fortunately, no one was hit. 'All right,' bellowed the sergeant, 'unload 'em, and I mean empty. Our war's over.'[6]

Sergeant Jim McEnery, meanwhile, had been put in charge of a K Company working party assigned to clean up the mess the Marines had made on the *President Jackson*. 'The guys were already nettled,' he remembered, 'because they didn't like MacArthur or the look and feel of Brisbane, and getting stuck with cleaning up after 2,500 Marines only added insult to injury.' The final straw was when the ship's captain described the clean-up as the 'worst' he had seen. Some men were so incensed they threw their rifles overboard. One muttered: 'If this is how it's going to be, just take us back to the 'Canal, for Chrissake!'[7]

Once on shore, they were loaded into trucks for the 32-mile journey down 'a narrow, winding road through flat, empty country' to Camp Cable. As the miles rolled by, a young carrot-headed Marine said in exasperation: 'Christ, we'll never make liberty in Brisbane from way out here in the boondocks!'

'That's the army for you,' groaned another. 'Fifty miles from no place, and not one broad in the county.'

They arrived to find the camp located 'in marshy land spotted with trees and ponds, and laced with streams'. The buildings and tents were widely dispersed to protect them from air attack, a precaution the Marines – used to living side by side in a combat area – considered ridiculous. 'Look at this damn lashup,' said a Marine officer, throwing his hands up in disgust, 'a mile to the head, and two miles to chow!'[8]

To Jim McEnery, the camp 'looked more like a city dump than a bivouac area', with trash from the previous occupants all around. K Company was housed in 'moldy pyramidal tents'. In the middle of McEnery's was a stagnant pool of water. 'If the water rose a few more inches,' he recalled, 'I'd have needed a life preserver.'

Oh well, he told himself, *what the hell?* He was so tired he could have slept on a bed of nails.[9]

Thurman Miller's chief memory of Camp Cable is acting as sergeant of the guard for K *and* L Companies, neither unit having enough fit men to cover the whole perimeter. During his rounds, he discovered two L Company Marines asleep at their posts, and sent both to the brig. But at their trial he was reprimanded by L's commander, Captain

Kramer, for posting men who were drunk. Miller was furious: he did not know the men and had not assigned them. Fortunately, his own skipper Captain Murray referred the matter to 'Red Mike' Edson, the regimental commander, who dismissed the charge after going through Miller's record book. 'This man's record is perfectly clean,' he told Murray. 'Don't put a mark on it.'[10]

Even liberty in Brisbane was a disappointment. It was 'dull', noted Lieutenant Thayer Soule, 'blocks of poorly constructed buildings with rusted iron roofs. There were no nightclubs, and the bars were under many restrictions . . . No doubt many men found what they were looking for in Brisbane, but my small group took a long, aimless walk around town, had a drink and dinner, then went to a movie.'[11]

With jangled nerves made worse by flocks of kookaburra birds, known as 'laughing jackasses', screeching through the trees, and even the replacements going down with malaria – some officers suspected the troops were infecting the local mosquitoes, which in turn were infecting the new arrivals – Major General Vandegrift proposed a move to southern Australia where the climate was cooler. Sent to scout out the city of Melbourne in the extreme southeast, two division staff officers were given 'a royal reception and promised every hospitality'.

The chief obstacle to the move was MacArthur's army staff: they could see no military value in having a veteran division in southern Australia and insisted that transport ships could not be spared. Fortunately 'Bull' Halsey came to the rescue. On hearing of the Old Breed's plight, he sent ships from New Caledonia – principally the former cruise liner SS *America*, which had been renamed USS *West Point* – as a thank-you for the 1st Marine Division's heroics on Guadalcanal. For the Old Breed, the ships arrived just in time. 'If we'd stayed in Brisbane,' claimed one Marine officer, 'well, we just wouldn't have been a division any more. It would have ended up with our having to disband and reform. Even for the short time we were there, it was a near disaster.'[12]

K Company sailed from Brisbane on the *West Point* on 9 January 1943 – a voyage described by one officer as 'probably the largest floating crap game ever held in the Pacific' as the Marines, with four months' pay burning a hole in their pockets, indulged in their favourite illicit pastime* – and arrived in Melbourne three days later.[13] The difference was like night and day. 'Melbourne,' noted Jim McEnery, 'is probably the most beautiful city I've ever been in, and after four months on Guadalcanal and three weeks at Brisbane, it looked like heaven on earth to me.' It helped, too, that the welcome from the citizens was one the Marines would never forget. They were hailed by the local newspapers as 'Saviours of Australia' and invited into the homes and hearts of thousands of people.[14]

Established on the northern bank of the Yarra River in the 1830s, and named after the peer who was then serving as British prime minister, Melbourne grew rapidly after the discovery of gold in Victoria in 1851, its population nearly doubling from 25,000 to 40,000 in just a few months. The new influx of wealth and people led to a grand programme of civic construction, with the Parliament House, Treasury Building, State Library, Gaol and university all begun in the 1850s and 1860s. Within twenty years, it had grown to become a major financial centre and the next largest city after London in the British Empire.

The de facto capital of Australia from federation in 1901 to the movement of the federal parliament to Canberra in 1927, Melbourne nevertheless retained its status as the richest and most important city in the country. It certainly impressed the men of the Old Breed. 'Around us,' wrote one, 'lay a city of wide streets, taxis, trolleys, department stores, bars, hotels, gas stations, street lights, soda fountains, factories, row after row of semi-detached houses and thousands of friendly people.' Ringing the city were the suburbs, 'geometrically arranged along asphalt roads lined with gum trees, modern-styled houses of stucco and brick with lush green lawns and carefully tended flower gardens'. Nearby were 'glistening white beaches crowded with bathers and multi-colored umbrellas, amusement parks with merry-go-rounds and spook houses'. In the bays and inlets were sailing yachts, and beyond the city was 'farm

* On the last day, one successful gambler asked his captain if he could look after a well-stuffed pillowcase for him. It contained $22,400. (Soule, *Shooting the Pacific War*, p. 129.)

and pasture land, rolling stretches of hot plains dotted with cattle, horses and sheep'. It reminded many Marines of home.

Little wonder that they regarded their time in Melbourne as one of the bright spots of the war. 'A campaign like Guadalcanal,' wrote a chaplain who joined the division later, 'dims everything else in a man's life. These fellows went to Australia possessing few memories except those of battle – and they wanted to shed those as quickly as they could. Melbourne . . . became to them the symbolic civilian environment. And it remained so until the end of the war.'[15]

The city, of course, did not have enough vacant housing to accommodate the entire division, and only Vandegrift's headquarters was stationed there. The various units were billeted in the city cricket ground – the famous MCG – and in camps further afield. The Devil Dogs were sent by rail to Camp Balcombe, near the coastal town of Mount Martha in the Mornington Peninsula, 40 miles south of Melbourne. The camp contained row upon row of lightweight, semi-cylindrical Quonset huts – prefabricated from corrugated galvanized steel – and 'outside toilets with running water, a place to wash our clothes, and even lights'.

Its facilities, climate and proximity to Melbourne made Camp Balcombe a welcome change from Camp Cable, and certainly from Guadalcanal, and the K Company men took full advantage. Initially put on a 'no duty' schedule because of their worn-out condition, they had plenty of free time to take a train ride into the city's Flinders Street Station where, just across the street, was a popular pub called Young & Jackson's. It was hard to miss: on the wall of the pub was Melbourne's most famous artwork, a painting of a reclining nude woman ('Chloe') by the French artist J. J. Lefebvre.

Having downed a couple of Foster's beers in the pub, the Marines would scatter in all directions, heading for their favourite hangouts. Jim McEnery spent a lot of time in a restaurant run by an old Russian lady. He would bring her cigarettes and chocolate from the camp Post Exchange (a general store known as the 'PX'), and, in return, she would cook him 'unforgettable meals' like borscht, a 'type of soup made out of beets'. She played the role of surrogate mother – he called her 'Mom' because she reminded him of his own – and sometimes, after a long night's drinking, let him sleep in the spare bedroom above the restaurant.[16]

The Russian lady's hospitality was replicated in homes across the region. Many Marines were invited to stay at farms where they 'picked grapes, pitched hay and herded sheep'. Everybody, wrote one veteran, 'wanted to get with a family, to take part in family life'. Given the run of a country home near Healesville, a sergeant was asked by his solicitous hosts if he wanted 'lunch in bed too'. He did.[17]

As it was summer in Melbourne, with the mercury nudging 100 degrees, the Marines frequented the city's many parks, beaches and fairground rides. They also chased the local women who, with their menfolk serving abroad, were only too happy to spend time with cash-rich young Americans. Jim McEnery dated a 'sweet' local girl, Marian Curtis, who lived with her family in a small town outside Melbourne. They invited him to stay over, and fixed up 'comfortable sleeping quarters' on their wide front porch. But the relationship did not develop because his drinking partner, another buck sergeant called Lou Gargano, was married with a kid, and had no interest in picking up girls. McEnery had known Gargano, a handsome Italian-American from Bayonne, New Jersey (just across the Hudson from New York City), since their time at New River. They had not seen much of each other on Guadalcanal because Gargano was in mortars, while McEnery served in 1st Platoon and at the company CP. But at Camp Balcombe they were both reassigned to 2nd Platoon and became best buddies.

During their trawls of the city bars, 23-year-old Gargano's movie star looks attracted a lot of Australian women. Yet, noticed McEnery, 'he never flirted with them' or paid them much attention. He was polite but nothing more. 'When this stinking war gets over,' Gargano assured his friend, 'all I want to do is settle down with my wife and little girl, maybe have another kid or two.'

This surprised McEnery. He knew that many servicemen had come to regret marrying their sweethearts before shipping out. Not Gargano. He stayed true to his wife and, with double-dating out of the question, McEnery saw less and less of Marian. He knew she would not be comfortable at his 'beer-drinking bull sessions' with Gargano and preferred not to lead her on. She had made it very clear to him that she was 'in the market for a husband' and, though he was fond of her, he was 'not anywhere near ready' to get married. He wrote later: 'I knew this stopover in Melbourne was going to end one day soon. When it did, I'd be going back into battle on some other damn island, and I didn't want to leave any Aussie war widow behind.' So he stopped calling and spent all his liberties drinking beer with Gargano or watching American movies.[18]

Thurman Miller dated a 'very lovely girl' who lived and worked in the city as a hat designer. But their relationship never went beyond 'just having a good time' because, early on, he told her of the sweetheart back home he intended to marry. Even so, he was often invited to dinner by her parents and once, much to his lasting shame, arrived drunk.[19]

Other Marines were less scrupulous, and on any given evening Melbourne's parks reverberated to the sound of amorous couples who had failed to find a room for the night. 'Goddamn,' muttered one young private, on seeing the naked bottoms of two of his colleagues rising and falling in rhythm, 'this is more than I can stand. I'm ready to grab any girl that passes by, even the one I had last night, and screw her ass off. Let's get out of here.'[20]

12

'The trick is to run just fast enough'

Camp Balcombe, January–March 1943

Shortly before leaving Brisbane, the men of K Company lost their second skipper in two months when Captain Clay Murray was transferred to another battalion. He was replaced by his XO, Charles T. Cobb, who had joined the outfit from I Company at the time of Captain Patterson's departure in early November. Still suffering from malaria and low spirits, Cobb was no more popular than his predecessors had been. 'He didn't seem to like me much,' noted McEnery. 'I never knew why, and the feeling was mutual.'[1]

Part of the problem might have been Captain Cobb's need to crack the whip as the company's training stepped up a gear in mid-January 1943. 'We were still physically weak,' remembered Thurman Miller, 'and the first month was light duty as we focused on disciplinary skills, resupply, and building up our strength. Then we added in more small-unit tactics and heavier physical conditioning. This intensive training was especially needed for the new guys.'

With most rifle companies at barely half strength – thanks to casualties, sickness and transfers to the United States – replacements began to trickle in. According to Miller, they performed well in the field but refused 'to conform to the image of parade-ground Marines' by talking in ranks, staying out of step and generally doing everything wrong. This infuriated Cobb who, at 8:00 a.m. each morning, would call Miller to his tent and chew him out 'over their attitudes'. Miller's response was that they would 'give a good account of themselves in combat'.[2]

Among the new arrivals was 19-year-old Private Nolen V. 'Bama' Marbrey, a 'green hayseed' from Huntsville, Alabama, a town best known for its cotton mills and arsenal in the Appalachian region of the Deep South. After boot camp, Marbrey had volunteered for the Marine Paratroopers' jump school at Camp Gillespie, near San Diego, where the minimum height and weight for recruits was 5ft 9in and 150lb. The course was brutal. 'They try to tear you down physically and mentally,' he recalled, 'then to build you back up. They want your brain and body and the bastards just about take you over, body and soul.'

Having got through the toughest part of the training, Marbrey was unlucky enough to break his leg on the second of six jumps needed to qualify for his wings, and was failed. Once fit again, he completed eight weeks of advanced infantry training at nearby Camp Elliott, an old navy base, before shipping out to the Pacific from San Diego in early 1943. 'For the majority of us,' wrote Marbrey, 'between eighteen and twenty years old, the beginning of a new adventure was at hand. Our spirits and morale were soaring.' A few days into their voyage, they were told their destination: Melbourne, Australia, where they would join the 1st Marine Division.

This prompted laughter and bemusement. Wasn't Australia where the English sent their convicts? Wasn't it full of kangaroos?

As for the 1st Marine Division, they all knew it had performed heroics at Guadalcanal and were pleased to be part of such a veteran outfit. 'Now maybe we'll get some professional training first hand,' mused one replacement.

'Yeah,' replied Marbrey, in his deep Southern drawl, 'I guess they know as much as anybody. I wonder how many divisions the Japs have got?'

'Oh, maybe two or three,' said the replacement. 'But most of them was killed on Guadalcanal, so all we have to do is kill the rest and go home. I figure we can do that in a couple of weeks. Then we can tour all the islands and screw all the hula girls.'

Later that day, in conversation with another Marine, Marbrey wondered aloud what kind of man he would be in combat. 'You ever wonder about that?' he asked.

'Yeah, Marb. I guess everybody does. They say you can't judge by your civilian life. My old man was in World War One and he said he was scared shitless. But in civilian life, he was mean as hell.'

After a month at sea, they landed at Melbourne and were directed to some waiting trucks. Before climbing in with his seabag, Marbrey reached down and grabbed a handful of dirt. 'It felt wonderful just to have it trickle from my hand,' he recalled. 'It was red, just like the dirt from Alabama.'

A couple of hours later, they drove through the gatehouse of Camp Balcombe and stopped in front of a building with a sign that read: 'Third Battalion Headquarters'. Hopping out with their seabags, they were called to attention by a first sergeant – or 'Top Kick', the senior non-commissioned rank in a rifle company – who rattled off eight names and told them to go to L Company, a collection of dilapidated buildings to his right. Marbrey was not on the list. When the Top Kick had finished, another appeared. He was red-faced and freckled, with a couple of scars. 'Right men,' he said, studying his clipboard. 'When I call your name, get your gear and go to K Company, down the street, past headquarters and wait there till you see my smiling red face.'

Marbrey was assigned to 2nd Squad, 2nd Platoon. Over the next few weeks, he and the other replacements got to know many of the old salts in the company, who would regale them with tall tales of combat on Guadalcanal. They quickly learned to distinguish a 'snow job' from a genuine story, and became 'experts at gleaning the wheat from the chaff'. The training, at this stage, was 'unhurried'. The squad leader showed endless patience when they screwed up, and 'everything ran like clockwork'.

During one liberty, Marbrey took the train to Melbourne with a company scout who explained: 'Now when the train stops at a place called Flinders Street Station, the objective is to get out of the double doors first and up the incline to the street. The walls along the incline are always lined up with women waiting for Joe.* If you run too fast up the incline, you don't have time to pick out a nice one, and if you run too slow, they are all gone with another Joe. The trick is to run just fast enough.'

Marbrey did as he was told, and spotted a nice-looking girl near the end of the line. He called to her, but she did not hear him. Instead his outstretched hand was grabbed by a less attractive woman and, before he could pull it back, they were on the street. His buddy was waiting for them and 'had picked a beauty'.

After a café meal of steak and eggs, the four of them went back to a room owned by the aunt of one of the girls. It contained two beds and a radio. After dancing for a while, they all got ready for bed. 'As we stripped,' remembered Marbrey, 'I turned my head discreetly, being the gentleman I was. I stole a glance just in time to see her panties disappear. Only they weren't panties, they were regulation green G.I. shorts. Oh Lord, I thought. Best not to think about it. Just relax and enjoy.'[3]

With light duties and a healthy diet of steak, eggs, gravy and milk, the Canal veterans of K Company soon regained their former vigour. Thurman Miller, for example, rapidly put on the 45lb he had lost. But with so many young Americans on the loose in Melbourne, drunk on beer and spirits, and flush with money, there was bound to be trouble. On one occasion a young Marine, not old enough to frequent bars, was refused a drink because of his age. 'We reminded the barkeeper,' wrote Miller, that the "kid" had manned his post on the Canal, just as the other men had done. "Now serve him or we'll tear your damn bar apart."' The kid got his drink.[4]

Fights became commonplace after units of the 9th Australian Division, famous for their exploits in the Western Desert of North Africa (including starring roles in the defence of Tobruk and the Battle of El Alamein),

* The term 'G.I. Joe' referred to most American servicemen. It came from cartoonist Dave Breger's popular comic strip of the same name that first appeared in *Yank* magazine in 1942.

returned to Melbourne in the spring of 1943. 'Ugly incidents between them and us occurred frequently,' remembered Second Lieutenant Thayer Soule, 'always at night, usually in a bar. We Marines had taken their girls. That was bad enough, but we Yanks had money to burn – better pay to start with, and a lot of back pay to boot.'[5]

The Aussie soldiers tended to fight in packs, but were never dirty: no bottles, sticks or chairs. Just a good old-fashioned fist fight with their mates by their side. One Australian colonel, expecting trouble, warned his Marine counterpart to keep his men off the streets of Melbourne on a certain night. The response of the Marine colonel was to give liberty to his entire regiment that day. 'I'll say one thing for the Aussies,' remarked a Marine, 'you couldn't keep 'em down. You could knock 'em down and knock 'em down again, and they'd keep on getting up for more – until their cobbers pulled them away.'[6]

Some of the bad blood was caused by a misunderstanding: the Marines had been re-clothed in army khaki, which made it impossible for the Australian veterans to distinguish them from the despised Army base troops who were also in town. It was partly to end this confusion that the Old Breed were issued a divisional shoulder patch that had been designed by Lieutenant Colonel Twining, Vandegrift's operations chief. It was a large red '1' in a blue diamond: running the length of the '1', in vertical white letters, was the word 'Guadalcanal'; surrounding it, scattered across the blue diamond, were the white stars of the Southern Cross. 'We were,' noted Thayer Soule, 'Army no longer.'[7]

It also helped international relations when the 1st Marine Division held a beer party for 9,000 men – half of them Australian – at the Melbourne Cricket Ground with no MPs present. Incredibly there were no fights and the popular tall-tale contest was won by an Aussie soldier who claimed to have captured a set of moose antlers by throwing turpentine on the animal's rear. 'All I had to do,' claimed the Aussie, 'was stand there till the moose rubbed himself down to his antlers.'

Thereafter, peace was restored and when the 9th Australian Division was eventually sent to fight in New Guinea there was, noted George McMillan, 'marked regret in the cantonments of the First'.[8]

13

New Arrivals

Camp Balcombe, March–June 1943

A couple of months into their time at Camp Balcombe, the men of K Company were ordered to fall in on parade. When everyone was present, Captain Charles Cobb appeared in full dress uniform and stood a few yards in front of the ranks. He stood silently for a moment, lost in contemplation. When at last he spoke, his voice trembled with emotion. 'This is a company of good men, and I wish you all the best of luck for the future. A new captain will take my place tomorrow. I am,' he said with a sob, 'being sent home to die.'

With tears streaming down his face, Cobb moved slowly up the ranks and personally shook hands with every member of the company. When that was done, he gave a final salute, turned on his heel, and walked back to his office. 'Fall out!' bellowed First Sergeant George H. Rose.[1]

Few were sad to see the back of the lachrymose Cobb. He had not been quite right – either mentally or physically – since joining the company and most were relieved that they would 'never have to go into battle' with him in command.[2] They prayed that his replacement – their fourth skipper in as many months – would be less self-absorbed than Lawrence Patterson, and more like Erskine Wells, the I Company commander who had won a Navy Cross leading a bayonet charge on Guadalcanal. This time, and much to their surprise, their prayers were answered.

From the moment 25-year-old Captain Andrew Allison 'Ack-Ack' Haldane took over K Company in Australia, his outstanding personal qualities – not least his selflessness, empathy, and willingness to take responsibility for others – were obvious. 'Ack-Ack was,' wrote Jim McEnery, 'one helluva great guy and an outstanding officer. He'd been a big football star at some college in New England, but he was a regular guy who got along fine with the enlisted men. He was firm with the troops but always fair, and he never raised his voice. As a fighting man, I think he was cut out of the same cloth as Red Mike Edson.'[3] McEnery could have paid him no greater compliment.

The younger son of first-generation Scottish immigrants, Haldane was born and raised in the blue-collar town of Lawrence, Massachusetts – located 30 miles north of Boston on the Merrimac River, and best known for the 'Bread and Roses' industrial strike of 1912 – where his father earned a paltry $10 a week in the local textile mill. In 1933, Haldane senior got promoted to supervisor and moved to a modest three-bedroom house in nearby Methuen where his youngest son Andy, a hugely talented athlete, excelled at baseball and football at high school. He was a mediocre student, however, and received financial support to study at two fee-paying prep schools before finally gaining a place at Bowdoin, a prestigious private liberal arts college in Brunswick, Maine, at the relatively late age of twenty in the fall of 1937. 'He was a poor boy,' noted Senator Paul H. Douglas of Illinois, a fellow alumnus and veteran of the 5th Marines, 'who came to Bowdoin [and] worked his way through.'[4]

Haldane first came to prominence at Bowdoin by starring in the baseball team and captaining the varsity football team in his senior year. Broad-shouldered and immensely strong, he played his sophomore and junior years as a hard-hitting fullback, a position that was generally used for short-yard plays. Yet he still managed to gain almost 400 yards in his sophomore season, the most for the team. During his final year as captain he switched to halfback, a position that allowed him to carry the ball 'on a larger variety of plays' and display 'surprising speed and shiftiness plus the power and drive for which he is already known'. With Haldane leading from the front, Bowdoin won the college football state championship in 1940.[5]

But he was far from a one-trick pony and won numerous non-athletic honours, including election as President of the Student Council and the award of the Wooden Spoon, the honorary gift to the most popular man in the senior class of '41. 'Andy became,' remembered a faculty member, 'the best-known and, I think, the most highly-regarded man in his college.' He continued:

> When I first saw him in action in [the president's] office, I was pleased – and surprised – by the ease and dignity with which he conducted the meeting. His control was not based on eloquence or intellectuality; it was based on his athletic ability, his physical and moral courage, his modesty, his campus judgement and his common sense.
>
> He remained unsophisticated, a bit gauche with his elders, unresentful of authority and rules, reliable in all respects and circumstances that didn't demand complicated cerebrations, apparently unacquainted with cynicism, captiousness and envy.
>
> In his college years, Andy was deeply – some people might say naively – loyal to everything and everybody that seemed to him to deserve loyalty. And, to my mind, he had rather good taste in loyalties.[6]

For Haldane, his time at Bowdoin was life-changing. It opened his horizons beyond small-town Massachusetts, and gave him the confidence and contacts to forge a successful career. In October 1941, having turned down a post-graduation try-out with the Cleveland Indians baseball team, he was appointed an assistant football coach at Bowdoin. His intention was to coach for a season before joining the US Marines. But, as the government prepared for war by rapidly expanding the armed forces, Haldane was called to service after just two weeks in the job. He was twenty-four.[7]

Passing out of the 7th Reserve Officers' Class (ROC) at Quantico, Virginia, as a second lieutenant in the spring of 1942, Haldane was posted to the 1st Marine Division as the leader of a machine-gun section in time to land on Guadalcanal. According to one of his men, PFC

William D. Reynolds, he was 'more of a hero in the bitter battle [for the island] than he was when he carried his ball club to state championships'. On one occasion, wearing his signature moustache and goatee beard, he was 'supervising wire-laying activities' when his men came under fire from Japanese snipers. Without hesitating, he grabbed the nearest machine gun and, though dangerously exposed, began to spray the surrounding trees and knock down 'several Japs'. With the threat eliminated, he told his men: 'Vacation's over. Let's get back to work.' It was this willingness to expose himself to the same dangers faced by his men that made him, said Reynolds, so 'immensely popular'.[8]

Haldane's close attachment to his alma mater is evident in the fact that, throughout his war service, he kept up a regular correspondence with Bowdoin President Kenneth C. M. Sills, Dean of Students Paul Nixon and football head coach Adam Walsh. On 24 November 1942, for example, President Sills wrote to the then Lieutenant Haldane, referring to the 'interesting letters' the young officer had written from Guadalcanal to Dixon, Walsh and other members of the Bowdoin faculty. 'It has been splendid,' noted Sills, 'to hear at second hand of your doings and the College is proud of you and so interested to hear that you have such a high opinion of your men; that I am sure is one qualification of a good officer.'

Haldane replied with a single-page V-Mail from the mosquito-infested Camp Cable near Brisbane on 6 January 1943, just two days before he and the rest of the 1st Marine Division were due to head south to Melbourne. He was unable to say exactly where he was – because of 'rigid' censorship rules – but the president could easily find out by reading the US newspapers. 'At present,' he added modestly, 'I am taking a back seat & it seems good to get a night's sleep now & then. Gosh I wish I could tell you more but I'm afraid I might make some slight infraction of the regulations which is very serious.'[9]

He wrote more candidly to his older sister Janet about the temptations on offer in Melbourne. 'The women here are very fast, he noted. 'They are big gals & they can handle themselves very well. These girls remind me a great deal of the American girls. The other night I met a shop welder and she had bigger arms than mine. Some of the boys come back with the weirdest takes. One of my men took out a wrestler & she wasn't bad at all. What a life.'[10]

When Haldane took over K Company from Captain Cobb a month or so later, he was still just twenty-five years old and only recently promoted to captain. Yet, despite his relative inexperience, he had an aura about him. It helped that he was physically imposing, of course, with his footballer's muscular physique, wide, pleasant face and square, slightly dimpled jaw (recently shorn of all facial hair). But it was more than that. To Thurman Miller, the new skipper possessed an unusual combination of qualities that made him 'humane and charismatic and courageous'. He added: 'He was only a couple of years older than most of us, but he seemed more grounded. For the rest of my time overseas I received top scores across the board [in my company evaluations], which meant something coming from an officer we all respected so much.'[11]

With the young, energetic and confident Andy Haldane at the helm, K Company's training stepped up a gear. 'Our training became more intense,' recalled Miller, 'and we went on longer marches. Soon a 20-mile march was routine. After a few months our commanders decided to test our recovery. On a Thursday at about noon they suddenly put out the word that weekend liberty call was at 1600 hours, or as soon as we got back to the base. We were 20 miles [away] with full packs. We began jogging.'

They got there with minutes to spare, having covered the whole 20 miles 'without the usual ten-minute break on the hour'.[12]

Haldane's appointment as skipper coincided with minor changes to the organization and strength of K Company, as part of a wider overhaul of Marine regiments in the wake of the Guadalcanal campaign to add more men and firepower. Each regiment expanded by seventy-four men from 3,168 to 3,242. This, in turn, meant a slight increase in the size of a rifle company from 183 men to 196. Most of these extra men were added to the weapons platoon, which grew in size from twenty-eight to thirty-eight men. A rifle platoon lost its automatic rifle squad, but the three rifle squads were expanded from nine to twelve men, giving the platoon a net gain of one man (from forty-two to forty-three). Each rifle squad now consisted of a squad leader (sergeant), assistant squad leader (corporal), two men carrying BARs, two assistant BAR men, and six riflemen (including one still armed with the Springfield '03 and accompanying grenade launcher).[13]

As part of this reorganization, Sergeant Jim McEnery took over one of the expanded rifle squads in 3rd Platoon, while Thurman Miller became platoon sergeant of 2nd Platoon. Their job was to pass on their knowledge to the new boys. 'We filled them in,' remembered Jim McEnery, 'on the tricks Jap snipers used, like tying themselves in the top of trees and waiting for a column of Marines to pass. And like cutting fire lanes a few feet wide at right angles to the Marines' line of march, then setting up machine guns to mow us down as we crossed the lane.'[14]

Recently assigned to the expanded mortar section of the weapons platoon was Private Romus Valton 'R. V.' Burgin, a 20-year-old farm boy from Jewett, Texas. Tall and beanpole thin, Burgin was the third of seven children, and the eldest son. Their father owned a 60-acre farm that used horse- and mule-power to grow corn, cotton, sugarcane and sorghum. Cotton was the *only* money crop, and Burgin had helped to pick it from the age of three. 'My mother cooked three meals a day for nine people,' wrote Burgin, 'and she worked in the field. The boys in the family, we did the housework just the same as the girls. My mother felt that if the girls can work in the fields, then the boys can do housework.'

Like many houses of the era, Burgin's had no electricity or indoor plumbing. Water was drawn from a 30ft-deep well in the yard that Burgin helped to dig. When the well dried up in a drought, the children fetched water from a nearby river. There was no icebox and most of the food was preserved in a smokehouse built of logs and covered in wooden shingles. Meals were cooked on a woodstove, and clothes washed in an iron tub with a scrub board.

Burgin's upbringing may not have been quite as deprived and dirt poor as, say, Thurman Miller's, but it was still tough and character-forming by modern standards. He enjoyed school: not for the lessons (he rarely scored higher than a C), but because he 'liked being around other folks and playing whatever they were playing'. He loved all sports, particularly track and field, and was voted football captain in his senior year of high school. 'I wasn't a big kid,' he recalled. 'I weighed 140 pounds. But I was fast and I could hit hard.'

On graduating in May 1941, he got a job in a Dallas warehouse for 30 cents an hour. 'I'd seen my dad work hard only to see the crop fail,' noted Burgin. 'I thought, "There's a better way to make a living than on the farm."'

Like many young men, he took the news of the Japanese attack on Pearl Harbor, and America's declaration of war, in his stride. Only later would he realize how much that single event changed the world, and his place in it. The first indication was his call-up to the military in November 1942, by which time he was working as a travelling salesman for a stationery company in Columbus, Ohio. He chose the US Marines because in recruiting posters it looked like a 'sharp outfit', a disciplined elite. 'I was from a farm,' he explained. 'I was used to hard work and discipline. The Army seemed sloppy to me.'

Though boot camp in San Diego was a shock, Burgin adapted quickly. He learned that a floor was the 'deck', walls were 'bulkheads', stairs were 'ladders', and the bathroom was the 'head'. He was taught how to make up his bunk and how to stow gear in his locker. There was a 'place for everything, and everything had to be in its place'. They did physical drill every day with their 8lb 11oz Springfield rifles. 'We'd stand holding that heavy rifle at arm's length, shoulder high – and hold it and hold it,' recalled Burgin. 'When they got through with us, our arms were so tired that the rifle felt like it weighed eighty pounds.' He eventually qualified Sharpshooter with both the rifle and .45 automatic pistol.

Boot camp was normally a twelve-week course. Burgin went through in six, an accelerated programme that was designed to break down the recruits both mentally and physically, before building them back up so they were able to kill without compunction. It worked. 'I can honestly say,' wrote Burgin, 'I could've cut a Jap's throat and never blinked an eye.'

Denied the usual week's leave, Burgin and his fellow boot camp graduates were sent straight to Camp Elliott, 20 miles north of San Diego, for advanced infantry training. On his first day, Burgin was told: 'You're going to be in the sixty mortars. Report to that tent over there.'[15]

Unaware that such a weapon even existed, Burgin strode over to an open pavilion where an instructor gave him and the other rookies a crash course on the assembly and operation of the 60mm M2 mortar. Based on a French design, it comprised four separate parts: a 28.6in long smoothbore barrel, breech cap and fixed firing pin (12.8lb); bipod with traversing and elevating mechanisms (16.4lb); baseplate for stability (12.8lb); and M4 aiming sight, with deflection and elevation scales, which was mounted on a bracket on the traversing head.[16]

Burgin discovered there were six men in a mortar squad: three ammo carriers, a gunner, assistant gunner and squad leader, usually a corporal.* In battle the gunner carried the base plate, his assistant the firing tube, an ammo carrier the tripod, and the squad leader the sight, which had a level indicator and was marked for degrees right and left. There were four main types of ammunition: a high-explosive round (weighing just under 3lb); a practice round, with a smaller charge, to measure range; an illuminating round, carrying a 100,000 candle-power unit suspended from a parachute, which provided bright light for twenty-five seconds while it fell to the ground; and a smoke round, containing white phosphorus which ignites when exposed to air, to create a screen for covering an attack or extracting casualties. All rounds contained four tabs of propellant at their base, about the size of a postage stamp and an eighth of an inch thick. You left them on or pulled them off, depending on how far you wanted to fire the round. To hit a target at 2,000 yards, the maximum range, you used all four; much closer targets required only a single charge.

During the next few weeks, Burgin and his squad practised setting up the mortar, over and over, until they could all do it in a matter of seconds and virtually in their sleep. Once assembled and dug in, they would put an aiming stake out in front of the mortar and zero in on

* Before Burgin joined K Company, the mortar section would gain a third squad, but they would be reduced in size from six to five men (losing an ammo bearer).

that. The corrections were made by the squad leader whose job was to observe from the front line, with the riflemen, about 25 or 30 yards ahead. Using a sound-powered phone, he would call in the 'range to the target, number of degrees right or left of the aiming stake', and give the order to fire. The gunner would make the necessary adjustments and his assistant drop in the round.

In battle, the mortar was deadly. A single high-explosive round could kill or maim anyone within a 45ft radius of its impact point. It also had the advantage, because of its steep trajectory, of being able to hit targets that larger-calibre artillery rounds and bullets could not reach. 'A man,' noted Burgin, 'can't hide from a mortar.'

In early March 1943, with his training complete, Burgin and the other members of the 9th Replacement Battalion were told they were shipping out. Later that day, they rode trucks to San Diego docks and boarded the USS *Mount Vernon*, a former ocean liner converted to a troop transport. The voyage to Melbourne, Australia – via Honolulu, Fiji and New Caledonia – took three weeks. Burgin was among the replacements sent to the 5th Marines at Camp Balcombe, a 'pretty place with green fields and gentle hills' that reminded him of Texas.

Initially assigned to the regiment's HQ and Service (H & S) Company – made up chiefly of communications, intelligence, administrative and support personnel – Burgin spent his first three months in Australia on KP duty. Not as a punishment, but just to keep him 'busy and because somebody had to do the work'. He made the best of it by doing a deal with the mess sergeant to work twenty-four hours straight, followed by a day of liberty. He would spend it in Melbourne, often with another replacement he had met on the voyage, Private Jim T. Burke from Clinton, Ohio. Before leaving camp, they would each buy three cartons of cigarettes, at 50 cents a go, and sell them for ten times that sum (or £2.50 Australian money). At a time when a pint of beer cost 12 cents, and steak and eggs 50 cents, this gave Burke – who had been overpaid and was now short on cash – enough money to enjoy his liberty.

In late April, they were walking down Collins Street in the centre of Melbourne when they spotted two pretty young women, a brunette and a blonde, and followed them into a milk bar.* 'The brunette's mine,' insisted Burgin.

'I'll take the blonde,' said Burke.

The girls, they discovered, were Florence Riseley and Doris Moran, both eighteen years old and living in the suburb of Albert Park. They had come into town to meet Florence's mother and three-year-old brother, who were from Tasmania and would be taking a train that evening. But with time to kill, they offered to show the Marines round the nearby Melbourne Museum, which included the stuffed remains of Phar Lap, the famous Australian racehorse that, said Doris, had been poisoned by 'you Yanks' while racing in the United States. Later, at the station, Burgin and Burke took turns giving Florence's brother a piggyback ride up and down the platform. It had the desired effect.

'They seem to be nice,' whispered Florence's mother to her daughter. 'Anybody who plays with a child like that can't be all bad.'

They double-dated once a week for the next three months, going to movies, riding in horse-drawn buggies and sitting on park benches, talking about their families and what they might do when the war was over. Florence said that her father had been gassed in France during World War I, and now worked as a steam shovel operator in a coal mine north of Melbourne. She also admitted she was sixteen, not eighteen, and had lied about her age to get a job in a factory making biscuits for the troops. Already promoted to assistant floor supervisor, she was being sent to night school by the company to study management. She seemed to be the complete package: 5ft 9in tall, 'witty and beautiful', and also 'very intelligent'. Burgin could hardly believe his luck.

He would have less time to spend with her after he was transferred from the 5th Marines' H & S Company to the mortar section of K/3/5 in June 1943. It would mean more training and less liberty. But he was glad to be back with a weapon he knew and, having entered the large Quonset hut that held both the machine gun and mortar sections, he was delighted to find his friend Jim Burke. They would serve in the mortars together.[17]

* A shop, popular in the 1940s, that sold candy and sodas.

14

Planning for Action

Southwest Pacific, March–December 1943

While K Company worked its way back to full strength, its next operation was being decided at high-level meetings in the United States, Australia and North Africa. Back in July 1942, the Joint Chiefs in Washington DC had authorized a series of offensive operations in the Pacific – including the capture of Guadalcanal and the Papuan Peninsula – that were essentially defensive in terms of strategy. 'The immediate aim of the Joint Chiefs,' wrote John Miller, Jr, in the official US Army history, 'was, not to defeat the Japanese nation, but to protect Australia and New Zealand by halting the Japanese southward advance from Rabaul toward the air and sea lines of communication that joined the United States and Hawaii to Australia and New Zealand.'

But by early 1943, with both the Guadalcanal and Papuan campaigns drawing to a successful close, 'Bull' Halsey and Doug MacArthur began preparing plans for a coordinated advance up New Guinea and the Solomons towards the Japanese stronghold of Rabaul on New Britain. The move was endorsed in January 1943 by the Anglo-American conference at Casablanca on the Atlantic coast of Morocco where Roosevelt, Churchill and their service chiefs* agreed, after much rancorous debate,

* Known collectively as the Combined Chiefs of Staff (CCS) Committee, a body that included the US Joint Chiefs of Staff and the British Chiefs of Staff. It had been set up in Washington DC in December 1941, in the wake of Pearl Harbor, to direct grand strategy for the Allies.

to delay the cross-Channel invasion of France until it was likely to succeed (which meant, in practical terms, 1944 at the earliest), and instead to assault the Mediterranean island of Sicily in the summer of 1943, and elsewhere to recapture Burma and make advances against the Japanese in the Pacific.

The priority of the British was, as ever, to concentrate their resources against Germany and use only limited forces against the Japanese until the Nazis had been completely overthrown. At the same time, they were wary of launching a cross-Channel invasion until sufficient landing craft were available and, more importantly, German morale and resources had been more seriously eroded. They preferred to attack Sicily next because it would safeguard Mediterranean shipping, tie up German troops, and threaten mainland Italy, possibly driving Hitler's Axis partner out of the war.

Their 'interminable operations in the Mediterranean' were opposed by General Marshall and Admiral King, who wanted instead 'to conduct a strategic offensive directly against Germany and to aid the Soviet Union', and at the same time to maintain 'constant unremitting pressure against the Japanese to prevent them from digging in and consolidating their gains'. Marshall warned that the American people would not stand for another Bataan, while King pointed out the strategic importance of an advance across the central Pacific to the Philippines, and raised the question of where to go after Rabaul was captured. Thanks to Roosevelt's support, the British got their way over Sicily. But the quid pro quo was that they were forced to back the American strategy to retake Burma, capture Rabaul, secure the Aleutians and advance west through the Gilbert and Marshall Islands in the central Pacific towards Truk and the Marianas. The central Pacific advances would follow the capture of Rabaul.[1]

Ironically, having won the Rabaul concession at Casablanca, Admiral King then questioned the need for such a potentially costly operation. Would it not be better, he suggested to the Pacific commanders, to bypass the Solomons and the Bismarck Archipelago and land instead on the Admiralty Islands, 400 miles to the northwest? Rabaul could then be neutralized by an air offensive, said King, but otherwise left to its own devices. No, responded MacArthur, Halsey and Admiral Nimitz, who all felt that bypassing Japanese strongholds would threaten America's overstretched supply lines. In any case, MacArthur told the Joint Chiefs, Rabaul was needed as a forward naval base and leapfrogging it would 'involve hazards rendering success doubtful'. There was also the question of whether American carrier forces, much weakened by the sea battles of 1942, could compensate for the lack of land-based air support. The favoured strategy of the Pacific commanders, therefore, was to advance step by step, constructing new air bases as they went.

Conceding defeat, King agreed to the new directive issued by the Joint Chiefs on 28 March 1943 for a two-pronged advance on Rabaul. This involved 'Bull' Halsey pushing northwest through the Solomon chain to the island of Bougainville, while MacArthur moved north along the coast of New Guinea before landing troops at Cape Gloucester on western New Britain. Collectively, the operation was known as Cartwheel.[2]

As amphibious specialists, the men of the 1st Marine Division would spearhead the Cape Gloucester landings in December 1943. But they would do it without Alexander Vandegrift, who had been promoted to lieutenant general and given command of the I Marine Amphibious Corps – made up of the 3rd Marine Division, the US Army's 37th Infantry Division and New Zealand's 8th Infantry Brigade – for the assault on Bougainville in November. He was replaced as commander of the 1st Marine Division on 8 July by his former deputy, Major General William H. Rupertus, fifty-three, an expert shot who had served on the Marine Corps rifle team. In the wake of Pearl Harbor, convinced that high standards of marksmanship and weapon maintenance were vital for success in combat, he wrote the Marine Rifleman's Creed. Part of it read:

> This is my rifle. There are many like it, but this one is mine.

My rifle is my best friend. It is my life. I must master it as I must master my life.

Without me, my rifle is useless. Without my rifle, I am useless. I must fire my rifle true. I must shoot straighter than my enemy who is trying to kill me. I must shoot him before he shoots me. I will . . .

Before God, I swear this creed. My rifle and myself are the defenders of my country. We are the masters of our enemy. We are the saviors of my life.

So be it, until victory is America's and there is no enemy, but peace![3]

Soon after taking command of the 1st Marine Division, Rupertus received the operation order for the Cape Gloucester campaign from the staff of Lieutenant General Walter Krueger's Sixth Army, the field force that MacArthur had activated to carry out the western portion of Operation Cartwheel. It was, thought Rupertus's staff, too complex and required a dangerous dispersal of force by landings at several points, rather than a concentration at one. The plan would go through several modifications before a final, improved version was agreed in late November.[4]

In the meantime, the training of the Old Breed increased in intensity, a particular emphasis being laid on marching and marksmanship with the new M1 Garand rifles that had just replaced the Marines' trusty bolt-action Springfields. Gas operated and semi-automatic, the M1 weighed 9½lb and could rapidly fire a whole clip of eight rounds by repeated pulls of the trigger. Once the last round had been fired, the clip was ejected upwards and the bolt lock opened, ready to be reloaded. This gave the durable, easy to maintain M1 a much higher rate of fire than either the Springfield or the bolt-action Arisaka Types 38 and 99 rifles used by the Imperial Japanese Army.

A mere Sharpshooter with the Springfield, R. V. Burgin qualified as Expert with the M1, the highest classification possible. Soon after, he took part in a battalion competition to see who was the fastest at stripping down and reassembling a machine gun, M1 and mortar. He won the mortar competition. 'I could put that mortar together and get it on target faster than anybody,' he recalled. 'I mean, I was the head dog. I made gunner immediately and was issued a .45 [pistol], which I wore from then on.' He was also promoted to private first class.[5]

Along with the new M1 rifles, the Devil Dogs were also issued a new broad-bladed knife known as a Ka-Bar, to be worn on a special sheath slung from the belt, for use either as a weapon or a utility tool. With its stacked leather handle (for better grip) and seven inches of phosphate-coated steel, it reminded Jim McEnery of 'the famed Bowie knife of the Old West'. The men were told: 'You can do many different things with this knife. You can open a can of C rations with it. You can chop up firewood with it. You can clean the mud off your boondockers with it. And, of course, you can slit a Jap's throat with it.'

In August, the men of K Company 'started making practice landings from rubber boats, and learning how to work closely with tanks'. Most of their liberties were cancelled, and leisurely weekends in Melbourne became a thing of the past.[6] Preparing to head out on one of the last liberties, R. V. Burgin noticed that the Marine in the bunk next to his was counting his money. His name was PFC Merriel A. Shelton, an olive-skinned 21-year-old former bartender from Jackson, Louisiana, who talked with a thick Cajun accent that became even harder to understand in moments of excitement. 'He was a little man,' remembered Burgin, 'and a character all right but not as goofy as everyone thinks.'

Both replacements and in the same mortar squad, Burgin and Shelton became good friends. Seeing the cash on Shelton's bunk – won at poker, a game the Louisianan excelled at – Burgin asked: 'How much money do you have there?'

'Oh,' said Shelton, counting his notes, 'I gots ten or twelve pounds.'

Then he picked up his change and weighed it in his hand. 'And I mus' have ten or twelve ounces here.'

Twigging that Shelton thought Australian currency was a 'weight thing', when really it was called pounds, shillings and pence, Burgin chuckled. 'I'll tell you what, Shelton,' he said, 'you're just a SNAFU* waiting to happen.'

Others heard the comment and laughed. From then on, Shelton was known as 'Snafu'.[7]

One evening, Captain Haldane ordered the whole company to collect its gear and prepare to move out. 'We hiked all night long with full packs and bedrolls carrying our M-1s,' remembered Jim McEnery. 'We'd march for fifty minutes, then get a ten-minute rest break.'

Next morning, after field cooks had served breakfast, they began the same routine: hiking all day at the same pace, never getting a break longer than ten minutes. When they finally stopped that evening to eat, an exhausted R. V. Burgin figured it would be for the night and began pitching a pup tent with Jim Burke. No sooner was it up than someone shouted, 'Fall in!' They scrabbled to get the tent down and back in formation before the column moved off for another all-night hike. Burgin recalled:

> We had a pace to maintain, and we wore our full transport packs, upper and lower part, with a bedroll. The whole thing weighed about forty pounds. We were carrying our M1s and I had that .45 strapped to my side and was carrying the butt plate for the mortar. Whenever they hollered 'break', I'd just lean back on that pack and instantly I was gone. I must have slept nine minutes out of every ten-minute break.

The following day, having reached their destination, they practised field exercises, crawling on their bellies under barbed wire, while tanks, artillery and machine guns fired live rounds over their heads, and planes bombed and strafed the ground in front. Finally, at 4:00 p.m., the firing

* A popular acronym in all branches of the US armed forces, it stood for 'Situation Normal, All Fouled Up'. In plain language, it was 'Situation Normal, All Fucked Up.'

stopped and the company began the long hike back to camp. Noticing an orchard of ripe apple trees en route, McEnery led his squad into it. They were enjoying a break in the shade, munching apples, when the owner of the orchard appeared. Expecting the worst, McEnery was surprised to see the farmer grinning.

'You Yanks,' he said, 'are welcome to anything I have. I've got a son in America, and everyone treats him marvellously over there. You can bed down here for the night if you want. I'll get you some blankets.'

Arriving back at Camp Balcombe, considerably later than the rest of the company, McEnery was chewed out by Lieutenant Daniel Dykstra, his new platoon leader, who was not 'nearly so charitable or understanding' as the farmer had been.[8]

Towards the end of September, K Company was allowed one final liberty before shipping out with the rest of the 5th Marines. The plan was to send the whole of the 1st Marine Division to a staging and training area on or near New Guinea, prior to the assault on New Britain in November. The destination of the 5th Marines was Milne Bay in eastern New Guinea.

Having already handed in their dress uniforms, shoes and hats, the Devil Dogs went into Melbourne wearing their khaki uniforms and boondockers. For R. V. Burgin, it was a last opportunity to say goodbye to Florence. He eventually found her with some girlfriends in St Kilda Park. Surprised to see him, she quickly guessed the truth and they clung to each other. Burgin was tempted to propose to her there and then. They had spent enough time together for him to know she was the one. But he also knew what lay ahead and 'didn't want to leave her a widow'. Instead he tried to reassure her. 'I'll be all right,' he kept saying. 'I'll come back for you when it's over.'[9]

Two days later, the men of K Company were roused at 6:00 a.m. and taken in trucks to the docks at Port Melbourne where – after a long wait – they and the rest of the 3/5 Marines embarked on the Liberty ship *B. F. Shaw*. Crewed by merchant seamen, these ships had been mass-produced to a simple design to carry cargo. They were 'never meant to carry troops,' noted Jim McEnery, 'and we were crammed into quarters that ranged from primitive to nonexistent'.

They were sharing the cargo hold with hundreds of crates of ammunition and supplies, artillery pieces, trucks, deflated rafts and other kit. They had two sleeping choices: to sling their hammocks, up to five high, between riveted bulkheads and girders; or bed down on the deck under ponchos and sections of two-man tents called shelter-halves. Their makeshift showers, toilets and the galleys were on the weather decks, 'which were sure to be awash with garbage, sewage, and seawater in rough weather'. The chow lines to these open-air galleys were 'slow and stretched for miles'.

Steaming north, they were ignorant of their precise destination. But the Canal veterans, at least, had their suspicions. We guessed, wrote McEnery, that it was 'another damn island, another damn airfield'.

They were right on both counts. To prepare, however, they were disembarked at Milne Bay on the eastern tip of New Guinea on 11 October. Their camp seemed like it had been 'scraped out the jungle'. Tents lined a single muddy street. It rained constantly, soaking the canvas, the ground and the Marines' clothes. 'When we went to lie down,' recalled R. V. Burgin, 'our cots would sink into the muck so that we soon found ourselves sleeping on the ground with only a layer of canvas beneath us . . . Between rains we dried out a little. They scattered some rock around, and that helped a bit.'

Despite the mud, they did their best to maintain Marine standards by washing themselves and their uniforms in a creek behind company HQ. If it was sunny, they dried their clothes before putting them on; if not, they wore them wet. Most days were spent training in the jungle: practising mock combat, marching and shooting on the ranges. 'It was,' recalled McEnery, 'a grim, gloomy, depressing place, and we were destined to be there for two and a half months.'[10]

Of course, when writing letters home, the Devil Dogs tried to be as upbeat as possible; they also omitted any details that would pinpoint their location or what they were about to do. R. V. Burgin, for example, in the first of hundreds of letters to Florence Riseley, wrote only that he was getting along fine and missed her.[11] Thurman Miller used his Red Cross stationery to compose a light-hearted ditty to his sweetheart Recie. It began: 'I'm sick of the Nip and the Tartar/I'm sick of their rice every day/These faraway spots on the map are/No place for yours truly to stay.'[12]

Their skipper Andy Haldane was unashamedly nostalgic as he replied to a letter from Kenneth Sills, the president of Bowdoin College, in late November. Sills had congratulated him on the name he was making for himself in the Marines, adding: 'You may be sure that you will get a very warm reception on the campus whenever you return.'

Haldane replied that he hoped he 'could get back & very soon', but there was 'a little more work to do' first. He continued:

> If ever I do get back you can be sure I will visit Bowdoin for there is a section of my heart set apart from the rest which carries an undying love for the school & its members.
>
> I can remember when I didn't know where my next dollar was coming from but now I am doing quite well for myself. I've often thought of what I could do after this war game is over and I've come to the conclusion that I would much rather be a civilian. It won't be long now for press reports as you know are very encouraging.

By mentioning 'press reports', Haldane was probably referring to the recent unopposed landings on Bougainville, the most northerly of the Solomons, that had cost the IJN a number of warships as it tried and failed to disrupt the operation; in Europe, meanwhile, Allied troops had captured Sicily and successfully invaded mainland Italy. Yet for all of Haldane's forced optimism, there is also a hint of sadness in his acknowledgement that he might not survive the war.[13]

Towards the end of their time on New Guinea, the K Company men rehearsed an assault landing in the bay in a new 2½ ton, six-wheel-drive amphibious vehicle known as a DUKW, or 'Duck'.* Thirty feet long

* Designed by Sparkman & Stephens and the General Motors Corporation, the

and eight wide, with room for 5,000lb of supplies or twenty-four Marines, it could get up to speeds of 50 miles per hour on land, but was 'slow and rough-riding in water'. R. V. Burgin, Jim Burke and the rest of the mortar squad discovered just how uncomfortable it was during their crossing of the bay in wind and rain. 'We couldn't see thirty yards,' noted Burgin, 'much less the other DUKWs. Our coxman lost his bearing, and then he lost his breakfast. I wasn't feeling so good myself. A wave of seasickness swept over everybody. The diesel blowing in our faces only made it worse.'

They then got stuck on a reef and, for two hours, the waves threatened to tear a hole in the steel hull. Fortunately, it was double-skinned and they finally limped to shore where some of the men were still so badly seasick they had to be hospitalized.[14]

As K Company prepared for the new campaign, the final details of the plan were still being thrashed out by the staffs of the Sixth Army and the 1st Marine Division who, in turn, were responding to decisions taken by the Joint Chiefs of Staff and their subordinate committees in Washington DC. Once the Combined Chiefs at Casablanca had approved an advance through the central Pacific, the Joint Chiefs got to work on a general strategic plan that would govern the way in which Nimitz's and MacArthur's forces were used until the end of the war. First presented to the CCS in mid-May 1943, it aimed to secure the 'unconditional surrender of Japan by air and naval blockade of the Japanese homeland, and, if necessary, by invasion'. There was a hope that naval control of the western Pacific might bring about surrender without invasion, or even without air bombardment. But if a bombing campaign and/or invasion became necessary, air and naval bases in the western Pacific would need to be secured. 'Therefore,' notes the official US Army history,

---

DUKW got its name from a manufacturer's code: D – the model year, 1942; U – the body style, utility (amphibious); K – for all-wheel drive; W – for dual rear axles. For any American looking at 'DUKW', it was hard not to pronounce this as 'Duck'.

'the United States forces were to fight westward across the Pacific along two axes of advance: a main effort through the Central Pacific and a subsidiary effort through the South and Southwest Pacific Areas.'

At Washington in May, the CCS confirmed their decision at Casablanca by approving Nimitz's plans for the capture of the Gilbert and Marshall Islands (as the opening phase of the central Pacific advance) and MacArthur's existing plans for Operation Cartwheel. But the Joint Chiefs then threatened to downgrade MacArthur's effort when they informed him in June that Nimitz's operations would begin in mid-November and require the use of both the 1st and 2nd Marine Divisions (then in the Southwest and South Pacific Areas, respectively), all the South Pacific's assault transports and cargo ships, and the major portion of Halsey's naval forces. MacArthur responded by emphasizing the strategic importance of his advance through New Guinea to the Philippines, and the need to retain the two Marine divisions for the assault on Rabaul. His protests were backed by Admiral Halsey.

Unbeknown to MacArthur at this stage, however, were the ongoing discussions in Washington DC as to the desirability of assaulting Rabaul. In the opinion of the Joint Strategic Survey Committee, it made sense to neutralize rather than capture Rabaul, while at the same time giving the central Pacific offensive priority over Cartwheel. Admiral William D. Leahy, Roosevelt's chief of staff and senior member of the Joint Chiefs, did not agree. A strong supporter of MacArthur, he 'argued strongly' against any curtailment of Cartwheel. Admiral King, meanwhile, was on the fence: he wanted to see Rabaul 'cleaned up' as soon as possible so that the Allies could 'shoot for Luzon'; but if Cartwheel did not move faster he favoured a curtailment.

The transfer of the Marine divisions was settled by a compromise: the 1st would remain under MacArthur's command, while the 2nd went to the central Pacific (where it would be used to assault Tarawa in the Gilberts in November 1943). Leahy, moreover, was outvoted in the Joint Chiefs by General Marshall and Admiral King who agreed with the Strategic Survey Committee that it was better to neutralize Rabaul rather than capture it. This was the recommendation that the Joint Chiefs made to the Combined Chiefs of Staff at an Allied conference in Quebec – codenamed Quadrant – in late August 1943. At the conference, the British Chiefs of Staff were broadly supportive of a single offensive drive across the central Pacific that would have sidelined Doug MacArthur's operations in the southwest Pacific. The British were hoping to release more resources for the planned invasion of Normandy the following spring. But they were opposed by President Roosevelt, who in turn had been swayed by General Marshall's demand for the US Army-led drive towards the Philippines to continue, and no doubt influenced by MacArthur's political heft and implicit threat to enter the 1944 presidential race.

The upshot was that the CCS directed MacArthur 'to seize or neutralize Eastern New Guinea as far west as Wewak and including the Admiralties and the Bismarck Archipelago. Neutralize rather than capture Rabaul.' A direct attack on Rabaul would, said the CCS, 'be costly and time consuming', while alternative anchorages and 'potential air and naval bases' were available at 'Kavieng and in the Admiralties'. With the capture and development of such bases Rabaul could be 'isolated from the northeast'.[15]

Though the chiefs had insisted on bypassing Rabaul, MacArthur still wanted to capture the smaller airfields on the western side of New Britain. Hence the plan to land the 1st Marine Division at Cape Gloucester. What the staffs of Krueger's Sixth Army and Rupertus's 1st Marine Division could not agree on, however, was the finer detail. In mid-October, Krueger's staff decreed that only a single regiment, the 7th Marines, would land in the Cape Gloucester area on D-Day (which had recently been moved to 26 December). The 7th was to be supported by an Army parachute regiment, the 503rd, which would drop in a patch of kunai grass southeast of the nearby airfield. 'The Marines,' noted George McMillan, 'were to drive through the jungle and join the parachutists, a piece of maneuver that looked better on paper to the Army staff than it did to the Marines who had already learned at Guadalcanal some sad lessons about maneuver in the rainforest.'

On 14 December, during a visit to the 1st Marine Division's HQ on Goodenough Island off New Guinea, Doug MacArthur asked Rupertus's staff what they thought of the plan. 'Well, General,' said Lieutenant Colonel E. A. Pollock, the 1st's operations chief, 'we don't like it.'

MacArthur looked surprised. 'Well, what is it, Colonel,' he asked, 'you don't like?'

'Sir, we don't like anything about it.'

The general turned to his subordinate Krueger, hoping for an explanation, but the Sixth Army commander stayed silent. Visibly angry, MacArthur turned back to Pollock. 'You had better speak to General Rupertus about your questions.'

'But I have,' said Pollock, undaunted. 'None of us like it.'

MacArthur had heard enough and stalked out of the tent. On reflection, however, he realized that the Marines were right and the plan had to change. Soon after the visit, he instructed Krueger to hold another joint conference with Rupertus and his staff to revise the plan. The final version permitted the 1st Marine Division to use all its regiments in the landing at Cape Gloucester on 26 December, with just one (the 5th Marines) held in reserve, while a subsidiary force landed at Arawe on the south coast to block the movement of reinforcements from the south. The army paratroopers were no longer involved. 'This plan,' said Pollock, 'was most acceptable. It kept the Division intact, and permitted the landing of a sizeable force against an enemy known to be numerically superior, and well established. This was in keeping with the views of the Division of initially placing an overwhelming force on the beach.'[16]

15

Green Hell

Cape Gloucester, 26 December 1943–2 January 1944

On Christmas Eve 1943, K Company left its camp at Milne Bay for the 100-mile journey up the coast of New Guinea to Oro Bay, the jumping-off point for Operation Backhander, the invasion of western New Britain. It was still at Oro with the rest of the 5th Marines when the landings began two days later on beaches either side of Cape Gloucester. The western supporting attack was made by the 2/1 Marines at Tauali. But the main effort was at Silimati Point, to the east, where two battalions of the 7th Marines – having spent Christmas Day at sea, playing poker and singing secular tunes like 'Pistol-Packin' Mama' – came ashore at Yellow Beaches 1 and 2.* As at Guadalcanal, the assaulting troops were mostly unopposed (bar some long-range machine-gun fire). But when they moved off the beach they entered a swampy jungle. 'Time and again,' noted a Marine, 'members of our column would fall into waist-high sink holes and have to be pulled out. A slip meant a broken or wrenched leg.'[1]

Once through the swamp, the 1/7 Marines secured the 450ft Target Hill that commanded the landing beaches, while the 2/7 Marines moved

* The beaches had been partly selected by reconnaissance troops known as 'Alamo Scouts' – made up of personnel from the Australian and US Navies, the US Marines and natives of the island – who had carried out a series of secret landings from September to December 1943.

deeper inland with the intention of setting up a beachhead perimeter. They encountered the first Japanese outposts at 700 yards, and at double that distance a sharp fight began 'that was not to end for five days'. Meanwhile the remaining two battalions of the 1st Marines, having landed at Silimati an hour after the 7th Marines, had turned west along the coastal track towards their main objective, Cape Gloucester airfield. They quickly ran into a cleverly disguised Japanese roadblock of four strong bunkers, armed with machine guns, and a system of rifle trenches. 'Two captains walked unsuspectedly into the Japanese lane of fire and were killed immediately,' wrote George McMillan. 'An amtrac [the new LVT-2, known as a 'buffalo'*] was brought up, but got stuck between two trees and the Japanese swarmed it. They shot one gunner, dragged the other over the side and knifed him to death.'

One of the dead gunners, Private Leslie E. Hansen, had a brother, Paul, on the amtrac who survived. When Major General Rupertus heard they were the sons of a widow who had already lost her older son in the war, he ordered Paul Hansen back to the United States.

By nightfall, the 1st Marines had cleared the roadblock and reached their first-day phase line. More than 13,000 men and 2,100 tons of supplies had already come ashore, and the main beachhead at Silimati – no more than a mile wide and 500 yards deep – was secure. Total casualties were just twenty-one killed (one by a falling tree) and twenty-three wounded. Japanese losses were around fifty dead.[2]

Few of the Marines who fought on New Britain had ever heard of this rugged, volcanic island: 'roughly crescent-shaped, 370 miles long, with an average width of 40 to 50 miles'. Bigger than all the Solomons combined, it was by far the largest land mass on which US troops fought in the Pacific, bar the main islands of the Philippines. 'Densely jungled,' noted the US Marines' official history, 'with a spine of

* The thinly armoured 'Water Buffalo', 26 feet long and 10 feet wide, was armed with up to four Browning machine guns and had room for three crew and twenty-four passengers.

seemingly impassable mountains, New Britain was one of the many Pacific islands which no European power bothered to claim for three centuries following its discovery.'[3]

Until 1880, that is, when the German Empire colonized the Bismarck Archipelago (named after Otto von Bismarck, the first German chancellor and architect of unification), northeastern New Guinea and the northern Solomons. In 1910, the Germans planned and built the town of Rabaul to serve as the region's administrative capital. But it and the rest of German New Guinea was seized by the Australians at the outbreak of World War I, the point at which the island of Neupommern ('New Pomerania') was renamed New Britain. The island was captured, in turn, by the Japanese in January 1942 and Rabaul was rapidly converted into a formidable advance base, boasting 'five airfields, a fine fleet anchorage, and the fanciest brothel east of the Netherlands Indies'. By the time the US Marines landed, the majority of the 100,000 Japanese troops on New Britain – under General Hitoshi Imamura, commanding the Eighth Area Army – were based in and around Rabaul, leaving around 9,500 men from the 65th Brigade to defend the Cape Gloucester area.

But if Japanese defenders at Gloucester were a little thin on the ground, the Marines also had to contend with a brutally inhospitable climate and terrain. The island, wrote the official campaign history, was hot and humid, with a 'rain forest' jungle that was typical of the Pacific tropics:

> Giant trees towering up to 200 feet into the sky above dense undergrowth lashed together by savage vines as thick as a man's arm and many times as tough, in the coastal area interspersed with occasional patches of kunai grass sometimes higher than a man's head, and hip-deep swamps. Decay lies everywhere just under the exotic lushness, emitting an indescribable odor unforgettable to anyone who has lived with it. Insect life flourishes prodigiously: disease-bearing mosquitoes and ticks, spiders the size of dinner plates, wasps three inches long, scorpions, centipedes. Vertebrate animals occur in less variety, the only dangerous creatures indigenous to the region being alligators and giant snakes of the constrictor species.

There were two seasons – 'wet and less wet' – with the monsoon generally beginning in mid-December, a detail not sufficiently noted by the planners.[4] It began to rain on D-Day, and in the early hours of the 27th a 'terrific storm struck the Cape Gloucester area', soaking even Major General Rupertus as he lay on his cot in the open air. The deluge continued for the next five days, making the swamps behind the shore line 'impassable for wheeled and tracked vehicles' and turning streams into 'raging torrents'. Sleeping in foxholes on the front line, pairs of Marines would put one poncho above them and another below, which was fine until the water level rose. 'If you could keep the water out,' recalled one veteran, 'then the heat of your body, wrapped in the poncho, would dry out your clothes during the night. Sometimes, when we weren't right on the lines, my buddy and I'd fix up a little lean-to, get a couple of saplings and stretch one of our ponchos on them, and cover ourselves with the other . . . You always got cold at night, even there in the tropics, because, I guess, we were always wet.'[5]

First to land on Guadalcanal, K Company and the rest of the 3/5 Marines were the last ashore at Cape Gloucester, on New Year's Day 1944 (D-Day plus 6). The other two battalions of the 5th Marines had reinforced the beachhead three days earlier and, at noon on 30 December, helped the 1st Marines to capture the Cape Gloucester airfield after a tough fight. Rupertus signalled Krueger: 'First Marine Division presents to you as an early New Year gift the complete airdrome of Cape Gloucester. Situation well in hand due to fighting spirit of troops, the usual Marine luck and the help of God.'[6]

A delighted Doug MacArthur received the news at his advance CP at Port Moresby. 'I extend my heartiest congratulations to your officers and men,' he wrote to Rupertus. 'I am filled with pride and gratitude by their resourceful determination in capturing Cape Gloucester. Your gallant Division has maintained the immortal record of the Marine Corps and covered itself with glory.'

Yet the battle was far from over. The airfield and its two strips were in a terrible condition – badly cratered from incessant bombing and shelling – and would take weeks to put into operation. For security, therefore, a defensive perimeter was thrown around the airfield, which was separated from the original beachhead by six miles of vulnerable coastal road. Rupertus took charge of the airfield defences, leaving assistant division commander Brigadier General Lemuel C. Shepherd, Jr, in command at Silimati Point. Shepherd's main task, communicated to him on 29 December, was to 'conduct operations to the Southeast in order to extend the beachhead perimeter and clear the enemy from the Borgen Bay area'.[7]

This was easier said than done. Japanese troops had set up strong defensive positions behind a number of streams, ridges and hills, and it would take a Herculean effort to winkle them out. The unenviable task was given to the 1/7 and 3/7 Marines and, from New Year's Day, the newly arrived 3/5 Marines, including Andy Haldane's K Company. When it landed at Yellow Beach 2, in the shadow of Target Hill, it was possible to cross the swamps on log roads that had been laid by US engineers. The weather, however, had not improved. As Jim McEnery recalled,

> By the time we'd been ashore ten minutes, all of us were soaked to the bone, and I don't think we ever dried out completely in the next four months we were there.
>
> I'd thought Guadalcanal was bad, but the weather at Cape Gloucester was the worst – and wettest – I ever saw anywhere . . . The ground – when you could find it for the water – was nothing but squishy red mud. It stuck to everything like glue – to our skin, our packs, our uniforms, our boondocker shoes. Within a few minutes after we landed, we were covered in it so thick you could hardly tell a Marine from a Jap.

It was immediately clear to McEnery that they had arrived in 'one of the most miserable places on the face of the earth'.[8]

There was little time to bemoan their bad luck because the 3/5 Marines had orders from Shepherd to move inland and take part in a two-battalion attack the following morning. Shepherd's intention was to hold fast on the left and centre of the beachhead perimeter, while the battalion on the right, the 3/7 Marines, moved forward into the jungle before wheeling left to attack southeast on a front of a thousand yards. The 3/5 would advance on its right flank. 'Because of the orientation of the old perimeter,' noted the US Marines official history, 'such a move would cause the line of advance to lie straight across the front of 2/7 [Marines], which for the past several days had been holding the center along the shore of a small [creek] across which the Japanese had been industriously digging in.'[9]

The main objective was the Aogiri Ridge, a 'jungle rise hidden by dense foliage' 1,000 yards to the southeast of the creek, where the Japanese 141st Regiment had constructed formidable defences. But first the 3/5 Marines had to get across the upper stretch of the creek. That afternoon, 1 January, the men of K Company advanced a couple of miles, cutting their way 'slowly' and 'painstakingly' through the 'vine-matted underbrush'.[10] They encountered no opposition. But as R. V. Burgin and the rest of the mortar section were digging in for the night beside a narrow stream, about fifteen Japanese soldiers emerged from the jungle, splashed across the water and charged towards the Marines, screaming 'Banzai!' and 'Marine, you die!'

As a gunner, Burgin carried the mortar base plate and was not armed with either an M1 rifle or the lighter M1 carbine. His only personal weapon was a .45 semi-automatic pistol which he drew and used to shoot a Japanese soldier in the chest as he ran towards him. 'He was about thirty-five or forty feet away from me,' remembered Burgin, 'still running when he went down. Other Marines were firing right and left and more Japs were stumbling, going down. The rest turned back to the woods. I don't think more than one or two got away.'

Though Burgin had just taken his first life, he felt only relief and pride. 'I did,' he noted, 'what the Marines had trained me to do – kill the enemy and don't let him kill you.' Thereafter, to ensure that the enemy never got that close again, he 'always carried an M1 *and* my pistol'.

Spooked by the sudden attack, Haldane ordered the company to dig new foxholes a little farther up the ridge. Nonetheless it was a nerve-wracking night – with land crabs rattling around in the leaves – and few slept. At one point the mortar section leader, 24-year-old Platoon Sergeant Johnny 'Big John' Marmet, a Canal veteran from Holmes County, Ohio, heard a sound near his foxhole and fired. Unfortunately, he hit one of his own men who had left his hole to take a piss. 'He was wounded, not killed,' wrote Burgin, 'but we had our first casualty.'[11]

Marmet was right to be cautious. That same night Private Nolen Marbrey, the young Alabaman who had joined 2nd Platoon, was woken by his foxhole buddy. 'Listen!' he hissed.

Marbrey did so, and could just make out a slight gargling sound to his left. It seemed very close. He quietly pulled out his Ka-Bar and cursed the fact that it was so dark. For the rest of the night, the two Marines sat back to back, 'knives poised for action'.

At dawn, as light filtered through the bush, they crawled out of their foxhole. In the next one, ten feet away, wrote Marbrey, 'sat a young Marine staring at his buddy, who was covered in blood. His throat had been cut. A few feet away lay a Jap with his face in the mud.' Marbrey's buddy turned the dead enemy soldier over with his foot. He had blood on his hands and 'looked as if his neck had been broken'.

A short while later, as the pair were eating a can of C rations* for breakfast, successive orders came from the company CP. *Stand by. Form a skirmish line and fix bayonets. Move out.*[12]

The plan of attack for 2 January was for the 3/5 and 3/7 Marines 'to advance abreast across the entire front' of the 2/7 Marines, including the creek. That way they would pinch out the Japanese positions in

* First introduced in 1940, the C ration (or Field Ration, Type C) was a prepared and canned combat meal that was issued when fresh food (A ration) or packaged unprepared food (B ration) was unavailable. It typically consisted of 16 ounces of 'meat' in three varieties: meat and beans, meat and potato hash, or meat and vegetable stew. Also issued was one bread-and-dessert can. A daily ration consisted of six cans – three meat and three dessert – each supplied with a key soldered to its base.

front of the 2/7 Marines and allow the left of the 3/7 to tie in with the right of the 1/7. The drive would then 'enter its second phase, changing direction more to the south' towards Aogiri Ridge.[13]

With his battalion advancing on a 500-yard front, the commander of the 3/5, Lieutenant Colonel David S. McDougal of Coronado, California, had all three rifle companies in the line: from right to left, I, L and K. As the men of Haldane's K Company moved out, moisture was dripping off the jungle foliage and 'a kind of gray-blue haze hung in the air, a spooky mist that hid everything beyond the closest trees'. R. V. Burgin was moving slowly through the thick jungle when he heard firing from the left. 'It turned into a pretty good firefight,' he recalled, 'until somebody up the line realized that we had run into the [3/]7th Marines. Before we got it stopped, one of our men had been killed.'[14]

They later discovered that they had been advancing parallel to the 3/7 until the latter was slowed by a pocket of Japanese resistance. Wheeling left with the rest of the 3/5 to face the creek, K Company appeared directly in front of the right wing of the 3/7 and was mistaken for the enemy. While the confusion was being sorted out, men from both companies fraternized. 'They looked beat!' recorded Nolen Marbrey. 'They hadn't shaved since they'd been on the island, and the mud was caked in their hair and whiskers. Eyes were bloodshot from fatigue and lack of sleep.'

One asked him: 'What outfit are you?'

'K-3-5,' said Marbrey.

'We're K-3-7,' the Marine replied, before patting him on the shoulder and turning to leave. A few steps on, he turned back and said: 'A few got through last night. Keep on your toes, and good luck.'[15]

That afternoon, K Company continued its advance towards the creek as part of a two-battalion operation. 'We were heading downhill,' remembered Jim McEnery, 'through a fairly open area – one of the few we'd seen – when [a] group of about ten Japs popped out of some brush to challenge us. PFC Slim Somerville hit them with short bursts from his BAR, and Corporal Leland Paine and I joined in with our M-1s until all the Japs went down.'

Shortly after this skirmish, the company scouts spotted 'another strip of dripping-wet, livid-green jungle' that marked the edge of the creek.[16] The channel looked to be only forty feet wide, and barely two or three feet deep. But its current was moving swiftly, its banks very steep and precipitous – up to twenty feet high in places – and as the men of K Company got closer they had no idea that the creek was, as Marine combat correspondent Sergeant Asa Bordages put it, a 'moat before an enemy strong point'. Bordages wrote: 'They couldn't see that the heavy growth across the creek was salted with pillboxes – machine-gun emplacements armored with dirt and logs, some of them several stories deep, all carefully spotted so they could sweep the slope and both banks of the stream with interlacing fire.'[17]

With the light fading, Captain Haldane sent a few scouts across the river to probe the Japanese defences. They included Private Roy R. 'Railroad' Kelly from Minneapolis, Minnesota, a BAR man in 1st Platoon. But realizing that it was too dangerous to continue the operation in the dark, Haldane called it off. 'We'll try again in the morning,' he said.

Kelly and the scouts withdrew across the stream. But as he was climbing back up the steep bank on the American side, Kelly felt a heavy blow to his back that knocked him off his feet. Fearing the worst, he felt for a wound but there was nothing. He got to his feet and continued back up the hill to a rise above the creek where Haldane had ordered K Company to dig in.[18]

Everyone was digging foxholes, with their rifles either lying on the ground or resting against a tree, when about fifty Japanese soldiers crept over the creek and attempted a surprise attack on the machine-gun platoon. 'They must have seen,' wrote Asa Bordages, 'that if they could reach those emplacements, if they could get those machine guns, they could swing them and smash the infantry company holding the next section of the line with enfilading fire.' Probably for this reason the Japanese did not yell or fire a shot as they charged with bayonets fixed.

Captain Haldane was in his CP, talking with his XO, Lieutenant Andy Chiswick from Newark, New Jersey, when they heard a Marine yell. 'They looked up,' reported Bordages, 'and saw the Japs racing towards the emplacements. They saw weaponless Marines scattering out of the way. Some were trying to reach their rifles. Some had no chance of getting to their weapons. The Japs were hardly thirty yards from the nearest gun and closing fast. Other Marines were firing.'

Haldane set off for the guns, 'blasting away' with his .45 automatic pistol as he ran. Chiswick followed, as did an assortment of company CP personnel, 'some with bare hands, some with clubs or entrenching tools snatched from the ground'. By now the lead Japanese had reached one gun and swung it round to enfilade the line. Before he could fire, he got a Marine bayonet in the chest. 'The enemy broke,' wrote Bordages, 'and the Marines cut them down. More than twenty dead Japs were scattered in the brush by the time it was quiet again.'[19]

Later, as he was opening his pack to get at his C rations, Roy Kelly discovered a spent bullet lying at the bottom. 'Boy,' he said, 'I'll bet them Japs think we're tough. They shot me in the back and I still got up and walked away.'[20]

16

Suicide Creek

Cape Gloucester, 3–4 January 1944

Next morning, 3 January, Captain Haldane ordered his 2nd and 3rd Platoons over the creek. They got as far as the near bank without incident. But as Thurman Miller's 2nd Platoon began sliding down the banks, their rifles held high over their heads, they were picked off one by one by Japanese snipers. 'Those still on the banks retrenched,' wrote Miller. 'Those clinging to the muddy walls of the creek took cover under fallen trees, unwilling to retreat without their dead.'[1] A second attempt to cross the creek was more successful, and some Marines scrambled onto the Japanese-held bank and into the jungle beyond. Asa Bordages reported:

> Then they got it. The jungle exploded in their faces. They hit the deck, trying to deploy in the bullet-lashed brush, trying to strike back. Marines died there, firing blindly, cursing because they couldn't see the enemy soldiers who were killing them. Or not saying anything. Just dying. The others could only hug the ground as bullets cut the brush above their heads, like a sweeping blade of fire. They couldn't even help the wounded.[2]

Marines on the American side of the creek tried to lay down covering fire for their trapped comrades. But the heavy tree cover made it impossible to use the mortars, and R. V. Burgin and his squad took cover to the left of K Company's front, close to where the 7th Marines were trying to cross. Nearby was a small break in the trees where they had set up a five-gallon water can with a canteen cup on top. Burgin crawled over to slake his thirst. But when Jim Burke tried to do the same, a shot rang out and the cup flew into the bush. Feeling something on his sock, Burgin looked down and saw 'a fragment of a bullet stuck there, still hot'.

Moments later, a shaken Burke slumped down beside him. 'I don't think I'm that thirsty,' he said.

With no direct line of sight to the creek, Burgin realized the sniper must be in the trees above, 'most likely tied in, as we'd learned from the Guadalcanal veterans'. They scanned the foliage but could see nothing but a green wall. Eventually Burgin went to get help from one of the company's .30-calibre machine gunners. The Marine 'set up his tripod', wrote Burgin, 'and swiveled his gun upward and cut loose, raking the trees back and forth. Bits of leaf and falling branches showered down. There was a sudden crack and a body dropped out of the canopy and jerked to a stop about twenty feet above the ground. When we left he was swinging there upside down with his rifle dangling beneath him.'[3]

Closer to the creek, meanwhile, the lead platoons were edging to the right, trying to find a place to cross where the fire was not so heavy, when a machine gun opened up. 'The fellow ahead of me stood up,' recalled Private Jim Anderson, an 18-year-old scout in the 3rd Platoon from Dallas, Wisconsin, 'and *rat-a-tat-tat*, he fell over. I crawled over to where he was lying. I looked at the fellow. He had three or four bullet holes in him. He was dead.'

The Japanese also opened up with mortars and rifles, and the Marines returned fire. Fighting his first battle, Anderson unwisely stood up to get a better view and was struck in the left side by two bullets. It felt like he had been hit by a baseball bat, and he knew right away he was badly wounded. Collapsing to the ground, he took off his equipment and began to crawl to the rear. 'Mortars were exploding on my left and right,' he noted. 'I got maybe twenty feet back and stopped to rest or pass out, I'm still not sure. Pretty soon a mortar shell lit up about fifteen feet away from me and put a lot of shrapnel in my left leg. At the same time a sniper was firing at me. He was missing me by only a foot or so every time he shot. I knew I was a dead man unless I moved.'

He kept crawling back up the hill and was eventually found by two corpsmen who patched him up and carried him on a stretcher to an amtrac. That took him, in turn, to the beachhead from where he was transferred to a hospital ship offshore. The medics on board saved his life by staunching the bleed from his serious stomach wound. Taken to New Guinea, he had operations to remove two bullets from his stomach and to patch up his foot. The bullets, he was told, had hit his cartridge belt before ricocheting into his side. He was very lucky to survive.[4]

Back at the creek, meanwhile, the platoons had got jumbled up as they tried to fight their way across. Thurman Miller found himself behind the same log as Lieutenant Daniel Dykstra of 3rd Platoon. Suddenly, after another burst of fire, Dykstra cried out, 'T.I., I'm hit! I'm hit!'

Glancing over, Miller could see that the officer's arm was a bloody mess: the entire elbow had been shot away. He reached for his first-aid pack and found only a compress. There was no sulfa powder* to go into the wound, and nothing to tie it up with. He stretched out Dykstra's arm as best he could, bandaged it with the compress, and secured two wooden splints with a piece of mosquito net. Moments later a corpsman appeared and, having applied a tourniquet to stem the bleeding, led Dykstra away. Though in great pain, the officer remained tight-lipped throughout.

Soon after, Miller saw movement across the creek and decided it was time to cross over. He stood up and yelled, 'Let's go, men!'

Jumping down the bank and into the water, he could hear bullets come

* Sulfa, or sulfanilamide, was a yellow antibiotic powder that was sprinkled on wounds by navy corpsmen and army medics to ward off infection. Combat bandages were coated with the drug. Though sulfanilamide had been developed in the 1930s by the German chemist Gerhard Domagk, it was used by both Axis and Allied troops and would save many thousands of lives. Domagk was later awarded the Nobel Prize in Physiology or Medicine for this breakthrough.

'brushing by' and see leaves falling around him. He glanced left and right, expecting to see the rest of 3rd Platoon, but no one had followed him because the Japanese had just begun a counter-attack of their own. Scrambling back up the bank, he found cover behind a rotten log.[5]

Not far away was Jim McEnery who, on seeing the severity of Dykstra's wound, had said a quick 'Our Father', the first of many that day. The noise of automatic fire was deafening, but McEnery 'couldn't see a damn thing to shoot at'. Just to his right, an arm's length away, Corporal Horace E. 'Tex' Goodwin from Dallas, Texas, had just set up his .30-calibre Browning machine gun on its tripod when he was shot in the chest by a sniper. 'His eyes were wide open,' remembered McEnery, 'and he looked straight at me for a second. It seemed like he was trying to say something, but then he fell without making a sound, and I could tell he was dead before he hit the ground.'

Convinced Goodwin had been shot by a sniper in the trees, McEnery scrambled away. As he did so, a corpsman ran to help Goodwin. Remembering the two corpsmen killed on Guadalcanal, McEnery pulled the corpsman to the ground. 'It's no use, Doc,' he told him. 'He's gone. You can't help him. You'll only get yourself killed if you try.'

Soon after, McEnery's buddy Lou Gargano, recently promoted to platoon sergeant, took a sniper's bullet through his canteen. Bruised but otherwise unhurt, he had dropped his rifle in the open, just a few feet from McEnery. 'Hey, Mac,' said Gargano, 'can you grab my carbine for me? I can't reach it.'

McEnery slithered forward on his belly and was close to the weapon when a Marine called out: 'Don't go there, Mac! They've got the range on you!'

Ignoring the warning, he grabbed the carbine and made a 'fast retreat without getting hit'. Handing the weapon back to Gargano, he asked: 'You okay?'

'Yeah,' said Gargano, still a little dazed. 'But I don't know what the hell I'm doing sitting here. Jesus, with the lieutenant down, I'm the platoon leader now.'

Getting to his feet, Gargano waved his men towards the trees lining the bank of the creek, 20 yards ahead. 'Stay low and take cover in the creek!' he yelled.

McEnery jumped up with his section and headed for the creek in a crouched run. Keen to be out of the line of fire, he went over the bank without looking, and sprained his left ankle and badly twisted his knee on some half-submerged rocks. He felt a sharp stab of pain and 'could almost hear the tendons popping in there', but somehow managed to stumble across to the far bank where he was joined on his left by Corporal Leonard 'Hook' Ahner, twenty, 'a lanky farm boy from rural Indiana' whose nickname came from his eagle-beak nose. As Ahner raised his head to take a peek over the bank, a bullet tore through the shoulder of his dungaree jacket without drawing blood. 'Well,' said the corporal, seemingly unfazed, 'that was a close shave.'

To McEnery's right was another corporal, Leland Paine, clutching his rifle and gasping for breath. 'Now right about here,' said Paine, 'is where I'd like to see John Wayne ride up and hit 'em with both barrels.'

Hardly were the words out of Paine's mouth when a bullet grazed his cheek. He touched the wound and frowned at the sight of blood on his fingers. 'Well, hell, Mac,' he said. 'I don't think old John's gonna show, do you?'

'No, man,' replied McEnery. 'Looks like we gotta fight this one on our own.'

Platoon Sergeant Gargano, by this time, was over to McEnery's left. 'We've got to get in position to return fire on these bastards,' he hollered. 'Start sending the men up the creek bank one at a time, and have them follow me.'

The firing was so heavy now that McEnery could hardly distinguish individual shots. But he did what Gargano asked of him. Buddy or not, 'he was the platoon leader now, and he was giving the orders'. Of the fifteen men that McEnery sent over the bank, around half came back wounded. He sent them towards the rear and, having disabled a number of their rifles (to prevent the Japanese from using them), he hobbled back himself.[6]

McEnery took advantage of a lull in the firefight as the Japanese pulled back from their forward positions. They were forced to do so because of the heroism shown by men of 1st Platoon, led by 27-year-old First Lieutenant William F. Reckus from Wilkes-Barre, Pennsylvania. Reckus had joined K Company as a newly commissioned second lieutenant in Australia in May 1943, having earlier fought on Guadalcanal as a non-commissioned officer with the 2nd Battalion's G Company. He was particularly close to Sergeant 'Dutch' Schantzenbach, one of his squad leaders and a fellow Pennsylvanian, and together they ignored the 'withering hostile machine-gun fire' to lead 1st Platoon over the creek and into 'an advantageous point for firing upon enemy gun emplacements'. Thanks to Reckus's 'sustained aggressiveness' and Schantzenbach's 'cool and aggressive leadership through the ensuing violent engagement', they were 'able to force desperately fighting hostile units to abandon their positions'.[7]

That the respite was temporary became all too obvious to Jim McEnery as he was stopped from heading back down the slope to the creek by a thumbs-down signal from Lou Gargano at the bottom. Realizing the route was unsafe, McEnery stayed where he was and took cover.[8] But nobody warned a heavy machine-gun platoon from the 3/5's M (Weapons) Company that headed straight down the slope a short while later. Led by 23-year-old Lieutenant Elisha Atkins from Belmont, Massachusetts, a fiercely intelligent Harvard graduate who was known to be 'very quiet and polite as hell', half the platoon was across the creek when the Japanese opened up with six automatic weapons at point-blank range. Atkins and a number of his men were shot. The others went to ground and, as the Japanese machine guns 'swept the brush just higher than a man lying flat', the survivors wriggled back to the creek where the 'screening bush' was their only protection from Japanese snipers perched in trees.

One poor Marine, riddled with bullets but still alive, was slumped over a half-submerged log. 'Here I am, Wills,' he kept calling to his sergeant. 'Over here.' Other wounded Marines were in the water pleading for help. But there was nothing that Sergeant Wills or anyone else could do. To move from the safety of the bank was certain death. 'All of them,' said Wills, 'were guys we knew, but we couldn't do a thing. We had to lay in the water and listen to them. It was the coldest damn water I ever saw. Their blood kept flowing into our faces.'

Their only hope was to creep downstream, close to the bank, 'and then make a dash, one by one, for the American shore'. But many of the casualties got caught in thick tangles of vines and brush as they crawled through the racing water. They included Lieutenant Atkins, known to his men by his call sign 'Tommy Harvard'. He was found by PFC Luther J. Raschke of Harvard, Illinois, who cut him free. 'I tried to help him along,' said Raschke, 'but he wouldn't come. He'd been hit three times. A slug had smashed his shoulder. He was losing blood pretty fast. But he wouldn't leave. He was trying to see that everybody got out first. He told me, "Go on, go on!" He wouldn't let anybody stop for him. He said, "Keep the line moving!" He made us leave him there.'

Raschke eventually got back to the safety of M Company's foxholes. But he could not stop thinking about the selfless and wounded young platoon officer he had left behind. Securing permission from his company commander to attempt a rescue, he and three volunteers crawled back down the slope to the creek. It was getting dark and they could hear nothing but the rushing of the water and the occasional Japanese voice. Raschke inched forward to the edge of the bank, his heart pounding. He knew that if he called out and the Japanese heard, they would all be killed. Yet he could not bring himself to abandon his officer a second time. He took a deep breath and whispered, as softly as possible, 'Tommy Harvard . . . Tommy Harvard.'

'I'm down here,' croaked a voice below him.

Suspecting a trap, Raschke asked: 'What's your real name?'

'Elisha Atkins,' the man replied.

It really was him. Raschke and the others crawled down to Atkins and pulled him out. 'God!' said the officer. 'Am I glad to see you.'

He was shivering violently from being so long in the ice-cold water, and weak from loss of blood, 'but still calmly Harvard as they carried him to the rear'.*[9]

* * *

* Having recovered from his wounds in the US, Atkins received a medical discharge. He trained as a medical doctor at the University of Rochester, and later became a professor of infectious diseases at Yale.

Repeated attacks by the 3/5 and 3/7 Marines had gained only temporary footholds on the Japanese bank of the creek. But as the light faded on 3 January, events were taking place on the right flank of the 3/7's sector that would alter the course of the battle. That afternoon, disappointed by the 3/7 Marines' faltering advance, William Rupertus had replaced its commander with the hard-charging Lieutenant Colonel 'Chesty' Puller. Tried and tested on Guadalcanal with the 1/7 Marines, Puller had begun the Gloucester campaign as the 7th Marines' XO. Now his job was to get the 3/7 over the creek, and he planned to do it by using armour. This was only possible because the engineers of the 17th Marines had worked night and day to build a corduroy causeway across the coastal swamps and through the jungle. But when three 30-ton Sherman M4 medium tanks – each one with a crew of five and armed with a 75mm gun and three machine guns – finally reached the creek in Puller's sector during the afternoon of the 3rd, they found its banks too steep to cross. The creek was a 'natural tank trap'.

With Puller directing operations, the engineers brought forward a bulldozer to cut away the jungle and push the near bank down into the creek bed 'to form a usable approach'. The Japanese responded by directing a hail of fire from a pillbox just 50 yards away at the bulldozer's operator, hitting Corporal John Capito in the face. 'Doc,' he told the corpsman who went to his aid, 'I'm hit . . . in the mouth.'

The bullet had gone through both of Capito's cheeks, cracking a tooth and blistering his lips. Another man climbed into the operator's seat, but he too was hit. Finally, two more volunteers – Staff Sergeant Kerry Lane and PFC Randall Johnson – crawled forward under heavy sniper fire. Staying on the ground in the lee of the bulldozer, they were able to work its levers with a shovel and an axe handle. Eventually Lane climbed into the seat to finish the job, and suffered the consequences with a bullet in the shoulder. Yet he bravely stayed at his post until the job was complete.[10]

'I hardly realized that I was wounded,' recalled Lane. 'I heard no noise, felt no pain . . . I was a little woozy after being hit in the left shoulder, and I was somewhat unsteady on my feet after crawling down from the bulldozer. My first reaction was to rally my platoon, which was hunkered down in the weeds at the edge of the creek so we could assist in directing the tanks across the fill.'

The only way to communicate with the three tanks, waiting on the American side of the creek, was by using the telephone in a box at the Sherman's rear. 'I've got to get on the phone,' Lane told his platoon commander, 'and direct them tanks across the fill. If I don't get them moving, we are all going to die in this damn creek.'

'You will never make it,' the captain replied. 'The machine gun fire is too much, and besides you're bleeding.'

Lane looked down at his tattered utility shirt and saw that it was 'soaked in blood'. He realized he needed medical attention. But he also figured it might be his last battle, and that others were counting on him. 'I ain't got time to worry about bleeding,' he told the captain, before instructing the other pinned-down engineers to give him covering fire as he 'staggered and crawled' across the fill to the lead tank on the opposite side of the creek.

Somehow he got across without further injury and, locating the phone at the back of the tank, told the guys inside 'to move forward' and he would guide them over 'the newly cut fill in the creek bed'. The tank commander agreed, and directed the two tanks in the rear 'to crank-up and follow him'.

But as it was getting dark a more senior officer – possibly Puller – intervened and delayed the attack until it could be properly coordinated the following morning. His job now done, Lane collapsed from loss of blood and was treated by a corpsman with morphine and plasma. Before he was stretchered to the rear, Lieutenant Colonel Puller told the corpsman: 'Take good care of this sergeant. He's one hell of a Marine!'[11]

At 8:00 a.m. on 4 January, after a fifteen-minute artillery bombardment, 'the first tank commenced a gingerly negotiation of the improvised ramp, wallowed through the shallow water and successfully mounted the opposite bank, infantrymen clustered around it in close support'. Two Japanese sappers tried to knock out the tank with magnetic mines, but were shot down before they could do so. Once all three tanks were across, they used their 'murderous' 75mm guns to make 'short work of the Japanese emplacements at close range, the supporting infantry disposing of those of the enemy who attempted flight'.[12]

Thanks to the extraordinary heroism of Lane and the other bulldozer drivers, the deadlock at the creek was finally broken.* By helping the tanks to cross, they made the Japanese position untenable. 'If they tried to hold against the frontal attack of the Third Battalion,' noted Asa Bordages, 'they would be hit by tanks and infantry from the flank. They'd be a nut in a nutcracker. They had to retreat or be crushed, and they retreated.'

By the time the 3/5 and 3/7 Marines surged across the stream later that morning, most of the surviving Japanese defenders had withdrawn and the bloody three-day engagement – aptly dubbed the Battle of Suicide Creek – was over. All that remained was to push through the Japanese positions, 'mopping up the remnants of resistance'.[13] Sorry to miss out on the triumphant advance was Brooklyn-born Jim McEnery who, having returned from the creek on the 3rd, was sent to a rear hospital to have his knee treated. 'Looks like you've got torn ligaments in there,' said a corpsman, 'and the more you try to walk on it, the worse it's gonna get. You ain't worth a damn on the line in the shape you're in anyhow.'

In hospital, McEnery was given a painkiller and had his left leg bandaged from mid-thigh down to his toes. He would remain there for over a week, and missed not only the conclusion to the Suicide Creek action, but also the desperate fight for Aogiri Ridge a few days later.[14] At Suicide Creek alone, K Company lost one officer (Daniel Dykstra) and forty-four men – seven killed and thirty-eight wounded – or almost a quarter of the strength it had landed with three days earlier. Total Marine casualties, 3/5 and 3/7 combined, were 36 dead, 218 wounded and 5 missing in action.[15]

* Lane and Capito were awarded Silver Stars for their 'conspicuous gallantry and intrepidity'.

'In the end,' wrote Thurman Miller, 'we made it across and cleared the enemy, but we paid a dear price; by the time we were across, the waters of Suicide Creek ran red.'[16]

17

'So long, Dutch'

Cape Gloucester, 3–8 January 1944

Even as the 3/5 and 3/7 Marines were fighting for possession of Suicide Creek, a sizeable Japanese force tried to recapture part of the American beachhead by assaulting Target Hill in the early hours of 3 January. 'The Japanese came up the steep slopes on steps they dug earlier in the evening,' noted George McMillan. 'As they had done so often on Guadalcanal, [they] alerted us by firing a green flare, and by the flare's light the Marines spotted them trying to clamber over the barbed wire laid twenty yards in front of the Marine machine-gun and rifle pits.'

For the next two hours the Japanese charged this wire, but never got past it. Their casualties were at least two hundred killed and wounded. Marine losses, by contrast, were just three dead and a dozen wounded.[1] The outcome could have been very different, however, if the Japanese had attacked a gap of 200 yards that existed between the defenders on the hill and another unit on low ground to its right. 'This lay in a natural avenue of approach,' noted the US Marines official history, 'exploitation of which would have enabled the Japanese to infiltrate in force and flank the hill.' Instead, either through 'ignorance or misconception', they chose to ignore the gap and attack the strongpoint on the hill. It led to disaster.[2]

Encouraged by the twin victories at Target Hill and Suicide Creek, Brigadier General Lem Shepherd ordered the advance to continue in a south-southeast direction towards the vital feature named in captured Japanese documents as 'Aogiri Ridge'. There was some confusion in Shepherd's CP as to the location of Aogiri. Was it Hill 150, directly south of Target Hill? Or, further on, the higher Hill 660 that rose steeply from the shores of Borgen Bay? It was hard to know because both lay in the path of the advancing troops, while the captured Japanese sketch map indicated only that Aogiri lay south of Target Hill. But the new attack – on a three-battalion front with, from left to right, the 1/7, 3/5 and 2/7 Marines – would soon find out.[3]

After a brief pause on 5 January, K Company's advance continued on the 6th in 'savage, slashing, torrential rain that struck you hard enough to hurt'. It turned the jungle into a muddy bog through which the Marines struggled to move.[4] 'Moving forward,' recalled R. V. Burgin, 'was like trying to walk through oatmeal. I was still carrying around that mortar base plate, but we couldn't use it much because of the trees, so 90 percent of the time I took my place up front with the riflemen.'

It was eerie going through jungle so thick that the field of vision was just three feet. Burgin knew there were Marines on either side of him, but he could not see them. He thought many times, *Hell, I'm the only man out here. I'm fighting this war all by myself.*[5]

As they marched ever deeper into the jungle, the only way to get ammunition and rations in, and wounded out, was by amtrac. 'On them, and them alone,' wrote Asa Bordages, 'the supply line depended. That line was life to the [3/5] battalion – as vital as the umbilical cord to an unborn child.' While avoiding sniper and mortar fire, the amtracs often got lost in the dense undergrowth and took hours to cover short distances. Stretcher parties had the same problem. One took nine hours to cover the 300 yards that separated the front line from the battalion aid post.[6]

The casualties continued to mount: 'Railroad' Kelly, the Minnesotan private who had narrowly escaped injury at Suicide Creek, was shot and wounded on the 6th. Pinned down in front of his platoon, he was rescued by the 'Mad Russian', PFC John Teskevich, who crawled out and dragged Kelly to safety, though not before the private had been struck by a second bullet. 'As far as I know,' said Mo Darsey, a witness, 'Teskevich never got a medal or other recognition for this feat.'[7]

A day later, First Lieutenant Andrew Chiswick, K Company's XO, was wounded and evacuated. His replacement was 27-year-old First Lieutenant Thomas J. 'Stumpy' Stanley from Brooklyn, New York. Of Irish parentage – his maternal great-grandfather had been killed at the First Battle of Bull Run in 1861 – Stanley was a tough, no-nonsense character who had worked in a steel sheet fabricating plant before accepting a football scholarship at Upsala College, New Jersey. Having graduated with a degree in Petroleum Geology in the summer of 1942, he joined the US Marine Corps and was commissioned a second lieutenant with an academic grade that placed him in the upper 20 per cent of the class of 248 men. Assigned to the 5th Marines at Melbourne in January 1943, soon after the regiment's arrival from Guadalcanal, Stanley served in the 2nd Battalion's H (Heavy Weapons) and E Companies, before he was moved to K Company as the new XO.[8]

Chiswick's injury was followed, at noon, by an ambush of the battalion commander, Lieutenant Colonel David S. McDougal, and his staff as they were setting up their advanced CP in an abandoned Japanese bivouac. 'The Marines dived for the deck with bullets cutting around them,' noted Bordages. 'Some crouched behind a big log. Some were in the open, with only weeds and bush for protection.' Among the wounded was McDougal, who was hit in the right shoulder as he fired his pistol at a machine gun. 'I guess I can't use that hand any more,' he said, switching the pistol to his left hand and continuing to fire.

Once the infiltrators had been overcome, McDougal was evacuated and his XO, Major Joseph Skoczylas, a varsity track star from Philadelphia, took over the battalion. But five hours later, Skoczylas was also wounded and 'Chesty' Puller of the 3/7 Marines took temporary charge of both battalions pending the arrival of a replacement from the 5th Marines. It was a desperate time for the 3/5. 'The enemy,' wrote Bordages, 'was hitting them from the front, from the flank, and snipers were picking men off from the rear. When night came the battalion had lost contact with the men on its left and was forced to form a tight circular defense.'[9]

Early next morning, 8 January, the 5th Marines' XO, Lieutenant Colonel Lewis W. ('Silent Lew') Walt from Wabaunsee County, Kansas, arrived to take over. Just thirty years old, a 'brawny, barrel-chested man with a square face and small but clear blue eyes', Walt had graduated from Colorado State University – where he was an honour student and president of the student body – with a BSc in Chemistry before joining the US Marines as a second lieutenant in 1936. Four years later, by then a captain, he volunteered for the 1st Marine Raider Battalion and won a Silver Star, rescuing two wounded men during his company's assault on Tulagi, Solomon Islands, on 7 August 1942. He later took command of the 2/5 Marines on Guadalcanal and landed with the same battalion at Cape Gloucester in December 1943, before his reassignment as regimental XO. His first act on reaching the 3/5 CP was typical of his hands-on approach to command: he scouted the battalion's circular perimeter, at one point 'slipping out as much as fifty yards in front of the line to see how the land lay'.

He was told by the men on the perimeter that each time they moved forward they lost colleagues to snipers. He replied: 'Give those trees a good spraying before we move out.'

They did so, with heavy machine guns, and brought down a batch of Japanese sharpshooters. But the enemy responded with heavy fire from two directions, pinning down Walt and his command group for more than ten minutes.

Walt's priority was to convert the 3/5's circular defensive position into a regular battle line. To that end he told Captain Haldane and the other company commanders to push out their flanks and link up with the other battalions. When that was done, he ordered the 3/5 to advance, following close behind the centre company with his own advanced CP. His mantra was: *When Walt attacks, he attacks with everything he's got – including himself.*[10]

When the assault began at 10:30 a.m., K Company was on the right of the battalion line. As it inched forward 'through undergrowth so thick with vines and crazy tangles of limbs and roots that neither side could see more than 10 yards ahead', the Japanese opened fire with mortars and machine guns.[11] 'It was,' said one Marine, 'like all the seams of hell busted at once.'

The company went to ground in 'a ragged line through the brush'. They did not know it yet, but they were just 100 yards from the base of Aogiri Ridge. It was not a big feature. 'From the base of one nose,' wrote Asa Bordages, 'across the crest and down the slope to the base of the opposite nose, it was perhaps 200 yards long. The ground in front of the ridge begins rising slowly, the pitch gradually increasing until it starts sharply upwards at an angle as great as 40 degrees. The last steep rise to the crest is only about 50 or 60 feet. Against the face of the ridge, hidden from them by the jungle, the Marines were advancing.'

All along the crest of the jungle-masked ridge, and sprinkled over its steep face, the Japanese had constructed 'an elaborate network of camouflaged bunkers and machine gun emplacements'. There was no approach that was not covered. They had even dug positions on the reverse slope, which descended into a small valley, and on a ridge to the rear from where they could provide covering fire. It was from this formidable position, manned by a battalion of veteran troops, that the Japanese were pouring a hail of mortar, machine-gun and rifle fire.

Aware it was suicide for his men to advance on their feet, Haldane told them to crawl. They did so, 'inching forward on their bellies, trying to get near enough to rush the machine guns'. Gradually they approached the gently rising ground that marked the start of the ridge. Some had guessed as much when they noticed enemy fire coming from above. But they could not see 'how long it was, how high it was, or how much the enemy had on it'.[12]

Among the first to discover the ridge were Lieutenant Bill Reckus and Sergeant 'Dutch' Schantzenbach of 1st Platoon. Since their heroics at Suicide Creek, both had added to their reputations on the slow advance south. Reckus, for example, had led an attack on a Japanese bivouac area in the face of 'heavy automatic fire', yet managed to extract his platoon without losing a man, and in spite of 'overwhelming odds'.[13] Now he and Schantzenbach were at the point of K Company's advance up the ridge, sheltering from enemy fire together behind a fallen tree, when the battalion XO, Major Robert H. Dillard, crept forward with orders from 'Silent Lew' Walt. The companies to the left of K Company were more advanced, Dillard told them. To straighten the line, therefore, K Company had to move forward or the battalion might disintegrate.

What Dillard did not say – and maybe did not know – was that the other companies were not facing Aogiri Ridge, but rather the less heavily defended lower ground to the east. But it would have made no difference. Walt wanted K Company farther forward, and that meant the rifle platoons braving a storm of fire from Aogiri's bunkers. Reckus could have ordered Schantzenbach's squad to attack while he stayed behind the log, directing operations. Other platoon leaders would have done just that. But to let his men face danger alone was not Reckus's style. He had been a corporal in combat. He knew good leadership from bad. He also knew his men were 'exhausted, the hope drained out of them'. It was up to him.

Hurling a grenade to distract the Japanese, Reckus leapt to his feet. 'Come on, Dutch,' he said to Schantzenbach. 'Let's show 'em how the boys from Pennsylvania do it.'

He ran forward at a crouch, followed by Schantzenbach. But Reckus had covered barely twenty yards when he was shot in the left shoulder and fell to the ground. Dragged behind cover by his sergeant, Reckus said: 'Well, Dutch, it don't look like the boys from Pennsylvania did so good.'

He was wrong. Inspired by their leader, Schantzenbach's men stormed up the slope, knocking out bunkers as they went. Eventually they too were driven to ground. But not before they had straightened the line. By then a corpsman had reached Reckus and was struggling to stem the flow of blood from his wound. 'Give me straight dope,' said the lieutenant. 'How bad am I hit?'

The corpsman suspected a severed brachial artery, which he knew would be fatal. But he tried to reassure the lieutenant. 'Don't worry, you'll be okay.'

Reckus could see from the corpsman's face that he was lying. 'Don't kid me,' he said.

They eventually brought in a stretcher and put Reckus on it. 'So long, Dutch,' he said, as they took him away. He died of his wounds the following day.

Ordered forward at the same time as Reckus's outfit was the neighbouring 2nd Platoon, commanded by 23-year-old First Lieutenant Lowell R. Toelle from South Bend, Indiana. The son of an auto factory foreman, Toelle had attended Butler University in Indianapolis where for three years he was starting left guard on the football team. A handsome, well-built all-American boy, he had originally enlisted in the Army Air Corps in the wake of Pearl Harbor, but later switched to the US Marines and was commissioned in January 1943. A month later he married Jeanne Steiner, a Butler classmate, and they set up house together in Indianapolis. But they were only allowed a brief spell of married life before Toelle was shipped to Australia in June as a replacement officer for K Company. He was an instant hit with the men of 2nd Platoon, who all called him 'Tully'. Thurman Miller, his platoon sergeant, recalled: 'We all liked him. He was an easy-going guy, and I always felt he had missed his calling.'[14]

In combat for the first time, Toelle was not as gung-ho as Reckus. Nor, for that matter, was Miller. Instead, they instructed one of the squad commanders, Sergeant Archie L. Thompson from Miami, Florida, to push forward up the ridge. Thompson was '23-years-old, clean cut, and a good man'. Recently married, he knew that he was being sent on a suicide mission, and said as much to Miller. The response brooked no argument: 'It's an order.'

Without another word, Thompson turned, gathered his squad and set off. 'That was the last I ever saw of him,' remembered Miller. 'Our lines were so close I heard him engage the enemy. I heard him cry out when he got hit. I heard him dying, and in the din of battle, the rattle of his breathing was sharp and unnatural. He had been shot in the throat, and the air sucked into the hole made the sound of snoring. He was about fifteen minutes dying.'

This incident should not reflect badly on either Toelle or Miller. Their responsibility was to the whole platoon, and neither was expected to lead a squad into battle. Miller, in any case, had tried something similar at Suicide Creek. Yet acts of reckless courage by officers can inspire exhausted troops, as Reckus's had done, and who can say that he was wrong and Toelle right? What is not in dispute is the lifelong guilt that Miller would feel for sending a good man like Thompson to his death. It became, wrote Miller, 'a personal thing for me, and for many years the sound of his dying would awaken me from sleep'.[15]

All that afternoon, the forward platoons held on at the foot of the ridge. But as darkness fell, Walt ordered them to withdraw to the position they had held that morning. There K Company was 'bent in an arc to give the battalion protection against attack on its open flank during the night'.[16]

18

Walt's Ridge

Cape Gloucester, 9–10 January 1944

At 10:30 a.m. on 9 January, after a heavy bombardment from Marine artillery pieces farther back, 'Silent Lew' Walt resumed his attack. His plan was for I and L Companies on the left to hold their ground, while K Company swung 'like a door until it was on a line and would then make a holding attack against the face of the ridge'. Meanwhile, on K Company's left, a reinforcement company from the 1/7 Marines would 'swing inward in an enveloping movement against the [eastern] nose of the ridge, flanking the enemy's position, rolling him up so that Captain Haldane's men could press home the frontal attack'.

That, at least, was the intention. It began well enough as the men of Captain Weber's C Company, 1/7, knocked out two enemy bunkers on the 'jungle-choked' nose of the ridge with white phosphorus grenades. But having advanced 50 yards – about a quarter of the length of the ridge – they were 'utterly pinned down' and could go no farther.

K Company, meanwhile, was advancing up the ridge against Japanese machine guns that had been 'cleverly concealed among the roots of trees and were well protected by snipers'.[1] Private Nolen Marbrey, the young Alabaman in 2nd Platoon, recalled:

> We edged higher up the hill, firing rounds at anything that moved above us and the sun was blazing away at our backs. When it was about noon, the firing lessened, and we halted. I figured we were

> resting before the final push, so I took cover behind a tree and pulled out my tin of rations. Using my knife for a spoon, I had taken a couple of bites when I felt my helmet move. My ears were ringing and my head tingled. I dropped the tin and hit the deck, trying to see where the shot came from. When it wasn't repeated, I took off my helmet and examined it. There was a crease along the top of it that scared the hell out of me.

Minutes later, as the attack continued, Marbrey shot and killed his first Japanese soldier. He found his victim 'lying on his side, still clutching his rifle'. The bullet had 'caught him in the mouth and exited through the back of his head'. He shouted excitedly to his buddies: 'Hey, Les, I got one! Hey, Jones, look!'

Moving on, Marbrey narrowly escaped injury from a Japanese grenade that exploded in the middle of a thick bush, showering him with 'bits of leaves and wood', but no shrapnel. 'I picked myself up,' he recalled, 'and started to run. The rest of the company had moved on up, and I didn't want to be down there by myself.'[2]

The men of K Company had been 'hammered all that morning', wrote Asa Bordages, and 'now they were charging, veterans and green kids together, flinging grenades, clawing, firing, tearing at the steep slope to reach the enemy, to get within bayonet thrust'. The fury of the charge almost carried the forward platoons to the crest of the ridge. But, recorded Bordages, 'they were stopped; pounded like a punch-drunk fighter who can only cover up and clinch, hanging on for no reason in the world except that he won't give up'.[3]

The high-water mark of the charge was reached by a 20-year-old private, Robert L. Gray of Los Angeles, California. 'With a large number of men in his platoon casualties and the rest pinned down by rifle, machine-gun and mortar fire,' read his medal citation, 'Private Gray, hearing the order to assault, unhesitatingly charged up the hill, killed at least two of the Japanese and destroyed a machine gun before he himself was mortally wounded by enemy fire.'[4]

Bordages's account of Gray's heroism is even more hyperbolic: 'He went forward ahead of the others, alone. He shot and stabbed his way past three machine-gun nests – shot and stabbed Japs in the foxholes in his path.' He was killed tackling a fourth machine gun, by which time his body 'lay almost thirty yards beyond the most advanced point the others had reached'.

Every member of K Company had played his part, particularly the skipper 'Ack-Ack' Haldane who, with 'utter disregard for his own personal safety', had 'fearlessly directed the attack' against the Japanese bunkers in the face of 'intense machine gun, mortar and sniper fire'.[5] His platoons, thanks to Gray, were just below the crest of the ridge. Weber's C Company were spread across the nose of the ridge, at angle of about 60 degrees from the forward elements of K Company. But there was a dangerous gap between the two that needed to be closed. Spotting this, Lieutenant Colonel Walt ordered the nearest platoon to swing forward on a pivot and link the companies. It was now, according to Bordages, that a young platoon leader – either Toelle or Dykstra's replacement, 25-year-old Lieutenant Edward C. Hempelman of Dayton, Ohio – protested that his men could not move another foot. 'Advance,' insisted Walt, 'or be relieved.'[6]

They advanced, and somehow found the will and strength to close the gap under heavy fire. But their position was still a precarious one. 'The assault elements,' noted the division's Special Action Report, 'had reached the limit of their physical endurance and morale was low. It was a question whether or not they could hold their hard-earned gains. It was then that Lieutenant Colonel Walt's leadership and courage turned the tide of battle.'[7]

Earlier, as he and Lem Shepherd watched the attack on the ridge from the jungle below, and bullets smacked into the base of the big tree they were hiding behind, Walt had promised: 'General, we are going to take that ridge and we are going to hold it.'

Now he had to act and, with no reserves available, Walt played his 'last card': an M3 37mm anti-tank gun that, at great risk, had been dragged through jungle the day before by another daring bulldozer driver. The gun fired armour-piercing, high-explosive and anti-personnel rounds, and Walt knew that if he could get it up the ridge it might tip the balance. Undaunted by the fact that it weighed half a ton, and even getting it to the base of the ridge through mud, deep jungle and enemy fire had taken a team of twelve more than an hour and a half, he gave the order to advance.

'A few Marines took hold to heave the gun forward,' wrote Bordages, 'but there weren't enough of them. The rest, sprawled on the ground in the brush, only stared and made no move to help. They just didn't believe the hill could be taken.'

Turning to his orderly, Walt said: 'Come on, Larson. Let's lend a hand.'

As Walt and Larson joined the others behind the gun, the air was thick with bullets pinging off the gun's shield and 'whipping the brush'. They all heaved together and the gun began to move. This prompted the rest of the team to join in. 'You saw the colonel out there,' explained one, 'straining a gut with the guys, and you figured, "Oh, what the hell," and got going again.'[8]

They advanced the gun a few yards at a time, before stopping to let the crew fire rounds of canister that blasted a narrow road through the jungle. As members of the team were killed or wounded, others ran forward to take their places. 'I was approximately ten feet away when a guy got hit, shot off the cannon,' remembered Thurman Miller. 'So I took his place. I joined them in pushing it a little ways then I got too far from my platoon so I rejoined them.'[9] Another who helped to haul the gun was R. V. Burgin of the mortars. He recalled:

> From time to time we'd stop and fire it to clear out a machine-gun nest or bunker. As we set up they'd fire at us and the bullets would sing off the quarter-inch steel shield on the front of the gun. We took turns, five or six of us at a time, wrestling that rascal up the hill in the mud. I pushed part of the way, slipping and sliding, vines snatching at my boots. As a reward they let me fire it.[10]

Eventually, by 'superhuman effort', the gun was 'manhandled up the steep slope and into position to sweep the ridge'. Three machine guns were sited to protect it, as were two foxholes manned by Marines with rifles and bayonets. Elsewhere, as night came on, the Marines were ordered to dig in and hold.

By now the Marine and Japanese lines were, in places, only ten yards apart. A section of the Japanese first line of defence – consisting of a chain of almost forty log and earth bunkers along the crest of the ridge – had been captured by Marines, giving them a foothold on the summit. But most of it was still intact, as was a second line of bunkers on the reverse slope. 'As the rainy night wore on,' recorded the official history, 'sounds of increasing activity from the [Japanese second line] indicated that they were preparing for the inevitable counter-attack. Colonel Walt got all available weapons into position to hold, including the 37mm, and all available men, including battalion headquarters.' It was, said Walt later, a 'desperate measure taken against overwhelming odds'. His advanced CP, at that point, consisted of just a runner and himself.[11]

Lieutenant Toelle's 2nd Platoon was dug in a few yards below the crest. They had hardly slept for two or three nights, and were exhausted. Some dozed while others kept watch. As they waited for the inevitable, Thurman Miller saw Toelle lift a large rock, eighteen inches in diameter, and put something under it. 'My wedding band, T.I.,' he said. 'I don't want those yellow bastards getting it off my finger if I get killed.'[12]

Shortly before 1:00 a.m. on 10 January, the Japanese began to chant in the dark: 'Marines, you die! Prepare to die!'

The Canal veterans had heard such taunts before. For the rookies, however – cold, wet and exhausted – the words were a terrifying portent of what was to come. Yet they kept their discipline, and not a shot was fired to give away their position.

Suddenly, at around 1:15 a.m., a lone voice shouted 'Banzai!' as the Japanese opened fire with all they had and the first counter-attack 'came screaming and howling up the reverse slope'. They were attacking on a front of just 100 yards, their main objective the 37mm gun in the centre of K Company's defences. 'The shrieking charge came close to the gun,' recorded Asa Bordages. 'Men fought it out with bayonets . . . But the gun didn't fire. If it fired once, if its position in the dark was revealed, the enemy's charge could converge on it.'

R. V. Burgin was in a foxhole with his buddy Jim Burke when the Japanese attacked. He had made up his mind not to let any enemy soldier get so close he would need to use his bayonet. But in the darkness, rain and confusion, a shape suddenly appeared at the edge of the foxhole. 'I was on my knees with my rifle pointed at him,' recalled Burgin, 'and I shoved my bayonet into his chest as hard and deep as I could, right beneath the breastbone. In one motion, I leveraged him off the ground and swung him over my shoulder, pulling the trigger all the way. I don't know how many shots I put into him – four or five anyway.'[13]

Having beaten back the first charge, the Marines could hear the Japanese chattering in the darkness, preparing another attack. It was an agonizing wait in the rain, compounded by groans from the wounded on both sides. Five minutes passed. Then maybe another five, before the Japanese launched their second assault with soldiers 'bent low, screaming death'. This time their 'hacking, frenzied' charge got within twelve feet of the gun. 'It was,' noted Bordages, 'hand to hand in the dark, in the pelting rain . . . Man against man. Smashing, clawing in the dark. Stabbing, clubbing. Slipping in the mud. Gasping, grunting, dying. Each man alone in the blackness, not knowing what was happening on his right or his left, but holding until he died [on] the ground where his feet were planted.' Eventually, this attack was also repulsed by Marines 'who died but would not step back'.

With ammunition running low, Platoon Sergeant Lou Gargano told the men of 3rd Platoon: 'Fix bayonets and drive them back.'

Around the same time, 'Dutch' Schantzenbach asked PFC Tom Rumbley: 'I wonder how much longer my luck's going to hold?'[14]

Thurman Miller, meanwhile, spent the short time between attacks crawling along and checking on his men. After the failure of the third assault, with his troops all but out of ammunition, he headed back the short distance to Haldane's CP where a gunnery sergeant named Manihan loaded his shoulders with three or four bandoliers of bullets. 'I made that trip,' he recalled, 'down and back up, real quick.'[15]

The fourth assault, the most violent yet, pierced the Marines' line, with some Japanese soldiers reaching Haldane's CP. Attacked by two Japanese, Sergeant Fred Miller was forced to use his rifle as a club until 'Ack-Ack' Haldane came to his rescue. 'He had some ammo left in his carbine,' remembered Miller, 'and so he just pumped rounds into them.'[16]

A Japanese major and two company officers got almost as far as Walt's foxhole, 50 yards behind the front line. But their charge was stopped by shrapnel from two short American 105mm shells that burst in a tall tree overheard. The major, recalled Walt, 'actually died three paces from where I was crouched .45 in hand waiting for him'. He was about fifty years old, of medium build, and holding a sword in one hand and a pistol in the other.[17]

After the fourth charge was beaten back, Walt discovered that the machine-gun platoon and most of the riflemen were out of ammunition. He used a field telephone to demand fresh supplies from his main CP at the foot of the ridge. 'Get up damn fast,' he insisted, 'or start setting up a line. They'll be coming through.'

The Marine in charge of the ammunition party was Platoon Sergeant St Elmo 'Pop' Haney, a 45-year-old ramrod-straight veteran from Chickalah, Arkansas, who had joined the Marine Corps at the tail end of World War I and served with the Devil Dogs in France. Discharged after the war, he taught history in a secondary school and even sold vacuum cleaners to make ends meet. But he missed the Corps and, after re-enlisting in 1927, was posted to China and later Pearl Harbor. A tall, leathery, teak-tough Marine, Haney was a stickler for discipline with some odd habits: he only addressed Marines by rank, never by name, and was fanatical about cleaning his gun and his body (conditions permitting). After serving on the Canal as one of K Company's platoon sergeants, he had been transferred back to the United States on account of his age and length of service. In the summer of 1943, however, he wangled a return to the Devil Dogs in Australia and was attached to company HQ with an undefined role. 'He wasn't assigned to any platoon,' remembered R. V. Burgin. 'He did not have a job. He was just there.'[18]

Haney's outstanding characteristics were courage and a fierce sense of duty. He needed both as he chivvied the exhausted line of load-carrying

Marines uphill through 'dark jungle undergrowth and driving rain'. Bordages wrote: 'They were out on their feet, staggering under their loads. They couldn't see one another to keep contact, but he had to keep them together, keep them going, get them to go faster, though already they were stumbling.'

With mortar rounds and grenades exploding all around, and bullets falling like rain, the caterpillar of Marines crawled slowly up to Haldane's CP. At least one of the detail was killed, and two more wounded, by Japanese infiltrators who were trying to cut the Marines' supply line. But most of the resupply got through to the CP safely and was quickly sent out to the platoons. 'There were places in the line they couldn't reach,' noted Bordages, 'because of the fire, and the ammunition had to be passed slowly from foxhole to foxhole. But it got there.'[19]

According to Walt, the ammunition arrived with just four minutes to spare. As the fifth and final banzai charge began – launched by a full company of Japanese troops, all veterans of the fighting on Bataan – Walt instructed his forward artillery observer to call down fire at successively reduced ranges, until the 105mm rounds were hitting a scant 50 yards in front of his lines. Inevitably some rounds fell short again, but the overall effect was to dislocate the Japanese assault. An enemy prisoner would later admit that the artillery barrage had 'caught the reserve company in a mass formation just ready to make the 5th assault'. The proof, wrote Walt, was a count of more than '150 mangled bodies in that immediate area the following day'. Those who did get as far as the summit were shot down long before they reached the Marines' line.

As dawn broke, the glassy-eyed and exhausted Marines moved forward to secure the whole ridge, mopping up pockets of resistance as they went. Later that morning, Walt's other companies captured the valley beyond, including 'a wide, firm, much used trail that showed on none of their maps'. This was the enemy's main supply line and the reason the Japanese had been so determined to hold Aogiri Ridge. But they had failed. 'Now they had no ridge,' noted the official history, 'and no reserve. As events would prove, they had shot their bolt.'[20]

When Brigadier General Shepherd inspected the battlefield a day later, he acknowledged the key role played by the temporary battalion commander. 'Henceforth we will call it,' he said, 'Walt's Ridge.'[21]

The capture of Walt's Ridge was one of the great military feats of the Pacific War. Lieutenant Colonel Walt's 'extraordinary heroism' was recognized by the award of a Navy Cross, though it might easily have been the Medal of Honor. Both in helping to push the 37mm gun up the hill without regard for his 'personal safety', and later in 'courageously leading his men against five counterattacks made by the Japanese', Walt displayed 'brilliant leadership and expert tactical knowledge', and 'contributed materially to the success of our forces in this area'.*[22]

Walt's pivotal role was later acknowledged by Lieutenant 'Stumpy' Stanley, K Company's XO. 'The whole affair,' wrote Stanley, 'was of heroic proportions and none of it could have happened if Lew Walt hadn't been there. I can think of no other man who could have pulled it off and made it work. The enlisted men performed in the traditional Marine Corps fashion and achieved, under Lew's leadership, the impossible. K-3-5 was, always, a very, very remarkable Company.'[23]

Walt returned the compliment. 'There has never been,' he told Stanley, 'a better group of fighters.'[24] This was confirmed by the award of an unusually high number of gallantry medals to K Company men. Captain Haldane and Platoon Sergeant 'Pop' Haney, for example, were both given Silver Stars. Haldane was commended for his 'brilliant leadership and indomitable fighting spirit', while Haney demonstrated 'daring initiative and selfless devotion to duty in the face of grave peril'.[25] The captain, moreover, was praised in an article by the combat correspondent Asa Bordages. 'His men held,' he wrote, 'taking their cue from Haldane. He was their captain, but he was one of them.'[26]

* Walt would later serve with distinction as III Marine Amphibious Force commander during the Vietnam War and was pivotal in forming Marine strategy between 1965 and 1967. He then became assistant commandant of the Marine Corps and retired with the rank of four-star general in 1971.

But the victory came at a high cost. Among the fatalities were all three rifle platoon commanders: Bill Reckus (1st Platoon), Ed Hempelman (3rd Platoon) and the recently married Lowell Toelle (2nd Platoon). 'The next morning,' remembered Thurman Miller, 'our company clerk came running up to me and said, "Tully got it last night." . . . To this day, I've always wondered why I didn't get his ring out from under that rock.'[27]

Reckus was awarded a posthumous Navy Cross for his 'extraordinary heroism' at Suicide Creek and Walt's Ridge. 'First Lieutenant Reckus,' read his citation, 'fought with sustained aggressiveness during six successive days of operations . . . Undaunted by grave hazards, he persisted in his valiant fight, selflessly leading a hand grenade assault against a heavily defended Japanese ridge until he fell, mortally wounded.'[28]

Receiving the same posthumous honour was Private Robert Gray, who had given his life to gain the first toehold on the crest on 8 January. The citation noted: 'His cool courage, spirit of self-sacrifice and unwavering devotion to duty were in keeping with the highest traditions of the United States Naval Service.'[29]

The other two platoon leaders, Toelle and Hempelman, were given posthumous Bronze Stars. Toelle was praised for showing 'great courage and leadership in repulsing several fierce counterattacks on a jungle ridge which had been captured from the enemy'. By his 'utter disregard for his personal safety,' said the citation, 'he was an inspiration to the men of his command'.[30] The medal and a Purple Heart were later awarded to Toelle's wife Jean in Los Angeles, where she was studying for a postgraduate degree.[31]

How Toelle and Hempelman were killed is unclear. They may well have died in hand-to-hand fighting during the five banzai charges that took place in the early hours of 10 January. It is also possible that they were victims of short rounds fired by American artillery as Walt risked everything to beat off the final Japanese attacks. Despite two artillery majors 'objecting vigorously as the range kept on being reduced until we were practically firing on our own troops', Walt was adamant and K Company paid the price.[32]

According to R. V. Burgin, two of his fellow mortarmen – PFC Robert McCarthy and Private Lonnie Howard – were killed when a short artillery round hit a tree and exploded. Howard, a replacement from Houston, Texas, had joined K Company in Australia and foresaw his death. 'Burgin,' he said during the afternoon of the 9th, 'if anything happens to me, I want you to have my watch.'

'You're crazy,' said Burgin. 'Nothing will happen to you. You'll be okay.'

'No, I'm serious,' he insisted. 'I want you to have my watch.'

After his death, Howard's body was taken away by corpsmen for burial and Burgin never did get his timepiece.[33]

Also killed by short rounds were Platoon Sergeant Lou Gargano, twenty-four, and Sergeants 'Dutch' Schantzenbach* and Norman E. Thompson, aged twenty-two and twenty-six respectively. All three were later awarded posthumous Silver Stars. The former's citation read:

> Courageously leading his men across a stream while subjected to withering hostile machine-gun fire, Platoon Sergeant Gargano skilfully directed his platoon through the ensuing attempt to gain heavily fortified enemy pillboxes . . . Displaying cool and aggressive leadership during a later strike against a hostile ridge, he enabled his men to capture and hold the enemy emplacement, with a minimum of casualties, fighting with unwavering determination until fatally injured while repulsing a hostile counter-attack.[34]

There was, of course, no mention in the citations that the real cause of death was friendly fire. But Gargano's friend Jim McEnery was told the truth when he was visited in hospital by Lieutenant Tom O'Neill, a

* Schantzenbach went to war with a favourite childhood book called *Hans Brinker or the Silver Skates* by Mary Mapes Dodge that he had been given as Christmas present when he was twelve years old. He wrote inside: 'This is my book. Norman Schantzenbach, December 25, 1933.' Decades later, the book was discovered in a Hawaiian used book store and eventually returned to Schantzenbach's son, Norman Jr, who was just three years old when his father was killed.

stalwart of K/3/5 on Guadalcanal who was now with L Company. 'We lost three real good men a couple of days ago,' explained O'Neill. 'It was a freakish thing. They were all hit by a short round fired by one of our own 105s. I thought you'd want to know.'

'Well, sure, I do,' said McEnery. 'Who was it?'

'Dutch Schantzenbach and Norm Thompson had come back to the platoon CP to hand out grenades to guys to take back to their squads when the round hit,' said O'Neill. 'They were both apparently killed instantly.'

The news shook McEnery. He had known Schantzenbach and Thompson since the New River camp in '41, and both were part of the company's 'heart and soul'. He thought back to Dutch 'leading a Higgins boat full of scared young Marines in singing "Roll Out the Barrel"' as they approached Guadalcanal; and no squad leader was 'more respected by the men he led than Thompson'.

Their deaths were bad enough. But who, he asked O'Neill, 'was the third one?'

The lieutenant looked away. 'Lou Gargano was a few feet from the others,' he said at last, 'but he got hit by a bunch of fragments and . . . well, he didn't make it, Mac.'

'Oh shit,' said McEnery, his mind refusing to accept that his good friend was dead. *How could a guy who went through what he did at Suicide Creek*, he asked himself, *be cut down by a short round from one of our own howitzers?*

He wanted to scream at O'Neill and tell him to quit kidding around. But the lieutenant's grave face betrayed the truth. 'Lou was gone,' recalled McEnery, 'and the realization hit me as hard as anything that ever happened to me. I couldn't stand to think about the wife and the baby daughter he'd never seen waiting for him at home. I thought I'd go nuts if I did, so I forced myself to think about something else.'[35]

19

Seek and Destroy

New Britain, January–February 1944

The twin battles of Suicide Creek and Walt's Ridge tore the heart out of K Company. It had landed at Cape Gloucester on 1 January with ten officers and 242 men. Ten days later, thanks to illness and battle casualties, it was down to just two officers and eighty-eight enlisted men.[1]

The night after the banzai attacks, PFC R. V. Burgin and Private Jim Burke were moved to the extreme right of the company line. 'There wasn't anyone beyond us,' recalled Burgin. 'It's a funny feeling when you know you don't have any support on your flank.'

Burke was digging the foxhole, while Burgin stood guard. Suddenly, through the underbrush, Burgin could just make out the shape of someone crawling towards them on his belly. As they had all been told not to leave their foxholes after dark for any reason, it had to be a Japanese soldier. He put his hand on Burke's helmet, pushing him down and pointing towards the shape with his .45 pistol. The shape got closer until Burgin could almost reach out and touch it. He aimed his pistol and was about to fire when he saw the helmet's silhouette and realized it was a Marine.

'Pssst, Burgin,' said a voice he recognized. 'You got any water? I'm thirsty as hell.'

'Yeah, Oswalt,' he replied. 'I've got some water.'

The ill-disciplined Marine was 20-year-old Private Robert B. Oswalt from Pasadena, California, another new guy. Burgin handed him a canteen and waited for him to take a slug. When he had finished drinking, Burgin said: 'Oswalt, what the hell are you doing out of that foxhole? Do you know I almost shot you right between the eyes?'

Oswalt's mouth fell open in shock.

'Let me tell you something,' continued Burgin. 'You get out of that damn foxhole again tonight, I *will* shoot you just on general principles.'[2]

The following day, K Company was taken out of the line and put in reserve. When it was 2nd Platoon's turn to be relieved, the replacement platoon leader asked, 'Who's in charge?'

'I guess I am,' replied Thurman Miller.

'Well,' said the lieutenant, 'we'd better do this a squad at a time.'

Miller shook his head. 'If you bring one squad, you'll replace my whole platoon.'

The lieutenant went pale.

Of the original forty-three men in 2nd Platoon, Miller was left with just thirteen, including himself. Some, like Lieutenant Toelle, had been killed. Most had been wounded and taken off the line. Taking the ridge, he wrote later, 'was about the worst fight I was ever in'.[3]

Moved back to a rest area near the airfield, the men of K Company were issued hammocks with built-in mosquito netting. Strung between two trees, they were suspended two feet above the ground. 'They'd keep you out of the mud,' recalled R. V. Burgin, 'if the rain hadn't rotted the strings. Sometimes at night you'd hear a *rip* and a *splat* and a lot of cussing. If it was raining you could drape a rubber tarp over you to keep dry, and you'd have a net to keep off the mosquitoes. You had to zip it open to get in and out.'

One afternoon, Burgin decided to play a prank on Private George Sarrett from Denison, Texas, who had joined K Company with thirty-four other replacements after Walt's Ridge. Sarrett was afraid of nobody: not the Japanese, nor the Devil himself. But land crabs – the large land-dwelling crustaceans that infested New Britain – were a different matter. Knowing this, Burgin waited until Sarrett was asleep in his hammock before he picked a crab up and slipped it in beside him. 'Sarrett came out of there with his KA-BAR knife,' wrote Burgin, 'slashing that mosquito net from one end to the other. Just – *whoosh* – and he was out of that hammock. Didn't make a sound.'[4]

Each morning when Thurman Miller climbed out of his hammock, he noticed he was covered in a strange pink substance. After a few days, determined to find out what it was, he searched through his pack and hammock and found a huge spider with the 'leg span of a small saucer'. The pink stuff was the spider's web.

They occasionally went down to the beach to wash. But unlike the picture-perfect sandy beaches of the Solomons, these were 'riddled with coral and generally dangerous to be in'. It was sun for ten minutes, if you were lucky, and rain the rest of the time. 'Our hammocks provided some shelter,' remembered Miller, 'but night and day during the rainy season huge storms came from all four directions. The wind toppled giant trees. In the quiet after the storm had passed, the trees trembled and one would slowly begin to fall, its roots loosened from the wet soil. More than a few Marines were killed by falling trees.'

One night, Miller was woken by 'brilliant lightning, roaring thunder and pouring rain'. Pulling his poncho a little tighter around himself, he thought back to when he was six years old and 'lying alone in his sickbed, gazing out in the darkness of a mountain storm'. *Will the storm of war swallow me up?* he wondered. *Will I ever see my parents again?* He eventually fell asleep once more, and in his dream heard the 'soft sound of a door opening, quiet footsteps, a calloused hand gently touching my fevered brow'. Peace settled over him, and he slept.[5]

K Company may have been out of the line, but its men were still susceptible to malaria, dysentery, dengue fever and 'jungle rot', a fungus that thrived in damp conditions and appeared on armpits, ankles and crotches, or anywhere that skin came into close contact with wet clothes. It looked, remembered Burgin, 'like little yellow pustules on your skin, each blister about the size of a match head'. The only treatment was an anti-fungal medication called gentian violet. The corpsmen would paint it on all the places the Marines had scratched raw. 'Everybody had that purple stuff on them,' noted Burgin. 'We were a colorful mess.'[6]

During this rest period, 'Ack-Ack' Haldane received a letter from

Kenneth Sills, the president of Bowdoin College. A report had just appeared in the local press about the Marines at Cape Gloucester, said Sills, and there were 'several allusions' to Haldane and his company. It referred, moreover, to Haldane and the other company commanders 'as the veterans who were leading the men'. Sills added: 'I assure you that all your friends here have read this account with the deepest interest and satisfaction. We often think of you and of all that you are doing for us and wish you the best of luck.'[7]

Haldane also received a message from Paul Nixon, Bowdoin's dean of students. 'One of our undergraduates,' wrote Nixon, 'has just brought me a picture of you and the account of Walt's Ridge in the Lawrence Daily Eagle. The picture makes you look as nice and friendly as a Baptist clergyman.'

In a response to a separate letter of congratulation from Andy Walsh, his former football coach, Haldane noted: 'I can sincerely say your instruction and guiding ways have helped me greatly in this task I have of leading men.'[8]

While K Company recovered from its mauling, the 7th Marines pushed on to Hill 660, capturing its summit after a bloody two-day fight at dusk on 14 January. Two companies of Japanese troops counter-attacked in the early hours of the 16th, but were destroyed by concentrated mortar fire. The fighting for the hills around Borgen Bay had cost the 1st Marine Division – chiefly the 3/5 Marines and the 7th Marines – 247 killed, 772 wounded and one missing in action. But an almost equal number were sick in hospital or the victims of accidents, including twenty-five men who were killed by falling trees.

A few days later, on 19 January, Major General Rupertus presided over the dedication of the division cemetery near the airfield. It rained, as usual, threatening to collapse the sharply spaded mounds of earth that marked each grave. Even the Stars and Stripes appeared limp and bedraggled as it was raised up the flagpole. But Rupertus was unconcerned. Baring his head, as did the others in his small party, he paid homage to the long list of dead (including three officers and sixteen enlisted men from K Company): 'These were our buddies. They took their hardships cheerfully – and died the same way. Their spirit was wonderful. Let us take a lesson from them.'[9]

By late January, most of the survivors of the Japanese 65th Brigade had withdrawn behind the Natamo River, south of Borgen Bay, having failed in their attempts to recapture the Cape Gloucester airfield. According to a division intelligence summary of prisoner interrogations, the Japanese were suffering just as badly in the harsh conditions as their American foe. 'Hunger, undernourishment, positive starvation, malaria, diarrhea, foot rot, skin disease, and all the rest,' it noted, 'brought a large proportion of the Emperor's troops to a condition of physical weakness, emaciation and inability even to walk, a condition that would make the victims of famine in India seem fairly robust in comparison. It was their physical inability that caused their collapse.'[10]

They did have one big advantage, though: familiarity with the terrain, which gave them the 'inestimable advantage of being able to choose their ground, whether to fight or to withdraw'. The Marines, on the other hand, 'must painstaking[ly] explore dozens of false leads in order to orient themselves, and this in jungled, mountainous, swampy terrain where the incredibly dense rain forest hid landmarks so thoroughly that a patrol might pass within a few yards of its objective without ever discovering it'.[11]

Major General Rupertus's tactics, as a result, were to seek out and destroy the enemy as he pushed south and east towards his second major objective: seizure of the line from Borgen Bay to the Itni River. This was largely achieved by mid-February, thanks to a number of long-range patrols. One in particular, led by Lieutenant Colonel 'Chesty' Puller (now restored as the 7th Marines' XO), encountered only the occasional Japanese straggler as it crossed the Itni at Gilnit and occupied Attulu Hill beyond.[12]

In early February, K Company and the rest of the 5th Marines and various attached units – 5,000 troops in all – were given a new amphibious mission: to make a series of landings on the north shore of New Britain in the hope of catching up with the retreating Japanese and cutting off their route to Rabaul via the coastal trail. The first landing by the 3/5 Marines (less I Company) was at Gorissi, 15 miles east of Borgen Bay, on 12 February. From there, a rifle platoon of K Company – assisted by local guides and some Army war dogs – reached the El River but found it impassable. A second platoon, therefore, 'leapfrogged the first by sea, landing beyond the next river to the east and arriving at Arimega Plantation on the 19th'. Karai-ai, a key Japanese supply point, 'now lay only a short jump ahead, and 3/5 seized it by a combined overland and overwater operation on 21 February'.[13]

Back with 3rd Platoon as the platoon guide, Sergeant Jim McEnery worked with a war dog on one patrol and was amazed at how it could pinpoint the enemy. 'It was almost like a bird dog setting a covey of quail,' he recalled, 'except that when the dog spotted the Japs, it let out this loud howl like a coonhound on the scent.' At one point the dog flushed about a dozen enemy soldiers from their hiding place. They tried to get away, but were killed with bayonets. The platoon became, as a result, very wary of ambushes. Fortunately, the Japanese were mostly too worn out to surprise the Marines.[14]

'We found a few stragglers,' wrote R. V. Burgin. 'They'd leave two or three behind with knee mortars and a machine gun. We called them knee mortars because they had a folding arch that looked like it could fit over your knee. They wouldn't use it that way, of course, because there was too much kick – it would break a man's leg – but we called it that anyway.'[15]

At one point, a patrol used a fallen tree to get across a creek. Most had made it safely across when the man in front of Burgin, 25-year-old PFC Andrew Geglein from Louisville, Kentucky, slipped and fell on the upstream side. Weighed down by his rifle and pack, Geglein disappeared in the chocolate-coloured water, and his colleagues assumed he would be washed under the log and come up the other side. They searched in vain. Eventually a Marine jumped in on the upstream side 'and groped along until he found Andrew hung up on the branches underneath'. They hauled him out, but he had drowned. Burgin thought: *That's a terrible way to lose your life when you're fighting a war.*[16]

Once K Company and the rest of the battalion had reached Karai-ai on 21 February, they were leapfrogged by the 1/5 Marines who captured Iboki Plantation three days later. All Japanese supplies had been 'systematically evacuated and the place deserted save for a handful of stragglers'. By 27 February, the regimental CP had been established at Iboki and 'all remaining elements of the 5th Marines, reinforced, were firmly established in the immediate area and patrolling in all directions'.[17]

The operations of the 5th Marines from Borgen Bay to Iboki were, noted Rupertus's new chief of staff, Colonel Oliver P. Smith,* 'an excellent example of successful shore to shore operations against scattered resistance'. Using just ten landing craft and jungle trails, they had 'transported and marched 5000 men with their attendant supplies and equipment for a distance of 60 miles around and over some of the worst jungle terrain in the world'. Sixty-six enemy prisoners were taken, and over two hundred killed during the advance.† There were only a handful of Marine casualties, the result of 'excellent patrol technique' and the 'use of war dogs'. It was a hugely impressive achievement.[18]

For a time it seemed as if the next job for the Devil Dogs – indeed the whole 1st Marine Division – would be an assault on Rabaul itself. Though such a strategy had been specifically ruled out as too 'costly and time-consuming' by the Combined Chiefs of Staff the previous August,

* Smith replaced Colonel Amor L. Sims as chief of staff on 3 February 1944. He had been selected for the post by Brigadier General Shepherd, an old friend, who was expected to take over from Rupertus as divisional commander at the earliest opportunity. But when Rupertus was informed by Vandegrift, the new commandant of the Marine Corps, that he 'would not be relieved for some time', he 'decided to get a Chief of Staff of his own choosing'. He therefore swapped Smith for Colonel John T. Selden. (Smith, 'Personal Narrative: New Britain', p. 12.)

† Such an unusually high ratio of Japanese POWs to killed in action – the average in the Pacific was more like 3 per cent – was probably because, by this point, the 65th Brigade was so totally starved, exhausted and demoralized that they began abandoning those comrades who could not keep up. These debilitated men were taken prisoner by Marines because they did not constitute a threat.

Doug MacArthur thought differently. In mid-February, therefore, he and Krueger met Rupertus at the Sixth Army HQ to discuss a proposed assault by the Old Breed and an Army combat team. Oliver P. Smith recalled:

> The rough plan was for the First Marine Division to land on the southwest side of the Gazelle Peninsula and move northeast over the mountains to attack Rabaul. The Army combat team was to land on the southeast side of the [peninsula] and proceed more or less north along the coast to Rabaul . . . On a small scale map the Scheme of maneuver looked all right. However, it ignored a few facts. There were 40,000 well-armed Japanese in the vicinity of Rabaul. To get to these 40,000 Japanese (enough for 3 divisions to assault) the First Marine Division would have to advance 25 miles over a 2700 foot mountain range on an indifferent track. The only way the Army combat team could reach Rabaul was by a coastal track which was flanked by high mountains.

All too aware of these difficulties, Smith persuaded Rupertus to let him propose an alternative plan. It recommended landing a 'minimum of 2 first-rate divisions' on the north coast of the Gazelle Peninsula, near Ataliklikun Bay, where they could 'tie into the road net and avoid the mountains' in the centre of the peninsula. It also recommended the support of a 'considerable Naval attack force, including battleships, carriers, cruisers, and destroyers'. After this 'brief estimate' was delivered to the Sixth Army HQ, Rupertus and Smith 'heard no more about attacking Rabaul'.[19]

20

Operation Appease

Talasea, March 1944

By the end of February 1944, the 1st Marine Division's original mission – to secure western New Britain – had been accomplished. But the original Backhander plan had envisaged a drive even farther east to the coastal settlement of Talasea on the Willaumez Peninsula, 'and this, combined with the pursuit of enemy forces fleeing to the sanctuary of Cape Hoskins and Rabaul', was the next objective. Sixty miles from Iboki, and 120 miles from Cape Gloucester, the peninsula jutted 25 miles north of the main body of the island 'like a crooked finger'. It contained, moreover, four coconut plantations and twelve mountain peaks, as well as a dirt airstrip at Talasea.

On 1 March, the task of seizing Talasea, as well as the huge Numundo Plantation on the eastern junction of the peninsula and the mainland, was given to the Devil Dogs. That same day, Colonel Oliver P. Smith swapped jobs with Colonel John T. Selden and became the new commanding officer of the 5th Marines.[1] It was a lucky break for K Company because the tall, softly spoken Smith was one of the finest Marine officers of his generation. Born in Texas, but raised in northern California where he attended UC Berkeley, Smith had joined the Marines as a second lieutenant in 1917. After a stint as the US naval attaché in Paris, he matriculated from the French École Supérieure de Guerre, the first Marine to do so, and returned to the United States to teach at the Marine Corps Schools at Quantico, Virginia, where he was known as the 'Professor' and an expert in amphibious warfare.

When war broke out, Smith was commanding a battalion of the 6th Marines in Iceland. He was assigned to Headquarters Marine Corps in Washington DC in May 1942 and, until his posting to the 1st Marine Division, was the XO of the Division of Plans and Policies. There was no doubting Smith's talent: he was intelligent, easy going and a brilliant staff officer. The one thing missing from his CV was combat experience, an omission his appointment as commander of the 5th Marines was destined to fill.

Smith was still chief of staff when the plan for Talasea – known as Operation Appease – was being put together. He was therefore in the unique position of having to draw up orders for a plan he would soon have to put into action. His task was complicated further by the fact that there was 'an absolute dearth of information about Talasea', both as to the number and location of enemy troops and the suitability of the landing beaches. According to intelligence reports, there were 'a lot' of Japanese in the area. Rupertus disagreed, and thought the Devil Dogs would simply 'walk ashore'.

With no adequate photo reconnaissance, Smith had to rely on the few available maps and the advice of Flight Lieutenant Rodney Marsland of the Royal Australian Air Force (RAAF), who owned a plantation on the Willaumez Peninsula. Marsland confirmed that at the narrowest part of the peninsula there was a channel leading through reefs to a beach near the Volupai Plantation. From there a trail led across the peninsula to the Bitokara Mission, and thence to Talasea. Smith decided, therefore, to land at 'Red' Beach near Volupai on 6 March, 'seize an initial beachhead and then, attacking in the direction of Volupai-Talasea, seize and occupy the Talasea area', before sending patrols south to the Numundo Plantation. Enemy troops in the area were estimated at 4–5,000, though Smith had 'reason to believe' that at least some of them had withdrawn to the Gazelle Peninsula.

Having only arrived at Iboki from Karai-ai in a 'somewhat bedraggled' state on 4 March, K Company and the rest of the 3/5 Marines were put in reserve. The operation was spearheaded by 500 men from the 1/5 Marines who were successfully landed from amtracs at 8:35 a.m. on 6 March. There was no air support because of bad weather, and the tiny beach – 100 yards long and 50 wide, backed by rainforest and swamp – could accommodate just three boats at a time. Fortunately, the initial opposition was light, and only five men were hit by Japanese rifle fire. But as the 1/5 moved inland, they were held up by Japanese machine guns and mortars. One 90mm round landed in the midst of an artillery battery, causing heavy casualties, while shrapnel from another struck the beachmaster and mortally wounded the regimental surgeon. Smith responded by pushing forward the 2/5 Marines, who by nightfall, assisted by medium tanks and a section of 37mm guns, had advanced 2,000 yards to the northern end of the Volupai coconut grove. There they set up an all-round defensive perimeter.

Smith's men had secured the beachhead and killed thirty-five Japanese soldiers, including three officers. But the enemy's heavy mortars had also taken their toll, and total Marine casualties were thirteen killed and seventy-one wounded (many of them artillerymen). In the emergency dressing station, wrote Smith, men were 'laid out on ponchos to keep them off the wet ground'. He added: 'They were dirty. There were piles of bloody dressings. The dead could be distinguished from the wounded by the fact that their faces were covered by ponchos.'[2]

Next day, 7 March, as the 2/5 Marines continued their advance up the trail towards Japanese strongpoints on Mount Schleuther, the 3/5 Marines landed and by nightfall had relieved the 1st Battalion on the beachhead perimeter. 'Compared to Cape Gloucester,' remembered Platoon Sergeant Thurman Miller, who had replaced Lou Gargano as the senior NCO in 3rd Platoon, '[the Willaumez Peninsula] was a paradise. It had civilization in the form of a German mission, a coconut grove, and very pretty beaches, with hot springs. The beaches were long and shallow, with pockets of warm water propelled from the volcano below.'[3]

On the 8th, the 2nd Battalion occupied Bitokara Mission and the abandoned airfield at Talasea Point. The 1st Battalion, meanwhile, had taken advantage of a captured Japanese map to move along a more southerly trail towards the Waru villages, on high ground west of the airfield. The villages were captured in a combined attack by the 1st and 2nd Battalions on 9 March. But it was largely a bloodless victory because, as a Japanese prisoner confirmed, the main body of defenders had withdrawn two days earlier, leaving a rearguard of 100 men to hold the villages. They had left the previous night.

A congratulatory message from Major General Rupertus to Colonel Smith was dropped from a Cub light plane. 'You and your regiment,' it read, 'have accomplished a magnificent job. Please inform your command that the Division and the Marine Corps are proud of you. The Fifth Marines have done it again. We like your guts.'[4]

With his chief objectives secure, Colonel Smith's remaining task was to send a patrol south to the Numundo Plantation at the base of the Willaumez Pensinula, a distance of more than 25 miles. Captain Haldane's K Company was selected for the job. It left Bitokara on 11 March with orders to reach Numundo in three days, a time estimate that was hopelessly optimistic.[5]

For the first five miles or so, K Company encountered little opposition. But a few miles further on, just north of the village of Patanga, the lead platoon was stopped in its tracks by rifle, machine-gun, mortar and artillery fire. The halt, however, was temporary. 'The Japanese would make a stand,' recalled Thurman Miller, 'and then retreat a quarter mile or so and reestablish their 75mm gun in a new position to slow us again.'[6]

This delaying action continued for four days as the Japanese opened fire from heavy vegetation and 'then withdrew effectively before the advance guard flankers could close in'.[7] K Company captured a few stragglers, but most were sick with malaria and starving. 'We tried to take them with us,' noted R. V. Burgin, 'but sometimes we had to leave them behind.'[8]

Miller was astonished when a group of prisoners fell to their knees and put their foreheads on the ground, expecting to be executed. He nudged one with the toe of his boot and motioned for him to stand.

The soldier did so. Miller knew he was master of the situation, that he had the power of life and death. He remembered:

> I looked at my men and saw nothing but hatred. I looked into my own heart and saw nothing but contempt. I stared at the Japanese soldier in front of me. Scarcely 2 feet separated us. For the first time I had come face-to-face with one of the enemy. Our eyes met. Just two men facing each other, both far removed from their homes, separated from their families. Each alone in a hostile land, each seeking to survive at the cost of the other's life.

Miller had been filled with the urge to kill. Yet, as he looked into the Japanese soldier's eyes, he realized that he, too, had been 'indoctrinated with hatred and a desire to kill, without hesitation or regret'. A sadness crept into Miller's heart, a sympathy for the man whose life he held in his hands. 'Ever so slowly,' he wrote, 'the pendulum began to swing, away from hatred, towards sanity. There surely were men in my platoon who did not share my thoughts, but reason, for me, had begun to return.' The prisoners were handed over to army men.[9]

Predictably, some Japanese took their own lives. Just beyond a creek, R. V. Burgin and his fellow mortarmen came across the black and bloated body of a Japanese officer, lying on his back with his knees up. He had a bayonet 'stuck in his body, and his hands were still curled round the grip'.[10]

The men of K Company, meanwhile, had suffered only minor casualties. This good fortune would not last, and one of the first fatalities was, predictably, a platoon leader: First Lieutenant James P. ('Jim') Lynch, Jr, 25, of Bala Cynwyd, Pennsylvania. A graduate of La Salle College, Philadelphia, and an employee of the Standard Oil Company, Lynch had been in the South Pacific for more than eighteen months when he joined K Company as a replacement officer. In a letter to his sister in the States, he joked that his 'boys were using a blow-torch to cook their cocoa in the trenches'.

But, according to McEnery, Lynch 'hadn't seen much action' and, on 15 March, made the 'mistake of walking right up to a line of Japanese foxholes, thinking they were all empty'. One was not, and the Japanese soldier inside 'shot Lynch dead'. He was the fourth platoon leader in K Company to die on New Britain, an attrition rate that underlined just how lethal it was to be a junior Marine officer on active service.[11]

Lynch's replacement as leader of the 3rd Platoon was 23-year-old Second Lieutenant William B. Bauerschmidt from Pottstown, Pennsylvania. Married to a fellow graduate of Bucknell University, he was the son of a World War I veteran and carried the same 'hog-leg' revolver that his father had used in France.[12] 'I could tell that he was fresh out of stateside and very green,' wrote Thurman Miller. 'It had always been our practice for two men to share their ponchos and make a small tent. I invited the lieutenant to share mine, but he informed me he was perfectly capable of caring for himself . . . Next morning, after the hard rains, there wasn't a dry thread on him.'

Miller's other piece of advice was for the officer to remove his badges of rank so the Japanese could not target him. Again, he refused – though, shortly after, Miller noticed that he had done just that. His inexperience in jungle warfare, however, was obvious and potentially dangerous. Spotting a waterfall on the side of the trail, Bauerschmidt 'yelled for the platoon to gather round and fill their canteens'. Nobody moved. Instead they looked to Miller for guidance. He held up two fingers and said: 'Two at a time.' He explained to Bauerschmidt that if they all huddled round the waterfall, a single grenade could wipe out the whole platoon. His way, only two would die. The officer nodded and, when all the canteens were filled, they moved on.[13]

This was not Bauerschmidt's only error. He would develop into 'a damn fine Marine officer', recalled Jim McEnery, 'but during his first few days with the platoon, he sent me out on a mission that could've easily gotten me killed'. Entering a small village, they saw a line of foxholes ahead that the locals insisted were all empty. Bauerschmidt was unconvinced. 'Hey, Mac,' he said to the platoon guide. 'Go up there and check out those foxholes. I'll cover you.'

McEnery knew he was taking a risk. That, after all, was how Lynch had been killed. But an order was an order. He moved forward, sweating

Second Lieutenant Arthur L. 'Scoop' Adams, commanding K Company's 1st Platoon at Guadalcanal. One of his men wrote: 'I would've followed him anywhere.'

Sergeant Thurman 'T. I.' Miller from Otsego, West Virginia, and his childhood sweetheart (and later wife) Recie Marshall.

Sergeants Lou Gargano (left) and Jim McEnery in Australia before the New Britain campaign.

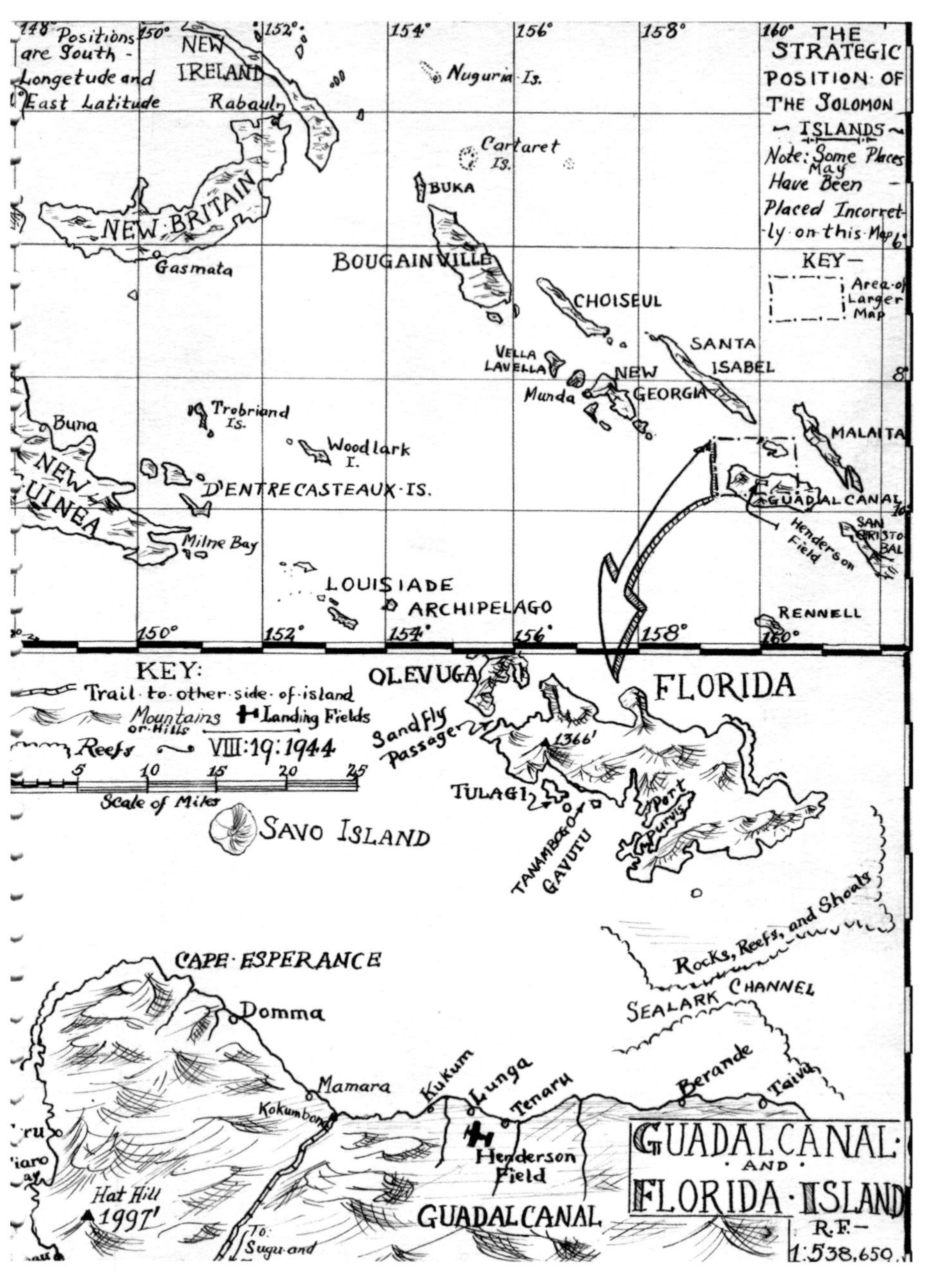

A hand-drawn map of the Solomon Islands campaign by Second Lieutenant Thayer Soule.

US Marines landing on the beach at Guadalcanal, 7 August 1942.

Marine machine gunner on Guadalcanal, cradling a .45 Thompson submachine gun.

Marine patrol crossing the Lunga River.

Marines lining up for food.

Marines moving to the front.

Marine mortar crew preparing for action.

Lieut. Gen. Thomas Holcomb (second left), commandant of the Marine Corps, is given a tour of Guadalcanal by Maj. Gen. Alexander A. Vandegrift, commanding the 1st Marine Division, in late October 1942.

Japanese prisoners of war.

Marine officers on the beach at Guadalcanal.

Marines leave Guadalcanal in early December 1942, having survived a brutal four-month campaign.

Lieutenant Andy 'Ack-Ack' Haldane, back row second from left with moustache, and fellow machine gunners with a captured Japanese flag on Guadalcanal.

Haldane instructs his XO, Lieut. Thomas 'Stumpy' Stanley, in the use of the new .30 Garand M1 semi-automatic rifle.

Marines land at Cape Gloucester on the island of New Britain, December 1943.

Marines wading on to a beach at Cape Gloucester.

freely, and breathed a big sigh of relief when he saw the foxholes were empty and the Japanese long gone. Later, Bauerschmidt apologized. 'That was a bad move on my part, Mac, and I'm sorry. I put you at risk, and I shouldn't have done it. We should've just grenaded the damn holes to be on the safe side.'[14]

During the evening of 16 March, the Japanese made their last stand against K Company at the village of Kilu, eight miles north of Numundo. While the two forces slugged it out, a Marine landing craft approached the beach. It carried Lieutenant Colonel Harold O. Deakin, the commander of the 3/5 Marines (since taking over from Walt on 12 January), who had been given permission by Colonel Smith to transport a section of 81mm mortars by sea to assist Captain Haldane. A Japanese 75mm field gun opened fire, bracketing the vessel but failing to hit it, and Deakin was able to land the mortars without casualties. They were used to drive the Japanese out of the village.

This was the last contact with the enemy. Patrols were pushed through to the Numundo Plantation – arriving on the 18th – and 1,500 yards further to the south and southwest, but no Japanese were encountered. K Company's total casualties were one dead and seven wounded.[15]

The Talasea operation was, Smith wrote later, 'the longest small boat shore-to-shore operation conducted by Marines in World War II'. It was conducted without either air or naval gunfire support, and no regiment 'ever had a longer or more tenuous line of supply'. Total casualties for the whole 5th Marines were 18 killed and 122 wounded, while those for the first two days exceeded the division's losses at the start of the Cape Gloucester campaign. During the course of a month, they killed 200 enemy soldiers and captured 150, and cleared an area the size of Guam (212 square miles).[16]

21

'The sickness, the rain, the spider'

New Britain, March–May 1944

Relieved at Numundo by I Company, Captain Haldane's men returned to the Bitokara Mission for some well-deserved rest and recreation. Colonel Smith considered it 'one of the most beautiful spots' he had seen in the tropics, and it was there that the Stars and Stripes were raised, on a flagpole made from the trunk of a slender royal palm tree, to mark the end of the battle.

Smith and his staff were billeted in the Mission House, a three-room structure with a complete theological library, a wide veranda and an outside kitchen. Under the house lived two Nisei (Japanese-American) interpreters and their orderlies, kept busy by a large cache of captured Japanese documents from which they were 'able to identify practically all the units on New Britain and adjacent islands'. Both interpreters had gone to high school in Honolulu: one acted and spoke like an American; the other was a typical Japanese, and often impersonated an enemy soldier to get information from prisoners.[1]

K Company pitched their jungle hammocks nearby. A delighted R. V. Burgin wrote:

> The mission was on a hill overlooking a small harbor, where we swam and fished. There were broad lawns and flowers and fruit trees, including a pepper tree. I'd never seen one before. It was about eight or ten feet high and absolutely loaded with those little

> tobasco peppers. We also saw banana trees, though no bananas. Nearby there was a native village. The place must have been a tropical paradise before the war.

The men were able to have their first proper bath since Melbourne in hot springs – a pool filled by clear running water that gushed at body temperature from rocks in the side of a hill – a mile south of the mission. But the food situation was dire. There was, remembered Burgin, 'never enough of it'. One meal consisted of a little piece of ham, some potatoes, cabbage and a big navel orange. He looked at it in his mess tin and thought: *What the hell? Do they think they're feeding a canary?*

In the event, he was not able to finish even this meagre meal because his stomach had shrunk so much during his time in the field. Food was a constant preoccupation. 'We'd go in for lunch,' remembered Burgin, 'and they'd serve soup so thin you could read a newspaper through it. At night we'd designate one man to go down to the chow dump, where they stockpiled all the food, and he'd bring something back to the battalion, a gallon can of peaches or fruit cocktail or something like that. Everybody got their canteen out to have some, including our lieutenant. I'll call him "Legs," because he was a tall, gawky guy.'[2]

Burgin's officer was Second Lieutenant Charles C. 'Duke' Ellington from Birmingham, Alabama. He had joined K Company as part of the recent beefing up of Marine rifle companies from six officers and 190 men to seven officers and 228 men. Ellington was that extra officer, put in charge of a slightly expanded mortar section, up from sixteen to twenty men. The other organizational change was that the mortar section was now part of company HQ, while the former weapons platoon had been renamed the machine-gun platoon. It consisted of an officer and forty-three men, with six machine-gun squads instead of three, arranged in three sections of two squads each. The rifle platoons were each given an extra three men, split among the three rifle squads who now had thirteen men instead of twelve: a squad leader and three four-man fire teams (fire team leader, BAR man, assistant BAR man and rifleman). Company HQ, thanks to the addition of the mortar section, now numbered three officers and fifty men.[3]

This added firepower – particularly the three extra machine guns – would be of huge benefit to K Company in the battles to come. But for the men of the mortar section, the arrival of a dedicated mortar officer was not a welcome innovation. For one thing it meant the supersession of their former leader, the combat-hardened veteran Platoon Sergeant Johnny Marmet, with a novice like 'Duke' Ellington. A married 30-year-old, Ellington had been in uniform since late 1940 when he was drafted from his job in Birmingham's Commercial Credit Corporation. But it was not until early 1944 that he got his first taste of active service, albeit at the tail end of the New Britain campaign.[4]

Ellington cut an awkward figure: tall, skinny and not remotely athletic, with grey eyes and brown hair. The chief objection that Burgin and others had towards him, however, was his self-serving nature. When an order came down that anyone caught stealing food would be court-martialled, Ellington called his section together and chewed them out. '*You* guys,' he told them indignantly, 'are going to have to stop stealing that food! They're going to court-martial *your* ass!'

The men were furious because they knew that Ellington had eaten as much stolen fruit as anyone. *What kind of officer is this?* wondered Burgin. The answer was obvious. He told the guys: 'Don't pay any attention. Let's go ahead and take the food, but make damn sure we don't get caught. Whenever he comes into camp, we just won't let him know it's here and he won't get any more.' They did, and he didn't.[5]

Fortunately for K Company, most of the other replacement officers were good men. By far the best of the bunch was 26-year-old First Lieutenant Edward A. 'Hillbilly' Jones from Whiteford, Maryland, a small rural town just a stone's throw from the Pennsylvania border. A popular and fun-loving youngster, Ed Jones was a chorist for the local Methodist church and a talented guitar player. He also became, after his father was disabled in the early 1930s, a surrogate dad and provider for his nine younger siblings. Leaving high school to join the Civilian Conservation Corps, he sent most of his pay home to his family so they could eat during the Depression. 'Don't worry, mom,' he promised. 'I'll always take care of you.'

In 1938, Jones joined the Marine Corps as a private and served three years on ships before the outbreak of war. He was, remembered his sister Anne, 'smart, handsome and a terrific singer'. Dubbed 'Hillbilly' because of his rural roots, he was universally liked by officers and enlisted men on account of his friendly, easy-going nature. He was also fearless in battle, winning a Bronze Star for singlehandedly knocking out a Japanese machine gun on Guadalcanal. Later in the campaign, he kept up unit morale on the front line by singing favourite songs like 'I want a girl, just like the girl that married dear old dad . . .'[6]

Given a second lieutenant's gold bars for his outstanding service on Guadalcanal, Jones began the New Britain campaign as battalion supply officer for the 3/5 Marines, serving alongside Rex McIlvaine, the former XO of K Company, who was a battalion liaison officer. But staff work was not for Jones and, after K Company had lost the bulk of its officers at Suicide Creek and Walt's Ridge, he took over the beefed-up machine-gun platoon. 'We *all* liked Hillbilly,' remembered R. V. Burgin. He was 'the kind of officer you always wanted to have somewhere near you in a battle. He was soft-spoken, always calm and reassuring. Nothing rattled him.'[7]

Not long after K Company's return to Bitokara, a base for two Patrol Torpedo (PT) boat squadrons was established at nearby Garua Harbor. Originally armed with four torpedoes to target Japanese warships, by now their main occupation was disrupting Japanese nocturnal barge traffic, so that their original armament of two pairs of Browning heavy .50 calibre machine guns and one 20mm had been augmented by combinations of 20mm, 37mm and even 40mm guns. Powered by three supercharged V12 petrol engines that were capable of generating speeds in excess of 40 knots, the PT boats were a deadly weapon that could disrupt enemy shipping as far afield as Cape Hoskins and the Gazelle Peninsula. Their base included a mother ship – a converted yacht that held their stores and supplies – and a floating workshop, dry dock and gasoline tank. The men of K Company were intrigued. 'I loved those PT boats,' recalled R. V. Burgin, 'and I wasn't alone. We'd all go down and visit with the crews and swap lies, always trying to outdo one another. They'd invite us on board and we'd sit at the turrets and fire the guns. Get a feel for what it was like to be on one of those things.'[8]

One member of K Company – 20-year-old field cook Sergeant Fred E. Miller from St Joseph, Missouri – went further by going out on a mission with a PT boat. Miller had got to know the crews well by trading Japanese souvenirs for cans of maple syrup and flour and eggs to make pancakes, and eventually persuaded one crew to let him ride with them up to Rabaul one night. He found it an exhilarating experience as the PT boat, one of six, fired its torpedoes and machine guns at Japanese shipping in Rabaul Bay, before making its escape at top speed. But when 'Ack-Ack' Haldane got to hear about Miller's unauthorized exploits, he was unimpressed. 'Miller,' he told him, 'if you're going to get your ass killed, I'd prefer you do it fighting with us. No more night excursions.'[9]

Haldane's intervention might have saved Miller's life. Soon after, while on patrol near Cape Hoskins, two PT boats searching for a Japanese schooner were mistakenly attacked by a flight of Australian Bristol Beaufort twin-engine medium bombers. The planes made a total of two strafing runs and one bombing run, killing one crew member who was trying to identify himself by holding aloft an American flag. It was carnage: torpedoes and gasoline exploded, partially destroying both boats. Of the original twenty-six crew members, eight were killed or missing; the others all wounded.

How had it happened? An investigation established that the PT boats were in enemy waters and the planes at 5,000 feet – too high to identify the craft as American – when they began their attack. The Australians were 'deeply sorry', of course, but that was scant consolation for the colleagues and families of the men who had lost their lives. The commander of the PT squadron, a Lieutenant Thompson of the US Navy who had attended the University of California, was 'very bitter'. But there was nothing to be done, noted Colonel Smith, beyond an insistence that 'PT boats should operate only at night, and . . . be sure that friendly night fighters know of their presence'.

Sadly, neither rule was adhered to a short time later when Thompson himself, commanding two boats off the Gazelle Pensinula, was jumped by two Marine Corsair fighter-bombers. This time the boats fought back and shot down one of the planes. But more planes appeared and, after a brief but vicious struggle, both boats were sunk, with Thompson among the many casualties. It was only when a seaplane landed to pick up the downed pilot that the PT boats 'were discovered to be friendly'. It rescued Thompson and the other survivors.[10]

In early April, Oliver Smith received word from Rupertus's staff that the 1st Marine Division would soon be relieved on New Britain by the US Army's 40th Division. The move was the consequence of an increasingly acrimonious dispute between Chester Nimitz and Doug MacArthur. Since the successful ousting of the Japanese from the Gilbert and Marshall Islands – including Tarawa, Kwajalein and Eniwetok – in a hard-fought campaign that had raged from November 1943 to February 1944, Nimitz had been focused on his next major objective: the capture of the Mariana Islands to provide airfields from which the revolutionary new B-29 Superfortress bomber – developed at a cost of $3 billion,* and capable of flying 1,600 miles at high altitude, out of the reach of enemy fighters – could strike at Japanese cities and industry.

The decision to assault the Marianas had been confirmed by the Combined Chiefs of Staff at the Cairo Conference in November 1943. But MacArthur still hoped to bend Nimitz's line of advance towards his own theatre where he intended to consolidate all available forces for the capture of Mindanao, the most southerly of the main Philippine islands. In March 1944, the Joint Chiefs gave MacArthur permission to advance north through the Admiralty and Celebes Islands towards Mindanao. The overall strategic plan was, at this stage, 'to secure a base in the strategic triangle formed by the Philippines, Formosa, and the coast of China'. Such a move would cut the lines of communication between Japan's home islands and her conquered lands in the Dutch East Indies and

* Since the cost of the Manhattan atomic bomb project was 'only' $2 billion, the B-29's development was the single most expensive arms programme of the war.

Southeast Asia, and provide bases for air attacks and future invasions, including the ultimate assault on Japan itself. After much debate, the Joint Chiefs agreed on a two-pronged strategy: Nimitz would attack through the central Pacific, while MacArthur advanced on the New Guinea–Mindanao axis in the southwest Pacific.

MacArthur's ultimate aim was to be appointed Supreme Commander of the whole Pacific, bringing both the Pacific Fleet and Nimitz's Marine and army divisions under his command. To this end he had opposed the decision to capture the Marianas and tried to keep the 1st Marine Division on New Britain until, as he put it, he had completed 'the Rabaul campaign'. He was to fail in both endeavours.

Once the Marianas were secure, Nimitz had been tasked by the Joint Chiefs with Operation Stalemate, the capture of the Palau Islands, Japan's main bastion in the western Carolines which lay 530 miles east of Mindanao. There were, for Nimitz, two justifications for Stalemate: 'first, to remove from MacArthur's right flank, in his progress to the Southern Philippines, a definite threat of attack; second, to secure for our forces a base from which to support MacArthur's operations into the Southern Philippines.'

To carry out Stalemate, Nimitz requested the return of the 1st Marine Division to his command. He was convinced that the 'substitution of a division without amphibious combat experience would seriously jeopardize the success of that venture'. When MacArthur insisted that he had nothing available to replace the 1st, Nimitz transferred the 40th Infantry Division from his own theatre. Backed by Admiral King, he told MacArthur to relieve the 1st 'as soon as practicable'. Reluctantly, MacArthur gave the necessary orders, though the final echelon – including the 3/5 Marines – did not leave the island until 4 May.[11]

Aboard one of the last transports was Oliver P. Smith, now assistant division commander* with the rank of brigadier general. 'We saw New

* Smith's predecessor, Brigadier General Lem Shepherd, had been appointed commander of the reactivated 1st Provisional Marine Brigade, including the 4th and 22nd Marines. The brigade fought on Guam in the summer of 1944 and

Britain Island disappear over the horizon,' he recalled, 'with few regrets.'[12]

The campaign had cost the reinforced division 310 killed and 1,083 wounded. Twenty-one of those fatalities – four officers and seventeen enlisted men – were in K Company. Given that there were twenty-seven rifle companies (not to mention other combat units) in the division, this was a disproportionately high toll for one company to suffer, and testament to the viciousness of the fighting at Suicide Creek and Walt's Ridge. By contrast, the 3/5's other two rifle companies, I and L, had eleven and ten men killed respectively.[13]

Was it all worth it? By the end of the campaign, noted the US Marines official history, the Japanese had withdrawn their remaining forces to the 'immediate vicinity' of Rabaul where they 'sat out the rest of the war in magnificent isolation, harassed by routine "milk run bombing," powerless to influence the issue that was being decided hundreds and thousands of miles to the west and north-west'. By neutralizing Rabaul, the campaign had secured MacArthur's right flank as he continued his advance towards the Philippines.[14]

Another factor, often overlooked, is the context of the campaign. When it was conceived, progress in the Pacific War was slow. The bitter struggle for Guadalcanal, the northern Solomons and New Guinea had made Allied commanders cautious. From this perspective, securing Cape Gloucester and its airfields (while denying them to the Japanese) made perfect sense. Whether, in retrospect, this was really necessary – given the proximity of Allied airpower on New Guinea – is an open question.

As for the 1st Marine Division, it had 'achieved a degree of perfection' in its conduct of 'jungle operations' that had probably never been equalled: 'from the landing beaches, to the adaption of amphibious techniques which carried patrols 130 miles along New Britain's northern coast'.[15] By this point, compared to the other combat divisions in the Pacific, the Old Breed was in a class of its own.

Such lofty considerations, however, were far from the minds of

---

was later expanded to become the 6th Marine Division, which Shepherd commanded on Okinawa.

Haldane's men as they left New Britain on the fast attack transport USS *Elmore* on 4 May 1944. Recently promoted to gunnery sergeant ('gunny'), Thurman Miller recalled:

> I looked back at the skyline with the live volcano in the background. The rugged coastline and the rain forest fell away; it was a place I would never see again, but its memories are constant in my soul. The sound of Sergeant Thompson dying. Tully hiding his wedding band. Suicide Creek, where the balance of power shifted so many times. Hordes of the enemy screaming '*Banzai!*' and coming on and on, proudly dying for their emperor. The sickness, the rain, the spider.

Miller discovered later that every morning his mother had gone into the bushes near her home to pray for the safe return of her son and his buddies. It might have done the trick because, as he left the shores of New Britain, he was convinced a 'higher power' was watching over him. 'I had been in some situations,' he wrote, 'out of which I could not have come but for the mercy of God.'

He had not emerged from the Green Hell unscathed, however. Every veteran, wrote Miller, leaves a part of himself on the battlefield. It was, for him, both figuratively and literally the case on New Britain. At 110lb, Miller was even more emaciated than he had been on leaving Guadalcanal. With wrinkled skin that 'hung like folds in drapes', he 'felt old and worn out'.[16]

22

'Whose bright idea was this anyway?'

Pavuvu Island, May 1944

Though many were little more than walking scarecrows, suffering from a variety of ailments that ranged from jungle rot to dysentery and malaria, Haldane's men were in high spirits as the USS *Elmore* headed southeast in calm seas and clear skies. According to the latest scuttlebutt – said to have come from Major General Rupertus himself – they were making for Melbourne, and Corporal R. V. Burgin was fairly bursting to see Florence again. Even those without Australian sweethearts were excited to return to the big city where they could eat, drink, chase women and try to forget the war for a while.

After chow, a large group would gather on deck to hear Lieutenant 'Hillbilly' Jones strumming his guitar. They sang along, often with more enthusiasm than skill, to popular songs that reminded them of home: 'Danny Boy', 'Nobody's Darling but Mine', 'San Antonio Rose' (a favourite of Texans like Burgin and George Sarrett), and 'Waltzing Matilda', the popular Australian bush ballad that had become the Old Breed's unofficial anthem during its last spell Down Under.[1]

As the voyage continued, those with a keen sense of direction might have wondered why the *Elmore* kept heading southeast, when Australia was due south. They got their answer on 7 May, three days in, when the ship's loudspeakers crackled into life. 'Now hear this,' said a crew member. 'This ship is bound for Pavuvu in the Russell Islands.'[2]

Pavu-where? the guys asked themselves. Nobody had heard of it. One thing was certain: they weren't returning to Australia.

'Anyone know anything about it?' asked one Marine.

'Boys,' replied a sailor, 'the name of that island is Pavuvu. P-A-V-U-V-U.' He lowered his voice in a conspiratorial whisper. 'And let me warn you, it's vacant, and I've even heard it's haunted. Humans can't live there. There ain't nothing but rats and crabs and crocodiles. You people won't be there a week before you're yelling for us to move you to another island.'[3]

Next day, as the sun was setting, they reached their destination: the largest of the Russell Islands, situated 40 miles northwest of Guadalcanal. They anchored in Macquitti Bay, in the north of Pavuvu, and the view from the *Elmore*'s deck was better than expected. There were 'palm trees', remembered R. V. Burgin, 'a lagoon and sandy beaches'. The shore was dotted with thin piers that ran out from tiny copra-drying sheds, part of the process that turns coconut kernels into oil. A plantation house, square-framed with a red corrugated-iron roof, sat high on stilts in the grove behind the beach.[4] It looked, to Nolen Marbrey, 'cool and serene and somewhat peaceful'. Was the sailor messing with them?

They found out the following morning when, in pouring rain, they transferred down rope ladders to Higgins boats and were taken to the beach. 'The top-kick's whistle began to blow,' wrote Marbrey, '[and] men began picking up back packs and gear. K Company slid out of the boats into the shallow water, sinking into the gray, "crawfishey" mud, and wading into shore.'

They could see a single pier and, behind it, a muddy road that gouged a passage through the palms. Once formed up, they trudged along the road to the main camp, located in the centre of a 600-acre coconut grove on the peninsula between Macquitti and Hooper Bays. The company street was lined on each side with six-man pyramid tents. A huge sign proclaimed: KING COMPANY WELCOME TO YOUR NEW HOME. Marbrey and his buddies looked at the sign in awe, wondering where the hell they had got the paint. 'It seemed,' he recalled, 'that new replacements had reached the island before us.'[5]

But, apart from the tents (and many of those were tattered and full of holes), there was no infrastructure to speak of and the ground was covered with layers of rotten coconuts, and beneath that mud. 'The place had been a plantation until the war started,' R. V. Burgin discovered, 'when the people who owned and worked it took off. Ever since, those coconuts had been falling off trees and rotting on the ground. Every now and then you'd hear one hit with a *thwack!* You learned to give the trees a wide berth. The smell was overwhelming. It was years before I could eat coconut again in any form.'[6]

They had hoped to find, wrote Sergeant Jim McEnery, 'at least a preliminary campsite with roads, bivouac areas, drill fields, water wells, electric generators'. Instead their 'rest camp' was comprised of a few 'ragged castoff Army tents and half-rotted canvas cots', pitched on 'a wasteland of oozy mud littered with millions of coconuts and besieged by armies of rats and land crabs'. Taking in the scene, they shook their heads and asked each other the same question: 'Whose bright idea was this anyway?'[7]

It later emerged that the people responsible for choosing Pavuvu as a rest camp were the staff of Major General Roy S. Geiger's III Amphibious Corps, the formation to which the 1st Marine Division had just been transferred from Krueger's Sixth Army. The original intention had been to send the Old Breed to recuperate on Guadalcanal where III Corps had its headquarters and where, since the capture of the island, a vast military base had been established. But that was ruled out because Geiger's staff feared a repeat of what had happened to the 3rd Marine Division, which had, in the wake of the hard-fought Bougainville campaign, been sent to Guadalcanal to rest, refit and retrain. In practice, the 3rd had been ordered by the island command to provide daily working parties of a thousand men, and it was decided that the 1st, already 'spent, used, burnt out' by the New Britain campaign, could 'ill afford such an oblique expenditure of manpower'.

Searching for an alternative, the corps staff flew over Pavuvu in a light plane and saw 'only the graceful shore line, the symmetrical rows of palms that must have given them a feeling of tidiness about the place that a closer view would have betrayed'. The island was therefore selected as a rest camp after a cursory aerial observation, and without a single member of staff having set foot there.[8]

In many ways, the island seemed ideal. Captured by the 3rd Marine Raider Battalion in 1942, it was just ten miles across (at its widest) and virtually uninhabited. The central and southern part was rugged, with peaks of up to 1,500 feet, and covered with rain forest. But the north 'consisted of a series of fingers on most of which were coconut groves'. The one between Macquitti and Hooper Bays had been chosen as the site of the Old Breed's camp.

For the early arrivals, however, the problems were obvious. There were no roads – the first was built by a battalion of Seabees* – and it would take more than a month to haul out and dump the morass of fallen coconuts. Yet the ground remained waterlogged because, as Brigadier General Oliver P. Smith put it, 'decayed coral rock underlay the coconut groves and the abundant rainfall did not readily drain through it'. Even when the sun shone, it struggled to penetrate the thickness of the groves, and 'the foot traffic of thousands of men churned the turf into mud'.

With no surface water on Pavuvu, seven wells had to be dug with a daily output of 200,000 gallons. This did not leave much for bathing. Basic issues like these had been overlooked by Geiger's staff, leaving the 1st Marine Division to find solutions. 'The camp was very compact,' noted Smith, 'and, with good roads, camp administration would have been simple. When we arrived, however, the camp was hardly more than a bivouac.'[9]

As the sun went down on K Company's first day on Pavuvu, it 'got dark in a hurry' and the men scrabbled around for some light. Fortunately Platoon Sergeant 'Pop' Haney, the eccentric and longest-serving member of the company, had the solution. 'Come here, Sergeant McEnery,' he told the New Yorker, 'and I'll show you a little trick I picked up.'

* Or 'CBs', the nickname for the US Naval Construction Battalions.

McEnery watched while Haney filled a canteen cup with beach sand and poked into it a six-inch length of tent rope. Next, he poured in a few ounces of gasoline, struck a match and touched it to the rope. 'And – *poof!* – like magic,' remembered McEnery, 'Pop Haney had made a crude little lamp that put out a fair amount of light – at least enough to eat by or write a letter by, maybe even to play cards by. It sure beat stumbling around in the dark like a bunch of moles.'

He exclaimed to Haney: 'Well, I'll be damned.'

'No you won't,' said the old-timer with a wink, 'not if you watch your step and learn a few more tricks.'[10]

Next morning, after a night of persistent rain, Thurman Miller swung his feet off his bunk into ankle-deep water. The quagmire in the company streets made walking impossible. You just had to 'chug along', remembered Miller, 'as best you could'. Desperate to write home, he went to a Red Cross station and asked for a pencil, paper and an envelope. They wanted 10 cents an item. 'I don't have any money,' said Miller. 'I haven't seen any pay for four months.'

'In that case,' replied the aid worker, 'we can't let you have them.'

An exasperated Miller next went to the tent that served as a library and asked to borrow a book. 'You have to deposit one,' he was told, 'to check one out.'

'To hell with it,' he responded, before stalking away.

There were, however, some lighter moments. Having received a shipment of alcohol, Haldane and the other officers gave a portion to the senior NCOs (top-kick down to platoon sergeant). This included Miller, who decided to pool his with another gunnery sergeant and drink a little each day. They opened their first bottle that night, a Sunday, intending to take it easy because it was Miller's turn to hold roll call the following morning. But not having consumed alcohol since leaving Australia, eight months earlier, they quickly lost track of time. Eventually Miller looked at his watch. 'Ten o'clock in the morning!' he wrote. 'I jumped up with a start. I looked out at the dawning and hurriedly put on my clothes.'

Stepping out into the company street, he bellowed: 'Company K outside for roll call!'

The men emerged from their tents in dribs and drabs.

'Get the lead out!' shouted Miller.

More appeared, but at the same glacial pace. Finally, with the company standing to attention, each platoon sergeant reported to Miller. 'First Platoon present and accounted for,' and so on, down the line.

When everyone had reported, Miller did an abrupt about-face, saluted smartly and opened his mouth to report to Captain Haldane. But there was no sign of the skipper. Miller looked back at the men. Many were in their underwear or shirtless, and looking at him as if he had lost his mind.

He exploded: 'What kind of Marines are you? Where the hell's the company? Even the officers are crummy!'

They stared back, not saying a word. Just then, Miller felt mud oozing between his toes. He looked down at his bare feet. The whole company started laughing, pointing, and laughing some more. Thanks to a bit of wine, Miller had carried out roll call at dusk on Sunday, not dawn on Monday. 'It was not the quantity we had consumed,' wrote Miller, 'but rather the tropical heat along with the fact we were not used to it.' A day later, two cartoons appeared on the company bulletin board. One showed Miller crawling up the company street; the other relieving himself while he leant against a coconut tree. 'They were good cartoons,' he noted. 'They looked exactly like me.'[11]

For R. V. Burgin, the worst things on Pavuvu were the rats and land crabs which had 'pretty much taken over the place'. The rats lived in the top of palm trees, where it was hard to get at them, and were mostly seen at night, 'skittering across the tents or sliding down the tent ropes'. The land crabs – the size of a fist and the colour of a bruise – were everywhere. They got into the Marines' bunks, clothes and footwear. Burgin would shake his boondockers before putting them on, and two or three crabs would usually fall out and scuttle sideways out of the tent. Some Marines got so fed up they went on a Sunday morning crab hunt, gathering hundreds of the little critters into a heap, pouring gasoline on it and striking a match. 'The stink from the burning crabs,' wrote Burgin, 'made us forget the rotting coconuts for a while.'

There were regular work details to help clear the thousands of fallen coconuts and dump them in a swamp. Now a corporal, Burgin was excused this menial work. He was expected to send out members of his squad, however, and they always came back stinking of sour coconut milk. They tried to wash off the smell in the rain, using Marine soap and a brush, but it never did the trick.

Other work parties were hauling crushed coral 'to pave the roads and lanes between the tents, trying to keep on top of the mud'. The Marines took some of the coral into their tents to make a dry floor under their cots. They also built platforms from scraps of wood to have somewhere dry to store their clothes, shoes and letters from home. Burgin used his to pin up Florence's photo. He soon had mail, including a parcel from his sister Ila that contained homemade strawberry jam and some cookies. Though broken in transit, the biscuits tasted delicious. Even more welcome was a bundle of letters from Florence. Burgin wrote to her whenever he could, sending the letters to Australia by airmail. The cost was 70 cents a letter, as opposed to nothing for surface mail, but he did not mind the expense. Her letters kept him sane, and he read them right away.

She was, she wrote, 'still working at the biscuit factory in Melbourne, putting in long hours'. Her little brother – the one Burgin and Jim Burke had carried piggyback at Melbourne train station – had chicken pox, but was getting better. She ended the letter by telling Burgin she loved him and was counting the days till his return. It was enough to move the hard-bitten Texan to tears. He missed her 'terribly', and kept getting flashbacks of things they had said and done in Melbourne: walks 'through the park full of flowers, buying fresh fruit from the little stand at Young & Jackson, just sitting on a bench in the sun'. At night, lying in his cot, Burgin would remember his twenty-first birthday when he 'drank a little too much and we sat in the dark movie theater and she cradled my spinning head in her arms and kept kissing me'. It made his heart ache for her, and he wondered if he should have married her before he shipped out, when he had had the chance.[12]

23

Changing Places

Pavuvu Island, May–June 1944

It was customary for US servicemen who had been overseas for two years and/or fought in two campaigns to be rotated home. If the rules had been followed, K Company would have lost the majority of its senior leaders after New Britain, including Captain 'Ack-Ack' Haldane, Lieutenant 'Hillbilly' Jones, Gunnery Sergeants Thurman Miller and Mo Darsey, Sergeants Jim McEnery and Corporal John 'the Mad Russian' Teskevich. In the event, only Miller and Darsey – the pair who had served the longest – were given the option. The others were told they would have to stay on for one more campaign because, thanks to heavy Marine casualties, there were not enough experienced officers and senior NCOs to go around.[1]

A total of 260 officers and 4,600 Marines from the 1st Marine Division returned to the United States in the late spring and summer of 1944, having served at least twenty-four months overseas. Yet a further 264 officers and 5,750 men who had also been abroad that long, and served in two campaigns, were forced to stay on – or volunteered – for one more battle. They were bolstered by a similar number who had completed at least a year of foreign service and fought at Cape Gloucester, as well as 5,000 or so replacements. It would, therefore, be a largely 'veteran division' that fought the next campaign.[2]

Having met the very high threshold, Miller was told that he was going home. 'But where was home?' he wondered. 'Back in the hills of

Appalachia? In a tent city in North Carolina? Could it have been somewhere in the "land down under" I had loved so much? Or had the Corps become my home?'

The question became even more pressing when, soon after hearing that he was about to ship out to the States, Miller was summoned by Captain Haldane. 'T. I.,' he said, 'I'll get right to it. If you stay for the next one, I'll make you Top Sergeant.'

Miller felt conflicted. He liked Haldane and they had always got on well. Yet lately he had been troubled by the thought that his luck, which had held so far, was 'running out'. He made his decision. 'Close Crop,' he said, using his personal nickname, on account of the skipper's shaved head, 'you keep your Top Sergeant's stripes. I'm going home.'

After Miller's refusal, Haldane asked Mo Darsey to stay on and he agreed.* Miller did not expect to see either of them again. A few days later he was told to pack up and prepare to leave at eight the following morning. It was no big deal: his bag had been packed and ready for weeks. That night, after dark, he was visited in his tent by Second Lieutenant Bill Bauerschmidt, the keen, error-prone but well-intentioned leader of 3rd Platoon. Despite their run-ins, Miller could see 'no malice' in the young officer's eyes. Instead he 'saw the look of an honest man who had found himself', tempered by battle, hardened by life in the jungle and 'wiser in his ways'. Miller recalled: 'He held out his hand and thanked me for the help I'd been. I told him I was only doing my job and it had been a pleasure knowing him.'

The following day, as he watched the island of Pavuvu recede from the deck of the troop transport USS *General John Pope*, Miller felt wretched. He tried to shake his gloom by gazing at the abundant marine life: whales blowing, dolphins leaping and sharks circling the fantail. It did no good, because in the 'churning wake' he could see the 'faces of the friends' he had left behind. Men, like Mo Darsey and Jim McEnery,

* Shortly before Peleliu, Darsey moved to another unit and David P. Bailey became K Company's first sergeant. Bailey had also fought on Guadalcanal and at Cape Gloucester with the 3/5 Marines.

he had known since the New River camp, almost three years earlier. Now he was leaving, while they would fight on.

Miller should have felt euphoric that he had survived two brutal campaigns and was returning to the woman he loved. Instead he was wracked with guilt for abandoning his fellow Devil Dogs before their great adventure was over.[3]

Arriving on the same ships that took Thurman Miller and the other long-service veterans home were thousands of wide-eyed replacements from the States. Among the first to reach the island was 20-year-old PFC Sterling Mace, a cocky young tearaway from Queen's, New York. 'We arrived at Pavuvu during the night,' recalled Mace. 'The next morning they walked us down the gangplank with only the clothes on our backs, helmets on our heads, and seabags on our shoulders. We didn't even have weapons.'

Raised in a small bungalow in the 'Little Italy' district of Queen's, Mace loved the colour and vibrancy of his tight community of 'one million immigrants and natives'. Money was scarce, as it was across America during the Depression, and young Sterling and his elder sister Mickey would get their clothes from a handout store and shoes that rarely fitted. Yet they could have been 'a lot worse off' – their dad even owned a car – and Mace's childhood memories were mostly happy ones. He got his first taste of military discipline when, at the age of sixteen, he and some friends were sent to the Citizens' Military Training Camp at Fort Dix, New Jersey, as punishment for stealing food from a boat. There he was taught to use a bayonet, fire the M1903 Springfield rifle, march, fall in and even walk through the tear-gas room. It was all good practice for the real thing.

A keen and talented sportsman, Mace was about to take the field to play halfback for his local football team – the Glen Morris Bonecrushers – when he heard news of the Japanese attack on Pearl Harbor from a car radio. The universal response, Mace remembered, was: '*Where in the hell is Pearl Harbor?* Nobody had the foggiest that 108,504 U.S. Servicemen would have to die in the Pacific Theater of Operations to answer that question, to make things right.'

Soon after the attack, he tried to follow a close buddy into the US Navy,* but failed the sight test because of his 'lazy' right eye. He got around this minor disability when he applied to join the US Marine Corps in late 1942, aged eighteen, by memorizing the eye chart. Sent to boot camp at Parris Island, South Carolina, he was shocked at the constant abuse from the drill instructors. 'Everywhere you go,' he recalled, 'it's shitbird-this and shitbird-that . . . You're a shitbird when they shear the top of your head so you look like a scalded dog. You're a shitbird for standing in the front of the line, and a shitbird for standing in the rear.' The one consolation was that no one recruit was victimized; they all were.

Having passed out of Parris Island, Mace was sent to Camp Lejeune (formerly New River)† in North Carolina for further training and to await deployment. He took advantage of a 24-hour pass to lose his virginity to a cheap hooker in nearby Sugar Hill. 'Alright. Come on boy. Let's go,' she tells him, as if the war might end 'any second', and with it her chances of 'turning a buck into bullion'.

It was almost a year later that Mace sailed from San Diego on overseas duty and, during the long voyage, became good pals with two other replacements: PFC Seymour 'Sy' Levy, a 17-year-old from Brooklyn; and PFC Bill Leyden from Valley Stream, a small town just outside New York City. He liked them for different reasons. Levy was a nice Jewish kid, well-built and good-looking with thick dark hair, who despite his age was still a pretty tough Marine. He tended to wear a white T-shirt and rolled-up dungaree pants, exposing the socks above his boondockers. Leyden, on the other hand, was a 'typical New Yorker, with the gift of the gab, full of ideas, always looking for a new angle, smart on his feet'. Tall, energetic and outspoken, with 'wavy hair and an infectious smile', he had a real eye for the ladies and 'could have sold a Cadillac to a bunch of blind Amish'.

* That friend, Sonny Campbell, was killed when his aircraft carrier, USS *Hornet*, was sunk in the Battle of the Santa Cruz Islands in late October 1942.

† The camp was renamed in late 1942 in honour of Major General John A. Lejeune, the recently deceased 13th Commandant of the Marine Corps.

Told they were joining the fabled 1st Marine Division, they hoped to find it in Australia. Instead they made a five-day stop at New Caledonia – a 'dump', in Mace's opinion, with its waterfront full of 'filthy concrete buildings and dirty garbage-infested roads, lined with sickly coconut trees' – before moving on to Pavuvu. 'It wasn't necessarily an eyesore,' wrote Mace, 'but it definitely didn't give the impression that it was an island resort either.'

Once on shore, Mace, Leyden and Levy were taken to a large bivouac area where a veteran NCO called the roll and gave them their assignments as riflemen in K Company, 3rd Battalion, 5th Marines: Leyden in the 1st Platoon; Levy and Mace in the 3rd Platoon. 'That was a nice luxury,' remembered Mace, 'since we all arrived together and we didn't know anybody.'

Before leaving the bivouac area, Mace and Levy were approached by some Old Breed veterans. 'Hey, fellas,' said a short blond-haired Marine, bare to the waist, 'wanna see somethin' great?' Unfastening a pouch from around his neck, he opened it to reveal a handful of gold bits, some roughly in the shape of teeth, but most just tiny fragments of yellow. 'So, whatcha think o' these, boys?' he asked, grinning. 'Pulled 'em out myself!'

After an embarrassed pause, Levy said: 'Yeah, those sure are . . . *great.* Boy, I bet there's a coupla hundred bucks' worth in there.'

The Marine frowned and pulled the drawstring on the bag. 'More like a coupla *thousand*!' he said, narrowing his eyes. 'But don't none of you boys be gettin' any funny ideas, ya hear? You'll get your own gold soon enough – or if ya don't, you can bet the Nips'll get you *first*.'

He grinned and stalked away, leaving Mace and Levy open-mouthed. They had heard the stories that the Japanese liked gold teeth, but did not believe for a minute that US Marines were systematically excavating them from the mouths of corpses. Here was evidence. 'Jesus Christ, Sy,' muttered Mace, 'who'd we fall in with? A buncha friggin' cannibals?'

Not quite, wrote Mace later, but they were not exactly 'Edisons and Einsteins, either'.

In fact, when he met up with his colleagues in 3rd Platoon a day later, Mace's first impressions were mixed. He liked the platoon leader Bill

Bauerschmidt, 'with his high-top lace boots that were never tied all the way but instead they flared at the tops'. Mace wrote: 'He had a hop to his walk, and his eyes tilted in like a boxer's. Bill carried his dad's World War 1 .45 service revolver into combat – engraved with the initials *WB* on its grip – dearly wanting to make his father proud. Beyond pride, Bill had no other choice. He had to be a fine officer, in order to counteract some of the deficiencies inherent in our platoon.'

Mace also thought highly of Platoon Sergeant Harry J. Spiece from Philadelphia, a 'great Marine' who, for his part, did not always appreciate the new arrival's 'wiseass New York ways'. He was less taken with his squad leader, Sergeant Anthony J. 'Tony' Palmisano, another replacement who was yet to see action. A 'dark, heavyset Italian, almost a little too fat', Palmisano was oddly unassertive. 'His heart,' concluded Mace, 'simply wasn't in it.'

Among the other 3rd Platoon replacements who made an impression on Mace were PFC Orley Uhls, 'a nice, quiet country boy from Illinois' with a 'warm smile' who would be the only Marine to leave a bar sober; Private Frankie Ocepek from Cleveland, Ohio, who 'loved humor – laughed at anything, 5' 6" and wielded a nineteen-pound BAR, thirty-four years old, black hair, graying at the temples, probably never had a bad word to say about anyone'; PFC Frank Minkewitz, 'a tall Polack, married, thinning hair, probably a draft board decision'; and PFC Gene Holland, 'artsy, a deep thinker, like something was in his mind always wanting out'. Holland's father had died when he was a child, 'so he was raised by his mother and sister'.

Mace admired many of the veterans in the platoon: Corporal John 'the Mad Russian' Teskevich, PFC Roy 'Railroad' Kelly (whose life Teskevich had saved at Cape Gloucester), and PFC Jesse Googe who had 'lied about his age to get into the Marines and served on Guadalcanal, maybe at sixteen'. One veteran that Mace did not hit it off with, however, was the platoon guide, Sergeant Jim McEnery. 'Jim was a snappy Marine,' remembered Mace, 'with a Leo Carillo pencil-thin mustache, coming at us with his unmistakeable Brooklyn accent, calling us out for a work detail.'

Despite the rain, McEnery lined them up in the company street. 'Alright, you Marines,' he said, 'when I say fall out, I mean fall out! We're on a working party here, you guys, so get your shit together and follow me!'

Walking behind the sergeant, Mace turned to his neighbour and said: 'Who the fuck is this big-shit Marine?' He would soon find out.[4]

At first, McEnery did not have much time for the new guys. Many would turn out to be 'top-notch Marines', he wrote later, 'but I swear some of them acted like real chowderheads when they first arrived'. Top of his list was Mace's buddy Sy Levy, whose 'mother had damn near disowned him for lying about his age to get in the Marines', and McEnery could see why. He was 'book smart enough' to get top grades in school, and liked to recite poetry by Rudyard Kipling in a mock British accent, but in other respects was hopelessly naïve and impractical. Hearing about the gasoline lamps that 'Pop' Haney had built, he tried to build one of his own in a Coke bottle. It exploded and set his tent on fire.

Despite incidents like this, McEnery liked Levy, a 'nice kid and a dedicated Marine who served as a morale booster for his fellow replacements and even for older guys like me'. But he had his doubts that Levy would hold up under the strain of combat, and spent extra time briefing him about things he would need to know.

Bill Leyden was a different proposition. Another New York smartass with Irish roots, he did 'dumb stuff' not because he did not know better (like Levy), but because he was always testing the boundaries. 'Leyden,' wrote McEnery, 'liked to think of himself as a daredevil, and he took pride in taking risks that other guys wouldn't. This made me kind of nervous because risk takers have a habit of dying young on a battlefield, and I knew he'd have plenty of chances to show how daring he was in the months ahead.'[5]

24

Operation Stalemate

Southwest Pacific, June–July 1944

On 2 June 1944 – four days before the Allies launched Operation Overlord in Normandy, northern France – the 1st Marine Division HQ received word of its next objective in the Pacific from a Joint Chiefs paper entitled 'Concept of the Palau Operation'. Codenamed Stalemate, it would take place 'after the Marianas campaign, with a target date of September 8'.[1]

As Major General Rupertus had yet to return from the States – where he was enjoying some leave and arranging the rotation of battalion commanders – Brigadier General Oliver Smith was in temporary command of the division. Palau, discovered Smith, is an archipelago of several large islands and more than one hundred small ones at the westernmost extremity of the vast Caroline Islands chain, lying just above the equator and roughly 500 miles from both the Philippines to the west and New Guinea to the south. It was its very remoteness, even from the rest of Micronesia, that had 'long retarded the islands' development and delayed knowledge of their existence to the outside world'. Since the early eighteenth century the islands had been ruled by foreign powers: first Spain, then Imperial Germany (which bought the Carolines, Marshalls and Marianas from the Spanish in 1899), and, most recently, Japan, after it had seized Germany's Pacific possessions at the start of World War I.

By 1941, the population of Palau was 6,200 natives of Micronesian stock and 16,000 Japanese civilians who had emigrated from the home islands. More than half the natives lived on the largest island, Babelthuap, while most of the Japanese were on the smaller islands to the south, such as Koror and Peleliu. The whole archipelago covered an area of 175 square miles and, apart from Angaur in the south and a couple of small atolls in the north, was encircled by a huge coral reef.[2]

The initial plan, outlined in the Joint Chiefs' paper, was to land on three of the larger islands: the US Army's XXIV Corps – consisting of the 7th and 96th Infantry Divisions – would capture Babelthuap; while the 1st Marine Division (with the US Army's 81st Infantry Division in support) seized first Peleliu and then nearby Angaur. The justification for the mission, according to Smith, was as follows:

> (a) There was a good airfield on Peleliu and an uncompleted airstrip on Babelthuap. Angaur was suitable for the construction of an airport. Planes based in the Palaus could support General MacArthur's invasion of the Philippines. Mindanao was only 550 miles from Peleliu.
> (b) Possession of the Palaus, together with the Marianas, which were being attacked first, would effectively cut off the by-passed Japanese bases in the Central Pacific.
> (c) Possession of the Palaus would give us a fair anchorage, Kossal Passage, at the north end of Babelthuap and a more limited anchorage at Koror.[3]

The man with overall responsibility for Stalemate, and the follow-up operations to capture the island of Yap (280 miles northeast of the Palaus) and the Ulithi atoll* (120 miles from Yap) – also part of the western Carolines – was Admiral 'Bull' Halsey, who had just relinquished command of the South Pacific Area to take over the US Third Fleet, with its temporary headquarters in Pearl Harbor. Yet when asked by the Joint Chiefs on 18 June if he would consider bypassing any of

* A ring of thirty islets surrounding an enormous lagoon that was almost 20 miles long and up to 10 miles wide.

the 'present selected objectives and proceeding at earlier date to Japan or Formosa' – a question also posed to Nimitz and MacArthur – he answered in the affirmative. His war diary noted: 'Admiral Halsey expressed the view that part or all of the immediate objectives in the western Carolines could be by-passed, and the operations against the Philippines could be accelerated.'

Since first hearing of the plan to capture the western Carolines at a conference with Admirals King and Nimitz in San Francisco in May 1944, Halsey had had his doubts. 'Ulithi had a useful anchorage,' he recalled, 'but I saw no need for any of the other islands. Yap's only value was as a minor staging point for aircraft. The Palaus threatened the route between New Guinea and the Philippines, but although they also offered an anchorage – Kossol Roads – and several sites for airfields, I felt that they would have to be bought at a prohibitive price in casualties. In short, I feared another Tarawa.'*

Halsey, however, was overruled by both Nimitz and MacArthur, who insisted that Stalemate should go ahead. Where he and Nimitz were in total agreement, however, was on longer-term strategy. 'Almost alone among senior admirals,' wrote Halsey, 'Chester and I advocated invading the central Philippines, building a major base, and jumping from there to the home islands of Japan, via Iwo Jima and Okinawa. Ernie King, on the other hand, strongly recommended by-passing the Philippines and occupying Formosa, which I considered more redoubtable and more useless than the Palaus.'

When Halsey's chief of staff, Rear Admiral R. B. 'Mick' Carney, protested to King that the Philippines were indispensable, the latter asked: 'Do you want to make a London out of Manila?'

'No, sir,' responded Carney. 'I want to make an England out of Luzon.'[4]

One high-profile gathering to agree the best long-term strategy to defeat Japan – though one not attended by the Joint Chiefs of Staff,

* The vicious three-day battle for Tarawa Atoll in the Gilbert Islands, in November 1943, had cost the 2nd Marine Division more than 3,000 casualties. Of the 4,800 Japanese and Korean defenders, only 136 surrendered; the others perished.

who suspected the president of electioneering – was the meeting between President Roosevelt, Nimitz and MacArthur in Pearl Harbor, in late July 1944. Nimitz presented King's proposal to the ailing president, who was in the midst of his fourth presidential campaign. It involved bypassing Luzon and the northern Philippines and launching the next major offensive against the island of Formosa (modern Taiwan) which, Nimitz explained, was ideally placed to cut off Japan's oil supplies by sea. Moreover, air forces based there could strike Japanese targets in China and the Japanese home islands themselves. Luzon was less useful, because if the more southerly island of Leyte were captured, the Allies would have an adequate anchorage in the central Philippines for the advance on Formosa.

Interestingly, this option was also the preference of the other Joint Chiefs – George C. Marshall and 'Hap' Arnold – who both felt it offered the quickest route to defeat Japan. Nimitz, as we have seen, was not convinced the plan would work, and preferred to take the western Carolines first, before invading the central Philippines and Iwo Jima. But, loyal to a fault, he argued for his superior's plan as if it were his own.

MacArthur responded with a masterly presentation, delivered without notes, that tapped into the president's political considerations. America had a moral obligation to free the Philippines, he said, and release Filipinos and Americans who were suffering untold hardships in Japanese concentration camps. Filipinos – and, indeed, the rest of Asia – might forgive America for abandoning them in 1942, but not for bypassing them in 1945. In any case, said MacArthur, Luzon was more important than Formosa in a strategic sense because with it went control of the South China Sea and Japan's communications to its southern possessions. Whereas bypassing Luzon would expose US forces on Formosa and elsewhere to devastating attacks from Japanese bombers stationed there. Nimitz agreed with this point and, when questioned by Roosevelt, said he could support either operation. This prompted Roosevelt to suggest a compromise: the recovery of Luzon with the forces available in the western Pacific, while a decision on Formosa could wait. In fact, no definite decision was taken because the Joint Chiefs continued to debate the merits of Luzon versus Formosa until October.[5]

What *was* decided on Hawaii was that Operation Stalemate would go ahead as planned. The command structure was as follows: Admiral Halsey (US Third Fleet) was in overall command, though he would not witness the landings because the fleet would be too far to the west, 'blanketing enemy airfields in the central Philippines'; Vice Admiral T. S. 'Ping' Wilkinson, commanding the Joint Expeditionary Force, was in charge of the amphibious phase; Major General Julian C. Smith was commander of all expeditionary troops; while Major Generals Roy Geiger (III Amphibious Corps) and John R. Hodge (XXIV Army Corps) had responsibility for the capture of Peleliu/Angaur and Babelthuap respectively.[6]

Geiger, fifty-nine, was one of the first Marine Corps aviators and had commanded the legendary Cactus Air Force on Guadalcanal with distinction. More recently he had led I Amphibious Corps' conquest of Bougainville. Yet his immediate concern in June 1944 was the recapture of Guam – an operation scheduled to begin in late July – and, as a result, his staff had 'very little time to think about the Palau operation'. Before embarking for Guam, Geiger's staff issued a brief and far from adequate operation plan. It was, therefore, left to Brigadier General Oliver Smith, the 1st Marine Division's acting commander, and his staff to come up with a more detailed and workable version.[7]

Colonel Harold D. 'Bucky' Harris, the intelligence chief, began by studying all the maps, aerial photos, and geographical and hydrographical information that were available for Peleliu and the adjacent islands. He learnt that Peleliu, located just inside the southwest tip of the huge Palau reef, was an oddly shaped coral-limestone island with two elongated arms of land that resembled the claw of a lobster. Approximately six miles long by two wide, it lay on a northeast–southwest axis and was composed of two distinct sections: the southern part, which was relatively flat and wide; and the bigger and more westerly northern arm, some 3,500 yards long and 1,000 wide, which consisted of 'an irregular series of broken coral ridges, narrow valleys, and rugged peaks'. This ridge system – the toughest nut to crack from a military perspective – derived its name from the 550ft Umurbrogol Mountain. Honeycombed with natural caves, and littered with crags, pinnacles and coral rubble, it was ideal terrain for defenders. The smaller and more easterly northern arm quickly tapered off into a series of islets, separated from each other and the longer northern arm by a complex of swamps and shoal coral.

In 1944, the island was heavily wooded with thick jungle scrub, and 'on the thin topsoil of the Umurbrogol ridges grew a sparse, scraggly vegetation that cloaked the contours beneath and defied all attempts at pre-invasion aerial reconnaissance'. With no rivers or lakes, the inhabitants relied mainly on rain water stored in cisterns.

The main military objective on Peleliu was the two-runway airfield, built in an X-pattern, that the Japanese had constructed in the centre of the southern lowlands. Surfaced with hard-packed coral, the airfield was suitable for both bombers and fighters, and included 'ample taxiways, dispersal areas, and turning circles'. To the west and south the airfield was flanked by scrub jungle, interspersed with wild coconut trees and the occasional grassy clearing; to the east a dense mangrove swamp; and to the north an extensive area of administrative buildings and, immediately beyond them, the sharp ridges of what would become known as the Umurbrogol Pocket.[8]

The most important decision for Smith, Harris and Colonel Fields, the operations chief, was choosing where to land. The obvious location was on the west side of the island where the reef was broad and shallow, varying in width from a mile in the north to 400 yards in the south, and the extensive beaches were composed of coarse-textured coral sands, not too steep, and trafficable by wheeled vehicles and tanks. Their preference – the 'best of a poor lot', according to Harris – was for the beaches overlapping the airfield and, on his return to Pavuvu on 1 July, Major General Rupertus concurred. That same day, Rupertus sent Fields to Pearl Harbor to obtain any extra intelligence and to assist with the planning there.[9]

Meanwhile the battle for the Marianas had begun with landings on Saipan by Lieutenant General Holland 'Howlin' Mad' Smith's V

Amphibious Corps on 15 June. With Japanese troop strength on the island at least 40 per cent higher than American intelligence estimates, the struggle to capture Saipan took far longer than anticipated, and it was not until 9 July that hostilities ceased. By then, almost the entire Japanese garrison of 31,000 men had perished, as well as many thousands of civilians (some jumping to their deaths from the so-called 'Suicide Cliff' near the northern tip of the island in the final days of the battle). American casualties of over 3,000 killed and 10,400 wounded – out of the 71,000 troops who landed – were the costliest of the Pacific War to date.

While the fighting raged on Saipan, a huge naval clash – known as the Battle of the Philippine Sea, the last of the five major carrier-versus-carrier engagements of the Pacific War – took place off the Marianas on 19–20 June between the US Navy's Fifth Fleet and the IJN's Mobile Fleet. It resulted in a decisive defeat for the Japanese, who forfeited three aircraft carriers (two sunk by submarines) and more than 600 aircraft in an aerial fight dubbed the 'Great Marianas Turkey Shoot'. American losses, by contrast, were just 120 planes and a battleship damaged.

Even as the Saipan tragedy was unfolding, Emperor Hirohito warned his hawkish prime minister, General Hideki Tojo: 'If we ever lose Saipan, repeated air attacks on Tokyo will follow. No matter what it takes, we have to hold there.'

Following Saipan's fall, not to mention the destruction of most of the IJN's remaining carrier airpower at the Battle of the Philippine Sea, the disgraced Tojo was forced to resign and Kuniaki Koiso, a retired general who had served as governor-general of Korea, replaced him. Behind closed doors there was a recognition by Koiso and his cabinet that the war could no longer be won, and that the best Japan could hope for was a negotiated peace that allowed it to retain at least some of its foreign conquests. In public, however, Koiso insisted that Japan would continue to fight the war with undiminished intensity. 'The government,' he announced on 22 July 1944, 'will firmly adhere to the nation's established foreign policy, and work for a thorough-going realization of the principles of the Greater East Asia, thereby carrying the Holy War to a complete victory and thus setting the Imperial mind at ease.'[10]

The knock-on effect of the protracted fight for Saipan was to delay the landings on the other Mariana Islands of Guam and Tinian until late July (with both in American hands by 10 August). This, in turn, meant that shipping and fire support for Operation Stalemate would not be available for the original date of 8 September. The landing was, as a result, rescheduled for 15 September. At the same time Babelthuap was dropped as an objective by Nimitz on the grounds that, larger and more rugged than Saipan, it would be extremely costly to capture and would in any case be neutralized by the seizure of Peleliu and Angaur. The plan now – rebranded Stalemate II – was for the 1st Marine Division (and a regiment of the 81st Division, held in reserve) to take both Peleliu and Ngesebus, an island just to the north where the Japanese had begun to construct an airfield, while the 81st Division (less one regiment) took care of Angaur once the situation in Peleliu was 'in hand'. The XXIV Corps, meanwhile, originally scheduled to capture Babelthuap, would instead land on 5 October on the small island of Yap, the Palaus' nearest neighbour, where there was a good airfield.

Initial intelligence reports indicated that there were 9,000 Japanese troops on Peleliu and not more than 4,000 on Angaur. In fact, as documents captured on Saipan in July revealed, there were 10,500 men of the formidable 14th Infantry Division on Peleliu – including 6,500 combat troops – commanded by Colonel Kunio Nakagawa of the 2nd Infantry Regiment. Angaur, by contrast, had only 1,400 defenders after the bulk of the 59th Infantry Regiment was withdrawn in late July to strengthen Babelthuap, where the main attack was expected. Unfortunately for the 1st Marine Division, the revised troop estimates 'arrived too late or lacked sufficient corroboration' to justify the alteration of existing tactical plans.[11]

In the early stages of the Pacific War, the Japanese high command had largely ignored the Palaus. But by September 1943, after reverses in New Guinea and the Solomons, Japanese planners began to construct an inner defence line that embraced the areas west of the Marianas,

Carolines and Western New Guinea. The line was created chiefly to buy time, with everything behind it supposed to be a defence in depth. Within this zone, decreed the IGHQ in Tokyo, each Japanese soldier would fight to the death.

With the enemy's capture of the Admiralties and Marshalls in early 1944, bringing all the Carolines within the effective striking range of Allied land-based bombers, the HQ of the Japanese Combined Fleet was transferred from Truk to the less vulnerable Palaus. But a successful air raid by US carrier-borne planes in late March forced them to move again to the Philippines, where a permanent naval base was being constructed. The Palaus, meanwhile, were bolstered on 24 April by the arrival from Manchuria of the veteran 14th Infantry Division – one of the finest in the IJA – commanded by Lieutenant General Sadae Inoue. The bulk of the troops were in Babelthuap, the largest island, while Inoue had his headquarters in Koror, the administrative centre. Assigned to defend Peleliu were Colonel Nakagawa's excellent 2nd Infantry Regiment, a battalion each from the 53rd Independent Mixed Brigade and the 15th Infantry, two naval anti-aircraft battalions, and supporting units of artillery, mortars, signals and light tanks. Confident his men would repel the invader, Nakagawa reported:

> All the officers and men carried in mind the meaning of our sacred war . . . and being a picked Manchukoan regiment that does not expect to return alive and will follow to the death an imperial order, devoted themselves to the endeavour of being the type of soldier who can fight hundreds of men . . . We vow with our unbreakable solidarity we will complete our glorious duty and establish the 'Breakwater of the Pacific'.

Though fewer than 12,000 troops were stationed on Peleliu and Angaur, they could easily be reinforced by some of the 25,000 troops on the other Palau islands, 'many specially trained in amphibious operations'.

Faced with a lack of cooperation on Peleliu from the naval garrison – commanded by a flag officer who was senior in rank to Nakagawa –

Lieutenant General Inoue sent his deputy, Major General Kenjiro Murai, to take nominal command of the island. Yet Colonel Nakagawa would continue to direct its defence, and all key orders were issued in his name. His chief handicap would be the absence of airpower: more than 150 planes were destroyed in the carrier raid of late March and, after the loss of the Marianas in the summer, the IGHQ effectively wrote off the doomed Palau garrison and concentrated its air defences in the Philippines. Nakagawa, however, was still expected 'to conduct a tenacious defense in the event of an American attack, thereby delaying utilization of the coveted airfields by the invaders'.

To achieve his aims, Nakagawa adopted new defensive tactics. Recent American assaults against well-fortified beaches had been extremely costly for the Japanese defenders because of the enemy's ability to unleash a devastating preparatory bombardment. This was not the case on Biak, near the western end of New Guinea, where the Japanese commander had prolonged the fighting in the early summer of 1944 by digging in part of his forces inland. Learning from this, and from the tough defence of Saipan, IGHQ in Tokyo ordered all island garrison commanders to prepare a main line of resistance 'far enough inland from the beach to minimize the effects of the pre-invasion bombardment'. This defence in depth was designed to wear down enemy forces who could be counter-attacked with reserves at the appropriate time.

These instructions were followed to the letter by Nakagawa, who utilized the rugged terrain 'to construct mutually supporting defensive positions' and divided the island into four sectors, each manned by a reinforced battalion, with a second in reserve. He also organized some companies as special counter-attack units with infiltration teams to knock out enemy tanks. Beaches were mined, offshore obstacles erected, anti-tank barriers constructed and barbed wire strung. 'Everywhere,' noted the Marine history of the campaign, 'the dominating terrain was utilized for the placement of artillery, previously zeroed-in on the beaches, to wreak havoc among the assaulting troops. All defensive positions took full advantage of man-made and natural cover and concealment, while yet dominating all invasion approaches.'

On Peleliu's southwest beaches, where the American invasion was planned, the natural offshore obstacles were augmented by tetrahedron-shaped tank obstacles and mines, while a long anti-tank ditch ran parallel to the coast. The beaches were covered by pillboxes and casemates of reinforced concrete, mounted with 37mm and 47mm anti-tank guns. Larger artillery pieces – including a 75mm gun which commanded the entire southern portion of the island – were dug into the dominating Umurbrogol ridges to the north of the airfield. There the Japanese had expanded natural caves and dug tunnels to 'deploy their troops and locate their weapons for a last-ditch stand'. Thus was created a 'mutually interlocking system of concrete pillboxes, entrenchments, gun emplacements, and riflemen's positions'. Food and ammunition had been stored, and no escape routes planned. The defenders would fight to the finish. Shortly before the landings began, Inoue told his men:

> This battle may have a part in the decisive turn of tide in breaking the deadlock of the 'Great Asiatic War'. The entire Army and people of Japan are expecting us to win . . . Rouse yourselves for the sake of your country! Officers and men, you will devote your life to the winning of this battle, and attaining your long cherished desire of annihilating the enemy.[12]

25

Sledgehammer

Pavuvu Island, June 1944

Twenty-year-old PFC Eugene B. Sledge's first sight of the island was from the deck of the troopship *General Howze* as it 'moved into an inlet bordered by large groves of coconut palms' on 2 June. Having departed San Diego with the 46th Replacement Battalion three months earlier, he was excited to be joining the legendary unit that had fought on Guadalcanal and New Britain. 'From the ship,' noted Sledge, 'we could see coral-covered roadways and groups of pyramidal tents among the coconut palms. This was Pavuvu, home of the 1st Marine Division.'

Told they would disembark the following morning, Sledge and the other rookies spent the afternoon hanging over the rail, talking to the 'hollow-eyed and tired' Marines on the pier. He was surprised at how friendly and unassuming the veterans were. 'They made no attempt to impress us green replacements,' he wrote, 'yet they were members of an elite division known to everyone back home.'

Too hot and hyped up to sleep, Sledge checked and rechecked his gear, 'making sure everything was squared away'. He eventually went up on deck to nap in the open air while two Marines sang and played some of the 'finest mountain music' he had heard on a fiddle and a mandolin.

At nine the following morning, carrying the 'usual mountain of gear', he and his fellow replacements trudged down the gangplank and were directed to a line of waiting trucks. They passed a line of veterans waiting to go home. 'Are we glad to see you,' said one. Tanned and worn out, they looked happy to be leaving. 'For them, the war was over,' wrote Sledge. 'For us it was just beginning.'[1]

Born and brought up in a comfortable upper-middle-class family in Mobile, Alabama, Sledge was the younger son of Dr Edward Sledge, a prominent local physician who had been elected president of the Alabama Medical Association in the late 1930s. His mother Mary Frank (née Sturdivant) was from an influential Selma family, and was daughter of the dean of women at Huntington College in Montgomery. Sledge grew up in Georgia Cottage, an elegant 1840 Greek Revival house in the more affluent quarter of Mobile, a small port city of fewer than 80,000 inhabitants. It was a comfortable life of 'servants and family retainers, and pastimes that included deer and dove hunting on private estates . . . and squirrel hunting in Baldwin County'.[2]

Having graduated from high school in 1942, Sledge entered Marion Military Institute with the intention of becoming an officer 'in some technical branch of the U.S. Army'. But, 'prompted by a deep feeling of uneasiness that the war might end' before he could 'get into overseas combat', he enlisted in the US Marine Corps in December 1942.[3]

Sledge's decision was influenced by his high school buddy Sid Phillips who, spurred on by news of the Japanese attack on Pearl Harbor, had joined the Marines a year earlier at the age of seventeen. Like many Southern boys, Sledge and Phillips were fascinated by Civil War history and had spent many a weekend tramping over the battlefields near Mobile in search of musket balls, shell fragments, buckles and other kit. At home, Sledge kept Civil War-era firearms and uniforms in a 'treasure room'.[4] Both were proud Southerners who identified closely with the region's strong military tradition. 'Whatever its historical origins or validity,' wrote Aaron Trehub, author of an essay on Sledge and the region's military culture, 'the notion that the South has a special relationship to the military history and culture of the United States is widely accepted, and the identification of the region with militarism and violence has a long pedigree.'

There was for Sledge, moreover, a strong personal connection: both his great-grandfathers had fought as Confederate officers in the Civil War; his father had served as a medical officer in the US Army in World War I, treating victims of shell-shock; and his elder brother Ed had become an officer in the US Army after Pearl Harbor.[5] For all these reasons, Sledge had wanted to sign up with Phillips. But he was forbidden to do so by his parents because he had to finish high school and, more importantly, had a heart murmur that his father had detected.[6] Sledge's future wife later confirmed that he had been afflicted by 'many childhood illnesses'. Yet Sledge himself made no mention of the heart murmur in any of his writing – which was extensive – and it certainly did not hold him back when he joined the Marines a year later. He did say, however, that his parents and brother Ed wanted him to stay in college for as long as possible – presumably to keep him out of harm's way – and his decision to leave Marion did not please any of them.

Sledge mollified his family, a little, by applying to join the new V-12 Navy College Training Program, which was designed to increase the number of commissioned officers by sending servicemen to colleges and universities across the United States. Once they had completed their bachelor's degrees, they were expected to enrol in a three-month officer candidate course. Sledge's brother Ed – by then a lieutenant in the US Army's 741st Tank Battalion – had promised that life would be 'more beautiful' as an officer. His parents, not surprisingly, were 'mildly distraught' at the thought of their son joining the Marines 'as an enlisted man – that is "cannon-fodder"'. They might have changed their minds if they had known that junior officers had the highest death rate of any rank in the Marines.

In Sledge's case, it never became an issue because he flunked out of the V-12 Program after just a single semester at the Georgia Institute of Technology in Atlanta. 'It was,' he wrote later, 'all but impossible to concentrate on academics. Most of us felt we had joined the Marines to fight, yet here we were college boys again. The situation was more than many of us could stand. At the end of the first semester, ninety of us – half of the detachment – flunked out of school so we could go into the Corps as enlisted men.'[7]

Sledge's implication is that he failed on purpose. He made the same claim, years later, in a letter to a friend. 'It has never entered my mind,' he insisted, 'that I "washed out of the V-12 program." To me, I got out of it the only way [I could], i.e., I purposely flunked out . . . We felt no sense of failure, but on the contrary, we felt we were doing our duty by getting into the war . . . There was no stigma or shame attached to it at all. I would do the same thing again.'[8]

At the time he gave a very different version of events in letters to his parents. On 9 September 1943, for example, Sledge admitted to his mother that 43 per cent of Marine trainees at Georgia Tech were failing some subjects and he was 'no exception'. He had, however, told the dean that he would try to 'do better'. He added: 'If it weren't for my promise to you I would have told him the opposite like many of the boys did. But you and Father always keep promises to me & so I'll do the same to you. But I'll really be glad to leave here.'

In his next letter, Sledge said he felt conflicted about not being on the list of Marines who were being sent to Parris Island. 'I hate to leave here by failure,' he explained, 'but I'll be glad to do so. When I'm through P.I. [boot camp] I'll really have self-confidence. I'll have reason for it. I'll be a man then, but this fooling around isn't good for anyone.' If he had chosen his own course, he added, he could have been an officer 'in no time'. But it was 'too late now'.

This implicit criticism of his parents provoked a stinging response from his mother that caused Sledge to backtrack hastily. 'I am thoroughly ashamed for saying what I did,' he wrote on 5 October, '& apologize. No one could ask for better parents than I have. It's just that I, like Sid [Phillips], want to get into the brawl & was really disappointed when I joined & was put into school. But I hope I don't have to stay here too long.'[9]

If these letters from Atlanta started alarm bells ringing in the Sledge household, the address on the next one confirmed their worst fears: San Diego, California. Written on 5 November, it contained Sledge's unconvincing explanation as to what had happened:

> The captain told me at the last minute that I might have to come to boot camp. As I had passed enough hours to stay, he asked me if I desired to stay & I said I did. He thought it over & said because I had been sent to the wrong school & couldn't transfer, I must go to San Diego. As I wasn't taking an engineering course I would have to take one next semester & with my past college courses wouldn't have a chance. So you see I don't feel bad about coming here.

He got a little closer to the truth in his follow-up letter, written on the 9th. 'There are,' he explained, 'about 1,000 college training boys like myself here. Many of them were gyped like I was . . . For yours and Father's sake, I will always be sorry I was a failure. But I have one consolation, that is if I had passed everything I would be here anyway. So you see I'm really not a failure.'[10]

Unwilling to admit to his parents that, contrary to his promises, he had deliberately failed the programme, Sledge was trying to muddy the waters. In truth, he resented their persistent refusal to let him join the Marines as an enlisted man – first with Sid Phillips, then when he dropped out of Marion – and it was only a matter of time before he defied them. The trigger point, he told a Marine officer many years later, was a throwaway jibe that had touched a sore nerve. He explained:

> I enlisted to fight. However, I was sent straight to Georgia Tech., given a pile of books and told that my duty was to study hard in order to become a Marine officer. I was told that Marines are Marines are Marines regardless of their billet . . . However, one day on liberty, four Marines, who were service troops at a nearby Navy installation, called me a 'college boy Marine'. I had never been so humiliated. Determined like myself not to sit out the war in college, over half of the Marine detachment at Tech. purposely flunked out at the end of the first semester and were sent to San Diego.[11]

During the train ride to the west coast, Sledge and his fellow drop-outs were in high spirits, as if they were heading 'for a picnic instead of boot camp – and war'. They played cards and practical jokes on each other, and waved, yelled and whistled at any females they passed. The other rail traffic was almost exclusively military, including flatcars loaded with tanks, halftracks, artillery pieces and trucks, and other troop trains going in both directions. At San Diego, they were taken by bus to the Marine Corps Recruit Depot ('boot camp') and given the traditional welcome: 'You'll be sorree!!'

Sledge joined fifty-nine other 'boots' in Platoon 984, under a solidly built, ramrod-straight drill instructor (DI) called Corporal Doherty. 'He glared at us,' recalled Sledge, 'like a wolf whose first and foremost desire was to tear us limb from limb. He gave me the impression that the only reason he didn't do so was that the Marine Corps wanted to use us for cannon fodder.'

For the next six weeks – shouting in an 'icy, menacing manner'– Doherty drilled the recruits mercilessly in the 'deep, soft sand' of a nearby beach, taught them to crawl with weapon in hand, and got them to practise early morning rifle calisthenics, a long series of tiring exercises that hardened their bodies and refined their hearing. They would rise at 4:00 a.m. and, having shaved, dressed and eaten, were at the mercy of the DI until taps at ten in the evening. Even then, they could be roused at any time for rifle inspection, close-order drill, or to run around the parade ground. Only later did Sledge understand the reason for this 'seemingly cruel and senseless harassment': to prepare him for the chronic lack of sleep that every front-line soldier has to endure. 'Combat,' he wrote, 'guaranteed sleep of the permanent type only.'

On the range, Sledge was disappointed to miss qualifying as Expert rifleman by just two points. Yet he wore the Sharpshooter's Maltese Cross-shaped badge with pride,* and was quick to remind his Yankee buddies that most of the high shooters in the platoon were 'Southern

* The Expert marksman badge, by contrast, was two crossed rifles in a laurel wreath.

boys'. Finally, after eight gruelling weeks, it was over. They were the honour platoon and Corporal Doherty had done his job well. 'We were hard physically,' wrote Sledge, 'had developed endurance, and had learned our lessons. Perhaps more important, we were tough mentally.'[12]

Late in the afternoon of 24 December 1943, they fell in without rifles or cartridge belts, and dressed in service greens, to receive three bronze Marine Corps Eagle, Globe and Anchor badges which they put in their pockets. They were then marched to an amphitheatre to hear the short and affable camp commandant tell them: 'Men, you have successfully completed your recruit training and are now United States Marines. Put on your Marine Corps emblems and wear them with pride. You have a great and proud tradition to uphold. You are members of the world's finest fighting outfit, so be worthy of it.'

Sledge was next posted to Camp Elliott for a two-month stint of combat training. It was the only period during his wartime service that he lived under a roof: in neat H-shaped wooden barracks, painted cream. The NCOs 'seemed relaxed to the point of being lethargic', and there was no yelling or screaming, a welcome change from boot camp. By lectures and demonstrations, he and the other newly minted Marines were introduced to a variety of weapons: mortars, machine guns, automatic rifles and anti-tank guns. Asked for his preference, Sledge selected the 60mm mortar. It was, the instructor told him, an 'effective and important infantry weapon' that could be used to 'break up enemy attacks' and 'soften enemy defenses'. They would be firing over the heads of their buddies, and so needed to know exactly what they were doing. A short round would kill and maim their own men.

Once familiar with the gun drill – 'during which the bipod was unstrapped and unfolded from carrying position, the base plate set firmly on the deck, the bipod leg spikes pressed into the [ground], and the sight snapped into place on the gun' – they tried live firing at empty oil drums on a hillside. When the first round 'burst with a dull *bang* about two hundred yards out on the range', Sledge suddenly realized how deadly a mortar could be. 'A cloud of black smoke appeared at the point of impact,' he recalled. 'Flying steel fragments kicked up little puffs of dust all around an area about nine by eighteen yards.'

Hand-to-hand combat training followed, mostly judo and knife-fighting. It never occurred to Sledge and his fellow trainees that war might kill or cripple them. Their chief concern was that they would be 'too afraid' to do their jobs under fire, and be branded 'yellow'. It was some relief, therefore, to hear from two Bougainville veterans that everybody gets scared in combat. 'Anybody says he don't,' said one, 'is a damn liar.'[13]

With his training complete, Sledge departed San Diego Harbor on the last day of February 1944 on the *President Polk*, a former luxury liner. A week later – referring to his elder brother who was in the UK preparing for D-Day – Sledge wrote to his parents: 'Edward is doing his job & I'll try to do mine. No one will ever say that your sons didn't do their part for their country. Just don't worry about me . . . The ship is good & the navy feeds us royally.'

Sent first to New Caledonia, he and the rest of the 46th Replacement Battalion spent five weeks learning about Japanese weapons, tactics and combat methods, and route-marching through the hills. Sledge also found time to write home, including a letter to his maternal aunt 'Ta Ta',* a dog breeder who had given him his beloved cocker spaniel Deacon. In an earlier note, 'Ta Ta' had tried to compliment her nephew by saying he looked like an RAF fighter pilot in his service photo. The prickly Sledge was furious. 'If a man told me that,' he informed his aunt, 'I'd grab him by the stacking swivel and blacken his sights. In other words push his face in. Not that I have anything against the RAF. But I'm in an outfit with 169 years of fighting spirit and tradition behind it and I don't care to be told that I resemble a "fly-fly glamour" boy.'

* Ta-Ta (pronounced Tay-Tay) – full name Octavia Sturdivant Wynn (born 1889) – lived with her husband Charles 'Pinkie' Wynn in a modest Cape Cod cottage in Selma, Alabama. She was a society editor and columnist for the *Selma Times-Journal*, and often wrote about history. (John S. Sledge, 'Clio's Confederates: The Women Who Gave Me My Path', *Alabama Heritage*, Fall 2017, 64–5.)

In another letter, he admonished his mother for sending him newspaper clippings of 'strikes, racial trouble, and political bickering'. He added: 'If there is one thing that makes a boy feel low over here, it is the thought of trouble back in the U.S.' In future he wanted to hear about 'peaceful happenings' like 'hunting, science, history, etc.'.

By now, Sledge knew he was bound for the 1st Marine Division and a possible reunion with his close buddy Sid Phillips, who had fought on Guadalcanal and Cape Gloucester as an 81mm mortarman with H (Heavy Weapons) Company, 2/1 Marines. 'I got a letter from Sid forwarded from Camp Elliott,' Sledge wrote to his mother on 11 April. 'He says he thinks he is about ready to go home but if I'm put in his outfit he will stay over here until we go home together. Boy it will be good to see him. I hope I am transferred to his outfit.'[14]

On 28 May, Sledge and the rest of the 46th Replacement Battalion left New Britain in the *General Howze* – the freshly painted, spick-and-span troopship was a great improvement on their previous vessel – and reached Pavuvu five days later. Once on shore, they were taken to a large parking area paved with coral and divided into groups by a lieutenant with a clipboard. To Sledge's group of a hundred or so, he said: 'Third Battalion, 5th Marines.' Sledge wrote later that if he had had an option – which of course he did not – he would have chosen the 'Fighting Fifth' because of its proud record in World War I and connection to the 'old Corps'. He added: 'I felt as though I had rolled the dice and won.'

This was artistic licence. At the time, as his letter to his mother made clear, he wanted to join Sid Phillips in H Company, 2/1 Marines. But it was not to be. Driven in trucks 'along winding coral roads by the bay and through coconut groves', Sledge and the others were dropped outside the 3/5 Marines' HQ. There an NCO assigned Sledge to K Company. Soon, Second Lieutenant 'Duke' Ellington appeared and asked the fifteen or so men who had received crew-served weapons training (mortars and machine guns) their preference. Sledge plumped for 60mm mortars and 'tried to look too small to carry a seventy-pound flamethrower'. It worked. Assigned to the 60mm mortar section, he moved his gear into the tent that housed the second squad, led by Sergeant R. V. Burgin.[15]

The squad had a distinctly 'Southern' flavour: Burgin and one of the ammunition carriers, George Sarrett, were from Texas; the gunner Corporal 'Snafu' Shelton from Louisiana. As an Alabaman and former alumnus of Marion Military Institute (like Ellington), Sledge should have felt right at home. Yet his privileged upbringing and college education set him apart from the other enlisted men, all of whom came from blue-collar backgrounds, and for a time Sledge was the butt of jokes. 'The only damn job you ever had at home,' Burgin told him, 'was feeding the dog.'[16]

He took the ragging in good heart, as was expected, and bellyached with the other replacements when they were sent on work details, hauling rotting coconuts and coral. Burgin had little sympathy. 'I had just come off of four months of battle,' he recalled, 'where I was sleeping in foxholes when it would be raining and I'd wake up the next morning with water up to my chin. They'd been sleeping on momma's white sheets in Marine Corps barracks. Now they thought they'd fallen into the hellhole of creation, and I guess from their point of view they had.'[17]

Slowly but surely, however, this 'quiet, studious young man from Alabama' was accepted into the squad. It became official when they gave him his predictable, but not entirely suitable, nickname of 'Sledgehammer'.[18]

26

'They really put on a show'

Pavuvu Island, June–August 1944

Corporal Sid Phillips was relaxing on his cot when he noticed, through the open tent flap, 'someone coming down the company street looking in each tent'. When the figure was three tents away, he recognized his good buddy Eugene Sledge. Running into the street, he hollered Sledge's childhood nickname, 'Ugin!'

They embraced and 'pounded on each other and rolled around wrestling on the ground shouting and screaming'. A large crowd gathered, thinking it was a fight. Phillips put the onlookers straight by introducing his friend, and then resumed the mock battle. For Sledge, it was a relief to find Sid 'just like he always was'. In the days to come, they spent much of their spare time together, talking about home and the war. Knowing how sensitive Sledge could be, Phillips did his best to conceal from him the truth about combat in the Pacific: the mud and rain; the hunger and exhaustion; and the sight, sound and smell of dead and dying men. He worried that Sledge would find the indignity and randomness of battlefield death hard to come to terms with. So he tried to underplay the danger and discomfort by saying that a Marine's greatest enemy was boredom.

Sledge took the bait, informing his parents that a Marine spent most of his time 'on his bunk reading a funny paper' and that he was 'just as safe now as if I were at home' – which was true.[1] At the same time he voiced his concern for his brother Ed whose unit, the 741st Tank Battalion, had landed on Utah Beach on D-Day. 'When you receive any word from him,' he wrote to his mother on 22 June, 'send me a cable gram or something saying he is all right. Now I know how you & Pop worry over us for I'm the same way about Ed.' With no definite news by 3 July, Sledge told his parents: 'Edward is constantly in my prayers day & nite. We were glad to hear that the casualties were fairly low . . . I guess you read about the Marines lost on Saipan. We really had heavy hearts when we heard of it.'

In the earlier letter, Sledge had mentioned that he and Sid spent every evening together, and were planning a post-war trip to the 'eastern battlefields of the Civil War'. Then came the news, in a letter dated 25 June, that Sid had left for home and Sledge was 'really glad', though it had been hard to say goodbye. A week later, with Phillips on his way back to the States,* Sledge begged his parents to give his friend 'a good time & good food'. It must have been a difficult time for the young Alabaman: parted from his best friend after an all-too-brief reunion. But if he felt lonely, he kept it from his folks, writing instead with news from other correspondents ('Bill Wacker . . . is going with a nice girl who's grandad owns a huge tract of timber'), requests for candy and cookies, and the occasional comment on political issues back in the US.[2]

What Sledge could not give his parents, of course, was any information about where he was and what he and the rest of K Company were doing. Work details apart, they were spending most of their time training for the next operation. He wrote later: 'We held numerous landing exercises – several times a week, it seemed – on the beaches and inlets around the island away from camp. We usually practiced from amtracs.†

* Despite having spent more than twenty-four months overseas and served in two campaigns, Phillips still had to win a regimental lottery to stamp his ticket. He left Pavuvu in late June 1944. (Makos, *Voices of the Pacific*, p. 148.)

† The models that Sledge and his buddies were practising in were the LVT-2 'Water Buffalo', capable of speeds of 20 mph on land and 6.5 knots on water, of carrying a payload of 7,000lb, and with an operational range of 50 miles, and the LVT-4, a slightly improved version of the LVT-2, with the engine further forward and a rear ramp door that allowed a safer exit. Carrying capacity improved from sixteen to thirty troops.

The newest model had a tailgate that dropped as soon as the tractor was on the beach, allowing us to run out and deploy.'

Scheduled to land on Peleliu in the second wave with the machine gunners, bazooka men and flamethrowers, the 60mm mortar squads were told to get off the beach as fast as possible. 'The Nips are going to plaster it with everything they've got,' warned their officers, 'so your chances are better the sooner you move inland.'[3]

During one of these beach landing exercises, 'Duke' Ellington told his men to set up their mortars in the wrong place. When he was chewed out by the new commander of the 3rd Battalion, Lieutenant Colonel Austin C. 'Shifty' Shofner, Ellington passed the buck. 'What the hell were you thinking, setting up that way?' he yelled at R. V. Burgin. 'They're supposed to be over there!'

Burgin was furious. When Platoon Sergeant Johnny Marmet asked him why, he replied: 'John, he's been riding us for the stuff he's been doing ever since New Britain. He's passing down the blame to me and everybody else for his own damn mistakes. You get that son of a bitch off of my ass or *I'm* going to get him off. And if I get him off, both of us are going to be sorry.'

Marmet took the hint. 'I'll take care of it,' he said.

And he did because, wrote Burgin, there were no more issues for a while.[4]

As well as landing exercises and field problems, the mortar men were given refresher courses in the use of all company small arms: M1 rifle, BAR, carbine, .45-calibre semi-automatic pistol, Thompson submachine gun, and flamethrower. Trying out the latter on a tree stump from a distance of 25 yards, Gene Sledge was shocked by intensity of the 'stream of red flame' and the 'loud splattering noise' as the napalm hit the stump. He felt heat on his face as a cloud of black smoke shot upwards. 'The thought of turning loose hellfire from a hose nozzle,' he wrote, 'as easily as I'd water a lawn back home sobered me. To shoot the enemy with bullets or kill him with shrapnel was one of the grim necessities of war, but to fry him to death was too gruesome to contemplate.'[5]

Sledge was more at home – and at ease – with the 60mm mortar, winning a platoon competition to test each man's proficiency with the weapon on 16 July. His reward was advancement from ammo carrier to assistant gunner, serving next to 'Snafu' Shelton on Burgin's no. 2 gun. It was from Cape Gloucester veterans like Burgin and Shelton that Sledge got his first real sense of what combat against the Japanese was really like. 'I don't remember how many Japs that we killed that night,' Burgin told him, referring to the close-quarter Battle for Walt's Ridge, 'but it was a bunch of them. A lot of Japs committed suicide that night.'[6]

One old salt that Sledge quickly gained a deep respect for was the eccentric Platoon Sergeant 'Pop' Haney. The young PFC first noticed Haney in the shower, scrubbing his genitals with a GI brush 'the way one buffs a shoe'. Given that the brush, with its tough, split-fibre bristles, was designed to scrub heavy canvas gear and dungarees, this method of bathing was 'truly impressive'. Haney's professionalism and sense of responsibility was no less emphatic. Like the time, Sledge remembered, when he threw coral gravel into a young replacement officer's face for neglecting basic safety measures on the pistol range. Accepting the admonishment, the officer 'took off rubbing his eyes and blushing visibly', while Haney resumed his seat as if nothing had happened.

Haney was similar in weight to Sledge – 135 pounds – but there the similarities ended. With 'sandy crew-cut hair and a deep tan', the sergeant was 'lean, hard, and muscular'. His barrel-chested, slightly hump-backed torso reminded the young mortarman of a Michelangelo anatomy sketch, with every muscle standing out in 'stark definition'. He had squinty eyes and small features, and his dark brown face resembled 'wrinkled leather'.

He lived in a pup tent set apart from the others, and did not appear to have any buddies. This was not because he was 'sullen or unfriendly'; he just lived in a world of his own. 'We all cleaned our weapons daily,' recalled Sledge, 'but Haney cleaned his M1 before muster, at noon chow, and after dismissal in the afternoon. It was his ritual. He would sit by himself, light a cigarette, fieldstrip his rifle, and meticulously clean every inch of it.' Then he would move on to his bayonet, and when that was done he would reassemble his weapon, fix his blade, and practise a few minutes of 'thrust, parry, and butt-stroke movements at thin air'.[7]

The closest Haney had to a friend in K Company was Sergeant Jim McEnery, the Canal veteran from New York, who would listen patiently while the platoon sergeant explained the importance of staying awake at night in a foxhole, or how to fight off an attacker. 'You gotta keep your bayonet sharp and in your hand when there ain't room to use your rifle,' he insisted. 'You gotta grab that fuckin' Jap and pull him up close and cut his damn throat as quick as you can.'

Sharing a bottle of whisky with McEnery, Haney always returned to the same theme: the 'old Corps', and how things were in France in 1918 where he served with the same company – K/3/5 – at Belleau Wood. 'You'd have done all right over there, McEnery,' he said, 'because you're careful, and you don't take a lot of stupid chances. Most of these punk kids, though, they'd never have made it in the old Corps.'[8]

Unaware of his recent heroism on Walt's Ridge, Sterling Mace and some of the other young replacements regarded Haney as a 'fossil' and a 'joke'. He was 'scrawny', wrote Mace, and his dungarees 'hung off him like a scarecrow's raiment'. They laughed when he talked to himself and fought imaginary enemies, asking: 'Who's he fightin' now, I wonder? Attila the Hun?' They assumed he had gone 'Asiatic' – the term Marines used for men who had been in the tropics for too long, and had lost their minds – and felt a mixture of pity and contempt.[9]

Sledge thought differently. He considered Haney as 'not a man born of woman, but that god had issued him to the Marine Corps'. For all his personal idiosyncrasies, he inspired Sledge and some of the other greenhorns because he represented a direct link to the 'old Corps'. To them, Haney '*was* the old breed' and they admired and loved him for it.

The man who would rise highest in Sledge's estimation, however, was his skipper Andy Haldane. Late one afternoon, as the company straggled back from the rifle range on a featureless trail lashed by a tropical rainstorm, a 'chilled and forlorn' Sledge was finding it difficult to keep his balance in the mud. Suddenly a big man appeared from the back of the column, walking 'with the ease of a pedestrian on a city sidewalk'. Pulling abreast of Sledge, he remarked, 'Lovely weather, isn't it, son?'

Recognizing his skipper, Sledge grinned and said, 'Not exactly, sir.'

Asked by Haldane how he liked the company, Sledge said he thought it was a 'fine outfit'. They then chatted easily for a few minutes about the Alabaman's family, home and education. 'As we talked,' recalled Sledge, 'the gloom seemed to disappear, and I felt warm inside. Finally he told me it wouldn't rain forever, and we could get dry soon. He moved along the column talking to other men as he had to me. His sincere interest in each of us as a human being helped to dispel the feeling that we were just animals training to fight.'

Jotting down his memories of war, Sledge was highly critical of a number of officers, 'Duke' Ellington included. But not Andy Haldane. He considered him to be the 'finest and most popular' officer he came across, and everyone in K Company felt the same. Haldane had a 'strong face full of character, a large, prominent jaw, and the kindest eyes' that Sledge ever saw. Though he insisted on strict discipline, he was a 'quiet man who gave orders without shouting'. He possessed a 'rare combination of intelligence, courage, self-confidence, and compassion' that commanded both respect and admiration. 'We were thankful that Ack-Ack was our skipper,' recalled Sledge, 'felt more secure in it, and felt sorry for other companies not so fortunate. While some officers on Pavuvu thought it necessary to strut or order us around to impress us with their status, Haldane quietly told us what to do. We loved him for it and did the best job we knew how.'[10]

Around Independence Day, 4 July 1944 – celebrated on Pavuvu with baseball and boxing competitions, track races and a stage show – Haldane chose one officer and ten men for a special assignment: to take a boat across to the neighbouring island of Banika and guard a storehouse for two weeks. 'One of us asked what we'd be guarding,' remembered R. V. Burgin, who was on the detail. 'Beer and soda pop, Haldane told us. A whole warehouse. It was like sending foxes to guard the chicken coop.'

Led by Lieutenant 'Hillbilly' Jones, the group was made up exclusively of veterans like Corporal Burgin, his singing partner George Sarrett and Corporal John Teskevich. In Burgin's opinion, 'everyone else was a top-notch Marine' and he 'felt proud to be in their company'. Arriving on Banika, a short 20-mile boat ride from Pavuvu, the men were housed in two six-man pyramid tents, on real wood platforms, and given light duties. They dined on a nearby ship at anchor, choosing from a menu and enjoying unheard-of luxuries like napkins and tablecloths. At the warehouse, they drank as much warm beer and soda as they liked.

Hillbilly, Burgin and a couple of other Marines spent one Saturday night downing homemade alcohol and grapefruit juice, telling jokes and singing songs. They got so sozzled that Burgin had to put the others to bed: but not before dousing their heads with water from a 250-gallon water tank. He woke up vomiting and did not eat for four days.[11]

The group returned to Pavuvu in time to see Bob Hope and his USO troupe* – singer Frances Langford, guitarist Tom Romano, comedian Jerry Colonna and dancer Patty Thomas – perform in front of 15,000 Marines in the open space behind the docks. Hope wrote later that flying from Banika to Pavuvu in a light plane, and circling low over his waiting audience, was one of the highlights of his Pacific tour. He and his troupe had already performed in Tarawa, Saipan, Bougainville and Tulagi, among other venues, and did not have Pavuvu on the schedule. But a special request from the 1st Marine Division's recreation officer persuaded Hope to make the short detour from Banika in a Piper Cub. With no airstrip available, they landed on one of the roads.

'Did you enjoy the flight?' Hope asked Colonna, on stage.

'Tough sledding.'

'Why tough sledding?'

'No snow,' said a deadpan Colonna. The Marines roared with laughter.

Hope kept the jokes coming by saying the island's land crabs reminded him of Bing Crosby's racehorses – 'they run sideways'. Pavuvu was so small, he added, 'the gophers have to take turns coming up'.

Frances Langford charmed the audience with a string of popular

* The United Service Organisations (USO) was founded in early 1941 to provide live entertainment for American servicemen and their families. Today it works in partnership with the Department of Defense (formerly War), but relies on private contributions and is not a government department.

songs. But the star turn was undoubtedly Patty Thomas who, dressed alluringly in a mini-skirt and halter top, invited Marines to guess the dance and then come on stage to try it out with her. The winner was the Marine who did the ballet.

Hope ended the two-hour show with his theme song, 'Thanks for the Memories', to raucous and sustained applause that continued as the performers took off, one by one, in their Piper Cubs. 'For days afterward,' remembered R. V. Burgin, 'we'd talk about that show. It really lifted our spirits.'[12]

So impressed was young replacement PFC Andy Stumpf that he mentioned the performers in a letter to his parents in Clark County, Washington:

> This morning we saw Bob Hope, Jerry Collona [sic], Frances Langford and Patty Thomas. They flew right over us in these little cub airplanes and landed. They really put on a show and I still can't figure out why they would come to a weather-beaten hole like this. We had a very crude stage and we sat on the ground. Frances sang a lot and the other girl danced. I was all eyes on her, as I have never seen anybody that was stacked up as nice as she was; she was really beautiful. And between Hope and Colonna, they were a scream, and how we enjoyed it! Both the girls were beautiful, and you can imagine a bunch of guys that haven't seen a girl for a year or so. It was the most enjoyment we've had – in fact it is the only one.[13]

Years later, on one of his last TV broadcasts, Hope described the show on Pavuvu as an incredibly moving experience. 'You knew when you walked out there,' he said, 'that a lot of those guys you'd never see again.'[14] He was right, of course, and a few months later – by which time the performers were back in the States – Hope received a copy of PFC Stumpf's letter from his mother. Her son Andy, she explained, had been killed soon after writing the letter 'in his first battle, at Peleliu'. She added: 'He was only nineteen, had never been away from home before and was lonely and homesick, as most of the boys are, and I can never thank you enough for having brought him those two hours of fun.'[15]

27

'This is going to be a short one, a quickie'

Southwest Pacific, July–September 1944

In late July 1944, Captain Andy Haldane received another letter from Kenneth Sills, the president of Bowdoin College, congratulating him on his Silver Star, the award of which had just been announced. 'I understand,' wrote Sills, 'that you and Ev[erett] Pope [another Bowdoin alumnus] are still on active duty. I assure you that we think of you very often and whenever anyone comes back from the war out your way everyone asks, "How is Andy getting along?"'

In his reply, Haldane told Sills that he and Pope were still in the Pacific,* but if they could 'get through the next one' they would soon be home 'to get a few days rest'. Meanwhile, all he could do was 'carry on'. He added, referring to the Peleliu campaign: 'This next one is going to be a peach. Woe is me!'

Haldane finished the short note with an excuse for his intermittent correspondence. 'Lately,' he explained, 'I've had no time to write letters for work comes before pleasure and I've got plenty of work. We have a new colonel and he is fresh from the States so you can imagine how he has us snapping. My health has been disgustingly good and malaria seems to have gone forever.'[1]

The colonel in question – or rather lieutenant colonel – was 'Shifty' Shofner, a 28-year-old native of Chattanooga, Tennessee, who had had

* Pope was commanding C Company, 1/1 Marines.

an eventful war. Captured as a captain with the 4th Marines at Corregidor in May 1942, he spent almost eleven months in Japanese prison camps before escaping and joining up with Philippine guerrillas, a feat that earned him a Distinguished Service Cross. He eventually made his way back to the United States, via Australia, and, having attended the USMC Command and Staff School, was promoted to lieutenant colonel. But there were doubts about his fitness for higher command. In his final report, for example, he received average marks for 'attention to duty, cooperation, intelligence, and judgement and common sense'; and, even worse, his commander indicated that he did not 'particularly desire to have him' in his unit.

Yet his superiors were convinced that these weaknesses were outweighed by Shofner's toughness and first-hand knowledge of the Japanese. He was dispatched to the 1st Marine Division and appointed the new CO of the 3/5 Marines, replacing temporary commander Major Walter S. McIlhenny who joined the regimental staff. Arriving on Pavuvu in early July 1944, Shofner immediately increased the 3/5's tempo of training, pushing the officers and men as hard as he could. They 'had to be drilled', he told them, 'so that they could do their job when exhausted, afraid, wounded, hungry and thirsty, and in shock from the violence of battle'.[2]

This did not make Shofner popular. He was overbearing and tactless in his dealings with company commanders – Haldane included – and the men complained about the frequency of 'weapons and equipment inspections, work parties, and petty cleanup details around the camp'. Sledge 'griped as loudly as anyone' about the living conditions and discipline, but later acknowledged that it was vital preparation for the rigours to come. Without it, he wrote, 'I doubt seriously whether I could have coped with the psychological and physical shock and stress' of combat. He added: 'The Japanese fought to win. It was a savage, brutal, inhumane, exhausting, and dirty business. Our commanders knew that if we were to win and survive, we must be trained realistically for it whether we liked it or not.'[3]

Shofner kept his job, in spite of his unpopularity, but his immediate superior was not so fortunate. Colonel William S. Fellers had served on Guadalcanal as the 5th Marines' XO and later as the divisional supply officer, excelling in the latter role during the Cape Gloucester campaign. When it was over, he had been out of the US for more than twenty-four months and should have rotated home. But, promised a regiment by both Vandegrift and Rupertus, he put off his return to replace Oliver Smith as the permanent CO of the Devil Dogs in late May 1944. Yet he, like Shofner, rubbed his subordinates up the wrong way with his irascible manner and unreasonable demands.

The bad feeling came to a head in mid-August when Lew Walt, the 5th Marines' XO, told his friend John T. Selden, Rupertus's chief of staff, that Fellers had lost the confidence of his officers and men. Having looked into the matter, Oliver P. Smith felt it was in the 'best interests' of the regiment and the division to relieve Fellers, and Rupertus agreed. Within a couple of days, Fellers was on a plane home and 'Bucky' Harris, the division's 41-year-old intelligence chief, took command of the 5th Marines. It would be, for the Devil Dogs, a fortunate turn of events. Fellers was running on empty, noted Smith, and might have 'cracked up' under the strain of regimental command on Peleliu. Harris was not, and would prove to be an inspired leader.[4]

Raised in Laramie, Wyoming, Harris had graduated from the US Naval Academy at Annapolis with a Bachelor of Science degree in June 1925, before joining the US Marines. He served at various foreign stations – including China and Nicaragua – and was attending the École Supérieure de Guerre in Paris, France, when war broke out in Europe. For helping to evacuate many fellow Americans, he was commended by the US ambassador to France. He then worked as an intelligence officer at Marine Corps Headquarters in Washington DC and in the South Pacific, prior to joining the 1st Marine Division as XO of the 1st Marines in late 1943.[5]

Having personally selected the landing beaches on the western side of Peleliu, Harris was well aware of their pros and cons. In the former category was the fact that they were 'within easy range' of naval gunfire and air support, while their extensive length allowed for a wide dispersal of landing craft 'that was highly desirable to cut down the effectiveness of Jap gunnery'. They would also allow for the early capture of the nearby Japanese airfield. On the flip side, the beaches were narrow, almost certainly heavily mined, in easy range of the Japanese guns on the central massif, and protected by a fringing reef to the west that varied in width from 100 to 1,000 yards. To cross the reef, therefore, would require the use of amtracs and DUKWs, rather than the bigger landing craft (LCIs and LSTs).* Even artillery would have to come in this way.[6]

The final plan for Operation Stalemate II – issued to the 1st Marine Division on 15 August – was for a landing of three regiments abreast (a total of five landing teams) on a beachhead 2,200 yards wide, 'followed by a drive straight across the island to seize the airfield and to divide the enemy forces'. When the time was right, a reinforced battalion would make a shore-to-shore assault against Ngesebus Island and capture its fighter strip.

The landings would follow nine days of strikes by carrier-borne planes and a three-day bombardment by naval ships.

The assault troops and guns would sail in LSTs to a point 4,000 yards off Peleliu, where they would be transferred to amtracs and DUKWs for the ride over the reef and on to the beaches. Tanks, meanwhile, would be dropped from LSTs at the edge of the reef and use 'deep water fording kits' to reach land. The intention was to get the first eight waves of amtracs – carrying the 4,500 men of the five assault battalions – ashore in just nineteen minutes. They would land, from north to south, on White Beach 1 and 2 (3/1 and 2/1 Marines respectively), Orange Beach 1 and 2 (1/5 and 3/5 Marines respectively), and Orange Beach 3 (3/7 Marines).

The job of the 1st Marines (now commanded by Colonel 'Chesty'

* Landing Craft Infantry (LCI), a small steel ship, 158 feet in length, with space for 200 men; and the much bigger Landing Ship Tank (LST), 327 feet long, and capable of disembarking 2,100 tons of amphibians (amtracs) in deep water and tanks on to beaches.

Puller) was to seize some of the 'high ground' north of the airfield. The 2/1 Marines on the right, in contact with the left flank of the 5th Marines, 'was to move through a swampy area behind its beach out along the northern end of the airfield, and then turn north into the ridges'. The 3/1 Marines, 'landing on the extreme left of the Division beachhead, and at the foot of some of the lowest ridges, was to charge right up onto them'. At the southern end – or right – of the beachhead, the 7th Marines was to 'drive across the island, then turn south and advance on and seize the southern promontories'. The key task of taking the airfield on D-Day, therefore, had been entrusted to 'Bucky' Harris's 5th Marines, landing in the centre of the beachhead. This meant that Haldane's K Company, having missed the assault landings at Cape Gloucester, was back in the firing line: it would storm the right of Orange Beach 2, while I Company assaulted the left.

Ideally, Harris would have preferred more than a fortnight to supervise the Devil Dogs' training and make his final preparations. This included the rehearsal of pillbox assaults with flamethrowers, bazookas, demolition packs, anti-tank guns, machine guns, rifles and hand grenades; night defence and firing of mortars; patrolling with war dogs; and physical conditioning. He briefed each battalion on its objective 'with a discussion of the terrain and the meager information we had on the enemy'. He also warned them that his study of air photos indicated that the Japanese had tanks and might use them to counter-attack the regiment's left flank. He would deploy anti-tank guns accordingly.[7]

Shortly before leaving Pavuvu for the final landing rehearsals at Cape Esperance on Guadalcanal, the 1st Marine Division was visited by Lieutenant General Vandegrift, now commandant of the Marine Corps. At a conference with the senior officers, he grinned at Harris and said: 'Bucky, after this operation I am ordering you home, and I'll give you a month's leave.' Harris was delighted, shipping most of his personal items home to his wife, and keeping only the 'barest essentials' for Peleliu.[8]

* * *

On 26 August, the 3/5 Marines boarded four LSTs – one for each rifle company, and one for Shofner's Battalion CP – and 'bade a not particularly fond farewell to the rat and crab capital of the Pacific', the start of a three-week voyage that would end on the beaches of Peleliu. K Company's vessel, LST-*661*, lacked cabin space for all the men, so the platoon leaders drew lots. 'The mortar section got lucky,' recalled Gene Sledge. 'We were assigned to a troop compartment in the forecastle with an entrance on the main deck. Some of the other platoons had to make themselves as comfortable as possible on the main deck under and around landing boats and gear secured there.'[9]

They reached Guadalcanal on the 27th and took part in a divisional landing exercise at Cape Esperance that lasted for three days. It went mostly as planned, though the beaches 'bore little resemblance' to the ones they would hit on Peleliu. There was also a feeling that the amtracs – carrying up to thirty-six men and a 37mm gun – were 'considerably overloaded'. But it was decided to leave the loads as they were because of the need to get as many troops on to the beach as quickly as possible.[10]

From 30 August to 3 September, the men were allowed to go ashore. Sterling Mace remembered a 'nice little party on the sand' with the other 3rd Platoon men, lounging around and swinging from a rope above the water. They drank beers and Cokes, and passed round the latest issues of *Leatherneck* magazine. 'Say, Mace!' said Corporal Ray Grawet from Chicago, Illinois, tapping a page of the magazine. 'Isn't this *you*?'

PFC Pete Candella laughed. 'Hey, it sure as hell is!'

'Here,' said Mace, 'lemme see that!'

It really *was* a photo of him and a few other Marines, taken in a railcar on their journey from the east to the west coast. He was stuffing himself with food.

'Boy,' said Grawet. 'Looks like we have a regular Hollywood Marine in our midst!'[11]

Jim McEnery and some of the other Canal veterans wanted to visit the Marine cemetery on the island to pay their respects to their fallen buddies. The news that there was no transport available caused a great deal of 'bitterness and resentment'.[12]

Before leaving Guadalcanal, the officers and senior NCOs of the division's three infantry regiments – the 1st, 5th and 7th – gathered in a movie area for a pep talk by Major General Rupertus who, having fractured his ankle in a fall from an amtrac on Pavuvu, was still using crutches. The operation, he told them, would not be another drawn-out affair like Guadalcanal or Cape Gloucester. It would be tough, but soon over. 'We're going to have some casualties,' he conceded, 'but let me assure you this is going to be a short one, a quickie. Rough but fast. We'll be through in three days. It might take only two.'[13]

It was a hopelessly optimistic prediction and one that would come back to haunt Rupertus. The 1st Marine Division was a veteran unit, but most of its previous combat experience had been in jungle warfare on Guadalcanal and New Britain. Peleliu required something very different: 'ridge and cave fighting against a defender who had been given three months to develop his defenses, painstakingly organized and integrated, in considerable depth, and of even greater strength than those which he had erected at Saipan and Tarawa'.

Marine intelligence had produced a remarkably accurate estimate of the number of Japanese troops on the island, but it knew little about their system of defence. Its large-scale maps, pieced together from aerial photographs, would be of little use in helping to navigate the ridges and caves in the centre and north of the island where one feature looked much like another. Only when American troops were on the ground would the extreme difficulty of capturing the island's larger northern claw – where thick scrub vegetation concealed 'sharp ridges and broken hill masses honey-combed with hundreds of natural caves, which the enemy had laboriously converted by means of interconnecting tunnels and shafts, reinforced concrete and steel, into an intricate mutually supporting underground fortress of truly formidable proportions' – become clear.[14]

* * *

On 4 September, *661* and the other twenty-nine LSTs carrying the division's assault companies weighed anchor and began the 2,100-mile journey to their objective. The trip was mostly in fine weather and, bar the occasional alert, largely uneventful, with no enemy planes or surface craft sighted.[15] On Pavuvu the troops had been briefed on their first-day objectives, and shown photographs, maps and a model of the island, but not told its name for security reasons. Now it was revealed: Peleliu.[16]

No one in K Company had heard of it. But their ears pricked up when they heard the island was 'infested with bugs and snakes, indigenous birds that made strange noises, and Japanese forces of an unknown quantity'. There was also no natural water source. Everything they drank, they would have to take with them.

'Well if it's so goddamn lousy,' said Sterling Mace to his squad leader Jim McEnery, 'what the hell are we taking it for?'

McEnery ignored the question, and the briefing continued.[17]

Before leaving Pavuvu, they had been told that the division would be reinforced to 28,000 men for the operation, making it the largest the Marine Corps had ever put in the field. When a replacement mentioned this on the voyage, a veteran put him straight. 'Use your head, buddy. Sure we got the 1st Marines, the 5th Marines, and the 7th Marines; them's infantry. Where the hell's all them people who is supposed to "reinforce" the division? Have you seen 'em? Who the hell are they, and where the hell are they?'

'I don't know,' replied the replacement, 'I'm just telling you what the lieutenant said.'

'Well, I'll tell you who them "reinforcements" is. They's all what they call specialists, and they ain't line company Marines. Remember this, buster. When the stuff hits the fan, and you and me are trying to live through that shootin' and the shellin', them damned specialists'll be settin' on they cans back at division CP on the beach, writin' home about how war is hell. Wake up, boy, them shavetail lieutenants is as useless as tits on a boar hog. The NCOs run things when the shootin' starts.'

The lighter moments included watching 'Pop' Haney's daily display of bayonet drill on the ship's fantail after morning chow, dressed only in khaki shorts, boondockers and leggings. 'For about an hour he went through his routine, complete with monologue,' recalled Gene Sledge, 'while dozens of Company K men lounged around on coils of rope and other gear smoking and talking.' Occasionally a sailor would wander by, open-mouthed, and ask if Haney was Asiatic. No, replied Sledge, we're all like that.[18]

To take his mind off what lay ahead, R. V. Burgin stood at the railing and watched the porpoises 'play in the wake of the ship', and 'the flying fish glide over the crests of the waves'. On the horizon lay dozens of big ships: aircraft carriers, battleships and cruisers. Closer in were the escorting destroyers and PT boats. They were all zigzagging as they sailed, changing direction every fifteen minutes to make it harder for a Japanese submarine to fix on a target. There was one alarm, prompting the PT boats to circle and drop depth charges, but no sign that they hit their mark.

As on the voyage from New Britain, Burgin and others would gather round 'Hillbilly' Jones while he played his guitar, singing favourites like 'Red River Valley':

From this valley they say you are leaving,
We shall miss your bright eyes and sweet smile,
For you take with you all of the sunshine,
That has brightened our pathway a while.[19]

Among the K Company men who took the opportunity to pen a last letter home was 'Ack-Ack' Haldane. 'I have been pretty busy alright, preparing for our next offensive,' he wrote to his high school sweetheart Phyllis Stowell on 5 September. 'Now however we are at sea again en-route to another enemy stronghold. This letter will not go out until after we hit our objective but at least you know that I gave you thought on the way up . . . Don't ever worry about me Phyllis for I'll be O.K. Just remember that I can't go wrong because after this blitz I'm coming back so wish me luck. I'll need it.'[20]

While the assault troops headed for Peleliu, the softening up of the target continued. The Palaus had been struck first by carrier planes from the US Fifth Fleet in March 1944, and more attacks were launched in

July and August. Land-based bombers continued the assault, and from 8 August to 14 September dropped more than 91 tons of fragmentation, demolition and incendiary bombs in night raids. From late August they were augmented by 394 daytime sorties by B-24 Liberators, dropping almost 800 tons of high explosives. By 5 September, photo reconnaissance confirmed the presence of just twelve Japanese fighters, twelve floatplanes and three observation aircraft in the Palaus. The enemy airstrips, moreover, were badly cratered and only extensive and lengthy repairs could make them operable.

These air strikes were followed on 12 September by a fierce bombardment of Peleliu's defences by the big guns of Rear Admiral Jesse B. Oldendorf's Fire Support Group, consisting of five old battleships, four heavy cruisers, four light cruisers and fourteen destroyers. Alternating with aerial strikes by carrier planes, this naval gunfire continued until the landings on 15 September, by which time more than 17,000 rounds – ranging in calibre from 5in to 16in – had been fired, a total of 2,255 tons of high explosive.

Meanwhile US Navy Underwater Demolition Teams (UDT) – the forerunners to the modern Navy SEALs – had begun removing underwater obstacles, blasting ramps for LSTs and pathways for DUKWs in the coral, clearing boulders from roadways, and placing buoys and markers. 'Clad only in swimming trunks,' noted the Marine official history, 'these underwater experts were constantly fired at by Japanese with rifles and machine guns during the dangerous process of destroying the underwater obstructions which [Oldendorf] described as "the most formidable which we encountered in the entire Pacific".'

While the UDTs performed their tasks well, the impact of three days of heavy naval gunfire was less effective. The original gunfire support plan had been for a two-day bombardment. When Geiger asked for an extra day, his request was granted. But as the allotment of ammunition was the same, it was simply fired over a longer period. Moreover, the bombardment was ended early by Oldendorf, who felt that all the targets on Peleliu worthy of naval gunfire had been destroyed. In truth, though the blizzard of shells had turned much of the island's interior into, as one Japanese soldier described it, a 'barren wasteland', the skilfully camouflaged and well-protected Japanese artillery positions – some sited in caves with steel doors – were mostly untouched. So too were the Japanese defenders, who had been 'placed in sheltered areas, from which they could emerge, unscathed and combat-ready, after the American barrage lifted'.[21]

As Peleliu was being ineffectively pounded from the sea, planes from Vice Admiral Marc A. Mitscher's Fast Carrier Task Force (part of 'Bull' Halsey's US Third Fleet) launched a series of strikes against airfields and other targets on the islands of Leyte, Cebu and Negros in the central Philippines. Over the course of three days – 12–14 September – the US Navy pilots flew 2,400 sorties and destroyed 200 enemy planes and a number of ships. Their own losses were just eight planes and ten pilots.

'Enemy's non-aggressive attitude [was] unbelievable and fantastic,' reported a euphoric Halsey to Nimitz on 14 September. For the previous two months he had been pressing Nimitz to cancel Operation Stalemate II in favour of an earlier invasion of Mindanao in the southern Philippines. Now, given the lack of opposition in the central Philippines, he made an even more radical proposal: to bypass Mindanao and use the troops slated for Stalemate II to strike at Leyte at the earliest opportunity. The Palau and Yap–Ulithi operations, he told Nimitz, did 'not offer opportunity for destruction of enemy forces commensurate with delay and effort involved'. Instead the forces assigned – including the 1st Marine Division – should be transferred to MacArthur's command and used to seize Leyte 'immediately and cheaply without any intermediate operations'.

If Nimitz had agreed, the Peleliu operation might have been postponed at the eleventh hour. But while Nimitz was prepared to pass on Halsey's recommendation concerning Phase II – the Yap–Ulithi operations – to the Joint Chiefs,* he ruled that Phase I, the capture of Peleliu and Angaur,

* Nimitz added a suggestion of his own: if MacArthur resisted the proposal to bring forward the Leyte operation, 'it may be feasible to take Iwo Jima in mid-October using the Yap force'. But what if, on the other hand, Nimitz had

'would have to go through as planned' because of 'commitments already made' (in other words, the invasion fleets were en route and could not be stopped). In a separate cable to King, Nimitz insisted that possession of Peleliu and Angaur was 'of course essential and it would not be feasible to reorientate the plans for the employment of the Palau attack and occupation forces as rapidly as Halsey's [signal] appears to visualize'.

Not surprisingly, MacArthur endorsed the new plan to bypass Mindanao for Leyte, and to bring forward the invasion of the latter to 20 October. The Joint Chiefs – in Quebec for an Allied conference with Roosevelt, Churchill and the British military chiefs – also agreed to Halsey's suggestion to cancel the Yap–Ulithi operations and redirect the Army's XXIV Corps to an earlier liberation of Leyte. When Halsey decided to capture Ulithi anyway, and 'as early as practical . . . with resources at hand', the only force available was Geiger's corps reserve, a single regimental combat team from the 81st Division. Its deployment would leave the Marines battling to secure Peleliu without any reinforcements 'should they be needed'.[22]

Halsey's intervention, and the resultant change of strategy, begs the question: was the invasion of Peleliu necessary? Nimitz, who had as clear a concept of the strategic situation in the Pacific as any Allied commander, was convinced that it was. By capturing it and its airfield, he would be able to dominate the rest of the Palaus and, in the words of historian Joseph H. Alexander, 'bottle up tens of thousands of troops on Babelthuap and throughout the western Carolines, including Yap'. Alexander added:

> As Nimitz had been insisting for months, U.S. forces might be able to take Ulithi without Yap, but it could not be done without first taking Peleliu. Possession of Peleliu's airfield – and construction

---

agreed to Halsey's suggestion to cancel the landing on Peleliu and used those troops to assault Iwo Jima in the autumn of 1944 before its defences had become so formidable? The 'two decisions in combination', writes Toll, 'might have saved thousands of American lives'. (Toll, *Twilight of the Gods*, pp. 126–7.)

> of a heavy bomber strip on the flat terrain of nearby Angaur – would permit Nimitz to support MacArthur, suppress Yap, protect Ulithi, and project reconnaissance and bombing missions far to the northwest as well.

Nimitz may also have been guilty of overconfidence. The most recent landing had been on the island of Tinian which the Marines had secured in just nine days, inflicting a casualty ratio of four to one against the defenders. He hoped that Peleliu would be 'another Tinian', and that the battle-hardened 1st Marine Division would capture it at an affordable cost. What Nimitz and the planners did not know, wrote Alexander, was that they would be facing on Peleliu 'one of the best-trained, best-led infantry regiments in the Imperial Army, or that in Colonel Kunio Nakagawa the Marines would fight against a commander surpassed only by Iwo Jima's Tadamichi Kuribayashi as their most redoubtable opponent of all time, a colonel with such an eye for terrain and such a gift for close combat that the Japanese government promoted him posthumously to lieutenant general'.

Nor did anyone appreciate, noted Alexander, 'the fact that the Japanese had just modified their counter landing tactics' and would introduce the American invaders on Peleliu to 'cave warfare, deep positions arrayed in honeycombed echelons, a new war of attrition'. Into the 'lethal landscape' of the Umurbrogol 'came an overconfident landing force, whose assault numbers barely equalled the defenders (much less the three-to-one ratio found necessary for success in earlier operations), whose operational reserves were too few and committed too readily to lower priority missions against Angaur and Ulithi, with preliminary naval gunfire support reduced nearly to Tarawa levels, and with insufficient tank and mechanized flame-thrower assets'.[23]

It would be a much tougher nut to crack than Nimitz had anticipated; but that does not mean, with the information available to him, it was a mistake to try.

28

'This is it, boys!'

Palau Islands, 14–15 September 1944

After evening chow on 14 September 1944, twelve hours before the invasion of Peleliu, Gene Sledge and his buddy PFC Robert Oswalt – the Marine almost shot by R. V. Burgin on Walt's Ridge – met on LST-*661*'s deck to chew the fat. 'What are you going to do after the war, Sledgehammer?' asked Oswalt.

'I don't know, Oswalt. What are you planning to do?'

'I want to be a brain surgeon. The human brain is an incredible thing; it fascinates me.'

Sledge was not surprised. He knew Oswalt to be exceptionally intelligent and thought brain surgery might suit him very well. As they spoke, the sun began to sink below the horizon. Sledge loved the Pacific sunsets: they were even more beautiful than those over Mobile Bay. Suddenly a thought struck him like a thunderbolt. *Will I live to see the sunset tomorrow?*

His knees almost buckled as panic swept over him. He grabbed the railing to steady himself, hoping his buddy had not noticed his temporary loss of composure. The ship's loudspeaker came to his aid: 'Now hear this! Now hear this! All troops lay below to quarters! All troops lay below to quarters!'

They returned to their compartment in the forecastle and, a short time later, Second Lieutenant 'Duke' Ellington appeared. 'At ease,' he told the mortar section, a frown on his worried face, 'I have something to say.'

When everyone was settled, he reminded them that tomorrow was D-Day and the fighting would be, in General Rupertus's assessment, 'rough but fast'. Three to four days. Then they could return to a rest area. He continued: 'Remember what you've been taught. Keep your heads down going in on the amtrac. A lot of unnecessary casualties at Saipan were the result of men looking over the side to see what was happening. As soon as the amtrac stops on the beach, get out on the double, and get off the beach fast.'

It was important, he added, for them to keep out of the way of amtracs heading back to pick up more men, and tanks coming in behind them. The Japanese would be plastering the beach with everything they had, so if they got pinned down on the beach, artillery and mortars would 'ruin' them.

They were to have their weapons ready. 'A round in the chamber of your small arms and lock your pieces. Have the canister containers of your high-explosive rounds untaped and stowed in your ammo bags ready for immediate use as soon as you are called on to deliver fire on the company front. Fill your canteens, draw rations and salt tablets, and clean your weapons. Reveille will be before daylight, and H hour will be at 0830. Hit the sack early. You will need the rest. Good luck and carry on.'

Once Ellington had departed, Johnny Marmet and the other NCOs began to hand out ammunition and rations. 'Imagine,' said one mortarman, 'only four, maybe three days for a battle star. I can put up with anything for no longer than that.'

The mortarmen sat on their bunks, cleaning their weapons and filling their combat packs. Sledge's contained a folded poncho, a pair of socks, a couple of boxes of K rations,* salt tablets, twenty rounds of extra carbine ammunition, two hand grenades, a fountain pen, a bottle of

* Designed for short-duration use during combat, the K (or 'paratrooper') ration was first introduced in 1942 and consisted of three boxed meals of candy, hard biscuits and canned processed meat, totalling 2,830 calories, for a single day's consumption.

ink, writing paper in a waterproof wrapper, a toothbrush and a small tube of toothpaste, some photos of his parents, some letters, and a dungaree cap. On to the outside of the pack he hooked his entrenching tool in its canvas cover.

His other equipment included an old toothbrush for cleaning his carbine, an M1 steel helmet with a camouflage cover, sage-green dungaree jacket and trousers, thin cotton socks, ankle-high boondockers and light tan canvas leggings (into which he had tucked his trousers). Because of the heat he wore no underwear or shirt.

On his web pistol belt he carried two canteens, two pouches (one with a field dressing, the other with two fifteen-round carbine clips and a brass compass in a waterproof case), a single grenade, a Ka-Bar knife in its leather sheath, and another heavy knife that his father had sent him (similar to a meat cleaver) for chopping through the wire braces on a crate of mortar rounds. His personal weapon was a semi-automatic M1 carbine, weighing under 6lb and accurate up to 300 yards. To its stock he had fastened an ammo pouch with two extra clips. He did not carry a bayonet because the carbine was not designed to hold one.

Once everything was packed and squared away, the men wrote final letters and chatted about anything but the war. Eventually the conversations trailed off and, one by one, the mortar section hit the sack. 'It was hard to sleep that night,' recalled Sledge. 'I thought of my home, my parents, my friends – and whether I would do my duty, be wounded and disabled, or be killed.'

He tried to convince himself that God loved him and would not let him die. Then again, he reasoned, God loves us all and many *will* die or be ruined physically and mentally. He broke out into a cold sweat, his heart pounding. 'You're a damn coward,' he told himself.

Finally, while reciting the Lord's Prayer, he fell asleep.[1]

In the early hours of 15 September, LST-*661* slowed and then stopped. It was the signal for Corporal R. V. Burgin, already awake, to get ready. He felt for his boondockers in the darkness and pulled them on. He sat there until Johnny Marmet came in. 'Okay, Burgin. Let's get 'em up.'[2]

The room was soon alive with men dressing, shaving and waiting to use the two toilets in the small head. One was occupied by 'Pop' Haney who sat there, without a care in the world, 'grinning and talking calmly to himself while smoking a cigarette'. Nervous rookies grumbled and scowled at Haney for taking his time, but because he was a platoon sergeant 'no one dared suggest he hurry'.[3] Haney was nominally attached to Haldane's company headquarters. Before leaving Pavuvu, however, he had asked Cape Gloucester veteran Sergeant Hank Boyes, a 24-year-old squad leader in the 1st Platoon from Trinidad, California, if he could land with him, and Boyes, having checked first with his platoon leader, Second Lieutenant John E. 'Moose' Barrett, Jr, said that he could.[4]

Those with the strongest stomachs headed for the galley and the traditional Marine Corps battle breakfast of steak and eggs. They included 18-year-old PFC Vincent Santos from San Antonio, Texas, who had been dubbed 'Speedy' after coming last in a Fourth of July foot race. 'When's the last time you got steak and eggs?' asked Santos, to no one in particular. 'And when's the next time you're going to get steak and eggs? So I'm making the best of it.'

After breakfast, they went out on deck. 'The brightest stars still hung in the sky,' remembered Burgin. 'There was already a soft glow in the east.' A Piper Cub appeared at a distance of 800 yards and a trigger-happy anti-aircraft gunner opened fire on it, the tracer lighting up the dark sky.

Marines started yelling. 'You damned idiot! That's one of ours!'

Luckily, the plane took evasive action and the gunner missed. Soon after, with dawn fast approaching, 'all hell broke loose' as Rear Admiral Oldendorf's fire support ships opened fire on Peleliu's beaches and the sector immediately beyond. 'The sea lit up like flashbulbs,' noted Burgin. 'Thunder rolled across the waves and rumbled back at us. A few minutes later the first planes from the carriers flew over, headed north, Hellcat fighters and Dauntless dive-bombers loaded with napalm and five-hundred-pound bombs. We could see pink and orange splashes in the distance and a few seconds later hear the *thump-thump* of the explosions.'[5]

Dawn broke 'calm and clear' at 5:52 a.m. to reveal the rugged outline of Peleliu's southwest coast. Filling the waters off White and Orange

Beaches, 'sharply silhouetted against the first rays of sunlight', were American warships 'as far as the eye could see'. Only a slight surf was running and visibility was almost unlimited in every direction. The only cloud in the sky was a long, low smudge of smoke across the northern horizon, east to west, caused by the exploding ordnance.[6]

Sledge was watching the scene with Corporal 'Snafu' Shelton, the Gloucester veteran who 'knew what to expect'. Shelton pulled out a pack of cigarettes and drawled, 'Have a smoke, Sledgehammer.'

'No thanks, Snafu,' said Sledge. 'I've told you a million times I don't smoke.'

'I'll bet you two bits, Sledgehammer, that before this day is over you'll be smokin' the hell outa every cigarette you can get your hands on.'

Sledge gave him a sickly grin. Just then, the ship's bell rang and the tannoy announced: 'Get your gear on and stand by.'

They headed back to the compartment where the other mortarmen were helping each other with packs, straightening shoulder straps and buckling on cartridge belts.[7] The scene was repeated across the ship as the rest of the company – Haldane's CP, Jones's machine-gun platoon and the three rifle platoons – prepared for battle. As a BAR gunner in 3rd Platoon, PFC Sterling Mace strapped on a cartridge belt with six BAR magazine pouches, three on each side, holding two twenty-round magazines apiece (a total of 240 rounds, twice the amount of ammo a rifleman would carry). Over his left shoulder he slung the BAR, weighing 19lb even without its bipod, which he had removed on Pavuvu because it made the weapon unbalanced.

A Marine appeared with a tin of black grease. 'Hey, Mace,' he said. 'You want some of this?'

'Sure, guy,' he responded, dipping two fingers into the grease. But instead of striping his face, like the others, he drew a Salvador Dalí moustache, complete with curlicues.

The second bell rang and they were told to go below deck. 'Well, that's us,' said squad leader Jim McEnery. 'We better get a move on, guys.'[8]

The mortarmen also set off. 'God,' mumbled R. V. Burgin in quiet prayer, 'I'm in your hands. Take care of me.'[9]

The men of K Company, heavily burdened with packs and weapons, filed slowly down the metal ladder to the tank deck in the belly of the ship where a line of growling amtracs were waiting, their exhausts belching noxious fumes and their tracks grinding back and forth. By platoons and sections they were directed to the back of the correct vehicle and waved inside.

'First Platoon, load!'

'Second Platoon, load!'

'Third Platoon, load!'

'Machine Gun Platoon load!'

'Mortar Section, load!'

Sledge was disappointed to see that their amtrac was not one of the new models with a stern ramp, and that to exit they would have to jump over its high sides where they would be more exposed to enemy fire. He was 'too scared and excited to say much, but some of the other guys grumbled about it'.

The lack of a tailgate was not the only problem. As one mortarman was about to climb aboard, he noticed the number on the side of the amtrac. 'Jesus! Thirteen. Now we're in the shit.'

'Don't worry, boys,' said R. V. Burgin. 'Thirteen's my lucky number.' Which was true: he was born on 13 August 1922; his father's birthday was also the 13th; and he had joined the US Marines on 13 November 1942. He was anxious and wary, like everyone else, but he never thought for a minute he 'wouldn't make it'.[10]

A few amtracs ahead was the one carrying Lieutenant Bill 'Zero' Bauerschmidt, Platoon Sergeant Harry Spiece, Jim McEnery, Sterling Mace and the rest of 3rd Platoon. Mace saw the driver crane his head and look back, 'maybe counting heads'. He could feel his throat sting 'with the choking vapors'. He looked at his buddy Sy Levy, just ahead of him, raised his thumb and shouted in encouragement: 'Three days!' Levy returned the thumbs-up, 'affecting a wan smile' as he did so.[11]

Moments later, the ship's big clamshell doors opened and the amtracs followed each other down the ramp and into the water, 'floating out into the bright morning sun'.[12]

It was 7:30 a.m. After circling for half an hour, the beach master dropped his red flag and the first wave of armoured amtracs – bristling with either 75mm or 37mm howitzers, and Browning machine guns – began their slow but steady approach to White and Orange Beaches. Up ahead were eighteen larger landing craft, equipped with 4.5in rocket launchers, that had taken up a position 1,000 yards offshore and were unleashing salvoes of rockets.[13]

K Company's amtracs were in the second wave. Waiting for the signal to head in, Gene Sledge had never felt such 'supremely agonising suspense'. He was in a cold sweat, his stomach tied in knots, a lump in his throat. His knees 'nearly buckled' as he clung to the side of the amtrac. 'I felt nauseous,' he wrote, 'and feared that my bladder would surely empty itself and reveal me to be the coward I was.' But the men around him looked no better than he did, and it was with a 'sense of fatalistic relief' that he welcomed the signal to move.[14]

First Lieutenant 'Stumpy' Stanley, commanding the assault wave (and riding with the 1st Platoon on the extreme left of the company's front), remembered the ride in as 'interminable'. He wrote: 'Just as we reached the line of departure an LCI, stationed on the immediate right, let go its full complement of rockets. The flashes of flame and smoke from the "shoot" completely enveloped the little craft. "My God!" I said. "That trawler has blown up!!!" I never had the chance to look back to see just what the hell had happened to it.'[15]

For Gene Sledge, it was a 'frightful spectacle'. He wrote:

> Huge geysers of water rose around the amtracs ahead of us as they approached the reef. The beach was now marked along its length by a continuous sheet of flame backed by a thick wall of smoke. It seemed as though a huge volcano had erupted from the sea, and rather than heading for an island, we were being drawn into the vortex of a flaming abyss. For many it was to be oblivion.

'Duke' Ellington pulled out a half-pint of whiskey and yelled, 'This is it, boys!' He offered the bottle to Sledge, who refused it. Even the smell might have caused him to pass out. So the lieutenant took a long pull himself and handed the bottle to others. Suddenly a large shell 'exploded with a terrific concussion' to their right front, sending up a large plume of water that doused the occupants. Then the amtrac lurched and halted, pitching the men into one another. The treads flailed and something scraped the hull. They were on the reef. For 'some terrifying moments' they were held fast, a sitting duck for enemy gunners. Sledge could see the Marine coxswain 'wrestling frantically with the control levers' while Japanese shells 'were screaming into the area and exploding all around us'.

Johnny Marmet leaned forward and pointed his .45 automatic at the coxswain's head. 'If you don't get this son of a bitch moving,' he yelled, 'I'm going to by God shoot you in the head!' It seemed to do the trick because, by 'pushing and pulling the controls like a madman', the coxswain was able to rock the amtrac free and they began moving again 'amid the geysers of exploding shells'.[16]

On the 1st Platoon's amtrac, a short way ahead, PFC Bill Leyden was wondering if he had what it took to do his job. Only eighteen, and untested in combat, he was supposed to be the first to exit the amtrac on the right-hand side. Would he live up to his own – and his buddies' – expectations? Or would he freeze? He squeezed his eyes shut and thought of his devout Catholic mother saying a prayer for him. *Hail Mary, full of grace, the Lord is with thee . . .*

Opening his eyes, he saw that his lanky friend and fire team leader, Corporal 'Hook' Ahner, from Huntingdon, Indiana, was looking at him. 'You scared, Bill?' asked Ahner, concern in his eyes.

'Nah, I'm okay,' responded Leyden, less than truthfully.

'Well if you ain't scared, you're the only guy here who ain't,' said Ahner with a grin. 'I'll go out first if you want me to.'

'No, I'm ready. I'm okay.'

Leyden glanced at his grim-faced squad mates: PFC Marion Vermeer from Washington state, PFC Roy Baumann from Upper Wisconsin, Corporal Ted 'Tex' Barrow from Texas (said to be the nephew of Clyde

Barrow, one half of the infamous 'Bonnie and Clyde' bank-robbing duo). He could not imagine anything worse than letting these people down. He would rather die than let Ahner do his job for him.[17]

From 3rd Platoon's amtrac, nearby, Jim McEnery could see other vessels well down the coastline, on either side, 'taking direct hits, bursting into flame, and spouting plumes of black smoke'. The 1st Marines were on their left, the 7th on their right, and it looked like both 'were catching hell'. Yet, for some reason, the 5th Marines in the centre of the beachhead 'weren't as bad off'.[18]

Most Marines were keeping their heads down, but Sterling Mace took a last look as they approached Peleliu. The water at the beach's edge looked eerily white and still, as yet 'untouched by Marines'.

'One minute!' shouted the coxswain. 'One! Minute!'

That was their cue to turn and face the exit ramp. Mace then made a final plea to the sibling who had died when he was four. *Sister Dorothy*, he muttered to himself, *be my guide*.[19]

29

'Move it! Move it!'

Peleliu, 15 September 1944

Third Platoon's amtrac clawed its way a few yards up the wet sand of Orange Beach 2, stopped and dropped its rear ramp. Jim McEnery was the first out, followed by PFC Joe Moskalczak, Frank Minkewitz, Sterling Mace and the others. Looking to his left, Mace could not see any Marines; instead there was a lone mongrel dog, 'wet, shaking from tail to muzzle'. A Japanese machine gun opened up, causing Mace to sprint to the right and take shelter behind another amtrac. Seeing him and others hesitate, Lieutenant Bauerschmidt shouted: 'Don't stand there like a bunch of dummies! Remember what you've been taught. Get off the beach as fast as you can. A beach is a bad place to be, so move it! Move it!'*

Joe Moskalczak, a 20-year-old former coal miner from Blakely, Pennsylvania, led the charge up the sandy incline. 'Near the top we hit the deck,' he recalled, 'because I heard the buzzing of machine gun bullets sailing overhead. I fired my rifle . . . Frank Minkewitz tried to fire his BAR, but it did not go off. So I grabbed my canteen and poured water over the action. Now it worked.'

* Japanese defensive tactics had changed since 1943. Then they had allowed the Americans to come ashore before launching banzai attacks at night. But heavy casualties had forced a rethink. Now their tactic was to defend the beaches before withdrawing into prepared positions, forcing the Americans to attack at a time and place of their choosing.

McEnery urged the men on towards a strip of dense scrub. A young private, running beside him, stumbled and fell. McEnery stopped to help, thinking he had been hit. But there was no blood. Instead the man started vomiting. 'God,' he said, 'I'm sick as a dog. I think it's the exhaust fumes from the tractor.'

The sergeant grabbed him by the shirt, hauled him to his feet and gave him a shove towards the 'strip of pale green undergrowth' ahead. 'You'll be okay,' he shouted. 'Just stay low and run, damn it, run! I'll be right behind you.'

Stopping at the edge of the scrub, McEnery tried to use his hand-held walkie-talkie to find out where the rest of K Company and the 3/5 Marines were. But all he could hear was a babble of voices, no one making any sense. He looked ahead and saw, to his horror, a group of Japanese soldiers trying to manoeuvre a 75mm field gun into position behind a pile of coral rocks. The gun was barely 30 yards away and, if not taken out, would cause carnage on the beach. He bellowed into the radio for artillery support, but there was no response. Instead, a Marine in his squad shouted, 'Hey, Mac, there's one of our tanks heading this way!'

He turned to see an armoured amtrac, its own 75mm cannon jutting out from its turret, grinding slowly towards him. *Thank you, Lord.*

The amtrac stopped beside him. 'We're looking for the Seventh Marines,' shouted the commander.

'They're not in this sector,' McEnery yelled back, 'but stay with us if you can. We need your help.' He pointed towards the pile of rocks and the Japanese gun. 'Can you take that thing out?'

The commander spotted the target and nodded. 'Consider it done, sergeant.'

He ducked down and, ten seconds later, the amtrac's cannon spouted flame as a round roared towards the pile of rocks. It was right on target, blasting the field gun onto its side and killing some of the gunners. A second round 'flung up a cloud of dust, chunks of coral, and several enemy bodies'.

Some of the survivors tried to run, but were cut down by Marines firing M1s and BARs. 'We went down to look at our enemy,' recalled

Joe Moskalczak. 'Someone said, "Look, this one is still breathing." With that, Seymour Levy ran a bayonet into him. He could not pull the bayonet out, so he fired his rifle to free it.'[1]

Bauerschmidt's 3rd Platoon was, at this point, holding the extreme right flank of the division's beachhead. That role had been assigned to the 3rd Battalion of the 7th Marines, which should have landed by now on Orange Beach 3. But the amtracs carrying the 3/7's two assault companies had been held up by 'serious underwater obstacles' and 'heavy enfilading fire from the right, causing the drivers to veer to the left'. As a result, one of the companies would eventually land on Orange Beach 2 and become intermingled with K Company. It would take time to sort them out and move the 3/7 men to the right. For its first thirty minutes ashore, therefore, and possibly for longer, K Company had no flank protection.[2]

Gene Sledge's chief memory as his amtrac stopped on the beach, and he followed 'Snafu' Shelton over its left side, was of a machine-gun burst of 'white-hot tracers' zipping through the air and 'almost grazing' his face. Jerking his head back, he lost his balance and fell awkwardly onto the sand 'in a tangle of ammo bag, helmet, carbine, gas mask, cartridge belt, and flopping canteens'.

By now, rounds were exploding all around him, their fragments slapping on the sand and splashing into the water a few yards behind. Machine-gun and rifle fire was growing in intensity, the bullets 'snapping viciously overhead'. Keeping low, Sledge scuttled to the edge of the beach where he threw himself to the ground. All he could see and hear were flashes and violent explosions. His mind was numb with shock.

Glancing back across the beach he saw a DUKW take a direct hit from a shell: pieces of debris flew into the air, while the carcass was engulfed by fire and dirty black smoke. No survivors emerged. Up and down the beach, and out on the reef, more amtracs and DUKWs were burning. A group of Marines were shot down as they emerged from one hulk, and Sledge could see their buddies trying desperately to save them as they struggled in knee-deep water. 'I shuddered and choked,' he recalled. 'A wild desperate feeling of anger, frustration, and pity gripped me.' Watching his helpless comrades being slaughtered, he felt 'sickened to the depths' of his soul, and kept asking God, 'Why, why, why?'

Getting up, he ran up the sloping beach towards a shallow depression that would give him some cover. Just beyond the edge of the beach he narrowly missed stepping on the pressure trigger of a large black and yellow land mine. His foot had missed it by inches. He reached the depression and, seeing a large white post with Japanese writing, felt a sense of pride that this was 'enemy territory' and that by capturing it they would 'help win the war'.

Moments later, Sledge was ordered by Burgin to move to the right and join the rest of the squad in what had been a small coconut grove before its trees were reduced by fire from both sides to a thicket of low ragged stumps. 'Still,' noted Burgin, 'they gave us some kind of cover. You couldn't dig in the hard coral, but there were plenty of shell craters, and we hunkered down to catch our breath. Bullets were singing over our heads. The small Jap grenade launchers we called knee mortars were popping and artillery was rolling.'

Amid the chaos, Sledge asked his squad mates for a cigarette. 'You're crazy, Sledgehammer,' replied Sergeant Burgin. 'You don't smoke.'

'I want a cigarette,' insisted Sledge.

Burgin gave him one, which he took with trembling hands.

'I toldja you'd start smokin', didn't I, Sledgehammer?' said a jubilant 'Snafu' Shelton, a big grin on his face.

Sledge kept looking to his right, expecting to see men from the 3/7 Marines, but the beach was empty. Eventually more Marines began to arrive directly behind them. Unfamiliar officers and NCOs were shouting, 'K Company, First Platoon, over here!' 'K Company, Mortar Section, over here!' It caused some confusion until they realized it was their namesake company in the 7th Marines.[3]

Landing soon after the assault platoons, 'Ack-Ack' Haldane and his headquarters personnel moved forward under intense artillery, mortar and machine-gun fire to a tank trap ditch where they took cover. Haldane could see that some of the heaviest fire was coming from the right flank where the 3/7 Marines was supposed to be. But as the amtrac carrying the radio communications had been hit on the way in, he was forced to rely on runners to communicate with his platoons, the battalion CP and the unit on his flank. The man he chose to find the 3/7 Marines was field chef Sergeant Fred Miller. 'Get over there,' he told Miller, 'and let them know where we're at and what's going on.'

Keeping as low as he could, Miller retraced his steps towards the beach before heading south. For the first 150 yards he did not see anyone. Then more amtracs started to arrive on Orange Beaches 2 and 3 with men that Miller assumed were from the 3/7. He moved inland, looking for a place to lie low, and spotted a big depression that had probably been made by a 16in naval shell. He made a run for it, and was just yards away when a machine gun opened up from a Japanese pillbox, two bullets catching him in the right thigh and left hand. Rolling the last yard or two into the depression, he took off his pack and dressed the thigh wound with sulfa powder and a compression pad. He then gave himself a shot of morphine.

Worried that the Japanese would try to finish him off, he prepared to make a final stand. *I'm still a deadly force*, he told himself, *because I've got that M1, a lot of ammo and two grenades. And so if they want to come out, they're going to bite some dust.*

After duelling with the pillbox for a few minutes, he spotted two Marines from the 3/7 and shouted for help. As they headed in his direction, he threw a smoke grenade to mask their approach from the pillbox. It worked and, once the two Marines had joined him in the shell hole, he felt like 'the most secure bastard in the world' and that they could 'handle anything'.

Later – once the pillbox had been neutralized and he had reported his company's position to the commander of K Company, 3/7 Marines – he was carried back to the beach and evacuated in an amtrac to the hospital ship USS *Bryan*.[4]

* * *

On Orange Beach 1, meanwhile, the two assault companies of the 1/5 Marines had met only scattered resistance and by 9:00 a.m. had advanced through coconut groves as far as their first objective: phase line 0-1, on the western edge of the airfield. There they tied in with Marines on both flanks: a company of the 2/1 Marines to the north; and I Company of the 3/5 Marines to the south. But when no order came from the regimental CP for them to advance to their second and final objective for the day – phase line 0-2, on the far side of the airfield – they set up a defensive position with mortars, machine guns, anti-tank guns and even three Shermans from Company B of the 1st Tank Battalion which were spread out and placed hull-down in shell craters.[5]

Part of the reason for the 1/5's cautious approach was the heavy opposition met by the 3/1 Marines, the battalion on the extreme left of the beachhead, which prevented it from reaching its first phase line, let alone its second. Though it did manage to capture a formidable Japanese defensive position on its flank, a jagged coral outcrop jutting into the sea called The Point, it failed to clear the enemy from a coral ridge 70 yards inland. 'Had the Japanese launched a major counterattack down the corridor between the ridge and the sea,' noted the US Marines official history, 'they might have succeeded in penetrating to the beaches, which were cluttered with men, gear, and supplies brought in by later waves. The effect upon the beachhead could have been disastrous; in fact, the possibility existed that the Marines might have been driven into the sea.'

Luckily, the counter-attack never came. Coming ashore on White Beach 2, the assault companies of the 2/1 Marines faced only moderate resistance and were able to reach their first phase line – about 350 yards inland – by 9:45 a.m. Here, in the wooded area facing the airfield, they linked up with the left of the 5th Marines. Because of the 'precarious situation on the left' of the beachhead, however, they were ordered to remain where they were until the following morning.[6]

'Bucky' Harris, the commander of the 5th Marines, landed in the fifth wave with the advance elements of the regimental CP. Spotting two groups of burning amtracs on the beach, he told the coxswain to head for the gap between them, in the hope that the 'flame and smoke would confuse the Jap gunners for a couple of minutes' and give them 'enough time to get off and head inland'. The tactic worked, and Harris was able to set up his CP in front of a 'long, wide and deep anti-tank ditch' flanked by a minefield.

Told about the confusion on the right of Orange Beach 2 where the K Companies of the 3/5 and 3/7 Marines were intermingled, Harris realized it would take some time to unscramble and reorganize them so that they could complete their objectives: which were to advance the 500 yards or so to the far side of the island, thus securing the southern tip, before linking up with I and L Companies and completing the capture of the southern half of the airfield. He recalled,

> Finally I got the CO of the 3rd Bn [Lieutenant Colonel Shofner] on the radio. He reported that his company commanders were sorting out their own platoons and had made some progress, but it would be some little time before he could make a coordinated move. He gave me the coordinates of his CP and I told him I would send him a wire party shortly so we could have phone communications. This was my last communication with the 3rd Bn.[7]

At around 9:00 a.m., having extricated itself from its sister company in the 3/7 Marines (which was moving to the right), Haldane's K Company resumed its advance across the island. But it was soon halted by a heavy Japanese mortar barrage.[8] 'Everyone hit the deck,' recalled Gene Sledge, 'I dove into a shallow crater. The company was completely pinned down. All movement ceased.' The shells kept falling, faster and faster, until Sledge 'couldn't make out individual explosions, just continuous, crashing rumbles with an occasional ripping sound of shrapnel tearing low through the air overhead amid the roar'. The air was thick with smoke and dust. Sledge's body 'shuddered and shook' as if he was having a 'mild convulsion'. Sweating profusely, he prayed, clenched his teeth and cursed the Japanese.

Nearby, 'Duke' Ellington was quivering with fear. Sledge, partially protected by the crater, felt sorry for him and anyone else 'out on that flat coral'. It was his first experience of shelling and he felt 'utter and absolute helplessness'. It seemed to go on for hours, but actually lasted only about thirty minutes. When it was over, by which time elements of the 3/7 Marines were in position on the right flank of K Company, the long-delayed move towards the first phase line began. Sledge got up shakily, covered in a layer of coral dust, and passed the walking wounded heading for the beach and evacuation. One was an NCO he knew and liked, holding a bloodied battle dressing over his upper arm. 'Hit bad?' asked Sledge.

The NCO grinned. 'Don't feel sorry for me, Sledgehammer. I got the million-dollar wound. It's all over for me.' He waved and hurried off.

The company was on high alert as it moved forward through the 'thick sniper-infested scrub'. Ordered to halt on the edge of open ground, Sledge saw his first Japanese corpses: a medic and two riflemen. The medic had evidently been killed by shellfire in the act of treating his comrades, because his medical chest lay open beside him, its various bandages and medicines 'arranged neatly in compartments'. He was on his back, his chest torn open and the 'glistening viscera' of his internal organs exposed to view. Sledge felt sick.

Observing the Alabaman's reaction, a 'sweaty, dusty' veteran slung his rifle, leaned forward and plucked a pair of horn-rimmed glasses from the face of the dead corpsman 'as casually' as a guest selecting an hors d'oeuvre at a cocktail party. 'Sledgehammer,' he scolded, 'don't stand there with your mouth open when there's all these good souvenirs lying around.'

He held up the glasses for Sledge to see. 'Look how thick that glass is,' he said. 'These sonsabitches must be half blind, but it don't seem to mess up their marksmanship any.'

The veteran proceeded to ransack the corpse, taking a Nambu pistol and its leather holster, and a neatly folded Japanese flag from inside the corpse's steel helmet, which he then threw away. The veteran's buddy appeared and started stripping the other two corpses. Sledge was shocked by their 'casual and calloused' attitude to the enemy dead, and wondered if it was only a matter of time before he was so dehumanized by war that he could 'field strip' the enemy with such nonchalance.

A few yards away, a corpsman was treating casualties in a 'small, shallow defile'. Sledge went over and found him kneeling over a young Marine who had just died from a neck wound. The victim had a pale 'handsome, boyish' face and did not look a day over seventeen. *What a pitiful waste*, Sledge told himself.

Sobbing quietly to himself, the tears streaming down his 'dusty, tanned, grief-contorted face', the corpsman held the dead Marine's chin tenderly in his left hand while he made the sign of the cross with his right.[9]

K Company continued to advance until, approaching the east side of the airfield, it was held up on the edge of a dense scrub forest by a Japanese artillery piece and some concrete and log pillboxes bristling with machine guns. R. V. Burgin could see six men working the artillery piece, and got his men to pick them off 'one by one'.[10] The pillboxes were a tougher nut to crack, and had already inflicted a number of casualties when Sergeant Hank Boyes – the squad leader in 1st Platoon who had allowed Haney to tag along with his outfit – spotted a lone Sherman tank. He ran over and tried the tank's rear telephone. Finding it out of order, he climbed up onto the tank and persuaded the commander to tackle the Japanese gun positions.

'In order to have a full field of vision,' read the citation for Boyes's Silver Star, 'he rode on the outside of a tank, completely exposed to all types of heavy hostile fire while effectively directing the tank's fire in destroying four strongly held artillery positions and their occupants. His leadership, courage and devotion to duty were in keeping with the highest traditions of the United States Naval Service.'[11]

30

'They're Nip tanks!'

Peleliu, 15 September 1944

At 10:00 a.m., having neutralized the pillboxes at the edge of the airfield, K Company tied in with I Company on the first phase line. When the push to the east resumed thirty minutes later, Haldane's men kept in contact with elements of the 3/7 on their right flank, but quickly lost touch with I Company which, like the 1/5 Battalion, had orders to hold its ground. L Company was used to fill the gap and 'mop up the southern edge of the airfield'.

As K Company 'continued to push through the scrub forest', Haldane had 'trouble maintaining contact between his platoons'. The thick undergrowth limited visibility to a 'few feet', and enemy snipers kept up a constant harassing fire. The US Marines official history noted:

> Flank elements had to take but a few extra steps to the side and contact became lost with neighbouring units. The [3rd] Battalion's control problem was further complicated because of the earlier loss of the LVT carrying practically all the wire and equipment of the 3/5's communication platoon. Although most of the Marines managed to wade ashore and join the battalion early in the afternoon, they had been able to salvage for future use little of the vital equipment.[1]

K Company's 1st Platoon, meanwhile, had 'encountered fierce rifle and machine gun opposition from enemy pillboxes located across a road parallel to the platoon's front which caused heavy casualties' in the two assault squads and 'completely halted their advance'.[2] It was now that the inexperienced platoon leader, Second Lieutenant 'Moose' Barrett, came to the fore. A 20-year-old native of Oak Park, Illinois, Barrett was the eldest of six siblings: five boys and a girl. His father John was an All-American high school football player who went on to play professionally for the Chicago Staleys (a precursor to the Bears). Inheriting his father's athleticism, Barrett had starred as a fullback for Georgetown University's football team before joining the US Marines in February 1943. With his powerful frame – 5ft 11in tall and 190lb in weight – Barrett was good enough to be drafted by the Washington Redskins of the National Football League (as the 210th overall pick). But military service had intervened and his only brief taste of professional football was a few games for the San Diego Bombers before he was shipped out to the Pacific.[3]

Dubbed 'Moose' on account of his imposing physique, Barrett was determined to lead his platoon by the same example he had set his college and high school football teams. With his men pinned down by fire from the Japanese pillboxes, he knew he had to act. His medal citation read:

> After a personal reconnaissance of his platoon's position, he left his assault squads under command of the platoon sergeant and led his support squad to the left in an attempt to outflank the enemy and attack from the rear. When a hostile mortar barrage caused heavy casualties and disorganized his flanking unit as he was leading it into position to cross the road, Second Lieutenant Barrett quickly rallied the remaining men and charged forward into the midst of the Japanese positions, launching a devastating close-range attack with hand grenade and carbine fire until he himself fell, mortally wounded. Continuing to direct his men despite his wounds until the hostile strong point was entirely annihilated, Second Lieutenant

> Barrett, by his inspiring leadership, outstanding fortitude and valiant fighting spirit, had enabled his platoon to continue its successful attacks on the enemy positions . . . He gallantly gave his life for his country.[4]

Badly wounded by shrapnel in the right leg, 'Moose' Barrett later died in the aid station from loss of blood. Thanks to his heroism – for which he was awarded a posthumous Silver Star – K Company was able to secure the north–south trail. Here it was joined, on its left, by I Company, which had been relieved at the first phase line by a company from the 2/5 Marines. Its right flank, however, was no longer in touch with the 3/7. Around this time, Shofner received a radio message from the 3/7's command post. It stated that its left flank unit was on a north–south trail that was 200 yards farther east than the one K Company had reached. Shofner immediately ordered I and K Companies to continue their attack to the east, thus enabling Haldane's men to link up with the neighbouring battalion. Both companies got almost as far as the eastern beaches, but there was still no sign of the 3/7. Instead, Haldane's men opened fire on Japanese soldiers who were wading along the reef at the mouth of the bay. 'OK, you guys, line 'em up and squeeze 'em off,' said a sergeant. 'You don't kill 'em with the noise. It's the slugs that do it. You guys couldn't hit a bull in the ass with a bass fiddle.'[5]

By now, Shofner had received clarification from the 3/7's CP that its left flank unit had been 200 yards west of K Company, and not east of it as previously reported. K Company's move forward, while the 3/7's flank elements held fast, had only widened the gap. Aware of this, Shofner ordered Haldane to bend his right flank back to tie in with the 3/7's left flank. But because his rifle platoons were already committed, Haldane only had HQ personnel available. In the event, these men were unable to extend their line far enough to the southwest to link up with the 3/7 by nightfall.

Shofner was also struggling to coordinate the movements of his three rifle companies. L Company, on his left flank, was able to continue its advance along the southern end of the airfield, while maintaining contact with the 2/5 Marines. But the exact whereabouts of I and K Companies were not known. They were out on a limb – in touch with neither L Company nor the 3/7 – and dangerously exposed to a Japanese counter-attack from either flank.[6]

Having reached the coast, Haldane's men headed back into the thick scrub to find the rest of the division. 'For some time,' recalled Gene Sledge, 'I completely lost my bearings and had no idea where we were going. The weather was getting increasingly hot and I was soaked with sweat.' He swallowed a few salt tablets and took frequent swigs from his water canteens. But he stopped doing this when an NCO warned him to conserve his supply because no one knew when they would get any more.

Eventually a sweating runner with a concerned face appeared from the rear. 'Hey, you guys, where's K Company's CP?'

They directed him to where they thought Ack-Ack's CP was located. 'What's the hot dope?' asked a mortarman.

'Battalion CP says we gotta establish contact with the 7th Marines, 'cause if the Nips counterattack they'll come right through the gap.'

'Jesus.'

The mortarmen joined the rest of the company in a clearing. There the rifle platoons formed up and took casualty reports, as the Japanese shelling became heavier, threatening the feared counter-attack. Fortunately, most of the bombardment fell to the rear, and K Company was able to move out in good order towards the airfield, the edge of which they reached at just before 5:00 p.m., having failed to find the 7th Marines. Sledge could see vehicles moving in the distance. 'Hey,' he said to a veteran, 'what are those amtracs doing all the way across the airfield toward the Jap lines?'

'Them ain't amtracs,' came the reply. 'They're Nip tanks!'

Just then, shell bursts appeared among the enemy tanks, fired by Shermans to the left of K Company's position. Haldane ordered his men to deploy: the riflemen formed a line along a trail at the edge of the scrub, using piled rocks and logs as cover, while the mortarmen set up their guns in a shallow crater just behind the trail. 'Stand by to repel counterattack!' bellowed an NCO. 'Counterattack hitting I Company's front!'

Sledge had no idea where I Company was, but assumed it was somewhere to the left. He sensed K Company was dangerously exposed and, if attacked, all would be lost. 'Snafu' Shelton confirmed his fears. 'They needta get some more damned troops up here,' he growled.[7]

Out on the airfield, they could see the Japanese tanks rolling southwest, parallel to the main runway, and behind them were running large groups of infantry. 'The tank battle,' remembered R. V. Burgin, 'was no contest. Those little Jap tanks were thin-skinned and fragile, and our own Shermans, plus fire from bazookas and artillery, just tore the whole column apart in minutes. The foot soldiers melted away. We blinked and they were gone. Afterwards, pieces of tank were scattered across the airfield like insect parts under a spider-web.'[8]

There were, in fact, two Japanese counter-attacks at the airfield. The first, by two columns of light tanks – thirteen in all – with infantry support, was directed at the centre of the 1/5 Marines who, thanks to Harris, were well dug-in on the eastern perimeter with anti-tank guns, heavy machine guns and Shermans in support. It was all over in barely fifteen minutes as the 1/5 Marines, supported by flanking fire from the 2/1 and 2/5 Marines, shot the Japanese tanks to pieces. Only two Marines were killed – crushed by Japanese tanks – and a handful wounded.* A second counter-attack, about an hour later, was made by a large force of Japanese infantry, led by two tanks. It headed in the same direction, and met the same fate.[9]

* Among the few US casualties was Gunnery Sergeant Mo Darsey, formerly of K Company. 'It was near sundown,' wrote his son, 'and they were in a shell hole for protection. The radio operator reported that a Japanese tank was running over Marines in shell holes and killing them. Daddy said they needed ammunition for their bazooka, which he was attempting to get when he was shot by a machine gun bullet. It hit his right hand and stomach, ripping off his first two fingers.' Darsey survived his wounds and was medically discharged in April 1945. (http://dublinlaurenshometownheroes.blogspot.com/2010/07/maurice-o-mo-darsey.html [accessed 22 January 2021].)

Sledge, meanwhile, had taken a round of high explosive from a canister in his ammo bag, and was holding it in his hand, waiting for the order to fire, when a machine gun cut loose. 'It sounded,' wrote Sledge, 'like one of ours – and from the rear of all places! As I peeped over the edge of the crater through the dust and smoke and saw a Sherman tank in a clearing behind us, the tank fired its 75mm gun off to our right rear. The shell exploded nearby, around a bend in the same trail we were on.'

He was about to fire the mortar when the tank's machine gun opened up again. 'Sledgehammer,' shouted a colleague, 'don't let him hit that shell. We'll all be blown to hell.'

'Don't worry,' Sledge snapped back, 'that's my hand he just about hit.'[10]

For Burgin, it was instantly clear what had happened. The Sherman was in support of the 3/7 Marines and, having spotted the mortar squad up ahead, assumed it was part of the Japanese counter-attack and opened fire. Worse still was 'Duke' Ellington's reaction. 'He turned and flat out ran,' remembered Burgin. 'That yellow son of a bitch, I thought, running like that. I brought my M1 rifle up and got him in my sights. My finger was on the trigger. He vanished behind a log.'

Having almost shot his officer, Burgin turned to deal with the tank. 'Secure the mortars!' he ordered, as he took off towards the Sherman, dodging from tree to tree and waving his arms.

'Knock it off! Knock it off!' he bellowed. 'You're gonna kill the whole damn bunch!'[11]

Someone must have heard him because the firing died away. Sledge breathed a sigh of relief. The fire from the tank had reduced him, in a matter of seconds, 'from a well-trained, determined assistant mortar gunner to a quivering mass of terror'. The thought of being killed by the enemy was bad enough, but to be shot by his own side was more than he could take.[12]

Not long after the second Japanese counter-attack at the airfield was beaten off, and as the light began to fail, the 3/5 Marines' CP received a direct hit from a large-calibre artillery shell. It killed a number of headquarters personnel and wounded the commander, 'Shifty' Shofner, who was hit by shrapnel in the abdomen and left arm. He looked down and 'could see the bones of his forearm, the skin and muscle torn away by shrapnel'. Having blacked out, he woke on a hospital ship to be told by a medic he was a 'lucky man' and would make a full recovery. He was, the man added, the 'sole survivor of his command group'. When Shofner asked about returning to his unit, the medic 'became evasive and suggested that he rest for a while'.[13]

'Bucky' Harris received the bad news in his own CP when a runner reported erroneously that a Japanese shell had killed Shofner, his XO, operations officer and communications officer. He passed the news on to the commander of the 2/5 Marines and 'told him he would have to take care of the left flank until the 3rd Bn was back in action'. He also dispatched his deputy, Lieutenant Colonel 'Silent Lew' Walt, to take over the 3/5 as Shofner's temporary replacement (a role he had performed so impressively at Cape Gloucester). On reaching the 3/5's CP, Walt discovered that Major Robert Ash, the battalion XO, had been killed by mortar fragments soon after landing, and that Shofner had been wounded by the later blast at his CP, but survived. 'As always,' recalled Harris, 'Lew did a masterful job. He soon had the companies unscrambled and moving out on their pre-assigned tasks. He got off a patrol to the south and soon had contact with the 7th Regtl. HQ. I phoned the 2nd Bn CO this information, so that before dark the 5th [Marines] was well in hand when I gave orders to halt and dig in for the night, putting up such barbed wire as might be needed for the more vulnerable sections of our line.'[14]

What Harris failed to mention was that Walt, accompanied by PFC George W. Poppe of the intelligence section, had chosen to make a personal and highly dangerous reconnaissance in the dark to find the 3/5's missing rifle companies. Using Poppe's situation map to navigate through the 'enemy-infested scrub' in the pitch dark, they first located L Company, a rifle platoon of which 'was still tied in with 2/5 on the airfield while the other two were preparing a perimeter defense for the night some 100 yards farther south in the jungle'. After 'ordering the two isolated platoons back to the airfield to set up a linear defense in conjunction with 2/5', he next discovered the 'long-lost flank of 3/7, which was already digging in for the night on the edge of the airfield some 400 yards in from the beach'.

It was not until 9:00 p.m., however, that Walt and Poppe found I Company, and 'only after a difficult passage through the jungle in the dark'. Isolated from other friendly forces, it had set up an all-round perimeter defence, some 200 yards south of the airfield and 300 short of the eastern shore. Walt sent it north to the airfield with orders to 'tie in on the right flank' of L Company. He found his last rifle company, K, another 100 yards to the southwest.[15] Lieutenant 'Stumpy' Stanley, K Company's XO who had spent the day with the assault platoons, recalled:

> There was no consternation or feeling of being alone on the part of K-3-5. Andy Haldane, now with us up front, in his cool, calm way directed the Company in attending [to] the job at hand. As darkness fell and the small arms fire slackened on both sides, Haldane ordered a perimeter defense. The terrain precluded digging-in, so as each man took his position, he built a personal parapet out of broken coral and debris. We had fought the entire day and our gains were fairly won. We intended to protect those gains.
>
> Somewhere up the line of command someone got the idea that K-3-5 was lost. We had no contact with B[attalio]n but we felt secure. Regiment felt otherwise. So it was that after a couple of hours, Lew Walt, with his runner, strode into our Company set-up. Calm as can be, he related the general situation to Haldane and myself and, without fanfare, ordered us to pull back so as to tie in with the screwed up 7th Marines on our right and with the rest of the 3-5 on our left.
>
> The move to the rear was performed without any undue fuss. To be sure, the now intense darkness of the tropical night made for much stumbling and fighting with tangled mangrove growth, all accompanied by the sub-rosa cussing that only a Marine can vent, but the movement was successful.[16]

According to the US Marines official history, K Company was sent back to the airfield to tie in between I Company and the left flank company of 3/7, 'thereby finishing the forming of a defensive line along the edge of the airfield'. In fact, I Company failed to locate its assigned position on the edge of the airfield in the dark, and instead deployed in the woods 'in front of the gap in the 5th Marines lines, thereby minimizing the danger'.[17] But, overall, Walt's bold initiative had made the battalion's position much more secure. 'We were isolated,' wrote Gene Sledge, 'nearly out of water in the terrible heat, and ammunition was low. Lt. Col. Lew Walt, accompanied only by a runner, came out into that pitch-dark, enemy-infested scrub, located all the companies, and directed us into the division's line on the airfield. He should have won a Medal of Honor for the feat!'

It was, for Sledge, an immense relief to complete his gun pit and register the mortar by firing two rounds of high explosive in their new position on the edge of the airfield. To slake his thirst, which was 'almost unbearable', he popped a couple of dextrose tablets in his mouth and took the last swig of his water. 'Artillery shells shrieked and whistled back and forth overhead with increasing frequency,' he wrote, 'and small-arms fire rattled everywhere.'[18]

Jim McEnery remembered that first night on Peleliu as 'one of the longest and uneasiest' of the war. 'What's going to happen tonight, Mac?' a rookie asked him. 'Are the Nips going to pull one of those banzai charges?'

'I don't know, kid,' McEnery replied. 'If they do, they'll let you know they're coming long before they get here, and we'll blow their asses off. Infiltrators are a bigger problem, 'cause you can't hear 'em coming. Just stay down, and keep your rifle and Ka-Bar ready.'[19]

Sergeant Tony Palmisano, Sterling Mace's squad leader, had not been seen since the landing. Mace assumed that Palmisano had been wounded or killed. It later transpired, however, that he had lost his nerve. 'The reason we never saw Palmisano on Peleliu,' wrote Mace later, 'was that as soon as we landed, he took another amtrac right back out to the ships, and there he stayed, having crapped out on the operation. Maybe he had cold feet, or maybe he simply realized, right there on the beach, that the Marine Corps wasn't for him.'

The sergeant, noted Mace, was later court-martialled for cowardice and given five years in the naval penitentiary on Mare Island.[20]

Major General William Rupertus spent most of D-Day watching the invasion of Peleliu from the open starboard deck of the fast-attack ship USS *DuPage*. Sitting on a folding canvas chair, he could see 'the burning amtracs along the beach', and hear 'fragments of warning' from the 'radios scattered around the deck aft of him'.

It soon became clear that things were not going to plan and, as each hour passed, Rupertus became increasingly determined to go ashore and see for himself. He was dissuaded by his chief of staff, Colonel Selden, who flagged up his lack of mobility (Rupertus still needed a cane to walk), the likelihood that he would 'know less' on land than he did aboard ship, and that his deputy, Brigadier General Oliver Smith, was already ashore. If reports to Smith were 'no fuller than they were', added Selden, 'it was fair to assume that the situation on the beach simply had not crystallized enough for full reports to be made'.[21]

Smith, who had set up the Advanced Division CP in a deep anti-tank ditch at the back of Orange Beach 2 at noon, messaged Rupertus at nightfall that 'all regiments were in contact and dug in for the night and that the attack would be resumed at 0800 the following morning'. It was not difficult to draw up the necessary orders, Smith wrote later, as it was simply a question of 'resuming the attack to capture objectives previously assigned'.

Rupertus had hoped to seize two phase lines on D-Day: 0-1, which included 300 yards of beachhead behind White 1 and 2, along with Orange 1 and 2, and all the island south of the airfield; and 0-2, which meant all of the airfield. What the division had actually captured on the first day was approximately phase line 0-1 north of Orange 3, and a wedge across the island east of Orange 3. The southern peninsula of the island, most of the airfield and all of the ridge line were still in enemy hands.

'Until several days later,' wrote Smith, 'when we got complete casualty reports from the transports, we did not fully realize what this shallow beachhead had cost.' It was 92 killed, 1,148 wounded and 58 missing.* Against estimated casualties of 500, these were 'very heavy losses' and could not be sustained for 'many days in succession without destroying the combat efficiency of the division'.

To prepare for the attack on the 16th, regiments were told to request the necessary naval, air and artillery fire support. The 1st and the 7th Marines confirmed that they were ready to resume the attack at 8:00 a.m. Only the 5th Marines wanted a delay because, as 'Bucky' Harris explained to Smith on the field telephone, his regiment was 'short of ammunition and water'. Smith refused. The shore party would do everything it could to resupply the 5th Marines during the night. But, either way, the attack would 'go off' as planned.

Just how precarious a foothold the division had on Peleliu was brought home to Smith that first night when a firefight erupted a short way down the anti-tank ditch, causing the brigadier general and his staff to 'hit the dirt'. In the morning, noted Smith, 'we buried three freshly killed Japanese'.[22]

* K Company's share of the division's D-Day casualties was relatively modest: two dead and thirteen wounded. That represented just over 6 per cent of the total company strength (7 officers and 228 enlisted men). Some rifle companies in the 1st Marines, by contrast, had lost 20 per cent of their strength. (AUA, Sledge Papers, RG96/96-038, Box 3, Folder 8, 1st Sgt David Bailey's Log of Casualties on Peleliu.)

31

'Everywhere shells flashed like giant firecrackers'

Peleliu, 16–17 September 1944

'Alright, Third Platoon,' said Sergeant Harry Spiece, catching the eyes of Jim McEnery and the other squad leaders, 'we're gonna make a run across that airfield. Second Battalion will be on our left; we're going to the right. We've got the shorter run, but you never know what's gonna happen.'[1]

It was just before 8:00 a.m. on 16 September 1944 – D-Day + 1 – and Oliver Smith's resumption of operations was about to begin. The 7th Marines, in the south, would 'secure the promontories'. The 1st Marines would scale the high ground north of the airfield, dubbed 'Bloody Nose Ridge'. But the most spectacular job, and the one that would look the most impressive in communiqués, 'was the seizure of the airfield, requiring companies of the 5th [Marines] to come out of their cover and walk unprotected across the naked, pocked, fire-raked landing strips'.[2]

Earlier, Second Lieutenant 'Zero' Bauerschmidt had joined McEnery behind his 'small pile of rocks and brush', and told him to get the platoon ready to move. 'It's time to do what we came here for,' said Bauerschmidt, 'and capture that damn airfield. We'll do this just like we practiced it on Pavuvu. Stay down till I give the signal. Then run at a crouch and keep moving. Try not to stop for anything. Put some distance between yourself and the guys around you, so you don't make as big a target.'[3]

Around the same time, a parched Gene Sledge had tried to fill up his empty water canteen from a small pool of milky-looking water that some K Company men had found nearby. But he thought better of it when one man started retching and a corpsman yelled, 'Don't drink that water, you guys! It might be poisoned.'

Back at his gun pit, Sledge was relieved to see that a shore party had just delivered water cans, ammo and rations. He poured a slug of water into his aluminium canteen cup, and was shocked to find it 'full of rust and oil' and stinking of diesel. He drank it anyway, and vowed never to slack on an oil-drum steam-cleaning detail again. 'As awful as the stuff was,' he wrote later, 'we had to drink it or suffer heat exhaustion. After I drained my cup, a residue of rust resembling coffee grounds remained, and my stomach ached.'

Sledge grabbed his gear and prepared for the attack. Already the supporting artillery, ships and planes were 'laying down a terrific amount of fire in front on the airfield and ridges behind'. K Company would move when it stopped.[4]

The plan of attack was for the 5th Marines to execute 'a turning movement northward, using the extreme left flank of the division as a pivot point'. All three battalions were involved. 'On the left was the 1st Battalion strung out along the woods' edge. The 2nd was deployed in the middle about halfway across the open terrain, and the 3rd was on the right at the southern fringe of the airfield.' The 3rd Battalion's job, with L Company on the left and K Company on the right, was to support the 2nd Battalion in its drive up the east side of the airfield. The attack, however, was slightly hampered by the fact that, a couple of hours earlier, a Japanese shell had hit the regimental CP, killing the communications officer Captain Kehoe and injuring 'Bucky' Harris and his operations officer, Major McIlhenny, the former commander of the 3/5. McIlhenny, a French-speaking Louisianan and heir to the Tabasco sauce fortune, was 'parleyvooing like crazy when they carried him away'. Despite hyperextending his knee, Harris refused to be evacuated. 'The regimental surgeon,' he recalled, 'was busy writing evacuations slips when I got dug out of the sand and he started to make one out for me. I ordered him to tear it up, saying I had spent a long time getting to command a regiment and was not going to get thrown out [on] the second day. Dr Smith grinned at me and tore up the slip, saying, "You are the boss."' Harris had his knee bound up with elastic bandages, and remained on duty.[5]

K Company's attack began at 8:00 a.m. 'Move out! Move out!' yelled Bauerschmidt, jabbing the air with his father's hog-leg revolver.

They went forward in a wave, then quickly spread out. As they advanced, Japanese guns opened fire from the ridges on the far side of the airfield, causing 'little mushrooms of dirt and smoke' to appear between the running Marines. The air was 'full of blue tracer bullets' from Japanese machine guns.

Running parallel to Jim McEnery were PFCs Sterling Mace and Seymour Levy. Just ahead of him was Corporal John Teskevich. The first man to fall was PFC Dan Lawler, an ammo handler in 'Hillbilly' Jones's machine-gun platoon, hit in the back by mortar shrapnel. 'Keep moving!' shouted McEnery, in case someone tried to help Lawler. 'Don't slow down.'

The sergeant ignored his own advice. Reaching the outer edge of the main runway, he realized his bowels were about to empty, so he stopped, pulled down his pants and 'took a crap right there in the middle of the runway while my platoon mates ran past, hardly seeming to notice me, and bullets smacked the tarmac a few feet away'. After the 'longest, most helpless-feeling thirty seconds' of his life, McEnery yanked up his pants and started running again.[6]

Up ahead, Sterling Mace ducked as a shell went off to his left and bits of coral peppered his back. Through blurred vision, he could see 'straw-colored sheets of haze and heat from the earth' and a Marine lying on his back, 'making like a beached fish, pulling for air, his chest a squeezebox'. The Marine was suffering from heat prostration – a victim of dehydration and the 100-degree heat – as were others to Mace's right, 'shivering and exhausted, with mottled grey and red visages'.[7]

For Gene Sledge, the crossing of the airfield was the 'worst combat experience' of the war: far more terrifying than the landing in amtracs, because here they were exposed, 'running on our own power through a veritable shower of deadly metal'. He wrote:

> The ground seemed to sway back and forth under the concussions. I felt as though I were floating along in the vortex of some unreal thunderstorm. Japanese bullets snapped and cracked, and tracers went by me on both sides at waist height. This deadly small-arms fire seemed almost insignificant amid the erupting shells. Explosions and the hum and growl of shell fragments shredded the air. Chunks of blasted coral stung my face and hands while steel fragments spattered down on the hard rock like hail on a city street. Everywhere shells flashed like giant firecrackers.

He saw Marines fall but kept going, his teeth gritted in anticipation of the shock of being hit. It seemed impossible that any of them could make it unscathed. Having ignored the temporary cover of several craters, he stumbled and fell when halfway across, just as a shell exploded to his left 'with a flash and a roar', a fragment missing his head by inches. Instead it struck 'Snafu' Shelton beyond him, bringing him down. He crawled over and was relieved to find 'Snafu' just winded and bruised, the fragment having spent much of its force before it hit the Louisianan's heavy web belt. Sledge found the piece of shrapnel, about an inch square and half an inch thick, still hot from the explosion, and dropped it into Snafu's pack. The pair then got to their feet and ran after the others.[8]

Sterling Mace and the rest of 3rd Platoon were among the first to reach the relative safety of the mangrove swamp on the far side of the airfield. 'Who's hit? Who got hit?' panted Mace as he took off his helmet. Others flopped down beside him, 'lying on their packs and sides, gulping air in great gasps'. Some lit cigarettes, others just gazed back over the ground they had crossed, 'unbelieving, shielding their eyes from the rays of the sun'.[9]

Even the Canal and Gloucester veterans looked shaken, a sight that Sledge found oddly comforting as he gazed down at his trembling hands, and almost laughed at himself 'with relief'. Incredibly, K Company had suffered just two wounded by shrapnel crossing the airfield: Lawler and a private in 2nd Platoon. Both were evacuated, before the company moved on to its next objective.[10]

The other assault companies had not got off so lightly, particularly those of the 1/5 Marines on the left. While a few of its riflemen were able to use the cover provided by the 'scrub growth and rubble along the northern fringe of the airfield', most had 'to brave the open runways in an open order formation with intervals of about 20 yards'. Their advance across the fire-swept terrain, noted the battalion commander, 'was an inspiring and never to be forgotten sight'. Reaching the main hangar area on the northeast side of the airfield, they faced stiff resistance from Japanese soldiers in the ruined buildings, a large V-shaped anti-tank ditch, and two stone bunkers that housed 20mm guns. It was finally overcome in fierce hand-to-hand fighting that exacted a heavy toll on the attackers.[11]

K Company, meanwhile, had continued its march northeast through the mangrove swamps, with the 3/7 Marines on its right. Haldane's men dug in for the night with their backs to the sea. Sledge had set up his mortar in a 'meager gun pit on a slight rise of ground', not far from 'a sheer rock bluff that dropped about ten feet to the ocean'. Despite being in thick undergrowth, there was a hole in the jungle canopy through which they could fire their mortar.

Having registered the gun by firing a couple of high-explosive rounds onto an obvious avenue of approach, they set up aiming stakes to mark other features on which they might fire. Then they dug shallow foxholes and settled down for the night, one man sleeping while his buddy kept watch. Every so often, a burst of gunfire or a bang from a grenade would disturb the quiet. The tension got to Gene Sledge as he peered into the darkness, his hand gripping Shelton's cocked .45 semi-automatic pistol 'at the ready'. Suddenly he heard movement in the dry vegetation ahead. The rustling sounds grew closer, then stopped. More noise, followed by silence. It had to be a Japanese infiltrator, he reasoned, crawling close enough to use a grenade or bayonet.

As he flipped off the safety, his heart thumping, a 'helmeted figure loomed up against the night sky' in front of him. He could not be certain if the helmet was American or Japanese. Aiming the pistol at the wearer's face, he pressed the grip safety and 'squeezed the trigger slightly to take up the slack'. Despite his fear, his hand was steady.

'What's the password?' said Sledge in a low voice.

No answer.

'Password!' he repeated.

'Sle-Sledgehammer,' stammered a voice.

He gently released the trigger.

'It's de l'Eau. Jay de l'Eau. You got any water?'

'Jay,' said Sledge, 'why didn't you give the password? I nearly shot you!'

'Oh, Jesus,' said de l'Eau, spotting the pistol. 'I thought you knew it was me.'*

Sledge's hand was trembling violently as he lowered the gun. He felt 'nauseated and weak and wanted to cry'. He had come within an ace of shooting one of his best buddies, a 21-year-old Gloucester veteran from Los Angeles who should have known better than to prowl around in the dark. Sledge was furious. After handing de l'Eau a canteen, he let rip: 'Just how in the hell could I tell it was you in the dark with Nips all over the place?'[12]

There were many Japanese infiltrators that night, and one of them threw a grenade that accounted for PFC Bob Oswalt, another 21-year-old Gloucester veteran, in the early hours of 17 September. Sledge learned of the tragedy as he passed Oswalt's shallow foxhole – now his grave – in the morning. 'A bright young mind,' he wrote later, 'that aspired to delve into the mysteries of the human brain to alleviate suffering had itself been destroyed by a tiny chunk of metal. What a waste, I thought. War is such self-defeating, organized madness the way it destroys a nation's best.'[13]

* * *

* Years later, when asked if he thought Sledge really would have shot him, de l'Eau joked: 'Yes, he probably would have, but I was three feet away, and Sledgehammer couldn't hit anything with that .45 beyond a distance of 2 feet, so I was safe.' (AUA, Sledge Papers, RG96/96-038, Box 2, Folder 23, Letter from de l'Eau to Sledge, 16 June 1988.)

By the end of 17 September, the 1st Marines had lost 1,236 men in three days – nearly half its strength – and its 'front line units were decimated'. The 3/1 Marines alone had just under 500 effectives, of whom 200 were headquarters and attached personnel. It was an early indication of the brutal and bloody struggle that lay ahead, as the 1st Marine Division shifted its focus from the airfield to the rugged Umurbrogol ridges to the north where the Japanese defenders had dug a formidable network of defensive positions into the coral rock, impervious to aerial bombing or artillery fire. It was against the outer layer of this rocky fortress – a 'contorted mass of decayed coral, strewn with rubble, crags, ridges and gulches thrown together in a confusing maze' – that the men of the 1st Marines had been hurled on 16 September, an attack that would continue for the next week.[14] Brigadier General Smith wrote:

> According to the map, the high ground north of the airfield consisted of a series of parallel ravines oriented northeast-southwest. The map was reconstructed from aerial photographs taken before the jungle covering was blasted from the terrain by naval gunfire, air, and artillery bombardments. When the bombardment stripped the terrain of its jungle covering, it was found to consist of rugged, pitted, upended coral formations. Ravines, which on the map and photographs appeared to be steep-sided . . . actually had sheer cliffs for sides, some of them 50 to 100 feet high . . . There were dozens of caves and pill boxes worked into the noses of the ridges and the ravines. It was very difficult to find blind spots as the caves and pill boxes were mutually supporting . . . We found later that some of the caves consisted of galleries of more than one level with several exits . . . These caves and pill boxes housed riflemen, machine gunners, mortars, rockets and field pieces.[15]

Moreover, as a report from the 1st Marines noted,

> There were no roads, scarcely any trails. The pock-marked surface offered no secure footing even in the few level places. It was

> impossible to dig in; the best the men could do was pile a little coral or wood debris around their positions. The jagged rocks slashed their shoes and clothes, and tore their bodies every time they hit the deck for safety. Casualties were higher for the simple reason it was impossible to get under the ground away from the Japanese mortar barrages. Each blast hurled chunks of coral in all directions, multiplying many times the fragmentation effect of every shell. Into all this the enemy dug and tunnelled like moles; and there they stayed to fight to the death.

As if the harsh terrain was not bad enough, the attackers also had to contend with a 'blazing sun' that reflected off the white sand and coral and turned the 'entire arena into a blazing furnace'.[16]

The 3/5 Marines, meanwhile – commanded since the afternoon of 16 September by Major John H. Gustafson, formerly XO of the 2/5, who replaced Walt – had been ordered to relieve the 1/5 Marines north of the airfield and launch an attack in support of the 1st Marines through low ground on the eastern side of Bloody Nose Ridge on the 17th. At the same time, the 2/5 Marines would clean out the jungle between 3/5's right flank and the eastern shore. For the attack, the 3/5 was deployed on a two-company front – L (left) and K (right) – with I Company in reserve.[17] 'As soon as we moved forward,' recalled Gene Sledge, 'we came under heavy flanking fire from Bloody Nose Ridge on our left. Snafu delivered his latest communiqué on the tactical situation to me as we hugged the deck for protection: "They need to git some more damn troops up here," he growled.'[18]

So severe was the enemy artillery and mortar fire that the 3/5 made only modest gains and its attack was called off late in the afternoon. K Company had just three casualties: one killed and two wounded.[19] The latter included young Sy Levy, injured as he and the rest of 3rd Platoon pushed through a jungle thicket.

Boom! 'What the hell was that?' asked Sterling Mace, swinging his BAR in the direction of the noise.

'Sounded like a grenade or maybe a booby trap,' replied Jim McEnery.

McEnery hurried towards the sound and found Levy on his knees, 'holding the lower part of his face with both hands', blood running down his neck. He was mumbling something, and seemed to be in shock.

'What happened to you, Sy?' asked McEnery.

There was no response. A corpsman arrived, and covered Levy's chin and lower jaw with a field dressing. 'There's shrapnel in there,' he told McEnery. 'Looks like several fragments. He needs to go to an aid station, maybe a hospital ship.'

While they waited for a stretcher to appear, Levy was barely conscious and still losing blood. 'Hey, cheer up, man,' said a Marine. 'That looks like a million-dollar wound to me. I think you just got yourself a ticket home.'

After Levy was evacuated, McEnery noticed Mace looking glum. 'You worried about your pal?' he asked.

'Nah, he'll be okay, I guess,' replied Mace. 'Actually I kind of envy him, but I'm gonna miss him, too, Mac. I mean, Christ, I may never see the crazy so-and-so again.'

'Yeah,' said McEnery, shrugging, 'well, probably not till after the war, anyway.'

They were both wrong.[20]

Later that day, after K Company had been ordered to dig in and hold its ground, Gene Sledge was sent on a work party to bring up ammo, food and water. They were struggling to unload a 55-gallon drum of water from an amtrac with a rope sling, while at the same time dodging mortar shrapnel, when a Marine appeared from the rear and asked: 'You fellows need any help?'

He was dressed like them – in green dungarees, leggings and a cloth-covered helmet – with a .45 semi-automatic pistol on his hip, but appeared to be much older, at least fifty, and was wearing glasses. When he took off his helmet to mop his brow, he revealed a mop of grey hair. Asked who he was and which unit he was with, he replied: 'Captain Paul Douglas. I was division adjutant until the barrage hit the 5th Marines' CP yesterday, then I was assigned R-1 in the 5th Regiment. I am very proud to be with the 5th Marines.'

'Gosh, Cap'n!' said one of the party, as he passed Douglas a box of ammo. 'You don't have to be up here at all do you?'

'No,' said Douglas, 'but I always want to know how you boys up here are making out and want to help if I can. What company are you fellows from?'

'From K Company, sir,' answered Sledge.

Douglas grinned. 'Ah,' he said, 'you're in Andy Haldane's company.'[21]

It turned out that Douglas was also a Bowdoin alumnus – class of 1913 – and knew of Haldane's exploits both as a ball player and a soldier. Douglas himself was quite a character. Born in Massachusetts in 1892, he had lost his mother when he was four and was raised by his stepmother in Maine. After graduating from Bowdoin and Columbia (with a PhD), he taught economics at a number of universities, including Chicago. He also worked as an economic advisor to various politicians (including Franklin D. Roosevelt, when governor of New York), and helped to draft state laws regulating utilities and establishing old-age pensions and unemployment insurance. After narrowly failing to win election to the US Senate as a Democratic candidate for Illinois on 1942, he enlisted in the US Marine Corps as a private at the age of fifty. Promoted to sergeant, he was eventually persuaded to take a commission and posted to the Pacific. A lifelong advocate of the working man, he felt right at home with the men of K Company.[22]

As they finished unloading the supplies, Sledge and the others agreed that there 'wasn't a finer company commander than Captain Haldane'.

Douglas nodded his approval. After he had said his goodbyes, a Marine asked the group: 'What's that crazy old grey-headed guy doing up here if he could be back at regiment?'

'Shut up! Knock it off, you eightball!' growled the NCO in charge. 'He's trying to help knuckleheads like you, and he's a damned good man.'

Back with his mortar squad, Sledge ate chow and drank a cup of hot bouillon made from dehydrated tablets and some of the polluted, oily water. Despite the heat, it was the 'most nourishing and refreshing' food he had eaten in days. After dark, he was joined on the edge of his gun pit by two likeable Canal veterans: Lieutenant 'Hillbilly' Jones, who had taken over 1st Platoon after 'Moose' Barrett's death, and Corporal John Teskevich, the 'Mad Russian'. They shared rations and talked, and the conversation was one of the 'most memorable' of Sledge's life.

Thanks to 'Duke' Ellington's antics, the young Alabaman did not have a lot of time for officers. The exceptions were Ack-Ack and Hillbilly, who was second only to the company commander in popularity among the enlisted men. Hillbilly was, noted Sledge, 'a clean-cut, handsome, light-complexioned man – not large, but well built', who had been an 'enlisted man for several pre-war years' and only received his commission after outstanding service on the Canal. He added:

> An Act of Congress may have made Hillbilly an officer, but he was a born gentleman. No matter how filthy and dirty everyone was on the battlefield, Hillbilly's face always had a clean, fresh appearance. He was physically tough and hard and obviously morally strong. He sweated as much as any man but somehow seemed to stand above our foul and repulsive living conditions in the field . . . His accent was soft, more that of the deep South, which was familiar to me, than that of the hill country.
>
> Between this man and all the Marines I knew there existed a deep mutual respect and warm friendliness. He had that rare ability to be friendly yet not familiar with the enlisted men. He possessed a unique combination of those qualities of bravery, leadership, ability, integrity, dignity, straightforwardness, and compassion. The only other officer I ever knew who was his equal in these qualities was Captain Haldane.

That third night on Peleliu, Hillbilly talked about his childhood and asked Sledge about his. It was more the quiet way he spoke, rather than the content, that soothed the mortarman. Sledge admitted his shame at feeling so afraid, and that some men seemed more able to cope.

'You've nothing to be ashamed of, Sledgehammer,' said the lieutenant. 'Your fear is no greater than anyone else's. You're just honest enough to admit its magnitude. I'm afraid, too. We all are. But the first battle is the hardest because you don't know what to expect. Fear dwells in everyone. Courage means overcoming fear and doing one's duty in the presence of danger, not being unafraid.'

Teskevich returned with some coffee and, as they sipped their joe in silence, Sledge felt almost lightheaded. He heard a loud voice say emphatically, 'You will survive the war!'

'Did y'all hear that?' he asked.

'Hear what?'

'Someone said something,' insisted Sledge.

'I didn't hear anything. How about you?' said Hillbilly to Teskevich.

'No, just that machine gun off to the left.'

They turned in soon after, and Sledge did not mention the voice to anyone else. But he was convinced that God had spoken to him, and resolved to make his life 'amount to something after the war'.[23]

32

'I never saw such agonized expressions'

Peleliu, 20–25 September 1944

While the men of the 1st Marines were battling to capture the high ground north of the airfield – a fight that Oliver P. Smith described as one of the 'bitterest' of the Pacific War – the Devil Dogs had the much more straightforward task of clearing the narrow peninsula and islands that represented the lower arm of the 'lobster's claw' to the east.[1]

On 20 September – D-Day + 5 – having crossed the causeway and pushed south through mangrove, jungle and swamp two days earlier – Haldane sent out patrols while the bulk of K Company took up a defensive position along a stretch of coast dubbed Purple Beach to guard against Japanese infiltration and reinforcements on the eastern shore. It was joined there by Seymour Levy, fresh out of hospital, his injured chin still wrapped in white bandages. 'He looked tired and pale,' recalled Jim McEnery, 'but he seemed to feel okay.'

Returning from a patrol, Sterling Mace was astonished to see his buddy. 'What the heck're you doing here?' he asked. 'I thought you'd be halfway to the States by now.'

'Aw,' mumbled Levy, grinning, 'I sneaked off the hospital ship and bummed a ride to the beach on a ferry. I just wanted to be back with the company. I missed you guys. Besides, it's where I belong.'

Mace shook his head. 'Jeez, Sy, you must be nuts. You know that?'[2]

The biggest combat patrol sent out that day was led by 'Hillbilly'

Jones. Composed of around forty Marines, it was a mixture of 1st Platoon, R. V. Burgin's mortar squad, a section of machine guns, a Doberman Pinscher war dog and its handler (both part of the 4th Marine War Dog Platoon, attached to the 5th Marines), and 'Pop' Haney, who was still tagging along with 1st Platoon. The patrol's senior NCO was acting Platoon Sergeant Hank Boyes. Their orders, remembered Burgin, were to move 'down to the tip of a long, narrow peninsula running along the southeast coast of the island'. Located just off the peninsula were two islands where a couple of thousand Japanese troops were believed to be holed up. When the tide went out, it would be easy for them to wade across, come up the peninsula, and take K Company by surprise. The patrol's job was to 'set up and watch for them'.[3]

It was not a mission that Gene Sledge, for one, was looking forward to. Having picked up extra rations and ammunition, and filed through the company lines exchanging parting remarks with friends, he felt like a little boy spending his first night away from home. It reminded him that K Company was where he wanted to be. 'It was not just a lettered company,' he wrote later, 'in a numbered battalion in a numbered regiment in a numbered division. It meant far more than that. It was home; it was "my" company. I belonged in it and nowhere else.' This sense of family was not 'misplaced sentimentality but a strong contributor to high morale'. It made a man feel he belonged, and that his buddies would look out for him, as he would for them. It was, Sledge felt, 'particularly important in the infantry, where survival and combat efficiency often hinged on how well men could depend on one another'.

Moving off through thick undergrowth, the scouts keeping a keen eye for snipers, they walked past 'numerous shallow tidal inlets and pools choked with mangroves and bordered by more mangroves and low pandanus trees'. Sledge, a keen ornithologist, noticed a pair of 'man-o-war' birds* – with hooked beaks and a huge seven-foot wingspan – nesting at the top of one low tree. Stopping to study them, he was rebuked by

* Known as 'man-o-war' or frigate birds because they force other birds to regurgitate recently eaten food, which they then steal.

Burgin. ‘Sledgehammer, what the hell you staring at them birds for? You gonna get separated from the patrol.’

Sledge saw Burgin’s point and moved on. They finally halted at the end of the peninsula where Hillbilly set up his CP in an abandoned Japanese bunker, built of coconut logs and coral rock. The men deployed around it, taking advantage of the relatively soft soil to dig foxholes that were deeper than usual. The mortar gun pit was sited 30 feet from the bunker and just a few feet from the swamp water that separated the peninsula from the first of the islands that were said to be crawling with Japanese. Visibility was limited to a couple of yards because of the ‘dense tangle of mangrove roots on three sides of the patrol’s defensive perimeter’. Nor were the mortarmen able to register their gun, for fear of giving their position away and losing the element of surprise. Instead they aimed it in the direction from which they expected the enemy to come, ate their rations, checked their weapons, and prepared for a long night.

It began to rain and, as he peered out into the inky blackness, Sledge had a sudden realization that he and the rest of the patrol were ‘expendable’, their lives of little value. It was a depressing thought and, to lighten the mood, he asked George Sarrett about his boyhood in Texas and experiences on New Britain. They were chatting in low tones when someone crawled up behind them and whispered, ‘What’s the password?’

It had been given out earlier and, as was typical in the Pacific, contained the letter ‘l’ which the Japanese tended to pronounce as an ‘r’, thus identifying them as non-American. They both responded with the correct word. ‘Good,’ said Haney. ‘You guys be on the alert, you hear?’

An hour later, Haney reappeared with the same question. They responded as before. ‘Good. You guys check your weapons? Got a round in the chamber?’

‘Yes.’

‘Okay, stand by with that mortar. If the Nips come through this swamp at high port with fixed bayonets, you’ll need to fire HE and flares as fast as you can.’

Twice more Haney did the rounds, prompting Sarrett to growl on the last occasion: 'I wish to hell Hillbilly would grab him by the stackin' swivel and anchor him to the CP.'

By now the men on the perimeter were, in Burgin's words, 'more than alert. We were forty twitching bundles of nerves. We jumped at every sound. A fish splashing out in the water, some animal snapping a twig or some bird ruffling its feathers – anything could set us off.'

Soon after Haney's fourth appearance, Sledge looked at the luminous dial on his watch. It was just gone midnight. A low voice sounded from the CP, 'Oh, ah, oh.' Then the same sound, only louder.

'What's that?' asked Sledge.

'Sounds like some guy having a nightmare. They sure as hell better shut him up before every Nip in this damned swamp knows our position.'

They could hear someone thrashing around in the CP. Burgin, who was closer, realized it was the dog handler. 'Oooooh! Oooooh! Dog! They're gonna kill me, dog! Help me!'

'Quiet that man!' ordered 'Hillbilly' Jones.

'Help me!' shouted the dog handler, who had lost his senses. 'Oh, dog! God! Help me! Help me!'

'Shut that man up!' hissed an increasingly desperate Hillbilly.

Several men tried to wrestle the deranged dog handler to the ground and keep him quiet, but he kept shouting. Eventually the corpsman arrived and gave him a shot of morphine. It only made matters worse. 'The Japs have got me! The Japs have got me! Save me, dog!'

More morphine was given, but it did no good. Hillbilly tried to soothe him. 'It's okay, son. You're going to be okay.'

The dog handler kept yelling.

Someone tried to knock him out with a punch, 'the sickening crunch of a fist against a jaw' audible to Sledge thirty feet away. The dog handler fought back 'like a wildcat, yelling and screaming at the top of his voice'.

Hyped up by the mortal danger they were all in, and clean out of options, a voice commanded: 'Hit him with the flat of that entrenching shovel!'

There was a horrible *thud*, then silence.

R. V. Burgin, whose foxhole was just a few feet from the drama, remembered sitting there 'for a long time, nobody talking'. He felt 'more rattled than if the Japs had come'.

'Christ a'mighty, what a pity,' said a Marine in the foxhole next to Sledge.

'You said that right,' responded his buddy, 'but if the goddamn Nips don't know we're here, after all that yellin', they'll never know.'

Dawn finally came, after a seemingly endless night, to reveal a shocking scene at the CP. The dead body of the dog handler was lying next to the bunker, covered with a poncho. Gene Sledge recalled: 'The agony and distress etched on the strong faces of Hillbilly, Hank, and others in the CP revealed the personal horror of the night. Several of these men had received or would receive decorations for bravery in combat, but I never saw such agonized expressions on their faces as that morning in the swamp. They had done what any of us would have had to do under similar circumstances. Cruel chance had thrust the deed upon them.'

In the CP itself, Hillbilly got on the radio to Major Gustafson at battalion headquarters.* 'John,' he said, 'we need to come out of here.'

Gustafson tried to dissuade him, but Hillbilly was adamant. 'No, John. I'm telling you we need to come out of here. We've had a situation here and everybody's nerves are shot. We need to get the hell out.'

'Okay,' said the major, after a short pause. 'I'll send a relief column with a tank so you won't have any trouble coming in.'

An hour later, the tank emerged from the thick undergrowth, flanked by K Company men. They loaded the handler's body on to the tank and returned with it through the 'dripping trees' to the company's lines. There were no repercussions, and little discussion afterwards. 'None of us was proud of it,' wrote Burgin, 'but the dog handler had endangered all of us . . . We'd done what we had to do. I was as close as anybody to what happened, three or four feet away. I'd seen who'd swung the

* Originally from North Carolina, Gustafson's radio call sign was 'Tarheel' (the nickname for people from that state).

shovel. I knew who did it. He did something that needed to be done. As long as any of us is alive, none of us will reveal who it was.'

Nor did they. The final oddity of the whole grim experience, according to Burgin, is that the Doberman was 'silent during the whole deal'.[4]

At 9:45 a.m. on 25 September, four days after the return of the ill-fated patrol to Purple Beach, the men of K Company were ordered to collect their gear and march to the nearest road, close to the village of Ngardololok, where trucks would be waiting to take them back over the causeway to the western portion of the island. They were marching along in single file when they met, coming the other way, the 'raggedest bunch of Marines' any of them had seen. They were 'unshaven and filthy from powder burns, bloodstained and near emaciated', with 'glazed and distant eyes' and 'battered dungarees salted white with sweat'.

Second Lieutenant Bauerschmidt shook his head slowly. 'Man,' he said to Jim McEnery, 'look at those guys. You can tell they've been through hell.'

'Yeah,' responded McEnery, 'I'd been kind of envying them because they were getting relieved and we weren't. But now that I see the poor devils, I sure as hell don't envy them anymore.'

The men they encountered were the remnants of 'Chesty' Puller's 1st Marines. 'We stopped and swapped news,' remembered R. V. Burgin. 'We found out they had lost about three-quarters of their regiment. What was left looked like ghosts of Marines. They went their way and we went ours, wondering what we were getting into.'[5]

Two days earlier, the 1st Marines had been withdrawn from the fighting in the ridges north of the airport and replaced by the 321st Infantry, part of the US Army's 81st Division that had just captured the neighbouring island of Angaur. 'We're not a regiment,' said a member of the 1st Marines as they trudged down from the high ground, 'we're the *survivors* of a regiment.'

He was right. In eight days of combat on Peleliu, the 1st Marines had lost 1,737 men: 299 killed and 1,438 wounded. As a proportion of battalion strength, that worked out at 71 per cent of the 1/1 Marines,

56 per cent of the 2/1, and 55 per cent of the 3/1. The 1/1 Marines had just seventy-four men left in its nine rifle platoons, and every platoon leader was a casualty. The regiment had killed, at the same time, an estimated 3,700 Japanese.

Among the more conspicuous acts of heroism was the capture and defence of a steep coral outcrop called Hill 100 by Captain Everett Pope – Haldane's former classmate and the commander of C Company, 1/1 Marines – and just twenty-five men. 'Attacked continuously with grenades, machine guns and rifles from three sides,' noted Pope's medal citation, 'and twice subjected to suicidal charges during the night, he and his valiant men fiercely beat back or destroyed the enemy, resorting to hand-to-hand combat as the supply of ammunition dwindled.'

Reduced to just eight defenders, Pope was finally ordered to withdraw. Though wounded by shrapnel, he got back safely and was later awarded the Medal of Honor, one of only eight given to the men of the 1st Marine Division for heroism on Peleliu.[6]

Many participants in the battle, and historians since, have criticized 'Chesty' Puller for the tactical inflexibility that cost his regiment so many casualties. The criticism is justified. What Puller cannot be accused of, however, is sending men to their deaths while he kept out of harm's way. One visitor to the 1st Marines' CP during the battle wrote:

> It was a hot day and Puller was stripped to the waist. He was smoking his battered pipe; characteristically he held the pipe between his incisors and talked out of the side of his mouth. His CP was located where the bluffs came very close to the road. This defilade was necessary because the Japanese were laying down considerable mortar fire, and considerable small-arms fire was passing overhead. While I was at the CP some Japanese snipers worked down to a position north of the CP where they could fire down into it. Puller organized a patrol and sent them out to get the snipers. In a few minutes there were bursts of fire and shortly after that the patrol returned.[7]

Eventually, however, the strain of battle was too much even for a Marine officer as hard-bitten as Puller. After the corps commander Major General Geiger had visited the 1st Marines' CP on 21 September, a member of Geiger's staff noted that Puller was 'very tired' and 'unable to give a very clear picture of what his situation was'. When Geiger asked him what he needed in the way of help, he said he was 'doing all right with what he had'.

Geiger moved on to the division CP and, having consulted the casualty reports, told Rupertus that, in his estimation, 'the First Marines were finished'. The regiment needed to be taken out of the line and replaced by army troops. Rupertus tried to avoid this by insisting that the island could be secured in another day or two with the troops available, a claim dismissed by the official historians as 'a patently impossible solution in view of the overall tactical situation'. But Geiger would not budge: the 1st Marines would be taken off the island and replaced by a regiment of the 81st Infantry Division. Why, then, was Rupertus so reluctant to use army units? It may have been 'rooted in earlier experiences', wrote the official historians, 'which did not always result in harmonious relations'. Or Rupertus may simply have 'distrusted a division that was new to combat and felt that the battle-hardened 1st Marine Division was capable of finishing the job it had undertaken without any help'. Either way, Geiger was right to intervene.[8]

Like Rupertus, 'Chesty' Puller found it hard to face facts. Even after the 1st Marines had been relieved and sent to recuperate on Purple Beach, Puller told his men that they would return to combat after a three-day rest. That was never the plan. 'There were no replacements available,' noted Brigadier General Smith, 'and losses in the rifle units had been so heavy, particularly among the officers and non-commissioned officers, that the units were no longer effective.'[9]

The decimated regiment was finally shipped out of Peleliu – having seen no more action – on 2 October. Taken aboard two hospital transports in steady rain and a heavy swell, one dishevelled Marine was asked by a spotless young naval officer if he had any souvenirs to trade. 'I brought my ass outa there, swabbie,' he replied. 'That's my souvenir of Peleliu.'[10]

33

'I'm hit! Christ, I'm hit!'

Sniper's Alley, 25–26 September 1944

Just after noon on 25 September, the men of K Company reached the road near Ngardololok and found trucks waiting to take them to the west coast. Their new mission, explained 'Ack-Ack' Haldane, was to secure the north of the island by advancing up the western coastal road that flanked the coral crags and crevices of Umurbrogol Mountain, the Japanese stronghold that lay beyond Bloody Nose Ridge.

The day before, the US Army's 321st Infantry had attacked north along that same West Road, supported by the 3/7 Marines. By noon, faced with only light small arms and mortar fire, the spearhead battalion of the 321st had advanced more than a thousand yards to the junction of the West Road and a trail leading eastwards. There stiff Japanese resistance was overcome, resulting in the capture of an anti-tank gun, three machine guns and a naval gun. While the main force pushed another few hundred yards up the road to Gorekoru, establishing a defensive line just beyond the village, elements of the 2/321st and 3/321st moved down the eastern trail and, after a 'brief but bitter engagement', captured Hill 100, the northern bastion in the Umurbrogol ridges that commanded the East Road. By nightfall the 3/321st had seized an escarpment south of Hill 100 and established contact with the 3/7 Marines to the southeast.

Early on the 25th, a strong combat patrol from the 321st – composed of infantry, tanks and flamethrowers – advanced 1,200 yards north of Gorekoru, killing thirty Japanese and destroying four pillboxes and two large supply dumps. Such weak resistance along the West Road was confirmation for Rupertus that the main Japanese strength was in the central ridges. He therefore ordered a swift drive to the north by the 5th Marines, while the 321st Infantry completed the bisection of the island, thus isolating the enemy in what would become the Umurbrogol Pocket. The route to the north lay open, and it was the Devil Dogs' job to secure it.[1]

As their trucks 'bumped and jolted' past the airfield, the men of K Company were amazed at the transformation since their last visit. 'Heavy construction equipment was everywhere,' wrote Gene Sledge, 'and we saw hundreds of service troops living in tents and going about their duties as if they were in Hawaii or Australia. Several groups of men, Army and Marines, watched our dusty truck convoy go by. They wore neat caps and dungarees, were clean-shaven, and seemed relaxed. They eyed us curiously, as though we were wild animals in a circus parade.'

Looking at his buddies in the truck, Sledge could understand why. They were 'armed, helmeted, unshaven, filthy, tired, and haggard'. The contrast with the 'clean comfortable noncombatants' was stark, and they tried to boost their morale by discussing the impressive show of American 'material power and technology'.[2]

Reaching the junction with the western road, they turned north and were soon hemmed in by the shore on their left and the 'rugged ridges of the Umurbrogols' on their right. They had not gone far when they started seeing 'dogfaces', army soldiers from the 321st. The trucks stopped just beyond Gorekoru where the closest ridge was in American hands. There they exchanged scuttlebutt with the 'dogfaces', who told them that the coastal road ahead was known as 'Sniper's Alley'.[3]

The plan was for the 5th Marines to pass through the 321st and continue the advance up the West Road to the north. All three battalions were involved: the 1/5 Marines in the lead, followed by the 3/5 and the 2/5. By the time K Company reached its drop-off point near Gorekoru, the 1/5 had already made good progress. Its spearhead company faced only light resistance from Japanese 'holdouts' until it reached Road Junction 15, the meeting of the West and East Roads that was less than a mile from the northern tip of the island, and defended by a small enemy force on a nearby ridge. A brisk firefight overwhelmed this force and allowed the 1/5 Marines to capture the junction and a radio station a little to the north.

The job of the 3/5 Marines – advancing with I Company on the right and K on the left – was to take out any pockets of resistance the 1/5 had missed, while also expanding its zone of operation towards the eastern shore, thus securing the terrain between the West and East Roads.[4]

'Looks like we'll be walkin' the rest of the way from here by ourselves,' said Corporal John Teskevich to Jim McEnery. 'That don't sound like such a hot idea to me.'

'Bauerschmidt says they're sending up some tanks to go with us,' responded McEnery. 'He says maybe we can hitch a ride on one of them, but that doesn't strike me as such a good idea, either.'

'Beats walking, though.'

'Maybe so,' said McEnery, 'but it makes you a good target, too, sittin' there on the deck of a tank.'

The night before, the two Canal veterans had talked about what they would do when they got back to the States. The 'Mad Russian' wanted to drink beer, hustle some broads, get in a 'fistfight or two', and – he was adamant about this – never go down a 'damn coal mine' again. He joked that time was running out for his old man to collect the $20,000 on his GI insurance. 'If he gets it,' he said with a chuckle, 'the Japs're gonna have to hurry.'[5]

It was mid-afternoon when a platoon of Shermans finally showed up and K Company got the order to move out. The tanks led the way through the flat and sparsely wooded terrain, followed by the rifle platoons, mortars, machine guns and company HQ. They could hear the 'chatter of Jap machine guns in the distance', and occasionally see a 'stream of blue tracer bullets' passing high over their heads and bound for some target in the American-held ridge to their right.

There were occasional rifle shots from the undergrowth and the odd casualty, but no serious opposition. By late afternoon, with the men tiring under heavy loads and the hot sun, Bauerschmidt waved one of the tanks over and motioned for some of his men to climb aboard. McEnery's squad was the closest. Tossing their weapons up, they helped each other to clamber up and perch beside the turret: Teskevich, Jesse Googe and Sy Levy on one side; McEnery and Sterling Mace on the other.

'Well it ain't a Caddy,' said Levy, grinning, 'but it'll do.'

'It's a goddamn limousine, is what it is, Sy,' replied Mace.

On Bauerschmidt's signal, the tank lurched forward, causing the outriders to cling to any fingerhold. The Sherman had only advanced 30 yards when a shot rang out and McEnery ducked instinctively. He glanced at the 'Mad Russian', who also seemed to have ducked. Looking closer, he could see Teskevich was 'doubled up with pain and clutching his belly'. Blood was oozing out between his fingers.

Another shot caused Googe to yell out: 'Ahhh, I'm hit! Christ, I'm hit!'

'Stop the tank!' bellowed McEnery. 'We got two men wounded.'

They lowered Teskevich to the ground, while the call went out for a corpsman. Googe sat nearby, holding his right arm which was slick with blood. The corpsman George Chulis appeared and, having examined Teskevich, took McEnery aside. 'The slug went all through his intestines,' he said, grim-faced. 'Nothing much I can do.'

'Then see about Googe,' said McEnery. 'I think his arm's busted.'

He looked back at Teskevich. His face was grey and the front of his dungarees 'solid blood'. Still conscious, he caught McEnery's eye and smiled. 'Guess I'm gonna make my old man rich, after all, Mac,' he whispered.

McEnery, choked with emotion, could think of nothing to say. He knew he would cry if he tried. He stayed with Teskevich until he died a few minutes later. Other K Company men looked over as they passed, shook their heads and quickly glanced away. Teskevich's eyes were still open, and he seemed to be smiling, as McEnery covered him with a poncho. They had served together since the fall of 1941. Most of the other 'originals' were either dead or back in the US: 'Scoop' Adams, Mo

Darsey, Thurman Miller, Weldon DeLong and 'Dutch' Schantzenbach. Now it was just McEnery.

'We better haul ass,' he told Mace and Levy, a lump in his throat. 'We got a long way to go.'[6]

K and I Companies followed in the wake of the 1/5 Marines as far as Road Junction 15. There they 'pivoted to the southeast and headed down [the] East Road', establishing night defences on the road and along the western slopes of Hill 80. That hill was the last link between the main Japanese position to the south and the Amiangal ridges, the northernmost hill mass on Peleliu.[7] During the advance, K Company was targeted by snipers, and by long-range harassing fire from artillery and mortars on high ground to the west and north and on Ngesebus Island, a few hundred yards off the northern tip of Peleliu. But there were no more casualties.

Tied in with the 1/5 Marines to their left and I Company to the right (which itself was flanked by the 2/5 Marines), Haldane's men dug in as best they could, with most of them 'finding some crater or depression and piling rocks around it' for protection. Ordered to carry a five-gallon can of water to the company CP, Gene Sledge came upon Andy Haldane 'studying a map by the light of a tiny flashlight that his runner shielded with another folded map'. Nearby sat the company's radioman, 'quietly tuning his radio and calling an artillery battery of the 11th Marines'.

Sledge put down the water can and sat on it, using the brief rest stop to observe his skipper. If he had been a better artist, he would love to have sketched the scene before him. 'The tiny flashlight faintly illuminated Captain Haldane's face as he studied the map,' he noted. 'His big jaw, covered with a charcoal stubble of beard, jutted out. His heavy brow wrinkled with concentration just below the rim of his helmet.'

Taking the phone from the radioman, Haldane requested a barrage of 75mm high- explosive rounds to be fired out to K Company's front. When the artilleryman at the other end queried the need for such a request, Haldane said firmly: 'Maybe so, but I want my boys to feel secure.'

Soon after, the shells came 'whining overhead and started bursting in the dark thick growth across the road'. Haldane's main concern was that the Japanese would try to infiltrate the company's lines during the night. It was to counteract this possibility that he arranged for the strafing of the undergrowth, and ordered his men to keep a sharp lookout.

Several hours passed without incident. Sledge was keeping watch from his hole, while 'Snafu' Shelton slept fitfully, grinding his teeth as he often did in the field. Directly ahead the white coral road was easily visible in the pale moonlight. Beyond was a 'wall of dark growth' that made identification of individual shapes impossible.

Suddenly, two figures jumped up from a shallow ditch on the other side of the road. 'With arms waving wildly,' recalled Sledge, 'yelling and babbling hoarsely in Japanese, they came. My heart skipped a beat, then began pounding like a drum as I flipped off the safety of my carbine.' One of the figures angled to Sledge's right, ran down the road a short distance, crossed over and disappeared into a foxhole on I Company's front. The other headed straight for Sledge, whirling a bayonet over his head.

Sledge hesitated. There was another foxhole between him and the intruder, and if either of the occupants rose up to tackle the enemy, he feared shooting a comrade in the back. *Why doesn't Sam or Bill fire at him?* he wondered.

With a 'wild yell', the intruder leapt into the first foxhole and a 'frantic, desperate, hand-to-hand struggle ensued, accompanied by the most gruesome combination of curses, wild babbling, animalistic guttural noises, and grunts'. The sound of men 'hitting each other and thrashing around came from the foxhole'.

Watching in horror, Sledge saw a figure jump out of the hole and head for the company CP. The figure had only gone a few yards when it was intercepted by a Marine who, holding his rifle 'by the muzzle and swinging it like a baseball bat', hit the infiltrator a 'smashing blow' in the head.

Off to the right, where the second Japanese had entered I Company's lines, came 'hideous, agonized, and prolonged screams that defied description'. These brutish yells unnerved Sledge even more than shocking events in his field of vision. Finally, a rifle shot was heard from the foxhole in front of Sledge, and a voice shouted, 'I got him!'

By now the screams from I Company's lines had ceased, and Sledge could hear moaning from the figure who had been clubbed with the rifle.

'How many Nips were there?' asked a sergeant in a nearby foxhole.

'I saw two,' said Sledge.

'There must'a been more,' suggested another Marine.

'No,' insisted Sledge. 'Only two came across the road here. One of them ran to the right where all that yelling was, and the other jumped into the hole where Sam shot him.'

'Well, then,' said the Marine, 'if there were just those two Nips, what's all that groanin' over here then?'

'I don't know, but I didn't see but two Nips, and I'm sure of it.'

A Marine in the next foxhole said: 'I'll check it out.'

He crawled past Sledge and over to the groaning man in the shadows, raised his .45 pistol and fired. The moaning stopped, and the Marine crawled back to his foxhole.

As it got light, Sledge glanced across at the body still on the ground. It seemed to be wearing Marine dungarees and leggings, and did not appear to be Japanese. He walked over to investigate and stopped a few yards short. 'My God!'

Asked by Marines nearby what was up, he said: 'It's Bill.'

A sergeant came over from the CP. 'Did he get shot by one of those Japs?' he asked.

Sledge stared blankly at the sergeant, sick to the stomach, unable to answer. He turned to face the man who had 'mistakenly shot Bill' through the left temple, thinking he was a Japanese infiltrator. As the realization of what he had done hit him, the man's 'face turned ashen, his jaw trembled, and he looked as though he were going to cry'. He went straight over to the CP to report what he had done. Haldane immediately sent for anyone who was dug in nearby and might have seen what had happened, including Sledge.

'At ease,' he told the young mortarman. 'Do you know what happened last night?'

Sledge went through the sequence of events, emphasizing that he had only seen two Japanese and had said so at the time.

'Do you know who killed Bill?' asked Haldane.

'Yes.'

'It was a tragic mistake,' said Haldane, 'that anyone could have made under the circumstances. You're never to discuss it or mention the man's name, understand?'

Sledge nodded.

'Dismissed.'[8]

The victim was 18-year-old PFC William S. Middlebrook, Jr, a 'nice young guy' from Houston, Texas, and the younger of two brothers to serve in the 1st Marine Division. His elder brother Robert, a veteran of Guadalcanal and Cape Gloucester, had been rotated home before Peleliu. The family were never told the truth about Bill's death. In line with the erroneous entry in the battalion muster roll – stating that Middlebrook had been 'killed in action against the enemy (wound, gunshot, head)' – his parents always believed that their son had died at the hands of a Japanese infiltrator, a deceit that Sledge was unwilling to expose when he wrote to Middlebrook's mother after the war. She replied: 'Thank every so much for your very nice letter. You told me so much that I didn't know . . . I got my last letter from him dated Aug. 12. The next I heard was when I got the telegram Oct. 5, saying he was killed in action . . . I only had two sons and Bill was my baby.'[9]

At the time, Middlebrook's death provoked strong feelings in the company. As far as Sledge and the other mortarmen were concerned, the 'villain in the tragedy' was Sam,* Middlebrook's foxhole buddy and fellow rifleman. When the incident occurred, he should have been on watch. Instead he had fallen asleep – 'an unforgiveable breach of trust' – and Middlebrook paid the price, as did the man who accidentally

* Sledge almost certainly used a pseudonym for 'Sam'. He was possibly fire team leader Corporal John Tamburri, who according to Middlebrook's mother was 'with my son when he lost his life' during a night attack. (AUA, Sledge Papers, Mrs Middlebrook to Sledge, 29 May 1947.)

shot him and had to live with that knowledge. Sam was 'visibly remorseful', remembered Sledge, 'but it made no difference to the others who openly blamed him'. When he 'whined and said he was too tired to stay awake on watch', he was sworn at by men who were 'equally tired yet reliable'.

The two Japanese infiltrators were probably members, wrote Sledge, of a 'close-quarter combat unit'. The one shot by Sam was wearing 'tropical khaki shorts, short-sleeved shirt, and *tabi* footwear (split-toed, rubber-soled canvas shoes'). His only weapon was a bayonet. The reason he entered Sledge's part of the line was probably to destroy the mortar. His comrade had angled towards a part defended by a machine gun. Both weapons 'were favorite targets for infiltrators in the front lines'.

Later that morning, Sledge visited I Company to hear what had happened to the other intruder. The man had, it transpired, jumped into a foxhole where he met an alert Marine. In the desperate hand-to-hand struggle that followed, the Marine was disarmed, but still managed to kill his opponent by thrusting his finger into his opponent's eye-socket. 'Such,' wrote Sledge, 'was the physical horror and brutish reality of war for us.'[10]

34

'Put the man out of his misery!'

Ngesebus Island, 28–29 September 1944

At dawn on 28 September, Haldane's men gathered up their gear and 'moved down to a narrow strip of sand on the extreme north tip of Peleliu, where thirty amtracs were waiting' to transport them across to the island of Ngesebus. Already naval guns, artillery and Marine aircraft were bombarding the island with 'an awesome array of firepower', including 14in shells from the battleship *Mississippi* and 6in shells from the light cruisers *Denver* and *Columbus*, and bombs, rockets and machine-gun bullets from the Corsair fighter-bombers of VMF-114, commanded by Captain Robert 'Cowboy' Stout, flying out of the repaired Peleliu airfield.

'Unless you'd seen it all before,' wrote Jim McEnery, 'it was hard to imagine how anything could live through such a massive bombardment. But the memory of the much larger fireworks display before our Peleliu landings was still fresh in our minds, and we remembered that most of the Jap defenders had come through that one untouched.'[1]

The decision to seize Ngesebus in a shore-to-shore operation had been taken by Major General Rupertus the day before. He knew that, with the north of Peleliu all but secure, Ngesebus and the Umurbrogol ridges were the last two major pockets of Japanese resistance. By capturing Ngesebus, he would not only secure the 5th Marines' flank, but also prevent the island from being used as a stepping-stone for Japanese reinforcements. The destruction of the Umurbrogol Pocket would then just be a matter of time.

Having grossly underestimated the strength of the Japanese opposition on Peleliu, Rupertus was under enormous pressure. He had hoped to capture the island in just two or three days. Thus far, the fierce fighting was almost a fortnight old and far from over. In that time, an estimated 8,000 Japanese soldiers had been killed, and only 103 captured (more than 90 of whom were Korean construction troops). That still left 2,300 men from the original Japanese garrison, bolstered by an additional 600 soldiers of the 2/15th Infantry Regiment who had been shipped down from Babelthuap a few nights earlier. The 1st Marine Division's casualties were less severe, but still very heavy: 768 killed, 3,693 wounded and 273 missing in action. When added to the 321st Infantry's losses of 279 men, the total number of American casualties was already more than 5,000.[2]

With the 1/5 and 2/5 Marines still in action in northern Peleliu, the job of capturing Ngesebus was given to the 3/5 which, since its largely bloodless capture of Hill 80 on the 26th, had been in regimental reserve. The plan was for the battalion to seize the island in twenty-four hours or less, supported by a company of armoured amtracs and Sherman tanks. 'That was a tall order,' noted McEnery, 'because, despite its small size, the island was a miniature of Peleliu itself – with low ridges down its center that were honeycombed with Nip caves and bunkers. It even had its own airstrip that was big enough for Zeros to use to attack positions on Peleliu.'

When Lieutenant Bauerschmidt briefed his 3rd Platoon, he said that the Japanese had 'over 500 troops in heavy fortifications on the island, plus dozens of mortars, several 75s and some large-caliber naval guns'. It would be, he promised, a 'hard fight'.[3]

The first air attacks were made by Corsairs at 6:30 a.m. on the 28th, hitting the airstrip with 500lb bombs and the rest of the island with rockets and bullets. 'Strafing runs were made just a few feet off the deck,' noted the VMF-114 squadron's war diary, 'and a hail of lead laid all over the island.' The air assault was followed at 7:00 a.m. by a huge bombardment from five battalions of artillery on Peleliu, and from big naval ships offshore, that continued with brief intervals until just before H-Hour at 9:05 a.m.[4]

The final strafing attack of the landing beaches was made by Corsairs as the amtracs moved into the water. 'The engines of the beautiful gull-winged planes roared, whined, and strained as they dove and pulled out,' observed Gene Sledge. 'They plastered the beach with machine guns, bombs, and rockets. The effect was awesome as dirt, sand, and debris spewed into the air.' The Marines of K Company responded by cheering, yelling, waving, and raising their clenched fists.[5]

Watching these events unfold was a posse of senior commanders – including Rear Admiral George Fort, Major Generals Julian Smith, Roy Geiger and William Rupertus, and Brigadier General Oliver Smith – who were keen to see 'at close hand a complete landing operation in miniature'. They had taken 'station under cover on a point of land' 1,400 yards from the southern shore of Ngesebus, where they had 'an unobstructed view of the landing beaches and most of the water gap'. They were also within range of Japanese quick-firing 37mm anti-tank guns. Fortunately, the enemy were unaware of their presence.[6]

The first waves of armoured amtracs – each armed with one 75mm cannon and two machine guns – hit the beaches on the southern shore of Ngesebus at 9:03 a.m., followed soon after by amtracs carrying the assault platoons of K and I Companies. 'Resistance was light,' noted Oliver Smith, 'although there was some mortar and small arms fire directed at the amphibian tractors. None was hit, although one stalled and the troops had to wade ashore. The medium tanks followed the last wave of LVTs [amtracs]. These tanks were not equipped with deep water fording kits, as the original kits had been discarded on D Day after the assault landing and not replaced.' But as the water between the two islands was just three feet deep, it was felt they could get across safely as long as they proceeded in column and avoided pot holes. Most of them did: of the sixteen medium tanks that set off, only three were lost in the crossing.[7]

In one of the first troop-carrying amtracs to hit the beach was Sterling Mace, with the rest of 3rd Platoon. He remembered an 'easy' landing, unlike the one on Peleliu itself. 'In the fifteen minutes it took to cross the six-hundred yard causeway,' he wrote, 'it was the USMC who spent all the ammunition. No guff from the Japs.' The ramp dropped at the water's edge and the platoon piled out 'like gangbusters'.[8]

Once again, 'Stumpy' Stanley was commanding the assault wave. The advice he had been given by Andy Haldane was to concentrate on 'getting the men off the beach' as quickly as possible. He did just that by yelling at the top of his voice, 'Move out! Move out!'

It seemed to have the desired effect. 'I could see both flanks clearly,' he recalled, 'and indeed the men were moving out.'[9]

Directly ahead of 3rd Platoon was a pillbox that Mace engaged with his BAR and McEnery with a couple of grenades. It was finally put out of action by two Marines armed with a bazooka and a flamethrower. When two Japanese defenders emerged with their clothes on fire, they were 'put out of their misery' by rifle fire. 'We penetrated the rest of the Japs' first line of defences without much further trouble,' remembered McEnery, 'and ran past the bodies of fifty or sixty dead Japs who'd probably been killed by the strafing Corsairs. We used grenades to silence a couple of Nip machine guns that were still being manned and quickly disposed of another pillbox, using the same combination of weapons as before.'[10]

One of the most advanced squads was led by Gunnery Sergeant Tom Rigney, a good-looking 'poster Marine' from New York City, who carried his tommy gun 'with pride'. Rigney and his men were moving past a couple of 'small cave-like openings' when shots rang out and a Marine was hit. To cover him, Rigney moved in front of the cave entrance and opened fire with his tommy. He was still in this exposed position when 'Stumpy' Stanley appeared. 'I yelled at him to get the hell away,' recalled Stanley, 'to move off a little to the side. At this time I was only about 20 feet from the group. I no sooner yelled at Tom when a burst of auto fire from the cave ripped into Rigney.' A 'competent, knowledgeable veteran of several campaigns', Rigney had made 'one fatal mistake' in his anxiety to ensure the company's rapid progress, and it had cost him his life.*[11]

* For showing 'daring initiative, indomitable fighting spirit and aggressiveness on behalf of his company's wounded', on both 15 and 28 September, Rigney was awarded a posthumous Silver Star. (https://valor.militarytimes.com/hero/38423)

Moving up behind Rigney's group, with nothing but the ocean on its flank, was Bauerschmidt's 3rd Platoon. Jim McEnery's job as platoon guide was to maintain contact with the 1st Platoon to the right. 'As we inched forward during that first hour ashore,' he recalled, 'I came across a Thompson submachine gun in perfect condition and about a hundred rounds of ammunition. The gun was just lying there behind a little knob of rock, and I had no idea at the time how it got there. Someone told me later that it was probably dropped by [Gunnery] Sergeant Tom Rigney.'[12]

Up ahead, McEnery spotted a Sherman tank being attacked by a swarm of Japanese infantry. 'We gotta get those Nips off that tank!' he yelled at Mace and Bill Leyden. 'Follow me!'

They were thirty feet away when they opened fire with rifles and tommy gun, sending Japanese bodies flying off the nearest tank 'in all directions'. Several were still on top of the turret, trying to wrest it open, when McEnery hit them with a second burst. Within ten seconds, the tank was clear of attackers, many of whom were now writhing on the ground. The sergeant told his men to finish them off. Moments later, another tank pulled up and the hatch swung open. 'I saw what you guys did back here,' said the tank commander to McEnery. 'Thanks for the help. Are you short of rounds for your tommy gun?'

'Yeah,' he replied. 'I'm practically out.'

'Well, here,' he said, handing down a box of .45-calibre ammunition. 'I got way more than I need.'

'Thanks, man. I promise to put this to good use.'

Hurrying after the rest of 3rd Platoon, McEnery test fired a few of the new bullets. They worked fine. He was spotted, however, by 'Ack-Ack' Haldane who was advancing with the company CP. 'Hey, Mac,' said Haldane, 'you'd better go slow on that ammo. Before we're done here, you may need every round you've got.'

McEnery flushed with guilt. 'Okay,' he replied, 'I'll save the rest for the Japs.'

Haldane waved at him and moved on.[13]

* * *

Meanwhile, Gene Sledge and the mortar section – moving inland a little to the right of 3rd Platoon – had been fired on by a Japanese Nambu machine gun at the edge of the airstrip, forcing them to dive for cover. Sledge was huddled behind a small coral rock with a buddy, PFC Louis Boeckemeier from Dumont, Iowa, the rounds zipping 'viciously overhead', when he heard a 'sickening crack like someone snapping a large stick'.

'Oh God,' screamed Boeckemeier as he lurched on to his right side. 'I'm hit!'

He had been shot in the left elbow, and was writhing and groaning in pain. Assuming the perpetrator was a bypassed sniper, and not the machine gun, Sledge dragged Boeckemeier round the rock, out of sight, and yelled for a corpsman. 'Doc' Kent Caswell crawled over, as did another Marine. While Caswell was inspecting the wound, the other Marine tried to cut off Boeckemeier's pack with his Ka-Bar and accidentally struck the corpsman with the razor-sharp blade, inflicting a nasty gash to the left of his nose. 'Despite considerable pain,' recalled Sledge, 'Doc kept at his work. In a quiet, calm voice he told me to get a battle dressing out of his pouch and press it firmly against his face to stop the bleeding while he finished work on the wounded arm. Such was the selfless dedication of the navy hospital corpsmen who served in the Marine infantry units.'

Soon after, the sniper was killed by a tank and it was possible to evacuate Boeckemeier on a stretcher. The mortar section moved on and eventually got orders to set up its guns on the far side of a seemingly empty Japanese bunker and prepare to fire. Though the bunker was undamaged, acting Gunnery Sergeant William Saunders assured the mortarmen that it was clear. Some of the men had thrown grenades through the ventilators, said Saunders, and he was sure there were 'no live enemy inside'.

While Corporal Burgin was 'getting the sound-powered phone hooked up to receive fire orders from Sgt. Johnny Marmet, who was observing', Sledge, 'Snafu' Shelton and the others began to dig in the guns a few yards from the bunker. As they did so, Sledge could hear low and excited

Japanese voices from inside the pillbox, and metal rattling against an iron grating. He grabbed his carbine and yelled, 'Burgin, they're Nips in that pillbox!'

'I think you're cracking up, Sledgehammer,' said the corporal. 'Saunders says it's clear.'

'I don't give a damn what Saunders told you,' said Sledge who, with the other members of his squad, was crouching in front of the bunker, watching several horizontal ventilator ports – eight inches long and two high, with steel bars like a jail cell – along its wall. 'There's Japs in this thing. I can hear voices.'

Burgin walked over and peered through one of the ports. He could see a pair of eyes staring back. Cursing in his best Texan style, Burgin shoved his carbine through the bars and loosed off two or three shots. 'The face vanished,' he recalled. 'I'm sure I hit him. There was a sudden commotion in the bunker, like you'd hear from a beehive if you slapped a hollow tree.'

He fired more shots, angling the barrel to reach all corners of the bunker. Bullets ricocheted off the walls. When the racket died down, Burgin could hear Japanese voices. Then an object came bouncing out the side entrance to his left. 'Grenade!' shouted Sledge as he dived behind the sand breastwork protecting the entrance.

It exploded, as did several more, but no one was injured because they were all hugging the deck. Most of the mortarmen moved to the front of the bunker – the beach side – while Vincent Santos and PFC John Redifer got on the roof. As Sledge was nearest the door, Burgin told him to look inside. He raised his head above the sandbank and saw, barely six feet away, a crouching Japanese machine gunner, his eyes 'black dots in a tan, impassive face topped with the familiar mushroom helmet'.

Sledge reacted first, jerking his head down so fast his helmet 'almost flew off'. A split second later a burst of bullets tore a furrow through the bank, just above his head, showering him with sand. 'My ears rang from the muzzle blast,' recorded Sledge, 'and my heart seemed to be in my throat choking me. I knew damned well I had to be dead! He just couldn't have missed me at that range.'

As his mind raced, he thought of how his folks had almost lost their youngest out of sheer stupidity: looking into a pillbox of Japanese without his carbine at the ready. 'You all right, Sledgehammer?' asked Burgin.

He managed a 'weak croak' in response.

After more hesitation – and a fruitless argument between Snafu and Redifer as to whether the Japanese had automatic weapons or not – Santos discovered a ventilator pipe without a cover and began dropping grenades down it, each one exploding 'with a muffled *bam*'. They stood up, assuming that no one could still be alive, and got their answer as two more Japanese grenades were tossed out, the explosions peppering the two PFCs in the forearms as they tried to protect their faces. They were patched up by Doc Caswell, 'his face swathed in bandages'.

Unwilling to take any more casualties, Burgin moved his men back 40 yards to a couple of shell craters, and sent a runner to the beach to fetch an armoured amtrac. As they waited for it to arrive, four or five Japanese soldiers exited the bunker and headed for a nearby thicket, but were shot down before they could get there. Eventually the amtrac appeared and fired three 75mm armour-piercing rounds into the side of the pillbox, blasting a hole four feet in diameter. Even before the dust had settled, a Japanese soldier appeared at the hole and drew back his arm to throw a grenade. Sledge had his carbine at the ready this time and, seeing the enemy, lined up the sights on his chest and began squeezing off shots. 'As the first bullet hit him,' he recalled, 'his face contorted in agony. His knees buckled. The grenade slipped from his grasp.' Others fired too, and the soldier 'collapsed in the fusillade, and the grenade went off at his feet'.

Sledge's immediate reaction was not relief, or even satisfaction, but revulsion. 'The expression on that man's face,' he wrote, 'filled me with shame and then disgust for the war and all the misery it was causing.'

His maudlin thoughts were interrupted by Burgin's order to keep firing until Corporal Bill 'Red' Womack from Mississippi appeared with his flamethrower. Womack was a 'brave, good natured guy', remembered Sledge, 'and one of the fiercest-looking Marines I ever saw', tall and broad-chested 'with a fiery red beard well powdered with white coral dust'. Stooping under the two heavy tanks on his back – filled with 70lb of flammable jellied gasoline – Womack got to within fifteen yards of the target, aimed the nozzle and pressed the trigger. There was a *whoooooooosh* as the flame leapt at the opening, some 'muffled screams, then all quiet'.

Burgin and another Marine entered the bunker and quickly realized why the occupants had been so hard to kill. It was subdivided, along its length, by concrete baffles with low offset openings, so that an explosion in one would not spread to another. The air was heavy with the smell of charred flesh. Blackened bodies and weapons were scattered here and there. One made a slight movement, causing Burgin to draw his .45 and fire, point-blank, into the back of the soldier's head.

Outside, Marines were stripping the packs and pockets of the dead Japanese for souvenirs. They went about it with ruthless efficiency, collecting gold teeth, flags, pistols, swords and *hara-kiri* knives. Too big to carry, rifles were smashed so they could not be fired. Even Sledge, who thought looting the dead was a 'gruesome business', helped himself to a bayonet and scabbard. But he drew the line when a Marine used his Ka-Bar to extract gold teeth from a badly wounded Japanese soldier who was kicking his feet and gurgling in protest. 'Put the man out of his misery!' shouted Sledge.

All he got in response was a 'cussing out'. Soon after, another Marine ran up and shot the Japanese soldier in the head, 'ending his agony'. Grumbling his disapproval, the scavenger 'continued extracting his prizes undisturbed'. It marked, for Sledge, a low point in the Pacific War: with decent men capable of such 'incredible cruelty' as they tried to survive 'amid the violent death, terror, tension, fatigue, and filth that was the infantryman's war'. On Peleliu, as the casualties mounted, time and life 'had no meaning', wrote Sledge, and the brutal fight for survival 'eroded the veneer of civilization and made savages of us all'.[14]

Sledge's unflinching honesty about the barbarism he witnessed is often cited as evidence that American troops were just as culpable as the Japanese. What is rarely mentioned, however, is that the Japanese brutality was calculated. Their officers and high command believed that their racial and spiritual superiority would overcome American materialism; that by dragging the fighting to the depths of revulsion they could break their 'softer' opponents' will to resist. They were wrong.[15]

The day had gone pretty well for the 3/5 Marines. All three rifle companies had landed: K and I in the first wave, with their line of advance to the northwest; L Company committed soon after with the task of pivoting to the right to attack the eastern shore of the island. Facing little opposition, L Company had completed its mission to seize the eastern part of Ngesebus within an hour and a half of landing. It followed that up, at 1:00 p.m., by sending a platoon to capture Kongauru Island off the northeastern tip of Ngesebus, a feat it quickly achieved in the face of limited opposition.

K and I Companies had 'found the going considerably tougher in their zone of advance, particularly along the battalion left [K's responsibility], where a series of ridges flanked the western shore of the island'. There the Japanese fought with tenacity from caves and dugouts, and had to be rooted out by Marines assisted by armour, flamethrowers, bazookas and explosive charges.[16] It was, remembered Jim McEnery, 'one long, continuous firefight' as they attempted to capture a 'maze of interconnected caves and pillboxes, all of them crawling with Japs'. At one point, with 3rd Platoon 'bogged down temporarily as K and I Companies moved up together', 'Pop' Haney jumped up and rallied the men. 'Come on! Come on!' he yelled at Second Lieutenant Bauerschmidt. 'We gotta keep movin'! We gotta move up!'

Bauerschmidt responded by leading his platoon up the hill to its front. McEnery thought he must have thrown forty or fifty grenades that day, and fired hundreds of rounds of .45 ammunition. Among the casualties was PFC Bill Leyden, the wiseass New Yorker, who was badly wounded in the face and neck by fragments from a Japanese grenade. It was thrown by an enemy soldier who had exited a cave and shouted: 'Kill me, Marine! Kill me!'

Leyden did just that, but not before the grenade exploded. Its shrapnel left Leyden's handsome face a 'bloody mess', especially the area around his left eye, and McEnery could only pray that he would keep his sight. 'Bill was barely eighteen,' he noted, and he could be a wise guy at times, but he was also a damn good Marine who fought as hard and well that day as any man I ever knew.'[17]

During the operation, the battalion CP received a direct hit from a shell that wounded Major Gustafson in the left arm, but not seriously enough to require his evacuation. By 5:00 p.m., when orders were given for all companies to dig in for the night, most of Ngesebus, bar a few hundred yards of the northwestern tip, was in American hands.[18]

Next morning, after a night of rain, K and I Companies resumed the attack. According to Jim McEnery, it took just over an hour 'to wipe out the last of the Jap caves' with the help of bazookas, flamethrowers and TNT demolition charges. In fact, it wasn't until 3:00 p.m. that the last remaining 75mm gun was knocked out by tanks and the island declared secure. By that time, K Company had lost another three killed and seven wounded. The latter included Corporal Richard Van Trump, Sterling Mace's fire team leader, who had had most of his lower jaw shot away.[19] Shortly before he was wounded, Van Trump sent Mace and another Marine forward to outflank a Japanese position. They never got the order to withdraw, and were left in that exposed position for more than forty-five minutes before they realized that nearby cries of mimicry – 'Hey, Zero, we're over here!' – were from the Japanese.* 'The speed we used high-tailing it out of there,' wrote Mace, 'was surely an Olympic record.'[20]

That afternoon, as K Company waited to be relieved by troops from the 2/321st Infantry, Gene Sledge and his buddies sat glassy-eyed and 'numbly looking at nothing'. The 'shock, horror, fear and fatigue of fifteen days of combat' was taking its emotional and physical toll. Feeling himself choking up, Sledge turned from the men facing him, put his face in his hands, and began sobbing. His body 'shuddered and shook'

* According to Mace, they must have overheard the many 'coded' conversations between Zero Bauerschmidt and Van Trump. (Mace, *Battleground Pacific*, pp. 125, 141.)

as the tears flowed. 'I was sickened and revolted to see healthy young men get hurt and killed day after day,' he recalled. 'I felt I couldn't take any more.'

A hand on his shoulder caused him to look up. It was 'Duke' Ellington. 'What's the matter, Sledgehammer?' he asked.

When Sledge tried to explain, the second lieutenant said: 'I know what you mean. I feel the same way. But take it easy. We've got to keep going. It'll be over soon, and we'll be back on Pavuvu.'

Ellington was not popular with his men. But his words of sympathy, on this occasion, gave Sledge the strength he needed to keep going.[21]

The two-day operation to capture Ngesebus had cost the 3/5 Marines just under fifty casualties, the bulk of whom – eight killed and twenty-four wounded – were in 'Ack-Ack' Haldane's K Company. Meanwhile, the battalion had killed or captured 470 Japanese. The army troops would account for another hundred or so of the enemy during the mopping-up phase.[22]

35

'Shit, they're behind us!'

Umurbrogol Pocket, 1–4 October 1944

'OK, you people,' said an officer to K Company's mortar section, 'stand by to draw rations and ammo. The battalion is going to reinforce the 7th Marines in the ridges.'[1]

Gene Sledge received the unwelcome but expected news with 'fatalistic resignation'. It was the morning of 1 October 1944 and K Company, with the rest of the 3/5 Marines, had been resting near Ngardololok in eastern Peleliu since its return from Ngesebus on the 29th. For all practical purposes, organized resistance in the north of Peleliu had also ended that day, though the 1/5 and 2/5 Marines continued mopping-up operations the following morning. Relieved by elements of the 321st Infantry, they returned to Ngardololok to join the 3/5 in a well-earned break from combat during the afternoon of the 30th.*

There remained just a single Japanese stronghold: the Umurbrogol Pocket, which by 1 October had been reduced to an area of roughly 1,500 yards by 550 in the ruggedest part of the island. Though these compressed ridges were barely 300 feet high, the sides were, as a rule, 'extremely steep and fissured'. Many had 'razor-back summits devoid of

* The 1/5 and 2/5 Marines assumed that only a handful of Japanese were still at large in the north. It would, in fact, take the army troops two more days to end resistance in northern Peleliu, 'and even then isolated Japanese continued to exist in dugouts whose entrances were partially blocked by debris'. (Garand and Strobridge, IV, pp. 217–18.)

any cover or concealment', and 'deep draws and gullies, the floors of which were often interspersed with coral boulders and outcroppings, were commonplace'.

Into these 'almost perpendicular' coral ridges the Japanese had blasted a series of interconnecting caves, varying in size from simple holes for two men, to tunnels large enough to hold artillery, 150mm mortars and ammunition. All the defensive positions had been carefully chosen, skilfully camouflaged and enjoyed excellent fields of fire. They were mostly immune from 'naval gunfire, bombardment by artillery and mortars, or bombing and strafing'. The dominant features within the pocket were: Walt Ridge, named in honour of the XO of the 5th Marines, which occupied and dominated the southeast corner, parallel to the East Road; Boyd Ridge, north of Walt, and separated from it by a depression 70 yards wide; Five Brothers Ridge; Main Valley or Wildcat Bowl, which was enclosed to the west by the China Wall, and to the southeast by a jagged ridge known as Five Sisters; and Death Valley, which separated the Five Sisters and China Wall from the coral ridges dominating the West Road. Almost all of the ridges extended from northeast to southwest.

The only way to nullify the caves in these features was to kill the occupants – including Colonel Nakagawa, the de facto commander of the Peleliu garrison, and an estimated 3,000 men – or seal their entrances, one at a time. On hearing that K Company was heading into the pocket, Sledge and his colleagues were 'resigned to the dismal conclusion that our battalion wasn't going to leave the island until all the Japanese were killed, or we had all been hit'.[2]

For the attacking troops, conditions in the pocket were uniquely awful: the ridges all looked the same, wrote Jim McEnery, and when one had been captured 'there were always three or four more just like it looming ahead of us'; bodies littered the terrain, Japanese and American, and the stench of death hung over the island like a 'suffocating fog'; and feasting on the hundreds of decomposing corpses were 'huge clouds of blowflies' that at times were so thick they 'blotted out the sun, and you had to fight them for every bite of food you ate'.[3]

The 3/5 was being sent to support the 7th Marines which, having failed to break into the pocket from the southeast a week earlier, had been ordered by Rupertus to try again. Attacking on a two-battalion front from the north on 30 September, the 7th made moderate gains, but at a heavy cost: the effective strength of the 1/7 was now down to just ninety men, while the 3/7 was below 50 per cent combat efficiency, partly the result of dysentery and battle fatigue. On 1 October, the day the 3/5 Marines relieved the 2/7 along the pocket's southwestern perimeter, the 1/7 and 3/7 attacked again from the north, but made little headway.

Rupertus's plan was for a major assault on the pocket on 3 October from multiple directions: the 2/7 from the east, towards Walt Ridge; the 3/7 from the northeast, towards Boyd Ridge; and the 3/5 from the south, towards the Five Sisters (with the 5th Marines Weapons Company in support).[4] For the duration of the operation, the 3/5 would come under the command of Colonel Herman H. Henneken of the 7th Marines, an arrangement that displeased his opposite number in the 5th Marines, 'Bucky' Harris. 'On the 1st of October,' Harris wrote later, 'my 3rd Battalion was transferred to the control of the 7th Regiment, which it was announced would make an all-out drive to erase the remaining Jap garrison. I did not share the optimism of Div. HQ, as this looked like it would be another assault on the frontal ridge that had already all but destroyed the 1st Regiment and had stopped an Army Regiment cold, there and round on the ridge on the west flank.'

He and his deputy 'Silent Lew' Walt decided to visit Major Gustafson to discuss the 3/5's role on the left flank of the attack. Harris recalled,

> We went over in my Jeep, as close as prudence dictated, then proceeded on foot, picking up [Gustafson] on the way. We found a likely spot where we could view his sector, and pointed out some details that might assist the Battalion, particularly Jap positions capable of enfilading his men. While engaged in this recon. job we were spotted by the Japs, who promptly sent a mortar [round] over that landed uncomfortably close. Luckily for us, it fell into a

sizeable pot hole of considerable depth. The blast was deafening, but Lt. Col. Walt and Major Gustafson wasted no time in moving to the rear, and even with a bum knee and sore foot, I was not too far behind them.

Gustafson headed back to his CP, and Harris and Walt were about to board their jeep and do the same when Major General Rupertus appeared. 'What are you doing here?' he asked, brusquely.

'I came to view the zone assigned to the 3rd Battalion,' replied Harris, 'and offer its CO, Major Gustafson, any suggestions and advice that might be helpful.'

'Harris,' said Rupertus, brusquely, 'if your advice is needed I will ask for it. Go back to your own outfit and stay out of the affairs of the 7th Regiment.'

Irked by this rude dismissal, Harris sensibly kept his thoughts to himself. Walt was no less angry, but Harris calmed him by saying their best bet now was to 'play zipper-lip'.[5]

On 1 October, having just relieved a company of the 2/7 Marines along a stretch of the West Road known as 'Dead Man's Curve' – close to where Teskevich and Googe had been shot a week earlier – K Company was ordered to clear snipers from some nearby ridges.

The 3rd Platoon was inching its way along a jagged ridge when Jim McEnery got a bad feeling. 'Watch it now, guys,' he said. 'There's no such thing as a comfort zone out here. Just take it easy and keep your heads down.'

Sterling Mace was crouching a little to McEnery's left, stuffing his pack and pockets with extra ammo, itching to use his BAR on the enemy. 'Oh crap, I didn't leave any room for my cigs,' he said, turning to his friend Seymour Levy. 'Hey, Sy, you got room in your pack for this fresh pack of butts? I got no place to put 'em where they won't get mashed.'

'Sure,' replied Levy, 'toss 'em over here.'

'You better be careful, Mace,' said PFC Frankie Ocepek, 'Levy's liable to smoke the whole pack when you're not looking.'

'He better not. It's the only pack I got.'

Levy just shook his head. He had been quieter than usual since the wound to his chin and, after Mace had moved on up the line with his BAR, he had an odd look in his eyes.

'Something eating you, kid?' asked McEnery.

Levy shrugged. 'I guess I'm just edgy, Mac. I hate being pinned down like this. It makes me feel . . . you know, trapped. Sometimes I feel like I can't stand it.'

'Just take it easy and keep your head down. You gotta be patient at times like this.'

A shot rang out, and someone yelled for a corpsman. McEnery could see Levy fidgeting. 'Keep your damn head down,' insisted the sergeant.

For a short while, Levy seemed back in control. He even struck up a conversation with a corporal. But a few minutes later, he grabbed his rifle and yelled: 'I'm sick and tired of this shit! I can't take it anymore!' He jumped up and was immediately shot in the forehead and killed by a Japanese sniper, his blood spattering McEnery's face.

Unaware his buddy had been hit, Mace appeared a few minutes later to get his cigarettes, by which time two Marines had risked their lives to get Levy's body back down the hill. 'Hey, Frank,' he asked Ocepek. 'Where'd Levy run off to?'

Ocepek looked down, unable to meet Mace's stare.

'Where the fuck is Levy, Frank?'

'Nobody wanted to tell you,' said Ocepek at last, his words barely audible. 'I'm sorry, Mace. He's *gone*. He took one in the head as he peered over the edge, to have a look. He just . . . he just said he was tired of this shit, and then he looked.'

'Goddammit!' Mace exploded, 'I'll kill all you Jap sonuvabitches! I'll shoot all you fucking bastards!' He began to move back up the line, pointing his BAR at the ridge, but was stopped by McEnery.

'You're one of the best BAR men in the platoon,' said the sergeant, with his hands on Mace's shoulders, 'and I ain't letting you get yourself killed for nothin', so just cool off. You can handle this, kid. Hell's bells, you *gotta* handle it.'

The pair had never got on. But McEnery's intervention was enough to calm Mace and save his life. The young BAR-man sank to his haunches and dropped his head. 'But why'd he have to come back?' he asked. 'Why couldn't the dummy just take his million-dollar wound and go home?'

'I don't know,' said McEnery. 'And now we'll never know.'[6]

Two days after Levy's death, 3rd Platoon was in action again as K Company took part in Rupertus's coordinated attack on the Umurbrogol Pocket. It was, remembered McEnery, a 'battalion-strength assault from the south against the five-headed monster we'd come to know as the Five Sisters'. Spearheaded by Haldane's men, it was launched at the same time that the 2/7 Marines attacked Walt's Ridge from the east, the very same feature 'where Captain Everett Pope's men had taken such terrible losses two weeks earlier', and proof that the fight for Peleliu was 'as disheartening as it was deadly'.[7]

K Company began its advance on 3 October, after an intensive early morning barrage of 155mm guns and the massed fire of 81mm mortars from five battalions had hammered Japanese positions in the pocket, causing Colonel Nakagawa to report that 'all through the night of the 2nd, the enemy fired 40,000 artillery shells from their positions on land and ships at our defense points'.[8]

Rising up on the left flank of K Company as it moved forward was a network of ridges that were thick with Japanese caves and pillboxes. 'We start off in a skirmish line,' remembered Sterling Mace, 'a zigzagging group of Marines, taking furtive steps through the morning mist toward a place that looks more ominous and foreboding than any other place we've been on Peleliu.' The valley was 'composed of nothing but heat-baked coral, littered with mangrove, bits of wood, discarded Marine gear, spent ammunition, and the scent of putrefaction and cooked blood'. At the end of the draw was a 60ft sheer cliff, its jagged teeth 'eating away at the sky'.[9]

The immediate threat to K Company, however, was from the caves to the left. 'We had tanks with us,' recalled Jim McEnery, 'but the terrain was so rough they could only fire at the [Japanese] positions from a distance, so we had to spend most of the morning using bazookas, flamethrowers, and TNT charges against the caves until we thought they were all shut down. But unfortunately, we missed some, and as we moved farther up the hill, we suddenly found ourselves in a meat-grinder, catching enemy fire from both front and rear.'[10]

The first fatality was Corporal Ray Grawet – 'real macho, open jacket, bare chest exposed, a .45 in his hand' – who made the mistake of inspecting the entrance of a large cave after a tank had blasted it with 75mm shell. He was promptly shot in the chest and killed. 'Quickly,' recalled Sterling Mace, 'they rush Ray out of the way, and the demolition Marines implode the cave, sealing up Raymond's killer.'

As stretcher-bearers carried Grawet's body back down the draw at the trot, Mace thought of the bulldog tattoo on the dead Marine's shoulder and wondered, *What's the rush?*[11]

Others hit around the same time as Grawet were PFC George Porrett – also killed with a gunshot wound to the chest – and acting Platoon Sergeant Hank Boyes of 1st Platoon (and winner of a Silver Star on D-Day for directing fire from the hull of a tank), who was wounded in the right hand by shrapnel.[12]

About noon, having reached the base of the Five Sisters, K Company was joined on the right flank by L Company, and together they renewed the attack. One platoon advanced with a tank into the ravine known as Death Valley that ran along the left flank of the Five Sisters, while the remainder of the two companies ascended the 'first, third, fourth, and fifth sisters numbering from West to East'.[13]

Second Lieutenant Bill Bauerschmidt's 3rd Platoon was climbing the side of the First Sister – on the flank of Death Valley – when a Marine yelled, 'Shit, they're behind us! Get down! Get down!'

The warning came too late for Bauerschmidt, who was hit low in the stomach by a Japanese bullet and fell heavily to the ground. McEnery scrambled over to him as other enemy rounds 'peppered the hillside'. What he saw made him sick. 'It was,' remembered McEnery, 'like Teskevich all over again. Same kind of wound in the same area. The lieutenant was already covered with blood from the waist down, but he was still trying to get that hog-leg .45 out of his holster.'

'I don't get it,' mumbled Bauerschmidt. 'The shot came from behind. Are our own men shooting at us?'

'No, sir,' said McEnery, 'we must've missed some.' The sergeant was about to say more, but Bauerschmidt was no longer conscious. It took some time for stretcher-bearers to appear and, thought McEnery, *Who could blame them?*

Bauerschmidt was beyond help and died a few minutes later. It was a tragic end for the young married Bucknell graduate. As an error-prone rookie he had almost got McEnery killed on patrol on New Britain. But that was all in the past. 'I'd never known an officer that I liked or admired more,' wrote McEnery. 'He'd been an outstanding platoon leader, but he'd been a good friend, too. He'd made us grunts feel like he was one of us, and I hated what had happened to him.'*

Yet, at that moment, there was only one thought in McEnery's mind: *A lot more of us are going to die if we stay where we are. Gotta move! Gotta move!*

He shouted to the rest of the platoon, 'We can't hold here! Fall back down the hill! Fall back!' Another Marine, PFC Lyman Rice from Zavalla, Texas, was shot in the head and 'killed instantly as he tried to retreat'.[14]

It soon became a general withdrawal as Major Gustafson – informed that both forward companies were facing 'very effective rifle fire' from positions that 'could not be located' – ordered the battalion to pull back to a line of defence only 100 yards forward of where it had jumped off that morning. With the move underway, McEnery remembered he had left his pack in a ditch and ran forward to recover it. The move almost cost him his life as he was spotted by a Japanese soldier who threw five hand grenades, a couple landing just a few feet from the ditch. Though unharmed by the explosions, McEnery did not dare shoot at his assailant because beyond him, in direct line of sight, was the company CP.[15]

* Bauerschmidt's wife Annabelle, his sweetheart from college, was later presented with her husband's posthumous Silver Star. He had shown 'brilliant initiative and great personal valor under extremely perilous conditions'.

That night, the company bivouacked on fairly level ground in full view of the Japanese in their lairs in the Five Sisters. As the ground was too hard to dig, most Marines were huddled behind makeshift barricades of wood and rock. 'Raids by individual enemy soldiers or small groups began as soon as darkness fell,' remembered Gene Sledge. 'Typically, one or more raiders slipped up close to Marine positions by moving during dark periods between mortar flares or star shells. They wore *tabi*, and their ability to creep in silently over rough rocks strewn with pulverized vegetation was incredible.'[16]

The company's defensive front was a U-shape, with the back open 'because there wasn't supposed to be anybody behind us'. Just after 10:00 p.m., Sterling Mace and his foxhole buddy PFC Charlie Allmann, 'a quiet guy, almost lethargic and built wiry', heard someone shout 'Corpsman!' Mace looked behind and saw two figures running towards them. 'Charlie,' he said, 'you see these guys coming? Are they stretcher-bearers or what?'

By all rights, Mace should have opened fire. But he hesitated, waiting for a word of assurance from Allmann, who kept quiet. Before he could change his mind, the figures had 'peeled off to the right' towards the machine-gun platoon. Dug in there was PFC Gil Amdur, a softly spoken 19-year-old from Rockford, Illinois. Hearing footsteps behind him, Amdur whispered, 'Who's out there? Gimme the password.'

He expected to hear the words 'Bull Run', but there was no response. He saw a shadow approaching his position and, like Mace, should have opened fire. Instead he issued another challenge. 'Goddammit, who's out th—'

Thud. Something had struck the ground beside him. Seconds later, the grenade exploded, riddling Amdur's upper body and face with shrapnel, and killing him instantly.

Mace could see the halo of a flash from the corner of his eye, 'coming from about forty yards behind Charlie and me where the machine guns are set up. *Fsssss!* There's a red glow in the night and a sharp thunderclap.' Alert to the danger, he did not hesitate when another group of dark figures approached his position, pulling the trigger on his BAR and emptying a full magazine into them. 'Some bend back unnaturally as they skid and fall,' he noted, 'while others collapse to the side or simply fold inward at the belly. All of them crumple together, touching one another, in a soft cloud of coral dust and the afterglow of my muzzle flash.' Mace would account for at least another four enemy before the night was over.[17]

Two other K Company men were wounded by grenades – one of whom, 34-year-old Frankie Ocepek, was hit by shrapnel in both legs and his right arm – as more Japanese infiltrators tried to break through the company lines and reach their own positions in the Five Sisters. None succeeded. One was still hiding out the following morning when he was stepped on by the mortarman Jay de l'Eau, who had left his position to relieve himself. Spotting the enemy, de l'Eau brought up his carbine and pressed the trigger. It misfired, so in desperation he threw the weapon at the Japanese soldier and ran.

The enemy leapt to his feet and threw a grenade which struck de l'Eau in the back. Fortunately, it was a dud and failed to explode. Undeterred, the Japanese drew a bayonet and took after de l'Eau 'at a dead run'. Panicking, the Marine 'spotted a BAR man and fled in his direction, yelling for him to shoot the enemy'. He did, after an agonising pause, firing most of his twenty-round magazine into the stomach of the enemy and almost cutting him in two. The terrified de l'Eau, meanwhile, had soiled his dungaree pants and had to waddle back to battalion to change them.[18]

Another Japanese infiltrator was shot and killed by Joe Moskalczak as he tried to run up the ridge. Searching the corpse, Moskalczak realized his victim was a corpsman and kept his medical equipment as a souvenir. That morning, twenty-seven dead Japanese were found inside the lines of the 3/5 Battalion, most of them in K Company's area.[19]

The coordinated attack on 3 October had resulted in only modest gains – the capture of Boyd and Walt Ridges, and the opening of the East Road – and it was resumed the following day. Once again, K and L Companies attempted to capture the Five Sisters but, after initial gains, were held up by heavy defensive fire and eventually withdrawn to the start line. Among the injured were Lieutenant 'Hillbilly' Jones and PFC Joe Moskalczak. Jones had been shot in the left hand as he advanced with 1st Platoon; despite the wound, he refused to be evacuated and instead 'directed the fire of friendly tanks against the enemy until his platoon was able to move and take its objective with a minimum of casualties'. Moskalczak was hit in the head, back and left leg by mortar shrapnel as he went to get food from a makeshift mess tent. 'I woke up in a tent on an Army cot,' he remembered. 'My gear was with me, my rifle and helmet. Looking at my helmet, I could put two fingers in the hole that was there, also my back had been hit.' He was evacuated to a hospital ship.*

That evening the whole battalion moved back to a bivouac area and was replaced in the front line by an armoured amtrac unit. As before, K Company had suffered the bulk of the battalion casualties: nine of the thirteen killed and twenty-three of the forty-three wounded.[20]

But losses were much more serious in the 7th Marines, which by the end of the fighting on 4 October 'could no longer function as an effective combat unit on the regimental level', and had to be relieved by the 5th Marines. The 3/7's I and L Companies had been reduced to a combined strength of just eighty men (from their original 470); the 1/7 Marines could barely muster a hundred men in total; while the 2/7 had only 30 per cent of its combat manpower.[21]

The battle's 'very heavy casualties' and 'infinitesimal gains' had confirmed the worst fears of 'Bucky' Harris and 'Silent Lew' Walt. But they gained no pleasure from knowing they were right. With the whole of the 7th Marines and his own 3rd Battalion 'no longer in any condition for an offensive role', wrote Harris, a 'sense of gloom and futility was rife'.[22]

* Moskalczak had earlier stripped from Japanese bodies two pistols with holsters, several flags (often found inside helmets), two wallets and the medic's instruments. All were stolen from his pack during the voyage back to the United States. He sold his last souvenir, a pair of Japanese shoes, to a Marine on a train in California for $3. (AUA, Sledge Letters, Box 2, Folder 36, Letter from Moskalczak to Gene Sledge, 9 March 1988.)

36

Hillbilly and Ack-Ack

Umurbrogol Pocket, 5–12 October 1944

Early on 5 October, Colonel 'Bucky' Harris was summoned by telephone to the division CP, sited in the shattered two-storey Japanese administration building at the northern end of the airstrip. Arriving by jeep, he was directed to a nearby tent where he found Major General Rupertus alone, tears coursing down his cheeks. 'Harris,' said his distraught commander, 'I'm at the end of my rope. Two of my fine regiments are in ruins. You usually seem to know what to do, and get it done. I am going to turn over to you everything we have left. This is strictly between us.'

Rupertus made no apology for his earlier rudeness on 1 October; nor did Harris expect him to. Yet by ceding control of the battle to Harris, the division commander was belatedly acknowledging that the battle tactics the 5th Marines had used to such good effect in the north of the island – a series of carefully planned, methodical advances, using every form of firepower available – might also work against the Umurbrogol Pocket. Harris's first act was to fly over the pocket in a Piper Cub reconnaissance plane, viewing the terrain from all angles. Then he returned to his CP and, while making notes on his operations map, explained to his deputy Lew Walt that they had been given the 'hot potato' of capturing the pocket with only their regiment 'plus anything left in the Division'.[1]

His new approach was to attack from the north and northwest – down the canyon between the western ridges and the single ridge to the east – in a 'slow but deliberate and inexorable advance', spearheaded by tanks, armoured amtracs and 'ronsons' (flamethrowers mounted on amtracs), that in 'due time would achieve the desired result at a minimum cost in personnel and materiel'.[2]

So it proved. Using every weapon available – including napalm strikes from the air, 1,000lb bombs, direct fire from artillery against cave mouths, tanks and half-tracks, flamethrowers, demolition charges, 37mm guns and infantry small-arms – Harris's men fought from ridge to ridge and slowly compressed the pocket. Among the features captured during the subsequent week of fighting were the ridge overlooking Dead Man's Curve on the West Road, Baldy Ridge and Hill 140, and the canyon between Boyd's Ridge and Hill 40. A number of tank–infantry sorties were made into Horseshoe Valley – in the heart of the pocket – which 'shot up cave defenses and killed numerous enemy'. But the captured positions proved to be untenable as the 'infantry was unable to remain in these extremely exposed positions after the tanks withdrew for refueling and rearming'.[3]

Despite its reduction in strength to around one hundred men – roughly 40 per cent of its original total – K Company took part in the latter stages of 'Bucky' Harris's assault on the pocket. Its first action was on 10 October when it was ordered to accompany a Sherman tank into the narrow Horseshoe Valley to locate 'the source of enemy rifle fire which had been harassing troops along the [west] road'. The job was given to 'Hillbilly' Jones's 1st Platoon, now reduced to just fifteen riflemen. As the morning wore on, the platoon failed to find any snipers and lost two men to injuries from mortar fire. Hillbilly was at the end of his tether. 'Like everybody else in the company,' wrote Jim McEnery, 'Jones was tired and on edge and these latest casualties didn't help matters. If they continued at this rate, his whole platoon could be wiped out before the day was over.'

Normally calm and level-headed, Jones was 'really depressed and sick' about the platoon's losses and 'desperate to get back at the Japs'. That was the reason, according to a member of his platoon, why he 'did what he did that morning'.[4] Having advanced up the 'shallow gulley', Jones was crouching behind one of the tanks, holding his tommy gun and watching the sniper-infested ridge through binoculars, when Major Clyde Brooks, the battalion operations officer, ran up and took cover beside him.

'Major Gustafson sent me over,' said Brooks, 'to see what we could do about those snipers. You got any ideas?'

'I'm thinking,' responded Jones, 'about climbing up on this tank to try to spot a target for the gunners to shoot at. They'd have a better chance of hitting something with a machine gun or a seventy-five than we do from the ground with rifles. What do you think?'

'It sounds awful damn risky to me.'

'Yeah, but I figure it's either that or sit here in this Nip shooting gallery for the rest of the day.'

Brooks mulled it over. 'Okay then,' he said at last. 'Give it a try, but watch yourself.'

Leaving his tommy gun on the ground, Jones clambered onto the tank's rear deck and tapped on the turret. Once he had the tank commander's attention, he said: 'I'm gonna try to find you a target for your .30-caliber or your seventy-five, so get ready.'

'Are you sure you want to do this?' yelled Brooks from the back of the tank.

Jones shrugged. 'So far, so good.'

The platoon leader was sitting behind the turret, scanning the terrain to the rear, when he was shot in the left side, below the ribs. He fell backwards and slid off the tank.

Watching from a distance of about thirty yards, Sterling Mace felt sickened at the sight of the Marine being hit. Unaware it was Jones, he assumed the Marine was a mortar spotter. But to his surprise, the man got to his feet and, having waved away the corpsman who had come to treat him, climbed clumsily back onto the tank.

'Hey,' said Mace to his neighbour, 'maybe he just fell off on his own the first time.'

Those closer to the tank knew the truth. Though badly hurt, his shirt soaked with blood, Jones wanted to finish what he had started. Another shot rang out and, this time, the bullet entered the left side of Jones's chest and pierced his heart. He was killed instantly. The 'handsome, guitar-strumming officer . . . was gone', noted McEnery, 'and every man in the company felt a sense of personal loss when they learned of Hillbilly's death'.[5]

Quickly on the scene, 'Stumpy' Stanley was shown a cave opening, about fifteen feet up the rocky side of the draw, that many of those present thought the shots had been fired from. He gave orders for the cave to be blown closed with ten 50lb boxes of TNT. 'The area was cleared,' he recalled, 'and we let the thing "go". The effect of the explosion was stupefying.'

Soon after, Stanley received orders from battalion to withdraw. He sent the men back, but remained with the Sherman tank which, having advanced deeper into the Horseshoe, had lost its right track. To discourage any more sniper fire, Stanley kept spraying all the openings he could see in the rock face with bursts from his tommy gun. By the time he followed the tank and its recovery vehicle out of the Horseshoe, an hour and a half later, he had gone through most of his supply of ten magazines, or 200 rounds, of .45 calibre ammunition.[6]

Later that day, Sterling Mace saw a body outside the aid station, covered with a poncho. 'Is this Hillbilly here?' he asked a Marine nearby.

'I don't know,' shrugged the Marine. 'I guess so.'

Mace lifted the poncho and saw that it *was* the popular Jones, his face 'perfectly set in an attitude of calm and ease'. There was not a blemish on him, though his skin gave off 'a clammy sheen, as if the last beads of sweat his body produced had not finished drying in his death'. His one minor physical imperfection was a slightly skewed nose – 'broken at one time, perhaps playing football or boxing in high school'.

'Yeah,' said Mace to no one in particular, 'that's him.'[7]

Jones was the third company officer to be killed on Peleliu, and the second while leading 1st Platoon. Like Barrett and Bauerschmidt before him, he was awarded a posthumous Silver Star. 'His aggressive fighting spirit and outstanding courage in the face of grave peril', noted the citation, 'were contributing factors in the success' of his company's operations on 4 and 10 October.[8]

Of the original seven company officers, three were dead and a fourth – Second Lieutenant Gene 'Mad Mac' McMahon, the 2nd Platoon leader – had been evacuated to a hospital ship on 4 October. That meant that all three rifle platoons and the machine-gun platoon were now commanded by sergeants.

Two days after Jones's death, K Company moved north with the battalion to relieve the 2/5 Marines in the vicinity of Hill 140, which had been captured the day before. The plan was for the battalion to continue the 2/5's southerly advance into the west flank of the pocket, thus securing the ridges that overlooked the West Road.

At around 10:00 a.m., while the relief was underway, Captain Haldane led a small patrol up to an OP on the nearest ridge. 'Being as he was an old machine gun hand,' recalled Jim McEnery, '[he] still liked to take a personal hand in making sure the company's .30-caliber weapons were in the most effective locations.'

He was accompanied by his personal aide Sergeant Dick Higgins, his runner Corporal Jim Anderson, and acting platoon leaders Jim McEnery and Johnny Marmet. Nearing the OP at the top of the ridge, the party crawled the last few feet and halted just below the ridgeline. Haldane was at the highest point, flanked by Higgins and Anderson. A few feet below him were McEnery and Marmet. They all held their breath as the captain crawled up to the edge of the ridgeline and raised his head a few inches above it to steal a look. He said: 'We need the guns as close as we—'

Haldane's sentence was cut short by the sharp report of a rifle shot. 'It sounded less like gunfire than somebody slapping his hands together,' remembered McEnery, 'but every one of us on the hill knew instantly what it was.' The bullet struck Ack-Ack in the forehead and killed him instantly. Those near him were spattered with gore.

'Oh, dear God, no!' whispered McEnery. He and Anderson stared at each other in 'shock and disbelief', while Higgins scrambled towards his stricken skipper. Someone pulled the aide back, 'to keep him from getting hit too', and he 'whirled around and ran back down the hill, screaming for a corpsman'.

It was far too late for that.

By the time McEnery's head had cleared, Marmet had gone back down the hill and two Marines were carrying Haldane's body away on a stretcher. That just left Jim Anderson, who was wiping blood off his face and shaking his head. 'I can't believe this,' he muttered. 'I saw it but I can't believe it.'[9]

Gene Sledge and the rest of the mortar section were heading into the ridges, up a 'narrow valley filled with skeletons of shattered trees jutting up here and there', when they met Johnny Marmet coming the other way. Sledge could tell from the expression on the platoon sergeant's face, and the way he was walking, that something was 'dreadfully amiss'.

Marmet was nervously clutching at the web-strap on his tommy gun, slung over his shoulder. This was a first: Sledge had never seen him show signs of nerves before, even under the heaviest fire, which the Canal veteran tended to regard as more a nuisance than a lethal threat. The sergeant's 'tired face was contorted with emotion, his brow was tightly knitted, and his bloodshot eyes appeared moist'. It was clear he had 'something fearful' to tell them. The mortarmen shuffled to a halt. Sledge's first thought was that the Japanese had landed thousands of reinforcements from the northern Palaus and they would 'never get off the island'; or maybe the enemy had bombed an American city or 'chased off the navy as they had done at Guadalcanal'. Running wild, his imagination never came close to the truth.

'Howdy, Johnny,' said a mortarman.

'All right, you guys,' responded Marmet, avoiding eye contact, 'let's get squared away here.'

Obviously flustered, he kept repeating, 'Okay, you guys. Okay, you guys.'

The mortarmen exchanged quizzical glances. Something was up.

Suddenly Marmet blurted out: 'The skipper is dead. Ack-Ack has been killed.'

Sledge was 'stunned and sickened' by the news. Chucking his ammo bag on the ground, he turned from the others, sat on his helmet and began sobbing.

Behind him, someone muttered, 'Those goddamn slant-eyed sonsabitches.'

Despite the 'steady stream' of casualties, Sledge had never contemplated Haldane's death. As their skipper, he 'represented stability and direction in a world of violence, death and destruction'. Now that he was gone, Sledge felt 'forlorn and lost'. It was the 'worst grief' he experienced during the whole war. He wrote:

> Captain Andy Haldane wasn't an idol. He was human. But he commanded our destinies under the most trying conditions with the utmost compassion. We knew he could never be replaced. He was the finest Marine officer I ever knew. The loss of many close friends grieved me deeply . . . But to all of us the loss of our company commander at Peleliu was like losing a parent we depended upon for security – not our physical security, because we knew that was a commodity beyond our reach in combat, but our mental security.

Some of the mortarmen threw down their gear. Others were cursing and rubbing their eyes. It was, wrote R. V. Burgin, 'more than a death in the family, losing Hillbilly Jones and Andy Haldane like that'. Both had served in three campaigns and, had they survived just a few days more, would have lived through the war. It was such a shame for their families. But Burgin would have a more personal reason to regret the death of Haldane because, as he found out later, the skipper was about to recommend him for the Silver Star for coordinating the destruction of the bunker on Ngesebus. It was an award that many who were present that day, Sledge included, felt he deserved; but it was not to be.*

* Haldane, on the other hand, was awarded a posthumous Silver Star (his second, and the fourth given to K Company officers killed on Peleliu). 'A splendid and

Eventually, having pulled himself together, Marmet said, 'Okay, you guys, let's move out.'

They picked up the mortars and ammo bags and, feeling as though their 'crazy world had fallen apart completely', they 'trudged slowly and silently in single file up the rubble-strewn valley'.[10]

---

fearless leader,' read the citation, 'Captain Haldane repeatedly led his assault company through intense hostile artillery and small arms fire to rout the enemy from strongly held positions with heavy losses. On 12 October, he personally directed a platoon of his men against a firmly defended cave on an important ridge, continuing his efforts until mortally wounded by Japanese sniper fire.'

37

The Lucky Few

13–29 October 1944

On 13 October, after mortars and artillery had plastered the enemy-held peaks to their immediate front, I and K Companies sent out small patrols to close up cave entrances with demolition charges. 'Everywhere we went on the ridges,' remembered Gene Sledge, 'the hot humid air reeked with the stench of death. A strong wind was no relief; it simply brought the horrid odor from an adjacent area. Japanese corpses lay where they fell among the rocks and on the slopes . . . in grotesque positions with puffy faces and grinning buck-toothed expressions.'

Marine dead, on the other hand, were removed on stretchers to the rear of the company's position and covered with ponchos. Yet they might lie there 'for some time and decompose badly' before they were collected by Graves Registration teams and buried in the division cemetery near the airfield.

The fighting was exhausting, costly and pitiless. Sledge wrote:

> The Japs fought like demons and shot our stretcher teams – the corpsmen and the wounded. We hated them with a passion known to few antagonists. Some writers blame it on racism. I don't believe that. The Code of Bushido by which the Japs fought fostered brutality. We never took prisoners, even when some few tried to give up. They often tried to throw a grenade at us. After taking a position we routinely shot both the dead and wounded enemy

> troops in the head, to make sure they were dead. Survival was hard enough in the infantry without taking chances being humane to men who fought so savagely.

After dark, Japanese infiltrators attempted to penetrate the battalion's lines, but were repulsed with heavy losses. 'It was,' noted Sledge, 'the usual hellish night in the ridges, exhausted Marines trying to fight off incredibly aggressive Japanese slipping all around . . . I was so tired I held one eye open with the fingers of one hand.'

I Company advanced farther on the 14th, and linked up with the left flank of a pioneer company, while K and L Companies held their ground. The last two K Company casualties – Platoon Sergeant Harry Spiece and PFC Earl Shepherd – were both wounded by mortar fire and evacuated that day. Later came the welcome news that the battalion would be relieved by army troops in the morning. Sledge was so determined not to have his throat cut 'at the last moment before escaping from the meat grinder' that he got even less sleep than usual.[1]

At 10:00 a.m. on the 15th, K Company turned over its position in the pocket to some 'grim-looking' men from the US Army's 321st Infantry. 'We didn't say much to them,' recalled Jim McEnery, 'and they didn't say much to us, but the expressions on their faces were worth a thousand words. They were scared shitless – understandably so – and as awful as we looked, they envied us.'

The survivors of K Company made their way down the hill, still under occasional small arms fire, and boarded trucks for a ten-minute ride to a bivouac area near the East Road called White Beach. It was like another world, and so quiet that McEnery thought he was going deaf. It had a cook-house, mess tent, showers, decked tents and even an outdoor movie theatre. They were able to shave, wash their hair and brush their teeth.

Ordered to establish a defensive perimeter facing the shore, they did so. But it was a formality. For K Company – and the rest of the 5th Marines – the fighting on Peleliu was finally over.[2]

* * *

From 6 to 14 October – the period 'Bucky' Harris was in command – the Umurbrogol Pocket was reduced in size by 30 to 40 per cent. The gains included the vital capture of Hill 140, which dominated much of the remaining enemy-held area; and all the high ground commanding the West Road, thus allowing the free and secure movement of north–south traffic.[3]

It was, noted Harris, 'slow and tedious' progress. Yet by 'dint of care' and 'improvisations', they were able to root out the Japanese defenders by using the tactics of 'blast, burn and bury'.* Almost daily, Harris would receive a phone call from Lieutenant Colonel Lewis J. Fields, Rupertus's operations officer, urging him to speed things up. The division commander was desperate to secure the whole of the island before the Old Breed was relieved by the 81st Division. But Harris would not be hurried. He reminded Fields that the 5th Marines had taken 80 per cent of the division's objectives on Peleliu, and that any 'impetuous haste' now would simply result in 'more casualties for no gain'.

Finally, on 14 October, two days after Rear Admiral Fort had declared that 'assault' operations on Peleliu were finally over, Harris received word that the 5th Marines was about to be relieved by Colonel Robert F. Dark's 321st Infantry. Harris had known Dark from their time together at the Infantry School in Fort Benning. 'He came to my CP,' recalled Harris, 'where I briefed him on the situation map, and I arranged to provide guides to lead his men up to relieve my 1st and 2nd Battalions. I also arranged for the prompt relief of the 3rd Battalion which would only require a small force.' He particularly warned Dark 'of the danger of advancing until you knew there were no Japs in rear of you and your flanks were secure'.

A few days later, Lieutenant Colonel Fields phoned Harris to give him the news that Dark's regiment had 'jumped off and advanced 600 yards'. Harris knew that the call was intended to 'needle' him, but kept his cool. 'Fine,' he replied, 'more power to them.'

Half an hour later, a panicked Fields called again. 'The general,' said

* The method was more typically known as 'blow torch and corkscrew'.

the division operations officer, 'wants you to get ready to put your men back in the line.' Dark's two assault battalions, he explained, had been counter-attacked from both flanks and driven back past their start line.

As requested, Harris alerted his 'weary warriors' and told them to get dressed, put fresh water in their canteens, see their weapons were oiled and cleaned, and wait for the order to move. It never came, because Fields called a third and final time to say that Dark had used his reserve battalion to stabilize the front and reoccupy his line of departure, and that the 5th Marines' assistance was no longer required. Harris stood down his men and gave each one an issue of two beers. 'I think,' he wrote later, 'this was one of the most popular orders I ever gave.'[4]

Although the 5th Marines took very heavy casualties on Peleliu, they would have been higher still but for Harris's outstanding leadership. Jim McEnery wrote:

> Harris refused to send us on suicide missions against those Jap caves like some of the other commanders had done. Instead, he played a patient waiting game, calling in artillery, tanks, mortars and air support, and giving them time to do their work before the infantry went in to clean up with flamethrowers, bazookas, and TNT . . . Most of us in K/3/5 who left Peleliu with breath in our lungs owe our lives to Colonel Harris.[5]

Gene Sledge later wrote to Harris: 'We in K-3-5 were very proud of the way you handled the 5th Marines on Peleliu. The battle was ferocious enough as it was, but we in the ranks deeply appreciated the fact that you tried to save lives while getting the job done. We knew little or nothing of command decisions, but we thought [Chesty] Puller was crazy and needlessly threw lives away, and that Rupertus didn't know what was going on up in those ridges.'[6]

During K Company's stay at White Beach, Sterling Mace and Gene Holland hitched a lift to the new division cemetery, located between Orange Beach 2 and the airfield, to pay their respects to their fallen comrades. They were met by row upon row of white crosses, 'all laid out neat, in perfect straight lines'. The outer edges were a bustle of activity as fresh holes were dug, and dead Marines were placed in them by men from the Graves Registration Service. They kept walking up and down the rows until they found the grave they were looking for: Sy Levy's.

Mace stared down at the fresh mound of earth, imagining Levy 'wrapped in a bag or something, sightless, unmoving, unfeeling'. All he could think to say was, 'Well, this is it.' Then, noticing something odd, he turned to one of the Graves Registration Marines. 'Hey, buddy.'

'Who, me?' said the Marine, leaning on his rake.

'Yeah, come over here. Look, this guy . . . this guy is Jewish. What's he got a cross for? Shouldn't he have a Star of David over here?'

The Marine shrugged. 'Well, ummm . . . we don't have a star like that. I don't know, *buddy*. I mean, what do ya want me to do about it? I just work here, okay?'

'Yeah, okay,' said Mace. He looked at Holland. 'Let's get the fuck outta here, Gene.'[7]

Back at White Beach, Gene Sledge was relaxing near the water when a buddy offered to show him a 'unique souvenir'. The Marine carefully unwrapped layers of wax paper – originally used to hold rations – and proudly held up his prize: a black and shrivelled human hand.

'Have you gone Asiatic?' asked a horrified Sledge. 'You know you can't keep that thing. Some officer'll put you on report sure as hell.'

'Aw, Sledgehammer,' responded the Marine, laying the hand on a rock, 'nobody'll say anything. I've got to dry it in the sun a little more so it won't stink.'

He explained that he had used his Ka-Bar knife to cut the hand from a Japanese corpse, assuming it would be a more interesting souvenir than gold teeth. 'What do you think?' he asked.

'I think,' said Sledge, 'you're nuts. You know the CO will raise hell if he sees that.'

'Hell no, Sledgehammer, nobody says anything about the guys collecting gold teeth, do they?'

'Maybe so, but it's just the idea of a human hand. Bury it.'

More Marines appeared, and all agreed the hand had to go. 'You dumb jerk,' growled a sergeant, 'throw that thing away before it begins to stink.'

Finally, and reluctantly, Sledge's buddy chucked the hand among some rocks. 'The war,' wrote Sledge, 'had gotten to my friend; he had lost (briefly, I hoped) all his sensitivity. He was a twentieth-century savage now, mild mannered though he still was. I shuddered to think that I might do the same thing if the war went on and on.'[8]

Around this time, Sledge penned his first letter to his parents from Peleliu. 'I know you both have worried an awful lot,' he explained. 'I wanted to write you many times but we were always in action except a little while & there was no mail service then. From now on I'll write as regular as I can.' He said nothing, of course, about his first gruelling experience of combat. Instead he asked about his brother, who had just been wounded in action – for the second time since landing in Normandy on D-Day – during the bitter Battle for Hürtgen Forest on the Belgian/German border. 'I hope Ed is all right,' he wrote. 'We were told that if a man was twice wounded, regardless of overseas time, he automatically went home. So I can't see why Ed hasn't been relieved . . . I hope he will be soon.'[9]

On 27 October, a week after William Rupertus had handed the command of the island to Major General P. J. Mueller of the 81st 'Wildcat' Division, K Company was trucked back to Purple Beach on the eastern shore to await embarkation. It looked to Sterling Mace very different from their first stay: 'ships moored everywhere, LSTs snug to the beach, a veritable swarm of swabbies, all ranks, milling about, laboring on their ships, huddled in circles playing cards, smoking'.[10]

They were bivouacked in a 'sandy, flat area near the beach' where they were reunited with their jungle hammocks and knapsacks (the lower part of the Marine's combat pack, which contained their spare uniforms). Many burned their old uniforms, which by now were falling to pieces. But as Gene Sledge's dungaree jacket was in reasonable condition, he decided to rinse it in the ocean, dry it in the sun, and keep it as a good luck souvenir. He also kept his boondockers, though the jagged coral had worn away most of the inch-thick cord soles, because his replacement shoes were in his seabag on a ship.[11]

When word arrived on 29 October that the whole 3/5 Battalion would ship out the next day, First Sergeant David Bailey arranged for a group photograph to be taken of K Company. Of the 235 men who had landed on D-Day, only 85 remained, a casualty rate of 64 per cent in barely a month of fighting.* In the photograph – one of the most famous and poignant of the Pacific War – the survivors are tightly grouped, some wearing T-shirts, others bare-chested, on a stretch of sloping beach with palm trees beyond. The two officers are lying down at the front – a smiling 'Duke' Ellington on the left, and a more serious 'Stumpy' Stanley to his right – and behind them the senior NCOs, including David Bailey and Johnny Marmet. The tall, skinny figure in the centre of the first row of standing Marines is R. V. Burgin, who would later claim to have 'absolutely no memory of having that picture taken'. To the far left of the row behind is the upright, moustachioed figure of Jim McEnery, a forage cap shielding his face from the bright sun. Gene Sledge, also wearing a cap, is standing two rows behind Burgin.

Photographs were also taken of the individual sections and platoons. The photo of the mortar section was of eighteen men, all kneeling and mostly grinning, including Marmet, Sledge, Burgin, Jay de l'Eau, 'Snafu' Shelton and George Sarrett. The picture of 3rd Platoon, on the other hand, was of just nine men (from an original forty-five) – McEnery, Sterling Mace, Gene Holland, Frank Minkewitz and Roy Kelly among them – the corpsman George Chulis and the surviving machine gunners attached to the platoon. 'Most of us smile,' wrote Mace. 'Make of that what you will. Perhaps we're pleased to be getting off the island. Maybe our smiles are what civilized men are supposed to do when a camera is pointed their direction . . . Or maybe we're laughing at a mysterious joke.'[12]

* Twenty-six men had been killed, and 124 hospitalized with battle wounds at various locations around the Pacific. (McEnery, *Hell in the Pacific*, p. 268.)

The 1st Marine Division's total casualties on Peleliu were a crippling 1,124 killed, 5,024 wounded and 117 missing in action: a total of 6,265. They had killed an estimated 10,695 Japanese soldiers, and captured another 302.* Yet it was not until 24 November that the Japanese commander, Colonel Nakagawa, sent a final message to Babelthuap from his last redoubt at the southern end of the 'China Wall':

> Our Defense Units were on the verge of being completely annihilated. Therefore the unit destroyed the 2nd Infantry regimental colours . . . Since 1800 the personnel left in this Defense Unit were Captain Nemoto and 56 men. This number split into 17 teams and decided to put on a last raid . . . Following the Commander's wishes, we will attack the enemy everywhere.

That night, Nakagawa and his nominal superior, Major General Murai, committed suicide. Two days later, the commander of the 323rd Infantry informed Major General Mueller that organized resistance on Peleliu had come to an end. By then, the 81st Division had lost 277 killed and 1,008 wounded, increasing total American casualties to more than 7,500. Incredibly, it was not until 21 April 1947 that the last Japanese servicemen – a lieutenant and twenty-six men – surrendered to the naval island commander. 'The news picture of the surrender,' noted George McMillan, 'showed the Japanese lieutenant bending low before an American naval officer, with his obviously well-fed command standing at rigid attention behind him.'[13]

The US Marines' official history of the campaign was quick to acknowledge the uniquely difficult circumstances in which the 1st Marine Division had been forced to fight. The terrain, for example, was 'completely at variance with anything previously encountered, for Peleliu

* Ninety-two of the 302 POWs were Japanese: seven army, twelve navy and seventy-three labourers. The remainder were non-Japanese labourers, including one Chinese, one Formosan, three unidentified and 206 Koreans. (Garand and Strobridge, IV, p. 276.)

contained some of the most rugged and easily defended ground yet seen by American forces in the Pacific'. In contrast to previous campaigns, the 'well-trained and dug in' Japanese defenders 'no longer expended men and equipment' in heroic but pointless banzai charges. They remained instead in well-supplied and cleverly sited cave positions in the island's high ground, waiting for the Americans to come to them.[14]

'That the Marines and soldiers eventually prevailed under these conditions,' wrote historian Joseph H. Alexander, 'is a tribute to their small unit leaders and individual rifelmen.'[15] The resultant cost in young American lives – 1,400 – was high. But it was only a fraction of the 10,900 Japanese dead, victims of Tokyo's fanatical determination to fight to the finish. Rear Admiral Fort, in tactical command at Peleliu, later described the capture of the island as 'the most difficult amphibious operation in the Pacific War'. Iwo Jima was twice the size of Peleliu, with double the defenders, yet that island required *three* Marine divisions to take it.

Admiral 'Bull' Halsey never deviated from his belief that Operation Stalemate II was unnecessary, and that its gains would be bought at a 'prohibitive price'. He wrote: 'I feared another Tarawa – and I was right.'

What, then, were those gains? They prevented the use of Peleliu and Angaur as bases for Japanese aircraft and submarines; and, by late November, Angaur-based US bombers were providing 'vital support to American troops on Luzon'. In addition, about 43,000 Japanese soldiers were 'effectively neutralized' in the northern Palaus, where they remained until the end of the war. Perhaps the greatest gain, however, was the use of Ulithi Atoll as an excellent fleet anchorage that would assume 'major importance' during later operations in the Pacific.

For the Marine Corps, the Peleliu operation was a vindication of the 'years of careful study and analysis' that had been spent developing its amphibious doctrine and proof that a seaborne assault on a heavily fortified island was 'feasible'. It would, moreover, help to prepare both the army and Marine Corps for what was to come.[16]

An often-forgotten bonus – pointed out by historian Joseph H. Alexander – was that the survivors of the cruiser USS *Indianapolis*, sunk by a Japanese submarine on 30 July 1945, were found by a search plane based at Peleliu. Had the plane taken off from another base, it is unlikely that these 316 men (from an original crew of 1,195) would have survived. Alexander added:

> The tactical lessons in cave warfare learned at such cost by the III Amphibious Force proved invaluable in the struggle for Okinawa a half-year later . . . Lacking all this hindsight, Nimitz made the best decision he could with the information available at the time. The subsequent unpleasant surprises and terrible costs were painful to bear, but the result was a clear victory. Nimitz succeeded in driving another stake into Imperial Japan's heart, a chilling warning that U.S. forces could prevail despite the most ingenious of defences and skilful of island commanders – even on a bad day.[17]

Yet such arguments cut little ice with the Marines who fought on Peleliu and survived. There were, wrote Jim McEnery, 'longer, costlier, and much better known land battles' in the Pacific. Yet Peleliu was 'uniquely horrible' because of its 'savage fighting, agonizing battlefield conditions, impossible terrain and logistics, physical misery, and psychological heartbreak'. It was, in his view, 'thirty days of the meanest, around-the-clock slaughter that desperate men can inflict on each other when the last traces of humanity have been wrung out of them and all that's left is the blind urge to kill'.[18]

38

'We were worn down and sobered'

Pavuvu Island, October–November 1944

Early on 30 October 1944, the men of K Company squared away their packs, picked up their gear, and headed down to the beach where they boarded amtracs for the trip over the reef to the troop transport SS *Sea Runner*, anchored offshore. All the while, Gene Sledge was 'distracted by an oppressive feeling' that, at the last moment, they would be turned around and thrown back into the line 'to help stop a counterattack or some threat to the airfield'.

Reaching the side of the *Sea Runner* in a heavy swell, weighed down with equipment, and weakened by illness and lack of sleep, the men found it hard to clamber onto and up the cargo net. Sledge felt 'like a weary insect climbing a vine', but kept going. Others stopped to rest, and were hauled the last few feet by sympathetic sailors. Having stowed his gear in a troop compartment below deck, Sledge went topside to enjoy lungfuls of 'fresh clean air' that 'wasn't heavy with the fetid stench of death'. Joined by a cigarette-puffing 'Pop' Haney, they stared for a while at the island's 'jagged ridges and shattered trees'.

'Well, Haney,' said Sledge, at last, 'what did you think of Peleliu?'

He was expecting Haney to give the old salt's usual line: I've seen worse. Instead, Haney replied: 'Boy, that was terrible! I ain't seen nothin' like it. I'm ready to go back to the States. I've had enough after that.'

For Sledge, none of them would ever be the same after what they had gone through. 'Something in me died at Peleliu,' he admitted.

'Perhaps it was a childish innocence that accepted as faith the claim that man is basically good. Possibly I lost faith that politicians in high places who do not have to endure war's savagery will ever stop blundering and sending others to endure it.' But he also learned important lessons on the island, chiefly the Marine's need to rely on and trust comrades and 'immediate leadership'. The other ingredients that had enabled him to 'survive the ordeal physically and mentally' were, in his view, the Marine Corps' discipline, esprit de corps and tough training. He realized, too, that to defeat an enemy as 'tough and dedicated as the Japanese', the Marines had to be 'just as tough'.

Yet Sledge was also self-aware enough to realize that, unlike many of his fellow enlisted Marines (the majority of whom had been brought up in poor homes where they had had to fend for themselves), his happy childhood and close family support had left him with a sensitivity and compassion for the sufferings of others that made it particularly hard for him to cope with the brutalizing effect of combat. 'As Wilfred Owen's poem "Insensibility" puts it so well,' he wrote, 'those who feel most for others suffer most in war.'[1]

Sailing in convoy the following morning, the *Sea Runner* took eight days to reach Pavuvu, where the 1st Marine Division would lick its wounds and absorb more replacements before the next operation. It was, for the survivors of K Company, a relaxing voyage. 'We had comfortable quarters below decks,' remembered Jim McEnery, 'and the *Sea Runner*'s galley served excellent chow.' They spent most of their time on deck, 'just bullshitting and breathing in the fresh air', and with no duties they slept as much as they liked.[2]

Since 'Hillbilly' Jones's death, there was no guitar player to sing along to, and even if there had been, the mood was too downbeat. 'I saw in the eyes of each survivor,' remembered 'Stumpy' Stanley, Haldane's successor as skipper, 'the price he paid for thirty days of unrelenting close combat on that hunk of blasted coral.' R. V. Burgin agreed: 'We were worn down and sobered. What we'd been through hadn't sunk in, and whatever it was we were heading to wasn't yet a reality.'

On 7 November – three days after Gene Sledge's twenty-first birthday

– the *Sea Runner* entered Macquitti Bay and dropped anchor. The shoreline of Pavuvu looked familiar from a distance. But as the men of K Company were being transferred by small boat from the ship to the island's new steel pier, and got closer to the beach, they 'hardly recognized the place'.

A sleek new canteen/clubhouse was under construction and there 'wasn't a rotten coconut or rat to be seen'. Even more shocking was the sight of Red Cross nurses – the first young, attractive women they had seen since their departure from Melbourne more than thirteen months earlier – standing behind decorated tables near the water's edge, and handing out doughnuts and paper cups of chilled grapefruit juice. 'A few overeager Marines rushed up to get in line at the tables,' remembered Jim McEnery, 'but a good many shied away and pretended to ignore the women. They sat down on the beach, kind of sulking and looking the other way. Others just stood and stared at the nurses like they were creatures from Mars.'[3]

Gene Sledge was among those who accepted the grapefruit juice, and then regretted it. His mind was 'so benumbed by the shock and violence of Peleliu that the presence of an American girl on Pavuvu seemed totally out of context'. He felt bewildered and resentful. *What the hell is she doing here?* he wondered. *She's got no more business here than some damn politician.*[4]

One Marine lightened the mood. 'Well, hell,' he said, 'I guess we'll have to wear swim trunks from now on when we take a dip.'

For Jim McEnery, the arrival of women was a good thing and proof that civilization had finally made it to Pavuvu. Certainly, the living conditions on the island bore no relation to their pre-Peleliu experience. 'Instead of a sea of mud,' wrote McEnery, 'there were neatly laid-out streets and roads built of packed coral, a fifteen-acre parade ground, ball fields and other recreational facilities.' They were billeted in brand-new tents with wooden decks and electric lights, and had access to 'modern showers, laundries, screened and well-lighted mess halls, plus a large PX stocked with all kinds of stateside goods' that included sodas, ice-cream, candy bars and a three-can-a-week beer ration.[5]

Waiting for them in the company's street were scores of 'self-conscious replacements' who appeared so relaxed and innocent of what lay ahead that Gene Sledge felt sorry for them.[6] On Jim McEnery's mind was the prospect that he and the other three-campaign veterans would not be sent home after all. 'There was always the chance,' he wrote, 'that somebody in Washington could change the rules, and that worried me a little. It meant I might end up in another killing spree on another damn island, so it was premature to think too much about going home.'

McEnery's qualms were allayed a few days later when it was announced that the Old Breed veterans who had served at least two years in the Pacific – a total of more than 4,800 men – were going home. They would, moreover, be given a thirty-day leave when they got there. Once Major Gustafson had signed the paperwork, it was a 'done deal', though the original departure date of 19 November was put back two weeks to 1 December. Once this was settled, McEnery went over to battalion headquarters and told the astonished sergeant major that he wanted to extend his enlistment for another two years.

'You need to wait till you get stateside,' insisted the sergeant major.

'No way,' responded McEnery. 'I want to do it now, before I leave.'

Convinced that there was 'no way' the Marine Corps was going to discharge a healthy NCO with his combat experience until the war was over, he decided to re-enlist now in the hope of being assigned as a drill instructor when he returned to the States. 'In its own way,' he wrote, 'it would be a job that was just as vital to the war effort as shooting at Nips and getting grenades thrown at you. But at the same time, it wouldn't be nearly as dangerous and dirty as the one I'd been doing for the past twenty-eight months.'

He and a large group of veterans – including 'Pop' Haney and Johnny Marmet – finally left Pavuvu on the navy transport USS *Wharton* on 1 December. Stopping at Guadalcanal, New Caledonia and Hawaii en route, it took three weeks to reach San Francisco. McEnery 'spent a lot of time at night looking up at the stars and thinking about the men we'd lost': Bill Landrum, Weldon DeLong, 'Dutch' Schantzenbach, Lou Gargano, John 'the Mad Russian' Teskevich, Seymour Levy, Bill

Bauerschmidt, 'Ack-Ack' Haldane and others. 'No matter how it happened though,' wrote McEnery, 'they were all just as dead. It made me fully aware – for the first time, I think – how lucky I was to be still breathing and heading home.'[7]

Shortly after K Company's return to Pavuvu, on an occasion when all the replacements were absent on work parties, First Sergeant David P. Bailey ordered the Peleliu veterans to 'Fall in!' As they 'struggled out of their tents into the company street,' recalled Gene Sledge, I thought how few remained out of the 235 men we started with. Dressed in clean khakis and with his bald head shining, Bailey walked up to us and said, "At ease, men." He was a real old-time salty Marine and a stern disciplinarian, but a mild-mannered man whom we highly respected. Bailey had something to say, and it wasn't merely a pep talk.'

Bailey began: 'You should all be very proud of yourselves. You fought well in as tough a battle as the Marine Corps has ever been in, and by doing so you've upheld the honor of the Corps. You people have proved you are good Marines.'

Dismissed, the veterans returned 'silently and thoughtfully' to their tents. None was more moved by Bailey's brief but heartfelt speech than Gene Sledge. 'His straightforward, sincere praise and statement of respect and admiration for what our outfit had done,' wrote Sledge, 'made me feel like I had won a medal.' It was 'not the loud harangue of a politician or the cliché-studded speech of some rear-echelon officer or journalist', but rather a 'quiet statement of praise from someone who had endured the trials of Peleliu with us'. His words 'meant a lot' to Sledge, and to his comrades too.

A more personal endorsement was provided one night, after lights out, by a Gloucester veteran in Sledge's mortar team who had been wounded on Peleliu. 'You know something, Sledgehammer?' he said from his cot.

'What?'

'I kinda had my doubts about you, and how you'd act when we got into combat, and the stuff hit the fan. I mean, your ole man bein' a doctor and you havin' been to college and bein' sort of a rich kid compared to some guys. But I kept my eye on you on Peleliu, and by God you did OK, you did OK.'

'Thanks, ole buddy,' replied Sledge, a lump in his throat. Those 'simple, sincere personal remarks of approval' from a veteran comrade meant as much to him as any medal for bravery, and he would carry them in his heart 'with great pride and satisfaction' for the rest of his life.

On a separate occasion, Sledge was lying on his cot after evening chow when he noticed the skipper 'Stumpy' Stanley carry a book and some papers over to the 55-gallon oil drum that served as a trash can in the company street. Most of the papers he just tipped inside. But one thick book he held up to study before slamming it into the trash in 'obvious anger'. Once Stanley had left, a curious Sledge walked over to take a look. The papers were mostly combat maps of Peleliu which he tossed back in (an act he later regretted). The book, on the other hand, was a large hardback, about a thousand pages long, and bound in dark blue. On its spine was the title and editor: *Men at War*, an anthology of war stories selected by Ernest Hemingway.*

This is good history, thought Sledge, *I wonder why Stumpy chucked it away*. He got his answer when he opened it up and saw written, 'in a bold strong hand', the name *A. A. Haldane*. A lump rose in his throat as he asked himself why he would want to read about battles when Peleliu had cost the company its much-admired skipper and many good friends. He, too, 'slammed the book down into the trash can in a gesture of grief and disgust over the waste of war'.[8]

In correspondence with his family, Sledge related none of these feelings or experiences. So intense had been the month-long battle for Peleliu that there was no facility to send or receive letters until the worst of the fighting was over, and the backlog was waiting for the survivors

* The stories included accounts of the battles of Waterloo, Austerlitiz, Thermopylae, Shiloh, the Alamo and others by authors as diverse as C. S. Forester, William Faulkner, Winston Churchill and Rudyard Kipling. First published in 1942, it was read by many American serviceman who wanted to feel inspired by great tales of war.

when they returned to Pavuvu. Sledge's letters in response contained only the occasional hint of what he had just gone through. On 10 November, for example, he chided his parents for begging him to write an air mail and assure them that all was well. He explained: 'As much of a turmoil as there was, your pleading for a letter didn't help a bit. You should know I write whenever I can. Also if I had been hurt you would have been notified. I know how you couldn't help worrying, but it was sure hard receiving mail & [being] unable to answer it, & then no one can seem to understand why.'

In his next letter, a few days later, he mentioned he had been on Peleliu – 'just another page of history now' – and that a news cameraman had taken pictures of him and his gunner 'Snafu' Shelton while they were 'firing furiously' on Ngesebus. 'So be on the lookout,' he told his dad, '& you may see me in the movies.' He also confirmed the arrival in the post of the Colt Springfield Armory .45 semi-automatic pistol his father had worn in World War I. 'Boy I was glad to get it & I'll bring it home when I've spent time here.'

On 23 November, he told his mother that radio reports about the high number of American casualties on Peleliu were 'very true, I'm sorry to say'. He went on to say that he had collected shells from one of the island's beaches and was having them made into a bracelet for her. 'I hope,' he wrote, 'because those dainty little shells came from such a dreadful place, that you won't fail to see their beauty & know they show you were in my mind continuously.'

Such emotive and unguarded comments like these were few and far between. Instead, Sledge's letters were mostly confined to family reminiscences ('Remember three years ago today you & I were dove hunting at the Wares' when we heard of the 'dastardly sneak attack on US bases'), requests for food and magazines (but *not* canned baby food because he was being teased about it), and the odd humdrum remark about what he was up to. 'As I look over at my bunk with a copy of Field & Stream & a box of cookies on it,' he wrote to his father on 7 December 1944, 'I feel the need to remove my shoes and relax. This rest snows me but I guess we really earned it.'[9]

R. V. Burgin was just as circumspect in his replies to Florence's letters from Australia. 'Our mail was censored,' he recalled. 'We couldn't write anything about where we were or where we'd been or what we were doing. Just, Hello, I miss you terribly, I love you, I hope to see you soon, Good-bye.' His letters, as a result, were short: two or three pages, at the most. Hers were longer, six pages or more, and full of news from Down Under.

On Thanksgiving Day – 23 November 1944* – Burgin wrote to Florence: 'I am a very happy yet a lonesome boy.' Apart from being relieved that he had survived two tough campaigns, he was delighted that 'Duke' Ellington, the mortar section leader who had caused him 'so much trouble for so long', had just been transferred to battalion headquarters and given command of the newly created Assault (Special Weapons) Platoon, equipped with flamethrowers, bazookas and demolition charges.[10] The move provoked very different feelings for Corporal Jay de l'Eau, who had also been assigned from the mortar section to the new platoon. 'I really hated to leave K Company,' he told Gene Sledge, 'even though I knew we would be attached in combat. While I never lost the feeling and pride of belonging to K Company I never was really part of it any more. We were kind of like orphans, we were no longer part of the family . . . I guess the other thing about the reorganisation that we from K Company did not like was that we inherited 1st Lieutenant 'Duke' Ellington . . . He was disliked. He was held in the same esteem as your "Mac".'[11]

The man de l'Eau was referring to was Ellington's successor as mortar section leader: 22-year-old Second Lieutenant Robert E. 'Mac' MacKenzie from Orono, Maine, 'a blond New England college kid fresh out of Officer Candidates School'.[12] When MacKenzie first joined K Company on Pavuvu, he was assigned to replace Bill Bauerschmidt as 3rd Platoon leader. He immediately asked Sterling Mace, Orley Uhls and some of the other platoon veterans to join him in his tent.

* A federal holiday in the United States that, since 1942, has been celebrated on the fourth Thursday in November.

'PFC Mace,' began MacKenzie, 'I understand you spent a considerable amount of time on Peleliu, in combat, is that correct.'

'That is correct, sir,' said Mace.

'Made the landing, did you? What was that like?'

Mace told him how the rifle platoons had come in first, with the machine guns and mortars following 'right behind'. He explained that there was a lot of shelling and machine-gun fire, and that one of the platoon leaders, Lieutenant 'Moose' Barrett, was killed that day.

'So,' said MacKenzie, making notes on a pad, 'the mortars and machine guns. The mortars came in right *behind* the first wave?'

'Sure,' agreed Mace. He was about to say something about that being 'standard operational procedure', but assumed that an officer would know that. First the riflemen go in, with the mortars and heavy weapons following close behind for immediate support. The setup, in Mace's eyes, was both practical and logical.

They talked some more, and eventually Mace and the others were dismissed. Soon after, remembered Mace, Second Lieutenant MacKenzie took over the mortar section. His place as 3rd Platoon leader was taken by Second Lieutenant Samuel A. 'Spud' Dunlap, a 'big guy' who was said to have played professional football for the Brooklyn Dodgers before the war.[13]

Most of the old hands in the mortar section were underwhelmed by their new officer, though the bar set by his predecessor had not been high. 'Mac,' remembered Gene Sledge, 'was blond, not large, but was well built, energetic, and talkative, with a broad New England accent. He was a conscientious officer, but he irritated the veterans by talking frequently and at great length about what he was going to do to the Japanese when he went into action.' Sledge felt embarrassed for MacKenzie because it was 'so obvious he conceived combat as a mixture of football and a boy scout campout'. He refused to listen to the veterans who suggested he had a shock coming. 'I hope to God,' a Texan mortarman told Sledge, 'that big-mouth Yankee lieutenant has to eat every one of them words of his when the stuff hits the fan.'[14]

One of the few veterans who got on well with MacKenzie – presumably because virtually anyone would, to him, have been an improvement on Ellington – was R. V. Burgin, Marmet's successor as platoon sergeant. He and MacKenzie eventually became good friends, but in the early days even Burgin was exasperated by the young officer's gung-ho attitude. 'The only thing in his mind,' noted Burgin, 'was what he had seen in the movies. It was just the rookie in him talking . . . Still I liked him.'

The mortar section had lost fewer men on Peleliu than the rifle and machine-gun platoons. Even so, the addition of a new gun on Pavuvu – bringing the total to three – meant that some replacements were needed. Burgin selected two from his home state: T. L. Hudson and Clyde Cummings. 'Just why in the hell do you want those particular two?' asked the sergeant in charge.

'Well,' said Burgin, 'in the first place they're Texans. In the second, both are good, strong young men. I need two good ammunition carriers and they can do the job.'

The sergeant laughed. 'Yeah, go on and take them.'[15]

Many more replacements were needed by the rifle platoons, particularly Dunlap's 3rd. 'Since it was only me and Charlie Allmann left of our original team,' remembered Sterling Mace, 'I got the [corporal's] stripe, and Charlie got a new fire team. By the time the replacements arrived to bolster our depleted ranks, my BAR was taken away from me and I was given an M-1 rifle and a new BAR man in PFC Eubanks.'

Just 19 years old – a year younger than Mace, whose twenty-first birthday was 2 February 1945 – Eubanks was a tall and lanky 'country bumpkin' from West Virginia. He was, noted Mace, the 'sort of guy who if you put him in a new suit, the suit would never fit'. His natural look was a 'pair of bibbed overalls with a piece of straw hanging out of his mouth – or maybe stumbling down a yellow brick road, with Dorothy and Toto in tow'. Yet none of this made him, in Mace's opinion, any less dedicated to the Marines, or less ready for action.

The other two new men who completed his fire team were the BAR assistant, PFC George Weisdack from Donora, Pennyslvania, and the scout PFC Robert 'Wimpy' Whitby from Solon, Ohio. A little older than Mace, Weisdack was 'short, good looking, with dark hair, and a

Marines evacuating a casualty at Cape Gloucester.

Dead Japanese soldiers in front of a tank.

Moving weapons and supplies in the Cape Gloucester mud.

Marines advancing behind a tank.

Captain A. A. Haldane receiving the Silver Star for 'brilliant leadership and indomitable fighting spirit' during the capture of Walt's Ridge, January 1944.

Captain Thomas 'Stumpy' Stanley, commanding K Company, calls in artillery support on Okinawa.

Hank Boyes (left) and Howard Nease on Pavuvu, early 1945.

K Company's mortar men on Okinawa a week after the battle was over. (Left to right) Dan Lawler, Gomez, Eugene Sledge (with pipe in mouth), Myron Tesreau, V. F. Vincent, Weisdack.

Photos taken from the packs of dead Japanese soldiers on Okinawa.

Survivors of K Company's Mortar Section with a captured Japanese flag on Okinawa, including George Sarrett (standing, far left), Vincent Santos (third from left), John Redifer (far right) and Jim Dandridge (kneeling, far left).

real pencil-thin mustache – a touch of the Hollywood look'. He was suffering, however, from a serious case of ringworm on his back – showing up as 'nickels and quarters . . . red-ringed and sprinkled with white powder' – that 'must have hurt like a sonuvabitch'. Weisdack endured the pain in silence, but Mace knew that it was only a matter of time before it took him out of the line.

'Wimpy' Whitby was unusual in that he was married with two young daughters, a 'real good *family* man' with a 'mortgage, and everything that went with a white-picket-fence life'. He was thirty-two years old, 5ft 7in tall, and a 'little chunky, with dark, sort of curly hair, already graying at the temples'. Hardly 'your prototypical poster model for the Marine Corps'.

As all three were untested in combat, they pestered Mace to tell them what it was like. Mace's response was cautious. He knew that if he was honest he would 'scare the crap out of them', and if he lied he would 'give them a false sense of security'. It was a lose-lose situation. 'Look, George,' he said, after Weisdack had posed the question during a game of cards, 'it's hard for me to tell you what it's like because each campaign is different. All ya gotta do is stay alert. Don't anticipate something taking place; just be ready when it does. And don't goof off, alright? Stay alert. Be a smart Marine. Everything after that will come to *you*. You don't have to come to *it*. You'll be alright, if ya don't think about it too much. Okay?'[16]

A replacement who joined 1st Platoon on Pavuvu was Private Harry Bender from Chicago. Just seventeen years old when he volunteered for the US Marine Corps in early 1944, and 5ft 3in tall – an inch shorter than the minimum height required – he was accepted because of an (erroneous) assumption that he would grow. He was, he remembered, 'the youngest, the shortest, and the orniest' in his platoon.

Surprised by the friendly reception from the platoon's veterans – they 'knew you proved yourself in combat' not 'training' – he became good friends with New Yorker Bill Leyden, now fully recovered from the shrapnel wound to his face that he had suffered on Peleliu. Bender's one flaw was that he complained too much. As an enlistee and not a draftee, this was something to avoid. 'If ever I started bitching about something,' remembered Bender, 'they'd ride you a little and say, "Shit, you asked for this shit." You get to the point when you don't complain anymore.'[17]

After several weeks back on Pavuvu, some of the enlisted veterans were interviewed for field commissions. R. V. Burgin, for example, was quizzed by three or four officers who asked him questions like what did he feel about ordering men into action when they might be killed, and did he plan to make the Marine Corps his career? His answers were 'I'm okay with that, I've done it before', and 'No'. But he said the wrong thing when he admitted sending $2,000 home to his family.

'Mmmm,' said one of the officers. 'You've been a private, a private first class, a corporal and a sergeant. You were making fifty-five dollars and you're now drawing sixty-five dollars a month. And you've sent two thousand dollars home?'

'Yes, sir.'

'Sergeant, do you shoot crap?'

'No, sir. I do not.'

It was the truth. The money had come mostly from poker winnings, but Burgin was not asked if he played that. Even so, he heard no more about a commission.[18]

Also interviewed – this time by an 'extremely handsome' lieutenant who exuded composure and modest self-confidence – was Gene Sledge. They got on well, and Sledge was typically honest. Asked why he had dropped out of the V-12 officer candidate programme, he explained how he had felt about joining the Marine Corps and being sent to college.

'How do you feel about it now that you've been in combat?' asked the lieutenant.

'It would be nice to be back in college. I saw enough on Peleliu to satisfy my curiosity and ardor for fighting. In fact, I'm ready to go home.'

The officer laughed, and then asked Sledge how he liked the Marine Corps and his unit. He said he was proud to be a member, and that being a 60mm mortarman was his first choice.

'How would you feel,' said the officer, more serious now, 'about sending men into a situation where you knew they would be killed?'

'I couldn't do it, sir.'

After a few more questions, the officer said: 'Would you like to be an officer?'

'Yes, sir, if it meant I could go back to the States.'

Again the officer chuckled and, a few friendly remarks later, brought the interview to a close. When Sledge told his buddies about it, one of them responded: 'Sledgehammer, damn if you ain't got to be as Asiatic as Haney. Why the hell didn't you snow that lieutenant so you could go into OCS?'

Sledge said something about the officer being too wise to fall for a snow job. But the real reason, he knew, was that he did not want to leave K Company:

> It was home to me, and I had a strong feeling of belonging to the company no matter how miserable or dangerous conditions might be. Besides, I had found my niche as a mortarman. The weapon and its deployment interested me greatly, and if I had to fight again, I was confident of doing the Japanese far more damage as a mortarman than as a second lieutenant. I had no desire to be an officer or command anybody; I just wanted to be the best mortar crewman I could – and to survive the war.[19]

39

Where Next?

Southwest Pacific, December 1944–February 1945

The battalion cooks and messmen had almost finished clearing up after the New Year's Eve dinner when a sentry shouted, 'Corporal of the guard, fire at post number three!'

One of the gasoline heaters in the galley had caught fire and, as the mess sergeant cursed and shouted orders, Gene Sledge saw two figures 'slide through the shadows' from the mess hall towards the company street. A few minutes later, by which time the galley fire had been extinguished, Sledge and his tentmates were invited to a party in a nearby tent. Sledge arrived to see Corporal Howard Nease, a Gloucester veteran from Greensboro, North Carolina, sitting on his cot with a 'huge, plump roast turkey' on his lap.

'Happy New Year, you guys,' said a grinning Nease.

As each man filed past him, the corporal sliced off huge slabs of succulent turkey and placed them in his outstretched hands. They drank beer and a potent home brew known as 'jungle juice', while a fiddler and a mandolin player struck up the 'Spanish Fandango'. Later Sledge and others howled with laughter as Nease explained how he and two buddies had lit the fire to distract the mess sergeant so they could enter the galley and 'liberate' two turkeys. Both the theft and the sharing of the booty were typical Nease. 'He was one of those wonderfully buoyant souls,' remembered Sledge, 'always friendly and joking, coolheaded in combat, and though much admired, very modest.'

It was the finest New Year's Eve party that most of them could remember, topped off at midnight when the 11th Marines fired an artillery salute.[1] Once the party was over, R. V. Burgin and one or two others carried the bones and carcasses over to I Company's street and dumped them in a trash can. 'Guess who got the blame the next day,' noted Burgin, 'for stealing the turkeys.'[2]

Next morning, young Private Harry Bender – who had helped Nease to steal the turkeys – was called to the office of the new company XO, 22-year-old First Lieutenant George B. 'Shadow' Loveday from San Gabriel, California. Loveday had served on Peleliu as the machine-gun platoon leader of I Company, 3/5 Marines. But he was not liked by the men of K Company. 'He was,' recalled Bender, 'a real prick. He asked me about the turkey, and didn't believe a damn word I said. Nothing was ever done about it.'[3]

Given the XO's unpopularity, it helped that the men approved of Haldane's successor, 'Stumpy' Stanley, who was, wrote his runner Corporal Jim 'Andy' Anderson, 'a fine gentleman and a good warrior'. He added: 'Captain Haldane was our number one commander, but Captain Stanley was a close second. Some officers treated you like a servant, but Captain Stanley, when he was going to tell you to do something, he would say, "Could you do this for me?" . . . He must have heard that from Haldane.'[4]

Shortly after the Old Breed had returned to Pavuvu in early November, Major General Pedro A. del Valle, a former commander of the 11th Marines, replaced William Rupertus as division commander. Few of the veterans were sad to see the back of Rupertus. Del Valle, by contrast, was a popular figure. The 51-year-old son of a former governor of Spanish Puerto Rico, he was a 'quick, dark man with luminous sharp eyes' who had commanded the Marine artillery with distinction on Guadalcanal. 'High combat morale,' noted Admiral Halsey, 'was characteristic of the units under del Valle.'[5]

To prepare his men for the next challenge, del Valle had them perform close-order drills, parades and reviews on the 15 acres of level ground that stood between Pavuvu's pier and the beach road. 'This was better than work parties moving rotting coconuts,' noted Sledge, 'and added a "spit and polish" to our routine that helped morale. A regular beer ration of two cans a man each week also helped.'

As the training was intensified – including two trips to Guadalcanal – the question on everyone's lips, veteran and rookie alike, was: where next? Among the many rumours was talk of landing on mainland China and the island of Formosa. There were clues in the nature of their training – which emphasized street fighting and cooperation with tanks in open country – and the issue of 'maps (without names) of a long, narrow island'. But no one had put two and two together until a friend of Gene Sledge's from L Company, 'who had also been in the V-12 program and was a Peleliu veteran', came excitedly to his tent with a *National Geographic* map of the northern Pacific. On it they identified the same 'oddly-shaped island' in the map without names as Okinawa, located 325 miles south of the southern tip of the Japanese home island of Kyushu. 'Its closeness to Japan,' remembered Sledge, 'assured us of one thing beyond any doubt. Whatever else happened, the battle for Okinawa was bound to be bitter and bloody. The Japanese never sold any island cheaply, and the pattern of the war until then had shown that the battles became more violent the closer we got to Japan.'[6]

In his letters home, however, Sledge was more concerned with the imminent danger to his brother Ed as the Germans counter-attacked in the Ardennes Forest (the so-called 'Battle of the Bulge').* 'I can't blame you,' he wrote to his mother on 7 January 1945, 'for being so disturbed about the German counter thrust. I am too. I certainly pray for his safety.' As for his own situation, he hoped to be 'home next Christmas'

* The attack – the last great German offensive of the war – by two panzer (tank) armies was launched on 16 December 1944 against weakly held US positions in the Low Countries. The objective was to reach the Belgian port of Antwerp. But after initial gains, the Germans were held up in front of the Meuse river and the battle was effectively over by Christmas, though it would take another month of hard fighting before the 'bulge' was flattened. Both sides suffered about 80,000 casualties, with an additional 30,000 civilians killed and wounded.

and was 'really planning on it'. He signed off: 'I'll be so glad when Ed & I are home so you both can quit worrying.' He and his parents were right to be worried about Ed, whose unit, the 741st Tank Battalion, was in the thick of the fighting. But he came through it, and was awarded the Bronze Star for gallantry on the first day of the battle.

A few weeks later, Sledge relayed better news to his parents from both Europe and the Pacific: the Russians were just 'seventy-three miles from Berlin', while MacArthur's campaign in the Philippines was 'going well for the army'.* He also thanked them for sending all three volumes of Douglas Southall Freeman's Civil War history, *Lee's Lieutenants: Gettysburg to Appomattox*. 'I know,' he wrote, 'I'll get many an hour of pleasure from them.'[7]

It just so happened that the commander of the Tenth Army, Lieutenant General Simon B. Buckner, Jr, was also reading *Lee's Lieutenants*, a history that featured his own father. Was Buckner looking for inspiration? For tips? His diary gives no clue, beyond the comment: 'A tragic epitaph to a nobly defended cause.'[8]

The decision to invade the island of Okinawa, 70 miles long and the most southerly of Japan's forty-seven prefectures, had been taken by the Joint Chiefs of Staff the previous October. It ended a long period of consultation and debate among the Allied leaders and their senior commanders, and represented a victory for the strategy advocated by Admiral Nimitz, that of taking a direct route to Japan.

The practical effect of President Roosevelt's visit to Pearl Harbor in late July 1944 had been to allow MacArthur to continue his advance up through the Philippines, while Nimitz edged closer to Formosa via the central Pacific, the first step being the capture of Peleliu. But much

* In fact, by the end of their January offensive, the Russians had advanced 300 miles and reached the River Oder, just 43 miles east of Berlin. In the Philippines, meanwhile, MacArthur had followed up his capture of Leyte (in late December 1944) with a landing on the main island of Luzon by Lieutenant General Walter Krueger's Sixth Army on 9 January 1945.

had changed by the time all organized resistance on that island had ended in late November.

From 11 to 16 September 1944, Roosevelt, Churchill and their Combined Chiefs of Staff met at Quebec for the Octagon Conference where they agreed, among other things, that Britain would become a full partner in the war against Japan after the defeat of Germany. Churchill's preference was for an advance across the Bay of Bengal and an operation to recover Singapore and the Malay Peninsula, lost in such ignoble circumstances in early 1942. Roosevelt disagreed. The Americans, he said, had been very successful in 'island-hopping' in the Pacific, and bypassing strong Japanese garrisons like Singapore which could be mopped up later. But he was prepared to accept Churchill's offer of naval support in the central Pacific, overruling Admiral King's unwillingness to share victory 'with an eleventh-hour entry'.[9]

Happy with this concession, Churchill and his chiefs of staff let the Americans decide the optimum route of advance in the Pacific. On 15 September, while the conference was still in progress, the Joint Chiefs authorized General MacArthur to bring forward his operation to capture the Philippine island of Leyte from 20 December to 20 October. But there was still an assumption that Nimitz would launch Operation Causeway – the invasion of Formosa – once the Philippines were secured. That, however, was about to change.

On 16 September, sensing an opportunity to ditch the Formosa operation in favour of a move directly north from the Philippines to the Ryukyu and Bonin islands, and from there to Japan, Nimitz asked his senior army commanders for their opinion. Lieutenant General Robert C. Richardson, Jr, commanding US Army Forces in the Pacific Ocean Area, was firmly in agreement. Regarding the occupation of Formosa as a costly diversion, he argued instead for a dual advance along the Luzon–Ryukyus and Marianas–Bonins axes. This would allow MacArthur to seize the island of Luzon after Leyte, and provide air and naval bases in the Philippines to block enemy shipping lanes and neutralize Formosa. But only the next step – possession of the Ryukyu chain of islands, extending 700 miles south of the Japanese home islands, and the Bonins further to the east – would enable extensive air operations against Kyushu and Honshu. These, in turn, would prepare the ground for amphibious landings.

Richardson was backed by Lieutenant General Millard F. Harmon, commanding US Army Air Forces, who pointed out that the acquisition of air bases could be achieved with far less cost in men and matériel in the Ryukyus than in Formosa. The final nail in Causeway's coffin was provided by Lieutenant General Buckner, the recently appointed commander of the US Tenth Army, who said that he lacked the supporting and service troops for such a large-scale operation.[10]

Nimitz repeated these arguments to Admiral King when they met in San Francisco on 29 September. The alternative to Causeway, said Nimitz, was to keep the pressure on the Japanese by taking, in turn, Luzon, Iwo Jima and Okinawa. Formosa, meanwhile, could be kept in check by a series of air strikes from carriers. Why Iwo Jima? asked King. Because, explained Nimitz, it would allow fighter protection for the huge B-29 bombing raids on the Japanese home islands that were planned for 1945.[11]

Convinced by Nimitz, King proposed to his fellow Joint Chiefs on 2 October that, because of insufficient resources in the Pacific Ocean Area and the unwillingness of the War Department to make additional resources available until after the defeat of Germany, operations against Luzon, Iwo Jima and Okinawa should precede the seizure of Formosa. They concurred and, a day later, Nimitz was ordered by the Joint Chiefs to 'occupy one or more positions in the Nansei Shoto [Ryukyu Islands], target date 1st March 1945'. The purpose was to establish bases from which to attack 'the main islands of Japan and their sea approaches' with air and naval forces; support further operations in regions bordering the East China Sea; and sever air and sea communications between Japan's home islands and its possessions to the south and west. But the first step was to 'capture, occupy, defend and develop Okinawa Island'.[12]

The selection of 58-year-old Lieutenant General Buckner to command the US Tenth Army – the joint army–Marines formation that had originally been tasked with the capture of Formosa – was an odd one. Born in Munfordville, Kentucky, Buckner was the son of a famous Confederate general of the same name who later became a state governor, though he failed in his 1896 nomination as vice-president of the United States. But at the time of his appointment to lead the Tenth Army, the younger Buckner had no experience of field command and, moreover, had never participated in a battle of any kind. Having graduated from the US Army's military academy at West Point in 1908, Buckner had risen steadily if unspectacularly through the ranks. He completed two tours of the Philippines, but missed active service in World War I, and spent much of the interwar period as a student or instructor at various military schools, including a stint as commandant of cadets at West Point. He was remembered there as a stern disciplinarian who allowed his cadets few luxuries. 'Buckner forgets cadets are born not quarried,' commented the parent of one aspiring officer.[13]

Lacking field experience, Buckner clung to US Army doctrine that artillery played the decisive role in combat. Infantry were needed to find and hold the enemy, he believed, but only artillery could destroy it. When war came a second time in December 1941, he was eager to put this theory into practice. But by then he was running the army's Alaska Defense Command, a relative backwater that saw only limited action. In 1943, for example, when amphibious landings recovered the Aleutian Islands of Attu and Kiska from the Japanese, both operations were navy-led.[14]

Salvation came in the summer of 1944 with his appointment to command the newly formed US Tenth Army with its headquarters in Hawaii. Senior navy admirals in the Pacific – notably Raymond A. Spruance, commanding the US Fifth Fleet (and in overall charge of the Okinawa operation), and Kelly Turner, commanding the amphibious task force – would have preferred the appointment of an experienced Marine general like Holland M. 'Howlin' Mad' Smith, who had led ground troops during the Gilbert and Marshall Islands campaigns, and at Saipan in June 1944. But they were overruled by Admiral Nimitz because Holland Smith's sacking of an army general on Saipan, Major General Ralph Smith of the 27th Infantry Division – the so-called Smith v. Smith controversy – had caused bad blood between the Marine Corps and the US Army. Nimitz chose Buckner for two reasons: he was the next senior army general available; and, though inexperienced, he was known to be a straight-shooter and even-handed, both useful traits in a man who would have to work closely with the navy and the Marines.[15]

It helped that Buckner had an excellent supporting cast: particularly his chief of staff, Brigadier General E. D. Post, who had served with him since West Point; and his deputy chief of staff (US Navy/Marines), Brigadier General Oliver P. Smith, the former 'Devil Dogs' commander who, more recently, had served as Rupertus's deputy on Peleliu. Smith's early impression of Buckner, after meeting him at army headquarters in Schofield Barracks, Pearl Harbor, in early November 1944, was mostly positive. 'He was,' noted Smith, 'in excellent physical condition: ruddy, heavy-set, but with considerable spring in his step. He had snow-white hair and piercing blue eyes: the eyes were almost hard.' Though he had had 'surprisingly little troop duty' and 'limited' experience in amphibious operations, he did not lack for 'character' and Smith had 'no reason to feel he would not continue to operate well in a joint undertaking [with the navy]'. While Buckner's 'methods and judgments were somewhat inflexible,' wrote Smith, 'you always knew where you stood.'[16]

Post, Smith and Buckner's other deputy chief of staff (US Army), Brigadier General Lawrence E. Schick, did most of the planning for the assault on Okinawa, codenamed Operation Iceberg. Their first priority was to gather all the geographical, meteorological and demographic information they could find on the island and its people from captured documents and prisoners of war, former residents and old Japanese publications. The bulk of their data came from aerial photographs which, taken by planes 1,200 miles from their bases, were frustratingly small-scale or incomplete. Yet the basic facts were not in dispute. Okinawa was the largest island in the Ryukyus, a chain stretching almost 800 miles in a long arc from Kyushu to Formosa, and forming a boundary between the East China Sea and the Pacific. Of these 140 islands, only 30 were inhabited in 1945. The climate was subtropical, with temperatures ranging from 60° to 83° Fahrenheit, heavy rainfall, high humidity and violent typhoons between May and November.

Situated roughly in the centre of the Ryukyus, Okinawa was 70 miles long and from 2 to 18 miles wide, running north to south, and covering an area of 485 square miles. Composed of porous coral rock, it was fringed with reefs: close to shore and rarely more than a mile wide on the western side; but much wider on the eastern side, where the coast was more sheltered.

When Commodore Perry's black ships first sailed into Naha Harbor on the west of the island in 1853, Okinawa was a semi-independent country that paid tribute to both China and Japan. Ryukyuan kings had ruled the surrounding islands from their capital at Shuri Castle, to the east of Naha, since the early fifteenth century. But after the entire Ryukyu archipelago was annexed by Japan in 1879, and the monarchy abolished, the Okinawan people became fully integrated into the Japanese governmental, economic and cultural structure. With a similar racial heritage to the Japanese, and resembling them in looks and physique, the Okinawan stock and culture had also been heavily influenced by the Chinese. In 1945 they spoke Luchan, not Japanese, and their predominant religion was an animistic cult that worshipped fire and hearth, and venerated ancestors.

Most of the 435,000 inhabitants were poor – subsisting on small-scale agriculture and fishing – and much of the useable land in the bottom third of the island was cut into small fields and planted with sugar cane, sweet potatoes, rice and soy beans. This was because northern Okinawa, the two-thirds of the island above the Ishikawa Isthmus, is rugged and mountainous, with a central spine 1,000 feet or more in height running the length of the region. Descending from both sides of this ridge are terraces dissected by ravines and watercourses, and ending at the coast in steep cliffs. Similar terrain is found on the Motubu Peninsula, jutting out to the west, where two mountain tracts are separated by a central valley. Covering the whole of this northern area in 1945 were pine forests and dense undergrowth, with only a few poor roads clinging to the western coast.

South of Ishikawa, on the other hand, is a more benign landscape of rolling hills, ravines and escarpments. At the time it contained three-quarters of the population, four airfields and the large towns of Naha, Shuri, Itoman and Yonabaru. Generally aligned east to west, the hills provided a series of natural lines of defence. There were more roads in the south, but most were country lanes unsuitable for motorized traffic. Drainage was poor, and heavy rains would quickly turn the deep, claylike mud into a quagmire.

The obvious place for a landing was the 9,000-yard stretch of the western coastline, a little south of Ishikawa, known as the Hagushi beaches. Divided by the Bishi River, the beaches ranged from 100 to 900 yards in length and from 10 to 45 yards in width at low tide. Composed of coral sand, they mostly had at least one exit road and were flanked by a low coastal plain which was dominated by rolling hills. The plain was also the site of two of the island's four main airfields: Yontan, north of the Bishi, and Kadena to the south.

American estimates of enemy troop strength on Okinawa grew slightly from 48,600 in October 1944 to 65,000 in March 1945. They correctly identified the main infantry formation units – the 24th and 62nd Divisions, and the 44th Independent Mixed Brigade (IMB) – as well as a regiment of tanks and large numbers of heavy artillery pieces and anti-tank guns. These forces were grouped, according to aerial photos, in at least three main areas of defence: Naha, the Hagushi beaches and the Yonabaru–Nagagusuku Bay area on the lower east coast. It was assumed, in the event of the landings being successful, that the main line of enemy resistance would be across the narrow waist of land south of Hagushi.[17]

The initial landing plan for Operation Iceberg – known as Plan Fox – was to put troops ashore at Hagushi on the west coast where, as Oliver Smith put it, 'a very limited advance would put in our hands the Yontan and Kadena Airfields'. The plan included the capture of the island of Keise Shima, just off the west coast of Okinawa, prior to the day of landing – codenamed Love Day* – to allow the siting of heavy artillery

* The day of landing was designated 'Love Day' to avoid confusion with Iwo Jima's 'Dog Day'.

to support the main landings. Eight infantry divisions were assigned to the operation:* the XXIV Corps of the US Army (7th, 27th and 96th Divisions); the III Amphibious Corps of the US Marine Corps (1st, 2nd and 6th Marine Divisions); and two extra US Army divisions, the 77th and 81st, in floating reserve. When support units were added, this brought the landing force strength up to 183,000. Buckner wanted an additional 70,000 service troops. He was refused on the grounds that the troops were not available and, even if they had been, both the shipping and beach capacity were inadequate.[18]

On 1 November 1944, Plan Fox and an 'alternate plan' to land on the southeast coast of Okinawa were presented to Vice Admiral Kelly Turner, commanding the amphibious task force and Buckner's immediate superior. Hugely experienced by this stage of the war – having led a string of successful amphibious assaults in the Pacific, including Guadalcanal, the Russell Islands, Tarawa and Makin, and the Marshall and Mariana Islands – Turner did not suffer fools gladly. When Buckner's staff told him that they had no confidence in the alternate plan, and were only presenting it because they thought there should be one, he loudly disagreed. From the navy's perspective the alternative was preferable because the approach was through open sea, whereas Plan Fox meant sailing through the Kerama Islands just west of Okinawa. Even with these islands in our hands, said Turner, the navigational aspects of the approach would be more difficult, and the weather conditions harder to predict. He therefore requested a reconsideration of the east coast landing and a possible feint at Hagushi. Despite Turner's request, wrote Oliver Smith, 'the Plan Fox Estimate was distributed to all hands on November 5th'.[19]

Love Day was delayed twice during the next month: from 1 to 15 March 1945, and then to 1 April 1945, the final date. This was partly

* Both army and Marine divisions were based on a triangular structure of 3 infantry regiments, 9 battalions (three per regiment), 27 companies (three per battalion), 81 platoons (three per company) and and 243 squads (three per platoon). They also included support units of artillery, engineers, armour, pioneers and service troops.

down to weather concerns, and partly to the availability of shipping. Vice Admiral Turner, meanwhile, had come around to Plan Fox after he requested an in-depth study that described the Hagushi beaches as the 'best' in Southern Okinawa 'for the purpose'. His proviso was that, in addition to Keise Shima, the Kerama Islands were also seized seven or eight days prior to Love Day 'to provide a much needed protected anchorage where supporting ships could be refueled and rearmed and thus assure uninterrupted support of the landing'.[20] This, of course, meant the allocation of part of an infantry division, the 77th, to take the Keramas, a diversion of resources that Buckner opposed, but could do nothing about. Turner 'scattered too much', he noted in his diary. 'I prefer greater concentration on the main objective.'[21]

Early in the New Year, Smith became aware of a seemingly minor decision of Buckner's that would have, in time, the gravest consequences: his plan for all Tenth Army general officers to wear metal stars on their combat helmets.* Smith heard about it from Major Frank Hubbard, Buckner's recently appointed aide, who came to take his order. Smith wrote of telling Buckner 'that in the type of warfare encountered in the Pacific, it had been found advisable for generals to hide their identity if they valued their skins . . . There were always hidden Japanese snipers to fire on persons carrying field glasses or other equipment identifying them as officers.'

According to Smith, a 'compromise was finally reached by which the helmet was untouched, but small white stars were painted on the liner; this on the theory that the helmet without the liner would be worn only in the rear areas'. That may have been true for Buckner's subordinates; but the general himself would insist on going through the campaign wearing a liner-less helmet with three distinctive metal stars.[22]

* One star denoted a brigadier general, two a major general, and three a lieutenant general (Buckner's rank).

40

'The Road to Certain Victory'

Okinawa, March 1944–February 1945

The man given the unenviable task of defending Okinawa against an American attack was 57-year-old Lieutenant General Mitsuru Ushijima, commanding the Japanese Thirty-Second Army. 'Tall and heavyset' with 'ruddy cheeks and a benign countenance', Ushijima had been born in Kagoshima on the island of Kyushu where his father was a samurai – a member of the high-born warrior caste that served the great feudal landowners – and later a career officer in the Imperial Japanese Army. Following in his father's footsteps, the young Ushijima graduated from the prestigious army academy in Tokyo with honours in 1908, and passed out of the Army Staff College eight years later.

Fiercely non-political, Ushijima had avoided any association with the ultranationalist cliques that were rife in the army, telling his instructors and students at the elite army's Toyama School – of which he was commandant for a period in the 1930s – to concentrate on their military service. He did just that, winning praise for leading his 36th Infantry Brigade to a series of victories over Chinese nationalist forces in the early years, 1937 to 1939, of the Sino-Japanese War. After garrison duty with the IJA's 11th Division in Manchuria, he returned to Japan in October 1939 as commandant of the Non-Commissioned Officers Academy. A vocal opponent of the surprise attack on Pearl Harbor – which he felt would prolong the war in China and weaken Japan vis-à-vis her true enemy, Soviet Russia – Ushijima was removed from his post in April 1942 for fear he was sending the wrong signals to his students. But thanks to the support of other senior generals who also had misgivings about the Pacific War, he was reinstated as commandant of the army academy, a post he held until he was ordered to take command of the Thirty-Second Army on Okinawa in August 1944.[1]

Ushijima was unlucky to inherit as his chief of staff a man who could not have been less like him in physical appearance, politics and military philosophy. Short and stout, Major General Isamu Chō was a fierce nationalist who in the 1930s had been active in the 'young officers' military clique that was calling for Japan's territorial expansion. Implicated in the massacre of at least 200,000 Chinese civilians and prisoners of war at Nanjing in the winter of 1937–8, and briefly arrested for his part in a coup d'état against the civilian government, the 50-year-old Chō was a ruthless and aggressive military strategist who thought attack the best form of defence. If it had been his decision, the Japanese troops on Okinawa would have planned to fight the invading Americans on the beaches. Instead, Ushijima took the advice of his talented operations chief, Colonel Hiromichi Yahara, forty-two, who was convinced the only way to defend Okinawa, given the inevitable imbalance in troop numbers and firepower, was to leave the beaches uncontested and instead concentrate Japanese strength in the south of the island.[2]

Plans put forward by Imperial General Headquarters in Tokyo in January 1945 had decreed that the battle for Okinawa would be won on the sea and in the air, and that the troops on the island would merely be needed 'to mop up enemy remnants after they landed'. Yahara knew this was nonsense and planned accordingly. Born to a modest family of farmers in the sparsely populated southwest of Honshu Island, the bespectacled Yahara had used brains and determination to advance his army career, passing out first from the War College. He had served as a regimental officer, worked undercover in Southeast Asia and, more recently, taught at the Imperial Japanese Army Academy in Tokyo under Ushijima. But it was his two years as an exchange officer in the United States, including six months with the 8th Infantry, that would serve him best on Okinawa as it gave him an insight into the American military mind.[3]

Reaching the island in March 1944, Yahara considered Okinawa an obvious future target for US forces as they advanced closer to Japan's home islands, 325 miles to the north, and argued for a significant troop build-up. 'I felt it was crucial,' he recalled, 'that we select those islands where we could expect the enemy to attack, place decisive troop strength there, and make adequate combat preparations while we still had the chance.' He eventually got his way, and various units were rushed to Okinawa until, by the late summer of 1944, the garrison had swelled to 105,000 men, backed by a further 20,000 half-trained Okinawan *Boeitai* (militia).[4]

At this stage, Yahara's strategy was to 'move in the direction of any enemy landings, launch an offensive, and destroy the enemy near the coast'. But when IGHQ decided in November 1944 to move the Thirty-Second Army's best unit, the 25,000-strong 9th Division, to the Philippines, via Formosa,* Yahara changed tack. Now with, he believed, too few troops to prevent a major landing, he concentrated the vast bulk of his forces in the southern third of the island, 'behind several heavily fortified lines north of army headquarters at Shuri Castle' in the centre of the island. Well protected in tunnels and caves, they could withstand any quantity of enemy bombs and gunfire. Or as Yahara put it: 'Against steel, the product of American industry, we would pit our earthen fortifications, the product of the sweat of our troops and the Okinawan people.'[5]

The change was controversial as it ran counter to the Imperial Japanese Army's operational doctrine of seeking out a 'decisive battle' rather than a 'war of attrition'. But Ushijima gave his approval, and for the next five months soldiers and civilians toiled night and day to prepare a defensive system across the narrow waist of southern Okinawa where, forward of Ushijima's HQ on Mount Shuri, 'several jagged lines of ridges and rocky escarpments' were turned into 'formidable nests of interlocking pillboxes and firing positions'. All were 'connected by a network of caves

* As it happened, the 9th Division never got to the Philippines, but remained instead in Formosa.

and passageways inside the hills' that allowed the defenders to move safely to the point of attack.[6]

For a brief moment in late January 1945 it looked as if help was on its way. IGHQ messaged that the 84th Infantry Division would be sent to Okinawa as a replacement for the 9th. But that same day the order was rescinded because IGHQ had had second thoughts about denuding Japan's home islands of troops when they might soon be under attack themselves. To raise spirits, Yahara wrote and disseminated a pamphlet titled 'The Road to Certain Victory', in which he argued that defensive fortifications would counteract the Americans' marked advantage in troop numbers and firepower.

Seemingly convinced, soldiers and civilians carried on the work of expanding existing caves, and building a network of tunnels and concrete machine-gun posts, with great enthusiasm. Lacking specialised tunnelling equipment, they used entrenching tools, picks and shovels to hack into the tough coral rock. Once through the outer crust, however, the soil was a soft red clay, and relatively easy to dig into. With no cement or iron to shore up the tunnels, each unit cut wooden beams from pine forests in the mountainous north, and moved them south in native boats called *sabenis*, often at night to avoid American air raids. By late March, more than 60 miles of underground fortifications and command posts had been constructed, as well as anti-tank minefields and gun emplacements.[7]

Efforts had also been made from January onwards, recalled Chō's secretary Shimada,

> to mobilize virtually the entire civilian manpower of Okinawa for use as Army auxiliaries. Additional Home Guard levies were made, designed to supplement the earlier conscriptions of the fall of 1944. Almost the entire student body of the Middle Schools, the Vocational Schools and the Shuri Normal School was organised into guerrilla units, the most prominent of which was the celebrated Blood-and-Iron-for-the-Emperor Duty Unit . . . The students were trained in infiltration tactics by a Capt[ain] Hirose, an expert on

guerrilla warfare who had been sent to 32nd Army from Imperial HQ for the express purpose of coordinating the activities of infiltration groups and similar irregular forces.[8]

Among the 2,000 Okinawan schoolboys, aged fourteen to eighteen, who were recruited into the Blood and Iron Student Corps was Shigetomo Higa, a fourth grader from Sikiyama in Shuri who attended the Okinawa First Prefectural Middle School. When Higa joined the school in 1941, it was 'quite free and relaxed'. But with the arrival of Principal Fujino a year later, the atmosphere became more militarist. In 1944, Shigetomo's five-year programme of study was cut short by a year as part of the Emergency Student Mobilization Outline: most classes were cancelled and Shigetomo spent most of his time on labour details constructing airfields and gun emplacements.

After the fall of Saipan in the summer of 1944, Shigetomo attended a lecture given by Lieutenant General Watanabe, Ushijima's predecessor as Thirty-Second Army commander. 'There is no doubt,' declared a tearful Watanabe, thumping the desk before him, 'that the enemy will land in Okinawa and, when that happens, every civilian must share the same fate as our soldiers, so I am asking you to be ready to die a glorious death in the name of the emperor.' Shigetomo was shocked by both the general's appearance and message. He had always assumed that Japan would win the war. Now, one of the country's senior generals was admitting that defeat was all but inevitable.[9]

Tokyo, meanwhile, was relying on a new secret weapon to defeat the Americans: kamikaze (or special attack) units.* There had been suicide attacks earlier in the war. At Pearl Harbor on 7 December 1941, a Japanese D3A had dived into the seaplane tender *Curtis*. The following October a crippled Japanese torpedo bomber was deliberately flown into the destroyer USS *Smith*, killing twenty-eight and wounding twenty-three.

* Literally 'divine wind', a form of suicide attack in which the pilot used his plane, rocket, torpedo or boat – usually packed with explosives – as a weapon.

In the same sea battle, at least two Japanese planes crashed into the carrier *Hornet*. There were, moreover, a number of instances from 1942 onwards of Japanese planes colliding with their American counterparts. But it was not until the autumn of 1944, during MacArthur's invasion of Leyte, that the Imperial Japanese Navy's Special Attack Corps was formed in the Philippines in a desperate attempt to counteract the superiority in aircraft carriers, battleships and planes enjoyed by the US Navy.

The first mission by the Shimpū Tokkōtai (Divine Wind Special Attack Units) was on 25 October 1944, during the naval Battle of Leyte Gulf, when five Mitsubishi Zeros, each carrying a 250kg bomb, attacked a cluster of US Navy aircraft carriers. Two planes were shot down, but the other three got through, damaging two carriers and sinking a third, the USS *St Lo* (a smaller Casablanca-class escort carrier), after fires caused the ship's magazine to explode. By the end of the following day, further kamikaze attacks had struck many more ships, sinking a total of five and damaging others.

On hearing of these first suicide attacks, the 43-year-old Emperor Hirohito, who had ruled Japan since the death of his father in 1926, asked: 'Was it necessary to go to this extreme?' But, he added, 'they have certainly done a good job.'[10]

These early successes caused an immediate expansion of the kamikaze programme to include all types of planes – fighters, bombers and even training aircraft, many flown by inexperienced pilots – as well as piloted flying bombs (Ōhkas),* motor boats packed with explosives (Shinyō) and human torpedoes (Kaiten). One of the earliest volunteers for the Kaiten Corps was Naoji Kōzu, a former student at the Tokyo Imperial University who had been conscripted into the Japanese Imperial Navy. Unlike the early members of the Shimpū Unit, he was never told he

* The largest Ōhka attack – featuring small single-seated wooden aircraft, laden with almost 4,000lb of explosives, and carried to within 13 miles of the target by a twin-engined bomber – was made against US aircraft carriers on 21 March 1945. All sixteen bombers and their Ōhka missiles were either shot down or lost before they reached their target.

would be going to a place 'from which I'd have absolutely no chance to return'. He only found out the truth when he was assigned to Hikari, the Kaiten base in southern Honshu, and saw the craft for himself. He recalled,

> The body was painted flat black. It overwhelmed a man. A small sail and a tiny periscope located at its center seemed to disturb the harmony of the whole. The rear third was a Type-93 torpedo. A maintenance officer described it to us dispassionately. 'The total length is fourteen point five meters. Diameter, one meter. The crew is one man. Explosive charge one point six metric tons. Navigation range seventy-eight thousand meters. Maximum speed thirty knots.'

The details aside, Kōzu only had to look at the position of the pilot, in a tiny cockpit in the centre of the Kaiten, to know it was a suicide weapon from which there would be no escape. Overcome with emotion, he could not speak. 'I felt,' he wrote, 'that I myself turned into something no longer human.' There was, he discovered, a way out of the corps: by failing to operate the Kaiten properly during test runs. But he never seriously considered that option because it would have meant someone else taking his place. 'I couldn't bear the idea of sacrificing someone else by quitting. I knew if I did, I'd regret it for the rest of my life.'[11]

By January 1945, the kamikaze units were at the centre of the IGHQ plans – codenamed Operation Ten-Go – to repulse the next phase of the American advance in the Pacific, probably against Okinawa. 'I firmly believed,' said Rear Admiral Sadatoshi Tomioka, chief of operations of the Naval General Staff, 'that Okinawa alone was the decisive battleground where we would be able to reverse the war situation'. The navy's strategy was to deliver such a severe blow to the attacking American forces that it would force them to the negotiating table. But the problem for the IJN – which was expected to do the bulk of the fighting both on the sea and in the air – was that its surface force was down to just a handful of battleships and no operational aircraft carriers, while its depleted stock of planes and pilots, particularly its special attack units, would need to be replenished before it could carry out a large-scale air operation. That was unlikely to be before May 1945.[12]

But the navy's warnings were ignored and on 6 February 1945, IGHQ issued the Ten-Go Air Operations Agreement for the navy and army to provide 2,000 and 1,350 planes respectively – those numbers to include 740 special attack planes – to hurl against the advancing US fleet. With the die cast, the IJN stepped up its preparations. 'Although the training could not be completed,' recalled Commander Yoshimori Terai, the air operations chief on the Naval General Staff, 'we intended to carry out the operations forcibly by employing special attack tactics.'[13]

The navy's intention was to slow down the American advance on Okinawa by launching a kamikaze attack against the carriers of the US Fifth Fleet in their anchorage at Ulithi Atoll in the Caroline Islands, the so-called Operation Tan No. 2, on 11 March 1945. But only two of the twenty-four twin-engine bombers, each carrying 800kg bombs, made it as far as Ulithi: one struck the stern of the aircraft carrier USS *Randolph*, just below the flight deck, killing 27 sailors and wounding 105; the other crashed into a road on the small island of Sorlen, mistaking a signal tower for a ship. As a result of this largely failed mission, noted Commander Terai, the IJN was 'forced to face the Okinawa Operations unprepared'.[14]

41

'In some ways it was bigger than D-Day'

From the Solomons to the Ryukyus, March 1945

Shortly before the kamikaze attacks on the US Fifth Fleet at Ulithi, the 1st Marine Division completed its preparations for the invasion of Okinawa with a week of amphibious manoeuvres off the coast of Guadalcanal, including a mock landing on 6 March 1945 that went 'exceptionally well'.[1] As K Company and the rest of the 3/5 Marines had been in the assault waves at Peleliu, they were assigned as regimental reserve and transported in the attack transport ship USS *McCracken* instead of LSTs. For the mock landing they went ashore in Higgins boats, rather than amtracs, and were picked up later that day.

Platoon Sergeant R. V. Burgin, PFC Gene Sledge and two of the 60mm mortar squads were in one of the last boats to leave the shore. Overloaded, and hampered by rough sea conditions, the boat began to ship water through an open view port. Even after the port's folding steel shutters were closed, water still sprayed over the bow ramp and in through various cracks. Up ahead, in the gathering twilight, they could see the stern of a transport at the tail of the convoy as it passed round the end of Guadalcanal. 'If we didn't catch up with that transport before dark,' remembered Sledge, 'we didn't know when we would get back to our ship.'

With water filling the bilges, the coxswain started the pumps to keep the vessel afloat. The situation was 'grim', and Sledge dreaded the thought of having to swim two miles through choppy water to the beaches if the boat sank. What irony, he thought, that after surviving Peleliu they might die 'by drowning on maneuvers in Iron Bottom Bay'. Slowly but surely, they gained on and caught the last transport and shouted to come aboard. Just in time, cables were dropped from a pair of davits and fastened to rings in the floor of the Higgins boat as it started to sink. A cargo net was lowered, and they scrambled up it, 'mighty relieved to be out of that small boat'. Transferred later to the *McCracken*, they were asked where they had been.

'We went to 'Frisco for a beer,' replied one of Sledge's party.

'Wise guy!'[2]

Returning to Banika for a few days to replenish supplies and fuel, the men were given liberty ashore to visit friends in hospital and drink at the canteens. Gene Sledge used the downtime to write and thank his mother for sending 'three beautiful Easter cards' and a press clipping about a new degree course in Forestry at the Alabama Polytechnic Institute in Auburn that he thought sounded 'interesting'. He also asked her to send some camellias to the divorced sister of Jay de l'Eau, his 'closest friend' in the battalion. The nearest he got to revealing the tension he must have been feeling, with a new operation imminent, was when he chided his mother for writing about 'casualties, set backs etc' (which was possibly a reference to the heavy losses that the Marines were taking on Iwo Jima). He explained: 'I hear enough about the war without reading it in letters from home. Don't ask me why they don't use certain weapons & tactics. I'm just one of the Americans fighting it & if I did know I couldn't tell you.'[3]

On 15 March, the 1st Marine Division left the Russell Islands in a convoy of ships bound for Ulithi Atoll. By the time they reached the lagoon six days later, Vice Admiral Marc A. Mitscher's Fast Carrier Task Force (part of Spruance's US Fifth Fleet) had just returned from a successful operation to bomb airfields and harbours in the Japanese home islands of Kyushu, Honshu and Shikoku.* The *McCracken* – again

* Mitscher's task force destroyed 528 Japanese planes, damaged 16 surface craft and hit scores of hangars, factories, warehouses and dock areas. 'The success of

carrying K Company and the rest of the 3/5 Battalion – anchored close to one of Mitscher's carriers, the 'terribly scorched and battered' 872ft USS *Franklin*, which had been bombed in a Japanese counter-attack on 19 March. A total of five flat-tops – including *Enterprise*, *Intrepid*, *Yorktown* and *Wasp* – were hit by Japanese bombs and kamikaze planes during the operation, but by far the heaviest casualties – 806 killed and 265 wounded – were suffered by the *Franklin*.*

'We could see charred and twisted aircraft on her flight deck,' remembered Gene Sledge, 'where they had been waiting with loaded bombs and rockets to take off when the ship was hit. It must have been a flaming inferno of bursting bombs and rockets and burning aviation gasoline. We looked silently at the battered listing hulk until one man said, "Ain't she a mess! Boy, them poor swabbies musta' caught hell."'[4]

The 1st Marine Division's convoy remained at Ulithi until 27 March, enough time for the men to go ashore on the tiny islet of Mog Mog for recreation and physical conditioning. After some cursory calisthenics, the officers handed out warm beer and Cokes, and the men enjoyed a game of baseball. They appreciated the opportunity to get off their cramped transport and stretch their legs. No one wanted to board the Higgins boat for the return to the ship at sunset.

It was during this spell at Ulithi that R. V. Burgin received news he had been dreading about his younger brother Joseph Delton ('J. D.'). 'He was,' remembered Burgin, 'almost four years younger than me, always quiet, not a hellraiser. But he would not be pushed around.' As boys they had fished together, and hunted possums at night with dogs and .410 shotgun. J. D. was present when Burgin shot his first deer. It was, therefore, no surprise for Burgin to receive a letter from J. D. in

---

the operation,' noted the official history, 'was indicated by the subsequent failure of the Japanese to mount a strong air attack for a week after the American landing on Okinawa.' (Appleman, *Okinawa*, p. 50.)

* Despite its catastrophic damage, the *Franklin* was towed back to Brooklyn Naval Yard, via Ulithi and the Panama Canal, where she was given a replacement hull and flight deck. But she never saw action again and after the war, unlike most of her sister carriers, was not converted for jet operations.

early 1944 asking his advice about joining the Marine Corps. He urged his brother not to. 'I thought he might have an easier time of it than I did,' he wrote, 'if he joined the Navy.'

Typically headstrong, J. D. enlisted in the US Army instead and, after basic training, was sent to France. The telegram, from Burgin's father, conveyed the tragic news that J. D. had been 'killed by German artillery in Alsace-Lorraine'. According to his officer, he died instantly and 'hadn't felt a thing'.[5]

By the time the bulk of the 1st Marine Division had left Ulithi on 27 March, Operation Iceberg – the largest amphibious operation of the Pacific War – was well underway. One awestruck Marine wrote:

> This is the largest open-seas armada in history. Seven divisions and the whole Pacific Fleet. 1,457 ships and half a million men. Think about this. All those ships and men have to arrive together at the right time and place thousands of miles from the USA. *Remarkable logistics.* The seven divisions all come from different places and all are on ships. An awesome sight. Then there were the warships: [aircraft] carriers, battleships, cruisers and lots of destroyers . . . I am sure the public did not realise the size of the Okinawa operation. In some ways it was bigger than D-Day.[6]

Either way, it was an astonishing logistical enterprise. For the assault echelon alone, more than 183,000 troops and 747,000 tons of cargo were loaded onto 430 assault transports and landing ships at eleven different ports, from Seattle to Leyte in the Philippines. They would be supported by 120,000 service troops and engineers. The closest Pacific base to Okinawa was at Ulithi, five days' sailing at ten knots. Yet the bulk of the resupply would come from the west coast of the United States, a distance of 6,250 nautical miles, or twenty-six days' sailing.[7]

Most of the 540,000 Allied servicemen – navy, air, Marines and army – who would fight in the campaign were American. They included the naval personnel of Spruance's US Fifth Fleet, the most powerful in history with more than twenty fast aircraft carriers, ten battleships and 1,200 aircraft. Yet a small but significant portion of the Fifth Fleet's sea and air assets were British and Commonwealth, in the form of Task Force 57 – otherwise known as the British Pacific Fleet – which comprised two battleships, four fleet carriers, five cruisers (one each from Canada and New Zealand), eleven destroyers (two from Australia) and 220 aircraft. It was the Royal Navy's most formidable strike force of the war.[8]

The first assault troops – men of the US 77th Infantry Division – had left Leyte on 18 March, and eight days later began landing on the Kerama Islands, a few miles west of Okinawa, where they faced minimal opposition. Within three days, the islands were in American hands, as were 121 prisoners and 300 suicide boats that were to have been used against the US fleet. A further 530 Japanese soldiers had been killed, at a relatively minor cost of thirty-one American dead and eighty-one wounded.[9]

Far more chilling – and a sign of things to come – was the discovery of more than six hundred dead civilians, the victims of Japanese propaganda that it was better to commit mass suicide than be raped and killed by the American invaders. Men of the 306th Infantry 'found a small valley littered with more than 150 dead and dying Japanese, most of them civilians. Fathers had systematically throttled each member of their families and then disembowelled themselves with knives or hand grenades.' Under a blanket lay a father, two small children, and both grandparents, 'all strangled by cloth ropes'. As American soldiers and medics did what they could, providing food and care for the survivors, an old man who had killed his daughter 'wept in remorse'.[10]

On 25 March, the day before the first troops landed on the Keramas, the softening up of Okinawa itself began with the long-range shelling of the southwest coast by the US Navy. This was to cover the work of minesweepers and frogmen whose job was to clear the approaches to the Hagushi beaches of mines and underwater obstacles. From 29 March, the bombardment proper began when the battleships, cruisers, destroyers and gunboats of Rear Admiral Deyo's Gun & Covering Force 'closed the range' and used their heavy guns to 'hit their objectives with increasing effectiveness'. In the seven days prior to the landing on 1 April, naval guns would fire 'more than 13,000 large-caliber shells (6-inch to 16-inch) in shore bombardment', a total of 5,162 tons of high explosives. This fire was supplemented by numerous strikes from carrier planes – mostly from Mitscher's Fast Carrier Force – who targeted barracks, gun positions, airfields and midget submarine bases with rockets, bombs and napalm.[11]

As the intensity of the bombardment increased, assault troops were converging on Okinawa from multiple directions: the 7th and 96th Infantry Divisions from Leyte, the 27th Infantry Division from Espiritu Santo, the 2nd Marine Division from Saipan, and the 1st and 6th Marine Divisions from Ulithi. It was, remembered Gene Sledge, an uneventful voyage north in the *McCracken*, though he was conscious of the cooler weather after the heat of Peleliu, and thankful they were wearing wool-lined field jackets.

On board, they received their first detailed briefings about the task ahead from the company officers. 'This is expected to be the costliest amphibious operation of the war,' announced a lieutenant. 'We will be hitting an island about 350 miles from the Japs' home islands, so you can expect them to fight with more determination than ever. We can expect 80 to 85 per cent casualties on the beach.'

A buddy leant over and whispered to Sledge: 'How's that for boosting the troops' morale?'

The officer continued with his warnings: about the difficulty of getting over a seawall in K Company's sector; the threat posed by a large Japanese gun, up to 150mm, said by intelligence to be sited on the right flank of the battalion area; and the possibility of a Japanese paratrooper attack on their rear at night. 'It's pretty certain the Nips will pull off a massive counterattack,' he said, 'probably supported by tanks, sometime during our first night ashore or just before dawn. They'll *banzai* and try to push us off the beachhead.'*[12]

* The planners were not aware that, by this time, the Japanese had abandoned this costly large-scale suicide tactic and replaced it with the defence-in-depth

Similar briefings were taking place in all the Old Breed's ships. The division would be one of four to land on the Hagushi beaches on Love Day. Geiger's III Amphibious Corps would land, two divisions abreast, on the left flank, north of the village of Hagushi at the mouth of the Bishi River; Hodge's XXIV Corps, also two divisions, would land on the right flank, south of Hagushi. The four divisions were to be, from north to south, the 6th Marine Division, 1st Marine Division, 7th Infantry Division, and 96th Infantry Division. The Old Breed would land, therefore, in the left centre of Hagushi's twenty-one beaches, between two of the island's best airfields, Yontan and Kadena. Of its two assaulting regiments, the 7th Marines would come in on the left and the 5th Marines on the right. As it was in regimental reserve, the 3/5 Marines would land after the 1st and 2nd Battalions on the extreme right of the Devil Dogs' sector. It would, therefore, form the right flank of the III Amphibious Corps and link with the XXIV Corps to the south.[13]

The plan was for both corps to drive across the island in a coordinated advance. The 6th Marine Division's first task was to capture the Yontan airfield and then advance to the Ishikawa Isthmus, the narrow neck of the island, securing the beachhead on the north by L + 15. The 1st Marine Division, meanwhile, would head across the island and drive down the Katchin Peninsula on the east coast, clearing most of it by the same L + 15 date. The 7th Division would seize Kadena airfield and advance to the east coast, cutting the island in two. The 96th Division would first capture the high ground commanding the beaches from the south and southeast, and then move rapidly down the coastal road towards the town of Chatan. By L + 10 it was hoped that the 96th would have secured a line across the isthmus from below Kuba and Futema.[14]

During the evening of 31 March – the night before the assault – the

---

that had proved so costly on Peleliu and, more recently, Iwo Jima, where the V Amphibious Corps (3rd, 4th and 5th Marine Divisions) had lost almost 7,000 killed and 19,000 wounded in bitter fighting from 19 February to 26 March 1945. Almost the entire Japanese garrison of 21,000 men perished in the battle.

men of K Company were reminded to 'move off the beach as quick as possible'. Though not landing in the assault waves, they would still 'get the hell kicked out of us' as they tried to move inland. 'We were advised to hit the sack early,' wrote Gene Sledge. 'We would need all the rest we could get.'[15]

A restless R. V. Burgin went on deck to ruminate. It had been sixteen months since he had said goodbye to Florence in a Melbourne park. In that time, he had survived two major campaigns, yet felt no closer to fulfilling his promise to return one day. In fact, every battle took him physically much farther away. How long would he be on Okinawa? And then where? Japan? As he looked out into the darkness, convinced the enemy was getting both weaker and more desperate, he could not see 'any end to it'.[16]

42

Love Day

Okinawa, 1 April 1945

Woken at 4:00 a.m. on 1 April 1945 – 'Love Day' (but also April Fool's Day and Easter Sunday) – the men of K Company joined a long chow line for a breakfast of steak and eggs, bread, fruit cocktail and coffee, the 'usual feast before a slaughter'. They then returned to their troop compartments, through a ship that 'seethed with activity', to square away their combat packs, weapons and ammunition.

Gene Sledge was one of the last men in his squad to use the head, which consisted of a row of permanent wooden seats over a metal trough, and through which ran a constant flow of seawater. He felt the familiar pangs of 'fear and apprehension' in his stomach as he settled on a seat. Next to him was a 'cagelike chute of iron mesh' that ran from ceiling to floor. Suddenly, the 'incredibly loud sound of clattering, clanking, scraping, and rasping metal' caused him to spring up from his seat in fear, convinced that a kamikaze plane had crashed into the ship above him. With his trousers round his ankles, he almost fell. As he reached down to pull them up, the loud noises began again – 'like a thousand cymbals falling down stone steps' – and he noticed dozens of empty brass 40mm shell cases cascading down the chute from the guns above. Realizing it was just anti-aircraft fire, his 'fright subsided into chagrin'.[1]

By the time he had collected his gear and joined the others on deck, dawn had revealed a 'long, low landmass silhouetted a few miles away with an umbrella of smoke hanging over it'.[2] The bombardment of the landing beaches – which had begun at 5:30 a.m. and would eventually fire almost 45,000 rounds of 5in or larger ammunition, 33,000 rockets and 22,500 mortar rounds, the 'heaviest concentration of naval gunfire ever to support a landing of troops' – was growing in intensity and American planes had joined in with 'strafing, rockets, and bombing'.[3]

It was a fine, clear day, with the temperature rising to the mid-seventies, and the threat from a kamikaze attack was obvious. 'All troops below!' bellowed a naval officer. 'No troops on deck! Captain's orders. Jap planes coming. We don't want Marines killed on our deck. Everybody get below.'

Reluctantly they returned to their troop compartments where they waited, festooned with battle gear and 'packed like sardines in the aisles between the racks', for the all clear. 'We could hear the racket above our heads,' remembered R. V. Burgin, 'and none of us wanted to be caught like pigs in a pen if a Jap plane or bomb came crashing through the deck.' The doors had been locked and there was no ventilation. It was hot and hard for the men to breathe. They shouted to be let out, and when no one responded, they took matters into their own hands by smashing open the hatch.

A naval officer spotted them as they spilled out onto the deck. 'All Marines,' he shouted, 'return to your quarters. No troops topside. That's an order!'

'Sir,' responded a Marine, 'we're going to hit that beach in a little while and a lot of us might not be alive an hour from now. We'd rather take a chance on gettin' hit by a Jap plane out here than go back in there and smother to death.'

The officer – a young ensign in khakis and with a .45 pistol on his hip – turned and strode away.

Soon after, Captain 'Stumpy' Stanley and some of the other K Company officers appeared and ordered the men to stand by for loading. Moving to the assigned areas along the bulwarks of the ship, they could see everything from battleships down to rocket and mortar boats, not to mention dive-bombers, 'plastering the beaches'. Meanwhile Japanese planes, 'their engines droning and whining', appeared over the huge fleet and Gene Sledge saw at least two shot down by a blizzard of anti-aircraft fire.

The men formed up at the railing, four abreast, and waited for the order to load. Sledge was tense and 'filled with dread about the landing'. But it was nothing compared to the paralysing fear he had felt before Peleliu, and he put that down to experience. As a combat veteran, he knew what to expect from the Japanese, and from himself.

On a sailor's signal, they began climbing over the rail and down the scramble net into the waiting Higgins boats, taking care not to stand on the hands and head of the man below. Once the boat carrying the mortar section was full, R. V. Burgin shouted, 'Shove off, coxswain. You're loaded.' They nosed away from the ship and joined other battalion boats circling slowly and waiting for the signal to move.[4]

At 8:20 a.m. – ten minutes before H-hour – pennants were hauled down from the control craft and the first wave of amphibious tanks, covering an almost unbroken eight-mile line, began to move towards the shore, a distance of 4,000 yards, at a speed of 4 knots. The tanks were preceded by gunboats firing rockets, mortars and 40mm guns. Following a minute behind the tanks were the first wave of assault troops in amtracs. More followed at ten-minute intervals, with Wave Six scheduled to leave before Wave One hit the beach.[5]

The men of K Company watched all this unfold from their Higgins boats. 'The first wave's goin' in now,' said 'Snafu' Shelton. 'Stand by for a ram.'

'Yeah,' said another mortarman, 'the stuff's gonna hit the fan now.'[6]

Eventually it was time for the men of K Company to head in to the beach by transferring from their Higgins boats to some of the returning amtracs. As one of these amtracs hooked up to the mortar section's boat, a voice shouted: 'The landing is unopposed!'

They looked at the man in amazement. 'The hell you say,' responded a Marine.

'It's straight dope. I ain't seen no casualties. Most of the Nips musta hauled ass. I just saw a couple of mortar shells fallin' in the water; that's all. The guys went in standin' up. It beats anything I ever saw.'

Once over their astonishment, everyone started laughing and joking. 'The release of tension was unforgettable,' remembered Gene Sledge. 'We sat on the edge of the amtrac's troop compartment singing and commenting on the vast fleet surrounding us. No need to crouch low to avoid the deadly shrapnel and bullets. It was – and still is – the most pleasant surprise of the war.'

Then something dawned on Sledge: *why would the Japanese let them walk ashore unopposed on an island just 350 miles from their homeland? They must be planning something. But what?*

By now the whole section was singing and Sledge's preoccupation was noticed. 'Hey, Sledgehammer, what's the matter?' asked a buddy. 'Why don't you sing like everybody else?'

Sledge grinned and joined in the chorus of 'Little Brown Jug' ('Ha ha ha, You and me, Little Brown Jug, Don't I love thee').

'That's more like it!'

As they moved closer to Yellow Beach 2, they could see hundreds of boats and amtracs unloading men and supplies. Directly ahead, clearly visible as they 'moved in dispersed combat formations like tiny toy soldiers on the rising landscape', were men from the 1/5 Marines who had arrived in the assault waves. To Sledge they 'appeared unhurried and nonchalant' as they climbed the gently sloping ground, through a scenic patchwork of small gardens and farm plots.

Apart from a couple of mortar rounds exploding in the water a 'considerable distance' to their left, there was no sign of enemy activity as K Company's amtracs hit the beach at around 10:40 a.m. They formed up on the sand, a short distance from where the Bishi Gawa River emptied into the sea, the corps boundary. On their side of the river, on a small promontory, were the remains of the gun emplacement mentioned in their briefings. The seawall had been 'blasted down into a terracelike rise a few feet high' over which they moved with ease.[7]

Having been told they were 'heading into a meatgrinder', Corporal Sterling Mace of 3rd Platoon was amazed by the 'bustle of activity' from 'tanks and bulldozers, scores of troops, and hundreds of tents being erected'. Even more unexpected was the sight of a camera crew setting up its gear, and in their midst the film star turned Marine William Lundigan. 'Say,' said PFC Eubanks, 'I seen that guy in that *Dodge City* picture and . . . what was the other one? *The Fighting 69th* too!'*

While other Marines whistled and shouted, 'Hey, Hollywood!', and Lundigan humoured them with a nod of his head, PFC Bob Whitby turned to his fire team leader. 'This is great, ain't it, Mace? Looks like a real piece of cake.'

'Yeah, looks like . . . maybe something like that. Hey, you just keep your head screwed on, alright, Wimp?' Mace was feeling apprehensive. Too many things 'just didn't add up'.[8]

The task of the 3/5 Marines was to follow the right assault landing team (1/5 Marines) inland, at a distance of 400 yards, and protect the regimental flank. Moving in columns on a two-company front – K on the left, I on the right, and L in support – the battalion passed 'fields that had recently been harvested and were ready for the plow'. The small farmhouses had thatched roofs, and 'looked tidy and well kept behind stone walls'. There was no initial sign of any civilians, but lots of livestock on the loose: goats, pigs, chickens and even horses. The latter were 'small and shaggier' than the ones R. V. Burgin was used to back home, 'more like a Shetland than a true horse'. They were also easy to catch, and one was soon employed by a mortar squad to carry its ammo.[9]

At around 3:00 p.m., while K Company was halted in column, the battalion commander Major Gustafson moved past it with a small team. He was heading for an observation post that was sited just to the rear of C Company, the reserve unit of the 1/5 Marines, when, according to the battalion special action report, he and his staff came under fire from a 'small group of the enemy, numbering possibly 4 or 5', who had been 'bypassed or overlooked' by the assault companies. In fact, according to Corporal George Poppe of the intelligence section, only a single shot

* A 1940 movie, starring James Cagney, about the World War I exploits of New York's 69th Regiment of Infantry. Lundigan played Private Timmy Wynn.

was fired by a sniper in a nearby tree – 'about the only one left in the vicinity' – and it hit Gustafson, standing next to Poppe, in the arm. Poppe and another Marine, armed respectively with a tommy gun and a BAR, stalked and killed the sniper who, they discovered, was female. 'The kill was yielded to me,' wrote Poppe, 'because Tarheel [Gustafson] was my friend, although the BAR man had greater firepower. It was Tarheel's million-dollar wound, although not serious, [and] the war was over before he was able to return to duty. He may have been an officer to the Corps, but he was an enlisted man at heart.'[10]

Major Roth, Gustafson's XO, took over as battalion commander and ordered L Company 'to move up abreast' of the 1/5's C Company and 'provide flank protection'. He then instructed the rest of the battalion to dig in for the night. It was 5:15 p.m.

Gene Sledge's squad set up in a recently harvested field of grain, the soft soil making it easy to dig a good gun pit. The other two mortars were sited nearby. 'We registered in on likely target areas to our front with a couple of rounds of HE,' wrote Sledge, 'then squared away our ammo for the night. Everybody was expecting a big counterattack with tanks because of the open nature of the countryside.'

Before settling in, Sledge and a few others went to investigate a nearby Okinawan farmhouse which they found neat, clean and empty. As they were leaving, a replacement called Jim Dandridge from Richmond, Virginia, stepped on some wooden planks that were rotten, pitching him into a stinking cesspool beneath. He scrambled out, 'bellowing like a bull and smelling worse'. He knew it would be some time before he could get a change of dungarees. But that did not stop his buddies from 'kidding him unmercifully about his odd taste in swimming holes'.

Back in their foxholes, they heard the drone of a plane and looked up to see a Zero fly over and head out to sea. Several ships immediately opened up with anti-aircraft fire. But they were unable to prevent the plane from diving into a troop transport. 'It was,' noted Sledge, 'the first kamikaze I had seen crash into a ship, but it wasn't the last.'

They had all been issued a K ration, a chocolate D-Bar and a small bottle of brandy. Despite his 'limited taste, appreciation, and capacity for booze', Sledge felt chilled enough to try the brandy. But one sip of the fiery liquid was enough: he traded it for a can of peaches, and put on his wool-lined field jacket to keep out the cold.

There was no Japanese counter-attack. Instead, bar the odd rifle shot or burst of machine-gun fire, all was quiet – a 'stark contrast to the rumbling, crashing chaos of D-Day night on Peleliu'. At midnight, Sledge was woken by 'Snafu' Shelton and handed the tommy gun they shared. After a few minutes on watch, he saw what looked to be a man crouching near some trees. Convinced the figure was a Japanese infiltrator, he raised the tommy gun, set it on full automatic, flipped off the safety, and squeezed off a short burst of fire, taking care to aim low to counteract the recoil. 'Flame spurted out of the muzzle,' recalled Sledge, 'and the rapid explosions of the cartridges shattered the calm.'

The noise woke Sergeant Burgin and the others. 'Everybody all right?' someone shouted. 'What happened? Who's firing?'

Sledge said he thought he had seen a Japanese crouching in the shadows, but did not know if he had hit anything.

By now everyone was 'on edge, waiting in silence and squinting into the darkness, trying to see whatever Sledge had seen'. Minutes went by 'with only an occasional pop and rumble in the distance'. Eventually they decided it was a false alarm and those not on watch went back to sleep.

At first light, the infiltrator was revealed as a 'small haystack that, seen from a certain angle in the darkness, just might look like a crouching man'. For the rest of the day, Sledge was given hell for firing, as a Peleliu veteran, at a 'straw Japanese'.[11]

K Company's experience was mirrored across the Tenth Army's beachhead which, by nightfall on L-Day, was eight miles long and, in places, three miles deep. Already more than 60,000 men were ashore, including all the reserve regiments and 15,000 service troops. In addition, numerous tanks and anti-aircraft units had been landed, as had all the divisional artillery and, by evening, guns were in position to support the forward troops. Kadena airfield, moreover, was serviceable for emergency landings. Casualties were unexpectedly light: 28 killed, 104 wounded and 27 missing.[12]

Still aboard Kelly Turner's command ship USS *Eldorado*, Lieutenant General Buckner was elated. 'From start to finish,' he jotted in his diary, 'the landing was a superb piece of teamwork, which we could watch from the fifty-yard line in the command room of the flag deck. We landed practically without opposition and gained more ground than we had expected to for three days, including the Yomitan [sic] and Kadena airfields. Arnold's 7th Div[ision] made the furthest gains and got halfway across the island . . . The Japs have missed their best opportunity on the ground and in the air.'[13]

Vice Admiral Turner was even more optimistic. 'I may be crazy,' he signalled his boss Admiral Nimitz, 'but it looks like the Japs have quit the war.'

Nimitz was not fooled and messaged back: 'Delete all after crazy.'[14]

The Japanese decision not to defend the beaches was, of course, deliberate. In line with Colonel Yahara's strategy to fight a battle of attrition, the best troops had been concentrated in fortifications farther south – from where Lieutenant General Ushijima and his staff watched the landings* – and the only minor threat the Americans faced on land that day was from the 1st Specially Established Regiment, whose job was to protect the Yontan and Kadena airfields. But its men – drawn from two air base battalions – had had little combat training and, already weakened by the shelling, put up little resistance before withdrawing north to join the Kunigami Detachment in the Motobu Peninsula.

A Japanese soldier posted in an elementary school, two miles from the beaches, described the pre-invasion bombardment as like 'a hundred

* Referring to the landings, Yahara wrote later: 'Advancing with such ease, they must be thinking gleefully that they have passed through a breach in the Japanese defences. They will be wrong . . . It is amusing to watch the American army so desperately intent in its attack on an almost undefended coast, like a blind man who has lost his cane, groping on hands and knees to cross a ditch.' (Yahara, *The Battle for Okinawa*, p. xii.)

thunders striking at once'. He was astonished when, at one point during the morning, a soldier from a small unit assigned to guard the beach appeared with news of the landings. The man then returned to 'guard his position to the death – and, indeed, everyone [Japanese] at the landing site died fighting'.[15]

Another watching Japanese soldier was horrified that the Americans were able to land untouched. 'What a great opportunity!' he thought. 'Why didn't our air force come and attack them?'[16] In fact, as Gene Sledge had witnessed, kamikaze planes and bombers did reach Okinawa on 1 April, damaging the battleship USS *West Virginia* and some troop transports. Others targeted the British Pacific Fleet, operating against airfields 200 miles to the south of Okinawa, with one striking the fleet carrier HMS *Indefatigable* and starting a fire that killed fourteen crew and wounded another fifteen.[17] Yet the kamikaze failed to sink the British ship or put it out of action for long, and within a few hours the *Indefatigable*'s planes were flying missions. This was largely down to the fact that British carriers had armoured flight decks.

'American carriers similarly struck,' wrote Vice Admiral Sir Philip Vian, commanding the British flat-tops, 'were invariably forced to return to a fully-equipped Navy Yard for repairs.' But then the US Navy had many more carriers and could afford the loss of those put out of action. They also had the advantage, noted Vian, of 'greater speed and endurance, and a more effective anti-aircraft armament'.[18]

43

'We were euphoric, undisciplined, and stupid'

Okinawa, 2–10 April 1945

On 2 April, the 1st Marine Division continued its mostly unopposed trek across the centre of Okinawa. 'There had been a conference the first night between [Major] General Del Valle and the regimental commanders,' noted George McMillan.

> They decided to forgo an artillery preparation in the morning, and when the troops moved out of foxholes at 0715, April 2, the weather was cool and the countryside still beautiful, but ominously quiet. When, by late afternoon and despite extensive patrolling over rugged terrain, 'our forces were still unable to locate the center of enemy resistance', with the line now inland 6,500 yards, [Major] General Del Valle held a press conference ashore. 'I don't know where the Japs are, and I can't offer you any good reason why they let us come ashore so easily,' he said in frank bewilderment. 'We're pushing on across the island as fast as we can move with men and equipment.'[1]

The 5th Marines advanced that day with all three battalions abreast. The 3/5 Marines, attacking on the right, 'met no resistance, captured several civilians, and [the] only casualties were five men in Love Company due to an accidental explosion of a hand grenade'.[2] It prompted many to ask: 'Where the hell are the Nips?'

Gene Sledge saw his first dead enemy soldiers in and beneath a large leafless tree, where they had probably been acting as artillery observers. One was 'hung over a limb', his intestines spread out over the branches like 'decorations on a Christmas tree'. The other lay on the ground, his missing leg a few feet away with the leggings and trousers 'still wrapped neatly around it'.[3]

Having just turned eighteen, Private Harry Bender was prepared for the sight of dead Japanese soldiers. What he actually came across, during the morning of the 2nd, were the corpses of two young girls, 'maybe nine and eleven', in the courtyard of an Okinawan shack. He was convinced they were victims of American bullets. 'I'm sure of it,' he said. 'There was no one else around. No adults. Just the two little dead bodies . . . You could see their wounds, where they'd taken fire. So this was very sobering, right early on.'[4]

Most of the living civilians the men of K Company encountered were old men, women and children. The adults seemed to be 'totally bewildered by the shock of the invasion', noted Sledge, and 'scared to death of us'. Not so the children: 'cute and bright-faced' with 'round faces and dark eyes', they soon lost their fear of the invaders when they were given candy. During one halt, Sledge and his squad watched an Okinawan woman nursing her baby, while her infant son played with her sandals. Bored of this, he climbed on to his mother and started interfering with the breast-feeding. She responded by removing her breast from the baby's mouth, pointing it at the infant and squeezing a jet of milk into his face. He screamed in shock and started rubbing the milk out of his eyes.

Amused by the spectacle, the mortar squad began roaring with laughter. 'The woman looked up,' wrote Sledge, 'not realizing why we were laughing, but began to grin because the tension was broken. The little recipient of the milk in the eyes stopped crying and started grinning, too.'

Moments later, the word came down the column: 'Get your gear on; we're moving out.'[5]

* * *

On 3 April, Del Valle upped the pace by sending the Division Reconnaissance Company to scout ahead of the assault troops. Its jeeps reached the east coast of the island by noon, and then covered the length of the deserted Katchin Peninsula. Meanwhile the forward assault platoons had also crossed the island on foot by 4:00 p.m., thus severing Japanese communications between the north and south of Okinawa. A day later, all three of the Old Breed's infantry regiments 'had units on the east coast and were patrolling to the rear, the trip across having been relatively uneventful, except for the arduous climb over the inland hills and for an occasional sharp fire fight such as the 3rd Battalion, 7th Marines had (on April 3) around the village of Hizaonna, where it claims to have killed 122 Japanese at a cost of only 35 Marines'.[6]

Moving with K Company through an 'extremely rugged' terrain of 'high, steep ridges and deep gullies', Gene Sledge was mightily relieved that the Japanese had abandoned the area as it was 'ideal for defense'. With no enemy to deal with, his squad were able to enjoy the view, the 'delicious odor' of pine needles, and even spend time rescuing an Okinawan horse from a flooded drainage ditch. 'We calmed him,' noted Sledge, 'slipped a couple of empty cartridge belts beneath his belly, and heaved him up out of the ditch.'

They arrived at the coast 'in an area of marshes' during the afternoon of 4 April, 'some eight to thirteen days ahead of schedule'. Their rapid advance was only possible because of the 'widely scattered opposition', a situation that nobody thought would last for long. Their suspicions were confirmed later that day when word reached them that the army divisions were 'meeting increasingly stiff opposition' as they tried to move south. 'We knew,' wrote Sledge, 'that sooner or later we'd be down there with them in the thick of it.'[7]

Until that day came, however, they were determined to enjoy their temporary stay of execution. 'We were euphoric, undisciplined, and stupid,' recalled Sterling Mace. 'We did everything wrong – including the officers. Everybody was guilty of something. Some of us were guilty of everything.' The misdemeanours included catching and butchering local livestock, and racing horses on the beach. Some officers tried to intervene, but to little effect. What were they going to do? asked Mace. Shoot us off the horses? 'Every veteran knew that we were coming into action again. So the rule of the day was to simply enjoy life, sitting on your keister, before it was your time to get killed.'[8]

On 6 April, the day after Lieutenant Colonel John C. Miller Jr had taken over the 3/5 Marines as Major Gustafson's permanent replacement, the battalion was ordered to move north to the town of Inubi, set up a perimeter defence there and patrol the vicinity. During the move, K Company suffered its first fatality. A day earlier, Sergeant Leonard 'Hook' Ahner, the 22-year-old veteran squad leader in 1st Platoon, and two of his men had caught, butchered and cooked a young hog, sharing it with the rest of the platoon. But as plenty of meat was still left, Ahner decided to take it with them in a pot suspended on a wooden pole. Ahner took the front of the pole, while his men took it in turns to carry the other end.

The platoon had covered a couple of miles down the dirt road to Inubi when there was a sharp, popping sound from a pouch on Ahner's left hip. The sergeant had earlier taken off the tape that most Marines wrap round the spoon of the grenade as an insurance, and forgotten to put it back on. The safety pin must have fallen out as Ahner walked and the popping sound meant the grenade had ignited and would explode in five seconds.

Bill Leyden looked back at his squad leader and friend, Ahner, and could tell from his terrified expression that he realised what was about to happen. 'I guess he knew what was coming,' remembered Harry Bender, another member of Ahner's squad, 'because he ran and jumped in a ditch to get away from us. The grenade went off in his pouch. There was a big explosion that killed him instantly. About six guys were wounded. Some of the shrapnel went into my pack.' Fortunately, most of these wounds were only superficial.

When 'Stumpy' Stanley heard the news, he came down the column and knelt by Ahner's still smoking body, shaking his head. Some of the 1st Platoon men were weeping. Others took out their grenades and threw them away. They knew it could just as easily have been them.

'We also knew,' said Bill Leyden, 'that man's first instinct would be to unbuckle his belt and fling it away from him to save himself. But typical of Hook, he thought of the rest of us first.'[9]

From Inubi, K Company sent out various platoon-sized patrols to blow up enemy caves and search for Japanese soldiers. One led by 3rd Platoon's 'Spud' Dunlap shot and killed three of the enemy on 9 April. 'These soldiers,' noted the battalion intelligence officer, 'were fully clothed and in good physical condition. Documents, machine gun taken from them were turned in to R-2.'[10]

A day later 'Mac' MacKenzie, the keen but untested leader of the mortar section, took Sergeant Burgin and thirty-four men to patrol Hizoanna, a village where K Company of the 3/7 Marines had been ambushed on the 3rd. 'So off we went,' remembered Gene Sledge, 'with Mac striding along like he was still in OCS back in Quantico, Virginia. The veterans among us looked worried. The new men, like Mac, seemed unconcerned.' The young officer did not help matters by boasting that, if any of the men were hit, he would charge the Japanese 'with his kabar in his teeth and his .45 in hand'.

Beside a stream they found the first evidence of the 3/7's scrape: a Japanese corpse in full combat gear. A little farther along they came upon 'bloodied bandages and wrappings, and knapsacks that corpsmen had cut from injured Marines'. Then more Japanese bodies, 'along with empty ammo boxes and clips and lots of brass'. Staining the ground were 'dark clots of blood'.

While an alert R. V. Burgin sent Sledge and another Marine forward to scout a section of sunken roadway, MacKenzie wandered into a nearby farmyard. Soon after, shots were heard from the farmyard and Burgin and the others immediately took cover. Fearing the worst, Burgin slowly raised his head to see his officer 'calmly standing in the open, taking aim with his carbine at the carcass of some dead animal'.

The men were horrified. They had orders to fire only at the enemy, and here was their officer 'plinking away with his carbine like a kid with a BB gun'. If he had been a private, wrote Sledge, 'the whole patrol would probably have stuck his head in a nearby well'. But as he outranked them, they had to grit their teeth. All except Burgin, who took MacKenzie aside and asked him: 'Lieutenant, what the hell did you think you were doing? Now every Jap in ten miles is going to know exactly where we're at.'

MacKenzie mumbled something about remaining alert while on patrol. 'I don't think being alert,' said Burgin, 'includes taking target practice at dead animals.'

In Sledge's view, 'Mac wasn't stupid or incompetent. He just didn't seem to realize there was a deadly war going on and that we weren't involved in some sort of college game.' Such naivety was, to a certain extent, understandable in a rookie. What Sledge found less forgivable was MacKenzie's disgusting habit, when he needed to pee, of finding a Japanese corpse, standing over it and urinating in its mouth. 'It was,' wrote Sledge, 'the most repulsive thing I ever saw an American do in the war. I was ashamed that he was a Marine officer.'[11]

On the same day that young MacKenzie displayed his inexperience on patrol, Sterling Mace was told by the company runner that 'Stumpy' Stanley wanted to see him in his tent 'right away'. Having clashed a couple of times with Stanley over minor disciplinary issues on Pavuvu, he was not expecting any good to come out of the summons. When he entered the tent, Stanley was not alone. Off to his left was another officer: 'A thin, older Marine – at least in his fifties – with graying hair' and sporting the gold oak leaves of a major on the collars of his dungaree jacket.

Mace snapped to attention and saluted.

'At ease, Mace,' said Stanley. 'This is Major Paul Douglas. He's got the idea that the Nips are cutting the communication lines between the Fifth and the Seventh. We're having the damnedest time reaching them by radio. So what I want you to do is take your fire team and escort Major Douglas. Find out what's going on, and check it out.'

'Yes, sir!'

It was the same Paul Douglas who had helped Sledge unload ammunition from an amtrac on Peleliu. Wounded later in that campaign, he had rejoined the 1st Marine Division on Pavuvu in time for its next operation.

Outside Stanley's tent, Douglas told Mace that his intention was to follow the telephone line from K Company to the neighbouring company in the 7th Marines and find out if it had been cut. They set off, five men in all, and found it reasonably easy going across 'open land, spotty shrubs, and here and there a few rocky patches of turf'. It was the scout 'Wimpy' Whitby who soon noticed that the telephone line was so badly frayed in places by rocks that the copper was exposed. 'Think we should tell the major?' asked Whitby.

Mace looked back at Douglas, who appeared to be idling in the rear, 'taking compass readings, or maybe bird-watching'.

He said: 'Nah, Wimp. Let's not upset the applecart here. The last thing ya wanna do is upstage an officer. He's the expert, so he'll get the medal for this.'

They continued on and, two hours into their trek, came across the entrance to a small cave, close to the cable they were following. Just as Mace and the BAR assistant George Weisdack were debating the cave's significance, Douglas strode up to the entrance, .45 automatic in hand, and fired a round into it. He then turned to Mace: 'Go in there and check it out.'

Is this guy for real? wondered Mace. He looked at his team, but as rookies they were taking their lead from him. 'Well,' he responded at last, 'pardon me, sir, but we just don't operate that way. If someone throws a grenade in there, I'll go in.'

Unfortunately, they did not have a single grenade between them (a legacy of the Ahner tragedy), so Mace had no option but to enter, nose around for a second, and come out. 'All clear, sir.'

'Good,' replied Douglas, re-holstering his pistol.[12]

While the 1st Marine Division was mopping up tiny pockets of resistance in the centre of the island, far more significant battles were taking place elsewhere on Okinawa and in the surrounding sea. On 7 April, for example, the Japanese superbattleship *Yamato* – the world's largest, with nine 18.1in guns capable of firing a 3,220lb shell more than 27 miles – was sunk after repeated attacks by hundreds of American dive-bombers and torpedo-bombers launched from Vice Admiral Mitscher's Fast Carrier Force. The *Yamato* had been intercepted on a one-way suicide mission from Honshu island to attack the US Fifth Fleet at Okinawa, and went down with most of its 2,767-strong crew. Also sunk or scuttled were a light cruiser and four destroyers, bringing the total cost of this pointless, ill-fated mission to more than 4,000 men. American losses were just ten planes and twelve men.

When Emperor Hirohito, who had authorized the operation, was told of the disaster he put his hand to his temple and swayed in shock. 'Gone?' he asked. 'She's gone?'[13]

On Okinawa itself, the toughest resistance was faced by the 7th and 96th Infantry Divisions when they encountered the first strong outposts of the multi-layered Japanese defensive system in the bottom third of the island known as the 'Shuri Line'. Forming the right wing of Major General Hodge's XXIV Corps, the 96th Division had the task of capturing the formidable Japanese fortifications on the 1,000-yard long Kakazu hill mass. The attacks began on 9 April and fizzled out three days later after minimal gains, the corps as a whole having lost around 2,900 men: 451 killed, 2,189 wounded and 241 missing.[14]

Lieutenant General Buckner now told Hodge to delay any further push until an additional infantry division, the 27th, had reached his front line. He had convinced himself that Hodge's two attacking divisions were outnumbered by the Japanese defenders – in fact the opposite was true – and was worried about the supply of artillery shells. The new assault should wait, he told Hodge, until troops and shells were available in sufficient quantities. To make doubly certain, he assured the corps commander that he would be reinforced by a fourth division, the 77th, when it became available after the capture of Ie Shima, an island off the northwest coast of Okinawa, in mid-April.[15]

It was around now that Major General Bruce, the 77th's commander, urged Buckner to let him 'try a landing behind the main Jap position in southern Okinawa'. Bruce had done something similar on Leyte with successful results. But Buckner quickly dismissed the suggestion on the grounds that a second landing would be difficult to resupply and might be isolated and destroyed. His preference was to continue to attack on a single front, using the 'fire and manoeuvre' tactics so beloved of US Army doctrine. This meant building up his troop levels and firepower before launching what was bound to be, given the narrowness of the island and the strength of the Japanese defences, a costly frontal attack on prepared positions.[16]

This pause in operations was, in the opinion of Buckner's deputy chief of staff, Oliver Smith, a mistake. 'The Army apparently didn't realize,' wrote Smith, 'what the capture of ground in cave and pillbox warfare costs in casualties; that in the final analysis [they] must be taken by infantry; that the artillery can blast away the camouflage and keep the enemy underground but cannot take positions; and that delay only serves to increase total casualties and exhaust the troops.'*[17]

The response of the Japanese to the halt in American operations in the south was to launch an attack of their own. The impetus was a radio message sent by General Rikichi Andō, commanding the 10th Area Army in Formosa, to Ushijima on 5 April, ordering the recapture of the Yontan and Kadena airfields. Despite the opposition of Colonel Yahara, who felt the 'ill-conceived plan for a counter attack' would simply fritter away Japanese lives and therefore shorten the campaign, Ushijima felt he had no option but to comply. First the attack was delayed, and then it was watered down to involve just a single brigade after dark on 12 April. But it made only modest gains before the six attacking battalions were forced to retire with heavy casualties.[18]

By 13 April, the heaviest fighting had switched from the south to the north of the island, where Major General Lem Shepherd's 6th Marine

* Smith's comments underline the cultural difference between the Marine Corps and the army. For Marines, the infantry is the key element in battle, with other arms playing a supporting role. For the army, artillery and armour are dominant. Marines believe the army relies too much on firepower; soldiers think Marines take unnecessary casualties.

Division was tasked with capturing the main Japanese stronghold in the Motobu Peninsula. 'Northern Okinawa,' wrote Sergeant William Manchester of the 2/29th Marines, 'was not defenceless. Motobu Peninsula, steep, rocky, wooded, and almost trackless, was dominated by two mountains, Katsu and 1,500 feet, three-crested Yae-Take. Entrenched on Yae-Take were two battalions under the command of a tenacious officer, Takehido Udo.'[19]

The original plan had been to leave the conquest of the north until after the seizure of southern Okinawa. But as the scale of the Japanese defences in the south became clear, Buckner decided to tackle both extremities at the same time: not least because it would secure the ports in the north from possible counter-landings by Japanese troops. On 3 April, therefore, as the 6th Marine Division approached the Ishikawa Isthmus, he removed all restrictions on its further 'advance northward'.

The 6th's regiments leapfrogged each other as they moved up the isthmus with almost no opposition, bar the odd Japanese straggler. By 7 April, the spearhead units had reached Nago, a medium-sized town at the southern neck of the Motobu Peninsula. Three days later, Marines had sealed off the peninsula and almost surrounded the rugged Yae-Take feature where Colonel Udo had concentrated the bulk of his 1,500 men. The battle began on 14 April as five battalions attacked Yae-Take simultaneously from east and west.[20] Late on the 15th, disappointed with the 29th Marines' lack of progress, Major General Shepherd arrived at the regimental CP to find the 29th's commander, Lieutenant Colonel Victor Bleasdale, in a 'highly-agitated' state and uncertain of the location of his battalions. He was relieved of his command by Shepherd and replaced with Colonel William J. Whaling, a veteran of both Guadalcanal and Cape Gloucester.[21]

With the command rejigged, the attacks resumed from three directions on 16 April. By the evening of the 17th, Colonel Udo's command post was in American hands and all organized resistance in northern Okinawa had ended, though fleeing soldiers would fight as guerrillas for weeks to come. Since landing, noted a special action report, the 6th Marine Division had 'moved 84 miles, seized 436 square miles of enemy territory, counted over 2,500 enemy bodies and captured 46 prisoners'. Its losses, meanwhile, were 236 killed, 1,061 wounded and seven missing.

Designed for amphibious assaults, Marine divisions were bigger than their army counterparts because they were expected to be largely self-sustaining from the beachhead. The successful conclusion of the 6th's mission in northern Okinawa was conclusive proof, if any were needed, that Marine divisions were 'capable of extended operations ashore'.[22]

44

'I burned the whole village to the ground'

Okinawa, 13–26 April 1945

On 13 April 1945, American troops on Okinawa received the shocking news that President Roosevelt, their Commander-in-Chief for the previous twelve years, had died of a stroke the day before and been replaced by Vice President Harry S. Truman. 'I could hardly believe it,' wrote Gene Sledge in the first letter to his parents since landing, 'but he was getting pretty old.'[1]

Roosevelt was, in fact, only sixty-three when he died, though he had been mostly confined to a wheelchair since contracting polio in 1921. More importantly, he was the only president that many young American servicemen could remember and was regarded as both a fine war leader and a vital member, with Winston Churchill and the Soviet dictator Josef Stalin, of the Allies' 'Big Three'. When Churchill heard the news, he felt he had been 'struck a physical blow'. He wrote: 'My relations with this shining personality had played so large a part in the long, terrible years we had worked together. Now they had come to an end, and I was overpowered by a sense of deep and irreparable loss.'[2]

Part of Churchill's concern, shared by most Americans, was that Roosevelt's 60-year-old successor was, like many vice presidents, a political lightweight. The son of a farmer and livestock dealer from Lamar, Missouri, Truman had had little formal education and, after service as an artillery officer in World War I, he became a county court judge and was eventually elected to the US Senate in 1934. He came to nationwide prominence in 1941 when he chaired a special committee on waste and corruption in government expenditure (the so-called 'Truman Committee') – described by *Time* magazine as 'one of the useful Government agencies of World War II' – but was still mystified when Roosevelt chose him as a running mate for the 1944 presidential election with the words, 'Boys, I guess it's Truman.'[3]

He was a compromise choice: older and less impressive than the other candidates, but with few enemies and unlikely to alienate voters. In the event, the Roosevelt–Truman ticket achieved a 432–99 electoral-vote victory in the election, defeating the Republican ticket of Governor Thomas E. Dewey of New York and running mate Governor John Bricker of Ohio. But the job of vice president was hardly an onerous one – Truman presided over the Senate Chamber and, in the event of a tie, had the casting vote – and Roosevelt kept him at arm's length. During his eighty-two days as vice president, he only twice visited Roosevelt on official business.[4]

While grieving the president's death, Lieutenant General Buckner also felt 'concern over his successor's lack of diplomatic experience'.[5] So did Sledge and some of his colleagues, who were 'curious and a bit apprehensive about how FDR's successor, Harry S. Truman, would handle the war'. They did not want anyone in the White House 'who would prolong it one day longer than necessary', and might have been even more concerned if they had known how ignorant Truman really was about the running of the war.[6] '[He] was very ill informed about military and political affairs,' remembered a member of the White House Map Room (the president's intelligence and communications centre). 'He had not been briefed by President Roosevelt or by others in the Cabinet on some of the most major decisions that were coming up; he just didn't know a darn thing about them. [So] he was very, very eager to soak up as much information as he could, as quickly as he could.'[7]

It helped that Truman had remained in the Army Reserve after World War I, rising to the rank of colonel, and kept abreast of the latest military thinking by attending summer camps with regular officers. He was, therefore, in a relatively strong position to deal with the issues of military strategy and operations that were bound to arise.

Unaware of Truman's latent military acumen, the Japanese commanders on Okinawa regarded Roosevelt's sudden death as a godsend. 'The staff officers were ecstatic,' noted Colonel Yahara. 'Many seemed convinced that we would now surely win the war.'[8]

Meanwhile, yet to do any serious fighting, the men of K Company were enjoying what they assumed would be the lull before the storm and the fact that, for the first time in the war, they were allowed to give family and friends some details about life in a combat zone. 'I am on Okinawa and doing fine,' wrote Gene Sledge to his parents on 15 April. 'My outfit has fared very well and we are all enjoying this nice weather. The days are windy and chilly and the nights are always cold. We wear woollen under top, wool shirt and jacket. So we have plenty of clothes.'

They also had plenty to eat, having killed and eaten two hogs and numerous chickens, as well as foraging eggs, potatoes and cabbage. 'This is,' Sledge added, 'a really beautiful island and a lot like North Carolina with pines along the ridges and streams in the valleys. There are a lot of small farms and little villages . . . The farmers have horses, cows, chickens, pigs and goats galore. It's really funny to see Marines pass by with horses carrying their loads. We had six in the section at one time . . . Of course I've done a lot of riding and so has everyone else.'

As for the inhabitants, most were about 5ft 2in high, with 'dark eyes, black hair and olive skin'. Their 'peculiar customs' included washing their feet before entering homes, and wearing 'wooden shoes on stilts about 1½ inches high and kimonos'. Sledge had managed to acquire a kimono and a 'beautiful sash' for his mother, and would send it home when he had the chance.

He wrote again a day later, comparing the beauty of Okinawa to the hell of Peleliu, and mentioning that they had all dreaded landing on a

Sunday, much less Easter. 'Gen. Stonewall Jackson never invited battle on Sunday,' noted Sledge, 'and said something like this: "He who presses battle on the Sabbath day invites God's wrath!" God must be with us for he has certainly treated us well and looked after us here.'

In a third letter, on 18 April, Sledge's optimism continued:

> Yes, this was quite a surprise to all of us the way things turned out here . . . It's as different from Peleliu as night is from day. There we stepped right in the hot spot and didn't get out till we left the island. [I] was eating supper several days ago & was rudely interrupted by a visit from several [Japanese] Zeros . . . It wasn't long before our [fighter] boys got on the ball & when we saw this we all of us came out & began cheering & yelling. Two enemy went down & the others headed for safer regions.[9]

Three days later, K and I Companies of the 3/5 Marines were sent to patrol and secure a small group of islands off the east coast of Okinawa (Operation Hot Day). Transported in amtracs from Ishikawa to the largest of the islands, Takabanare, K Company landed at 12:10 p.m. without opposition 'on a narrow, clean, sandy beach with a large rock mass high on our left'. Over the next couple of days, its patrols criss-crossed the island and found only a few civilians and no enemy.[10] In one village, a cute kid approached Sterling Mace and, putting his hand to his mouth, said: 'Candy! Candy!'

'Listen,' responded Mace. 'See that guy over there.'

He was pointing at his sergeant, R. D. 'Blowtorch Willy' Wilson. The kid nodded.

'Hey, you're a real smart kid! Now, listen carefully, okay? You go over and tell that man exactly what I tell ya, and I'll give you some candy, alright?'

He told the kid what he wanted him to say, and repeated it until he had it 'down pat'. The kid then strolled over to where Wilson was sitting on his helmet, about twenty yards away. 'Hey, little guy, you want some candy?' asked the sergeant. 'Is that it? Candy?'

The kid looked up, smiled and said: 'Fuck you, Wilson!'

'What?'

'Fuck you . . . Sergeant Wilson!'

As his shock wore off, Wilson noticed Mace doubled-up with laughter. 'Mace, you shithead!' he said, before cracking up himself.

The kid got his reward.[11]

The rest of their stay on Takabanare was uneventful: they set up a defensive position on the steep rocky hill overlooking the beach, and spent their time eating K-rations, swimming and lazing in the sun. After a few days they returned to their bivouac on Okinawa and resumed patrolling in the centre of the island.[12] In one field, Corporal Mace and his fire team came across a group of dead civilians they assumed had been machine-gunned from the air. 'All of them,' wrote Mace, 'have splotches of dried crimson decorating their pajama tops. Fear and surprise still tattoo their faces. Here and there, scattered among the dead are their belongings.' Not for a minute did Mace and his men think that the perpetrator was Japanese: they 'have only one purpose in the air, and that is to get to our ships'.

On a separate occasion, Mace and his men – Fire Team 3 of 3rd Platoon – were at the back of a full company patrol as it wound its way through a deserted Okinawan village. Out of sheer badness and boredom, Mace snuck into one of the houses, put a tiny ball of composition C under a thatched roof and lit it. A few hundred yards down the road, Whitby glanced back and noticed a spiral of black smoke over the village. 'Say, Mace,' he asked, 'what the hell is that?'

'That?' said Mace. 'That's beautiful country, Bob. Beautiful goddamn country.'

He wrote later, with some regret: 'For all I know, I burned the whole village to the ground. I don't know what made me do it. I don't know why I didn't feel anything.'[13]

As the month wore on, word began to filter back to the men of the 1st Marine Division that the army troops were struggling to break through the Japanese defences in the south. 'Scuttlebutt ran rampant,' wrote Gene Sledge, 'about our future employment down there.'[14]

The rumours were accurate. Bolstered by 324 pieces of artillery – ranging from 105mm to 8in howitzers – Hodge's XXIV Corps had attacked with three infantry divisions abreast on 19 April. Moderate gains were made by the newly arrived 27th Infantry Division in the west, where the town of Machinato was captured; but elsewhere the attack was 'brought to a stop by intense mortar and machine-gun fire', including the destruction of thirty American tanks and self-propelled guns in front of Kakazu Ridge. 'At no point,' noted the official historian, 'had there been a breakthrough. Everywhere the Japanese had held and turned back the American attack. Even in the west, where the front lines had been advanced a considerable distance by the 27th Division, the area gained was mostly unoccupied low ground.'[15]

The offensive continued for another four days, but made little headway against enemy fortifications that stretched from just below Machinato to Ouki on the east coast. The Japanese defenders fought doggedly, limiting American gains to 'yards daily and in some places, such as Kakazu, denying any gain'.[16] A disappointed Lieutenant General Buckner wrote to his wife: 'The Japs here seem to have the strongest position yet encountered in the Pacific, and it will be a slow tedious grind with flamethrowers, explosives placed by hand and the closest of teamwork to dislodge them without very heavy losses.'[17]

Knowing this, it seems astonishing that Buckner did not reconsider his earlier decision to veto a second landing in the south. While he could not know the extent to which the Japanese had denuded their protection of the southern beachheads – moving all but 5,500 service troops to reinforce their main position at Shuri – he was soon aware from intelligence gleaned on the battlefield that troops of the Japanese 24th Division had been moved north. He was also receiving advice from a number of senior commanders that a landing was advisable. With the Ie Shima battle drawing to a close, Major General Bruce again offered to land his 77th Division on the beaches north of Minatoga with a view to linking up with American forces north of Shuri within ten days. But Buckner and his staff rejected the offer on the same grounds as earlier:

that the beaches were too restricted for resupply and might result in a second Anzio.*

Buckner also felt, from his observation of the battle thus far, that the 27th Division was performing poorly, and that the other divisions of XXIV Corps were badly depleted and needed a rest. Given that, at this stage, he had been warned by Nimitz not to commit either the 1st or 6th Marine Divisions to the battle because they might be needed for other operations, while the 2nd Marine Division was back in Saipan, pending a landing north of Okinawa, it seems logical that he wanted to use the 77th Division to bolster XXIV Corps. Yet this imperative disappeared on 26 April when Nimitz informed him that Phase III of Operation Iceberg, the occupation of islands north of Okinawa, had been postponed indefinitely by the Joint Chiefs of Staff in Washington, 'thus freeing the III Amphibious Corps for full use on Okinawa'.[18]

Around the same date, Major General Hodge urged Buckner to attempt a landing in the south on the basis that soldiers of the Japanese 24th Division had been identified in the front line, leaving the south more thinly defended than hitherto. But, again, Buckner refused. Instead, a day later, he issued orders for the 1st Marine Division to move south and replace the disappointing 27th Division in the front line. This was typical of Buckner's cautious, artillery-dominated approach to battle. It was a missed opportunity and one that would have costly consequences.[19]

According to his Marine deputy chief of staff, Oliver Smith, Buckner 'had hoped to complete the campaign in the south without committing the [III Amphibious Corps]'. This was partly US Army pride, and a belief that the rotation of his four army divisions would do the job. But when the 27th Division quickly wore itself out 'mentally and physically' – losing 3,500 men in fifteen days – he knew it had to be relieved. The

* In January 1944, in an effort to outflank German defences in southern Italy, part of General Mark Clark's Anglo-American Fifth Army had landed at Anzio south of Rome. A furious German counter-attack nearly destroyed the beachhead. Thereafter, the British and American force at Anzio failed to break out of the beachhead for more than four months.

excuse he gave to war correspondents was that the 27th's original assignment was as a non-combat garrison division and, with the fighting over in the north, he could now revert to that plan. He said much the same thing to General Greiner, the 27th's commander, who was 'obviously relieved'. But Smith was not fooled. Buckner relieved the 27th, he wrote, 'because he had lost confidence' in it.[20]

45

'Hit the deck and dig in!'

North of the Asa River, 1–3 May 1945

On 1 May 1945, K Company boarded trucks at Inubi and headed south over dusty roads, passing 'many bivouacs of service troops and vast ammunition and supply dumps, all covered with camouflage netting'. Nearing the front, they drove through artillery positions strewn with empty shell cases and the ground badly cut up by Japanese counter-battery fire.

Eventually the trucks stopped and the men piled out 'in driving rain and started forward single file' on the right side of a narrow coral road. Up ahead, they could hear the 'crash and thunder of enemy mortar and artillery rounds, the rattle of machine guns, and the popping of rifles'. Their own artillery rounds whistled overhead. 'Keep your five-pace interval,' ordered an officer.

Soon they met a column of men heading in the opposite direction. They were army troops from the 105th Infantry of the 27th Division, the unit they were relieving.* The soldiers looked exhausted, hollow-eyed and tight-faced. One lanky fellow caught Gene Sledge's eye and said: 'It's hell up there, Marine.'

* It may be significant that the 105th Infantry had had two battalions severely mauled in the great Japanese banzai attack on Saipan. Built back up for service on Okinawa, these units were never likely to be as proficient as others that had suffered fewer casualties, and which therefore retained a large cadre of combat-savvy NCOs.

'Yeah,' said Sledge, 'I know. I was at Peleliu.'

R. V. Burgin witnessed an act of disobedience among the 'Doggies' that told him everything he needed to know about their morale. Given an order by his sergeant, a soldier responded: 'Fuck you. Do it yourself. I'm not doing it.' Such behaviour by a Marine, noted Burgin, would have cost him his teeth and a night in the brig.[1]

K Company kept moving south and the shattered terrain reminded Sterling Mace of the 'black-and-white photos of Belgium during World War I – muted earth tones, scant vegetation, pitted and pocked ridges from the constant shelling – and in the many shell holes along the ground lay the detritus of war in its myriad forms. Empty crates of ammunition, spent shell casings, burned-out military vehicles of all types, discarded personal equipment.' At one point they passed rows of army dead, 'covered in ponchos, lying on stretchers, most of them shoeless, their buddies having scavenged the best pairs for their own use'.[2]

They eventually approached a 'low, gently sloping ridge' where K Company would go into the line. The noise of battle grew louder. Mace and his squad were 'nervously scanning the bombed-out hills' before them when the 'ground felt like it had been lifted a foot'. As artillery rounds screamed in, they broke into a zigzagging run, clods of earth bouncing off their helmets. Mace saw a foxhole and dived into it. Others did the same, 'peeking out over the rims of their holes, and *flash*!' A shell erupted, sending a wall of brown earth into the air.

Meanwhile the mortar section, ordered off the road to the left in dispersed order, was running at the double as Japanese rounds of all sizes 'whizzed, screamed and roared' around them. 'The ground sloped upward,' remembered Burgin, 'and we spread out to present a scattered target. Soldiers were streaming by. It was the worst pounding we'd received since the airfield on Peleliu.'

Nearing the crest of the ridge, he yelled, 'Hit the deck and dig in!' Sledge and Shelton began work on the gun pit, while the ammo carriers dug two-man foxholes in soft claylike soil. As they worked, word spread of the company's mounting casualties. The dead included the popular Corporal Howard Nease, who had shared the stolen turkey on New

Year's Eve, and a young replacement called Private Westbrook, 'a friendly curly-headed blond and one of the youngest men in the outfit'.

Nease's death hit everyone hard, particularly a Gloucester veteran who had joined the company at the same time. 'Howard's luck just run out, that's all,' he remarked gloomily. 'Ain't no damn way a guy can go on forever without gittin' hit.'

The mortar section took out their anger and frustration on their pugnacious lieutenant, 'Mac' MacKenzie, who kept excavating his deep one-man foxhole after the others had finished theirs and the Japanese fire had begun to slacken. 'Now that Nease and Westbrook have been killed, ain't it about time you took your kabar and .45 and charged them Nips, Mac?' asked 'Snafu' Shelton.

Other veterans reminded Mac of his earlier bravado, with Sledge offering to lend him his Ka-Bar. But the officer simply grunted and carried on burrowing 'like a badger'. When he had dug the hole deep enough, he began laying wooden boards from ammo boxes over the top, leaving one small opening through which he could squirm. Then he shovelled six inches of soil on top of the boards, and crawled inside.

Meanwhile, George Sarrett had inched up the little slope to take a look over the crest. No sooner had he raised his head than a Japanese machine gun opened fire from the opposite ridge, narrowly missing the mortarman. In his eagerness to duck, Sarrett 'lost his balance, slid back down the slope, and landed on top of Mac's dugout causing the roof to cave in'.

Emerging from the debris, MacKenzie complained: 'You ruined my foxhole!'

Sarrett apologised, but the rest of the section just 'smirked and grinned'. They had heard the last of their officer's bravado.[3]

By nightfall on 1 May, the relief of the 27th Division by the 1st Marine Division was almost complete. A day earlier, two battalions of the 1st Marines had taken over from the 165th Infantry on the extreme left of the Tenth Army's line, a sector that ran from the west coast, below Machinato airfield, to a point close by the village of Miyagusuki. On

1 May, the 3rd and 2nd Battalions of the 5th Marines extended the divisional line farther east by replacing, respectively, the 105th and 106th Infantry. The initial objective of the 1st Marine Division was to reach the Asa River, north of the island capital of Naha. But between it and the river was a series of hills and ridges on which the Japanese had prepared their defensive positions in depth.[4]

On 30 April, and again on 1 May, while the 5th Marines were moving into the line, the 1st Marines tried to push south, but on each occasion they made minimal gains at a heavy cost. The plan for 2 May was to continue the advance. By this date, three divisions were facing the Japanese in southern Okinawa: from west to east, the 1st Marine, 77th Infantry (which had replaced the 96th on 30 April), and 7th Infantry. Lieutenant General Buckner visited the commanders of both new divisions – Pedro Del Valle and Andrew Bruce – and got the impression that they expected 'to show their superiority over their predecessors by a rapid breakthrough of the enemy position'. They would soon realize the Japanese defences were a much tougher nut to crack than they had imagined.[5]

Both divisions attacked on 2 and 3 May: the 1st Marine in the direction of the Asa River, 1,500 yards to the south and running from the village of Dakeshi to the coast; and the 77th up the Maeda escarpment, a 'huge, forbidding, sheer cliff' in the centre of the island. 'They were promptly stopped,' noted Buckner in his diary, and 'learned some valuable lessons . . . From now on they will be more valuable as all-round fighters.'[6]

The terrain over which both divisions would have to fight was particularly formidable. The official historian of the 1st Marine Division noted,

> The Japanese had carefully prepared all the terrain leading into Shuri and utilized every mound, hummock, hill, and ridge to emplace troops and weapons. In some instances the burial vaults of Okinawans were opened up to make positions for machine guns, 47mm anti-tank guns and mortars. Caves were dug with connecting passageways so that ammunition could be brought up for emplaced

> weapons. Special emphasis was placed on coordinated fields of fire. By carefully using the natural arrangement of the hills and ridges, gun positions were made mutually supporting. On the reverse slope[s] . . . the enemy dug caves for protection of mortar squads, to store food and ammunition, or to provide places of safety for defenders of the hills when our artillery, naval gunfire and aerial bombing made the forward slopes and crests untenable.

The Japanese were further helped by the fact that 'each piece of defensive ground was higher progressively and afforded the enemy excellent observation of all troop movements and activities to his front'. As the pressure intensified, the Japanese commander was able to 'withdraw his troops to prepared positions on the next hill', thus contracting his defensive perimeter and making his fortress ever more formidable. 'Nowhere on the island,' noted the divisional historian, 'could be found more suitable ground for a real war of attrition.'[7]

K Company got its first taste of the strength of the Japanese defences on 2 May when it was ordered to advance, as part of the general attack, towards the Asa River. 'Rain ushered in a gloomy dawn,' remembered Gene Sledge. 'We were apprehensive but hopeful. There was some small-arms fire along the line, and a few shells passed back and forth during early morning.'

After a hasty breakfast of K rations and coffee (heated on a tripod with a hexamine tablet*), the mortar section was ordered to join in the general barrage of the enemy lines by artillery, ships' guns, 81mm mortars and machine guns. Shells 'whistled, whined, and rumbled overhead', the friendlies bursting before the ridge to the front, and the enemy's in K Company's area and to the rear.

At 9:00 a.m., the mortar section was ordered to cease fire so that the

* Invented in Germany in 1936, the hexamine solid fuel tablet was ideal for combat troops because it burned with a high energy density, was smokeless and left no ash.

assault platoons could advance. Burgin and the others were to be ready to pick up the mortars and advance at a moment's notice. 'Noise that had been loud now grew into a deafening bedlam,' remembered Sledge. 'The riflemen hardly got out of their foxholes when a storm of enemy fire from our front and left flank forced them back. The same thing was happening to the battalions on our right and left.'[8]

For the assaulting 2nd and 3rd Platoons, the brief advance was a nightmare as mortar rounds fell like rain and machine-gun bullets came zipping in from the left, spinning up puffs of dirt. 'Stay loose!' yelled Sterling Mace to his team. 'Don't stop!'

It took the heavily loaded Marines fifteen seconds to cross the 40 yards of open ground from the crest of the ridge to the next piece of cover, a low embankment, and in that time both platoon leaders, Second Lieutenants 'Spud' Dunlap and Sorterios 'Sam' Menzelos – the 22-year-old son of Greek immigrants who had studied at the University of California, Berkeley – were wounded.[9] R. V. Burgin, who had moved up with the riflemen to 'spot' targets for the mortars, was finding it 'impossible to get a clear picture of what we were firing at'. He wrote:

> Beyond our ridge lay a shallow valley, then another ridge. Whenever our men started to move forward, there was one particular Jap machine gun that would open up. Other enemy machine-guns were firing that morning, but this one had us pinned down . . . Our three [mortars] were about twenty-five or thirty yards behind me. I was communicating by phone. I could hear that machine [gun] chatter and I could hear the bullets zing by. I knew about where they were coming from, maybe four hundred yards across the valley and somewhere on our right. The valley was flat and open, but the opposite slope was thick with brush. I could not spot him to save my life.

Burgin eventually worked out that the machine gunner would only fire when the Marines had got past a certain point, and that something must be blocking his view. But as the men were headed towards the left, and he was firing from the right, they had failed to spot him when he fired. Burgin's plan was to draw his fire and observe the muzzle flash. That would make him a target, of course, but it was a risk worth taking. 'Just before I got to where I judged I would be walking into the gunner's field of view,' he wrote, 'I turned and took a step or two backward, watching the distant ridge. Instantly I saw a flash on the far hillside. Mud spattered at my feet and I felt something whack my trouser legs. But I had seen him!'

Ducking back into cover, he grabbed the phone to call in the coordinates. The first round exploded a few yards to the left, so he called in the correction. This time the round was right on target. 'There was a flash and a geyser of smoke and dirt. I watched that machine gun fly forward and the gunner do a kind of backflip through the air.'

Burgin punched the air in celebration. When he looked down, he noticed three holes in his dungaree trousers, but no wounds. Fortune had favoured the brave.*[10]

While this duel was taking place, Sledge and three other mortarmen were ordered to help evacuate the casualties. He remembered: 'With bullets snapping and popping overhead, we ran along for about forty yards, keeping just below the crest of the ridge. We came to a road cut through the ridge about eight feet below the crest; an officer told us to stand behind him until we were ordered to go out and bring in a casualty.' This was the exact spot where Nease and Westbrook had been hit by machine-gun bullets the day before.

While they waited, the survivors from two K Company rifle squads – including Mace – came back through the cut. They 'all wore wide-eyed, shocked expressions that showed only too vividly they were men who had barely escaped chance's strange arithmetic'. Clinging to their weapons, they 'slumped to the mud to pant for breath before moving behind the ridge toward their former foxholes'. The torrential rain added to the misery.

* For this selfless act of courage – deliberately exposing himself so that he could locate and destroy the Japanese machine gun – Burgin was awarded the Bronze Star.

Sledge prayed he would not have to step out into the road to collect a casualty. He knew that as most of the attacking troops had withdrawn, the Japanese would concentrate their fire on the stretcher-bearers. His prayers were answered when Gunnery Sergeant Hank Boyes, who had won the Silver Star on Peleliu, came through the cut and announced that 'everyone had made it back: casualties had been brought back farther down the line where the machine-gun fire hadn't been as heavy'.[11]

Granted a reprieve, Sledge and the others returned to their foxholes where they heard the welcome news that all further attacks had been postponed until the following day. But, with the rain and Japanese shells still falling, the general outlook was gloomy and depressing. 'Across the muddy fields,' noted Sledge, 'we saw our soaked comrades crouching forlornly in their muddy holes and ducking, as we did, each time a shell roared over.'

When the barrage eventually subsided, the men 'squatted thankfully' in their holes and grumbled about the weather. They were distracted by the alarming sight, to their left rear, of a team of stretcher-bearers taking a casualty back between two low ridges where they were in full view of the Japanese. Just before the team reached the cover of some trees, they were fired on by enemy riflemen, the bullets 'kicking up mud and splashing in the puddles of water' around them. Sledge and his squad requested permission to fire 60mm phosphorus rounds to give the team some cover. They were refused: to fire across the company front might hit friendly troops.

They watched helplessly as the stretcher-bearers struggled across the muddy field with bullets falling all around. 'It was,' remembered Sledge, 'one of those terribly pathetic, heartrending sights that seemed to rule in combat: men struggling to save a wounded comrade, the enemy firing at them as fast as they could, and the rest of us utterly powerless to give any aid.' For the mortarmen, it was an agony 'worse than personal danger'.

In desperation, the four carriers dropped all their personal kit apart from their weapons. They struggled forward, helmeted heads bent low, like beasts of burden. Just when it seemed they might reach safety the two at the back were hit by a burst of fire and fell, dropping the rear of the stretcher. Sledge and the other watching Marines gasped in horror. But they soon started cheering as the two unwounded carriers grabbed the stretcher casualty and supported him with one arm, while using the other to help a wounded carrier. With the onlookers cheering them on, the five men 'limped and hobbled into the cover of the bushes, bullets still kicking up mud all around them'. Sledge's 'relief and elation' was matched only by his 'deepening hatred for the Japanese'.

That evening, they received confirmation that K and L Companies would attack again in the morning. As extra ammo, rations and water were being distributed, Gene Sledge could see 'Stumpy' Stanley briefing the officers and senior NCOs. The former included the replacements for Dunlap and Menzelos: young men with 'enthusiastic, animated expressions' who were 'very conscientious and determined to do their best or die in the effort'. To Sledge, they 'appeared almost tragic in their naïve innocence and ignorance of what lay ahead for us all'.

After Stanley had dismissed his junior officers, they returned to their platoons to brief their men. 'Mac' MacKenzie was 'crisp and efficient' as he told Burgin and the other mortar section NCOs that the 'coming offensive would need the full support' of the 60mm mortars. They, in turn, told the men their tasks. 'We would get maximum support from heavy artillery and other weapons,' remembered Sledge. 'Casualties would be given swift aid. So we prepared our equipment and waited nervously.'

That evening, Sledge had a long heart-to-heart near his gun pit with a friend from one of the rifle platoons. Drawing nervously on a cigarette – while Sledge puffed from his tobacco pipe – the young replacement Marine admitted he was 'terribly afraid about the impending attack'. He was, he added, 'appalled and depressed' by the fighting that day and did not see how he could survive a repeat. He poured out his 'innermost secrets' – mentioning his parents and a girl back home he hoped to marry – and said the thought that he might never return to those he loved had left him in a state of 'near desperation'.

The conversation reminded Sledge of the way 'Hillbilly' Jones had 'comforted and helped' him through the 'first shock of Peleliu', and he tried to do the same for his friend by assuring him that everyone was afraid. He knew, of course, that riflemen were the most vulnerable in an attack. Yet he did his best to cheer the man up. Eventually, 'somewhat relieved, or resigned to his fate', the friend stood up, shook Sledge by the hand, and returned to his foxhole.

When it attacked the following morning, K Company's 1st Platoon was able to advance 300 yards to the next ridge line (thanks in part to the mortar section's destruction of the Japanese machine gun), the only 5th Marines unit to make any impression on the enemy defences that day.[12] But, 'hit so hard' by Japanese mortar and machine-gun fire from the front and both flanks, 1st Platoon took heavy casualties – including the officer, platoon sergeant, platoon guide and nine riflemen, all wounded – and was eventually forced to withdraw. Once again, Gunnery Sergeant Hank Boyes was in the thick of the action. A combat correspondent wrote,

> On orders from the company commander, Boyes organized the platoon's withdrawal. He then remained behind and, armed with smoke grenades, climbed to the top of the [ridge] and threw them so that stretcher bearers could come in under the smoke and take the wounded out. Boyes held his exposed position even after he felt the heat of a Jap bullet which went through his [forage] cap. Then a mortar shell tore through the sleeve of his jacket and leg of his pants.

Despite shrapnel wounds in his left leg, Boyes kept throwing smoke grenades until all twelve casualties had been evacuated. Even then he refused to go to hospital himself. 'Corpsman took care of it every day,' he wrote later, 'so I did not leave "K" Company.'[13]

Most of the men who witnessed Boyes's heroism that day were convinced it was worth another Silver Star at the very least. But Stanley refused to recommend the award because 'an officer didn't see it happen'.[14]

Sterling Mace helped to bring in one of the wounded – Sergeant John P. Heeb from Rushville, Indiana – on a poncho. Heeb had his dungaree jacket pulled up to his chest, and his pants around his ankles, exposing his terrible injury. 'Where there isn't blood,' wrote Mace, 'I can see the chalk white of his skin, appearing nearly transparent, so blanched I can make out a web of blue veins beneath the skin, sending blood through his heart, and out of a hole in his groin where his genitals used to be.' Robbed of his manhood, Heeb was a 'goner'. This island, noted Mace, 'will end up emasculating every one of us'.[15]

For at least one of the casualties, however, the cloud of injury had a silver lining. It was the Marine who had bared his soul to Gene Sledge. 'He wore a triumphant look of satisfaction,' remembered Sledge, 'shook hands with me heartily, and grinned as a stretcher team carried him by with a bloody bandage on his foot. God or chance – depending on one's faith – had spared his life and lifted his burden of further fear and terror in combat by awarding him a million-dollar wound.'[16]

46

'We gotta get the hell outta here'

Death Valley, 4–9 May 1945

Moved into battalion reserve after the failure of its attack on 3 May, K Company spent the night in the rear close to the aid station. The men were hoping for a quiet night. But Gene Sledge had not been asleep for long when he was roused by his foxhole partner. 'Sledgehammer, wake up. The Nips are up to something.'

Unholstering his pistol, Sledge heard an NCO shout: 'Stand by for a ram, you guys. One hundred percent alert!'

From the south came the sound of heavy artillery and small arms fire. It seemed to be coming from beyond the division's left flank, where the army troops were located. The firing directly to the front had increased too, as had the frequency of artillery fire overhead. 'What's the dope?' asked Sledge nervously.

'Beats me,' said his buddy, 'but something sure the hell's going on up on the line. Nips probably pulling a counterattack.'

As they waited for confirmation, heavy machine-gun and mortar fire broke out some distance to their right rear, where the 1st Marines' defences ended at the coast. From their little mound they could see streams of machine-gun tracers 'darting straight out to sea under the eerie light of 60mm mortar flares'. It could only mean one thing: a Japanese amphibious attack. 'The Nips must be pullin' a counterlanding,' said a Marine, 'and the 1st Marines givin' 'em hell.'

Sledge and others pondered the possibility of the Japanese getting ashore on their right flank while separate attacks engaged their front and left, and it soon became clear that the 'entire division might be isolated'. As if that thought was not bad enough, the next order instructed: 'Stand by for possible Jap paratroop attack! All hands turn to. Keep your eyes open.'

Sledge was no more afraid of Japanese paratroopers than of their veteran infantry. But the threat of being surrounded and unable to defend himself 'chilled' his soul. 'It was,' he remembered, 'a long night made worse by the uncertainty and confusion around us. I suffered extremely mixed emotions: glad on the one hand to be out of the fighting, but anxious for those Americans catching the fury of the enemy's attack.'[1]

The huge counter-attack launched that morning by the Japanese was an attempt to turn the tide of the campaign. Its architect was the aggressive Major General Chō, who had managed to convince his boss, Ushijima, that now was the time to strike a decisive blow. Colonel Yahara opposed the move, arguing that his defensive strategy had limited the Americans to gains of just a hundred yards a day and was working well. But the majority of the senior commanders supported Chō's argument that it was better to risk all in a sudden attack, than face certain defeat and death. Ushijima duly ordered an all-out offensive for 4 May, referring to it as an 'honourable final death attack'.[2]

Kamikazes began the attack on American shipping at dusk on 3 May, with seven suicide planes hitting the destroyer *Aaron Ward*, killing forty-five and wounding forty-nine, but failing to sink the vessel.[3] These attacks were followed by attempted landings on the west coast by several hundred men of the 26th Shipping Engineer Regiment, armed with anti-tank guns, heavy machine guns, light arms and thousands of satchel charges. But, miscalculating their position, they moved inshore at Kuwan, a point just behind the front line and heavily defended by men of the 1st Marines. They were shot to pieces by the defenders, with one platoon burning out six machine-gun barrels and using fifty boxes of ammunition. 'The whole thing was a godsend,' noted one Marine officer. 'If the Nips had landed above us, they would have faced no opposition.'[4]

Another attempted landing on the east coast, by the 23rd Shipping Engineer Regiment, was destroyed by American fire from the coast and ships in the bay. The two failed amphibious attacks had cost the Japanese 500 men and all their landing craft.[5] Other major assaults in the centre of the island, after a huge artillery bombardment, made some initial ground before they too were halted. The Japanese air attack on 4 May was the most successful, sinking four ships and damaging thirteen others, and killing and wounding more than 1,100 US sailors.[6]

But overall the offensive was a costly failure. Ushijima admitted as much when he told Yahara: 'Your judgement was correct . . . Now I am determined to stop this offensive. Meaningless suicide is not what I want.' The main force was now largely spent, admitted Ushijima, but some of the fighting strength was left, and they were getting 'strong support from the islanders'. He added: 'With these we will fight to the southernmost hill, to the last square inch of land, and to the last man. I am ready to fight, but from now on I leave everything up to you. My instructions to you are to do whatever you feel is necessary.'

Yahara summarized the cost of the failed two-day Japanese offensive as follows: the 24th Division had lost two-thirds of its 'fighting strength'; the 5th Artillery Group's ammunition was 'almost expended', with each gun limited to just ten rounds a day for the rest of May; two Shipping Engineer regiments had been 'totally annihilated'; the Thirty-Second Army had lost 'five thousand seasoned soldiers, killed and wounded'; and, if the offensive had not gone ahead, they could have 'prolonged the Okinawa battle for another month and saved thousands of lives'.[7]

To staunch the bleeding, he reverted to his original strategy of a defensive battle of attrition. This meant replacing some of the lost combat infantrymen with service and support troops. 'One man in ten,' stated the order, 'will continue with rear-echelon duties. The remaining nine men will devote themselves to anti-tank combat training.'[8]

K Company was still in battalion reserve as the news of the failure of the Japanese counter-offensive filtered through over the next two days. The 5th Marines, by this time, had pivoted to the right 'in order to flank the high ground in its left zone of action from the west, rather than to try to take it by frontal attacks from the north'. The feature in question was the 'Awacha Pocket', named after the village that lay just to its north. One of the keys to reducing the pocket was a north–south valley along its eastern flank – known to the Marines as 'Death Valley' – and an oblong feature beyond called 'Wilson's Ridge'.

It would take the 5th Marines more than a week to capture Wilson's Ridge and Death Valley. Most of the early advances by the 1/5 and 2/5 Marines were designed to manoeuvre companies into positions 'from which the Ridge could be overrun and the Valley cleared'. The task was made more difficult by the 'crazy pattern' of Japanese defences. 'With caves and pillboxes on front and reverse slopes,' noted the US Marines official history, 'as well as flanking slopes, the enemy was always in a position to deliver fire, regardless of our direction of attack, until we had occupied physically every foot of important ground and methodically destroyed and sealed all enemy positions.'[9]

Dug in to the north of Death Valley, the 3/5 Marines was used chiefly in a supporting role. K Company's mortar section, for example, was 'emplaced on the slope of a little rise about seventy-five yards behind the front line'. There they sat in the pouring rain, while supplies of ammunition, rations and water could only reach a dump on the far side of a shallow draw to their rear. It was exhausting, nerve-wracking work ferrying the boxes and cans forward through knee-deep mud and often under artillery fire. 'Such activity drove the infantrymen,' wrote Sledge, 'weary from the mental and physical stress of combat, almost to the brink of physical collapse.'

On 8 May, the working parties had already made a couple of trips across the draw when a Nambu light machine gun opened up from the left. Midway across, Sledge immediately 'took off at a run, slipping and sliding on the mud, to the protected area where the supply dump was placed'. Bullets 'snapped viciously around him', but he made it safely. To allow him to return, PFC John Redifer threw a phosphorus grenade to give some smoke-screen protection. 'Thick clouds of white smoke billowed forth,' remembered Sledge, 'and hung almost immobile in the heavy, misty air. I grabbed a metal box of 60mm mortar ammo in each hand. Each of the other men also picked up a load. We prepared to cross.'

As the Nambu was still firing down the draw, Sledge and the others hesitated. But he could see Redifer standing out in the open, throwing more grenades, and 'felt like a coward'. Finally, someone said: 'Let's go, on the double, and keep your five-pace interval.'

They set off into the 'smoky, murky air', heads lowered and teeth gritted as bullets zipped past them. Sledge expected to be hit, but preferred to take his chances than 'be yellow in the face of [Redifer's] risks to screen us'. If he had been shot while they cringed in safety, Sledge knew it would have haunted him for the rest of his life.

They made it across and, having dumped the ammo, went to thank Redifer. He was more concerned with solving the problem of supply than talking, and soon headed back across the draw when he heard the engine of a tank. He returned leading a big Sherman, and arranged for the tank to move 'back and forth across the draw, always between us and the enemy machine gun'. They kept this up, 'hugging the side of the tank like chicks beside a mother hen', until all the ammunition had been brought across.

Just as they were finishing, the XO 'Shadow' Loveday appeared. A tall, skinny man, he was the 'sloppiest Marine' Sledge had ever laid eyes on. 'His dungarees hung on him like old, discarded clothes on a scarecrow,' remembered the Alabaman. 'His web pistol belt was wrapped around his waist like a loose sash on a dressing gown; his map case flopped around; and every pack strap dangled more "Irish pennants" than any new recruit had in boot camp.'

Even worse than his slovenly appearance, however, was Loveday's disposition: 'Moody, ill-tempered and highly excitable.' He gave a demonstration of this now by chewing out Redifer with yells, gestures and curses for 'exposing himself unnecessarily to enemy fire'. Any other officer would have considered Redifer's actions brave and meritorious. But Loveday was 'so incredibly illogical' he had taken the opposite view. Having vented his rage, he strode off 'grumbling and cursing the individual and collective stupidity of enlisted men'. Redifer 'just looked off into the distance', while the others 'growled mightily'.[10]

That same day, American troops on Okinawa were told the 'momentous news' of Germany's unconditional surrender to the Allies on 7 May 1945, and the formal declaration on the 8th of Victory in Europe, or VE Day. 'At noon,' wrote Lieutenant General Buckner in his diary, 'every gun of our land and ship support batteries fired one round at the enemy. We then tuned in to the Jap radio frequency and announced in Japanese that the volley was in celebration of the victory.'[11]

The typical reaction in K Company to the news from Europe was: so what? 'Germany's surrender had come too late for [my brother],' wrote R. V. Burgin, 'and for a lot of other good men. But there were no signs that Japs would follow Germany's lead. For most of us, the end of fighting half a world away meant very little, except that maybe the flow of supplies would pick up and we'd get some help.'[12] Sterling Mace agreed. 'The news didn't change the position of our lines,' he noted, 'or the texture of the mud, the tint of the sky, or the amount of ammunition each of us carried in our pouches. Nor did it change what we knew was coming – that we'd be making another assault on the Japanese soon, and more Marines would surely die in the process.'[13]

To most of the Marines in K Company, 'Nazi Germany might as well have been on the moon'. But a few, like Sledge, had brothers with the forces in Europe and were obviously relieved. 'The news I'm waiting for,' he wrote to his mother a few days later, 'is a letter from you that Ed is on his way home. I don't think you need worry about him coming over here. I'm pretty sure he will go stateside for good, and I sure hope it's soon too.'[14] (Sledge's brother Ed would finish the war as a major with a Silver Star, Bronze Star and three Purple Hearts.)

At noon on 9 May, K and I Companies attacked south with tanks along the flanks of Death Valley after a huge preliminary bombardment by ship's guns and heavy artillery, and air strikes by Corsairs and dive-bombers. K

Company's mortar section fired in support, with R. V. Burgin observing and directing the salvoes. 'I watched our riflemen and tanks start across the valley,' he recalled, 'only to be brought up short by Jap fire. They were using their 90mm mortars, with big shells that made a strange fluttering sound as they came tumbling down. I ordered the mortars to fire phosphorus shells to provide a smoke screen for the attack.'[15]

It was, for Sterling Mace, another 'foul-up' of an attack that got barely fifty yards before it was held up by heavy enemy fire. 'All you can do,' he wrote, 'is grit your teeth and tuck your head, swerving, like a drunk, at a jagged run, as you're pelted by the mud, crud, and unidentifiable gunk that for all you know could be bits of your buddies flying by.'

Mace was at the point of attack with his squad leader, Sergeant Chase. They were both on the ground, taking cover from exploding rounds. 'Chase,' shouted Mace. 'We gotta get the hell outta here.'

The sergeant glanced briefly at Mace, before getting to his feet and heading to the rear.

'Hey!' yelled Mace. 'Where the hell are you going?'

'I got hit in the arm!' responded Chase, still running and not looking back.

Bullshit! thought Mace. He was lying next to the sergeant and had heard nothing. He glanced back over his shoulder and Chase had vanished. *Screw it. I never liked you anyway, ya sonuvabitch.*

Mace kept trying to move forward, and was almost killed when an 8in Japanese shell exploded nearby, bursting both his eardrums and leaving him badly concussed. 'Rolling over in the bottom of the hole,' he remembered, 'I exhale in one great puff, as if I've been gut-punched, almost expecting smoke to spew from my mouth. It's over. I check my body for blood.'

Helped back to the start line, he wanted to remain with the company but was eventually persuaded to go back to the battalion aid station by the corpsman, George Chulis. 'Leaning my M-1 against the wall of my foxhole,' he recalled, 'I climbed out and gazed at my surroundings one last time – watching the Marines, here and there, slosh around in the muck, observing them across a panoramic view that used to be my home, too. The sky was hard with white marbling grained across it, white clouds that didn't stand a chance any more than I did. And their faces? There were less than a handful of Marines who had made the Peleliu landing – Orley Uhls, Blowtorch Willy, Hank Boyes, Roy Kelly – fewer still who served on Cape Gloucester.'

By that time, 'Wimpy' Whitby had also been evacuated with combat fatigue. 'Facts are facts,' wrote Mace. 'Wimpy got stung with the same shell that left two gaping holes through my ears. It just so happened that the round that ended Bob's combat effectiveness was fired from a pen, and not a Nip counterbattery.'[16]

Gene Sledge, who had narrowly avoided injury from Japanese shell fire as the mortar section supported the attack, witnessed the return of the survivors. 'It was,' he remembered, 'the same tragic sight of bloody, dazed, and wounded men benumbed with shock, being carried or walking to the aid station in the rear. There also were the dead, and the usual enquiries about friends. We were all glad when the word came that 3/5 would move into reserve for the 7th Marines.' K and I Companies lost forty-nine men that day.[17]

Among the casualties was 53-year-old Major Paul Douglas, who once again had managed to convince 'the higher-ups to let him leave his post as division adjutant and go forward'. He was helping to bring in the wounded on stretchers when he was hit by a machine-gun bullet that severed a nerve in his left shoulder. In great pain, he said to the stretcher-bearers: 'Leave me here. Get the young men out first. I have lived my life, please let them live theirs.' He was brought in, anyway, and later evacuated to a hospital ship.*[18]

That evening, having moved to the right in support of the 7th Marines fighting to capture Dakeshi Ridge, Sledge sat on his helmet in the mud and read a letter from his parents. It contained the grim news that his

* Douglas spent thirteen months in the Bethesda Naval Hospital recovering from his wound, though he never regained complete function of his left shoulder and arm. He later served for many years as a United States senator for Illinois and died in 1976.

'beloved spaniel' Deacon, having been hit by a car, had dragged himself home and died in the arms of Sledge's father. 'He had been,' noted Sledge, 'my constant companion during the several years before I had left home for college. There, with the sound of heavy firing up ahead and the sufferings and deaths of thousands of men going on nearby, big tears rolled down my cheeks, because Deacon was dead.'[19]

47

'Hell's own cesspool'

Wana Draw and Half Moon Hill, 11–24 May 1945

At 7:00 a.m. on 11 May, the Tenth Army launched its biggest general offensive of the campaign. 'Progress along the line,' noted Lieutenant General Buckner in his diary. 'Visited both corps CPs and put a little pressure on corps commanders.'[1]

It was the first time that Hodge's XXIV and Geiger's III Amphibious Corps – the latter having taken over the right sector of the front on 5 May – had attacked side by side. Their aim was to envelop the main Japanese defences in front of the town of Shuri from both east and west, while a strong holding attack was maintained in the centre. Buckner and his staff were convinced that the Japanese front was weakest in the western half of the island, and that the fresher Marine divisions there had a real opportunity to break through. 'It will be,' he explained on 10 May, 'a continuation of the type of attack we have been employing to date. Where we cannot take strong points we will pinch them off and leave them for the reserves to reduce. We have ample firepower and we also have enough fresh troops so that we can always have one division resting.'[2]

The four divisions attacking were, from left to right, the 6th Marine Division (which had left the Motobu Peninsula a few days earlier), 1st Marine Division, 77th Infantry Division and 96th Infantry Division. As well as eliminating the last organised resistance in the Awacha Pocket – which it managed during the first day of the offensive – the 1st Marine

Division's main objective was the capture of the 'Shuri Heights', a catch-all term that included Shuri Castle (beneath which lay the underground headquarters of the Japanese Thirty-Second Army), but also the Japanese positions on the key features of Dakeshi Ridge, Wana Ridge, Wana Draw and Hill 55, and the ruined towns of Dakeshi and Wana, all of which protected Shuri from the northwest.

The first feature to fall was Dakeshi Ridge to the 7th Marines on 13 May. But Wana Ridge proved to be a much tougher proposition. On four successive days – 16–19 May – two battalions of the 7th Marines assaulted the ridge without success. Relieved by the 1st Marines on the 19th, the regiment had lost a thousand men since 10 May and was later awarded the Presidential Unit Citation for its part in the battle.[3]

Meanwhile the 5th Marines – having taken over from the 1st Marines on 14 May – made slow but gradual progress in their flanking attack on Hill 55 and the neighbouring Wana Draw. The former was captured by the 2/5 Marines on 20 May and Wana Ridge finally fell to the 2/1 Marines two days later. For most of this period, the 3/5 Marines was in regimental reserve and missed the worst of the fighting. However, that did not prevent the battalion commander, Lieutenant Colonel Miller, from being wounded by shell fire on the 17th. He was replaced by Major Frank Poland.

K Company, too, was often far enough forward to take and inflict casualties. On one occasion, as the company attempted to capture a low ridge, R. V. Burgin noticed that American artillery fire seemed to be having little effect on the Japanese defenders. 'Something had to be running just beyond the crest that was sheltering them,' he decided, 'something like a gully or a trench. The Japs could lay up in there protected from our artillery, then pop out and start firing when we moved up the slope.'

He knew that mortars, which dropped from a steep angle, might be able to hit this trench. So he picked up the sound-powered phone and ordered his section to fire a sixty-round bombardment, adding: 'Register one gun to fire from right to left, the second to fire left to right, and the third to fire all along the crest of the ridge.'

Unfortunately, his officer 'Mac' MacKenzie heard what he was up to and grabbed the phone. 'You can't do that,' he told Burgin. 'We don't have enough ammo.'

They argued for a while. But when MacKenzie refused to budge, Burgin called the company CP and explained what he wanted to do. 'Can you spare us the ammo?'

'No problem,' they replied.

MacKenzie came back on the line. 'I *order* you not to fire!' he yelled.

Burgin ignored him. 'Mortar section,' he instructed, 'fire on my command! Commence firing!'

The guns fired – *bump-bump-bump* – as MacKenzie 'ranted and raved'.

When the barrage was over, K Company took the ridge without a shot being fired. Burgin checked the target area and found 'fifty freshly killed Japanese soldiers in a narrow ravine, all dead from wounds obviously caused by our mortar fire'. The event illustrated to Sledge the 'value of experience in a veteran like Burgin compared with the poor judgement of a "green" lieutenant'.[4]

A few days later, on 20 May, K Company was backing up the 2/5 Marines' advance through Wana Draw when it was hit by a heavy artillery bombardment. Up front observing, R. V. Burgin and Jim Burke had just taken cover in two shell holes when there was a huge explosion. Burgin felt the force of it go 'right through' him, and was then buried by rocks and dirt. He clawed his way out, bruised and spluttering, but relieved to have survived such a close call. That afternoon he was sitting on his helmet, enjoying a meal of ham and lima beans from a can, when another big shell landed fifty yards away. 'Just a flash and a *crack!*' he remembered. 'The impact knocked me off my helmet and at the same time I felt something sting the back of my neck.'

Stunned, he sat on the ground for a moment, before reaching up to brush away whatever was on his neck. He felt something 'hard and sharp' before it fell to the ground. It was a jagged piece of metal, the size of a finger. He reached down to pick it up, but it was too hot to touch. When it had cooled a little, he examined it and put it in his pocket. By now, blood was trickling down his neck from a wound that was 'starting to really hurt'. Examined by a corpsman, he was given a shot of morphine and told to walk the few hundred yards back to the battalion aid station. Feeling light-headed, he stumbled along as best he could while the battle raged all around. From the aid station he was transferred to a field hospital where they diagnosed severe concussion – from the shell that had buried him – and said he was fortunate that the fragment had narrowly missed his thyroid gland.

He took the opportunity to write to Florence in Australia: 'Just a few lines to let you know that I was hit Sunday May 20th, but don't worry, Darling, I am not suffering and haven't been at all . . . I sure wish I had you here, Darling, to change the bandages & give me about a million sweet kisses a day or more. I am sleeping on nice white sheets with the softest pillow. It sure beats a wet foxhole.'[5]

For the men he left behind, Burgin's absence was keenly felt. He was, wrote Sledge, 'a Texan and as fine a sergeant as I ever saw . . . We would miss him.'[6]

On 22 May, the 3/5 Marines was ordered to extend the divisional front by relieving a battalion of the 4th Marines – part of the heavily depleted 6th Marine Division* – on a feature known as Half Moon Hill. The relief began at 10:50 a.m. on the 23rd and was completed in the early afternoon.[7] 'We shouldered our weapons and gear,' remembered Gene Sledge, 'and the column telescoped its way circuitously through muddy draws, slipping and sliding along the slopes of barren hills to avoid observation and consequent shelling by the enemy. It rained off and on.'

Nearing their destination, 'the Japanese dead, scattered about in most areas since May 1, became more numerous'. Even more depressing,

* During the week-long battle (11–18 May) to capture Sugar Loaf Hill, at the apex of a triangle of mutually supporting defensive positions that included Half Moon Hill and the Horse Shoe, the 6th Marine Division had lost 2,662 men and a further 1,289 cases of combat fatigue. The casualties included three battalion commanders and nine company commanders.

however, was the sight of so many Marine corpses. It was a strong Marine tradition, Sledge knew, to recover their dead, 'sometimes even at considerable risk, to an area where they could be covered with a poncho and later collected by the graves registration people'. But so incessant were the Japanese artillery and mortar bombardments that this had not been possible.

As Sledge and the rest of K Company trudged through the mud to their new position, they could see six Marine corpses 'lying facedown against a muddy slope where they apparently had hugged the deck to escape Japanese shells'. Lying side by side, scarcely a foot apart, they were clutching rusted rifles and showed every sign of being 'new replacements, fresh to the shock of combat'. Bizarrely, one was wearing a shiny gold watch, an oddity when most combat soldiers made do with 'plain, simple luminous-dial, waterproof, shockproof wristwatches' with green cloth wristbands. How odd, thought Sledge, for a Marine to wear such a 'flashy, conspicuous' watch; and odder still that 'some Japanese hadn't slipped out during a dark night and taken it'.

While artillery rounds swished and whined overhead in both directions, Sledge and the mortar section dug in below a low rise of ground, 100 yards back from the rifle platoons on the western side of a 'barren, muddy, shell torn ridge named Half Moon Hill'. The Japanese, meanwhile, still occupied caves in both of the southward-facing tips of the crescent.

Situated on the right flank of the battalion (and also the division), the men of K Company were facing south. Away to their right, beyond a narrow-gauge railroad track, lay the ridge known as the Horse Shoe. A short distance to their right rear was the feature, now in American hands, that had cost the 6th Marine Division so many lives: Sugar Loaf Hill. 'Stumpy' Stanley had set up his CP in the sunken railroad bed to the right of the mortar section's position. 'A nice tarpaulin,' noted Sledge, 'was stretched over the CP from one side of the railroad embankment to the other. This kept the post snug and dry while torrents of chilly rain kept shivering riflemen, machine gunners, and mortarmen soaked, cold, and miserable day and night in open foxholes.'

After siting the mortar, registering in on the aiming stakes, and preparing ammunition, Sledge had a good look around. 'It was,' he wrote, 'the most ghastly corner of hell I had ever witnessed. As far as I could see, an area that previously had been a low grassy valley with a picturesque stream meandering through it was a muddy, repulsive, open sore on the land. The place was choked with the putrefaction of death, decay, and destruction.' In a shallow defile to his right lay the corpses of twenty more Marines, each on a stretcher and covered with a poncho. Other bodies lay in shell craters, 'half submerged in muck and water, rusting weapons still in hand'. Swarms of flies hovered around them.

'Why ain't them poor guys been covered with ponchos?' asked Sledge's foxhole buddy. The answer came in the form of a huge explosion from a Japanese 75mm round, fired from gun positions on Shuri Ridge. If anyone moved from their holes, the shelling began immediately. 'Thus it was perfectly clear,' noted Sledge, 'why the Marine dead were left where they had fallen.' He added:

> For several feet around every corpse, maggots crawled about in the muck and then were washed away by the runoff of the rain. There wasn't a tree or bush left. All was open country. Shells had torn up the turf so completely that ground cover was non-existent. The rain poured down on us as evening approached. The scene was nothing but mud; shell fire; flooded craters with their silent, pathetic, rotting occupants; knocked-out tanks and amtracs; and discarded equipment – utter desolation.

All around was the stench of death. Sledge's only escape from the 'monstrous horror of it all' was to look up and 'watch the leaden gray clouds go scudding over, and repeat over and over' to himself that the 'situation was unreal' – a nightmare – and that he would soon awake and find himself 'somewhere else'. He had been depressed by the waste of human life on Peleliu; but this was far, far worse. 'We were,' he wrote, 'in the depths of the abyss, the ultimate horror of war . . . Men struggled and fought and bled in an environment so degrading I believed we had been flung into hell's own cesspool.'[8]

Other men referred to the place as the 'sea of death, because there were dead Marines laying down there in the water'. The hill, remembered 1st Platoon's Harry Bender, 'had the smell of death all around it – a sickening sweet smell, like something was rotting. Seeing those goddamn maggots in the bodies, boy, that was hard.'[9]

Soon after taking over the position on Half Moon Hill, 'Stumpy' Stanley went forward from the company CP to ensure that the men on the front line were in the right place 'and in a state of alert and readiness'. He was just approaching 1st Platoon, near the sunken railroad on the extreme right flank of the company, when a huge 150mm shell landed to his left, between two foxholes. He wrote:

> Immediately I went to the spot to check on the men. I found five bodies totally devastated. All five appeared to be dead. However, a Corpsman, who quickly arrived to give assistance, told me that one man was still alive but in deep shock. He was severely wounded, suffering multiple shrapnel wounds, blast and concussion damage. His body was placed on a stretcher and several of my men carried it to a nearby Battalion Aid Station. I did not expect this man to live.[10]

The lone survivor was PFC Bill Leyden, the wisecracking New Yorker. When the round exploded, he was sitting on the edge of his foxhole, barely 50 yards from the railway cut, while his squad leader Corporal Marion Vermeer and another rifleman, Private Roy Bauman, were lying inside. Having narrowly missed Leyden's back, the round struck the ground between his foxhole and another twenty feet to his left, manned by Privates Louis Verga and Archie Steele. Both were standing up at the time.

Another eyewitness to the tragedy was Gene Sledge. Having gone forward to observe for the mortars – the role normally performed by the absent Burgin – he was occupying the foxhole to the left of Verga's and Steele's. 'Shrapnel tore through the air,' he remembered, 'and hit the mud around my hole. Two bodies were thrown aside from Leyden's foxhole, and the third up into the air. (The latter, I learned later, was Leyden.) In the foxhole next to me Verga and Steele [were] slumped over, apparently dead or seriously wounded.'

Sledge was about to run over to help when a sergeant shouted: 'Sledgehammer, get back to your mortar. You may need to give fire on that Jap gun.'

He had not been back at the mortar position long when the five casualties were brought past on stretchers. Bauman and Steele 'appeared to be dead'. Verga was 'gasping for breath, and imploring God to stop the pain'. He died soon after. Vermeer was semi-conscious, but recognized Sledge when he spoke to him. 'Do you think I'll ever walk again?' he mumbled.

Sledge looked down and saw that one of Vermeer's legs had been severed above the ankle. He bit his tongue, choked, and assured Vermeer that one day he would. Moments later he saw him die. The last of the five, Leyden, was unconscious and assumed to be 'dying'. It was, for Sledge, 'one of the most brutal nerve-shattering experiences' of his war (and it had some tough competition).

It helped Sledge a little to hear later that Leyden had survived. How that was possible, given his exposed position on the edge of his foxhole, was a mystery even to Leyden. 'Considering what happened to Vermeer and Baumann,' he wrote later, '[it] makes me shudder and wonder what the hell I'm doing here?'

When the New Yorker regained consciousness at the battalion aid post, his buddy 'Tex' Barrow was by his cot. 'Leyden, you're rugged,' said the Texan, over and over. He realized later that his friend thought he was 'on the way out'. So did Leyden. 'I remember,' he wrote, 'seeing them pull the blankets over the guys on my right, one at a time, and when they got to me I thought they were going to do the same. They looked at me and continued down the line.'

The next thing he remembered, he was on the bottom row of a jeep carrying four stretchers. The guy above 'was moaning like hell' and his blood was 'splashing down' on Leyden. Taken to an army hospital on the edge of Yontan airfield, the New Yorker must have thought he was out of danger. As luck would have it, the airfield was the target of a suicide attack that night by plane-borne Japanese 'Giretsu' commandos. Of the nine Japanese planes sent on the mission, only one managed to land on the runway. But its fourteen heavily armed commandos still caused havoc by shooting and blowing up no fewer than thirty-three American planes, and killing two servicemen and wounding another eighteen. Leyden himself was almost a casualty as stray bullets and shrapnel 'tore up' his hospital tent. He recalled: 'I thought to myself, "For Christ's sake, not now. What a way to go!"'[11]

On 24 May, a day after the tragedy, some of the mortarmen were helping to carry ammo up from the rear when they passed close to the company CP. 'Hey, you guys,' yelled one, 'looka there; Stumpy's in bad shape!'

Looking across, they could see their skipper 'Stumpy' Stanley, 'just outside the edge of the tarpaulin, trying to stand by himself'. He was incapable of doing so, and had to be supported by two men. 'He looked haggard and weary,' remembered Gene Sledge, 'and was shaking violently with malarial chills. He could barely hold up his head. The men supporting him seemed to be arguing . . . He was objecting as best he could, but it was a feeble effort, because he was so sick.'

Having first caught malaria on New Britain, Stanley had suffered periodic attacks ever since. This one was particularly severe. 'Po' Stumpy,' said 'Snafu' Shelton, who was on the work party, 'got that goddamn bug so bad he can't hardly stand up. But looka there; he's all man, by God. He don't wanna be 'vacuated.'

'He's a damn good Joe,' commented another Marine.

The company generally – particularly its veterans – 'thought highly of Stumpy and respected him greatly'. He was a decent skipper and they had 'confidence in him'. But malaria had made it impossible for him to stay on his feet. A combination of the 'chilly rain, the emotional stress, and the physical exertion and strain of those days' would have been enough to bring even a fit man to his knees. For Stumpy, malarial chills were the last straw. He was evacuated that day and, as the last of the Peleliu officers, his departure was for Sledge the end of an era. 'He was the last tie to Capt. Andy Haldane. For me, Company K was never the same after that day.'[12]

With Stanley gone, the unpopular XO 'Shadow' Loveday became the new skipper. But for Sledge and many others, the man really in charge was Hank Boyes, the acting first sergeant since William Saunders had gone sick – without telling anyone* – in early May. 'Although we had an exec (a 1st Lt who had become titular skipper),' wrote Sledge, 'he wasn't able to command or lead because he apparently had combat fatigue, but he was brave as hell, and wouldn't turn in.' Boyes picked up the slack. In a joint statement, written years later, Sledge and some other veterans claimed that in the final weeks of the campaign Boyes had 'acted simultaneously as Gunnery Sgt, 1st Sgt, and Company Commander'. They continued:

> His selfless devotion to K-3-5 caused him to refuse twice a battlefield commission. He was a model of strength, determination, heroism, and leadership as the Company suffered over one hundred percent casualties on a shell-torn, muddy battlefield.
>
> He led us through the valley of the shadow of death, never faltering even though survival seemed impossible. We owe our lives to his superb courage and leadership.

With typical modesty, Boyes would later insist that he had been given too much credit and Loveday too little. They had covered well for each other, he told Sledge, and 'never had a disagreement'. The reason a lot of K Company men thought he was the 'boss man' was because Loveday

* In a letter to Sledge of 3 July 1992, Boyes described Saunders as a '*deserter* in action'. He added: 'K-3-5 went with no strength in leaders. I might say that they did the very best that they were capable of doing which was not good enough for the men that almost believed in them.' (AUA, Sledge Papers, RG96/96-038, Box 2, Folder 13.)

'had to spend most of his time on the line, and at the battalion', while he was at the company CP taking care of all the daily needs of the men. Those needs included rations, ammo, water, weapons, radios, telephones, jeeps, stretchers, incoming communications, mail, chaplains, replacements and casualties. It was, therefore, a 'full-time job' and he was 'very proud to have had the opportunity to serve so many fine men'.[13]

48

'Wild-eyed expressions of shock and fear'

Maggot Ridge to Shuri Castle, 25–29 May 1945

At daybreak on 25 May, Gene Sledge and George Sarrett climbed up to the crest of Half Moon Hill to man the mortar OP. Looking directly south, the ridge sloped sharply down from the crest to a big road embankment, 300 yards away, that ran parallel to the company's lines. Providing access to the embankment was a broad culvert, clearly visible to the Marines across the open, well-drained 'amphitheater' of land that was enclosed on its flanks by the southward-extending arms of the Half Moon, and at its base by two shallow ditches, about 50 yards apart. The ditches were closer to the embankment than to the American lines.

K Company had been warned by the 4th Marines, the previous occupants of the position, that the Japanese tended to emerge at night from caves in the reverse slopes of the crescent's arms. It was one of the mortar observer's jobs, therefore, to register the guns on various key points, including the reverse slope of the road embankment and the entrance to the culvert. Sledge had just done this when the Japanese responded with a heavy bombardment of their own. 'It was,' he remembered, 'an awful pounding. Each big shell fluttered and swished down and went off with a flash and an ear-splitting crash. Shrapnel growled through the air, and several men were wounded badly.'

Once the barrage was lifted, and the casualties taken away, an 'uneasy quiet' settled along the line. It was broken by a loud shout: 'There goes one!'

A single Japanese soldier, carrying his bayoneted rifle and wearing a full pack, had emerged from the culvert and was heading for the cover provided by the tip of the southern end of the left crescent. The Marines opened fire with rifles, BARs and machine guns, cutting him down before he could reach safety. They cheered when they saw him fall.

As the day wore on, more Japanese soldiers tried to reach the reverse slope of the left crescent, but none got through. Sledge played his part by calling for mortar strikes on the slope and the road embankment, and could see that some of the Japanese were killed by 60mm rounds. He was, nonetheless, itching to have a shot himself using the M1 rifle and ammunition that were kept in the OP. Eventually the Japanese stopped coming and Sledge was ordered to cease fire. He took the opportunity to visit a friend in the neighbouring machine-gun emplacement. The gunner was called 'Kathy' – after a chorus girl he had had an affair with in California – and had joined K Company after Peleliu. While Sledge was admiring a full-length eight-by-ten picture of the real Kathy in a 'scanty costume', protected by a waterproof plastic map holder, someone yelled: 'There comes another one.'

Sledge was on his way back to the OP when he saw that Sarrett had the phone in his hand and the guns were still 'secured'. So he returned to the machine-gun emplacement, grabbed a spare M1 rifle and started firing as the last of ten Japanese soldiers came out of the culvert. Instead of heading for cover, they formed a skirmish line and 'started trotting silently' across the bare ground towards K Company's position. It was suicide – but they came on anyway. Every Marine along the line was 'yelling and firing'. Within seconds, eight of the enemy soldiers were hit and bowled over. The remaining two turned and headed back for the culvert. Only a few Marines were still firing now, and it looked as if the soldiers might reach safety. Then one of them pitched forward, close to one of the shallow ditches, leaving just a single soldier on his feet. 'Kathy' got his sights zeroed in on him as the order came down the line: 'Cease firing!'

But the machine gun was making so much noise that 'Kathy' failed to hear the order, and kept firing. A burst of eight shots hit the middle of the Japanese soldier's pack and 'tore into him between his shoulders'. One tracer must have hit his vertebrae or other bones because it deflected up into the air. The Japanese fell forward and did not move. 'I got him,' yelled 'Kathy', clapping Sledge on the back, and shaking hands with the assistant gunner, 'I got the bastard.'

More shots rang out, aimed at the soldier hit near the ditch. He had managed to crawl into the shallow depression and was trying to make his way along it. But it was not deep enough to hide him completely, and machine-gun tracers were ricocheting off the ground 'like red arrows' as he struggled along.

Sickened by the bloodlust, one Marine shouted: 'Knock it off, you guys! The poor bastard's hit already and ain't got a snowball's chance in hell.'

'You stupid jerk,' responded another Marine. 'He's a goddamn Nip, ain't he? You gone Asiatic or something?'

The shots continued and eventually found their mark, prompting another outbreak of shouts and cheers. They were stilled by the appearance of the red-faced skipper, 'Shadow' Loveday, who was running along the line, slipping and sliding, and shouting, 'Cease firing, you dumb bastards!'

He stopped at each foxhole to hurl invective at its occupants, punctuating his curses by taking off his forage cap and hurling it into the mud. As he passed the machine-gun emplacement, 'Kathy' was still celebrating his kill. 'Knock it off, you damn fool!' yelled Loveday. Noticing Sledge, he scowled: 'You're supposed to be observing for the mortars; put that goddamn rifle down, you bastard.'

So infuriated was Sledge by his skipper's 'asinine conduct and comment' that he considered braining him with the rifle's stock. Instead he answered rashly: 'The guns are secured, sir. We were all sent out here to kill Nips, weren't we? So what difference does it make what weapon we use when we get the chance?'

Loveday's snarl turned into 'surprise then doubt'. He cocked his head to the side as if considering Sledge's comment. Then, without another word, he turned on his heel and continued along the ridge crest, 'cursing and yelling' as he went. Sledge resolved to keep his mouth 'shut in the future'.

At dusk, he and Sarrett were ordered back to the mortar gun pits. Another Marine would man the OP for the night. Getting down the muddy slope, however, was easier said than done. Japanese corpses, barely covered with mud, lay all around. The ridge was a 'stinking compost pile', and if a Marine slipped down the back slope he was 'apt to reach the bottom vomiting'. Sledge had seen one man slide all the way down, 'only to stand up horror-stricken as he watched in disbelief while fat maggots tumbled out of his muddy dungaree pockets, cartridge belt, legging lacings, and the like'. He and a buddy had then shaken and scraped them away 'with a piece of ammo box or a knife blade'.

They tried not to talk about such things. 'They were too horrible and obscene,' wrote Sledge, 'even for hardened veterans.'[1]

As dawn broke on 27 May 'with a thin fog and a pelting rain', Gene Sledge was woken by the voice of his foxhole buddy, 'Snafu' Shelton. 'Halt, who goes there?' demanded Shelton. 'What's the password?'

Sledge grabbed the tommy gun off his lap while Shelton raised his .45 automatic. About 20 yards away they could see two shadowy figures who appeared to be wearing American helmets. Instead of stopping and identifying themselves, they made straight for the company CP. 'Halt or I'll fire!' yelled Shelton.

The figures kept going, so he squeezed off a couple of shots but missed. Soon after, Shelton and Sledge heard some grenade explosions and a Marine announce proudly that he had killed two Japanese. When they went to check, they saw that the two dead Japanese were wearing Marine helmets but their own uniforms. One had 'no face and little head remaining'; the other was not quite 'as badly mangled'.

Later, having returned to their foxhole, the two mortarmen were asked by Hank Boyes why, if they were keeping watch, they had let the Japanese soldiers go past them. 'Hell,' responded Shelton, 'I saw 'em go right by here, but I reckoned they was headed for the company CP.'

Boyes looked nonplussed. 'What do you mean, Snafu?'

Shelton swelled with indignation. 'You remember when they made me bury that Nip I shot on Peleliu when them two was headed for the CP?'

'Yeah,' said Boyes, 'so what?'

'Well, I told them then if they made me bury 'im, then by God, next time I seen a Nip headin' for the CP I wasn't gonna stop 'im!'

Sledge groaned. 'Oooh, shut up, Snafu.'

He expected Boyes to explode. While always treating the men with 'respect and compassion', the gunnery sergeant would come down hard on anyone who failed in his duty. On this occasion, however, he let Shelton's apparent negligence go. 'You'd better not let that happen again!' he warned, before turning and stalking back to the CP.

The conditions they were expected to fight and die in on Half Moon Hill – a feature known to some of the men as 'Maggot Ridge' – were as bad as any that K Company had experienced since landing on Guadalcanal in August 1942. It was not unusual for replacements to get hit before the regulars even knew their names. 'They were forlorn figures,' wrote Sledge, 'coming up to the meat grinder and going back right out of it like homeless waifs, unknown and faceless to us, like unread books on a shelf. They never "belonged" to the company or made any friends before they got hit.'[2]

Among the few exceptions was Carlisle L. Tiller, Jr, a 26-year-old office worker from Richmond, Virginia. Married with a three-year-old daughter, Tiller had been called up in the summer of 1944 and, 'being a bit gung-ho and probably not too smart either', he failed to mention that he could type and was trained on heavy weapons. He landed on Okinawa with a replacement battalion and was assigned to K Company in early May. 'Although I was a machine gunner,' he recalled, 'the [2nd] Platoon was short of riflemen and my lieutenant said he wanted me in a rifle platoon for the next day's push, and he would put me in the machine gun squad after [that]. Well, he was wounded in that action and I never told his replacement – an M-1 is a lot easier to carry than a machine gun.'

One night on Half Moon Hill, Tiller was hunkering down in his foxhole during a particularly heavy mortar and artillery bombardment when a 'big fellow' from the mortar section appeared, crawling on his belly and looking for the 'guy from Richmond, his home town too'. It was Jim Dandridge, the Pavuvu replacement who had fallen into the septic tank at the start of the campaign. 'He was directed to my foxhole,' remembered Tiller, 'and we spent a good part of the night talking.'

On another occasion on Half Moon, Tiller's foxhole buddy Private Wellman fell asleep when he was supposed to be on lookout. The error was noticed by another Marine who, in his own breach of protocol, had left his foxhole 'for a call of nature'. Tiller wrote: 'He did his thing on our parapet without disturbing either of us. Next morning everyone had a good laugh, claiming a Nip slipped up during the night and crapped right in our faces.'

The turnover of officers and runners in 2nd Platoon was particularly high, and Tiller took over the latter job after no fewer than six of his predecessors were hit. Tiller had just started to dig a foxhole in what appeared to be a well-protected position when Lieutenant 'Pack' Pakradoorni, one of many replacement platoon leaders, 'decided it was better suited for the platoon CP'. So Tiller dug a separate foxhole nearby, and had just moved in when a mortar round struck the 'newly designated CP', severely wounded 'Pack' in the leg and the corpsman in the neck. 'I still have a vivid recollection,' wrote Tiller, 'of seeing "Doc", blood gushing, bandaging his own throat. I think they both pulled through.' Tiller was himself wounded by a grenade fragment – but only superficially – and he was 'back on the line in a few days'.[3]

Such wounds from shrapnel or blast concussion were, remembered Gene Sledge, all too common on Half Moon Hill, and the victims' 'bloody battle dressings' and 'dull expressions of shock and pain' made the 'horror and hopelessness of it all more vivid as we struggled through the chilly driving rain and deep mud to evacuate them'.

Some of the concussion cases 'wore wild-eyed expressions of shock and fear', while others looked like 'idiots or simpletons knocked too witless to be afraid anymore'. But even more distressing for Sledge was the sight of those who had succumbed to combat stress: with symptoms ranging from a 'state of dull detachment' to 'quiet sobbing', and even 'wild screaming and shouting'. Exposure to prolonged artillery fire was usually the cause. There were, in addition, numerous cases of malaria, pneumonia and trench foot. Sledge estimated that his feet were soaking wet for more than two weeks, causing an 'unforgettable sensation of extreme personal filth and painful discomfort'.

Receiving regular supplies of mail – which came up in canvas bags with the ammo and rations – was vital for morale. As well as letters from family and friends, they got the occasional note from former K Company buddies. At first, these surviving veterans spoke of their relief at being out of danger and back home with 'wine, women, and song'. But later they 'often became disturbingly bitter and filled with disillusionment', with some expressing a desire to return to the company. It seemed that nothing could take the place of 'old friendship forged in combat'.

Food usually consisted of a can of cold C rations and, if they were lucky, a cup of hot coffee. But it was hard to warm up anything with their little heat tablets because of the constant rain. They ate to stave off hunger, and for no other reason. Sledge's nostrils were 'so saturated with the odor of decay' that the thought of eating made him gag.

In the mud and constant shelling, field sanitation was impossible. Each man would relieve himself in a grenade canister and ammo carton, and then throw his waste out 'into the already foul mud around his foxhole'. Sleep was 'almost impossible in the mud and cold rain', but Sledge and others would wrap their ponchos around themselves and doze while their foxhole mates kept watch.[4]

K Company's torment on Half Moon Hill finally ended on 28 May when the 3/5 Marines attacked south against little opposition, and advanced several hundred yards.[5] 'Moving through the mud was still difficult,' recalled Gene Sledge, 'but we were all glad to get out of the stinking, half-flooded garbage pit.'

A day later, they attacked again towards Shuri Ridge and made even more rapid progress, as did the 1/5 Marines which captured the ruins of Shuri Castle and the abandoned underground headquarters of the

Japanese Thirty-Second Army before noon. 'We were close to Shuri Castle,' remembered Jim Anderson, the company runner, 'but never actually went into it. I was within half a mile of it. To me it looked like partial ruins on the top of the hill.' The battle for it, remembered Harry Bender of 1st Platoon, was 'nothing' compared to the earlier fight for Half Moon Hill. 'We just blasted it for a while and eventually it fell.'

When Sledge and the other Southerners in K Company learned that the 1/5 Marines had raised the Confederate flag on the castle's shell-torn ramparts – the 'very heart and soul of Japanese resistance' – they 'cheered loudly'. The Yankees among them 'grumbled', while the 'Westerners didn't know what to do'.[6]

This sudden collapse of Japanese resistance was deliberate. As early as 22 May, well aware that the Shuri defences would soon be overwhelmed, Colonel Yahara had managed to persuade his superiors to order a strategic withdrawal to the Kiyan Peninsula in the extreme south of the island. Not only was it protected by natural fortifications facing north, but it also had the advantage of good road communications, many natural caves, and a number of underground bunkers and tunnels.

The plan was for the bulk of the surviving Japanese forces to withdraw by 29 May, leaving only a skeleton force to block any enemy pursuit. But first, tens of thousands of Okinawan civilians would be forced to head south. That these Okinawans would be heading into a trap – penned into the southern tip of the island where many were bound to perish as the Thirty-Second Army fought its desperate last stand – was not something that concerned the Japanese military in the slightest, for it was not only a duty, but also an honour, to die for the emperor.[7]

There were plenty of indications that the Japanese were carrying out a withdrawal. On 26 May, for example, American reconnaissance planes had reported the extensive movement of troops and civilians from the front lines to the south of the island. The columns were targeted by strafing attacks and naval bombardment, and Buckner ordered both his corps to 'initiate without delay strong and unrelenting pressure to ascertain probable intentions and keep him [the Japanese] off balance'. Yet this was precautionary, and on 28 May the Tenth Army intelligence chief, Colonel Louis B. Ely, told a staff meeting that it 'now looks as though the Japanese thinks holding the line around north of Shuri is his best bet'.

A day later, Buckner said at another staff meeting that it appeared as if the Japanese were trying to withdraw to the south, but had made the decision too late. Only during the evening of the 30th, however, after discussions with his opposite numbers in the III Amphibious and XXIV Army Corps, did Ely conclude that the 'enemy was holding the Shuri lines with a shell, and that the bulk of the troops were elsewhere'. There were, he estimated, around 5,000 troops in what he hoped would be the Shuri pocket; but he was unaware of the exact whereabouts of the bulk of the Japanese forces. At another staff meeting on 31 May, Buckner insisted that General Ushijima had 'made his decision to withdraw from Shuri two days late'.[8]

This was not the case. The main movement of the remaining Thirty-Second Army combat units out of the inner Shuri defence zone took place in late May – with some setting off as early as the 26th – and by early June a new defensive line had been established, unbeknown to Buckner, on the Yaeju-Dake and Yuza-Dake hill masses. The retreating Japanese suffered casualties from strafing attacks and naval bombardment, while some of their rearguard troops were eventually overwhelmed, but the movement itself was largely unmolested by ground forces because Buckner and his staff failed to acknowledge it was taking place until it was too late to intervene.

It was only on 31 May, as the 'entire enemy line' appeared to be 'crumbling', that Buckner showed some vigour by ordering Hodge's XXIV Corps to drive southeast to the coast to 'prevent the enemy from retiring' to the Kiyan Peninsula. That day he also urged Geiger's III Amphibious Corps to 'secure the port and airfield of Naha', and complained incessantly when there were delays. But it was too little, too late.[9]

The Japanese were already manning their new defences, and would be joined by the surviving rearguard troops over the next couple of days. Their fighting strength before the retreat was estimated by Colonel Yahara at 40,000 men. Of these, 30,000 got back to the Kiyan Peninsula. They were: 24th Division – 12,000; 62nd Division – 7,000; 44th Mixed Brigade – 3,000; 5th Artillery Group – 3,000; others, including Okinawan Home Guard – 5,000. Yet Yahara knew all too well that mere troop numbers did not tell the whole story. The Thirty-Second Army's main strength – the 24th and 62nd Divisions, and 44th Mixed Brigade – 'had lost 85 per cent of its original complement' and was now made up chiefly of 'untrained, rear-area soldiers and Okinawan defense conscripts'. The Artillery Group had lost half of its guns, while the infantry had only a fifth of its machine guns and one tenth of its heavy weapons. Just as serious was the total lack of cable and radio communications, and the loss of all construction equipment to improve the new defensive positions. The Thirty-Second Army had also lost touch with the Naval Base Force which, after a premature retreat, had returned to the Oroku Peninsula where its 2,000 remaining men would fight their own last stand.

But Yahara was undismayed. 'Our defense policy,' he wrote, 'was to fight to the end with all our strength at the main defense fortifications of the [Yaeju] and [Yuza] hills. If the enemy launched landing operations on the southern beach, we would destroy them there.'[10]

49

The Final Stretch

Tsukazan to Kunishi Ridge, 3–18 June 1945

On 3 June, having made rapid progress against 'light resistance', the 3/5 Marines established positions on high ground near the village of Tsukazan, the original location of the Japanese Thirty-Second Army's headquarters. A day later, it and the rest of the badly depleted 5th Marines was relieved by the 1st Marines and placed in corps reserve.[1]

The situation elsewhere was still very fluid. To the west the 6th Marine Division had crossed the Asato estuary from Naha in amtracs on 3 June and landed on the northern shore of the Oroku Peninsula, which was defended by the remaining 2,000 men of the Naval Base Force. Yet it would take more than ten days for the Marines to subdue the Oroku defenders in their underground positions.

While this operation was underway, it was the task of the 1st Marine Division to keep pace with the two forward divisions of Hodge's XXIV Corps as they advanced south towards the new Japanese stronghold in the Kiyan Peninsula. At first it was unable to do so because its supply system had collapsed in the poor weather, forcing it to rely upon air drops and carrying parties to get food and ammunition to its front-line troops. This inevitably slowed its advance and, by the end of 3 June, the gap between it and the neighbouring 96th Division was 3,000 yards, thus exposing the latter's 383rd Infantry to harassing fire from its right flank. To fill the void, Hodge sent forward the 77th Division's 305th Infantry. But the 1st Marine Division – urged on by Buckner – also made ground on 4 June when the 2/5 Marines attacked southwest and captured Hill 57 and the high ground south of Gisuchi. This reduced the gap to the XXIV Corps to 1,000 yards.

Further east, the 7th Division had reached the southeast coast near Hyakana at the base of the Chinen Peninsula, the deepest incursion by the Tenth Army to date, an achievement described by Buckner as 'magnificent'. He was particularly pleased to receive from the 7th's commander, Major General Arnold, 'a bottle of seawater and beach sand and a picture of two soldiers bathing their feet on the southern shore'.[2]

For the next few days, as Buckner's two corps continued their drive to the south, the 5th Marines had the task of mopping up enemy resistance in the western sector. But there was little contact with enemy soldiers and the men of K Company were able to rest up and take advantage of the improved weather by drying out their clothes. When Gene Sledge took off his soaked and muddy boondockers for the first time in a fortnight, he discovered 'slimy, stinking socks' and bits of dead flesh. Unwilling to wash the putrid socks – a thick woollen army issue that he had traded for a candy bar in April – he 'spaded dirt over them as though covering up a foul corpse'.

They were supplied by air with food, water and ammo, and were able to enjoy 10-in-1 rations* as a welcome change from C and K rations. Sledge and his foxhole buddy George Sarrett were even sent on a routine mission to the west coast with a message about supplies. Having delivered the message, they were returning through the outskirts of a shattered and seemingly deserted town when they were targeted by a Japanese machine gun. Fortunately, the bullets missed – the gunner had given them too much lead – and they were able to take cover until a patrol from K Company arrived and killed the Japanese. 'You guys OK?' asked

* Introduced in 1943, and also known as a B ration, the 10-in-1 was a field parcel containing various canned meats and stews, a butter-substitute spread, powdered coffee, pudding, jam, evaporated milk, vegetables, biscuits, cereal, beverages, candy, salt and sugar. Also included were a tin opener, toilet paper, towels and water-purification tablets.

a grinning Marine. 'The gunny figured you'd run into trouble when you didn't come back and sent us out to look for you.'[3]

It was also during this period of rest that R. V. Burgin, recovered from his neck wound and 'eager to get back to K Company', got a clean bill of health from his doctor. 'It had been,' he wrote later, 'twenty days since I'd been wounded. I asked around if anybody knew the location of Third Battalion's K Company, and the next day I hitched rides on Army trucks headed south towards the front.' In his pocket he carried the shell fragment that had almost taken his life. He found the company several miles further south than he had left it. It had lost thirty-six men in the fighting around Shuri Castle and was in a 'bad way'. Even with fifty replacements – one officer and forty-nine men – it could only muster about one hundred men and three or four officers, about 40 per cent of its original complement. The scuttlebutt was that the 5th Marines 'would not be sent into combat again'.[4]

For the final phase of the battle, Lieutenant General Buckner had shifted the XXIV Corps' axis of advance to the southwest, thus giving the 96th Division the responsibility for tackling the two most formidable Japanese positions on the Yaeju-Dake and Yuza-Dake hill masses. They were, noted the official history, 'physical barriers which, together with Hill 95 on the east coast, formed a great wall across the entire XXIV Corps sector from Gusichan to Yuza'. The highest point of the entire four-mile-long cliff was Yaeju-Dake, which rose 295ft from the valley floor. Yuza-Dake 'stood at the west end of the line and then tapered off into Kunishi Ridge, which extended across the III Amphibious Corps' sector'.[5]

Buckner's decision was a curious one: it left the bulk of the heavy fighting to army troops, while the Marines were given what appeared to be the less onerous tasks of capturing Oroku (6th Division) and assaulting the Kunishi Ridge (1st Division). In fact, neither would be straightforward. By 10 June, the two forward regiments of the 1st Marine Division – the 1st on the left and the 7th on the right – were barely 1,500 yards north of Kunishi Ridge and subject to observation and harassing fire from the Yuza-Dake peak to the east. That day, the 1/1 Marines lost 125 men killed and wounded in an assault on a small hill west of Yuza town. The 7th Marines had far fewer casualties as it reached high ground near the village of Tera on the 10th, while the 2/1 Marines took Hill 69, west of Ozato, a day later.

The problem, now, was the nature of the ground. Only 1,000 yards separated the 1st Marine Division's front line between Tera and Ozato from Kunishi Ridge. But the intervening terrain was generally low and flat, offering an attacker little cover as he advanced. The 7th Marines were the first to move forward on 11 June, but heavy Japanese machine-gun fire promptly drove back the two assault battalions. That night they tried again, with C and F Companies leading off. Both reached the western edge of Kunishi Ridge with little difficulty. But as dawn broke on 12 June, their foothold was targeted by a storm of mortar, artillery and machine-gun fire. The regimental commander tried to reinforce the men with two tanks, but one was knocked out and the other driven back. When two support companies tried to cross the open ground under the cover of smoke rounds, they were also forced to retire with heavy casualties.[6]

Later more tanks were able to supply the men on the ridge with plasma, water and ammunition. They also took reinforcements – six to a tank, fifty-four in total – and brought back twenty-two casualties. That night, two more companies moved up in support. At daylight on the 13th – by which time there were elements of six companies occupying the lower end of Kunishi Ridge – the battle resumed. 'The Marines ahead of us were pinned down,' wrote one officer, 'and we got many of the bullets fired at them. There were a number of casualties. About noon, tanks came up and did some good work, taking some of the pressure off. We expanded our toehold a little, then a little more. By this time, all of us were engaged.'

Most of the 7th Marines' incoming fire was from the front and left flank. To protect its flank, therefore, the 2/1 Marines was ordered to seize the higher, eastern edge of Kunishi Ridge. Two under-strength companies (E and G) attacked that night, 13/14 June, and, despite a number of casualties, had four platoons on the ridge shortly after daybreak. Yet there was a sizeable gap to the 7th Marines' lodgement, away to the right, leaving the Japanese defenders 'in front and on both flanks in protected positions where they could shoot at almost anyone' in the 2/1 Marines' perimeter. Casualties 'mounted alarmingly' and were 'carried down in ponchos like sacks of meal'. Lieutenant Bruce Watkins, commanding E Company, called for tanks and tried to evacuate the wounded on their hulls. But they were picked off by snipers 'on the long grass to our flanks and rear', so he loaded them instead through the escape hatch. 'This was a rough way to handle badly wounded men,' noted Watkins, 'as the tank had to straddle them and then they were pulled through a small hole about eighteen inches square. However it was the only way.'

Shortly before dark, Watkins radioed his battalion commander and asked for more troops to extend the line. 'Without a longer front,' said Watkins, 'we'll continue to receive fire from both flanks and rear.'

'Negative,' replied his boss, 'there's no help available. You're just going to have to hang on.'

Soon after there was an air drop of ammunition and water – but most of it fell on the Japanese side of the ridge. Watkins recalled: 'I was a little bitter at this point. Our situation had all the elements of Custer's last stand.' He tried to encourage his platoon commanders by saying reinforcements might arrive the following day. In fact, F Company did come forward in the night, but Watkins chose to 'spread them out as a secondary line in the flat behind us'. Then, if the Japanese broke through, they could fall back on this line.

By dawn, Japanese pressure had contracted Watkins's defensive position into a 'semi-circle bowed towards the front with a diameter of about 150 feet'. Meanwhile the Japanese had moved into better firing positions, and many of Watkins's men were 'shot in their foxholes half asleep before they could find better cover'. But still the remains of three platoons 'hung doggedly to their position, unable to move either forward or back'. Salvation came in the form of a radio message from the battalion commander that they would be relieved by the 2/5 Marines that night.[7]

Earlier that day, the 3/5 Marines had also moved back into the combat zone when it replaced the 1/1 Marines on Hill 69. I and L Companies were forward on the hill, with K Company guarding a bailey bridge over a river a short way to the rear. 'It was,' remembered Gene Sledge, 'a beautiful place, cool and peaceful, so out of context with the screaming hell close above it.'[8]

As night fell, however, there was intense activity. 'Lots of flares,' noted Lieutenant Wilson Brockinton, the 24-year-old commander of 1st Platoon, 'lots of small arms firing, lots of killing, more so of civilians than of Jap infiltrators, and very little sleep.'* Born in Charleston, South Carolina, Brockinton had joined K Company as a replacement officer a week or two earlier. During a lull in company duties on 16 June, he and a few others clambered up a nearby hill to view the battlefield. From there they had a 'clear view of Hill 69 and Kunishi Ridge, where the [2/5] Marines, presumably supported by tanks and rocket launching vehicles, could be seen battling their way forward onto that ridge. Little did we know that in a few short hours we would be on that same "killing ground".'[9]

At noon on the 17th, by which time G and E Companies of the 2/5 Marines were facing fierce Japanese resistance in their attempts to capture the remaining 800 yards of the eastern end of Kunishi Ridge, K Company was ordered to move up in support. It began the move in daylight, but completed the final approach to the ridge under the cover of darkness. Moving at night was 'something the old salts of Gloucester and Peleliu didn't like at all', noted Gene Sledge. 'We were stubborn in our belief that nobody but the Japanese, or damned fools moved around at night. The new replacements who had come into the company a few days before seemed so pitifully confused they didn't know the difference. But moving up under the cover of darkness was the only sane way to approach Kunishi Ridge.'

* A total of twenty-eight civilians were picked up by the company in the vicinity of the bridge on 16 June, to add to the sixty-six who had been found by 'Duke' Ellington's 81mm mortar platoon in a cave a day earlier. (3/5 Marines Special Action Report, 22 April to 23 June 1945.)

They 'moved slowly and cautiously across dry rice paddies and cane fields', while up ahead artillery and mortar rounds were exploding on and around the ridge. They could hear, too, the 'familiar popping of rifles, rattle of machine guns, and banging of grenades'. For Sledge, the knowledge that this was 'probably the last big fight before the Japanese were wiped out and the campaign ended' made it even harder to contemplate. As he plodded along, his heart pounding and his throat 'almost too tight to swallow', he felt a sense of panic rising. 'Having made it that far in the war,' he wrote, 'I knew my luck would run out. I began to sweat and pray that when I got hit it wouldn't result in death or maiming. I wanted to turn and run away.'[10]

K Company was ordered by the commander of the 2/5 Marines to dig in about 250 yards north of the base of the ridge, and to make ready for an attack early the next morning 'with all three rifle platoons abreast'. It led, wrote Lieutenant Brockington, to the 'inescapable conclusion that a frontal attack on this well manned, well entrenched enemy stronghold, would be disastrous in its results. Why not, instead, if friendly troops were already ensconced on the top of the ridge, attack along its crest?'[11]

Sledge and the mortarmen were positioned to keep watch for Japanese trying to infiltrate from the left rear. 'We didn't set up our weapons,' he recalled, 'the fighting was so close-in with the enemy on the reverse slope and in the ridge that we couldn't fire high-explosives.' American 105mm artillery, meanwhile, was firing across the ridge and into the town of Kunishi to prevent the enemy from sending up reinforcements. But a couple of rounds fell short and exploded in the company's line. 'Corpsman!' yelled a Marine.

'Goddammit,' yelled a platoon leader into his walkie-talkie.

'What's the word on those short rounds?' asked someone at the company CP.

'Says they'll check it out.'[12]

In fact, it was thanks to the company runner Jim Anderson that the error was corrected. Asked by 'Shadow' Loveday if he could get back to the artillery and tell them to stop, he replied: 'I'll give it a whirl.'

Crawling part of the way on his stomach, he was challenged a few times but not shot. He eventually reached the guns and said to a lieutenant: 'Your artillery is falling on our front lines.'

'Oh, you're crazy,' replied the officer.

'No, sir,' said Anderson. 'With all due respect, you're going to kill somebody if you continue firing.'

After checking the coordinates, the artillery officer realized his error and the short rounds stopped.*[13] But it was already too late for three 1st Platoon men: Private Harry Bender, his BAR-man Bill Tyler, and a replacement sergeant, 'a banana Marine who'd been in Panama but hadn't seen any combat'. As the ground was too hard to dig foxholes, they had constructed a shelter by stacking pieces of coral around the side of a pillbox. Bender was on watch, as the other two slept. 'Sure enough,' he remembered, 'one shell came right at us, exploded above us, and splattered down on us. The sergeant was killed outright. Tyler was alive, but he was hit in his skull. I was sitting up and took shrapnel in the upper front part of my legs. My back. My arm. It blew my helmet off, too, and I was combing tiny pieces of shrapnel out of my hair for a while, too. Hot metal.' Evacuated back to a field hospital, both of the wounded men survived.[14]

The night-time drama, however, was far from over. 'The Japanese,' recalled Gene Sledge, 'were throwing grenades all along the line, and there was some rifle and machine-gun fire. On the right we began to hear American grenades exploding well within our lines.' One Marine said: 'Hey, you guys; Nips musta gotten hold of a box of our grenades. Listen to that, wouldja?'

'Yeah,' replied his buddy, 'them bastards'll use anything they can get their hands on.'

Later they discovered the truth: that some of the new men had been 'removing each grenade canister from a box of grenades, pulling the sealing tape from the canister, and then throwing the unopened canister

* On Lieutenant Loveday's recommendation, Anderson was later awarded the Bronze Star for his night-time excursion.

at the enemy'. The Japanese had simply opened the canister, taken out the grenade, pulled its pin and thrown it back. It was, noted Sledge, 'just one of many examples of the poor state of combat readiness of the latest group of new replacements'.[15]

The men of the three rifle platoons were roused at 3.30 a.m. to eat breakfast and prepare for the attack. Lieutenant Brockinton remembered,

> There we were at 0430, strung out in a long line abreast, our platoon in the centre, crossing that miserable canefield, which separated the K-3-5 CP and the base of that awful ridge, all hands anticipating heavy mortar/small arms weaponry, at the least, from the defenders. However, none came – and our artillery was still loosing a galling fire on the forward slope of the ridge and its crest. Could it be that the enemy had abandoned the Kunishi Ridge defense line? Or had we caught the enemy off guard with an early morning attack? As it developed, neither was true.

Having reached the far side of the canefield, the platoons began scrambling up the forward slope. As 1st Platoon neared the crest, it was fired on by Japanese defenders who had appeared from caves on the reverse slope. More bullets were coming in enfilade fire from the right. Lieutenant Brockinton dived for cover, while two men to his left 'darted forward to a position amongst some jagged coral rocks'. Moments later, both of these men – a BAR-man and a corporal – 'were slumped forward over their weapons, obviously dead'. Corporal Arthur, a recent replacement on his second overseas tour, was mortally wounded soon after, 'struck between the eyes, and dying in the arms of the platoon leader'.

It seemed to Brockinton 'as if the enemy had gained a definite edge in building up its small arms fire, pinning down all of the K Company men in sight'. Then, suddenly, 'there appeared on the scene' another replacement in 1st Platoon, Corporal Gonzales from Texas, who had previously served with the 2nd Division on Tarawa and at Saipan. Wielding a tommy gun, he was 'knocking out' defenders left and right, as was Corporal Lindner from New Jersey, a member of the neighbouring platoon, easily recognisable by his 'bushy, reddish hair and beard'. It was 'because of the performance of these two corporals', wrote Brockinton, 'that a base of fire was forthcoming from those around them, the ones who, to that time, had not been hit'. It was enough to drive the enemy off the heights.

The company had already suffered a number of casualties, and sporadic small arms fire and the tossing of grenades would be exchanged for much of the morning. But, for the most part, the mission to lodge K Company riflemen on the crest of the ridge 'had been accomplished'. Orders were passed to 'dig in', anticipating a counter-attack. But none came, and the 'remainder of the morning and most of the afternoon were spent in fighting the heat, the flies and an awful thirst, it being difficult to replenish our water supply'.[16]

Not needed for the attack, the mortar section helped to recover the casualties. They were brought down to the base of the ridge, 'to a point where tanks could back in out of the view of snipers on the ridge crest'. Among the injured was stretcher-bearer 'Tex' Cummings, one of the two ammo carriers that Burgin had selected on Pavuvu, who had been shot in the back as he moved up the ridge. He and the other badly wounded were tied onto stretchers, and the stretchers fastened to the rear deck of the tanks. The walking wounded went inside. 'Then the tanks took off in a cloud of dust,' remembered Gene Sledge, 'along a coral road to the aid station. As many men as possible fired along the ridge to pin down the snipers, so they couldn't shoot the wounded on the tanks.'

Sledge went up with one stretcher team to evacuate a Marine who was lying exposed above a sheer coral ledge. As the others hung back, he scrambled up onto the ledge and noticed the entrance to a small cave. Expecting to 'see a muzzle flash spurt forth', he felt strangely at peace with himself and not 'particularly afraid'. Luckily, there was 'no sound or sight of the sniper', and they were able to get the casualty down safely.

Having evacuated another casualty, Sledge was passing the company CP among some rocks at the foot of the ridge when he overheard the skipper, 'Shadow' Loveday, talking quietly to Hank Boyes. Loveday, remembered Sledge, 'said his nerves were almost shattered by the constant strain, and he didn't think he could carry on much longer'. The veteran Boyes was 'trying to calm the officer', who was sitting on his helmet, 'almost sobbing' and 'frantically running his hands through his hair'.

At first, Sledge felt compassion. He had been in the 'same forlorn frame of mind more than once, when horror piled on horror seemed too much to bear', and without Loveday's extra responsibility as skipper. But his empathy quickly turned to anger when he heard Loveday blurt out in desperation: 'What's the matter with those guys up on the ridge? Why the hell don't they move out faster and get this thing over with?'

Sledge snapped. Forgetting his rank, he strode into the CP and said to Loveday: 'I'll tell you what's the matter with those guys on the ridge. They're gettin' shot right and left, and they can't move any faster!'

Loveday looked up with a 'dazed expression'. Boyes turned round, expecting to see the battalion commander at the very least. Recognizing Sledge, he looked surprised and then angry. Before anyone could speak, the Alabaman backed away and left, well aware that he had overstepped the mark. He never regretted his outburst, though he did accept that Loveday was not himself that day. 'I think,' he wrote later, 'that Shadow had probably cracked due to the severe, prolonged stress and strain on Okinawa, but he was too brave to turn in. I think his periodic irrational outbursts, loss of temper and verbal abuse of the Marines under his command were simply manifestations of the fact that he was, in truth, a casualty.'[17]

In the afternoon, Sledge and some other mortarmen were resting among rocks near the crest of the ridge, having just passed up water and ammo to the riflemen above, when a Peleliu veteran suddenly began 'babbling incoherently', grabbed his rifle and shouted: 'Those slant-eyed bastards, they've killed enougha my buddies. I'm goin' after 'em.' He jumped up and headed for the crest that, even then, was covered by Japanese machine-gun fire, the bullets 'striking rocks' and whining off into the air.

'Stop!' yelled Sledge, grabbing for his trouser leg and missing.

A sergeant had more luck, tripping the man and bringing him down. He 'sprawled on his back, sobbing like a baby'. There was a dark stain on the front of his trousers where he had pissed himself. 'Take it easy, Cobber,' said the sergeant, trying to calm him but making sure he could not get up. 'We'll get you outa here.' Eventually a corpsman arrived and led the 'sobbing, trembling man out of the meat grinder to an aid station'.

'He's a damn good Marine, Sledgehammer,' insisted the sergeant. 'I'll lower the boom on anybody says he ain't. But he's just had all he can take. That's it.'[18]

Finally, at around 6:00 p.m., the remnants of the rifle platoons on the ridge were relieved by a unit of the 2/5 Marines. 'Down the forward slope we went,' remembered Lieutenant Brockinton, 'and back across part of the canefield, until we reached the company CP area, a completely exhausted group of riflemen, overcome by heat, thirst, dehydration, fatigue and pure exhaustion.'[19]

K Company's total casualties for the twenty-two hours it had spent on or near the ridge were a crippling fifty men and one officer: five killed, twenty-three wounded and the rest suffering from battle fatigue, heat exhaustion and blast concussion. This brought its total strength down to fewer than sixty men, around a quarter of its original complement of 235.[20]

'Every casualty now,' remembered R. V. Burgin, 'was a painful reminder that even though the Japs were down to their last caves, and the battle for Okinawa was almost over, any one of us could still go home wounded or crippled for life, or in a coffin. We were all thinking the same thing: If Okinawa was this bad, how bloody was it going to be fighting the Japs on their home ground? We knew we would soon have that to face.'[21]

50

End Game

Kiyan Peninsula, 18–30 June 1945

K Company's assault on Kunishi Ridge on 18 June was its last meaningful action of the campaign. It was also the day that effective Japanese resistance on Okinawa came to an end. Colonel Yahara realised as much when he received word in the Thirty-Second Army headquarters cave at Mabuni Hill, on the south coast, that both flanks of the defensive line had 'collapsed simultaneously': on the right, tanks and troops of the US 7th Infantry Division overran the 44th Mixed Brigade's command post on Hill 89 and then captured 'a low-lying hill some 1,500 metres east of Mabuni'; and on the left, 'enemy Marines' broke through the lines of the 89th Regiment and appeared at Makabe village, northeast of the 24th Division command post. With American tanks having penetrated 'deep' into the Japanese defence zone, not far from Komesu village, just two miles west of the headquarters cave, Yahara knew the collapse of the 'entire army was imminent'.[1]

So, too, did Lieutenant General Ushijima. He dictated a final order:

> My Beloved Soldiers,
>
> You have fought courageously for nearly three months. You have discharged your duty. Your bravery and loyalty brighten the future.
>
> The battlefield is now in such chaos that all communications have ceased. It is impossible for me to command you. Every

> man in these fortifications will follow his superior's order and fight to the end for the sake of the motherland.
>
> This is my final order.
>
> Farewell.

Major General Chō, after reading the draft, added in red ink: 'Do not suffer the shame of being taken prisoner. You will live for eternity.'

Once Ushijima had added his signature, the final order was ready to be sent out. For Yahara, whose official duties had now ended, there was a feeling of 'sudden bliss at being free of all worldly burdens'.[2]

Even as the Japanese commanders were acknowledging defeat, an event took place on the battlefield to the north that would give them a brief cause for celebration. At 8:30 a.m. on 18 June, Lieutenant General Buckner had left Tenth Army headquarters with an aide to see how 'his boys' were doing. He decided to visit the Marines as they had made the biggest leap forward on the 17th, whereas the 'doggies' of XXIV Corps had made 'no progress'.

The regiment he chose to visit was the newly arrived 8th Marines, part of the 2nd Marine Division, whose CP was on the reverse slope of Mezado Ridge, southeast of Kunishi. He arrived at noon and was escorted up to the regimental OP on the forward slope of Hill 52, which had a 'commanding view of the valley between Mezado Ridge and Ibaru Ridge'. Yet it was also 'exposed to Japanese field glasses scanning north from the northerly crest of Ibaru Ridge' and there was 'scant natural cover' for camouflage.

The OP was composed of two coral boulders with a gap of about a foot separating them. Buckner stood behind the gap, and watched the 'whole panoply of war' as riflemen from the 2/8 Marines moved up the valley towards the Ibaru Ridge. Colonel Clarence R. 'Bull' Wallace, the 8th's commander, and one or two others were more securely positioned behind the boulders.[3]

After Buckner had been watching events for some time, Wallace suggested that it might be prudent to replace his distinctive general's helmet with one a little less conspicuous. Buckner refused. 'I haven't come up to the front,' he said softly, 'to hide.' He added: 'I want the Japanese to realize that further resistance is futile, and perhaps such a realisation will persuade them to encourage the Okinawan civilians who are with them to surrender.'

Not long after this comment, Wallace's radio operator told his boss that he had just intercepted a message from Captain Pickett, the 1/8 Marines' operations officer, who, when looking back at the OP, could see the three stars on Buckner's helmet 'plainly visible'. Overhearing this exchange, a smiling Buckner took off the offending item and placed it on the coral rock beside him. He then replaced it with a helmet with no badge of rank provided by a member of Wallace's staff. 'Those people down there have enough to worry about,' Buckner commented good-humouredly, 'without me adding to their problems.'

A few minutes later – by which time it was 1:15 p.m., and Buckner had been enjoying the spectacle from the OP for about an hour – a Japanese round of unknown calibre (possibly from a 47mm anti-tank gun) exploded without warning at the foot of the gap between the two boulders, hurling shrapnel and pieces of coral rock into Buckner's right breast.* Wallace and one of his officers were standing on either side of Buckner, but neither was wounded. The only other minor casualty was Buckner's aide, who had suffered a perforated ear drum.

Buckner was carried in a poncho back over the crest to the relative safety of the reverse slope, where he was put on a field stretcher and given plasma by a doctor. But it was obvious to those present that he 'was beyond medical help'. As his life ebbed out of him, Buckner tried to stand but was unable to do so. Close to death, he reached out his right hand as if he wanted to be helped to his feet. For a moment, no one responded. Then PFC Harry Sarkisian, 'a very intellectual, courageous Marine', grasped the outstretched hand with both of his and held it tightly until Buckner died.[4]

* 'It was the opinion of most of the observers present,' recorded Captain Haley of the 8th Marines, 'that the Japanese, with their excellent sighting instruments, had picked up the three stars on the helmet and dropped an artillery shell or mortar shell in the Observation Post.' (Haley, 'The General Dies at Noon', p. 31.)

He was buried 'with the simple rites of a soldier fallen in battle' in the 7th Division cemetery, near the Hagushi Beaches, at 9:00 a.m. the following day. Promoted posthumously to the rank of general, Buckner was the most senior American soldier to be killed in action during World War II. His death sparked a race to replace him that was won, temporarily, by Major General Geiger, who became the first Marine to command an army. But this accolade was short-lived because, having consulted Doug MacArthur, General Marshall selected 62-year-old General Joseph W. 'Vinegar Joe' Stilwell as Buckner's permanent replacement.[5]

On 21 June, having learned of Buckner's death from American radio broadcasts, the Imperial GHQ in Tokyo congratulated Ushijima and his Thirty-Second Army for killing 'the enemy commander' and delivering 'deadly blows against his eight divisions of troops'. It was, wrote Yahara, 'the greatest news of the entire operation. We had managed to kill the enemy leader before our own commanding general committed ceremonial suicide. It seemed as if our forces had actually won a victory.'

Chō, like Yahara, was elated. But not Ushijima. 'He looked grim,' remembered Yahara, 'as if mourning Buckner's death. Ushijima never spoke ill of others. I had always felt he was a great man, and now I admired him more than ever.'[6]

In the early hours of the following morning, 22 June, Ushijima and Chō committed ritual suicide – the so-called 'death with honour' that was expected of defeated Japanese commanders – by plunging short swords into their bellies before they were beheaded. 'What a splendid last moment!' recalled Yahara, with no hint of irony. 'It marked the glorious end to our three months of hard battle, our proud 32nd Army, and the lives of our generals.'[7]

After its relief on Kunishi Ridge, K Company made a 'series of rapid moves south', following in the footsteps of the 8th Marines, and 'stopping only to fight groups of die-hard Japanese in caves, pill-boxes, and ruined villages'. On 20 June, for example, assisted by tanks, it cleaned out caves in Komesu Ridge, killing an estimated 175 Japanese. 'We were fortunate,' noted Gene Sledge, 'in not suffering many casualties in the company. The Japanese were beaten, and the hope uppermost in every veteran's mind was that his luck would hold out a little longer, until the end of the battle.'

They used 'loudspeakers, captured Japanese soldiers, and Okinawan civilians to persuade the remaining enemy to surrender'. When one group refused to leave a burial vault, 'Mac' MacKenzie jumped in front of the door and shouted in Japanese, 'Do not be afraid. Come out. I will not harm you.' Then he fired a complete twenty-round magazine from his tommy gun through the door, before moving on. Wearily familiar with MacKenzie's antics, Sledge and the other veteran mortarmen shook their heads and followed on. Soon after, half a dozen Japanese soldiers came out of the vault with guns blazing, and were shot down by Marines from another unit.

Later that day, the 3/5 Marines became one of the first American units to reach the end of the island. 'It was,' remembered Sledge, 'a beautiful sight even though there were snipers around. We stood on a high hill overlooking the sea. Below to our left we saw army infantry advancing towards us, flushing out and shooting down enemy soldiers singly and in small groups. Army 81mm mortar fire kept pace ahead of the troops, and some of our weapons joined in coordination.'

They got a 'bit edgy' as the mortar fire came closer. Eventually a battalion officer ordered a radioman to tell the army officer in charge 'that if they didn't cease fire immediately', the Marines would return fire. The army mortars 'stopped shooting'.[8] It was clear to R. V. Burgin that the fighting was almost over. 'Whatever Japs were left by now,' he wrote, 'were dug in behind us. It was only a matter of rooting them out of their hiding places. And they still prowled by night. Some of them got through our lines and we could see them wading out in the surf, where they made excellent targets.'[9]

Towards the end of 21 June, K Company was told that the island had been declared secure. 'We each received two fresh oranges with the compliments of Admiral Nimitz,' remembered Gene Sledge. 'So I ate mine, smoked my pipe, and looked out over the beautiful blue sea.

The sun danced on the water. After eighty-two days and nights, I couldn't believe Okinawa had finally ended. I was tempted to relax and think that we would board ship immediately for rest and rehabilitation in Hawaii.'[10]

Burgin thought the same. Replying to a packet of letters from Florence in Australia, he assured her that he was out of hospital and feeling fine. He added: 'I wish that we would have got married when I was there, and now you would be going to the States this month . . . Why didn't you drag me to the altar when I was there and marry me? Darling, I sure hope it won't be long until you can come to me & the war is over so we can cuddle in a little home of our own.'[11]

He was pretty certain that, having completed three campaigns and more than two years overseas, he would soon be going home. But before that, like the rest of K Company, he had one last task on Okinawa. 'Get your gear on,' instructed an officer, 'check your weapons. We're moving back north in a skirmish line. You people will mop up the area for any Nips still holding out. You will bury all enemy dead. You will salvage U.S. and enemy equipment. All brass above .50 in size will be collected and placed in neat piles. Stand by to move out.'

At 1:05 p.m. that day, 22 June, temporary Tenth Army commander Major General Geiger announced that all organised resistance on Okinawa had ceased. While representatives of various army and Marine units stood in formation, the band of the 2nd Marine Aircraft Wing played 'The Star Spangled Banner', and the colour guard of MPs raised the American flag over Okinawa. As the flag neared the top of the pole, a sudden breeze swept it out 'full against a blue and quiet sky'.[12]

There was, in truth, still a fair amount of mopping-up to do before the island was properly secure. One intelligence summary, dated 23 June, estimated that 4,000 Japanese soldiers were still at large on the island. Many were hiding in 'the hills and crags along the coast south and northeast of Mabuni', while others were 'attempting to escape to the northern part of the island' where food was reported to be 'plentiful' and 'better hiding places' were 'available'. According to debriefed prisoners of war, Japanese soldiers had been 'ordered to dress as civilians, and attempt to move individually or in groups of 2–5, to the vicinity of Nago for [the] purpose of conducting guerrilla warfare'.[13]

The mopping-up operation began on 23 June, the day General Stilwell landed on the island to take command, with the two corps assigned respective zones of action and three phase lines they needed to reach. The first sweep to the south produced the greatest results, with cave positions 'systematically sealed up by flame throwers and demolitions', and 'several bloody skirmishes' as well-armed groups tried to break through the American lines and head north. Extensive patrolling found a number of soldiers hiding in cane fields and rice paddies. When the American soldiers turned north, however, fewer and fewer of the enemy were discovered and the third and final phase line between Naha and Yonabaru was reached with 'comparative ease' on the 30th, three days ahead of schedule. The mop-up had killed an estimated 8,975 Japanese soldiers and captured a further 2,902, while 906 non-military labour personnel were also taken. American casualties were 783.[14]

Gene Sledge and the other K Company veterans could accept the risk of dying in combat while the battle raged. The possibility of being shot 'by some fanatical, bypassed Japanese holed up in a cave', on the other hand, was much harder to contemplate. So too was the order to bury enemy dead and salvage brass and equipment. 'By lawd,' said one Marine, 'why the hell we gotta bury them stinkin' bastards after we killed 'em? Let them goddamn rear-echelon people get a whiff of 'em. They didn't hafta fight 'em.'

Angry and frustrated, they 'complained and griped bitterly'. It was, thought Sledge, 'the ultimate indignity to men who had fought so hard and so long and had won'. For the first time, he saw several of his veteran comrades 'flatly refuse to obey an order' and, but for the intervention of cooler heads, they would have been 'severely punished'.[15]

Even recent additions to the company found the burial duty demeaning. John B. Dillon, an 18-year-old private from rural west Montana, wrote:

> I'm sure there is nothing in the world that stinks as bad as a human body that has decomposed for a few days in the hot sun. Those that had been roasted by the flame throwers were especially repulsive. What do you do with a body that is hanging in the crotch of a tree by one leg and covered with maggots? I can tell you one thing. Digging 'holes' for a corpse quickly degenerated into a few shovels of dirt thrown in the direction of the body. The stench permeated our clothes, our few personal belongings, everything we had. I couldn't eat a bite of food for several days.[16]

Gene Sledge took time out during the 'mopping-up' phase to give his folks the good news. 'Well,' he began, 'at last you can stop worrying. Things are quiet now & it is a relief after three months of it. I surely am glad it's over for it really was a grind. All that I'm waiting for now is to get to camp. By the time you get this we will probably be there. I can't help but keep thinking of all those packages that will be waiting there for me. We really have a lot to be thankful for & God has certainly watched over me all the time.'[17]

On hearing the battle for Okinawa was over, Winston Churchill sent President Truman a congratulatory cable. 'The strength of will-power, devotion, and technical resources applied by the United States to this task,' wrote the British prime minister, 'joined with the death-struggle of the enemy, of whom 90,000 are reported to be killed, places this battle among the most intense and famous in military history.'[18] Hanson W. Baldwin, the Pulitzer Prize-winning military editor of *The New York Times*, agreed:

> Never before had there been, probably never again will there be, such a vicious sprawling struggle of planes against planes, of ships against planes. Never before, in so short a space, had the Navy lost so many ships; never before in land fighting had so much American blood been shed in so short a time in so small an area: probably never before in any three months of the war had the enemy suffered

> so hugely, and the final toll of American casualties was the highest experienced in any campaign against the Japanese. There have been larger land battles, more protracted air campaigns, but Okinawa was the largest combined operation in a 'no quarter' struggle fought on, under and over the sea and land.[19]

Baldwin was correct. Okinawa was by far the bloodiest battle of the Pacific War, and one of the costliest in America's history. The Americans lost thirty-six ships (and a further 368 damaged), 763 planes and just under 50,000 men,* a quarter of whom were killed and missing, and the rest wounded. There were also more than 26,000 non-battle casualties, many suffering from combat fatigue or what today we would diagnose as PTSD.[20] The 1st Marine Division's share of casualties, alone, was 7,665 men killed, wounded and missing.[21]

The scale of Japanese and Okinawan losses was even more horrific. When the fighting ended on 30 June, 100,000 soldiers and home guard (including 15,000 Okinawans), and 125,000 Okinawan civilians – totalling a third of the pre-war island population – had lost their lives. A further 7,400 soldiers were taken prisoner, many of them impressed Okinawans. Local survivor Masahide Ōta, who fought against the Americans and later became governor of the island, put the blame for so many civilian deaths squarely on the Japanese military:

> The Japanese Imperial Army's objective was not to protect the local Okinawans, but instead to engage the Americans in combat for the longest time possible in order to earn time for further defensive preparations on the home islands. Rather than putting efforts into evacuation or the creation of a safe zone for civilians, the Okinawan

* American battle casualties were 49,531: 12,520 killed and missing, and 36,631 wounded. Army losses were 4,582 killed, 93 missing and 18,099 wounded; Marine losses were 2,938 killed and missing, and 13,708 wounded; and navy losses were 4,907 killed and 4,824 missing. Non-battle casualties were 26,211: 15,613 for the army and 10,598 for the Marines.

> people were used as a source of labor to build shelters, tunnels and other emplacements, to supplement combat units and to tend to wounded soldiers . . .
>
> The Japanese Army's heartless approach to ejecting local civilians from caves was matched by their killing hundreds, maybe even thousands, of their own soldiers who were too badly wounded to retreat southward from hospital shelters.[22]

As the battle neared its end, atrocities by individual soldiers were commonplace. 'Knowing that death was imminent,' writes Thomas Huber, author of an account of the battle from the Japanese perspective, 'the soldiers freely committed rape. In some cases, fearing discovery, [they] forced parents to kill their crying babies, or the soldiers killed the infants themselves. Sometimes, they killed Okinawans seeking to share a cave, fearing they were spies . . . The no-surrender policy for the mass of soldiers was dehumanizing and had the unintended consequence of victimizing large numbers of Japanese civilians.'[23]

The behaviour of the Japanese was, for Masahide Ōta, in marked contrast to that of the American military, who had from the start of the campaign provided 'food, clothing, and shelter to displaced residents in areas that it had already secured'. They had 'planned ahead and prepared for this contingency and their kindness in this respect no doubt saved tens of thousands of Okinawans from death by starvation'. Writing in 2013, four years before his death, Ōta acknowledged the recent ill-feeling by Okinawans towards the large US military presence on the island, but added that it could never erase the fact that the immediate post-war years 'were marked by strong feelings of gratitude among Okinawans towards the United States for its efforts to avoid a humanitarian disaster'.[24]

51

'We sure have a lot to be thankful for'

Motobu Peninsula, 27 June–17 August 1945

On 27 June 1945, PFC Gene Sledge was among half a dozen K Company men trucked north to prepare a rest camp for the 1st Marine Division in the Motobu Peninsula. They were nervous about leaving their buddies, but it turned out to be 'good duty'.

During the long and dusty ride to the peninsula, they passed areas they had fought through. Transformed with roads, tent camps and supply dumps, they were barely recognisable. 'We had come back to civilization,' wrote Sledge. 'We had climbed up out of the abyss once more. It was exhilarating. We sang and whistled like little country boys until our sides were sore.'

They eventually reached their designated camp ground: a potato field, not far from rocky cliffs that overlooked the island of Ie Shima (where Ernie Pyle, America's best-known war correspondent, had been killed by a Japanese bullet on 18 April). Their job was to keep an eye on the company gear. Having set up a bivouac, they spent the next few 'quiet, carefree days basking in the sun by day and mounting one-sentry guard duty at night'. They were like 'boys on a campout'.

Eventually the battalion arrived and all hands were required to complete the camp. 'Pyramidal tents were set up,' remembered Sledge, 'drainage ditches were dug, folding cots and bed rolls were brought to us, and a canvas-roofed mess hall was built.' Every day, old comrades returned from hospital, 'some hale and hearty but others showing the effects of only partial recovery from severe wounds'. By now, rumours that the division would rehabilitate in Hawaii had faded. But that could not diminish the 'indescribable' sense of relief that the 'long Okinawa ordeal' was finally over.

Even so, there were 'few familiar faces' left in K Company. Only twenty-six of the sixty-five Peleliu veterans who had landed on 1 April were still with the company at the end of the battle. They included Gene Sledge, R. V. Burgin, 'Snafu' Shelton, Hank Boyes, Jim Burke, John Redifer, Vincent Santos, George Sarrett, Orly Uhls and Jim Anderson. Most of the Old Breed's infantry units had suffered 'over 150 per cent losses through the two campaigns'. K Company's casualties were even more severe. 'I doubt,' wrote Sledge, 'there were even ten old hands who had escaped being wounded at one time or another on Peleliu or Okinawa.' He was one of them.[1]

R. V. Burgin remembered little of his time in the rest camp on Okinawa. After thirty months of combat, and the loss of countless men – including charismatic leaders like 'Hillbilly' Jones and 'Ack-Ack' Haldane – he was 'wiped out' and 'numb'. He slept with Florence's picture under his pillow and thought constantly 'of the days when we have a home of our own, and children to call us Mother and Dad'. He was pretty certain he had accumulated enough points to return home. The problem was Florence, and how to get her from Australia to Texas where they had agreed to set up home together. When travel was possible again, wives with children would get priority, then wives without children, and only after they had been accommodated would fiancées like Florence be allowed to make the trip.

'I just talked to my company commander about the papers,' he wrote to Florence in mid-July, 'and he is going to see about them in the morning. I hope I can get them fixed up before I go home. Oh how I hope & pray I can. I want to have your name on the list, knowing it won't be too long before you can come home to me forever, Darling, & I do mean forever.'

They had not seen each other for almost two years and the longing to do so was keenly felt by both of them. Florence was also concerned that her fiancé had downplayed the seriousness of his neck wound. 'Really, Darling,' he wrote to reassure her, 'it didn't hurt me. I hardly have a scar to show for it. I have been hurt a lot worse in a football game, and never stopped playing.'[2]

In his letters home, Gene Sledge described the beauty of the camp's position: on high ground, near the sea, with mountains in the distance. 'There are,' he wrote, 'several streams & large virgin pine trees everywhere. I see numerous crows & doves daily . . . During the daylight hours a cool breeze always blows through our tent & at nite it's very cool. So I am really catching up on sleep I missed in the past months.'

Of real concern to him, however, was the announcement in late July of a new points system for those in naval service. 'No points are given for overseas or combat time,' he told his parents. 'In short we won't be released until the war is over.'[3] For most of the Gloucester veterans – men like Burgin, Sarrett, Boyes, Shelton and Anderson – this was not a problem. They would be going home anyway. But for Sledge and the other Peleliu veterans, the news was quite a blow. He recalled: 'Ugly rumors circulated that we would hit Japan next, with an expected casualty figure of one million Americans. No one wanted to talk about that.'[4]

They were more than rumours. At 3:30 p.m. on 18 June,* a few hours after Lieutenant General Buckner had been killed on Okinawa, President Harry Truman met with his senior military advisors in the White House to discuss the next step in the war against Japan. In attendance were his Joint Chiefs of Staff: General George C. Marshall, Fleet Admiral Ernest King and Lieutenant General Ira Eaker (representing General of the Army 'Hap' Arnold, USAAF, who was recovering from a heart attack). Also present were Fleet Admiral Bill Leahy, Truman's military chief of staff, Secretary of the Navy James Forrestal, Secretary of War Henry Stimson and Assistant Secretary of War John J. McCloy.

'I've called this meeting,' explained Truman, 'for the purpose of hearing

* Or, more accurately, 4:30 a.m. on Tuesday 19 June in Okinawa, given the time difference of minus 11 hours between Washington DC and Naha.

more details about the proposed campaign against Japan set out in Admiral Leahy's memorandum to the Joint Chiefs of Staff four days ago. General Marshall, what are your thoughts?'

The US Army chief of staff began by saying the situation in Japan was 'practically identical' to that in Europe prior to D-Day. To bring Japan to its knees – as Germany had been – a ground invasion was necessary. The location and date, said Marshall, had been agreed by the Joint Chiefs and the senior military commanders in the Pacific, General MacArthur and Admiral Nimitz, as Kyushu Island, the most southerly of the Japanese home islands, on 1 November 1945. That would give enough time to 'smash practically every industrial target worth hitting in Japan as well as destroying huge areas in the Jap cities'; the Japanese Navy, 'if any still exists', would by that point be 'completely powerless'; and American air and sea power would have 'cut Jap reinforcement capabilities from the mainland to negligible proportions'. To delay any longer than 1 November, however, would risk a delay of 'up to 6 months' because of winter weather.

The Kyushu option was, said Marshall, 'essential to a strategy of strangulation' and appeared to be 'the least costly worthwhile operation following Okinawa'. It would act as a stepping stone to an invasion of the Tokyo Plain on the neighbouring Honshu Island. As for likely casualties, Marshall gave a number of comparative examples. At Luzon, there had been 31,000 American casualties to 156,000 Japanese (mostly killed), a ratio of 1:5. More recently – at Iwo Jima and Okinawa – the ratio of American to Japanese casualties was 1:1.25 and 1:2 respectively. Clearly, the closer they got to Japan proper, the harder the defenders fought. 'It is a grim fact,' commented Marshall, 'that there is not an easy, bloodless way to victory in war and it is the thankless task of the leaders to maintain their firm outward front which holds the resolution of their subordinates.'

After reading out a supportive telegram from Douglas MacArthur, Marshall said it was his personal view that the Kyushu operation was 'the only course to pursue'. Airpower alone was 'not sufficient to put the Japanese out of the war', any more than it had been to defeat the

Germans. The invasion of Kyushu would be no more difficult 'than the assault in Normandy' and he was convinced that all US servicemen in the Pacific needed to be 'indoctrinated with a firm determination to see it through'.

Admiral King backed up Marshall by saying that 'Kyushu followed logically after Okinawa' and was a 'natural set-up'.* When Admiral Leahy was asked for his opinion, he said that the troops on Okinawa had suffered about 35 per cent casualties of the total number involved, and that he expected a similar proportion to be lost on Kyushu. King, on the other hand, thought the losses would be 'somewhere between' the Luzon and Okinawa figures, by which he probably meant a loss-to-kill ratio of around one American to every three Japanese.

To help with the grim calculations, Marshall explained that 766,700 American troops would assault Kyushu. They would be opposed by a Japanese force of at least eight divisions, or 350,000 men.† Further reinforcement of those defenders was possible, but 'becoming increasingly unlikely'. That would mean, if King's estimate was correct, at least 120,000 American casualties on Kyushu, and possibly double that. But that was just the start, because Truman knew from the Joint Chiefs of Staff memorandum that a second, far bigger invasion of Honshu, in the vicinity of the Tokyo Plains, was scheduled for the spring of 1945, and it might be the autumn of that year before Japan finally surrendered.‡

* Despite his outward support for a ground invasion, King was highly sceptical and believed, as did many in the US Navy, that air bombardment and a close blockade were better and less costly options. The huge losses on Okinawa convinced both King and Nimitz that even the plan to capture Kyushu in November would be an unnecessary waste of American lives. They were biding their time in the hope of persuading Truman to cancel the operation. (Richard B. Frank, *Downfall: The End of the Imperial Japanese Empire* (New York: Random House, 1999), pp. 33–7, 142, 147–8.)

† In fact, there were more than 900,000 Japanese defenders on Kyushu. A further 3.4 million Japanese servicemen were on Honshu.

‡ The overall plan for the invasion of the Japanese home islands was known as Operation Downfall. It had two parts: Operation Olympic (Kyushu), scheduled

The potential total casualties for both invasions – involving more than five million American servicemen – were more than a million men.

Fully aware that the capture of Kyushu would not necessarily end the war, Truman suggested that the operation would simply create 'another Okinawa closer to Japan'. The Joint Chiefs agreed that this was so.

After more discussion, Truman summed up. He had called the meeting because he wanted 'to know definitely how far we could afford to go in the Japanese campaign'. He had hoped there might be a possibility of preventing an Okinawa from one end of Japan to the other'. But they had told him otherwise and he was now 'quite sure that the Joint Chiefs should proceed with the Kyushu operation'. It is telling that, while Marshall's presentation had explicitly linked the Kyushu (Operation Coronet) and Honshu (Operation Olympic) landings together, Truman only gave authorization for the former.[5]

There was, in any event, a possible alternative to a ground invasion: to drop the newly developed atom bomb. Truman had known about the bomb since his first day as president – 12 April – and had since been told that its first crucial test firing in the New Mexico desert would take place in July. He also knew that the Interim Committee set up to advise on the future use of the bomb had recommended on 1 June that, if it worked, the atom bomb 'should be used against Japan as soon as possible', against a 'war plant surrounded by workers' homes' and without prior warning. To follow any other course, argued the committee, would be to put at risk the 'major objective of obtaining a prompt surrender from the Japanese'. This view was mirrored by a panel of distinguished physicists – including J. Robert Oppenheimer – who had reported to the Interim Committee on 16 June: 'We can propose no technical demonstration likely to bring an end to the war; we see no acceptable alternative to direct military use.'[6]

The sticking point was whether or not the bomb would work. Until

---

for 1 November 1945; and Operation Coronet (Honshu), spring 1946. A total of more than six million Allied troops – five million Americans and one million British and Commonwealth – were due to take part.

that was known, the planning for the Kyushu invasion on 1 November would continue. But everything changed on 16 July when Truman received word in Berlin, where he was attending the inter-Allied Potsdam Conference with Josef Stalin and Winston Churchill, that the 'first full scale test' of 'the atomic fission bomb' in the New Mexico desert had been 'successful beyond the most optimistic expectations'. The memo added: 'We now had the means to insure [the war's] speedy conclusion and save thousands of American lives.'[7]

On hearing of the successful test in New Mexico, Churchill felt only relief. He wrote later:

> Up to this moment we had shaped our ideas towards an assault upon the homeland of Japan . . . I had in my mind the spectacle of Okinawa island, where many thousands of Japanese, rather than surrender, had drawn up in line and destroyed themselves with hand-grenades after their leaders had solemnly performed the rite of hara-kiri. To quell the Japanese resistance might well require the loss of a million American lives and half that number of British . . . Now all this nightmare picture had vanished. In in its place was the vision – fair and bright it seemed – of the end of the whole war in one or two violent shocks.[8]

There were now two pressing questions for Truman and his advisors to consider. What should the warning to Japan say? And, if it was ignored, which cities should be targeted? On the latter question, Truman agreed with the Interim Committee's advice to use the bomb 'on a war plant surrounded by workers' homes', telling Stimson that, in line with the 'laws of war', the bomb should be dropped on a 'war production center of prime military importance'. Various cities were considered, including Kyoto, the old imperial capital. But it was removed from the list when Stimson pointed out its importance to the Japanese as a 'cultural and religious shrine'. The final shortlist, agreed by Truman after consultation with Stimson, George Marshall and 'Hap' Arnold, was: Hiroshima, Kokura, Niigata and Nagasaki. 'The order of selection,' wrote Truman, 'was in accordance with the military importance of these cities, but allowance would be given for weather conditions at the time of the bombing.'[9]

He noted in his diary: 'I have told . . . Stimson to use it so that military objectives and soldiers and sailors are the target and not women and children. Even if the Japs are savages, ruthless, merciless and fanatic, we, as the leader of the world for the common welfare, cannot drop this terrible bomb on the old Capitol or the new [Tokyo].'[10]

Soon after, Truman signed the final ultimatum to Japan, known as the Potsdam Declaration. It called upon Japan to agree to immediate unconditional surrender or face 'prompt and utter destruction'.[11] When Tokyo ignored the ultimatum, Truman gave the order to drop an atom bomb on Hiroshima, 'an Army city' and 'major quartermaster depot' with warehouses full of military supplies.

Truman's decision to authorize the use of the atom bomb was directly influenced by the bloodbath on Okinawa. He feared that an invasion of Japan would cost the US military more than a million dead and wounded. It would also kill countless Japanese soldiers and civilians. 'My object,' wrote Truman, 'is to save as many American lives as possible but I also have a humane feeling for the women and children of Japan.'[12]

The first atom bomb – 'Little Boy' – was dropped by the US B-29 Superfortress *Enola Gay* on Hiroshima on 6 August.* When the Japanese government failed to respond, preparations were made to detonate a second bomb, 'Fat Man'. On 9 August, the day after Russia had declared war on Japan, 'Fat Man' was exploded over the Kyushu port of Nagasaki. A total of around 210,000 Japanese were killed outright in the two explosions, or died from their wounds and radiation sickness; an appalling

* A day later, on 7 August, alarmed by intelligence reports of a large Japanese troop build-up on Kyushu, Marshall asked MacArthur if he still supported a ground invasion. MacArthur replied yes on 9 August, adding that he did not believe the intelligence (it was in fact accurate). King hoped to use this exchange to persuade Nimitz to withdraw his support for an invasion. But Japan's surrender, a few days later, made what would have been an ugly Navy v. Army showdown unnecessary. (Frank, *Downfall*, pp. 211–13, 271–7.)

statistic, but less than the number killed on Okinawa, and a fraction of those who would have died if the US had invaded mainland Japan. Such a desperate course of action was no longer necessary.

On 10 August, the Japanese government declared a willingness to accept the terms of the Potsdam Declaration as long as Emperor Hirohito could keep his throne and remain above the authority of the occupation commander, thus giving him a veto over post-war reforms. The Allies refused, though Hirohito was allowed to stay on in a subordinate role.* Even then there were hardline elements in the military who tried to scupper a deal. But they failed to win the support of Hirohito and the coup failed. Japan agreed to surrender unconditionally on 14 August, much to the delight of the American servicemen on Okinawa who were poised to invade.

Hearing about the first bomb and Russia's declaration of war, Gene Sledge had dared to hope that war might soon be over. 'Everyone is laying bets on what is going to happen,' he wrote to his parents on 9 August. 'I'm just praying that the terrible mess will soon be over because I don't want any more good American blood lost. I'll soon be twenty-two and I'm no closer to getting set for post war than I was a year ago. So I'm hoping I can get back to civilian life very soon.'

Two days later, by which time negotiations had begun, he felt more optimistic. He wrote: 'For a long time I've been praying that we would all be united at Georgia Cottage for Christmas of 1945. From today's news it may be an answered prayer. We all have our fingers crossed & are praying that the war will really be over in a matter of days.'[13]

A little after noon local time, 15 August, Emperor Hirohito announced Japan's surrender in a radio broadcast. The men of K Company received the news with an 'indescribable sense of relief', but tinged with sadness. 'We thought,' noted Gene Sledge, 'the Japanese would never surrender.

* The decision to keep Hirohito as emperor was probably justified in the short term: to assist with the disarming of Japanese troops and the prevention of armed insurrection. But in the longer term it was a mistake not to force him to accept some responsibility for war crimes by abdicating.

Many refused to believe it. Sitting in stunned silence, we remembered our dead. So many dead. So many maimed. So many bright futures consigned to the ashes of the past. So many dreams lost in the madness that had engulfed us. Except for a few widely scattered shouts of joy, the survivors of the abyss sat hollow-eyed and silent, trying to comprehend a world without war.'[14]

On 17 August, Sledge wrote to his mother: 'I can imagine how happy you & Pop are that the war is over. I'm just as happy as you are. We sure have a lot to be thankful for that Ed & I came through no worse than we did . . . I got in the corps to help win the war – it's won and I can't get out any too fast to suit me.'[15]

Harry Truman's decision to drop the bombs still divides opinion today. But the men of K Company were in no doubt that it was the right thing to do. 'Some people say,' wrote R. V. Burgin, 'it was awful us using it. But if they think that was awful, I don't think people have a damn clue what would have happened if we'd hit Japan . . . We would have killed *millions* of Japanese, and there's no telling how many of us would have been wounded or killed, going in.'[16]

Postscript

'We'd forged a bond that time would never erase'

Returning home, summer 1944–July 2020

During almost three years of distinguished active service – from August 1942 to June 1945 – K Company, 3/5 Marines, fought in some of the bloodiest battles of the Pacific War: Henderson Field, Matanikau River, Point Cruz, Suicide Creek, Walt's Ridge, Peleliu airfield, Ngesebus Island, the Umurbrogol Pocket, Asa River, the Awacha Pocket, Wana Draw, Half Moon Hill and Dakeshi Ridge. By performing prodigious feats of valour in these and other actions, K/3/5 officers and enlisted men were awarded numerous gallantry meals, including Navy Crosses, Silver and Bronze Stars. Many were awarded posthumously to the ninety K/3/5 men who were killed in action; several hundred others received Purple Hearts for injuries received in combat, with some maimed for life. 'There has never been,' declared General Lew Walt, twice K Company's battalion commander, 'a better group of fighters.'[1]

Each individual death was a personal tragedy for family and friends who might grieve for the rest of their lives. In 2018, more than seven decades after First Lieutenant 'Hillbilly' Jones's death on Peleliu, his sister Anne was still mourning 'the loss of her beloved brother'. She 'can't help but wonder', noted her daughter-in-law, 'what Ed would have become if his life hadn't ended at Peleliu'.[2]

A more immediate sense of grief and loss is evident in the letter Mr and Mrs Sydney Haldane wrote in early November 1944 to Bowdoin president Kenneth Sills and his wife, soon after learning of their son

Andy's death in battle:

> Dear Friends,
>
> Please accept our very sincere thanks for the comforting letter of sympathy which we received in a time of deep sorrow. Our hopes were high for Andy's safe return to his home and friends, but that has all been changed. We shall always remember your kindness to Andrew while he was a student at Bowdoin College. We know that he felt he could never repay the College for all it had done for him in every way. Your splendid tribute to our son as an athlete, warrior and gentleman will be cherished by us, for always. Our interest in Bowdoin College is still warm and we feel it will be lasting.[3]

They could not know it, but plans would soon be afoot for 'a group of Bowdoin College men serving in the same Marine Division' to raise a sum of money to buy a cup to 'honor the memory' of their son. Among those involved was the same Major Paul Douglas, from the class of '13, who had so impressed Sledge and other K Company men on Peleliu and Okinawa. He and the others eventually raised the considerable sum of $275, which was used to purchase a large silver cup – thereafter known as the Haldane Cup – to be awarded each year to the Bowdoin College senior who had 'outstanding qualities of leadership and character'.

At Bowdoin's Commencement in 1951, when he was awarded an honorary Doctor of Laws degree by his alma mater, the major, who by then was Senator Paul H. Douglas of Illinois, spoke movingly about Haldane:

> He was a poor boy who came to Bowdoin, worked his way through . . . and went into the Marine Corps as a second lieutenant immediately upon graduation, as I find to my great joy some members of the graduating class are doing this year . . . When the first forces were assembled for the expedition to Guadalcanal, Andy was one of them . . . he then led a company on New Britain and at Peleliu.

> I want to tell you something about Andy because his was the type of life that we can all imitate. Andy went through three [campaigns]. His company in the Fifth Marines, which was my regiment also, always took more ground than any other company in the Division.
>
> He was a tiger in attack . . . but he was always wounded and always wound up each engagement 20 or 30 pounds less than when he began because he would give his rations away. He would give his blankets away, he would give his shirts away; and we always had to protect him at Peleliu to see that he got enough food.

The award of the Haldane Cup to a graduate that year, added Douglas, was to carry out the intention of 'those of us who were in his Division who loved him so dearly' and wanted to keep his memory alive.[4]

Many years later, an even more heartfelt and moving tribute to Haldane was given by one of his Marines, Gene Sledge, who had just received a letter from Haldane's nephew, a chief warrant officer in the US Marine Corps. Sledge replied:

> Your letter of 7 October [1980] arrived today. It was like a bolt out of the blue! For years I have tried to locate relatives of Capt. Haldane, but have had no luck. I certainly am delighted to know he has a nephew . . .
>
> I loved Capt. Haldane as much as I did my own father. Every one of the 235 Marines in K-3-5 who hit Peleliu felt the same way about him that I did. Some of them had fought with him at Cape Gloucester and Guadalcanal. When I came into the company after Gloucester the old salts told us new men that we were lucky as hell to be in K-3-5 because it was Ack-Ack Haldane's company – he was the finest company commander in the USMC they said. There has never been any doubt in my mind they were correct! When he was killed on Hill 140 on Peleliu, I cried like a baby – so did just about every one of the 80 odd survivors of K-3-5 at the time. The guys who were too emotionally wrung out to cry

> after 30 days of fierce combat on Peleliu, just cursed and yelled at the Japs like they had cracked up. It was the worst loss we experienced during the war, even though we all lost many, many close friends . . .
>
> Captain Haldane knew the name of every man in the company before Peleliu, new men like myself as well as old salts. He was modest, quiet, kind, compassionate and gentle – but he was brave, rugged, tough, and 'all man' in combat. He was a strict disciplinarian, but never yelled at anybody to my knowledge. We always did our best because we felt obligated to measure up to what the Skipper expected of us. He had all those characteristics of a fine human being mingled with those attributes of a born leader – a combination which comes along once in a million. He was – along with my father – the most admirable man I ever knew . . .
>
> As Andy's nephew, you have a lot to be proud of. He would be proud of you and the fact that you are in the Corps, and a CWO.[5]

Even those K/3/5 men who returned home safely were far from unscathed. They included Gunnery Sergeant Thurman Miller, one of the 'originals', who arrived back in West Virginia in the summer of 1944. 'Mom hugged me and cried,' he wrote. 'Dad gripped my hand tightly. My sisters hugged me, and all I could think was how good it was to see them again . . . Mom and Dad had aged considerably, stricken with worry over me. My heart went out to them. A great lump came into my throat, and that was strange to me. I had yet a streak of tenderness in me; love remained in my hardened heart.'

Soon after his return, he married his childhood sweetheart Recie Marshall, a striking young woman with long auburn hair and the 'most extraordinary brown eyes'. They moved to Camp Lejeune in North Carolina where Miller instructed new Marine recruits to prepare for combat. He enjoyed the work, but found the recruits, almost all of whom were draftees, to be softer and less willing to follow rules than the men he had served with. The final straw was being told that all

NCOs would have to take a course in field fortification. He decided to switch to the Officer Candidate Applicant (OCA) battalion – where he served under his former platoon commander Captain Rex McIlvaine – and became chief instructor of the next class of '77-day wonders'. Even this job was tough sledding. 'How could I generate the proper mood of hatred,' he wrote, 'just when I was returning to some semblance of normal life? How could I prepare them to fight? I could make them tough in a physical sense, but how could I tell them to kill, when I was tired of killing, of seeing human blood, brains, and bones mingled with bayonets, packs, and ammunition.'

He devised a simple and effective plan for the officer candidates to follow. 'We jettisoned everything,' he recalled, 'except the essentials, how to kill the enemy and keep oneself and one's command from being needlessly killed. We were supposed to be officers and gentlemen, but we had no time for the latter.' At the same time, Miller felt a keen responsibility not to pass those men he considered to be poor leadership material, whatever their family pedigree or political connections. It was a principled position that would cause no end of headaches for his superiors.

For the most part, Miller enjoyed his work with the OCA battalion. Yet during this period, and for many years after, he suffered recurring nightmares, hallucinations, sickness and misery. More than once he considered suicide. That he got through these dark moments was chiefly thanks to his wife Recie, who took care of him, talked to him and bore his children. 'I owe her my life,' he wrote later, 'for she gave me purpose and a reason to live.'

In the summer of 1945, having passed the exam for first sergeant, Miller was ordered to ship out to Okinawa to rejoin the 1st Marine Division for the final reckoning with Japan. He had all his booster shots for overseas duty, and Recie 'was packed to go home to Otsego'. It was not a campaign he was looking forward to. 'Knowing the fierceness of Japanese soldiers,' he noted, 'a ground war on their turf was likely to be protracted and ruthless and would cost many American lives.'

But it was not to be. He wrote:

> The awakened giant of America had perfected the ultimate weapon. I read of this destruction and death with a knot in the pit of my stomach. *My God, what have we done? What does it mean to 'split an atom'?* I had thought that war could not be more devastating – the worst damage that humans could inflict on each other. Now we had found the means to erase the human race from the face of the earth. I recalled the words of Jesus: *I am come to send fire on the earth; and what will I, if it be already kindled?*

The war was over, and he would live. Discharged a couple of months later, he and Recie moved back to Otsego, where work was hard to find. Over and over he was asked: 'What can you do? What are your skills?'

The honest answer – 'I'm a trained killer' – was not what they were looking for. His only option was to become a coal miner, one of the toughest and most hazardous peacetime occupations. 'Cave-ins were frequent,' he recalled, 'and the families of men who were hurt or killed on the job were often left destitute. Before mechanization, when there was a big roof fall in the mine, the first question asked by the bosses was "Did any mules get hurt?" Mules were expensive; another miner could always be hired.'

After two years of general labour, Miller got the slightly cushier job of working on the maintenance crew. He ended up a master mechanic and electrician, and worked underground for twenty-five of his thirty-two years in the industry. He and Recie eventually had three children – two boys and a girl – and raised them in a house Miller built close to where he had grown up. He also found God. Despite not being raised a Christian, he joined a gospel choir soon after the war and 'those spiritual songs got me thinking about the hereafter'. He was a devout Christian for the rest of his life.

For many years he was not in contact with his surviving Marine buddies 'for lack of time, lack of money, and a fear of revisiting those days'. But eventually he was visited at home by Mo Darsey, who persuaded him to attend a 1st Marine Division reunion in Milwaukee. There he 'reconnected with R. V. Burgin and many other reserves who joined us in Australia'. Darsey, he realized, was his brother. 'While I am in this world,' he admitted, 'Mo will always be in my heart. He was right. "Because of the hell we went through on Guadalcanal, there is a bond that doesn't exist between any other people."'

Miller's grandson Jeffrey later served in the Marine Corps at Camp Lejeune and Okinawa. Before he left for the latter, Miller gave him one of the Globe, Eagle and Anchor emblems he had carried on Guadalcanal. 'Thus, a part of me would ultimately reach the place where I would have eventually fought had the war lasted.'

In 2013, he published *Earned in Blood*, a memoir of his tough childhood in the Appalachian Mountains of West Virginia, his four years as a Marine, and his post-war struggles as a coal miner and sufferer from malaria and PTSD. It provides the reader, wrote eminent military historian Richard B. Frank, 'with a vivid panorama, painted with directness and honesty, of an exceptional personal journey through peace and war – a peace and war both without and within'.

On the book's final page, Miller was in no doubt that the sacrifice in the Pacific was worth it:

> We were referred to as the Greatest Generation, and truly our generation was called on to do the impossible with the unavailable, to go to the unknown and perform tasks never before asked of a people. We answered the call, we went, we conquered; we came home and rebuilt a nation and contributed to rebuilding a world. New and unforeseeable challenges await. We leave it in the hands of our youth, and I ask, Are you ready? Are you willing?

Miller died in 2017 at the age of ninety-seven.[6]

Platoon Sergeant Jim McEnery was a Marine until November 1946, having volunteered to stay on as a drill instructor at Parris Island on his return to the States in late 1944. After his discharge, he went back to Brooklyn and held down a variety of jobs that included running his own 'successful auto trim business in Hempstead, Long Island'. Later, he took a position as a maintenance foreman at Rutgers University in New Jersey, and worked there until his retirement in 1981.

In 1947, he had met, fallen in love with and married a friend of his sister's, Gertrude Johanson. After the birth of their only child, Karen, they tragically lost four babies who were born with fatal birth defects.

McEnery never regretted his time in the Marines. It gave him 'a totally different perspective on life' and taught him 'a lot of practical lessons that were worth a fortune later on'. They included the ability to 'adapt to conditions that most people would find unbearable'. For many years he grieved for the 'friends and comrades who didn't make it'. But he never lost sleep over the enemy soldiers he killed in battle.

He regarded the men he had 'fought beside and shared foxholes with' as family, and made it a point to stay in close touch with as many as possible. For many years he talked regularly on the phone to wartime buddies like 'Slim' Somerville and Thurman Miller, his old platoon guide on Guadalcanal. 'They're as close to me as brothers,' he wrote, 'and they will be for as long as we live.' He 'never missed' a K/3/5 or 1st Marine Division Association reunion, and would travel all over the country to see his old buddies.

In 2012, having retired with his wife to Ocala, Florida, McEnery published his war memoir *Hell in the Pacific*. 'I don't want Americans of the twenty-first century,' he explained, 'to forget what happened at Guadalcanal or Cape Gloucester or Peleliu. I want the memory of those tragic times and terrible places to live forever.'

He died later that year, aged ninety-two.[7]

Also arriving back in the States in late 1944, after serving with K Company in three Pacific campaigns, was the grizzled 46-year-old veteran Platoon Sergeant St Elmo 'Pop' Haney. He remained in the US Marines as an instructor and later joined the 1/7 Marines in China, finally retiring with the rank of gunnery sergeant in 1947, almost thirty years after his original enlistment. He later graduated from Chillicothe Business College in Missouri and, in 1949, married Ethel Tirey, three years his senior and too old to bear children. They lived together in Bentonville, Arkansas, until Ethel's death in 1972. Haney died seven years later, at the age of eighty.[8]

In 1983, unaware of Haney's death, 'Stumpy' Stanley tried to track him down, stating:

> I am writing this on behalf of the men who served with you in K-3-5 during the Guadalcanal, New Britain and Peleliu campaigns in WWII. All of us were wondering where you reside and what you have been up to in the years since the end of the war with Japan.
>
> Over the years, some of the old timers have been working on reassembling K-3-5 for the annual 1st Marine Division Association reunions. Today, we have about 140 men on our Muster Roll . . . Please drop me a line so I can get in touch with you to fill you in more completely as to our activities. Hoping to hear from you soon.

At the same time, Stanley wrote a short appreciation of Haney's service for the other K Company veterans. He was, noted Stanley, a 'true Marine in the Old Breed style' who was already advanced in years when they first met in Australia in early 1943. 'Despite his age, he carried his full share of the load, [and despite] being sent Stateside after each campaign, he managed to work his way back to combat with the Company . . . Haney is something of a legend in K-3-5.'[9]

Evacuated back to the States, via Guam, with 'psychoneurosis anxiety' and 'combat fatigue', Corporal Sterling Mace was recovering in Bainbridge Naval Hospital in Maryland when he heard the war was over. 'The navy boys hugged one another and smiled,' he remembered. 'There was laughter aplenty. But I couldn't get up. It was as if I were a part of the mattress, the bedding, the flooring, the earth . . . The war was finally over . . . and it felt so damn good . . . but it didn't feel like anything without the ones who made the end possible.'

A week later, he visited the mother of one of those men, Seymour Levy, in her corner apartment in Brooklyn, New York. She was, he noted, 'a very nondescript, middle-aged Jewish woman' who was trying hard not to cry. Eventually she asked: 'What happened out there, Sterling? How did my Seymour die?'

He replied: 'Seymour died, Mrs Levy. He died very quickly, *instantly* even. I'm really sure . . . that is, I don't think it was possible for him to feel any pain, when it happened.'

Crying now, she reached across the table and grabbed Mace's hands. 'Was it worth it?' she queried. 'What you boys did over there. Why Seymour didn't come home. Was it worth it?'

'Mrs Levy,' said Mace, in a quandary over how to answer, 'I was just a Marine. That's all. Just like Seymour . . . like a bunch of us, we were only doing our jobs.' After rambling for a while, he told her what she needed to know: 'I promise you it was worth every last bit of it.'

She had her hands over her mouth, but seemed to be saying: *Yes, I understand.*

When Mace left the apartment, he 'didn't feel any different. Nothing there had purged my soul of pain. There was no balm for a bleeding host.'[10] Years later, he admitted how difficult the visit had been. 'I went to see her and she was completely broken,' he wrote to Gene Sledge. 'You see he enlisted against her wishes and then he was killed on her birthday. Well I don't have to tell you that was the last time I visited anybody with a situation like that.'[11]

Mace was honourably discharged from the Marine Corps as a corporal in late October 1945. A few months later, he married auburn-haired Joyce Sellers and together they had three children: a boy and two girls. Taking advantage of the GI Bill – which paid for discharged servicemen to go through college – Mace attended the Jean Morgan School of Commercial Art, graduating in 1950. Thereafter he worked for the Long Island State Park Commission and was the operations manager at Jones Beach Theater for more than twenty-seven years.

He often thought about the war and attended the inaugural 1st Marine Division Association reunion at the Hotel Astor in Manhattan, New York City, in 1947, though he did not recognise a single Marine 'without his helmet and filthy dungarees'. Years later, when Bill Leyden and Jim McEnery started the New York chapter of the Old Breed Association, Sterling Mace became its secretary.

He eventually moved with his wife to Florida and became head of security at various resort hotels. In 2012, in retirement, he published *Battleground Pacific*: a moving and brutally honest, if somewhat erratically structured, account of his time as a young Marine at war. It ends with a 'better' answer to Mrs Levy's question. 'Yes, ma'am. It was worth it. After all, there never *has* been another World War.'

Mace was ninety-six when he died in July 2020.[12]

It was not until mid-September 1945, after another bout of malaria, that Platoon Sergeant R. V. Burgin was told he was going home. He was one of the lucky ones. Many of the other K Company veterans – including Gene Sledge, Jim Burke, Hank Boyes, 'Snafu' Shelton, George Sarrett and Vincent Santos – had been assigned to occupation duty with the 1st Marine Division in northern China. Burgin spent the day 'going from tent to tent' to say goodbye to the 'guys I'd fought alongside, all my old buddies'. When the division convoy left for China on the 26th, he was on his own.

Burgin finally left Okinawa on the attack transport USS *Lavaca* on 16 October, arriving at San Diego three weeks later. Discharged from Camp Pendleton in late November, he caught a train to Dallas, Texas, and moved in with his sister Ila. During Christmas with his parents in Jewett, his father tried to convince him to become a farmer. But having seen his father 'work too long and too hard for too little', he decided to return to Dallas to find a job.

He applied to join the Post Office and put in for disability pay – on account of his recurring malaria and other ailments – and was granted 60 per cent retroactive to his discharge. He also received the welcome news that he had been awarded the Bronze Star for his role 'in wiping out the machine-gun nest on Okinawa'. His parents drove up from Jewett for the ceremony in Dallas' Oak Cliff YMCA, the only time they saw their son in Marine uniform.

Burgin had to wait until late January 1947 – by which time he was working as a postman in east Dallas – to be reunited with his Australian fiancée Florence Riseley. He had started the process of bringing her to the States in the summer of 1945, and it finally ended eighteen months later with her arrival at Dallas Union Station. 'Florence,' he wrote, 'looked just like I remembered her, only better. We hugged like any couple in love who hadn't seen each other for years.' They were married two days later.

In November, Florence gave birth to the first of four girls, all of whom would be 'smart and successful'. Meanwhile Burgin worked his way up the Post Office to the job of superintendent of registered mail. 'Each step of the way,' he noted, 'I found my old Marine experience stood me well. It was like being a section leader . . . Like my old San Diego drill instructors, I never had to yell at anyone to get anything done.'

For thirty-five years, Burgin pushed the war out of his mind. He would occasionally joke with other former Marines in the Post Office about the 'funny things that had happened'. But they 'never really talked about the war'. Instead he 'just held it all back'. Then in 1979 he got a phone call. He recalled: 'Stumpy Stanley, our old company commander, Bill Leyden and a few others from the First Marine Division had been sitting in a New York bar having a drink. One of them said, "We should get everybody together again." Before they split up, each promised to call other Marines he knew from the war and pass the word along.'

After Burgin was approached, he got in touch with the guys he knew, including Jim Burke, John Redifer and Johnny Marmet. In 1980, Burgin was one of twenty men from K Company who went to the 1st Marine Division Association reunion in Indianapolis. He attended the reunions every year after that, and quickly got to the point where he could 'talk about the war any time, any place, with anybody'.

In 2010, in the wake of the HBO mini-series *The Pacific* – in which his character is played by actor Martin McCann – Burgin published a memoir of his wartime service, *Islands of the Damned*. 'What sticks with me now,' he wrote, 'is not so much the pain and terror and sorrow of war, though I remember that well enough. What really sticks with me is the honor I had of defending my country, and of serving in the company of these men. They were good Marines, the finest, every one of them.'

Burgin died in 2019 in Lancaster, Texas, at the age of ninety-six.[13]

In early 1946, after four and a half months' duty in northern China, Gene Sledge rotated home. 'It was time,' he wrote, 'to say goodbye to old buddies in K/3/5. Severing the ties formed in two campaigns was painful. One of America's finest and most famous elite fighting divisions had been my home during a period of the most extreme adversity. Up there on the line, with nothing between us and the enemy but space (and precious little of that), we'd forged a bond that time would never erase. We were brothers. I left with a sense of loss and sadness, but K/3/5 will always be part of me.'[14]

Sledge returned to Mobile for an emotional reunion with his parents and brother. He was one of the very few veterans of K Company not to be awarded a Purple Heart (to signify a wound in combat). His psychological wounds, however, would take many years to heal, and he had a hard time readjusting to civilian life. 'As I strolled the streets,' he explained later, 'civilian life seemed so strange. People rushed around in a hurry about seemingly insignificant things. Few seemed to realize how blessed they were to be free and untouched by the horrors of war. To them, a veteran was a veteran – all were the same, whether one man had survived the deadliest combat or another had pounded a typewriter while in uniform.'[15]

He later credited his father, who had worked with shell-shock cases in the previous war, for helping him to get through his mental turmoil:

> He told me when I came home that every man who saw combat had suffered varying degrees of agony. He said that he knew what the 1st Marine Division [had] experienced at Peleliu and Okinawa was the worst any man could have experienced – thus I had had it rough, but should never forget how lucky I had been to come out of it with not even a scratch. Therefore, time would heal the

> agony of the vivid memories if I followed two rules very strictly: 1. Never feel sorry for myself – my luck had been incredible, and keep that in mind. 2. Either use alcohol sparingly, or not at all – it can ruin the best of men. Also, don't get bitter about people who had cushy jobs – life never was fair, and I was lucky any way you look at it.[16]

Enrolling at Alabama Polytechnic Institute, Sledge was asked by a clerk at the registrar's office if the Marine Corps had taught him anything useful. He replied: 'Lady, there was a killing war. The Marine Corps taught me how to kill Japs and try to survive. Now, if that don't fit into an academic course, I'm sorry. But some of us had to do the killing – and most of my buddies got killed or wounded.'[17]

After gaining a BSc in business administration, Sledge worked for a few years in Mobile's insurance and real estate business. But it was not for him and, in 1953, he returned to Auburn to take a graduate degree in botany and, after that, completed a doctorate in biology at the University of Florida. In 1962 he began teaching biology at Alabama College (later the University of Montevallo), and from 1970 to his retirement twenty years later was a professor specializing in zoology, ornithology and comparative vertebrate anatomy. He later credited his study of science 'as one of the primary factors which enabled me to cope with postwar depression'. He explained: 'The beauty, orderliness, and symmetry of science is an exhilarating experience.'

In 1952, Sledge had the 'good fortune' to marry Jeanne Arceneaux, a 'wonderful girl', and the couple had two sons: John and Henry. Encouraged by his wife, Sledge began compiling a memoir of his war experiences as a means of helping him to cope with what he had been through. He had actually begun the process on the island of Pavuvu in late 1944 when he kept notes in a small pocket Bible. 'This had to be done on the sly,' he told a fellow Marine in 1982, 'because, as you know, keeping personal diaries was forbidden by Division order. My purpose was to write an accurate description of my experiences for the family I assumed (correctly it turned out) I would have if I survived. I was prompted to write primarily by the fact that most of the letters and records which my grandfathers wrote while officers in the Confederate Army had been lost. Therefore, as soon as I got home I wrote out a detailed outline.'

Over the years, he gathered more historical material and wrote up 'various episodes'. But it was not until the 1970s that he began to piece the story together properly. 'One strong motivating factor to me,' he explained, 'was that, in my opinion, most accounts in military history I had read were stereotyped and impersonal. Most memoirs (with rare exceptions) stopped short of "telling it like it was". I simply wanted my family to know exactly what the price of freedom is.'[18]

According to his son John, Sledge was 'truly driven' to complete the memoir and would write at a frenetic pace, as if 'taking dictation', and even work in the middle of the night, which was 'very unlike him otherwise'.[19] When the 850-page typed manuscript was finished, Sledge sent it to Lieutenant Colonel John A. Crown, the former commander of I/3/5 on Peleliu, for accuracy. Crown was impressed and suggested that Sledge write an article on Peleliu for the *Marine Corps Gazette*. It duly appeared as 'Peleliu: A Neglected Battle', a three-part essay that was published in consecutive issues of the monthly journal from November 1979 to January 1980. Encouraged by the favourable response from veterans – Sterling Mace described the piece as 'magnificent . . . I was there every step of the way' – Sledge approached a couple of presses with a view to publishing the whole manuscript. 'They replied that the story was interesting,' he remembered, 'but everything had already been written on the subject that needed to be.'

Hurt by the rejection, Sledge said to himself: *To hell with it – it was enough of an emotional strain just describing on paper the sacrifices and loss of so many fine buddies*. At least now he would not have to edit the huge manuscript, something he was dreading. While his wife Jeanne was still keen for it to be published, Sledge was content 'to ask the USMC History Section if they wanted a copy for their files'. It was now that Bob Smith, the editor of the *Marine Corps Gazette*, intervened by urging Sledge to contact publishers Presidio Press a second time. On the first occasion, Sledge had sent a letter but no manuscript. He included it with the follow-up correspondence and the response from Presidio was a thumbs-up. But the manuscript, they said, was far too long and would need to be edited. The job – 'mostly cut and paste, the deletion of episodes' – was chiefly done by Bob Smith, with Sledge giving each chapter a final pass before it was sent to Presidio.[20]

Sledge's working title for the book was 'A Marine Mortarman in World War II', later changed to 'Into the Abyss'. But it was published by Presidio in 1981 as *With the Old Breed: On Peleliu and Okinawa* – a nod to George MacMillan's classic 1949 history of the 1st Marine Division in World War II, *The Old Breed*. Dedicated to the 'memory of Capt. Andrew A. Haldane, beloved company commander of K/3/5, and to the Old Breed', it is an unflinching portrait of war, told through the eyes of an intelligent and sensitive young man from a comfortable middle-class family who was thrown into the maelstrom of a pitiless conflict. Sledge made no bones about the mutual hatred felt by both sides. 'This collective attitude,' he wrote, 'Marine and Japanese, resulted in savage, ferocious fighting with no holds barred. This was not the dispassionate killing seen on other fronts or in other wars. This was a brutish, primitive hatred, as characteristic of the horror of the war in the Pacific as the palm trees and the islands.'[21]

He describes in gory detail the merciless killing, the looting of dead Japanese, the retention of body part 'souvenirs' that included ears and, in one instance, a hand, and even the forcible removal of gold teeth from a wounded but still living enemy soldier. Sledge himself is dissuaded from taking gold teeth from a corpse by a corpsman who warns him that they might carry disease. Only later does Sledge realize that the corpsman was trying to help him retain some of his humanity. The incident is, noted one commentator, the 'moral turning point' of the book.

As much as it emphasizes the horror and waste of war, *With the Old Breed* is also a homage to the US Marine Corps, and is 'distinguished by Sledge's pride in his military service and his admiration for the bravery and sacrifices of his comrades'. The commentator added: 'Sledge does not flinch from describing the ugliness of war, but the ugliness is offset by examples of nobility, comradeship, and common decency.' [22] It was in many ways the perfect book for its time. America was still reeling from its humiliating withdrawal from Vietnam a few years earlier, leaving the Communist regime of North Vietnam to take control of the whole country. *With the Old Breed* provided a welcome tonic, recounting a tough but ultimately successful campaign against another formidable Asian enemy.

The acclaim from critics was universal. 'Of all the books about the ground war in the Pacific,' wrote John Gregory Dunne in *The New York Review of Books*, 'it is the closest to a masterpiece.' Celebrated British military historian John Keegan agreed: 'His account of the struggle of a gently raised teenager to remain a civilised human being in circumstances which reduced comrades – whom he nevertheless loved – to "twentieth-century savages" is one of the most arresting documents in war literature, all the more moving because of the painful difficulty someone who is not a natural writer found in re-creating his experience on paper.'[23]

Particularly flattering for Sledge was the praise heaped on the book by cultural historian Paul Fussell, himself a World War II veteran, who described it as 'one of the finest memoirs to emerge from any war'. Sledge responded: 'Thank you for all the nice things you said about With the Old Breed. Your opinion, like Keegan's, means a great deal to me. I've received hundreds of letters and phone calls from people in all walks of life – all complimentary, fortunately. All the infantrymen (of three wars, I might add) say, "You told my story. That's the way it was; I felt the same way."'[24]

One correspondent, having lauded the book, asked the author if he would ever go back to Peleliu. Sledge replied:

> I would find a visit to Okinawa very interesting – even though it was such a terrible battle for the 1st Marine Div. that few of us survived unhurt. However, I don't think that I could ever bear to return to Peleliu.* Everything about that fight, and that battlefield,

* Sledge was true to his word. His son Henry recalled: 'I had the opportunity to go to Peleliu in 1999 to retrace my dad's footsteps. The tour group was overjoyed

> was so ferocious and unreal that I'm afraid something in me would snap if I ever saw that place again – regardless of what it looks like now. Okinawa was so bloody that my company (K-3-5) lost, including replacements, over 100% casualties during the campaign. But Okinawa was just another one of conventional war's tragic slaughter fields. In my mind it is long over now, we won, and it helped shorten WW II. On Peleliu K-3-5 suffered 64% casualties (we got no replacements during the battle the way we did later on Okinawa). But there was an eerie, ferocious aspect to the Peleliu battle which to my mind made it seem unreal – it was the absolute essence of the depths of Hell. It did something to a man's heart and soul that no other experience in WW II could do.[25]

He was, he told a friend, overwhelmed by the reaction to *With the Old Breed*. 'The published reviews have been very good. I've gotten letters from veterans, historians, amateur historians, and the general reader – and all are very pleased with the book. The veterans, to a man, are vehement in their statements that it was the most accurate and realistic account they have ever read about what it was really like up on the front line.'[26]

The opinions that mattered most to Sledge, however, were those of his fellow K Company veterans. They, too, were united in their praise. Jay de l'Eau, twice married and the father of three children and two stepchildren, wrote from his home in Walnut Creek, California in October 1982:

> How does one begin a letter to an old friend after 36 years of silence? . . . Thank you for writing the book. In telling your story you have told the story of many of us. Your descriptions of the events where I was involved are excellent. I know it will be a

---

to have a Sledge on the trip. They told me that if my father wanted to go, they would provide the trip all expenses paid. When I said that to him, he replied wryly, "You tell them I've already had an expenses paid trip to Peleliu!"' (Henry Sledge's email to the author, 3 November 2021.)

> treasured resource for historians and all those interested in what it was like to be a combat Marine in the Pacific War. I truly feel honored for having been included . . . It brought back so many memories, funny, sad, frightening. The comradeship we had, the friends we knew, the losses we suffered. I put the book down and went for a walk.[27]

Former First Sergeant Hank Boyes, who had married an Australian after the war and settled in rural New South Wales (where he ran a successful logging and cattle business), was sent an autographed copy of the book by Sledge. 'Thank you so very much,' replied Boyes,

> We of 'K' Company have been honored to have a man of your ability to tell the story of our every day experience in and out of combat. You have exposed the sterling quality of every Marine in 'K' Company and have made us realize that we are the *fortunate few*. Your real description takes me minute by minute, step by step across the airfield on Peleliu: the heat, shortage of water, the sound of battle, the extreme fear, and excitement that we all experienced, each in his own way. It is so well told. I read 'With the Old Breed' with an unbelievable amount of tension and fear. I find it compulsive reading and hard because it is so very real.
>
> . . . On behalf of 'K' Company, Bev and our family, we thank you for a superb accomplishment.[28]

A few days later, Sledge received a second congratulatory letter from Boyes's wife Bev. 'I found [the book] very difficult to read,' she wrote, 'as I am sure I am one of many who never realized what terrible, extreme conditions you all endured. So many, many events I never knew about. It helps me to understand "Hank" even more (even after 29 years of marriage!). I am sure many wives will feel the same after reading your fine account of events. It is a very important part of the U.S.A. history, not to be forgotten nor we pray ever repeated. It means so much to the K-3-5 men that others know of their supreme effort.'

Hank had also found it hard to read, she explained, because it forced him to relive many things he had 'tried to block out of his memory over the years'. Yet he was very proud of the book and honoured to have featured in it. 'I know he gave his best,' she added, 'as you all did.'[29]

Another K Company veteran who received an autographed copy of the book from Sledge was Jim McEnery. The inscription read: 'With profound admiration for one of the best Marines and bravest NCOs I ever saw under fire. It was guys like you, Jim, that acted as an example to some of us "boots" and kept us going when things got rough.' McEnery was deeply touched, and grateful that the book had done much 'to immortalize the men of K-3-5'.[30]

Graduate school had taught Sledge how to write. But so personal was the subject matter in *With the Old Breed* that it 'wrung him out emotionally'. On many occasions he was on the verge of giving it up. But every time he 'thought of the suffering and loss of fine guys on Peleliu, and then read the short shrift that history has given that battle', it made him determined to complete the story. 'It became,' he admitted in 1982, 'a personal crusade to see that First Marine Division survivors could have their story told by one of their own who was there – all 30 days of it. Okinawa has gotten the recognition it deserves, but I think I was able to add something from the yardbird's foxhole perspective there.'[31]

Sledge's proudest moment was being presented with a 'plaque of appreciation' by his surviving K/3/5 buddies at a reunion in 1982. 'Captain Haldane's sister was at the reunion,' he recalled, 'and presented it to me – there wasn't a dry eye in the room of over 40 veterans and their wives. Such recognition from those Marines who lived and suffered the story of the book is the ultimate honor to me.'[32]

In 2001, after a long battle with stomach cancer, 77-year-old Eugene Bondurant Sledge finally 'reported for duty to the Man Upstairs'.[33] He is buried near his parents and brother in Mobile's Pine Crest cemetery. A year later, his follow-up memoir *China Marine: An Infantryman's Life after World War II* was published posthumously by the University of Alabama Press. But he is best remembered for his first book *With the*

Old Breed, which was used as source material for Ken Burns's PBS documentary series *The War* (2007) and the HBO mini-series *The Pacific* (2010), in which Sledge's character is played by Joseph Mazello. 'In all the literature on the Second World War,' wrote Burns, 'there is not a more honest, realistic or moving memoir than Eugene Sledge's. This is the real deal, the real war: unvarnished, brutal, without a shred of sentimentality or false patriotism, a profound primer on what it was actually like to be in that war.'[34] Actor Tom Hanks, who co-produced *The Pacific* with Steven Spielberg, added: 'More than a legend . . . Sledge turned the extremes of the war in the Pacific – the terror, the camaraderie, the banal and the extraordinary – into terms we mortals can grasp.'

Sledge would have been elated. He told a friend in 1982:

> I wanted to chuck W.T.O.B. aside on more than one occasion, it was a very unpleasant subject to write about. But I felt that so much macho nonsense had been written by people who little knew the reality of war, that I was obligated to 'tell it like it was for those who fought' whether anybody ever read it outside my family or not. I really never dreamed it would be published. So, now that it is finished I'm delighted that the book seems to present a clearer picture of what my buddies, and thousands like them, did for our country.
>
> There is no such thing as 'the glory of war' in reality. That's fiction and armchair historian's stuff. There is only the 'horror of war', to the men who fight. Unfortunately, until heaven prevails, somebody has got to be ready to defend our country or we'll lose it.[35]

Acknowledgements

The idea for a book following the fortunes of a single company of US Marines though the Pacific War – one of the most pitiless and brutalizing combat theatres in history – came while I was researching the story of the final American campaign on the island of Okinawa, *Crucible of Hell* (published in 2020). That battle was the vicious endgame of the Pacific theatre, not that the participants knew it at the time. What intrigued me was how they had got to that point. Where and why had it all begun? Who was involved? And what was the physical and mental toll taken on the young Marines and their families, both during the war and after.

Many people helped with the research and writing of this book. I would particularly like to thank historian Richard B. Frank who read, commented on and hugely improved the manuscript; Henry Sledge (son of Eugene), who also read and commented on the manuscript, and wrote the generous Foreword; David Miller (son of Thurman), who provided many photos and gave me permission to quote from his father's excellent memoir *Earned in Blood*; Steve Moore who provided photos of, and letters written by, his uncle Andy Haldane; Garret Shetrawski, a former US Marine officer, who is writing a biography of Andy Haldane and generously shared some of his research and photos with me; and Leighton Hughes. Thank you.

The research for this project was completed in three continents: North America, Europe and Asia. Among those who provided vital assistance are Aaron Trehub, the former Head of Special Collections & Archives, Auburn University Libraries, AL; John C. Varner of Auburn University Libraries; Roberta B. Schwartz of the George J. Mitchell Department of Special Collections and Archives, Bowdoin College Library, Brunswick, ME; Dr Keith Gorman, Director of the Booth Family Center for Special Collections, Georgetown University Library, Washington DC; Lynn Conway of Georgetown University Library; John Lyles of the US Marine Corps Archive, Quantico, VA; David Holbrook of the Dwight D. Eisenhower Presidential Library and Museum, Abilene, KS; David Clark of the Harry S. Truman Presidential Library & Museum, Independence, MO; Tsugiko Taira of the Haeburu Town Museum in Okinawa; and the staffs of the Prefectural Peace Museum and the Himeyuri Peace Museum in Okinawa, the UK National Archives and the Imperial War Museum in London, and the US National Archives and Records Administration in College Park, MD.

Lastly, I'd like to thank my literary agent Caroline Michel; my publisher Arabella Pike and her excellent team at William Collins, notably Katherine Patrick, Jo Thompson, Iain Hunt, Julian Humphries, Matt Clacher and copy-editor Steve Gove; Claiborne Hancock of Pegasus Books in the US; and, last but not least, my wife Louise, and daughters Nell, Tamar and Tashie, who would prefer it if my subject matter was not quite so grim.

Notes

Introduction

1 Jim McEnery with Bill Sloan, *Hell in the Pacific: A Marine Rifleman's Journey from Guadalcanal to Peleliu* (New York: Simon & Schuster, 2012), p. 232.
2 E. B. Sledge, *With the Old Breed: At Peleliu and Okinawa* (New York: Presidio Press, 1981; repr. 2007), p. 344.
3 Foreword by Richard B. Frank in Thurman Miller, *Earned in Blood: My Journey from Old-Breed Marine to the Most Dangerous Job in America* (New York: St Martin's Press, 2013), p. xiii.
4 Auburn University Special Collections and Archives (AUA), Sledge Papers, RG96/96-038, Box 2, Folder 4, E. B. Sledge to William L. Cain, Jr, 14 July 1982.

1 'I would've followed him anywhere'

1 Miller, *Earned in Blood*, p. 64.
2 McEnery, *Hell in the Pacific*, p. 15.
3 Miller, *Earned in Blood*, p. 36.
4 Miller, *Earned in Blood*, p. 65.
5 Max Hastings, *Finest Years: Churchill as Warlord 1940–1945* (London: HarperPress, 2009; repr. 2010), p. 239.
6 Richard B. Frank, *Tower of Skulls: A History of the Asia-Pacific War, July 1937–May 1942* (New York: W. W. Norton, 2020; repr. 2021), p. 521.
7 Samuel Eliot Morison, 'American Strategy in the Pacific Ocean', *Oregon Historical Society*, 62/1 (March 1961), pp. 4–56 (p. 30).
8 John. J. Stephan, *Hawaii Under the Rising Sun: Japan's Plans for Conquest*

After Pearl Harbor (Honolulu, HI: University of Hawaii Press, 1984), pp. 109–15.

9 Winston Churchill, *The Second World War – Volume 4: Hinge of Fate* (London: Cassell & Co., 1951), pp. 212–26; Ian W. Toll, *The Conquering Tide: War in the Pacific Islands 1942–1944* (New York: W. W. Norton, 2015; repr. 2016), pp. 7, 9.

10 Toll, *The Conquering Tide*, p. 9.

11 Quoted in George McMillan, *The Old Breed: A History of the First Marine Division in World War II* (Washington: Infantry Journal Press, 1949), p. 27.

12 Toll, *The Conquering Tide*, p. 10.

13 Field Marshal Lord Alanbrooke, *War Diaries: 1939–1945*, ed. Alex Danchev and Daniel Todman (London: Weidenfeld, 2001), pp. 283, 364.

14 Alanbrooke, *War Diaries*, p. 359.

15 Clark G. Reynolds, 'Admiral Ernest J. King and the Strategy for Victory in the Pacific', *Naval War College Review*, 28/3 (Winter 1976), pp. 57–64 (pp. 58–9).

16 Toll, *The Conquering Tide*, pp. 11–12.

17 John Miller, Jr, *Guadalcanal: The First Offensive* (Washington DC: Office of the Chief of Military History, 1995), pp. 1–3.

18 Miller, Jr, *Guadalcanal: The First Offensive*, pp. 8–17.

19 Toll, *The Conquering Tide*, pp. 14–15.

20 McMillan, *The Old Breed*, pp. 17–21.

21 Miller, *Earned in Blood*, p. 63.

22 McMillan, *The Old Breed*, p. 20.

23 Thayer Soule, *Shooting the Pacific War: Marine Corps Combat Photography in WWII* (Lexington, KY: University Press of Kentucky, 2000), p. 45.

24 Richard B. Frank, *Guadalcanal: The Definitive Account of the Landmark Battle* (New York: Penguin Books, 1990; repr. 1992), pp. 31, 50.

25 Frank, *Guadalcanal*, pp. 52–3.

26 'Germans call 'em Teufel Hunden: Recruiters Report a New Nickname for Marines', *Boston Daily Globe*, 14 April 1918, p. 13. There is, however, no evidence of this name – which should in any case be *Teufelshunde* – in German records.

27 MacMillan, *The Old Breed*, pp. 2–3.

28 Richard Overy, *Blood and Ruins: The Great Imperial War 1931–1945* (London: Allen Lane, 2021), p. 461.

29 Overy, *Blood and Ruins*, p. 465; George W. Garand and Truman R. Strobridge, *History of U.S. Marine Corps Operations in World War II – Volume IV: Western Pacific Operations* (Historical Division, USMC, 1971), pp. 16–17.

30 McMillan, *The Old Breed*, p. 6.

31 https://www.battleorder.org/usmc-rifle-co-1941 [accessed 15 July 2020]
32 College Park, MD, US National Archives and Records Administration (USNARA), NWMDM-D/994011, 5th Marines Record of Events, 7 August to 9 August 1942.

2 'Where I'm going will either make or break me'

1 Toll, *The Conquering Tide,* pp. 20–1.
2 USNARA, NWMDM-D/994011, 5th Marines Record of Events, 26 June to 7 August 1942.
3 Miller, *Earned in Blood*, p. 60.
4 Richard Tregaskis, *Guadalcanal Diary* (New York: Random House, 1943; repr. 1962), pp. 24–5.
5 Tregaskis, *Guadalcanal Diary*, pp. 30–1.
6 McEnery, *Hell in the Pacific*, p. 2.
7 Miller, *Earned in Blood*, p. 61.
8 Miller, *Earned in Blood*, pp. 5–24.
9 Miller, *Earned in Blood*, pp. 25–9.
10 Lori Copeland, 'Project 100,000: Harvesting Poverty's Labor Force for War' (Master's thesis, University of Kentucky, 2008), pp. 39–40.
11 Ed Price, 'More Than Our Share of Heroes', *Now and Then*, 4/3 (Fall 1987), pp. 8–9, in https://files.eric.ed.gov/fulltext/ED313196.pdf [accessed 28 July 2021]
12 McEnery, *Hell in the Pacific*, p. 36; Sledge, *With the Old Breed*, p. 11.
13 Miller, *Earned in Blood*, pp. 25–35.
14 McMillan, *The Old Breed*, pp. 7–9.
15 McEnery, *Hell in the Pacific*, pp. 21–40.
16 Miller, *Earned in Blood*, pp. 37–8.
17 http://dublinlaurenshometownheroes.blogspot.com/2010/07/maurice-o-modarsey.html [accessed 16 July 2020]; Miller, *Earned in Blood*, pp. 36–7.
18 Miller, *Earned in Blood*, p. 44; Adam Makos, *Voices of the Pacific: Untold Stories from the Marine Heroes of World War II* (New York: Berkley Caliber, 2013; repr. 2014), p. 153.

3 'Will I run? Will I be afraid?'

1 Miller, *Earned in Blood*, p. 62.
2 Tregaskis, *Guadalcanal Diary*, pp. 36–9.
3 Tregaskis, *Guadalcanal Diary*, p. 40.
4 McMillan, *The Old Breed*, p. 30.

5 McEnery, *Hell in the Pacific*, pp. 1–3.
6 Gordon L. Rottman, *World War II US Marine Infantry Regiments* (Oxford: Osprey, 2018), p. 10; McEnery, *Hell in the Pacific*, p. 9.
7 Miller, *Earned in Blood*, pp. 66–7.
8 McEnery, *Hell in the Pacific*, pp. 6–8.
9 Miller, *Earned in Blood*, p. 67.
10 Frank, *Guadalcanal*, p. 61.
11 McEnery, *Hell in the Pacific*, pp. 10–12.
12 Tregaskis, *Guadalcanal Diary*, p. 44.
13 Frank, *Guadalcanal*, pp. 62–3; McMillan, *The Old Breed*, p. 39.
14 McMillan, *The Old Breed*, p. 31.
15 5th Marines Record of Events, 7 August to 9 August 1942.
16 McEnery, *Hell in the Pacific*, p. 13.
17 Frank, *Guadalcanal*, p. 69.
18 McEnery, *Hell in the Pacific*, pp. 9, 14–20.

4 'You think we'll ever get off this damned island?'

1 McEnery, *Hell in the Pacific*, p. 47.
2 McMillan, *The Old Breed*, p. 39.
3 McEnery, *Hell in the Pacific*, p. 48.
4 Tregaskis, *Guadalcanal Diary*, pp. 49–50.
5 Frank, *Guadalcanal*, p. 80; McMillan, *The Old Breed*, p. 40.
6 McMillan, *The Old Breed*, p. 39; 5th Marines Record of Events, 7 August to 9 August 1942.
7 Tregaskis, *Guadalcanal Diary*, pp. 52–5
8 McEnery, *Hell in the Pacific*, p. 52; 5th Marines Record of Events, 7 August to 9 August 1942.
9 McEnery, *Hell in the Pacific*, p. 52.
10 Toll, *The Conquering Tide*, pp. 20–1, 41–53; Frank, *Guadalcanal*, pp. 104–21.
11 Frank, *Guadalcanal*, pp. 124–6; McMillan, *The Old Breed*, pp. 48–9.
12 McEnery, *Hell in the Pacific*, pp. 57–9.
13 Frank, *Guadalcanal*, pp. 126–7.
14 5th Marines Record of Events, 7 August to 9 August 1942.

5 The Goettge Patrol

1 McMillan, *The Old Breed*, p. 52; Frank, *Guadalcanal*, pp. 129–30; Tregaskis, *Guadalcanal Diary*, p. 82; Quantico, VA, United States Marine Corps

Archives (USMCA), COLL/3654, Box 2, Folder 17, Vandegrift Conference, 1 February 1943, 'The Goettge Patrol', p. 1.
2 Soule, *Shooting the Pacific War*, pp. 67–9.
3 McMillan, *The Old Breed*, p. 52; Frank, *Guadalcanal*, pp. 129–30; Tregaskis, *Guadalcanal Diary*, p. 82; USMCA, 'The Goettge Patrol', p. 1.
4 Soule, *Shooting the Pacific War*, p. 69.
5 McMillan, *The Old Breed*, p. 53.
6 Tregaskis, *Guadalcanal Diary*, pp. 82–3.
7 McMillan, *The Old Breed*, pp. 54–5.
8 USNARA, NWMDM-D/994011, 5th Marines Record of Events, 10 August to 20 August 1942.
9 Tregaskis, *Guadalcanal Diary*, p. 83.
10 5th Marines Record of Events, 10 August to 20 August 1942.
11 Soule, *Shooting the Pacific War*, p. 71.
12 Miller, *Earned in Blood*, p. 78.
13 McEnery, *Hell in the Pacific*, pp. 64–8.
14 Miller, *Earned in Blood*, pp. 78–9.
15 McEnery, *Hell in the Pacific*, p. 68.
16 Miller, *Earned in Blood*, pp. 81–4.
17 McEnery, *Hell in the Pacific*, p. 69.

6 'Boy, they were a sight for sore eyes!'

1 Toll, *The Conquering Tide*, p. 64.
2 McEnery, *Hell in the Pacific*, p. 75.
3 5th Marines Record of Events, 10 August to 20 August 1942.
4 McEnery, *Hell in the Pacific*, p. 77; Toll, *The Conquering Tide*, pp. 70–1.
5 Toll, *The Conquering Tide*, pp. 72–3; Frank, *Guadalcanal*, pp. 143–52.
6 McMillan, *The Old Breed*, pp. 61–3.
7 Tregaskis, *Guadalcanal Diary*, p. 116.
8 Auburn University Special Collections and Archive (AUA), Sledge Papers, RG96/96-038, Box 1, Folder 29, Captain Nikolai Stevenson, 'Guadalcanal Remembered', pp. 8–9.
9 Frank, *Guadalcanal*, pp. 156–7; McMillan, *The Old Breed*, p. 64.
10 McEnery, *Hell in the Pacific*, p. 84.
11 Toll, *The Conquering Tide*, pp. 82–3; Frank, *Guadalcanal*, p. 193.
12 McEnery, *Hell in the Pacific*, p. 84.
13 Frank, *Guadalcanal*, pp. 195–6.
14 USNARA, NWMDM-D/994011, 5th Marines Record of Events, 21 August to 18 September 1942.

15 Tregaskis, *Guadalcanal Diary*, p. 180.
16 Frank, *Guadalcanal*, pp. 228–41; McMillan, *The Old Breed*, pp. 73–81.
17 https://valor.militarytimes.com/hero/2345 [accessed 11 August 2020]
18 Frank, *Guadalcanal*, p. 242.
19 McMillan, *The Old Breed*, p. 81.
20 McEnery, *Hell in the Pacific*, pp. 86–8.
21 AUA, Sledge Papers, RG96/96-038, Box 3, Folder 21, K/3/5 Muster Roll, September 1942.
22 McEnery, *Hell in the Pacific*, pp. 88–9.

7 'A pesthole that reeked of death, struggle and disease'

1 McEnery, *Hell in the Pacific*, p. 98.
2 McMillan, *The Old Breed*, p. 82.
3 Miller, *Earned in Blood*, pp. 88–9.
4 Miller, *Earned in Blood*, pp. 92–3.
5 Toll, *The Conquering Tide*, p. 64.
6 Miller, *Earned in Blood*, p. 90.
7 AUA, Sledge Papers, RG96/96-038, Box 3, Folder 21, K/3/5 Muster Rolls, August–September 1942.
8 McEnery, *Hell in the Pacific*, pp. 114–15.
9 Toll, *The Conquering Tide*, p. 64.
10 Miller, *Earned in Blood*, p. 91.
11 Miller, *Earned in Blood*, p. 92.
12 McMillan, *The Old Breed*, pp. 88–9.
13 https://missingMarines.com/weldon-f-delong/ [accessed 18 August 2020]; McEnery, *Hell in the Pacific*, pp. 120–1.
14 Miller, *Earned in Blood*, pp. 93–4.
15 McEnery, *Hell in the Pacific*, pp. 113–14.
16 Miller, *Earned in Blood*, pp. 123–5.
17 Lieutenant Colonel Frank O. Hough, Major Verle E. Ludwig and Henry I. Shaw, *History of the U.S. Marine Corps Operations in World War II – Volume 1: Pearl Harbor to Guadalcanal* (Historical Branch, USMC, 1958), pp. 309–11; Frank, *Guadalcanal*, pp. 261–2; McMillan, *The Old Breed*, pp. 89–90; Tregaskis, *Guadalcanal Diary*, pp. 193, 196; McEnery, *Hell in the Pacific*, p. 100.
18 Tregaskis, *Guadalcanal*, pp. 196–202.
19 Frank, *Guadalcanal*, pp. 252–5, 267–8.
20 Frank, *Guadalcanal*, p. 274.
21 Frank, *Guadalcanal*, p. 274; McMillan, *The Old Breed*, p. 91.

8 'Thirty hours of pure hell'

1 Hough et al., *History of the U.S. Marine Corps Operations*, I, pp. 318–19.
2 McEnery, *Hell in the Pacific*, p. 104.
3 Frank, *Guadalcanal*, p. 284.
4 McEnery, *Hell in the Pacific*, p. 105.
5 Miller, *Earned in Blood*, p. 114–15.
6 Hough et al., *History of the U.S. Marine Corps Operations*, I, p. 320.
7 McMillan, *The Old Breed*, p. 95.
8 McEnery, *Hell in the Pacific*, p. 106.
9 Frank, *Guadalcanal*, pp. 287–8; Hough et al., *History of the U.S. Marine Corps Operations*, I, pp. 320–1; McMillan, *The Old Breed*, pp. 95–6.
10 McEnery, *Hell in the Pacific*, p. 108.
11 Frank, *Guadalcanal*, p. 313; McEnery, *Hell in the Pacific*, p. 109.
12 Toll, *The Conquering Tide*, pp. 134–5.
13 McMillan, *The Old Breed*, pp. 102–3; McEnery, *Hell in the Pacific*, pp. 111–12; Frank, *Guadalcanal*, pp. 315–16.
14 Miller, *Earned in Blood*, pp. 108–9.
15 McEnery, *Hell in the Pacific*, pp. 112–13.
16 Frank, *Guadalcanal*, pp. 317–19.
17 McEnery, *Hell in the Pacific*, p. 113.
18 Toll, *The Conquering Tide*, pp. 141–2; Frank, *Guadalcanal*, pp. 324–30.
19 Frank, *Guadalcanal*, p. 333.
20 Toll, *The Conquering Tide*, p. 146; William F. Halsey, *Admiral Halsey's Story* (New York: McGraw-Hill, 1947), p. 117; Douglas MacArthur, *Reminiscences* (New York: McGraw-Hill, 2001; repr. 2001), pp. [see Part Six: World War II: The Allied Offensive 1943–1944]; E. B. Potter, *Nimitz*
21 Frank, *Guadalcanal*, pp. 404–8.
22 Toll, *The Conquering Tide*, pp. 153–4; Frank, *Guadalcanal*, pp. 400–1.
23 Miller, *Earned in Blood*, pp. 123–7; AUA, Sledge Papers, RG96/96-038, Box 3, Folder 21, K/3/5 Muster Rolls, October–November 1942; McEnery, *Hell in the Pacific*, p. 114.

9 'It was just a crazy thing to do'

1 McEnery, *Hell in the Pacific*, p. 117.
2 Frank, *Guadalcanal*, pp. 411–13.
3 McEnery, *Hell in the Pacific*, pp. 118–19; Frank, *Guadalcanal*, p. 413.
4 Frank, *Guadalcanal*, p. 413.
5 McEnery, *Hell in the Pacific*, pp. 120–3; https://www.findagrave.com/

memorial/31509381/charles-jack-kimmel [accessed 10 September 2020]; Miller, *Earned in Blood*, p. 114.

6 https://www.findagrave.com/memorial/31509381/charles-jack-kimmel
7 McEnery, *Hell in the Pacific*, pp. 121–2.
8 https://www.findagrave.com/memorial/180017294/erskine-w_-wells [accessed 10 September 2020]
9 McEnery, *Hell in the Pacific*, p. 122.
10 https://www.findagrave.com/memorial/180017294/erskine-w_-wells
11 https://missingMarines.com/weldon-f-delong/ [accessed 10 September 2020]
12 McEnery, *Hell in the Pacific*, pp. 123–5.
13 Frank, *Guadalcanal*, pp. 414–16; https://valor.militarytimes.com/hero/7679 [accessed 14 September 2020]
14 McMillan, *The Old Breed*, pp. 125–6.
15 Toll, *The Conquering Tide*, pp. 159–60; McMillan, *The Old Breed*, p. 127; Frank, *Guadalcanal*, pp. 422–3; https://www.usni.org/magazines/naval-history-magazine/2016/april/dear-admiral-halsey [accessed 14 September 2020]

10 'We've got the bastards licked!'

1 K/3/5 Muster Roll, November 1942.
2 McEnery, *Hell in the Pacific*, pp. 133–4.
3 K/3/5 Muster Roll, November 1942.
4 McEnery, *Hell in the Pacific*, p. 134; Clay McNitt Murray obituary, 13 June 2015, https://tulsaworld.com/obituaries/localobituaries/clay-mcnitt-murray/article_0a30b372-a4be-5aff-ab1d-440b489417b1.html [accessed 16 September 2020]
5 Miller, *Earned in Blood*, p. 128.
6 Sledge, *With the Old Breed*, pp. 128–31; Toll, *The Conquering Sea*, pp. 160–6; Frank, *Guadalcanal*, pp. 436–59.
7 Halsey, *Admiral Halsey's Story*, p. 127.
8 Frank, *Guadalcanal*, pp. 472–92; Halsey, *Admiral Halsey's Story*, pp. 129–32.
9 McEnery, *Hell in the Pacific*, pp. 127–8.
10 McMillan, *The Old Breed*, pp. 134–5.
11 McEnery, *Hell in the Pacific*, p. 132.
12 USNARA, NWMDM-D/994011, 5th Marines Record of Events, 19 September to 9 December 1942.
13 Frank, *Guadalcanal*, p. 522.
14 Miller, *Earned in Blood*, pp. 141–2.
15 McMillan, *The Old Breed*, pp. 139–40.
16 McMillan, *The Old Breed*, pp. 135–6.

17 Miller, *Earned in Blood*, pp. 131–2; McEnery, *Hell in the Pacific*, p. 137.
18 McMillan, *The Old Breed*, pp. 136–7.
19 Frank, *Guadalcanal*, pp. 613–14.
20 Toll, *The Conquering Tide*, p. 187.
21 McMillan, *The Old Breed*, p. 137.
22 Frank, *Guadalcanal*, p. 614.
23 McMillan, *The Old Breed*, p. 137.
24 Frank, *Guadalcanal*, p. 616.
25 Miller, *Earned in Blood*, p. 134.

11 'Saviours of Australia'

1 Miller, *Earned in Blood*, p. 140.
2 Soule, *Shooting the Pacific War*, p. 124.
3 McEnery, *Hell in the Pacific*, p. 138.
4 McMillan, *The Old Breed*, p. 146.
5 Miller, *Earned in Blood*, p. 141.
6 Soule, *Shooting the Pacific War*, p. 124.
7 McEnery, *Hell in the Pacific*, p. 139.
8 Soule, *Shooting the Pacific War*, p. 124.
9 McEnery, *Hell in the Pacific*, p. 140.
10 Miller, *Earned in Blood*, p. 143.
11 Soule, *Shooting the Pacific War*, pp. 125–6.
12 McMillan, *The Old Breed*, pp. 147–8.
13 Soule, *Shooting the Pacific War*, p. 129.
14 McEnery, *Hell in the Pacific*, p. 141.
15 McMillan, *The Old Breed*, pp. 148–9.
16 McEnery, *Hell in the Pacific*, p. 142.
17 McMillan, *The Old Breed*, p. 150.
18 McEnery, *Hell in the Pacific*, pp. 142–5.
19 Miller, *Earned in Blood*, pp. 144–5.
20 USMCA, COLL/1194, A/10/L/3/4, Nolen V. Marbrey, 'WWII: A War Story', p. 66.

12 'The trick is to run just fast enough'

1 McEnery, *Hell in the Pacific*, p. 134; K/3/5 Muster Roll, November 1942.
2 Miller, *Earned in Blood*, pp. 145–6.
3 Marbrey, 'WWII: A War Story', pp. 1–64.
4 Miller, *Earned in Blood*, p. 147.

5 Soule, *Shooting the Pacific War*, p. 138.
6 McMillan, *The Old Breed*, p. 151.
7 Soule, *Shooting the Pacific War*, p. 139.
8 McMillan, *The Old Breed*, pp. 151–2.

13 New Arrivals

1 Marbrey, 'WWII: A War Story', p. 75.
2 McEnery, *Hell in the Pacific*, p. 134.
3 McEnery, *Hell in the Pacific*, p. 146.
4 AUA, Sledge Papers, RG96/96-038, Box 2, Excerpts from a memo written 'To Future Committees of Award of the Andrew Allison Haldane Cup', undated.
5 *The Lewiston Daily Sun*, 18 May and 25 October 1940.
6 AUA, Excerpts from a memo written 'To Future Committees of Award of the Andrew Allison Haldane Cup'.
7 *The Lewiston Daily Sun*, 7 and 25 October 1941.
8 *The Lewiston Daily Sun*, 14 October 1943.
9 Brunswick, Maine, Bowdoin College Library (BCL), George J. Mitchell Department of Special Collections & Archives, Kenneth C. M. Sills Administrative Records, 1889–1969, Box 4, Folder 64, Sills to Haldane, 24 November 1942, and Haldane to Sills, 6 January 1943.
10 PP, Haldane Family Papers, Andy Haldane to his sister Janet, 31 January 1943.
11 Miller, *Earned in Blood*, p. 144.
12 Miller, *Earned in Blood*, pp. 147–8.
13 Rottman, *World War II US Marine Infantry Regiments*, pp. 21–2.
14 McEnery, *Hell in the Pacific*, pp. 148–9.
15 R. V. Burgin with Bill Marvel, *Islands of the Damned: A Marine at War in the Pacific* (New York: NAL Caliber, 2010), pp. 21–47; Makos, *Voices of the Pacific*, pp. 78–9.
16 AUA, Sledge Papers, RG96/96-39/Box 1, Info on Mortar, 60mm M2 on mount M2.
17 Burgin, *Islands of the Damned*, pp. 47–56; Makos, *Voices of the Pacific*, pp. 83–4.

14 Planning for Action

1 John Miller, Jr, *Cartwheel: The Reduction of Rabaul* (Washington DC: Office of the Chief of Military History, 1959), pp. 1–8.
2 Toll, *The Conquering Tide*, pp. 223–4.

3 http://www.lejeune.usmc.mil/2dmardiv/aabn/Rifleman.htm [accessed 10 October 2020]
4 McMillan, *The Old Breed*, pp. 161–70.
5 Burgin, *Islands of the Damned*, p. 51.
6 McEnery, *Hell in the Pacific*, p. 149.
7 Makos, *Voices of the Pacific*, pp. 85–6.
8 McEnery, *Hell in the Pacific*, pp. 149–50; Burgin, *Islands of the Damned*, pp. 59–60.
9 McMillan, *The Old Breed*, pp. 110–11; Burgin, *Islands of the Damned*, pp. 60–1.
10 McEnery, *Hell in the Pacific*, pp. 150–2; Burgin, *Islands of the Damned*, pp. 66–71.
11 Burgin, *Islands of the Damned*, p. 67.
12 Thurman I. Miller, *War and Work: The Autobiography* (New York: Writers Club Press, 2001), p. 98.
13 BCL, Box 4, Folder 64, Sills to Haldane, 11 November 1943, and Haldane to Sills, 29 November 1943.
14 McEnery, *Hell in the Pacific*, pp. 150–2; Burgin, *Islands of the Damned*, pp. 66–71.
15 John Miller, Jr, *Cartwheel: The Reduction of Rabaul*, pp. 222–5; Toll, *The Conquering Tide*, pp. 235, 240.
16 McMillan, *The Old Breed*, pp. 168–70; Lieut. Colonel Frank O. Hough and Major John A. Crown, *History of the U.S. Marine Corps Operations in World War II – Volume II, The Campaign on New Britain* (US Marine Corps Historical Branch, 1952), pp. 11–20.

15 Green Hell

1 McMillan, *The Old Breed*, p. 173.
2 McMillan, *The Old Breed*, pp. 182–5; Hough and Crown, *History of the U.S. Marine Corps Operations in World War II*, II, pp. 48–54.
3 Hough and Crown, *History of the U.S. Marine Corps Operations in World War II*, II, p. 2.
4 Hough and Crown, *History of the U.S. Marine Corps Operations in World War II*, II, pp. 1–10.
5 McMillan, *The Old Breed*, pp. 176–9.
6 McMillan, *The Old Breed*, p. 191.
7 Hough and Crown, *History of the U.S. Marine Corps Operations in World War II*, II, pp. 87–9.
8 McEnery, *Hell in the Pacific*, pp. 156–7

9 Hough and Crown, *History of the U.S. Marine Corps Operations in World War II*, II, p. 96.
10 Miller, *Earned in Blood*, p. 158.
11 Makos, *Voices of the Pacific*, pp. 105–7; Burgin, *Islands of the Damned*, pp. 72–3.
12 Marbrey, 'WWII: A War Story', pp. 106–7.
13 Hough and Crown, *History of the U.S. Marine Corps Operations in World War II*, II, pp. 96–7.
14 Burgin, *Islands of the Damned*, pp. 73–4.
15 Marbrey, 'WWII: A War Story', pp. 107.
16 McEnery, *Hell in the Pacific*, p. 157.
17 Asa Bordages, 'Suicide Creek', Part 1, *Collier's: The National Weekly*, 26 May 1945, p. 12.
18 Interview with Fred E. Miller, 3 June 2013, Veterans History Project, Library of Congress, in https://memory.loc.gov/diglib/vhp/bib/loc.natlib.afc2001001.05670 [accessed 17 June 2020]
19 Bordages, 'Suicide Creek', Part 1, p. 59.
20 Interview with Fred E. Miller, 3 June 2013, Veterans History Project.

16 Suicide Creek

1 Miller, *Earned in Blood*, p. 159.
2 Bordages, 'Suicide Creek', Part 1, p. 12.
3 Burgin, *Islands of the Damned*, pp. 74–5.
4 Makos, *Voices of the Pacific*, pp. 110–11, 114.
5 Miller, *Earned in Blood*, pp. 159–60; Makos, *Voices of the Pacific*, p. 112–13.
6 McEnery, *Hell in the Pacific*, pp. 157–61.
7 https://valor.militarytimes.com/hero/8306 [accessed 28 October 2020]; https://valor.militarytimes.com/hero/38594 [accessed 23 October 2020]
8 McEnery, *Hell in the Pacific*, p. 162.
9 Bordages, 'Suicide Creek', Part 1, p. 61.
10 Hough and Crown, *History of the U.S. Marine Corps Operations in World War II*, II, pp. 97–8; Bordages, 'Suicide Creek', Part 1, pp. 61–2; Dick Camp, 'The Jungles will run red with blood', *Leatherneck Magazine*, January 2019, p. 35.
11 Lane, *Guadalcanal Marine*, pp. 306–7.
12 Hough and Crown, *History of the U.S. Marine Corps Operations in World War II*, II, p. 98.
13 Bordages, 'Suicide Creek', Part 1, p. 62.
14 McEnery, *Hell in the Pacific*, pp. 167–8.

15 AUA, Sledge Papers, RG96/96-38, Box 1, Cape Gloucester Casualties, 1–31 January 1944; Camp, 'The Jungles will run red with blood', p. 35.
16 Miller, *Earned in Blood*, p. 161.

17 'So long, Dutch'

1 McMillan, *The Old Breed*, pp. 195–6.
2 Hough and Crown, *History of the U.S. Marine Corps Operations in World War II*, II, pp. 93–5.
3 Hough and Crown, *History of the U.S. Marine Corps Operations in World War II*, II, p. 99.
4 Bordages, 'Suicide Creek', Part 1, p. 62.
5 Burgin, *Islands of the Damned*, pp. 77–8.
6 Bordages, 'Suicide Creek', Part 1, p. 62.
7 Miller, *Earned in Blood*, pp. 167–8.
8 AUA, Sledge Papers, RG96/96-038, Box 1, Folder 8, Stanley to Gene Sledge, 22 December 1981.
9 Asa Bordages, 'Suicide Creek', Part 2, *Collier's: The National Weekly*, 2 June 1945, p. 21; Hough and Crown, *History of the U.S. Marine Corps Operations in World War II*, II, p. 101.
10 McMillan, *The Old Breed*, p. 197; Bordages, 'Suicide Creek', Part 2, pp. 21, 28.
11 Miller, *Earned in Blood*, p. 161.
12 Bordages, 'Suicide Creek', Part 2, p. 28.
13 1st Lt William F. Reckus's citation for a Navy Cross, at https://valor.militarytimes.com/hero/8306 [accessed 28 October 2020]
14 'Officer's Body to be Returned for Interment', *South Bend Tribune*, 13 February 1949; Miller, *Earned in Blood*, p. 163.
15 Miller, *Earned in Blood*, p. 163.
16 Bordages, 'Suicide Creek', Part 2, p. 28.

18 Walt's Ridge

1 Hough and Crown, *History of the U.S. Marine Corps Operations in World War II*, II, p. 102; Bordages, 'Suicide Creek', Part 2, p. 30.
2 Marbrey, 'WWII: A War Story', pp. 109–11.
3 Bordages, 'Suicide Creek', Part 2, p. 30.
4 http://www.victoryinstitute.net/blogs/utb/1944/01/09/robert-l-grays-navy-cross-citation/ [accessed 29 October 2020]

5 Citation for the award of the Silver Star to Captain Andrew A. Haldane, at https://valor.militarytimes.com/hero/39523 [accessed 30 October 2020]
6 Bordages, 'Suicide Creek', Part 2, p. 30.
7 Hough and Crown, *History of the U.S. Marine Corps Operations in World War II*, II, p. 102.
8 Bordages, 'Suicide Creek', Part 2, p. 30.
9 T. I. Miller, in Makos, *Voices of the Pacific*, p. 117.
10 Burgin, *Islands of the Damned*, p. 78.
11 Hough and Crown, *History of the U.S. Marine Corps Operations in World War II*, II, pp. 102–3.
12 T. I. Miller, in Makos, *Voices of the Pacific*, pp. 118–20; Miller, *Earned in Blood*, p. 163.
13 Burgin, *Islands of the Damned*, p. 79.
14 Bordages, 'Suicide Creek', Part 2, p. 30.
15 T. I. Miller, in Makos, *Voices of the Pacific*, p. 119.
16 Interview with Fred E. Miller, 3 June 2013, Veterans History Project.
17 Hough and Crown, *History of the U.S. Marine Corps Operations in World War II*, II, p. 104.
18 AUA, Sledge Papers, RG96/96-038, Box 1, Folder 8, Service Records of Gunnery Sergeant St Elmo Haney; Miller, *Earned in Blood*, p. 35; R. V. Burgin in Makos, *Voices of the Pacific*, p. 116.
19 Hough and Crown, *History of the U.S. Marine Corps Operations in World War II*, II, p. 104; Bordages, 'Suicide Creek', Part 2, p. 32.
20 Hough and Crown, *History of the U.S. Marine Corps Operations in World War II*, II, pp. 104–5.
21 Bordages, 'Suicide Creek', Part 2, p. 32; Hough and Crown, *History of the U.S. Marine Corps Operations in World War II*, II, p. 103.
22 https://valor.militarytimes.com/hero/8534 [accessed 3 November 2020]
23 AUA, Sledge Papers, RG96/96-038, Box 1, Folder 8, Tom 'Stumpy' Stanley to Lt. Col. James Rogers, 21 August 1980.
24 AUA, Sledge Papers, RG96/96-038, Box 1, Folder 8, General Lewis B. Walt to Tom 'Stumpy' Stanley, 5 June 1981.
25 https://valor.militarytimes.com/hero/39523 and https://valor.militarytimes.com/hero/36681 [both accessed 3 November 2020]
26 Miller, *Earned in Blood*, p. 167.
27 T. I. Miller, in Makos, *Voices of the Pacific*, p. 121.
28 http://www.victoryinstitute.net/blogs/utb/1944/01/03/william-f-reckus-navy-cross-citation/ [accessed 30 October 2020]

29 https://valor.militarytimes.com/hero/7862 [accessed 30 October 2020]
30 https://www.findagrave.com/memorial/135011300/lowell-raymond-toelle#view-photo=197065281 [accessed 31 October 2020]
31 *The Indianapolis Star*, 22 October 1944.
32 Hough and Crown, *History of the U.S. Marine Corps Operations in World War II*, II, p. 104.
33 R. V. Burgin, in Makos, *Voices of the Pacific*, p. 121.
34 https://valor.militarytimes.com/hero/36463 [accessed 31 October 2020]
35 McEnery, *Hell in the Pacific*, pp. 169–71.

19 Seek and Destroy

1 Miller, *Earned in Blood*, p. 167.
2 Burgin, *Islands of the Damned*, pp. 80–1; R. V. Burgin, in Makos, *Voices of the Pacific*, p. 122; https://www.findagrave.com/memorial/127544164/robert-barry-oswalt [accessed 5 November 2020]
3 Miller, *Earned in Blood*, p. 168; T. I. Miller, in Makos, *Voices of the Pacific*, p. 123.
4 Burgin, *Islands of the Damned*, p. 83.
5 Miller, *Earned in Blood*, pp. 168–70.
6 Burgin, *Islands of the Damned*, p. 84; R. V. Burgin, in Makos, *Voices of the Pacific*, pp. 125–6.
7 BCL, Kenneth C. M. Sills Administrative Records, 1889–1969, Box 4, Folder 64, Sills to Haldane, 20 January 1944.
8 Faria Nasruddin, 'War hero Andrew Haldane '41 to be featured in biography', *Bowdoin Orient*, 8 December 2017, https://bowdoinorient.com/2017/12/08/war-hero-andrew-haldane-41-to-be-featured-in-biography/ [accessed 5 March 2021]
9 McMillan, *The Old Breed*, pp. 200–7; AUA, Sledge Papers, RG96/96-038, Box 1, Folder 2, List of Dead from the 3/5 Battalion during the Cape Gloucester and Talasea Campaigns.
10 Hough and Crown, *History of the U.S. Marine Corps Operations in World War II*, II, pp. 110–11; McMillan, *The Old Breed*, p. 211.
11 Hough and Crown, *History of the U.S. Marine Corps Operations in World War II*, II, p. 113.
12 McMillan, *The Old Breed*, pp. 215–16.
13 Hough and Crown, *History of the U.S. Marine Corps Operations in World War II*, II, p. 126.
14 McEnery, *Hell in the Pacific*, pp. 173–4; *The Philadelphia Inquirer*, 18 April 1944.

15 Burgin, *Islands of the Damned*, p. 85.
16 Burgin, *Islands of the Damned*, p. 95.
17 Hough and Crown, *History of the U.S. Marine Corps Operations in World War II*, II, pp. 126–7.
18 USMCA, Oliver P. Smith Papers, COLL/213, A/30/D2/4, Box 53, Folder 1, 'Personal Narrative: New Britain, Russell Islands, Palau, Peleliu', p. 9.
19 USMCA, Smith, 'Personal Narrative: New Britain, Russell Islands, Palau, Peleliu', pp. 11–12.

20 Operation Appease

1 Hough and Crown, *History of the U.S. Marine Corps Operations in World War II*, II, pp. 126–7, 152.
2 Smith, 'Personal Narrative: New Britain, Russell Islands, Palau, Peleliu', pp. 12–28; Hough and Crown, *History of the U.S. Marine Corps Operations in World War II*, II, p. 159.
3 Miller, *Earned in Blood*, pp. 174–5.
4 Smith, 'Personal Narrative: New Britain, Russell Islands, Palau, Peleliu', pp. 31–2, 5.
5 Hough and Crown, *History of the U.S. Marine Corps Operations in World War II*, II, p. 167.
6 Miller, *Earned in Blood*, p. 174.
7 Hough and Crown, *History of the U.S. Marine Corps Operations in World War II*, II, p. 167.
8 Burgin, *Islands of the Damned*, p. 88.
9 Miller, *Earned in Blood*, pp. 176–7.
10 Burgin, *Islands of the Damned*, pp. 90–1.
11 McEnery, *Hell in the Pacific*, pp. 173–4; *The Philadelphia Inquirer*, 18 April 1944.
12 McEnery, *Hell in the Pacific*, p. 175; *The Mercury (Pottstown)*, 26 October 1944.
13 Miller, *Earned in Blood*, p. 175.
14 McEnery, *Hell in the Pacific*, p. 175
15 Hough and Crown, *History of the U.S. Marine Corps Operations in World War II*, II, p. 167.
16 Smith, 'Personal Narrative: New Britain, Russell Islands, Palau, Peleliu', p. 46.

21 'The sickness, the rain, the spider'

1 Smith, 'Personal Narrative: New Britain, Russell Islands, Palau, Peleliu', pp. 34, 38–9.
2 Burgin, *Islands of the Damned*, pp. 91–2.
3 https://www.battleorder.org/usmc-rifle-co-1944 [accessed 13 November 2020]
4 https://www.ancestry.com.au/search/?name=Charles_Ellington&birth=1913&death=1944 [accessed 13 November 2020]
5 Burgin, *Islands of the Damned*, p. 92.
6 Bill Sloan, *Brotherhood of Heroes: The Marines at Peleliu, 1944* (New York: Simon & Schuster, 2005), pp. 27–8; 'Treasured uncle was a "genuine American hero"', in https://eu.southcoasttoday.com/article/20040425/News/304259989 [accessed 13 November 2020]; 'Live and Learn: On Memorial Day, thinking about what might have been', in https://eu.southcoasttoday.com/news/20180526/live-and-learn-on-memorial-day-thinking-about-what-might-have-been [accessed 13 November 2020].
7 Burgin, *Islands of the Damned*, pp. 109–10.
8 Burgin, *Islands of the Damned*, p. 93.
9 Interview with Fred E. Miller, 3 June 2013, Veterans History Project.
10 Smith, 'Personal Narrative: New Britain, Russell Islands, Palau, Peleliu', pp. 43–4.
11 Smith, 'Personal Narrative: New Britain, Russell Islands, Palau, Peleliu', p. 50; Toll, *The Conquering Tide*, pp. 438–9; McMillan, *The Old Breed*, pp. 226–7; Hough and Crown, *History of the U.S. Marine Corps Operations in World War II*, II, p. 182; Garand and Strobridge, *History of U.S. Marine Corps Operations in World War II*, IV, pp. 51–2; Robert Ross Smith, *The War in the Pacific: The Approach to the Philippines* (Washington DC: Center of Military History, US Army, 1953; repr. 1996), pp. 1–6.
12 Smith, 'Personal Narrative: New Britain, Russell Islands, Palau, Peleliu', p. 50.
13 Hough and Crown, *History of the U.S. Marine Corps Operations in World War II*, II, p. 183.; AUA, Sledge Papers, RG96/96-038, Box 1, Folder 2, List of Dead from the 3/5 Marines during the Cape Gloucester and Talasea campaigns.
14 Hough and Crown, *History of the U.S. Marine Corps Operations in World War II*, II, pp. 182–7.
15 Hough and Crown, *History of the U.S. Marine Corps Operations in World War II*, II, pp. 182–7.
16 Miller, *Earned in Blood*, pp. 180–1; Miller, *War and Work*, p. 107.

22 'Whose bright idea was this anyway?'

1 McMillan, *The Old Breed*, p. 229; Burgin, *Islands of the Damned*, p. 109.
2 Burgin, *Islands of the Damned*, p. 97; McEnery, *Hell in the Pacific*, p. 185.
3 Marbrey, 'WWII: A War Story', pp. 148–9.
4 McMillan, *The Old Breed*, pp. 229–30; Burgin, *Islands of the Damned*, p. 98.
5 Marbrey, 'WWII: A War Story', pp. 150–1.
6 Burgin, *Islands of the Damned*, pp. 98–9.
7 McEnery, *Hell in the Pacific*, pp. 187–8.
8 McMillan, *The Old Breed*, pp. 230.
9 Smith, 'Personal Narrative: New Britain, Russell Islands, Palau, Peleliu', pp. 51–2.
10 McEnery, *Hell in the Pacific*, pp. 189–90.
11 Miller, *War and Work*, pp. 108–9.
12 Burgin, *Islands of the Damned*, pp. 101–2.

23 Changing Places

1 Miller, *Earned in Blood*, p. 186.
2 Smith, 'Personal Narrative: New Britain, Russell Islands, Palau, Peleliu', pp. 79–80.
3 Smith, 'Personal Narrative: New Britain, Russell Islands, Palau, Peleliu', p. 50; Miller, *Earned in Blood*, pp. 186–8; Miller, *War and Work*, pp. 111–12.
4 Sterling Mace and Nick Allen, *Battleground Pacific: A Marine Rifleman's Combat Odyssey in K/3/5* (New York: St Martin's Griffin, 2012), pp. 4–44.
5 McEnery, *Hell in the Pacific*, pp. 190–2.

24 Operation Stalemate

1 Smith, 'Personal Narrative: New Britain, Russell Islands, Palau, Peleliu', p. 62.
2 Garand and Strobridge, *History of U.S. Marine Corps Operations in World War II*, IV, pp. 54–7.
3 Smith, 'Personal Narrative: New Britain, Russell Islands, Palau, Peleliu', p. 62.
4 Halsey and Bryan, *Admiral Halsey's Story*, pp. 194–7.
5 Jean Edward Smith, *FDR* (New York: Random House Inc., 2007; repr. 2008), pp. 621–2; Edwin P. Hoyt, *How They Won the War in the Pacific: Nimitz and his Admirals* (New York: Weybright and Talley, 1970), p. 412; Jonathan W. Jordan, *American Warlords: How Roosevelt's High Command led America to Victory in World War II* (New York: NAL Caliber, 2015), pp. 383–4.
6 Halsey, *Admiral Halsey's Story*, pp. 194–7.

7 Smith, 'Personal Narrative: New Britain, Russell Islands, Palau, Peleliu', pp. 62–3.
8 Garand and Strobridge, *History of U.S. Marine Corps Operations in World War II*, IV, pp. 57–8; Ross Smith, *The War in the Pacific: The Approach to the Philippines*, p. 457–9.
9 Smith, 'Personal Narrative: New Britain, Russell Islands, Palau, Peleliu', p. 63; AUA, Sledge Papers, RG96/96-038, Box 1, Folder 27, Brigadier General Harold D. 'Bucky' Harris to Captain T. 'Stumpy' Stanley, 11 July 1981.
10 Toll, *The Conquering Tide*, pp. 464–535.
11 Smith, 'Personal Narrative: New Britain, Russell Islands, Palau, Peleliu', pp. 63–4; Ross Smith, *The War in the Pacific: The Approach to the Philippines*, pp. 460–3.
12 Garand and Strobridge, *History of U.S. Marine Corps Operations in World War II*, IV, pp. 66–76.

25 Sledgehammer

1 Sledge, *With the Old Breed*, pp. 33–4.
2 Aaron Trehub, 'Eugene B. Sledge and Mobile: 75 Years After "The War"', *Mobile Bay Magazine*, 21 August 2020.
3 Aaron Trehub, 'William March and Eugene B. Sledge: Mobilians, Marines, and Writers', in *The Alabama Review*, 66/1 (January 2013), pp. 30–66 (pp. 34–5).
4 Hugh Ambrose, *The Pacific* (New York: NAL Signet, 2010; repr. 2011), p. 11.
5 Trehub, 'William March and Eugene B. Sledge: Mobilians, Marines, and Writers', pp. 43–4, 58.
6 Ambrose, *The Pacific*, p. 11; Makos, *Voices of the Pacific*. p. 149.
7 Sledge, *With the Old Breed*, pp. 5–6; interview with Jeanne Sledge, Disc 6, Special Features, *The Pacific*, HBO miniseries, 2010.
8 AUA, Sledge Papers. RG96/96-038, Box 1, Folder 34, Sledge to James G. Schneider, 25 February 1986.
9 AUA, Sledge Papers. RG96/98-091, Box 1, Folder 1, Sledge to his parents, 9 and 28 September, and 4 October 1943.
10 AUA, Sledge Papers RG96/98-091, Box 1, Folder 2, Sledge to his parents, 5 and 9 November 1943.
11 AUA, Sledge Papers, RG96/96-038, Box 1, Folder 25, Sledge to Lt. Col. Robert W. Smith, 1 February 1980.
12 Sledge, *With the Old Breed*, pp. 7–15; AUA, Sledge Papers, RG96/98-091,

Box 1, Folder 3, Sledge to his cousin Lizzie, 11 December 1943.
13 Sledge, *With the Old Breed*, pp. 15–22.
14 AUA, Sledge Papers, RG96/98-091, Box 1, Folder 4, Sledge to his parents, 7 March, and 11 and 22 April. 1944; Sledge to 'Ta Ta', 9 April 1944.
15 Sledge, *With the Old Breed*, pp. 33–5.
16 Ambrose, *The Pacific*, p. 344.
17 Burgin, *Islands of the Damned*, p. 104.
18 McEnery, *Hell in the Pacific*, p. 192; Burgin, *Islands of the Damned*, p. 104.

26 'They really put on a show'

1 Ambrose, *The Pacific*, pp. 344–5.
2 AUA, Sledge Papers, RG96/98-091, Box 1, Folder 5, Sledge to his parents, 22 June, 25 June and 3 July 1944.
3 Sledge, *With the Old Breed*, pp. 41–2.
4 Burgin, *Islands of the Damned*, pp. 107–8.
5 Sledge, *With the Old Breed*, p. 42.
6 Ambrose, *The Pacific*, pp. 373–5.
7 Sledge, *With the Old Breed*, pp. 43–4.
8 McEnery, *Hell in the Pacific*, pp. 197–8.
9 Mace, *Battleground Pacific*, pp. 38–41.
10 Sledge, *With the Old Breed*, pp. 45–6.
11 Burgin, *Islands of the Damned*, pp. 112–14.
12 McMillan, *The Old Breed*, pp. 249–50; Burgin, *Islands of the Damned*, pp. 114–16; Smith, 'Personal Narrative: New Britain, Russell Islands, Palau, Peleliu', p. 72.
13 https://www.nationalww2museum.org/war/articles/mail-call-moving-letter-within-letter [accessed 7 January 2021]
14 Burgin, *Islands of the Damned*, p. 116.
15 https://www.nationalww2museum.org/war/articles/mail-call-moving-letter-within-letter [accessed 7 January 2021]

27 'This is going to be a short one, a quickie'

1 BCL, Box 4, Folder 64, Sills to Haldane, 24 July 1944, and Haldane to Sills, 25 July 1943.
2 Ambrose, *The Pacific*, pp. 351–2, 378.
3 Sledge, *With the Old Breed*, pp. 46–8.
4 Smith, 'Personal Narrative: New Britain, Russell Islands, Palau, Peleliu', pp. 76–7.

5 AUA, Sledge Papers, RG96/96-038, Box 1, Folder 31, Brigadier General Harold D. Harris Service Record.
6 AUA, Sledge Papers, RG96/96-038, Box 1, Folder 31, unpublished memoir of Brigadier General Harold D. Harris, p. 125.
7 McMillan, *The Old Breed*, pp. 264–5, 279; Smith, 'Personal Narrative: New Britain, Russell Islands, Palau, Peleliu', pp. 70–5; Harris, unpublished memoir, p. 127.
8 Harris, unpublished memoir, p. 127.
9 USNARA, NND994011, Record of Operations of the 3/5 Marines, 26 August to 7 November 1944; McEnery, *Hell in the Pacific*, p. 205; Sledge, *With the Old Breed*, p. 49.
10 Harris, unpublished memoir, p. 127; Sledge, *With the Old Breed*, p. 49; Record of Operations of the 3/5 Marines, 26 August to 7 November 1944.
11 Mace, *Battleground Pacific*, p. 45.
12 McEnery, *Hell in the Pacific*, p. 206; Sledge, *With the Old Breed*, pp. 49–50.
13 McMillan, *The Old Breed*, p. 269; McEnery, *Hell in the Pacific*, p. 206.
14 Roger Willock, *Unaccustomed to Fear: A Biography of the Late General Roy S. Geiger* (Princeton: privately published, 1968), pp. 268–9.
15 Record of Operations of the 3/5 Marines, 26 August–7 November 1944.
16 Burgin, *Islands of the Damned*, pp. 116–17.
17 Mace, *Battleground Pacific*, p. 47.
18 Sledge, *With the Old Breed*, 50–3.
19 Burgin, *Islands of the Damned*, p. 120.
20 PP, Haldane Family Papers, Haldane to Phyllis Stowell, 5 September 1944.
21 Garand and Strobridge, *History of U.S. Marine Corps Operations in World War II*, IV, pp. 101–4.
22 Garand and Strobridge, *History of U.S. Marine Corps Operations in World War II*, IV, pp. 64–6; Ian W. Toll, *Twilight of the Gods: War in the Western Pacific, 1944–1945* (New York: W. W. Norton, 2020), pp. 125–9.
23 Colonel Joseph H. Alexander, 'What Was Nimitz Thinking?', *Proceedings* magazine, 124 (1998), at https://www.usni.org/magazines/proceedings/1998/november/what-was-nimitz-thinking [accessed 7 January 2022]

28 'This is it, boys!'

1 Sledge, *With the Old Breed*, pp. 53–8.
2 Burgin, *Islands of the Damned*, pp. 121–2.
3 Sledge, *With the Old Breed*, p. 58.
4 AUA, Sledge Papers, RG96/96-038, Box 2, Folder 13, Boyes to Sledge, 28 January 1980.

5 Burgin, *Islands of the Damned*, p. 122.
6 Garand and Strobridge, *History of U.S. Marine Corps Operations in World War II*, IV, p. 106; Burgin, *Islands of the Damned*, pp. 122–3.
7 Sledge, *With the Old Breed*, p. 59.
8 Mace, *Battleground Pacific*, pp. 49–50.
9 Burgin, *Islands of the Damned*, p. 123.
10 Sledge, *With the Old Breed*, p. 59; Burgin, *Islands of the Damned*, pp. 4–5.
11 Mace, *Battleground Pacific*, pp. 50–1.
12 Burgin, *Islands of the Damned*, p. 5.
13 Garand and Strobridge, *History of U.S. Marine Corps Operations in World War II*, IV, pp. 106–8.
14 Sledge, *With the Old Breed*, pp. 63–4.
15 AUA, Sledge Papers, RG96/96-038, Box 1, Folder 8, Tom Stanley to Gene Sledge, 17 December 1981.
16 Sledge, *With the Old Breed*, pp. 63–4; Burgin, *Islands of the Damned*, pp. 6–7.
17 Sloan, *Brotherhood of Heroes*, pp. 1–2.
18 McEnery, *Hell in the Pacific*, p. 208.
19 Mace, *Battleground Pacific*, p. 54.

29 'Move it! Move it!'

1 McEnery, *Hell in the Pacific*, pp. 208–10; AUA, Sledge Papers, RG96/96-038, Box 2, Joseph Moskalczak to Eugene Sledge, 9 March 1988.
2 Garand and Strobridge, *History of U.S. Marine Corps Operations in World War II*, IV, p. 116.
3 Sledge, *With the Old Breed*, pp. 65–7.
4 Interview with Fred E. Miller, 3 June 2013, Veterans History Project.
5 Garand and Strobridge, *History of U.S. Marine Corps Operations in World War II*, IV, pp. 115–16.
6 Garand and Strobridge, *History of U.S. Marine Corps Operations in World War II*, IV, pp. 110–16.
7 AUA, Sledge Papers, RG96/96-038, Box 1, Folder 31, Harris, unpublished memoir, pp. 129–30.
8 Garand and Strobridge, *History of U.S. Marine Corps Operations in World War II*, IV, p. 116.
9 Sledge, *With the Old Breed*, pp. 68–71.
10 Burgin, *Islands of the Damned*, p. 7.
11 AUA, Sledge Papers, RG96/96-038, Box 2, Folder 13, Boyes to Sledge, 5 May 1980; https://valor.militarytimes.com/hero/35441 [accessed 19 January 2021]

30 'They're Nip tanks!'

1 Garand and Strobridge, *History of U.S. Marine Corps Operations in World War II*, IV, pp. 116–17; Record of Operations of the 3/5 Marines, 26 August to 7 November 1944.
2 https://valor.militarytimes.com/hero/35223 [accessed 20 January 2021]
3 Georgetown University Library (GUL), Booth Family Center for Special Collections, John F. Barrett Papers, undated obituary.
4 https://valor.militarytimes.com/hero/35223 [accessed 20 January 2021]
5 Garand and Strobridge, *History of U.S. Marine Corps Operations in World War II*, IV, pp. 117–18; Record of Operations of the 3/5 Marines, 26 August to 7 November 1944; Sledge, *With the Old Breed*, p. 72.
6 Garand and Strobridge, *History of U.S. Marine Corps Operations in World War II*, IV, pp. 117–18; Record of Operations of the 3/5 Marines, 26 August to 7 November 1944.
7 Sledge, *With the Old Breed*, pp. 73–4.
8 Burgin, *Islands of the Damned*, p. 14.
9 Garand and Strobridge, *History of U.S. Marine Corps Operations in World War II*, IV, pp. 122–6.
10 Sledge, *With the Old Breed*, pp. 74–5.
11 Burgin, *Islands of the Damned*, p. 14.
12 Sledge, *With the Old Breed*, pp. 75–6.
13 Ambrose, *The Pacific*, pp. 405–6.
14 Harris, unpublished memoir, pp. 129–30.
15 Garand and Strobridge, *History of U.S. Marine Corps Operations in World War II*, IV, pp. 118–19; AUA, Sledge Papers, RG96/96-038, Box 2, Folder 37, George W. Poppe to Sledge, 12 December 1983.
16 AUA, Sledge Papers, RG96/96-038, Box 1, Folder 8, Tom 'Stumpy' Stanley to Lieut. Col. James Rogers, 21 August 1980.
17 Garand and Strobridge, *History of U.S. Marine Corps Operations in World War II*, IV, pp. 118–19.
18 Sledge, *With the Old Breed*, pp. 77–8.
19 McEnery, *Hell in the Pacific*, p. 215.
20 Mace, *Battleground Pacific*, pp. 228–9.
21 McMillan, *The Old Breed*, pp. 276–9.
22 McMillan, *The Old Breed*, p. 297; Smith, 'Personal Narrative: New Britain, Russell Islands, Palau, Peleliu', pp. 19–34.

31 'Everywhere shells flashed like giant firecrackers'

1 Mace, *Battleground Pacific*, p. 78.
2 McMillan, *The Old Breed*, pp. 300–1.
3 McEnery, *Hell in the Pacific*, pp. 215–16.
4 Sledge, *With the Old Breed*, pp. 83–4.
5 Garand and Strobridge, *History of U.S. Marine Corps Operations in World War II*, IV, pp. 139–41; McMillan, *The Old Breed*, p. 291; AUA, Sledge Papers, RG96/96-038, Box 1, Folder 27, Harris to Captain T. J. 'Stumpy' Stanley, 11 July 1981.
6 McEnery, *Hell in the Pacific*, pp. 216–17.
7 Mace, *Battleground Pacific*, pp. 80–1.
8 Sledge, *With the Old Breed*, pp. 85–6.
9 Mace, *Battleground Pacific*, pp. 81–2.
10 Sledge, *With the Old Breed*, pp. 86–7; AUA, Sledge Papers, RG96/96-038, Box 3, Folder 8, 1st Sgt David Bailey's Log of Casualties on Peleliu.
11 Garand and Strobridge, *History of U.S. Marine Corps Operations in World War II*, IV, p. 139.
12 Sledge, *With the Old Breed*, pp. 89–91.
13 1st Sgt David Bailey's Log of Casualties on Peleliu; Sledge, *With the Old Breed*, p. 91.
14 McMillan, *The Old Breed*, p. 306.
15 Smith, 'Personal Narrative: New Britain, Russell Islands, Palau, Peleliu', pp. 45–6.
16 McMillan, *The Old Breed*, p. 306.
17 Garand and Strobridge, *History of U.S. Marine Corps Operations in World War II*, IV, p. 141; Record of Operations of the 3/5 Marines, 26 August to 7 November 1944.
18 Sledge, *With the Old Breed*, p. 93.
19 1st Sgt David Bailey's Log of Casualties on Peleliu.
20 McEnery, *Hell in the Pacific*, pp. 223–4.
21 Sledge, *With the Old Breed*, pp. 95–6.
22 Paul Douglas, *In the Fullness of Time: The Memoirs of Paul H. Douglas* (New York: Harcourt, 1972), pp. 107–30.
23 Sledge, *With the Old Breed*, pp. 97–8.

32 'I never saw such agonized expressions'

1 Smith, 'Personal Narrative: New Britain, Russell Islands, Palau, Peleliu', p. 46.
2 McEnery, *Hell in the Pacific*, pp. 225–6.

3 Record of Operations of the 3/5 Marines, 26 August to 7 November 1944; Burgin, *Islands of the Damned*, p. 138.
4 Sledge, *With the Old Breed*, pp. 105–11; Burgin, *Islands of the Damned*, pp. 138–41.
5 Burgin, *Islands of the Damned*, pp. 143–4; Mace, *Battleground Pacific*, p. 103; McEnery, *Hell in the Pacific*, p. 227.
6 McMillan, *The Old Breed*, pp. 318, 457; Smith, 'Personal Narrative: New Britain, Russell Islands, Palau, Peleliu', p. 56.
7 McMillan, *The Old Breed*, pp. 311–12.
8 Garand and Strobridge, *History of U.S. Marine Corps Operations in World War II*, IV, pp. 185–6.
9 Smith, 'Personal Narrative: New Britain, Russell Islands, Palau, Peleliu', p. 56.
10 McMillan, *The Old Breed*, p. 320.

33 'I'm hit! Christ, I'm hit!'

1 Garand and Strobridge, *History of U.S. Marine Corps Operations in World War II*, IV, pp. 192–201.
2 Sledge, *With the Old Breed*, p. 112.
3 Burgin, *Islands of the Damned*, pp. 144–5.
4 Garand and Strobridge, *History of U.S. Marine Corps Operations in World War II*, IV, pp. 201–2.
5 McEnery, *Hell in the Pacific*, pp. 226–9.
6 Mace, *Battleground Pacific*, pp. 109–11; McEnery, *Hell in the Pacific*, pp. 229–31.
7 Garand and Strobridge, *History of U.S. Marine Corps Operations in World War II*, IV, p. 202.
8 Sledge, *With the Old Breed*, pp. 114–17.
9 Sledge, *With the Old Breed*, p. 118; AUA, Sledge Papers, RG97/96-005, Box 1, Folder 9, Mrs W. S. Middlebrook to Sledge, 29 May 1947.
10 Sledge, *With the Old Breed*, pp. 117–19.

34 'Put the man out of his misery!'

1 McEnery, *Hell in the Pacific*, pp. 238–9.
2 Garand and Strobridge, *History of U.S. Marine Corps Operations in World War II*, IV, pp. 209–11.
3 McEnery, *Hell in the Pacific*, pp. 237–8.
4 Garand and Strobridge, *History of U.S. Marine Corps Operations in World War II*, IV, pp. 210–11.

5 Sledge, *With the Old Breed*, p. 120.
6 Smith, 'Personal Narrative: New Britain, Russell Islands, Palau, Peleliu', p. 88.
7 Garand and Strobridge, *History of U.S. Marine Corps Operations in World War II*, IV, p. 212; Smith, 'Personal Narrative: New Britain, Russell Islands, Palau, Peleliu', p. 89.
8 Mace, *Battleground Pacific*, p. 121.
9 AUA, Sledge Papers, RG96/96-038, Box 1, Folder 8, Tom 'Stumpy' Stanley to Gene Sledge, 23 May 1980.
10 McEnery, *Hell in the Pacific*, pp. 240–1; 1st Sgt David Bailey's Log of Casualties on Peleliu; Mace, *Battleground Pacific*, p. 43.
11 Tom 'Stumpy' Stanley to Gene Sledge, 23 May 1980; Mace, *Battleground Pacific*, p. 43.
12 McEnery, *Hell in the Pacific*, pp. 240–1; 1st Sgt David Bailey's Log of Casualties on Peleliu.
13 McEnery, *Hell in the Pacific*, pp. 241–3.
14 Sledge, *With the Old Breed*, pp. 121–31; Burgin, *Islands of the Damned*, pp. 160–8.
15 For an excellent discussion of the racial element of the Pacific War, see John A. Lynn, *Battle: A History of Combat and Culture* (New York: Basic Books, 2003), chapter 7: 'The Merciless Fight – Race and Military Culture in the Pacific War'.
16 Garand and Strobridge, *History of U.S. Marine Corps Operations in World War II*, IV, p. 212.
17 McEnery, *Hell in the Pacific*, pp. 243–4.
18 Garand and Strobridge, *History of U.S. Marine Corps Operations in World War II*, IV, p. 212; Record of Operations of the 3/5 Marines, 26 August to 7 November 1944.
19 McEnery, *Hell in the Pacific*, pp. 243–5.
20 Mace, *Battleground Pacific*, pp. 137–41; AUA, Sledge Papers, RG96/96-038, Box 3, Folder 28, Mace to Sledge, 28 February 1980.
21 Sledge, *With the Old Breed*, pp. 136–7.
22 Garand and Strobridge, *History of U.S. Marine Corps Operations in World War II*, IV, p. 214; Record of Operations of the 3/5 Marines, 26 August to 7 November 1944; 1st Sgt David Bailey's Log of Casualties on Peleliu.

35 'Shit, they're behind us!'

1 Sledge, *With the Old Breed*, p. 138.
2 Garand and Strobridge, *History of U.S. Marine Corps Operations in World War II*, IV, pp. 219–22; Sledge, *With the Old Breed*, pp. 138–9.

3 McEnery, *Hell in the Pacific*, pp. 246–7.
4 Garand and Strobridge, *History of U.S. Marine Corps Operations in World War II*, IV, pp. 224–9.
5 AUA, Sledge Papers, RG96/96-038, Box 1, Folder 31, Harris, unpublished memoir, p. 137; Folder 27, Harris to Stanley, 11 July 1981.
6 McEnery, *Hell in the Pacific*, pp. 249–51; Mace, *Battleground Pacific*, pp. 150–6.
7 McEnery, *Hell in the Pacific*, p. 251.
8 Garand and Strobridge, *History of U.S. Marine Corps Operations in World War II*, IV, p. 230.
9 Mace, *Battleground Pacific*, p. 165.
10 McEnery, *Hell in the Pacific*, p. 253.
11 Mace, *Battleground Pacific*, p. 169; Makos, *Voices of the Pacific*, pp. 230–1.
12 1st Sgt David Bailey's Log of Casualties on Peleliu.
13 Record of Operations of the 3/5 Marines, 26 August to 7 November 1944; Garand and Strobridge, *History of U.S. Marine Corps Operations in World War II*, IV, pp. 231–2.
14 McEnery, *Hell in the Pacific*, pp. 253–4.
15 Record of Operations of the 3/5 Marines, 26 August to 7 November 1944; 1st Sgt David Bailey's Log of Casualties on Peleliu; McEnery, *Hell in the Pacific*, p. 254.
16 Sledge, *With the Old Breed*, p. 142.
17 Mace, *Battleground Pacific*, pp. 43, 175–8.
18 Sledge, *With the Old Breed*, pp. 142–3.
19 AUA, Sledge Papers, RG96/96-038, Box 2, Folder 36, Joseph Moskalczak to Gene Sledge, 9 March 1988; Record of Operations of the 3/5 Marines, 26 August to 7 November 1944.
20 Record of Operations of the 3/5 Marines, 26 August to 7 November 1944; 1st Sgt David Bailey's Log of Casualties on Peleliu; Citation for the award of the Silver Star to 1st Lieut. Edward A. Jones, in https://www.findagrave.com/memorial/62109739/edward-allison-jones [accessed 16 February 2021]; AUA, Sledge Papers, RG96/96-038, Box 2, Folder 36, Joseph Moskalczak to Gene Sledge, 9 March 1988.
21 Garand and Strobridge, *History of U.S. Marine Corps Operations in World War II*, IV, p. 236.
22 Harris, unpublished memoir, p. 137.

36 Hillbilly and Ack-Ack

1 Harris, unpublished memoir, pp. 137–8.
2 Garand and Strobridge, *History of U.S. Marine Corps Operations in World War II*, IV, p. 237.
3 Smith, 'Personal Narrative: New Britain, Russell Islands, Palau, Peleliu', pp. 102–5.
4 Record of Operations of the 3/5 Marines, 26 August to 7 November 1944; McEnery, *Hell in the Pacific*, p. 259.
5 McEnery, *Hell in the Pacific*, pp. 260–1; AUA, Sledge Papers, RG96/96-038, Box 2, Folder 10, Sergeant Fred E. Harris to Sledge, 8 November 1995; Mace, *Battleground Pacific*, pp. 196–8; Record of Operations of the 3/5 Marines, 26 August to 7 November 1944; McEnery, *Hell in the Pacific*, p. 259.
6 AUA, Sledge Papers, RG96/96-038, Box 1, Folder 8, Tom 'Stumpy' Stanley to Gene Sledge, 'Thoughts on Bucky's Notes', 17 August 1991.
7 McEnery, *Hell in the Pacific*, pp. 260–1; Sergeant Fred E. Harris to Sledge, 8 November 1995; Mace, *Battleground Pacific*, pp. 196–8.
8 https://www.findagrave.com/memorial/62109739/edward-allison-jones [accessed 5 March 2021]
9 McEnery, *Hell in the Pacific*, pp. 262–4; Jim Anderson in Makos, *Voices of the Pacific*, p. 239.
10 Sledge, *With the Old Breed*, pp. 150–1; Burgin, *Islands of the Damned*, p. 181.

37 The Lucky Few

1 Record of Operations of the 3/5 Marines, 26 August to 7 November 1944; Sledge, *With the Old Breed*, pp. 152–3, 164; Eugene B. Sledge, 'Peleliu 1944: Why Did We Go There?', *Leatherneck Magazine*, September 1983, pp. 72–4.
2 McEnery, *Hell in the Pacific*, p. 266; Burgin, *Islands of the Damned*, pp. 182–3.
3 Smith, 'Personal Narrative: New Britain, Russell Islands, Palau, Peleliu', pp. 106–7.
4 AUA, Sledge Papers, RG96/96-038, Box 1, Folder 8, Harris to Captain Stanley, 11 July 1981.
5 McEnery, *Hell in the Pacific*, p. 258.
6 AUA, Sledge Papers, RG96/96-038, Box 3, Folder 31, Eugene Sledge to Brig. Gen. Harold D. Harris, 25 March 1981.
7 Mace, *Battleground Pacific*, pp. 212–13.
8 Sledge, *With the Old Breed*, pp. 166–7.

9 AUA, Sledge Papers, RG96/98-091, Box 1, Folder 5, Sledge to his father, 24 October 1944.
10 Mace, *Battleground Pacific*, p. 215.
11 Record of Operations of the 3/5 Marines, 26 August to 7 November 1944; Sledge, *With the Old Breed*, pp. 166–7.
12 AUA, Sledge Papers, RG96/96-038, Box 1, Folder 2, Photos of K/3/5 on Peleliu; Box 3, Folder 35, Jay de l'Eau to Sledge, 1 May 1985.
13 Garand and Strobridge, *History of U.S. Marine Corps Operations in World War II*, IV, pp. 253, 264–5, 284; McMillan, *The Old Breed*, pp. 340–1.
14 Garand and Strobridge, *History of U.S. Marine Corps Operations in World War II*, IV, pp. 266–7, 284–8.
15 Alexander, 'What was Nimitz Thinking?'
16 Garand and Strobridge, *History of U.S. Marine Corps Operations in World War II*, IV, pp. 266–7, 284–8.
17 Alexander, 'What Was Nimitz Thinking?'
18 McEnery, *Hell in the Pacific*, pp. 231–2.

38 'We were worn down and sobered'

1 Sledge, *With the Old Breed*, pp. 168–72.
2 McEnery, *Hell in the Pacific*, p. 271.
3 McEnery, *Hell in the Pacific*, p. 272.
4 Sledge, *With the Old Breed*, p. 178.
5 McEnery, *Hell in the Pacific*, p. 273.
6 Sledge, *With the Old Breed*, p. 179.
7 McEnery, *Hell in the Pacific*, pp. 270, 274–6; McMillan, *The Old Breed*, p. 349.
8 Sledge, *With the Old Breed*, pp. 179–82.
9 AUA, Sledge Papers, RG96/98-091, Box 1, Folder 5, Sledge to his father, 24 October, 15 November and 7 November 1944; to his mother, 23 and 29 November, 12 December 1944; to his parents, 10 November and 17 November 1944.
10 Burgin, *Islands of the Damned*, pp. 193–4.
11 AUA, Sledge Papers, RG96/96-038, Box 2, Folder 23, Jay de l'Eau to Sledge, 31 October 1982.
12 Burgin, *Islands of the Damned*, pp. 193–4.
13 Mace, *Battleground Pacific*, pp. 229–32.
14 Sledge, *With the Old Breed*, p. 190.
15 Burgin, *Islands of the Damned*, pp. 192, 194–5.
16 Mace, *Battleground Pacific*, pp. 227–8, 231.

17 Private Harry Bender, in Makos, *Voices of the Pacific*, pp. 248–9.
18 Burgin, *Islands of the Damned*, pp. 195–7.
19 Sledge, *With the Old Breed*, pp. 185–6.

39 Where Next?

1 Sledge, *With the Old Breed*, pp. 182–3.
2 Burgin, *Islands of the Damned*, p. 200.
3 Private Harry Bender, in Makos, *Voices of the Pacific*, p. 250.
4 Jim Anderson, in Makos, *Voices of the Pacific*, p. 246.
5 McMillan, *The Old Breed*, p. 346.
6 Sledge, *With the Old Breed*, pp. 184–8.
7 AUA, Sledge Papers, RG96/98-091, Box 1, Folder 6, Sledge to his mother, 7 January 1945; to his parents, 2 February 1945.
8 Abilene, KS, Dwight D. Eisenhower Presidential Library and Archive (DDE), Simon Bolivar Buckner Papers, 1908–17 and 1941–45, Box 1, A92-16, Buckner Diary, 28 March 1945.
9 Andrew Roberts, *Masters and Commanders: How Roosevelt, Churchill, Marshall and Alanbrooke Won the War in the West* (London: Allen Lane, 2008), pp. 518–20.
10 Roy E. Appleman, James. M. Burns, Russell A. Gugeler and John Stevens, *Okinawa: The Last Great Battle* (Washington DC: Center of Military History, US Army, 1948), pp. 1–4.
11 Hoyt, *How They Won the War in the Pacific*, pp. 425–7.
12 Appleman et al., *Okinawa*, p. 4; London, UK, The National Archives (TNA), ADM/234, Piece 368, Naval Staff History, Battle Summary No. 47, 'Naval Operations Okinawa', 1950, pp. 1–2.
13 'Buck's Battle', *Time* magazine, 16 April 1945.
14 Nicholas Evan Sarantakes (ed.), *Seven Stars: The Okinawa Battle Diaries of Simon Bolivar Buckner, Jr., and Jospeh Stilwell* (College Station: Texas A&M University Press, 2004), pp. 10–11.
15 USMCA, Oliver P. Smith Papers, COLL/213, A/30/D/3/1, Box 54, Folder 1, 'Personal Narrative: 10th Army and Okinawa', p. 2.
16 Smith, 'Personal Narrative: 10th Army and Okinawa', pp. 2–8.
17 Appleman et al., *Okinawa*, pp. 7–10, 14, 17.
18 Smith, 'Personal Narrative: 10th Army and Okinawa', pp. 11–13.
19 Smith, 'Personal Narrative: 10th Army and Okinawa', pp. 12–13.
20 Smith, 'Personal Narrative: 10th Army and Okinawa', p. 13.
21 DDE, Buckner Diary, Saturday, 11 November 1944.
22 Smith, 'Personal Narrative: 10th Army and Okinawa', p. 32; USMCA,

COLL/185, A/14/F/3/3, Lieut. Col. J. Frederick Haley Papers, 'The General Dies at Noon', pp. 5, 24.

40 'The Road to Certain Victory'

1 Colonel Hiromichi Yahara, *The Battle for Okinawa: A Japanese Officer's Eyewitness Account of the Last Great Campaign of World War II* (New York: John Wiley & Sons, 1995), pp. xi, 18.
2 Yahara, *The Battle for Okinawa*, pp. 16–18.
3 Frank B. Gibney, 'Two Views of Battle' in Yahara, *The Battle for Okinawa*, pp. xv–xvii, 24.
4 Yahara, *The Battle for Okinawa*, pp. 5–16.
5 Yahara, *The Battle for Okinawa*, pp. 20–4.
6 Thomas M. Huber, 'Japan's Battle for Okinawa, April–June 1945', *Leavenworth Papers*, Number 18 (199), p. 7; Yahara, *The Battle for Okinawa*, p. 35.
7 Huber, 'Japan's Battle for Okinawa', pp. 12–13.
8 Interrogation Report of POW Akira Shimada, 24 July 1945, in Yahara, *The Battle for Okinawa*, p. 223.
9 *Descent into Hell: Civilian Memories of the Battle of Okinawa*, trans. Mark Ealey and Alastair McLauchlan (Portland, ME: MerwinAsia, 2014), pp. 44–53.
10 Albert Axell and Hideaki Kase, *Kamikaze: Japan's Suicide Gods* (London: Pearson Education, 2002), p. 52.
11 Naoji Kōzu, 'Human Torpedo', in Haruko Taya Cook and Theodore F. Cook, *Japan at War: An Oral History* (New York: W.W. Norton, 1992), pp. 313–16.
12 Rear Admiral Sadatoshi Tamioka, Doc. No. 5072, in General Headquarters, Far East Command, Military Intelligence Section, General Staff, *Statements of Japanese Officials on World War II (English Translations): Vol. 4*, 1949–50, pp. 316–22.
13 Commander Yoshimori Terai, *Statements of Japanese Officials: Vol. 4*, pp. 316–22.
14 Commander Yoshimori Terai, *Statements of Japanese Officials: Vol. 4*, pp. 316–22.

41 'In some ways it was bigger than D-Day'

1 McMillan, *The Old Breed*, pp. 252–3.
2 Sledge, *With the Old Breed*, pp. 193–5.
3 AUA, Sledge Papers, RG96/98-091, Box 1, Folder 7, Sledge to his mother, 11 March 1945.

4 Sledge, *With the Old Breed*, pp. 196–7.
5 Burgin, *Islands of the Damned*, pp. 206–7.
6 USMCA, William A. Looney Memoir, 1942–5, COLL/5276, A/5/J/6/4, 'Okinawa', pp. 1–2.
7 Appleman et al., *Okinawa*, p. 36.
8 David Hobbs, *The British Pacific Fleet: The Royal Navy's Most Powerful Strike Force* (Barnsley, UK: Seaforth Publishing, 2011; repr. 2017), pp. 126–8.
9 Appleman et al., *Okinawa*, pp. 53–6.
10 Appleman et al., *Okinawa*, p. 58; Shigeaki Kinjo interviewed by Michael Bradley, in '"Banzai!" The Compulsory Mass Suicide of Kerama Islanders in the Battle of Okinawa', *The Asia-Pacific Journal*, XI, 22/3 (June 2014).
11 Appleman et al., *Okinawa*, pp. 64–5.
12 Sledge, *With the Old Breed*, pp. 197–8.
13 McMillan, *The Old Breed*, p. 355.
14 Appleman et al., *Okinawa*, p. 32.
15 Sledge, *With the Old Breed*, p. 200.
16 Burgin, *Islands of the Damned*, p. 208.

42 Love Day

1 Sledge, *With the Old Breed*, pp. 200–1.
2 Burgin, *Islands of the Damned*, p. 212.
3 Appleman et al., *Okinawa*, p. 69.
4 Burgin, *Islands of the Damned*, pp. 212–14; Sledge, *With the Old Breed*, pp. 202–4.
5 DDE, Buckner Diary, 1 April 1945; Ernie Pyle, *Last Chapter* (New York: Henry Holt & Co., 1946), pp. 99, 101.
6 Sledge, *With the Old Breed*, p. 204.
7 Sledge, *With the Old Breed*, pp. 205–6; Burgin, *Islands of the Damned*, pp. 215–18.
8 Mace, *Battleground Pacific*, pp. 222–4.
9 USNARA, RG127, Box 261, 3/5 Marines Special Action Report, 1–22 April 1945; Burgin, *Islands of the Damned*, pp. 218–19.
10 3/5 Marines Special Action Report, 1–22 April 1945; AUA, Sledge Papers, RG96/96-038, Box 2, Folder 37, George W. Poppe to Sledge, 12 December 1983.
11 Sledge, *With the Old Breed*, pp. 208–10; Burgin, *Islands of the Damned*, pp. 221–2.
12 Appleman et al., *Okinawa*, p. 75; Toll, *Twilight of the Gods*, p. 573.

13 Buckner Diary, 1 April 1945.

14 Quoted in Laura Homan Lacey, *Stay Off the Skyline: The Sixth Marine Division on Okinawa* (Dulles, VA: Potomac Books, 2005; repr. 2007), p. 45.

15 Quoted in Feifer, *Tenozan*, p. 141.

16 Quoted in Feifer, *Tenozan*, pp. 143–4.

17 London, Imperial War Museum Archives (IWM), 14048, Private Papers of N. B. Gray, 'Memoirs' and 'Diary', 1 April 1945; Hobbs, *The British Pacific Fleet*, p. 138.

18 Sir Philip Vian, *Action This Day: A War Memoir* (London: Frederick Muller, 1960), pp. 178–9.

43 'We were euphoric, undisciplined, and stupid'

1 McMillan, *The Old Breed*, p. 362.

2 3/5 Marines Special Action Report, 1–22 April 1945.

3 Sledge, *With the Old Breed*, p. 211.

4 Harry Bender, in Makos, *Voices of the Pacific*, pp. 292–3.

5 Sledge, *With the Old Breed*, pp. 211–12.

6 McMillan, *The Old Breed*, pp. 362–3

7 Sledge, *With the Old Breed*, pp. 213–14.

8 Mace, *Battleground Pacific*, pp. 236–7.

9 Sloan, *The Ultimate Battle*, pp. 58–60; Harry Bender, in Makos, *Voices of the Pacific*, pp. 295–6.

10 USNARA, RG127, Box 261, 3/5 Marines Reconnaissance Patrol Reports, 9 April 1945.

11 3/5 Marines Reconnaissance Patrol Reports, 9 April 1945; Sledge, *With the Old Breed*, pp. 215–19; Burgin, *Islands of the Damned*, pp. 223–5.

12 Mace, *Battleground Pacific*, pp. 243–4.

13 Feifer, *Tenozan*, pp. 3–14, 33; Samuel Eliot Morison, *History of the United States Naval Operations in the Pacific: Volume 14 – Victory in the Pacific, 1945* (New York: Little, Brown, 1975; repr. 2012), pp. 200–2.

14 Appleman et al., *Okinawa*, pp. 125–6.

15 Buckner Diary, 8 and 9 April 1945.

16 Buckner Diary, 11 April 1945.

17 Smith, 'Personal Narrative: 10th Army and Okinawa', pp. 82–3.

18 Huber, 'Japan's Battle for Okinawa', pp. 31–2; Yahara Interrogation Report, 6 August 1945, in Yahara, *The Battle for Okinawa*, p. 213.

19 William Manchester, *Goodbye, Darkness: A Memoir of the Pacific War* (New York: Little, Brown, 1980; repr. 2002), p. 356.

20 Appleman et al., *Okinawa*, pp. 138–44.

21 Manchester, *Goodbye, Darkness*, pp. 140–3.
22 Appleman et al., *Okinawa*, pp. 148.

44 'I burned the whole village to the ground'

1 AUA, Sledge Papers, RG96/98-091, Box 1, Folder 8, Sledge to his parents, 14 April 1945.
2 Churchill, *The Second World War*, VI, pp. 412–13.
3 A. J. Baime, *The Accidental President* (New York: Mifflin Harcourt, 2017; repr. 2018), pp. 41–89.
4 Harry S. Truman, *Year of Decisions*, 2 vols (New York: Doubleday, 1955; repr. 1965), pp. 15–21.
5 DDE, Simon Bolivar Buckner Papers, 1908–17 and 1941–45, Box 1, A92-16, Bucker to his wife, 14 April 1945, in 'Lt. Gen. Simon Bolivar Buckner: Private Letters relating to the Battle of Okinawa', ed. A. P. Jenkins, in *Ryudai Review of Euro-American Studies*, 42 (1997), pp. 63–113 (p. 82).
6 Sledge, *With the Old Breed*, p. 222.
7 Independence, MO, Harry S. Truman Presidential Library & Museum (HST), 'Oral History Interview with George M. Elsey', 7 July 1970, www.trumanlibrary.org/oralhist/elsey7.htm [accessed 12 November 2018]
8 Yahara, *The Battle for Okinawa*, p. 45.
9 AUA, Sledge Papers, RG96/98-091, Box 1, Folder 8, Sledge to his parents, 15, 16 and 18 April 1945.
10 Sledge, *With the Old Breed*, pp. 222–3; 3/5 Marines Special Action Report, 1–22 April 1945.
11 Mace, *Battleground Pacific*, pp. 246–7.
12 Sledge, *With the Old Breed*, p. 223.
13 Mace, *Battleground Pacific*, p. 251.
14 Sledge, *With the Old Breed*, p. 223.
15 Appleman et al., *Okinawa*, pp. 184–5, 207.
16 Appleman et al., *Okinawa*, p. 248.
17 Buckner to his wife Adele, 22 April 1945, in 'Private Letters', pp. 85–6.
18 Appleman et al., *Okinawa*, pp. 258–60.
19 Appleman et al., *Okinawa*, p. 262.
20 Smith, 'Personal Narrative: 10th Army and Okinawa', pp. 99–100; DDE, Buckner Diary, 29 April 1945.

45 'Hit the deck and dig in!'

1 Sledge, *With the Old Breed*, pp. 226–7; Burgin, *Islands of the Damned*, pp. 230–1.
2 Mace, *Battleground Pacific*, p. 271.
3 Sledge, *With the Old Breed*, pp. 228–31; Mace, *Battleground Pacific*, p. 269; Burgin, *Islands of the Damned*, pp. 231–2.
4 Appleman et al., *Okinawa*, pp. 267–8.
5 DDE, Buckner Diary, 2 and 3 May 1945; Appleman et al., *Okinawa*, p. 268.
6 Appleman et al., *Okinawa*, p. 274; Buckner Diary, 2 and 3 May 1945.
7 Stockman, *The First Marine Division on Okinawa*, p. 5.
8 Sledge, *With the Old Breed*, pp. 231–2.
9 Mace, *Battleground Pacific*, pp. 266–7.
10 Burgin, *Islands of the Damned*, pp. 233–5.
11 Sledge, *With the Old Breed*, pp. 232–3.
12 Stockman, *The First Marine Division on Okinawa*, pp. 15–16; Sledge, *With the Old Breed*, pp. 232–8.
13 AUA, Sledge Papers, RG96/96-038, Box 2, Folder 13, Hank Boyes to Sledge, 5 and 22 May 1980 (enclosing a USMC press release by Sgt Walter Wood, a Marine Corps Combat Correspondent).
14 AUA, Sledge Papers, RG96/96-038, Box 2, Folder 13, Sledge to Brigadier General Ortho Steele, 6 October 1986 (requesting a retrospective gallantry award for Boyes).
15 Mace, *Battleground Pacific*, pp. 274–5.
16 Sledge, *With the Old Breed*, p. 239.

46 'We gotta get the hell outta here'

1 Sledge, *With the Old Breed*, pp. 238–41.
2 Huber, 'Japan's Battle for Okinawa', pp. 81–3; Yahara Interrogation Report, 6 August 1945, in Yahara, *The Battle for Okinawa*, p. 214; Appleman et al., *Okinawa*, p. 283.
3 Morison, *Victory in the Pacific*, pp. 251–2.
4 Appleman et al., *Okinawa*, pp. 287–9; Stockman, *The First Marine Division on Okinawa*, p. 11; USMCA, COLL/5223, A/26/J/7/2, Richard Bruce Watkins, 'Brothers in Battle: One Marine's Account of War in the Pacific', p. 39.
5 Appleman et al., *Okinawa*, pp. 287–9.
6 Appleman et al., *Okinawa*, p. 296; Huber, 'Japan's Battle for Okinawa', pp. 87–8; Morison, *Victory in the Pacific*, pp. 266–7.

7 Yahara, *The Battle for Okinawa*, pp. 41–4.
8 Yahara, *The Battle for Okinawa*, p. 44; Appleman et al., *Okinawa*, p. 303.
9 Stockman, *The First Marine Division on Okinawa*, pp. 16–18.
10 Sledge, *With the Old Breed*, pp. 244–8.
11 Buckner Diary, 8 May 1945.
12 Burgin, *Islands of the Damned*, pp. 241–2.
13 Mace, *Battleground Pacific*, pp. 293–4.
14 Sledge, *With the Old Breed*, p. 242; AUA, Sledge Papers, RG96/98-091, Box 1, Folder 8, Sledge to his parents, 17 May 1945.
15 Burgin, *Islands of the Damned*, p. 244.
16 Mace, *Battleground Pacific*, pp. 295–310.
17 Sledge, *With the Old Breed*, pp. 250–1; USNARA, NWMDM-D/994011, 3/5 Marines Special Action Report, 22 April to 23 June 1945.
18 McMillan, *The Old Breed*, pp. 383–4; AUA, Sledge Papers, RG96/96-038, Box 5, Folder 18, Paul E. Ison, 'Opinion: thoughts on the death of a man who didn't fear it'.
19 Sledge, *With the Old Breed*, pp. 251–2.

47 'Hell's own cesspool'

1 Buckner Diary, 11 May 1945.
2 Appleman et al., *Okinawa*, pp. 311–12.
3 Appleman et al., *Okinawa*, p. 330.
4 Burgin, *Islands of the Damned*, pp. 247–9; Sledge, *With the Old Breed*, pp. 254–5.
5 Burgin, *Islands of the Damned*, pp. 250–5.
6 Sledge, *With the Old Breed*, p. 267.
7 3/5 Marines Special Action Report, 22 April to 23 June 1945.
8 Sledge, *With the Old Breed*, pp. 268–73.
9 Harry Bender, in Makos, *Voices of the Pacific*, p. 313.
10 AUA, Sledge Papers, RG96/96-038, Box 3, Folder 1, Thomas J. Stanley deposition, 20 August 1982.
11 AUA, Sledge Papers, RG96/96-038, Box 3, Folder 1, Bill Leyden to Sledge, 28 February 1980; Eugene Sledge deposition, 26 October 1982.
12 Sledge, *With the Old Breed*, pp. 273–4.
13 AUA, Sledge Papers, RG96/96-038, Box 2, Folder 13, Hank Boyes to Sledge, 28 January 1980, 5 May 1980, 3 July 1982, Sledge to Boyes, 31 March 1980, and K Company veterans to Boyes, 4 April 1984; Box 1, Folder 27, Hank Boyes to 'Stumpy' Stanley, 17 March 1981.

48 'Wild-eyed expressions of shock and fear'

1 Sledge, *With the Old Breed*, pp. 274–82.
2 Sledge, *With the Old Breed*, pp. 284–6, 291.
3 AUA, Sledge Papers, RG96/96-038, Box 1, Folder 8, Carlisle L. Tiller Jr to Captain Tom J. Stanley, 28 April 1985.
4 Sledge, *With the Old Breed*, pp. 286–92.
5 3/5 Marines Special Action Report, 22 April to 23 June 1945.
6 Sledge, *With the Old Breed*, pp. 298–300; Jim Anderson and Harry Bender, in Makos, *Voices of the Pacific*, p. 319.
7 Yahara, *The Battle for Okinawa*, pp. 62–82.
8 Appleman et al., *Okinawa*, pp. 389–92.
9 Buckner Diary, 31 May 1945.
10 Yahara, *The Battle for Okinawa*, pp. 111–12.

49 The Final Stretch

1 3/5 Marines Special Action Report, 22 April to 23 June 1945; Sloan, *The Ultimate Battle*, p. 273.
2 Appleman et al., *Okinawa*, pp. 424–5, 432; Buckner Diary, 3 June 1945.
3 Sledge, *With the Old Breed*, pp. 315–20.
4 Burgin, *Islands of the Damned*, pp. 255–7; Hank Boyes to Sledge, 5 May 1980.
5 Appleman et al., *Okinawa*, p. 434.
6 Stockman, *The First Marine Division on Okinawa*, pp. 49–55.
7 Watkins, 'Brothers in Battle', pp. 49–52.
8 Sledge, *With the Old Breed*, p. 322.
9 AUA, Sledge Papers, RG96/96-038, Box 3, Folder 32, 'Lt Brockinton's K/3/5/ experience, June 1945', p. 2.
10 Sledge, *With the Old Breed*, pp. 323–4.
11 'Lt Brockinton's K/3/5/ experience, June 1945', pp. 2–3.
12 Sledge, *With the Old Breed*, p. 324.
13 Jim Anderson, in Makos, *Voices of the Pacific*, p. 329.
14 Harry Bender, in Makos, *Voices of the Pacific*, pp. 326–7.
15 Sledge, *With the Old Breed*, pp. 324–5.
16 'Lt Brockinton's K/3/5/ experience, June 1945', pp. 3–5.
17 Sledge, *With the Old Breed*, pp. 326–7; Burgin, *Islands of the Damned*, p. 259; AUA, Sledge Papers, RG96/96-038, Box 1, Folder 33, Sledge to Col. R. D. Bianchi, 9 June 1982.
18 Sledge, *With the Old Breed*, pp. 327–8.

19 'Lt Brockinton's K/3/5/ experience, June 1945', pp. 3–5.
20 Hank Boyes to Sledge, 5 May 1980.
21 Burgin, *Islands of the Damned*, p. 260.

50 End Game

1 Yahara, *The Battle for Okinawa*, p. 133; Appleman et al., *Okinawa*, pp. 456–8.
2 Yahara, *The Battle for Okinawa*, p. 134.
3 Post to Adele Buckner, 19 June 1945, in 'Private Letters', p. 109.
4 Haley, 'The General Dies at Noon', pp. 26–34.
5 Sarantakes (ed.), *Seven Stars*, pp. 86–7; Smith, 'Personal Narrative', pp. 135–6.
6 Yahara, *The Battle for Okinawa*, pp. 143–50; Appleman et al., *Okinawa*, pp. 468–70.
7 Yahara, *The Battle for Okinawa*, pp. 153–6; 'Interrogation of Testuo Nakamuta, General Ushijima's cook', June 26, 1945; Appleman et al., *Okinawa*, pp. 470–1.
8 Sledge, *With the Old Breed*, pp. 331–5.
9 Burgin, *Islands of the Damned*, pp. 260–1.
10 Sledge, *With the Old Breed*, p. 337.
11 Burgin, *Islands of the Damned*, p. 261.
12 Appleman et al., *Okinawa*, p. 471.
13 G-2 Periodic Reports, 7th Infantry Division, 'Summary of Information', 23 June 1945.
14 Appleman et al., *Okinawa*, p. 473.
15 Sledge, *With the Old Breed*, p. 338.
16 USMCA, COLL/2106, A/11/L/7/5, John B. Dillon, 'China Marine', p. 89.
17 AUA, Sledge Papers, RG96/98-091, Box 1, Folder 7, Sledge to his parents, 24 June 1945.
18 Churchill to Truman, 22 June 1945, in Churchill, *The Second World War*, VI, p. 542.
19 Quoted in Feifer, *Tenozan*, p. vii.
20 Appleman et al., *Okinawa*, p. 473.
21 Sledge, *With the Old Breed*, p. 342.
22 Ota Masahide, 'Introduction: The Battle of Okinawa', 7 January 2013, in *Descent into Hell*, pp. xvii–xix.
23 Huber, 'Japan's Battle for Okinawa, April-June 1945,' pp. 117–18.
24 Masahide, 'Introduction: The Battle of Okinawa', pp. xvii–xix.

51 'We sure have a lot to be thankful for'

1 Sledge, *With the Old Breed*, pp. 341–3.
2 Burgin, *Islands of the Damned*, pp. 264–5.
3 AUA, Sledge Papers, RG96/98-091, Box 1, Folder 7, Sledge to his parents, 6 and 31 July 1945.
4 Sledge, *With the Old Breed*, p. 343.
5 HST, Miscellaneous Historial Documents Collection, No. 736, 'Minutes of Meeting held at the White House on Monday, 18 June 1945 at 1530,' at https://www.trumanlibrary.org/whistlestop/study_collections/bomb/large/documents/index.php?documentdate=1945-06-18&documentid=21&pagenumber=1 [accessed June 28, 2019]; Truman, *Year of Decisions*, I, pp. 458–9.
6 Truman, *Year of Decisions*, I, pp. 101–5; https://www.trumanlibrary.gov/library/research-files/notes-meeting-interim-committee [accessed 7 April 2021]; Science Panel's Report to the Interim Committee, 16 June 1945, https://www.atomicheritage.org/key-documents/interim-committee-report-0 [accessed 7 April 2021]
7 HST, Brigadier General Leslie Groves, 'Memorandum on Alamogordo Air Base atomic fission bomb test', 18 July 1945; Baime, *The Accidental President*, p. 284.
8 Churchill, *The Second World War*, VI, p. 552.
9 Truman, *Year of Decisions*, I, p. 463.
10 HST, Papers of Harry S. Truman, Truman Diary, 25 July 1945.
11 Churchill, *The Second World War*, VI, pp. 556–7.
12 Harry S. Truman to Richard Russell, 9 August 1945, https://www.trumanlibrary.gov/library/research-files/harry-s-truman-richard-russell [accessed 7 April 2021]
13 AUA, Sledge Papers, RG96/98-091, Box 1, Folder 7, Sledge to his parents, 9 and 11 August 1945.
14 Sledge, *With the Old Breed*, p. 343.
15 AUA, Sledge Papers, RG96/98-091, Box 1, Folder 7, Sledge to his parents, 17 August 1945.
16 R. V. Burgin, in Makos, *Voices of the Pacific*, p. 335.

Postscript

1 AUA, Sledge Letters, RG96/96-038/Box 1, General Lewis B. Walt to Tom 'Stumpy' Stanley, 5 June 1981.
2 Susan Pawlak-Seaman, 'Live and Learn: On Memorial Day, thinking about

what might have been', https://eu.southcoasttoday.com/news/20180526/live-and-learn-on-memorial-day-thinking-about-what-might-have-been [accessed 14 September 2020]

3 BCA, Kenneth C. M. Sills Administrative Records, Box 4, Folder 64, Mr and Mrs Sydney Haldane to Mr and Mrs Kenneth Sills, 5 November 1944.

4 AUA, Sledge Papers, RG96/98-038, Box 2, Folder 1, Geoffrey R. Stanwood to Captain Thomas J. Stanley, 5 May 1980.

5 AUA, Sledge Papers, RG96/96-038, Box 1, Folder 25, Sledge to Chief Warrant Officer S. J. Moore (Andy Haldane's nephew), 10 October 1980.

6 Miller, *Earned in Blood*, pp. xvii, 189–232; T. I. Miller, in Makos, *Voices of the Pacific*, pp. 361–2; https://www.dignitymemorial.com/obituaries/beck
ley-wv/thurman-miller-7636698 [accessed 12 April 2021]

7 McEnery, *Hell in the Pacific*, pp. 280–92.

8 https://www.findagrave.com/memorial/36614363/stelmo-murray-haney [accessed 13 April 2021]

9 AUA, Sledge Papers, RG96/96-038, Box 1, Folder 8, Tom J. Stanley to Platoon Sergeant Haney, April 1983; Data Sheet on Haney, April 1983.

10 Sterling Mace, in Makos, *Voices of the Pacific*, p. 325; Mace, *Battleground Pacific*, pp. 317–25.

11 AUA, Sledge Papers, RG96-96-038, Box 3, Folder 3, Sterling Mace to Gene Sledge, 28 February 1980.

12 Mace, *Battleground Pacific*, pp. 328–30; https://morganfuneralhome.com/tribute/details/1204/Sterling-Mace/obituary.html [accessed 12 April 2021]

13 Burgin, *Islands of the Damned*, pp. 267–85; R. V. Burgin, in Makos, *Voices of the Pacific*, p. 340; https://www.dallasnews.com/news/obituaries/2019/04/11/r-v-burgin-author-and-lancaster-Marine-portrayed-in-hbo-s-the-pacific-dies-at-96/ [accessed 12 April 2021]

14 Sledge, *With the Old Breed*, pp. 343–4.

15 Eugene Sledge, in 'A World Without War', Episode 7, *The War*, PBS documentary series by Ken Burns and Lynn Novick, 2007.

16 Sledge to William L. Cain, Jr, 14 July 1982.

17 E. B. Sledge, *China Marine: An Infantryman's Life after World War II* (Tuscaloosa, AL: University of Alabama Press, 2003), p. 135.

18 Trehub, 'William March and Eugene B. Sledge', pp. 35–6; Sledge to William L. Cain, Jr, 14 July 1982; AUA, Sledge Papers, RG96-038, Box 2, Folder 4, Sledge to George B. Clark, 16 March 1982.

19 Trehub, 'William March and Eugene B. Sledge', pp. 36–7.

20 Sledge to George B. Clark, 16 March 1982; AUA, Sledge Papers, RG96/96-038, Box 3, Folder 28, Sterling Mace to Sledge, 28 February 1980.

21 Sledge, *With the Old Breed*, p. 40.
22 Trehub, 'William March and Eugene B. Sledge', p. 47.
23 https://www.nybooks.com/articles/2001/12/20/the-hardest-war/ [accessed 14 April 2021]; John Keegan, *The Second World War* (London: Century Hutchinson, 1989; repr. 1997), p. 502.
24 AUA, Sledge Papers, RG96/97-005, Box 1, Folder 14, Sledge to Paul Fussell, 5 December 1984.
25 AUA, Sledge Papers, RG96/96-038, Box 2, Folder 9, Sledge to Eric Mailander, 6 July 1982.
26 Sledge to William L. Cain, Jr, 14 July 1982.
27 AUA, Sledge Papers, RG96/96-038, Box 2, Folder 23, Jay de l'Eau to Sledge, 31 October 1982.
28 AUA, Sledge Papers, RG96/96-038, Box 2, Folder 13, Hank Boyes to Sledge, 22 March 1982.
29 AUA, Sledge Papers, RG96/96-038, Box 2, Folder 13, Bev Boyes to Sledge, 25 March 1982.
30 McEnery, *Hell in the Pacific*, p. 287.
31 Sledge to George B. Clark, 16 March 1982.
32 Sledge to Paul Fussell, 5 December 1984.
33 McEnery, *Hell in the Pacific*, p. 287.
34 Sledge, *With the Old Breed*, p. i.
35 Sledge to William L. Cain, Jr, 14 July 1982.

Bibliography

Primary Sources, Unpublished

Auburn University Special Collections and Archives (AUA), Auburn, Alabama
Papers of Eugene B. Sledge

Bowdoin College Library (BCL), George J. Mitchell Department of Special Collections & Archives, Brunswick, Maine
Kenneth C. M. Sills Administrative Records

Dwight D. Eisenhower Presidential Library and Archive (DDE), Abilene, Kansas
Simon Bolivar Buckner Papers
Vernon E. Megee Papers
Records of the 7th Infantry Division, 1944–48
Records of 27th Infantry Division, 1942–45
Records of the 77th Infantry Division, 1942–46

Georgetown University Library (GUL), Booth Family Center for Special Collections, Washington DC
Papers of John F. Barrett

Harry S. Truman Presidential Library and Museum (HST), Independence, Missouri
Eben A. Ayers Papers
George M. Elsey Oral History Interview, 7 July 1970
Brigadier General Leslie Groves, 'Memorandum on Alamogordo Air Base atomic fission bomb test', 18 July 1945
Miscellaneous Historical Documents Collection
Notes on the Interim Committee Meetings, 1945
President's Secretary's File, 'Notes regarding June 18, 1945 meeting', 7 June 1954
Public Papers: Statement by the President on the Death of Ernie Pyle, 18 April 1945
Papers of Harry S. Truman

Imperial War Museum Archives (IWM), London
Private Papers of W. A. Franklin
Private Papers of N. B. Gray

The National Archives (TNA), Kew, London
ADM 234/368: Naval Staff History, Battle Summary No. 47, 'Naval Operations Okinawa', 1950
ADM 358/4439: HMS *Indefatigable* – 1 April 1945, enemy action during the Allied invasion of Okinawa, Japan
CAB 106/95: Despatch on the contribution of the British Pacific Fleet to the assault on Okinawa by Admiral Sir Bruce A. Fraser, 26 May 1945

The National Archives and Record Administration (NARA), College Park, Maryland
Records of Tenth Army, 1944–45
Records of Marine Units, 1914–49

Private Papers (PP)
Haldane Family Papers

US Marine Corps Archives (USMCA), Quantico, Virginia
Howard W. Arendt Papers

Marius L. Bressoud Jr Papers
Jeptha J. Carrell Papers
John B. Dillon Papers
Christopher S. Donner Papers
J. Frederick Haley Papers
William A. Looney Papers
Nolen V. Marbrey Papers
Oliver P. Smith Papers
Richard Bruce Watkins Papers
Vandegrift Conference, 1 February 1943, 'The Goettge Patrol'

Primary Sources, Published

Published Documents, Diaries, Letters and Memoirs

Alanbrooke, Field Marshal Lord, *War Diaries: 1939–1945*, ed. by Alex Danchev and Daniel Todman (London: Weidenfeld, 2001)

Burgin, R. V., with Bill Marvel, *Islands of the Damned: A Marine at War in the Pacific* (New York: NAL Caliber, 2010)

Churchill, Winston S., *The Second World War*, 6 vols (London: Cassell, 1948–54)

Cook, Haruko Taya, and Theodore F. Cook, eds, *Japan at War: An Oral History* (New York: W. W. Norton & Co., 1992)

Crandell, Yoshiko Sakumoto, 'Surviving the Battle of Okinawa: Memories of a Schoolgirl', *Asia-Pacific Journal*, 12/14 (2014), 1–31

Descent into Hell: Civilian Memories of the Battle of Okinawa, trans. by Mark Ealey and Alastair McLauchlan (Portland, ME: MerwinAsia, 2014)

Douglas, Paul, *In the Fullness of Time: The Memoirs of Paul H. Douglas* (New York: Harcourt, 1972)

Feifer, George, *Tenozan: The Battle of Okinawa and the Atomic Bomb* (New York: Houghton Mifflin, 1992)

Goldstein, Donald M., and Katherine V. Dillon, eds, *Fading Victory: The Diary of Admiral Matome Ugaki 1941–1945*, trans. by Masataka Chihaya (Pittsburgh, PA: University of Pittsburgh Press, 1991)

Green, Bob, *Okinawa Odyssey: The Battle for Okinawa* (Houston, TX: Bright Sky Press, 2004)

Halsey, William F., and J. Bryan III, *Admiral Halsey's Story* (New York: McGraw Hill, 1947)

Higa, Tomiko, *The Girl with the White Flag: An Inspiring Story of Love and Courage in War Time*, trans. by Dorothy Britton (Tokyo: Kodansha Int., 1991)

Inoguchi, Captain Rikihei, and Commander Tadashi Nakajima, *The Divine Wind: Japan's Kamikaze Force in World War II* (Annapolis, MD: United States Naval Institute, 1958; repr. 1994)

Jenkins, A. P., ed., 'Lt Gen. Simon Bolivar Buckner: Private Letters relating to the Battle of Okinawa', in *Ryudai Review of Euro-American Studies*, 42 (1997), 63–113

Lane, Kerry L., *Guadalcanal Marine* (University of Mississippi, 2004)

MacArthur, Douglas, *Reminiscences* (New York: McGraw-Hill, 2001; repr. 2001)

Mace, Sterling, and Nick Mace, *Battleground Pacific: A Marine Rifleman's Combat Odyssey in K/3/5* (New York: St Martin's Press, 2012)

Manchester, William, *Goodbye, Darkness: A Memoir of the Pacific War* (New York: Little, Brown & Co., 1980; repr. 2002)

McEnery, Jim, with Bill Sloan, *Hell in the Pacific: A Marine Rifleman's Journey from Guadalcanal to Peleliu* (New York: Simon & Schuster, 2012)

Miller, Arthur, *Timebends: A Life* (New York: Grove Press, 1987)

Miller, Thurman, *War and Work: The Autobiography* (New York: Writers Club Press, 2001)

——, *Earned in Blood: My Journey from Old-Breed Marine to the Most Dangerous Job in America* (New York: St Martin's Press, 2013)

Mitsuru, Yoshida, *Requiem for Battleship Yamato* (Washington: University of Washington Press, 1985; repr. ebook, 1999), trans. by Richard H. Minear

Nichols, David, ed., *Ernie's War: The Best of Ernie Pyle's World War II Dispatches* (New York: Simon & Schuster, 1987)

Overy, Richard, *Blood and Ruins: The Great Imperial War 1931–1945* (London: Allen Lane, 2021)

Pyle, Ernie, *Last Chapter* (New York: Henry Holt & Co., 1946)

Robbins, Masako Shinjo Summers, 'My Story: A Daughter Recalls the Battle of Okinawa', *Asia-Pacific Journal*, 13/8 (23 February 2015), pp. 1–22

Sarantakes, Nicolas Evan, ed., *Seven Stars: the Okinawa Battle Diaries of Simon Bolivar, Jr., and Joseph Stilwell* (College Station, TX: Texas A&M University Press, 2004)

Simpson, William P., *Island "X" – Okinawa* (W. Hanover, MSS: The Christopher Publishing House, 1979)

Sledge, E. B., 'Peleliu 1944: Why Did We Go There?', *Leatherneck Magazine*, September 1983, 72–4

——, *With the Old Breed: At Peleliu and Okinawa* (New York: Presidio Press, 1981; repr. 2007)

——, *China Marine: An Infantryman's Life after World War II* (Tuscaloosa, AL: University of Alabama Press, 2002)

Soule, Thayer, *Shooting the Pacific War: Marine Corps Combat Photography in WWII* (Lexington, KY: University Press of Kentucky, 2000)

Statements of Japanese Officials on World War II (English Translations): Vol. 4, 1949–50

Stimson, Henry L., *On Active Service in Peace and War* (New York: Harper & Brothers, 1947)

Terkel, Studs, *The Good War: An Oral History of World War Two* (New York: The New Press, 1984)

Tregaskis, Richard, *Guadalcanal Diary* (New York: Random House, 1943; repr. 1962)

Truman, Harry S., *Year of Decisions*, 2 vols (New York: Doubleday & Co., 1955; repr. 1965)

Vian, Sir Philip, *Action This Day: A War Memoir* (London: Frederick Muller Ltd, 1960)

Yahara, Colonel Hiromichi, *The Battle for Okinawa: A Japanese Officer's Eyewitness Account of the Last Great Campaign of World War II* (New York: John Wiley & Sons, Inc., 1995)

Newspapers and Journals

Boston Daily Globe
Collier's: The National Weekly
The Indianapolis Star
Leatherneck Magazine

The Lewiston Daily Sun
The Mercury (Pottstown),
New York Times
North Jersey Herald & News
The Philadelphia Inquirer
San Francisco Chronicle
South Bend Tribune
Time Magazine

Secondary Sources

Books and Articles

Alexander, Colonel Joseph H., 'What Was Nimitz Thinking?', *Proceedings Magazine*, 124 (1998)

Ambrose, Hugh, *The Pacific* (New York: NAL Signet, 2010; repr. 2011)

Appleman, Roy E., James M. Burns, Russell A. Gugeler and John Stevens, *Okinawa: The Last Battle* (Washington, DC: Center of Military History, US Army, 1948)

Astor, Gerald, *Operation Iceberg: The Invasion and Conquest of Okinawa in World War II* (New York: Dell, 1996)

Axell, Albert, and Hideaki Kase, *Kamikaze: Japan's Suicide Gods* (London: Pearson Education, 2002)

Baime, A. J., *The Accidental President: Harry S. Truman, the Bomb and the Four Months That Changed the World* (New York: Houghton Mifflin Harcourt, 2017; repr. 2018)

Beevor, Antony, *D-Day* (London: Penguin, 2006)

Belotte, James, and William Belotte, *Typhoon of Steel: The Battle for Okinawa* (New York: Harper & Row, 1970; repr. 1984)

Bradley, Michael, '"Banzai!" The Compulsory Mass Suicide of Kerama Islanders in the Battle of Okinawa', *Asia-Pacific Journal*, 11/22 (2014)

Camp, Dick, 'Assault on Sugar Loaf Hill', *Leatherneck*, 100/9 (September 2017)

Doss, Frances M., *Desmond Doss: Conscientious Objector* (Nampa, ID: Pacific Press, 2005)

Edward Smith, Jean, *FDR* (New York: Random House Inc., 2007; repr. 2008)

Frank, Richard B., *Downfall: The End of the Japanese Imperial Empire* (New York: Random House, 1999)

——, *Guadalcanal: The Definitive Account of the Landmark Battle* (New York: Penguin Books, 1990; repr. 1992)

——, *Tower of Skulls: A History of the Asia-Pacific War, July 1937–May 1942* (New York: W. W. Norton, 2020; repr. 2021),

Garand, George W., and Truman R. Strobridge, *History of U.S. Marine Corps Operations in World War II – Volume IV: Western Pacific Operations* (Historical Division, USMC, 1971)

Hastings, Max, *Finest Years: Churchill as Warlord 1940–1945* (London: HarperPress, 2009; repr. 2010)

Hastings, Max, *Nemesis: The Battle for Japan, 1944–45* (London: HarperCollins, 2007)

Herndon, Booton, *The Hero of Hacksaw Ridge* (Coldwater, MI: Remnant Publications, Inc., 2016)

Hersey, John, *Hiroshima* (New York: Penguin Group Inc., 1973; repr. 1985)

Himeyuri Peace Museum: The Guidebook (Itoman, Okinawa: 2016)

Hobbs, David, *The British Pacific Fleet: The Royal Navy's Most Powerful Strike Force* (Barnsley, UK: Seaforth Publishing, 2011; repr. 2017)

Hoffman, Jon T., *Chesty: The Story of Lieutenant General Lewis B. Puller, USMC* (New York: Random House, 2001)

Hough, Lieutenant Colonel Frank O., Major Verle E. Ludwig and Henry I. Shaw, *History of the U.S. Marine Corps Operations in World War II – Volume I: Pearl Harbor to Guadalcanal* (US Marine Corps Historical Branch, 19?)

Hough, Lieutenant Colonel Frank O., and Major John A. Crown, *History of the U.S. Marine Corps Operations in World War II – Volume II: The Campaign on New Britain* (US Marine Corps Historical Branch, 1952)

Hoyt, Edwin P., *How They Won the War in the Pacific: Nimitz and his Admirals* (New York: Weybright and Talley, 1970)

Huber, Thomas M., 'Japan's Battle of Okinawa, April–June 1945', *Leavenworth Papers*, No. 18 (199), 1–141

Hull, Michael D., 'Modest Victor of Midway', *World War II* magazine, 13/1 (May 1998), 36–43

Jordan, Jonathan W., *American Warlords: How Roosevelt's High Command Led America to Victory in World War II* (New York: NAL Caliber, 2015),

Keegan, John, *The Second World War* (London: Century Hutchinson, 1989; repr. 1997)

Lacey, Laura Homan, *Stay Off the Skyline: The Sixth Marine Division on Okinawa* (Dulles, VA: Potomac Books, Inc., 2005; repr. 2007)

Leckie, Robert, *Okinawa: The Last Battle of World War II* (New York: Penguin, 1996)

Lynn, John A., *Battle: A History of Combat and Culture* (New York: Basic Books, 2003)

Makos, *Voices of the Pacific: Untold Stories from the Marine Heroes of World War II* (New York: Berkley Caliber, 2013; repr. 2014)

McMillan, George, *The Old Breed: A History of the First Marine Division in World War II* (Washington: Infantry Journal Press, 1949)

Miller Jr, John, *Cartwheel: The Reduction of Rabaul* (Washington DC: Office of the Chief of Military History, 1959)

——, *Guadalcanal: The First Offensive* (Washington DC: Office of the Chief of Military History, 1995)

Mitcham Jr, Samuel W., and Friedrich von Stauffenberg, *The Battle of Sicily: How the Allies Lost their Chance for Total Victory* (New York: Orion Books, 1991)

Morison, Samuel E., 'American Strategy in the Pacific Ocean', *Oregon Historical Society*, 62/1 (March 1961), 4–56

——, *History of the United States Naval Operations in the Pacific: Volume 14 – Victory in the Pacific, 1945* (New York: Little, Brown, 1975; repr. 2012)

Nelson, William F., *Appointment at Ie Shima* (privately published, 2014)

Nichols Jr, Major Charles S., and Henry I. Shaw, *Marines in World War II – Okinawa: Victory in the Pacific* (Washington DC: Historical Branch, 1955)

Potter, E. B., *Nimitz* (US Naval Institute Press, 1977)

Prange, Gordon W., Donald M. Goldstein and Katherine V. Dillon, *Pearl Harbor: The Verdict of History* (New York: McGraw-Hill, 1985)

Reilly, Robin L., *Kamikaze Attacks of World War II* (Jefferson, NC: McParland & Co., Inc., 2010)

——, *Kamikaze, Corsairs and Picket Ships: Okinawa, 1945* (Havertown, PA: Casemate, 2008)

Reynolds, Clark G., 'Admiral Ernest J. King and the Strategy for Victory in the Pacific', *Naval War College Review*, 28/3 (Winter 1976), 57–64

Roberts, Andrew, *Masters and Commanders: How Roosevelt, Churchill, Marshall and Alanbrooke Won the War in the West* (London: Allen Lane, 2008)

Ross Smith, Robert, *The War in the Pacific: The Approach to the Philippines* (Washington DC: Center of Military History, US Army, 1953; repr. 1996)

Rottman, George L., *World War II US Marine Infantry Regiments* (Oxford: Osprey, 2018)

Sloan, Bill, *Brotherhood of Heroes: The Marines at Peleliu, 1944* (New York: Simon & Schuster, 2005)

——, *The Ultimate Battle: Okinawa 1945 – The Last Epic Struggle of World War II* (New York: Simon & Schuster, 2007)

Stephan, John J., *Hawaii Under the Rising Sun: Japan's Plans for Conquest After Pearl Harbor* (Honolulu, HI: University of Hawaii Press, 1984)

Stockman, James R., *The First Marine Division on Okinawa: 1 April–30 June 1945* (Quantico: History Division US Marine Corps, 1946)

Toll, Ian, *The Conquering Tide: War in the Pacific Islands 1942–1944* (New York: W. W. Norton & Co., 2015; repr. 2016)

——, *Twilight of the Gods: War in the Western Pacific, 1944–1945* (New York: W. W. Norton & Co., 2020)

Trehub, Aaron, 'Eugene B. Sledge and Mobile: 75 Years After "The War"', *Mobile Bay Magazine*, 21 August 2020

——, 'William March and Eugene B. Sledge: Mobilians, Marines, and Writers', in *The Alabama Review*, 66/1 (January 2013), 30–66

Tuchman, Barbara, *Stillwell and the American Experience in China, 1911–45* (New York: Macmillan, 1971)

Willock, Roger, *Unaccustomed to Fear: A Biography of the Late General Roy S. Geiger* (Princeton, NJ: privately published, 1968)

Academic Theses

Copeland, Lori, 'Project 100,000: Harvesting Poverty's Labor Force for War' (Master's thesis, University of Kentucky, 2008)

TV Documentaries and Dramas

The War, PBS documentary series, 2007
The Pacific, HBO miniseries, 2010

Websites

https://www.battleorder.org/usmc-rifle-co-1941 [accessed 15 July 2020]
https://files.eric.ed.gov/fulltext/ED313196.pdf [accessed 28 July 2021]
http://dublinlaurenshometownheroes.blogspot.com/2010/07/maurice-o-modarsey.html [accessed 16 July 2020]
https://valor.militarytimes.com/hero/2345 [accessed 11 August 2020]
https://missingMarines.com/weldon-f-delong/ [accessed 18 August 2020]
https://www.findagrave.com/memorial/31509381/charles-jack-kimmel [accessed 10 September 2020]
https://www.findagrave.com/memorial/180017294/erskine-w_-wells [accessed 10 September 2020]
https://missingMarines.com/weldon-f-delong/ [accessed 10 September 2020]
https://www.usni.org/magazines/naval-history-magazine/2016/april/dear-admiral-halsey [accessed 14 September 2020]
http://www.lejeune.usmc.mil/2dmardiv/aabn/Rifleman.htm [accessed 10 October 2020]
https://memory.loc.gov/diglib/vhp/bib/loc.natlib.afc2001001.05670 [accessed 17 June 2020]
https://valor.militarytimes.com/hero/8306 [accessed 28 October 2020]
https://valor.militarytimes.com/hero/38594 [accessed 23 October 2020]
http://www.victoryinstitute.net/blogs/utb/1944/01/09/robert-l-grays-navy-cross-citation/ [accessed 29 October 2020]
https://valor.militarytimes.com/hero/39523 [accessed 30 October 2020]
https://valor.militarytimes.com/hero/39523 [accessed 3 November 2020]
https://valor.militarytimes.com/hero/36681 [accessed 3 November 2020]
http://www.victoryinstitute.net/blogs/utb/1944/01/03/william-f-reckus-navy-cross-citation/ [accessed 30 October 2020]
https://valor.militarytimes.com/hero/7862 [accessed 30 October 2020]
https://www.findagrave.com/memorial/135011300/lowell-raymond-toelle#view-photo=197065281 [accessed 31 October 2020]

https://valor.militarytimes.com/hero/36463 [accessed 31 October 2020]

https://www.findagrave.com/memorial/127544164/robert-barry-oswalt [accessed 5 November 2020]

https://bowdoinorient.com/2017/12/08/war-hero-andrew-haldane-41-to-be-featured-in-biography/ [accessed 5 March 2021]

https://www.ancestry.com.au/search/?name=Charles_Ellington&birth=1913 &death=1944 [accessed 13 November 2020]

https://eu.southcoasttoday.com/article/20040425/News/304259989 [accessed 13 November 2020]

https://eu.southcoasttoday.com/news/20180526/live-and-learn-on-memorial-day-thinking-about-what-might-have-been [accessed 13 November 2020]

https://www.nationalww2museum.org/war/articles/mail-call-moving-letter-within-letter [accessed 7 January 2021]

https://valor.militarytimes.com/hero/35441 [accessed 19 January 2021]

https://valor.militarytimes.com/hero/35223 [accessed 20 January 2021]

https://www.findagrave.com/memorial/62109739/edward-allison-jones [acccessed 16 February 2021]

https://www.findagrave.com/memorial/62109739/edward-allison-jones [accessed 5 March 2021]

https://www.trumanlibrary.org/whistlestop/study_collections/bomb/large/documents/index.php?documentdate=1945-06-18&documentid=21&pagenumber=1 [accessed June 28, 2019]

https://www.trumanlibrary.gov/library/research-files/notes-meeting-interim-committee [accessed 7 April 2021]

https://www.atomicheritage.org/key-documents/interim-committee-report-0 [accessed 7 April 2021

https://www.trumanlibrary.gov/library/research-files/harry-s-truman-richard-russell [accessed 7 April 2021]

https://eu.southcoasttoday.com/news/20180526/live-and-learn-on-memorial-day-thinking-about-what-might-have-been [accessed 14 September 2020]

https://www.dignitymemorial.com/obituaries/beckley-wv/thurman-miller-7636698 [accessed 12 April 2021]

https://morganfuneralhome.com/tribute/details/1204/Sterling-Mace/obituary.html [accessed 12 April 2021]

https://www.nybooks.com/articles/2001/12/20/the-hardest-war/ [accessed 14 April 2021]

Index